CONTEMPORARY AMERICAN
PROTESTANT THOUGHT

THE AMERICAN HERITAGE SERIES

THE AMERICAN HERITAGE SERIES

under the general editorship of
Leonard W. Levy and Alfred Young

CONTEMPORARY AMERICAN PROTESTANT THOUGHT, 1900–1970

EDITED BY WILLIAM ROBERT MILLER

THE BOBBS-MERRILL COMPANY, INC.
INDIANAPOLIS · NEW YORK

FOREWORD

This anthology attempts to assemble the most characteristically American contributions to twentieth-century Protestant thought. To the editor, this is a tradition that embraces modernism, the social gospel, liberalism, neo-orthodoxy, and the various encounters of Christian thought with process philosophy, pragmatism, psychology, and the social sciences. Above all, it is a tradition that stresses social commitment.

Thus the purpose of the volume, as William Miller writes in his introduction, is to survey the "major creative contributions to the ongoing stream of development" of Protestantism. It is neither "to allot equal time to each conceivable claimant, nor to give representation in proportion to denominational or factional blocs." The emphasis is on the "forward currents."

William Miller died before this book was published, shortly after he completed the final editing. In his early forties, an accomplished essayist, biographer, and editor, he was at the beginning of a new phase of his career that would have taken him on deep scholarly explorations into American religious history.

This book reveals, in our opinion, the special strengths he brought to interpreting the "forward currents" of Protestantism. Intellectually, he stood within them; indeed he was quick to acknowledge the successive influences on his own thinking of Paul Tillich, Nels F. S. Ferré, H. Richard Niebuhr, and Reinhold Niebuhr. His strong social commitments are partially suggested by his work with the Fellowship of Reconciliation (1956–62) and by the titles of his recent books: *Nonviolence: A Christian Interpretation* (1966); *The New Christianity* (1967); *Martin Luther King* (1968); and *Goodbye Jehovah* (1969). A committed man, at the same time he was a true "free lance" (by occupation he was a writer), who stood outside of any formal church or academic affiliation. The result was a refreshing independence of judgment in matters denominational and theological.

This volume also shows William Miller's gifts as a writer and as a popularizer in the best sense. He departed from the pattern of short headnotes in other volumes of the American Heritage Series to introduce each selection with a lengthy interpretive biography of the author. Frequently this is based on his personal knowledge of the man, sometimes on correspondence with him. For a number of living figures they are the first such sketches to appear in print. They are always incisive. The volume thus presents a unique intellectual portrait gallery of major twentieth-century American Protestant thinkers, as well as a sampling of their writing.

Within the American Heritage Series the volume takes its place alongside a number of other books that document the major themes of American religious thought. These include volumes on Puritan political thought, the Great Awakening, the churches and the city, Catholic thought on social questions, Unitarianism, the tradition of non-violence, and American theology as a whole. Still others are planned.

This book is one of a series created to provide the essential primary sources of the American experience, especially of American thought. The series, when completed, will constitute a documentary library of American history, filling a need long felt among scholars, students, libraries, and general readers for authoritative collections of original materials. Some volumes will illuminate the thought of significant individuals, such as James Madison or John Marshall; some deal with movements, such as the Antifederalist or the Populist; others are organized around special themes, such as black nationalism or military thought. Many volumes will take up the large number of subjects traditionally studied in American history for which surprisingly there are no documentary anthologies; others will pioneer in introducing new subjects of increasing importance to scholars and to the contemporary world. The series aspires to maintain the high standards demanded of contemporary editing, providing authentic texts, intelligently and unobtrusively edited. It also has the distinction of presenting pieces of substantial length which give the full character and flavor of the original. The series will be the most comprehensive and authoritative of its kind.

ALFRED F. YOUNG
LEONARD W. LEVY

Contents

Contents   *xiii*

Acknowledgment

I would like to acknowledge my vast indebtedness to many authors whose work I have drawn upon. To them must be added a number of scholars who reviewed my initial and later outlines, suggesting wise omissions and additions, referring me to source materials, and helping the book along in other ways. Among them must be mentioned Robert T. Handy, Edwin Scott Gaustad, Martin E. Marty, Sidney E. Mead, and John E. Smith. In the nature of the case, with sometimes conflicting opinions, I cannot blame any of them for the result; I can only say that without their comments the result would have been poorer. To each of the living authors who provided biographical and other information for the headnotes concerning them, many and profound thanks—this includes the late Harry Emerson Fosdick, who died before the volume was finished, and it extends to include Mrs. Edgar Brightman and Mrs. Reinhold Niebuhr. I must thank Arthur S. Link for referring me to the articles by Woodrow Wilson from which I chose those in this volume, and I must exculpate him as well as anyone else for my own interpretive bias in this case as in others. Special thanks are due to Robert F. Beach and the staff of the Union Theological Seminary Library; to my wife, Louise, who assisted me in parts of my research; to my son Brian and daughter Janice, who contributed their sweated labor, pasting and cutting hundreds of xeroxes, including many selections omitted in the final compilation.

This book was interrupted and greatly slowed down by months of hospitalization and convalescence for heart attacks suffered in April and June 1969. I thank God that I recovered to complete it, and I thank my friend, Helen Elizabeth Reddick, for the part she played in helping me to do both in difficult circumstances. Finally, I wish to give special thanks to the series editor, Alfred Young, for urging upon me a number of minor additions which added clarity and some considerable excisions which have spared you, the reader, at least a few occasions for dozing.

New York City
April 1970

Introduction

More than perhaps any other, the opening of the twentieth century symbolized, almost to the very year, a historical pivot, the closing of one era and the beginning of another. The rapid industrialization of the United States was largely accomplished and with it the rise of large urban centers. In polite parlance, the Western frontier had been officially closed, meaning that the last of the Indian wars was over and the enemy rendered powerless. Across the vast continent sped railroad trains over tracks laid within mere decades. The years ahead would see astonishing extensions of the march of technology—the automobile, aircraft, radio, scientific medicine and warfare—yet their foundation in a scientific worldview was already a fact, and such battles as remained to secure this worldview were in the nature of mopping-up operations.

The period of culmination, 1875–1900, has been called a critical one for religion—and specifically for Protestant thought. Rote orthodoxy and its arid literalism tried vainly to stem a rising tide of liberalism; yet in its very origins and nature, American religion hewed to the experiential and experimental rather than seeking to conserve ancient traditions. The faith of pioneers modulated into that of practical-minded townsfolk and city dwellers. As Kenneth Boulding has pointed out, "experimental religion legitimates change,"[1] and as religious establishments began to totter in Britain and Europe, the free churches of America not only grew numerically but partly provided a

---

[1] Kenneth E. Boulding, *The Meaning of the Twentieth Century* (New York: Harper, 1964), p. 117.

setting for bold theological innovation. Typified by the new and daring approaches of the newly gathered faculty at the University of Chicago, the intellectual circuitry of a transformed twentieth-century Christianity was just beginning to be laid. Representatives of outworn orthodoxy continued to hang on, as at Princeton, but by 1900 their day was over, their influence increasingly confined to backward rural areas. What was then known as "the new theology" was not so new that it came as a shock any longer to churchgoers of average education. Missionary encounters with other world religions, the German higher criticism of the Bible, the acceptance of geological and biological evolution—these and other influences went into the making of the new theology.

Most of the men who figured prominently in the religious thought of the early twentieth century were born between 1840 and 1863. Even the youngest of them experienced the impact of astounding and rapid change, not just as an idea but as facts of daily life: electric lights, telephones, a whole wave of successive innovations. Starting with vast resources and an experimental habit of mind, America, in half a century, sprang to the leadership of industrial nations. During the same period Germany underwent a parallel development that is instructive for its contrasts. The Germans excelled in precision, in organization, and systematization, as reflected not only in their chemical, optics, and machine tool industries but also in their theological scholarship. The Americans benefited from these disciplines, but their own national character expressed itself differently—in enterprise, in audacity of invention, in pluralism and pragmatism and democracy. As Joseph Haroutunian observed, "The American, who has lived not by the grace of the Establishment but by the trans-actions of his fellow men, does not have either the European's feeling of Truth or his obsequiousness before it. The given to an American has become either a habit or a problem."[2] The German sacrificed many other val-

---

[2] Joseph Haroutunian, "Theology and American Experience," *Criterion*, III (Winter 1964), p. 6. Also reprinted in *Dialog*, IV, 3 (Summer 1965), together with a critique by Bernard E. Meland.

ues for the sake of "Truth," order, efficiency. The American was more typically attuned to operational methods—not so much how things fit together in a system but how to get them to function for a desired purpose, how to get results. Whether God is Jonathan Edwards's sovereign deity or some more abstract or immanent entity, it is a living God with whom the American Protestant has entered into some kind of dynamic relationship, which is to say that he somehow finds God in experience, in life. He has little interest in a deistic Great Being of nature or cosmos, God as an onotological infinite, source of existence or supreme lawgiver. Even the most absolute idealist like Royce turns out to be a pragmatist in comparison with, say, Hegel or even Scheler. This is the chief reason why it is a mistake to try to reduce even the most derivative types of American theological liberalism to their German influences. The American version differed from the German even when it most closely followed it, for there was a selectivity of emphases that can hardly be overlooked and that is not simply to be accounted for in the fact of derivation. Not till the rise of neo-orthodoxy in the 1950s did American theologians succeed (and then only some of them and not for long) in de-Americanizing and fully Germanizing their theology. Broadly speaking, liberalism became normative in America, outlasting what had been a phase in Germany. Its progressivism and optimism were of a distinctive kind, rooted in an experiential faith in the pioneers' ability to build a nation where none had been before.

In earlier generations, the experiential character of American Protestantism was visible chiefly in a revivalism that stressed a deeply felt conversion experience coupled with adherence to moral scruples, a sense of personal salvation, and one or another literalistic, uncritical version of Calvinism, not only as doctrine but as a guide to personal piety. A series of theological departures from this background could be noted, from Horace Bushnell to Ralph Waldo Emerson, but it was only in the last third of the nineteenth century that a significant turn occurred in the development of American religious thought.

The relationship between, on the one hand, theology, philosophy of religion, Christian personal and social ethics and, on the other hand, the religious predilections of the average minister or churchgoer, is complex. At the turn of the century, when it was numerically dwindling, Congregationalism remained in the ascendant in the quality of its theological institutions and in the contributions of its theologians, while the numerically preponderant Baptists and Methodists contributed little writing of intellectual quality. Most Lutheran churches and their theologians retained the character of immigrant enclaves. Not until after World War II did they produce theologians like Carl Braaten, Martin Marty, and Robert Jenson, who could be said to be participants in the American experience on the level of religious thought.

To say this is to indicate an interpretive bias that seems to me inescapable. The purpose of this volume is not to allot equal space to each conceivable claimant, nor to give representation in proportion to denominational or factional blocs. What I have tried to produce, rather, is a survey of major creative contributions to the ongoing stream of development, showing the variety and vitality of a succession of thinkers. Not all are equally profound or laudable, but together they give a fair picture of the growth of Protestant thought in twentieth-century America. If there is any lack of balance in these pages, it arises from my decision to trace the forward currents. For example, in the debate between fundamentalism and modernism it has seemed sufficient to state the issues and give a selection only from Harry Emerson Fosdick, because his modernism, and indeed his whole career, represents a notable contribution to these currents. A selection from a fundamentalist spokesman like J. Gresham Machen might be of some documentary interest, but it would represent little more than a retrograde movement of slight intellectual import, a throwback to an earlier era. More recently, the writings of Edward John Carnell, Carl F. H. Henry, and other evangelicals have acquired a measure of intellectual respectability, and in omitting them I may be displaying a more overt bias; but whatever their merits, they seem to me peripheral to the significant trends. For a similar reason, and with deep regret because of my personal indebtedness to his thought, I have not included any selection by Paul Tillich, since, after three decades in America, he remained a German theologian, and this is not a survey of European ideas. Such European influences as are found in the selections in this volume will be seen sufficiently in writers who were rooted in the American ethos and experience.

The twentieth century represents, in both Europe and America, the coming of age of that technological civilization to which we have already referred. And for reasons rooted deep in its own past, from the establishment of the Puritan commonwealth in seventeenth-century New England to the golden age of invention and industry and the consolidation of a transcontinental nation barely two and a half centuries later, the American version of that civilization differed markedly from the European. We must, so far as we can, view the course of twentieth-century American Protestant thought in the political and cultural context of its time, beginning at the threshold of the new century.

THE PROGRESSIVE ERA

The decades of rapid industrial growth after the Civil War had resulted in social evils that could no longer be moralized away with platitudes about the depravity of the poor or the boundless opportunities on the frontier. Among theologians and religious leaders, capitalistic apologetics were giving way to a growing sense of social charity and mission; by the late 1880s a movement for civic reform and betterment was taking shape. One of its moderate representatives, Theodore Roosevelt, was elected Vice President in 1900. When President McKinley, a conservative, was assassinated the following year, Roosevelt was placed in a position to pursue a progressive policy, curbing the power of monopolistic corporations and offering a "square deal" to a nation for years victimized by vested interests and corrupt political machines.

The onset of Rooseveltian progressivism was no isolated development. In a sense it was fortuitous, but it set a new tone and created a new socio-political ambiance, giving further impetus to currents already in motion in American life—not only those moving for social reform but a whole complex of ideas and forces considered liberal, liberating, constructive, or progressive—in short, modern. The progressive political impetus took varied forms, but it lasted for nearly two decades and marked a definite departure from the old century—a departure confirmed in culture and technology by the beginnings of aviation, motion pictures and the mass-produced automobile, each of which was a dramatic step in extending man's control over his environment.

As it moved into the new century, Protestant thought became secular and this-worldly, to an extent not contemplated by the earlier proponents of the new theology. Liberal theologians related to the church admitted that a "startling discrepancy" existed between the historic faith and "the principles of its founder."[3] William Adams Brown offered an American amendment to Hegel's dialectic of history, accounting for the imperfections of historic religion in "the struggle of a spiritual principle with a resisting, and often hostile, environment."[4] Charles W. Eliot, the Unitarian educator, was president of Harvard University from 1869 to 1909, transforming it from a sectarian and provincial institution into a bastion of higher learning and free inquiry. "Millions of Americans," he said in 1909, "find in Masonic organizations, lodges of Odd Fellows, benevolent and fraternal societies, granges, and trades unions, at once their practical religion, and the satisfaction of their social needs. So far as these multifarious organizations carry men and women out of their individual selves, and teach them mutual regard and social and industrial cooperation, they

---

[3] William Adams Brown, *The Essence of Christianity* (New York: Scribner, 1902), p. 301.
[4] *Ibid*, p. 304.

approach the field and functions of the religion of the future."[5] Christianity, he maintained, had become "paganized." The future religion would promote truth and freedom as well as love and hope; "the love and hope will be thoroughly grounded in and on efficient, serviceable, visible, actual and concrete deeds and conduct,"[6] as exemplified in the achievements of modern medical science. The religion of which Eliot spoke was "twentieth century religion"—not Christianity but a force which would "progressively modify the creeds and religious practices of all the existing churches."[7] Yet four years later he would speak in the same fashion of "twentieth century Christianity," affirming "the leadership of Jesus" and the validity of his ethical teaching. "The American democracy . . . is to a large extent unchurched," but it "may be profoundly influenced by a church which, possessing no privileges, knows how to stir the hearts of the common people."[8]

Often the secular accent tended to reduce Christianity to shallow moralizing. Washington Gladden, offering the Sermon on the Mount as "the basis of social reconstruction," represents Jesus as a social philosopher whose teachings about the brotherhood of man provide a simple alternative to both capitalism and socialism, a solution to the complex problems of industrial society. "Is the economic fact or the spiritual fact fundamental in human society?" asks Gladden. "Are we competitors, or are we brothers?"[9] Like Josiah Strong and other champions of the Social Gospel, he writes the stuff on which benign church resolutions are made, progressive in rhetoric and intent but lacking in socio-historic or psychological insight —a superficial adaptation of small-town, middle-class, individual morality to modern urban conditions.

---

[5] Charles W. Eliot, "The Religion of the Future," *Harvard Theological Review*, II, 4 (October 1909), p. 405.

[6] *Ibid*, p. 403.

[7] *Ibid*, p. 406.

[8] Charles W. Eliot, "Twentieth Century Christianity," an address to the General Conference of Unitarian and other Christian Churches, October 6, 1913. In *American Unitarian Tracts*, 1919, p. 7.

[9] Washington Gladden, *Christianity and Socialism* (New York: Macmillan, 1905), p. 57.

Both Gladden and Eliot were born in the 1830s. Josiah Strong and William James were born in the following decade. The differences are less those of age than of circumstance. Both Gladden and Strong were ministers; however liberal, they moved within a more conservative and intellectually circumscribed setting than that of Harvard. The new religious sensibility took root and flourished freely in the universities but only secondarily and more cautiously at church-related theological schools. The rise of both privately endowed and publicly supported universities, often lacking departments of religion but seldom of social sciences, was an important factor in shaping the American religious mind after the Civil War, and along with it arose not only secular scholarship but a secularized morality, intellect, and social conscience attuned to the modern world. It was often consciously religious, Christian, and Protestant, although estranged from churchly traditions. Sometimes it consciously repudiated the church or denied that it was religious, yet affirmed values which were clearly the result not only of a Christian tutelage but of deep-rooted Calvinist family traditions. The secular liberalism of John Dewey was to no small extent shaped by his upbringing in Burlington's White Street Congregational Church; his ethics and his faith in democracy as a community of sharing benefited both from his religious background and his liberation from it. The social conscience of Max Eastman was also formed by religion—both his parents were Congregational ministers—and his espousal of revolutionary socialism was likewise pragmatic, moral, and undogmatic. Herbert Croly's *The Promise of American Life* (1909) was more truly rooted in the Edwardsian vision of the Kingdom of God than were many of the tracts of the Social Gospel. Socialist muckrakers like Upton Sinclair excoriated the churches for their complicity in the capitalist system and its inhumanities, but they often did so from moral impulses as Christian as those actuating Strong and Gladden.[10] Van Wyck Brooks' *The Wine of the Puritans* (1908) typified

---

[10] See Upton Sinclair, *A Personal Jesus* (New York: Evans, 1952).

the modern secular protest against the restrictions in the American religious heritage. It was an exaggerated overreaction that did the actual Puritans considerable disservice, but it was aimed not so much at the men of 17th century America as at their Victorian descendants. Another voice from the progressive literary world was Randolph Bourne (1886–1918), who, in the name of socialism, counterposed love and cooperation to the churches' teaching of moralistic duty and service: "The Protestant Church in its tenacious devotion to the personal ideal of a Divine Master—the highest and most popular Christian ideal of today—shows how very far it still is away from the ideals and ethics of a social democracy, a life lived in the Beloved Community."[11] Some radical Christians, like Norman Thomas, forced to a choice between the two, left the ministry and opted for a secular version of the Christian concerns that had formed their social commitment. John Jay Chapman, son of a president of the New York Stock Exchange, articulated views shared by many thoughtful educated men of the Progressive Era: "The old dogmas of the church are crude and somewhat ugly attempts to state certain mysteries of religious experience in such a manner that they can be used as badges of organization work and as political whips. The seminaries hammer at dogmas as if they outranked the Gospels. For this reason we dislike them. After we have once had experience of the truths to which they refer, however, we can no longer regard them as nonsense, or as hocus-pocus. They are attempts to define things which Christ expressed by his life—i.e., his relation to God, his relation to men, his mediation in every sense of the word."[12]

The Harvard of Charles W. Eliot, benefiting from the example of Berlin and other German universities, became for many years a prodigious influence in the shaping of American religious thought, particularly through the teachings and writ-

---

[11] Randolph Bourne, *The History of a Literary Radical and Other Papers* [1919] (New York: S. A. Russell, 1956), p. 303.
[12] John Jay Chapman, *Notes on Religion* (New York: Laurence Gomme, 1915), p. 83.

ings of William James, Josiah Royce, George Santayana, Ralph Barton Perry, William Ernest Hocking, and Alfred North Whitehead. More than a third of the writers represented in the first half of this volume, from H. C. King to Charles Hartshorne, studied at Harvard. Many of those who did not were nevertheless indebted to the Harvard thinkers.

Eliot was not alone in his pioneering educational efforts. Before him, the nonsectarian work of Horace Mann did much to open both New England and the nation to an educational perspective in which the Pilgrims became everybody's forefathers, denominational frictions were minimized, and champions of liberty, whether deist or Baptist, took their places in an ecumenical pantheon of heroes. Schools of denominational origin such as Williams and Oberlin, under the presidencies of urbane men like Mark Hopkins and Henry Churchill King, achieved distinction on much the same terms, foregoing doctrinal orthodoxy and promoting genuinely liberal education. The differences between King's Oberlin and the Cornell of Andrew D. White at the opening of the twentieth century were not great, either in standards of scholarship or in theological bias and interest, despite the fact that Oberlin maintained a theological faculty and Cornell did not. Even such former citadels of orthodoxy as Yale and Andover reorganized themselves in a liberal direction, becoming less mere training schools for the clergy and more like forums for the free exchange of religious ideas. This institutional change, as much as any specifically theological development fostered the liberal temper of early twentieth century religious thought in America. By comparison, the local churches remained conservative and faction-ridden—the less so, of course, as they were touched by the broadly progressive intellectual currents, which bore along a rising wave of liberal Protestant thought. And Protestant it was, with few exceptions, from the unlabeled "common faith" of John Dewey to the rigid moralism of Woodrow Wilson and the ostensibly secular radical criticism of Randolph Bourne and Van Wyck Brooks.

Harvard and Yale were becoming democratized, Americanized, upgraded in their standards of scholarship, ecumenized and secularized.[13] Of perhaps equal importance was the founding of the University of Chicago, an institution that embodied all these features. From the beginning of the twentieth century onward, Chicago rivaled Harvard as a creative center for religious studies, and the "Chicago school" more than any other, including Harvard, developed the distinctively American style in religious thought—democratic, pragmatic, pluralistic, attuned to modernity and change.

Chicago and Harvard were, at the dawn of the century, both American rather than regional, ecumenical rather than sectarian. Yet inescapably Harvard invited such adjectives as lofty, detached, proper, upper-class, while the Chicago keynotes were more socially conscious, democratic, experimental. New and robust, William Rainey Harper's University arose in what was then the newest of America's great cities and a nexus of encounter among diverse and lively regional cultures, linking the Great Lakes to the Midwestern plains and the great Western wheatfields, cornfields, and cattle ranges, while developing its own urban, machine-age style of life in their midst. The spirit of the city was well expressed in the blunt, rugged poetry of that same Carl Sandburg who wrote of Lincoln and of brawny cornhuskers. And the spirit of religious studies at the University was like the city's. If Peirce and James laid the foundations for a modern version of hard-headed Yankee practicality, it was men like John Dewey and George Herbert Mead who developed it into a scientific method designed for application in the field. Religious studies at Chicago were imbued with their method, taking the measure of modern man in his actuality and seeking a functional interpretation of religion geared to his situation. In Chicago's Shailer Mathews, Gerald Birney Smith, Edward Scribner Ames, and others who

---

[13] In a sense, the ecumenizing and secularizing may be seen as two sides of the same process—a thrust toward two kinds of "worlding," toward the *oikumene* of the common life and toward engagement with the *saeculum* or empirical world. The movement of "Americanization" in education was a "worlding" in both senses, and more—a movement up and away from regional Yankeedom, through and beyond both the parochial New England and the sectional Northern meaning of the term.

followed them, we find a modernism in religion that is no mere attempt to adjust the gospel to the urban age by taking account of evolution and other modern knowledge but an enterprise of rethinking religion in terms of the theories and findings of Deweyan psychology and Mead's social behaviorism. Walter Rauschenbusch towered above most exponents of the Social Gospel in his understanding of history and the difference between the social crisis of the Progressive Era and earlier epochs. But his theological liberalism remained essentially evangelical, a variant of progressive orthodoxy with a keen ethical edge. Shailer Mathews, in contrast, strikes a dynamic and functional note in his interpretation of the mind of biblical times and that of modern man. "The really vital religious issues," he wrote, "are those set by the social order itself, and these cannot be answered by the use of exclusively theological methods and presuppositions, but by the test of life itself. . . . If theology would not die of intellectual dry rot, it must become biological and social."[14] The Mathews of 1910 represented not so much an achievement as a tendency which was to come to fuller fruition later; this is true of the Chicago school in general. Yet its sudden emergence in the Progressive Era was symptomatic and catalytic beyond its immediate impact. Its answers were sometimes inadequate, lacking in depth; but the questions it chose to confront and its commitment to the social sciences and to a general scientific concept of process helped considerably in extending the pragmatic thrust of William James and in paving the way for important later developments. Following James, this theology sought both to understand the religious experience of the early Christian community and to reconstruct the idea of God along lines that would accord with the facts of life as disclosed by science. It moved beyond the German historico-critical method onto its own terrain, setting itself the task not only of ascertaining but interpreting the data of the Bible—and interpreting it not only in terms of the ancient community but of the modern, American, democratic community and its possibilities.

---

14 Shailer Mathews, *The Gospel and the Modern Man* (New York: Macmillan, 1910), p. 59 f.

The Chicago school only exemplifies a broad movement of the Progressive Era that found expression, in greater or lesser degree and in varying forms, in all the religious thinkers worth considering in that period—the quest for images of man, God, and society adequate to the promise of American democracy in an industrial, urban age. Some emphasized individual character more than social structure, but the common vision and impulse was open-hearted, generous, and optimistic. Whether understood in Roycean terms of loyalty or Rauschenbusch's solidarity, salvation was seen as social. Whether it was Jamesian pluralism or Wilsonian moralism, each man's truth leagued itself with the forces of democracy. Appeals to authority, established order, and orthodoxy were anachronisms that no longer found a hearing among serious thinkers. Individualism was by no means dead, but it was chastened or rationalized to the public interest, and the wealth to which it might still lay claim had set against it the claims of philanthropy and the income tax. Even when American troops were sent to Mexico and France, their errands were conceived not in terms of national honor and glory but of social salvation and the realization of Christian ideals on a world scale.

THE OPTIMISTIC DECADE

The protean hopes of social Christianity and its secular counterparts were sidetracked during America's participation in World War I, and the world that emerged from the holocaust was a troubled and disillusioned one. Adherents of the Social Gospel were split several ways by the impact of the war, the Bolshevik seizure of power in Russia and the ensuing Red Terror, as well as waves of strikes in the United States. Worn out by the moral ordeal of World War I and fearful of violent revolution at home, middle-class Americans turned against Wilson's internationalism. Although leading churchmen supported the League of Nations, most of their followers did not. The Interchurch Report on the great 1919 steel strike, published in 1920, was widely endorsed by denominational journals and by 1923 led to the end of the 12-hour day in the steel mills. During the Red scare of 1920, A. C. McGiffert, Henry Sloane Coffin, Ralph W. Sockman, Harry Emerson Fosdick, and other prominent liberal New York clergymen vigorously protested the expulsion of duly elected Socialist members of the state assembly, but their protest fell on deaf ears. A large number of Socialists, including their national leader, Eugene V. Debs, had opposed the war, and to many naive patriots this was tantamount to treason. Like Max Eastman, some had both opposed the war and supported the Bolsheviks, against whom a small contingent of American troops had been sent to fight. Many radicals were hastily rounded up and readied for deportation without trial. The New York East Conference of the Methodist Church went materially to their aid, and *The Congregationalist* bucked the current by publishing a sympathetic series, " 'Reds' I have Known." But leading Methodist, Congregational, and other laymen, lacking any ties to the Social Gospel movement and feeling their interests threatened, took exception to these moves. In the course of the decade, social reform rapidly lost popularity. By 1926 the Detroit Chamber of Commerce was able to persuade the local YMCA and most local churches to withdraw invitations they had extended to labor leaders who had come to attend the AFL Convention that year.

By 1919, many of the great voices of the Progressive Era were stilled by death—Bowne, Clarke, Gladden, James, Rauschenbusch, Royce, Strong—and those who arose, particularly in the area of social thought and action, found themselves facing a new and different situation. The war had given great impetus to industry, spurring labor organization, bringing Negroes to the Northern cities for the first time in large numbers, drawing recent immigrants into mines and mills and factories. The war had also redrawn much of the map of Europe, reduced Germany and Austria from crowned empires to shaky republics, and drastically altered international relations. The United States was now a world power, yet uncertain of its role. At the very time it gained this power, it turned inward.

Church leaders at the close of the Progressive Era were excessively optimistic about America's chances of joining the League of Nations; they themselves were being drawn into international cooperation through the Geneva Conference on Life and Work in 1920. In the same week the League was founded, Prohibition became the law of the land, and a large contingent of the Social Gospelers devoted their major efforts during the decade to promoting and defending it, while soft-pedaling other issues. Indeed, with the simultaneous resurgence of the Ku Klux Klan and its spread into the Midwest, Prohibition moved from left to right on the political spectrum, carrying many of its adherents toward the unsavory nativism of the 1928 Presidential campaign, which reactivated dormant anti-Catholic sentiment. As Paul Carter has observed, "the humanitarian concern for the drunkard as victim was replaced by righteous indignation at the drinker as criminal."[15] The prohibitionists of the 1920s confirmed with a vengeance the inhumane, moralistic legalism of Anthony Comstock and his anti-vice crusade of the 1870s. Their position was in short, reactionary, reverting to a type of repression that had little in common with the social ideals of Rauschenbusch and did much to widen the gulf between religion and the secular mind. Harry Elmer Barnes, in *The Twilight of Christianity* (1929), had abundant reasons to hope for the churches' extinction, and H. L. Mencken was provided with ammunition for a running tirade on the foibles of a benighted and fatuous religion.

In an age of radio, dirigibles, and motion pictures, not to mention Ford's Model T, the Democratic Party would nominate for Vice President the eloquent William Jennings Bryan, formerly secretary of state, who veritably symbolized the confusions of the age. His Christian pacifism caused him to part company with Wilson when war came; but Bryan's pacifism and his Populist progressivism were grounded in a simple moralistic faith that brooked no reforms in biblical studies. He epitomized the tragicomic rift in the Protestantism of the

---

15 Paul A. Carter, *The Decline and Revival of the Social Gospel* (Cornell University Press, 1954), p. 38.

1920s, lending his declining prestige to the Fundamentalist cause in their fight against evolution and modernism. At the same time, pacifism was becoming a leading feature of the modernist social outlook. A serious cultural lag was developing. Until the late 1920s, the clergyman was its chief victim. Despite the earlier rise of such theological schools as Yale, Chicago, Union, and Oberlin, many others remained sectarian, provincial, and backward; their students were not college-trained. Half a century earlier, even the average minister was better educated than most people, and his low salary was offset by gifts in kind as well as prestige. Now he was caught in a trap of shabby gentility, dependent on the favors of tradesmen, and vulnerable to Fundamentalism's strident defenses. Moreover, the tradesman often preferred Fundamentalism for its social conservatism, although in everyday life he was increasingly using the new gadgets of scientific technology and had pragmatic reverence for what science could do. Here, perhaps, we may discern the roots of the tendency to compartmentalize religion and to trivialize it by failing to take it seriously except on the level of pious fantasy. Hollywood helped to promote this trend with its anachronistic biblical spectacles, fostering a popular religious culture divorced from reality in such films as *The Ten Commandments* (1924), *Ben Hur* (1926), and *King of Kings* (1927). For the Protestant masses, the technological miracle of cinematography provided a form of theological education that was quite the opposite of serious theology rather than a popularization of it. Even most ministers were oblivious to the publication of Sigmund Freud's *The Future of an Illusion* while they drenched themselves in that very illusion. The Christ they saw was projected from their own image, the conventional Boy Scout and Rotarian, and Rotarians and Boy Scout leaders found it easy to speak of emulating a Christ who was made to order for them. A typical bit of Americana printed without comment in Mencken's *American Mercury* was a headline from a small-town newspaper: "George H. Shaw Lauds Christ in Rotary Talk." Somehow Christianity wasn't turning out the way Charles W. Eliot had predicted. The optimism of a misplaced faith, which defined man at his best as a complacent Babbitt, gave a nice irony to the title of a book by Mencken's colleague, George Jean Nathan, *Land of the Pilgrims' Pride,* and led Herbert Asbury, a secularized, "emancipated" descendant of the founder of American Methodism, to title his autobiography *Up From Methodism.*

Asbury would scarcely have guessed, or perhaps did not wish to contemplate, what some of the more modern Methodists were up to. The personalist philosophy of Borden Parker Bowne, paralleling that of H. C. King, had implanted itself at Boston University and was to inspire a new generation of theologians, the most distinguished of whom was Edgar Sheffield Brightman. Others included A. C. Knudsen, Herbert Alden Youtz, and Bishop Francis J. McConnell. Youtz and McConnell in particular carried forward the quest for a democratic idea of God in such books as McConnell's *Democratic Christianity* (1919). Throughout the 1920s and into the New Deal era, McConnell was an indefatigable champion of the rights of labor—not merely a preacher of the Social Gospel but a man who leaped to the defense of Tom Mooney and other victims of the class struggle. More controversial was Harry F. Ward of Union Theological Seminary, whose *The New Social Order* (1919) was among the boldest attempts by American Protestants to come to grips with the problems of the twentieth century. Ward, continually under fire from conservative Methodists, eventually came to identify his vision of the Kingdom of God with the fortunes of the Soviet Union, but in mid-1920s he stood closer to Shailer Mathews and the Chicago theology than to any partisan position[16] None of these social perspectives, however, added anything of importance to what Rauschenbusch had written; in retrospect he has outlasted the vagaries of McConnell and Ward. Brightman, less involved in the social struggle and more deeply committed to the theological and philosophical task, represents Method-

---

[16] See Donald B. Meyer, *The Protestant Search for Political Realism, 1919–1941* (University of California Press, 1960), pp. 145–153. Meyer's is the best available book on social Christianity in this period, but it may profitably be augmented with Robert Moats Miller, *American Protestanism and Social Issues, 1919–1939* (University of North Carolina Press, 1959).

ism's most enduring contribution of the 1920s and is a figure of larger importance for today.

The same kind of gravitational force that polarized Harry Ward away from conservative churchmen was felt by others though in different ways. Among the most notable was Abraham Jacob Muste, a young pacifist minister who led some 30,000 textile workers to victory in a four-month strike in Lawrence, Mass., in 1919. After further strike experiences in Utica, Paterson, and Passaic, he became head of the Brookwood Labor College in 1921 and later a figure in revolutionary politics. Like Norman Thomas's, his socio-political stance was a secular outgrowth of what had begun as a deeply Christian commitment.

During the war both Muste and Thomas belonged to the pacifist Fellowship of Reconciliation, which rapidly became the vital center of social Christianity for a decade or more. Rauschenbusch joined it the year he died; McConnell belonged to it; so did Fosdick and Brightman. By the late 1920s and early 1930s, its leading figures included the chief exponents of Christian socialism; its magazine, *The World Tomorrow*, edited by Kirby Page, Reinhold Niebuhr, and Devere Allen, rivaled *The Christian Century* in influence. Kirby Page, a minister of the Disciples of Christ, was an absolute pacifist whose book *The Sword or the Cross* (1921) argued simply and persuasively for a perfectionist "ethic of Jesus" as a practical solution to the problem of war. When the futility of the carnage of World War I became apparent, many liberal Protestants flocked to Page's banner. Charles Clayton Morrison, the founder-editor of *The Christian Century* and the publisher of Page's book, was among the many who proclaimed the goal, expressed in his own volume, *The Outlawry of War* (1927). Their optimism seemed vindicated when Frank Kellogg, a former trust-busting attorney now Secretary of State, drafted the Treaty of Paris. Ratified by the world's leading nations through the League, it pledged them all henceforth to abstain from warmaking. The pacifist mood seemed to envelop both secular and pious America; the following year's most acclaimed new novels were Ernest Hemingway's *A Fare-*

well to Arms and Erich Maria Remarque's *All Quiet on the Western Front,* which had already sold more than a quarter of a million copies in Germany.

Even as Morrison was ending all wars, however, the German economy was collapsing, and fascism was gaining ground there and in other European countries. Those who were most politically oriented were, understandably, the first to become aware of these rumblings, particularly if they were internationally minded Socialists or Communist sympathizers, for it was the European left that, in the 1920s, was most directly threatened by the rise of Hitler, Mussolini, and their kind. Among Protestant social idealists, these far-off events sparked various responses. Some shrugged them off or failed to notice them. Many pacifists cited fascism as one more indication of the consequences of the war, to be alleviated by redemptive sacrifice by the United States.

Most pacifists and other liberals, it should be noted, were middle-class idealists with little knowledge of sociology and no real acquaintance with labor problems. Even a man like A. J. Muste, seasoned in class conflict, moving into a revolutionary commitment, was somehow able to cling to an optimistic view of human nature that envisioned the inevitable triumph of the righteous oppressed. It remained for a handful of men to see the issues as they were—hardheaded social critics capable of scrutinizing their own and their associates' motives as well as those of their opponents: critics not only of society's ills but of proposed remedies. They were, at that time, pacifists and socialists whose commitment was based on a pragmatic assessment rather than a utopian vision, and their assessment took prominently into account a generally Marxist critique leavened by Freud, finding that man acts not from simple but complex motives which reflect his class interests, partisan biases, and national goals—no matter what he likes to think his objectives are.

Their leading representative was Reinhold Niebuhr, a man whose idealism was strongly tempered by his many-sided experiences in industrial Detroit, where he had seen the growth of both corporate interests and organized labor and had experienced the struggle between them in a more complex and searching way than had been the case with most devotees of social justice like Muste. Like Walter Lippmann, John Dewey, and a few others, Niebuhr sufficiently transcended his own involvements to be able to discern with penetrating insight the ironies inherent in them and to grasp the total context. A brilliant mind, nurtured in a more traditional theology than his FOR colleagues, yet more exposed than most of them to the direct impact of both automotive technology and mass-production methods, he sounded a new note in the evolving Social Gospel. "The applied sciences," he wrote in 1927, "have created an impersonal civilization in which human relations are so complex, its groups and units so large, its processes so impersonal, the production of things so important, and ethical action so difficult that personality is both dwarfed and outraged in it."[17] Niebuhr's major impact was not felt until the 1930s, but already in the decade of modernistic optimism and bourgeois illusions, he was pointing toward an important new statement of the contemporary human condition and the problematic of social salvation.

A perusal of the footnotes or indexes of Niebuhr's books, not to mention his numerous articles and reviews, suggests the vastness of the intellectual reservoir in which his thinking took shape, and any attempt to reduce it to a manageable handful of academic or other sources can only result in misinterpretation. A full-scale study of his thought in relation to other currents in the period of his maturation would, however, provide a valuable perspective on the salient strengths and anomalies of American Protestant thought in that crucial period of transition. One of the most striking features of Niebuhr's thought is a keen grasp of the identity between what Karl Marx described as "ideological" thinking and what Sigmund Freud called "rationalization"—ways of justifying human self-interest, disguising selfish motives or human inadequacies as objective, generous, or adequate. Niebuhr com-

---

[17] Reinhold Niebuhr, *Does Civilization Need Religion?* (New York: Macmillan 1927), p. 5 f.

bines a socio-political realism with a psychological realism. There are traces of this in James and Rauschenbusch, and it plays an incipient role in the shaping of the Chicago school. Edward Scribner Ames falls considerably short of Niebuhr's awareness of the factor of self- and group-interest; yet his psychologically informed and socially oriented religious pragmatism certainly represents a move in that direction. Shailer Mathews's *The Validity of American Ideals* (1922) reflects the same kind of limited and middle-class cultural optimism that circumscribes Ames' vision; if it misfired it was nevertheless reasonably well aimed, a move toward critical realism regarding man in society. The biblical studies of Shirley Jackson Case were in much the same vein.

Surely Niebuhr, before he left New Haven for Detroit, received some part of his intellectual equipment from Douglas Clyde Macintosh, who studied theology and philosophy at Chicago and took his doctorate there. Macintosh's first book, *The Problem of Knowledge*, appeared in 1915, in the year Niebuhr took his M.A. under him. In this and subsequent works he unfolded a viewpoint that rejected both the non-empirical rationalism of orthodoxy (e.g., Timothy Dwight, Samuel Hopkins, Charles Hodge) and the romantic subjectivism of Bushnell, Ritschl, and their followers. Under Ames at Chicago he discovered the alternative of empirical science, theology conceived as a theory based on the data of religious experience, and he found support for his inquiry in the common-sense realism of David Hume.

Developing his perspective in the rather different atmosphere of Yale, Macintosh preserved some of the characteristic Chicago emphases, such as the Deweyan rhetoric of "adjustment," while in many points of doctrine hewing to a more conventional faith in a transcendent and conscious personal deity, general and special providence, and immortality, each of which he sought to defend pragmatically. Macintosh's avowed realism is epistemological rather than socio-political. Following Ames and William James, he revises Schleiermacher's and Smyth's conceptions of the relation of religious feelings of awe, wonder, and absolute dependence to the reality of God, finding that this reality is also rooted in an awareness of values that have universal and ultimate validity. It is value that provides the basis of reverence, and God is that ultimate reality that is the source of value. Man is constitutively oriented toward value, because he must function in accordance with the principle of reality or suffer actual losses of value. Hence, says Macintosh in *Theology As an Empirical Science*, man's experience of value is a religious perception, for it is "awareness of the presence and activity, within experience, of a Power that makes for a certain type of result in response to the right religious adjustment,"[18] i.e., behavior and attitude in accordance with faith and trust in God.

The "theological laws" that comprise scientific theology are admittedly inexact, but according to Macintosh experience does disclose such laws. Prayers are invariably answered if by "prayer" is meant not only a formula of words but "right religious adjustment." God is a constant, while men and their responses are variables, and specific moral results may be expected from man's faithfulness and repentance, for God as Holy Spirit responds to such adjustment. Human actions are therefore crucially important, though not self-sufficient, and it is here above all that critical realism must operate. Macintosh chooses monism rather than dualism, realism rather than idealism, and distinguishes between naïve and critical realisms. Mysticism, for Macintosh, exemplifies naïve realism, for it affirms the truth of man's direct experience of God while denying that ordinary experiences are equally real. Critical realism takes account of the fact, moreover, that perception and its object do not stand in a simple, obvious relation to one another but in existential unity. That is, perception occurs in a complex of experience, and so it is with the perception of God as an objective reality.

Every science begins with presuppositions, untested assumptions, such as axioms or theorems. The experiential validity of the religious life depends on man's relation to a God who is

---

[18] D. C. Macintosh, *Theology As an Empirical Science* (New York: Macmillan, 1919), p. 32.

real and not merely apparent; hence theology, recognizing that validity, presupposes the objective reality of God as a scientific fact. This does not make it a fact, but the assumption holds good unless and until it proves insupportable. The analysis of experience, according to Macintosh, provides not only confirmation of that assumption but knowledge of what God does, and these provide a reliable basis for formulating theological laws of experience that are not merely subjective. Beyond what may be scientifically ascertained, pragmatic considerations apply, for man must act. In *The Reasonableness of Christianity* (1925), Macintosh advances the pragmatic principle as a criterion of rational faith, distinguishing it from the scientific principle. Like James, he does not maintain that false ideas are good if they produce good results, but that beliefs that are unverifiable are validated by their results if they provide a basis for action on behalf of basic human purposes. The pragmatic principle relates scientific theology to the "normative" theology of a particular faith such as Christianity. For Christianity, the normative principle is Christocentric. Jesus, as the primary example of right religious adjustment, is the normative revelation of God's will for man, showing the religious and moral unity of that will. The transcendent God of normative faith is the same as the immanent God of empirical theology; hence the revelation of this God in Christ is not incompatible with scientific knowledge, and it finds pragmatic verification in the life of the dedicated Christian.[19]

Henry Nelson Wieman followed Macintosh with a much more Deweyan emphasis in *Religious Experience and Scientific Method* (1926), defining God as "that object, whatsoever its nature may be, which will yield maximum security and abundance to all human living when right adjustment is made."[20] Regarding both human personality and God as processes of nature, he sees their relation in those organic wholes of experience in which value arises. Friendship is one

---

19 See D. C. Macintosh, *The Reasonableness of Christianity* (New York: Scribner, 1925), pp. 149–153.
20 Henry Nelson Wieman, *Religious Experience and Scientific Method* (New York: Macmillan, 1927), p. 381.

such organic whole produced by a concatenation of growth processes that Wieman calls "progressive integration." Man does not make friendships; he can only assemble the various conditions they require, and "God is the integrating process that arises out of the interaction of all these factors when the right relations are established between them.[21] This is done by observation and experiment. Wieman's empirical conception underwent notable growth in the years to follow, but his early work remains interesting, both in its brashness of statement and its modernistic individualism. Drawing upon Pierre Janet's *Principles of Psychotherapy*, in one essay of 1927, he identifies salvation as adaptation to conditions favorable to growth. "If by salvation we mean the progressive fulfillment of the deepest need of human nature, then religion provides the only way of salvation. . . . It is the need of bringing to fulfillment that multiplication of responses which arise in a man over and above his established habits. It is to develop a growing system of habits. It is to interact with ever more of the world round about him. This is the life of aspiration. To succeed in it is to be saved. To fail is to become a lost soul."[22] Each of the examples he gives shows adaptation as an adjustment of the self to the demands of situation and environment; never in this context does he propose that the latter be changed.

As the optimistic decade drew to a close, there were still a few men like Charles E. Jefferson, whose *Christianizing a Nation* (1929) echoed the simple social moralism of Josiah Strong. Many more contented themselves with individualistic piety. Walter Lippmann, in *A Preface to Morals* (1929), probed deeper and discerned a turbulent chaos where formerly there had been firm ancestral certitudes. "Among those who no longer believe in the religion of their fathers, some are proudly defiant, and many are indifferent. But there are also a few, perhaps an increasing number, who feel that there is a vacancy

---

21 Wieman, "A Workable Idea of God," *Religious Education*, XXIII (1928), p. 965.
22 Wieman, "How Religion Cures Human Ill," *Journal of Religion*, VII (May 1927), p. 275 f.

in their lives."[23] To fill that vacancy, Lippmann proposed a perennial "religion of the spirit." "In the realm of the spirit, blessedness is not deferred: there is no future which is more auspicious than the present; there are no compensations later for evils now. Evil is to be overcome now and happiness is to be achieved now, for the kingdom of God is within you."[24] But the God whose kingdom was to be sought did not resemble that of Christianity so much as that of Epikouros, and Lippmann in effect counseled a stoical retreat from mundane controversies into a tolerant skepticism. His mature man "would be strong, not with the strength of hard resolves, but because he was free of that tension which vain expectations beget."[25] As an autopsy of the 1920s, the book had a certain sad and wise humanistic grandeur; as a preface to the 1930s it was a counsel of calm detachment, an almost ascetic aloofness to the "worldling's" concern with success and progress.

Within the battlements of theological modernism, at the height of the controversy, Gerald Birney Smith surveyed the major trends of the period and concluded on a note of crisis: "Suddenly God ceases to be a principle of explanation." The philosophically construed universe had given way to a scientific one, and God as either King or Absolute had no place in it. "While many interesting changes in doctrine have occurred, it would seem that even more interesting developments are ahead."[26] Such terms as "the new orthodoxy" and "the new morality," in the 1920s, took their place alongside "the new theology" which was now a half century old, and the physicist-inventor, Michael Pupin, authored a book titled *The New Reformation*. All of these uses of the word "new" reflected the pervasive impact of science, which had indeed opened a chasm

---

[23] Walter Lippmann, *A Preface to Morals* (New York: Macmillan, 1929), p. 3.
[24] *Ibid*, p. 329.
[25] *Ibid*, p. 330.
[26] Gerald Birney Smith, "A Quarter-Century of Theological Thinking in America," *Journal of Religion*, V (November 1925), p. 594. See also Shailer Mathews, "Twenty Five Years," *Journal of Religion*, VII (1927), p. 376 ff.

between the modern period and its past—the chasm that provided the occasion for T. S. Eliot's *The Waste Land* (1922), a title which in retrospect aptly describes the American religious terrain of the decade, barren and fallow under the winds of myopic optimism and scantly illumined by sparse and flickering lanterns of thought. When the American economy ground to a halt after the Wall Street crash in October 1929, the rock upon which most of American theology was built was shaken to its foundations. Yet so insulated were most theologians that it took much time and many polemics before they began to grasp the dimensions of this new and different kind of crisis.

THE AGE OF CRISIS

The 1930s began with an ongoing economic crisis that had already plunged several European countries into severe difficulty. Italy had gone fascist in 1922, and similar movements were afoot in France, Belgium, Poland, Germany, and elsewhere. In the course of the Depression decade they arose in Britain and the United States but were undercut by democratic social reforms, while the Moscow-dominated Communist movement first vied with the fascists in a bid for revolution, later allying themselves in "popular fronts" with liberals and democratic socialists.

The year 1933 marked a kind of turning point for two of the most advanced industrial nations. In January, Franklin D. Roosevelt was inaugurated President of the United States, and Adolf Hitler was appointed chancellor of the Republic of Germany. In March, both the New Deal and the Hitler dictatorship had begun. For a dozen years to follow, Hitler offered a solution to the economic crisis, and to a large extent applied it, through a policy of racism and conquest that finally led to war and Germany's unconditional defeat at a formidable cost. During the first half of that period, as Hitler built his Third Reich, the Roosevelt Administration applied a trunkful of improvised remedies with partial success, finally achieving prosperity through war.

"Can German and American Christians Understand Each Other?" asked H. Richard Niebuhr in a *Christian Century* article of July 23, 1930. The question was to prove portentous for the decade. A prior question was whether American Protestants understood themselves and the depths of their crisis. In Europe, the "crisis theology" of Emil Brunner and Karl Barth had garnered much support within the seminaries and among outstanding churchmen, especially in Germany. In large measure, Barth and his colleagues represented a break with the religious socialist movement, which in Germany and Switzerland had arisen before World War I. Broadly speaking, at the beginning of the 1930s there were the following groupings on the German theological scene: 1) the "Barthian" theologians of the Word, or "neo-orthodox"; 2) a related group comprising Rudolf Bultmann, Friedrich Gogarten and others; 3) various liberals of the old school; 4) Paul Tillich and others who remained religious socialists but had revised their thinking in the light of the war and social crisis; 5) conventional religionists somewhat ill-at-ease in a secular republic, accustomed to the authority of the Kaiser. Of these groups the last was by far the largest, but to some Americans the first, second and fourth were of greater interest, for they seemed to offer alternatives to the inadequacy of the bourgeois liberalism which they all attacked and which in the United States too now seemed increasingly inadequate.

Barth was little known in the United States except to those who read German. Among those who were well attuned to Barth, Brunner and Tillich were H. Richard Niebuhr, Walter Lowrie and a few others. In 1928, Douglas Horton of Harvard brought out an English translation of Barth's *The Word of God and the Word of Man,* a book originally published in 1925. In it Barth declared that "the greatest atrocities of life [are] the capitalistic order and war,"[27] and he proceeded to indict the

---

[27] Karl Barth, *The Word of God and the Word of Man* (Boston: Pilgrim Press, 1928), p. 18.

bourgeois church, with its fatuous theology, for indulging in wanton distortion of the truly Christian revelation, which shows God as standing in judgment over all human vanities. God, he insisted, was "wholly other" than man, and man's task is not to reason from experience but to heed God's word as disclosed in the Bible. Barth did not call for a return to old orthodoxies but for a new orthodoxy that accepted the findings of recent scholarship and combined them with a commitment to the historic church and its creeds. It was in short a new and sophisticated "reconstruction" of theology on a radically different basis from that of the liberals.

The liberals, particularly the Americans, had come to regard the church in a rather vague light. Those most committed to social Christianity often found the church itself a stumbling block and channeled their efforts through church-related social action agencies or fellowships unaffiliated with the churches. Since the late 1920s, however, the nascent ecumenical movement, especially its Faith and Order branch, was bringing American Christians into closer contact with the more formal traditions of European Christendom. Under the impact of the Depression, churches were closing along with banks for lack of funds and serious commitment. Moreover, the trivialization of normative religion before the 1929 crash left the churches ill equipped to face the situation that now prevailed. American Protestantism had invested much of its hopes and energies in the Volstead Act, and the Wickersham Commission in 1931 reported that the "noble experiment" was worse than a failure; it had spurred the rise of gangsterism. In that same year, nearly a hundred people died of starvation at four New York hospitals, and many of the voluntary agencies Gladden and Strong had worked to create had had to concede that the crisis was far beyond them. When the New Deal began, the number of unemployed stood at 15 million. It was no time for panaceas, least of all yesterday's.

Walter Marshall Horton, in a book begun before the crash, could still speak of *Theology and the Modern Mood* (1930). Then a professor of systematic theology at Oberlin, he was broadly in sympathy with the critical realism of D. C. Macintosh, and he was also the author of *A Psychological Ap-*

proach to Theology (1930). As the Depression continued, he gravitated in the general direction of Barth—*Realistic Theology* (1934), *Contemporary Continental Theology* (1936). It is perhaps no accident that Horton, like most of those who first responded to the new German theologies, was a member of the Fellowship of Reconciliation. Reinhold Niebuhr, its chairman, responded coolly to Barth but in general welcomed the note of realism in him as well as in Brunner and Tillich. Henry Pitney Van Dusen spoke of "The Sickness of Liberal Religion" in *The World Tomorrow*. H. Richard Niebuhr introduced Americans to the differences between Barth's and Tillich's realisms in Macintosh's symposium, *Religious Realism* (1931), while Wilhelm Pauck was already asking—*Karl Barth: Prophet of a New Christianity?* (1930). Yet it was Tillich rather than Barth whom H. R. Niebuhr found the more congenial, for Tillich's approach to society and culture was not unlike his own.

The most vigorous endorsements of Barth came from men who were not part of Niebuhr's circle—above all, Walter Lowrie, whose book *Our Concern With the Theology of Crisis* (1932) not only took up the cudgels for Barth but joined a scathing attack on liberalism to a general and knowledgable introduction to the whole spectrum of the new German theologies, with additional attention to a 19th century Danish forerunner, Søren Kierkegaard, to whom Lowrie subsequently devoted major attention as translator and biographer. In a lengthy, Kierkegaardian subtitle to *Our Concern*, he referred to "the crisis of society and of the church understood as the crisis of the individual before God."

Some such connection there might be, indeed, between individual, church and society. The emphases varied, and no real consensus emerged until the 1940s; meanwhile a loose set of alliances and interactions took shape under the hammer of events both at home and abroad. The Depression itself was enough to demand changes. It made Americans receptive to the German accents, but also to indigenous currents. *The New Masses*, a Communist journal, for a time became the leading literary magazine, featuring stories by such men as John Dos Passos, James T. Farrell, Richard Wright and John Steinbeck, men who never heard of Barth. Commenting on them, one historian observes, "The new realism engendered by bread lines, labor conflicts, and slums was definitely 'hard-boiled' "— to a degree eclipsing that of the Progressive Era.[28] At every turn American culture underwent change of this general kind. Pollyanna was out. Anything smacking of irrelevance or undue optimism was intellectually suspect and had to prove itself. The main drift was toward a new kind of Americanism, including a tough-minded re-examination of the American past. Parrington's realistic *Main Currents in American Thought* went to press before the Depression, but it dominated the 1930s with its highly secularistic negative view of the Puritans, just as scholars were about to begin rescuing them from the Victorians. Joseph Haroutunian's *Piety Versus Moralism: The Passing of the New England Theology* (1932) was among the first to give Jonathan Edwards his due, and it was soon followed by Perry Miller's *Orthodoxy in Massachusetts* (1933), neither of which was inspired by Barth or Tillich.

The religious situation in the United States in the early 1930s was complex. Most intellectuals had gone the way of Walter Lippmann, if indeed they did not make a personal religion of the New Deal or Communism—one or another type of secular humanism held sway among the majority. Whatever were the operative beliefs of the ordinary citizen, a statistical fact was the erosion of church involvement.[29] Articulate and committed Christians entered the decade for the most part as modernists and soon found themselves in quest of realism of some sort or degree. Those who were alert to the international scene were the most vexed, for they had learned to detest war, and many were pledged to avoid another at all costs, while at the same time they were acutely aware of the inhumanity of Hitlerism. Still another question for them was the plight of the unemployed and labor's struggle to organize. In 1932 there were fewer than three million union members in the

---

[28] Harvey Wish, *Contemporary America* (New York: Harper, 3d ed., 1961), p. 511.
[29] See Robert T. Handy, "The American Religious Depression, 1925–1935," *Church History*, XXIX (1960), pp. 3–16.

United States, and dedicated unionists were out to organize whole new industries. Could pacifists like Niebuhr claim to be realists if they balked at violence on behalf of labor's rights or if they ignored the violence of Nazism? Niebuhr himself wrestled with such questions well before Hitler achieved power, and his *Moral Man and Immoral Society* (1932) sounded a keynote of pragmatic realism that would reverberate for long afterward. At the same time, his brother's translation of Tillich's *The Religious Situation* appeared. The following year saw the German publication of the latter's massive book, *Die sozialistische Entscheidung* (The Socialist Decision), followed by Hitler's takeover and Tillich's dismissal from his university professorship and flight into exile. Thanks to the Niebuhr brothers, he found refuge in New York and was given a professorship at Union Theological Seminary. Others followed; soon there was a growing community of anti-Nazi German exiles in America, including distinguished men from various professions—novelist Thomas Mann, playwright Bertolt Brecht, composer Paul Hindemith. Many of the best minds in theology, philosophy, and the social sciences were suddenly transplanted at the height of their prestige, often overshadowing their American colleagues. One result was the confirmation of the rising trend toward the European ideas. Most of the exiles were determinedly European in their thought and culture, bred to a certain disdain for American ways, which demonstrably lacked their own punctilious thoroughness. Their American hosts were impressed and tended to cast themselves in the role of fledglings awaiting indoctrination. Events had already persuaded them of the worthlessness of their own antecedents, and they repented and erased their past, rather uncritically but perhaps understandably.

In 1933 Karl Barth's by now legendary *Römerbrief* of 1919 was translated as *The Epistle to the Romans.* Its appearance in America was matched by the publication of a strident article by Edwin A. Lewis, a former English Methodist missionary then professor of systematic theology at Drew. Liberalism, he said, once "helped to break the strangle-hold of terms and phrases which had become in all too many cases merely empty shibboleths,"[30] but now it had led to shame, weakness, and defeat. The Social Creed of the Federal Council, he charged, had been substituted for the Apostles' Creed, and a merely human Jesus for the Christ of faith. It was on the whole a more Christocentric and incarnational statement than Barth would have approved, but it affirmed the Barthian thrust toward doctrinal revitalization and renewal of theology independent of any help from philosophy. Lewis' article drew much fire from fellow Methodists, impelling him to return to the attack even more vehemently with a book, *A Christian Manifesto* (1934).

John Dewey's humane and reasonable *A Common Faith* (1934) could only seem the height of absurdity to excited churchmen like Lewis, the more so as they followed the course of the ongoing German church struggle. For Barth had uttered his ringing "No!" not only to the *Kulturprotestantismus* of the Weimar Republic but to Nazism's totalitarian claims. While the majority of German Christians accommodated themselves to Hitler's racist ideology, Barth and his comrades resisted, gathering at Barmen in 1935 and issuing a declaration on the basis of which they constituted themselves the Confessing Church, pledging allegiance to the Word of God as revealed in Christ. Among those who ranged themselves with him were Martin Niemöller, Heinrich Grüber, and Dietrich Bonhoeffer. Soon afterward, Barth was deported to his native Switzerland. Niemöller, Grüber, and others were later imprisoned. They were all men of conviction and courage, and their stand added weight to the position of their American sympathizers, for they acted not from "principles of Jesus" but as confessional churchmen. An American book that year mirrored the spirit of Barmen—*The Church Against the World*, with essays by H. R. Niebuhr, Wilhelm Pauck and Francis Pickens Miller. There were others, too, who were moved to explain and to temper their continuing liberalism. Rufus

[30] Edwin A. Lewis, "The Fatal Apostasy of the Modern Church," *Religion in Life*, II (Autumn 1933), p. 483.

Jones's *Rethinking Religious Liberalism* and William Adams Brown's *Finding God in a New World* both reflected the Barthian challenge, as did Harry Emerson Fosdick's *Christian Century* article, "Beyond Modernism," and the changing vocabulary of Henry Nelson Wieman. The whole theological center of gravity had shifted.

H. Richard Niebuhr had not become a Barthian, though he undoubtedly responded to the German church struggle. His own confessional leanings and his concern for the church as the primary locus for Christian action had roots in his own heritage, and he had been a leader in the developments that resulted in the formation of the Evangelical and Reformed Church in 1934. He was involved with the church in its larger quest for unity, too, almost to the exclusion of other involvements.

His brother Reinhold exerted influence in ecumenical circles also, but he had palpable stature in the FOR and the Socialist Party, and less directly the labor movement. In 1935 these commitments formed a major crisis. John L. Lewis and other militant labor leaders were preaching industrial unionism in contrast to the AFL's traditional stratified craft unions. In this context an irreconcilable split developed in the FOR, with Niebuhr and his associates resigning when a referendum committed FOR members to nonviolence in the labor struggle. *The World Tomorrow* ceased publication, reappearing later as *Fellowship;* and meanwhile Niebuhr became editor of a new journal, *Radical Religion,* under the auspices of his Fellowship of Socialist Christians. In leaving the FOR, Niebuhr reaffirmed his stubborn opposition to war, but Italy's invasion of Abyssinia and the outbreak of civil war in Spain forced him to reconsider this position as well, and from these tragic necessities to explore more deeply man's nature and the dynamics and meaning of history. The resulting "Niebuhrian" position owed something to the Europeans but much more to the exercise of a pragmatic realism arising from his own encounter with crises. As it emerged, it was called Christian realism by its proponents, largely to distinguish their position from the "religious realism" they once shared with liberals such as Wieman. The core of the Christian realist group was fairly distinct, centering at Union Theological Seminary and including such men as John C. Bennett and Henry Van Dusen, as well as the exiled German religious socialists, Paul Tillich and Eduard Heimann, who could hardly be called Niebuhrians.

Subscribers to *Radical Religion* totaled only a fraction of those who had read *The World Tomorrow,* and Niebuhr's views advanced against heavy odds, but those men who were ranged on both sides of the debate included key figures in the ecumenical and church social action movements as well as eminent pastors and professors—virtually the whole of American Protestantism's social conscience. The distinctive character of Niebuhr's dialectic can best be understood in its origin as a means of adjudicating the conflicting claims that events made upon that conscience. Niebuhr's was not a simple Machiavellian political realism of power, but a dialectic that acknowledged that attainable goals were compounded through an adjustment between visionary ideals and the realities of power. "No easy answers" became a hallmark of this approach, a complex situational ethic whose nemesis was the "simple moralism" of an untempered, untimely social idealism demanding a perfection that was in fact impossible.

Tillich also represented a dialectical approach to religion and culture, but a more formal, less commonsensical one employing categories and concepts drawn from the philosophy of Schelling and Dilthey, ultimately rooted in Boehme, Eckhart, and Plotinus. Tillich defined cultures as theonomous, autonomous, and heteronomous—or, roughly, religious, humanistic and mixed—and discussed the historic process as moving from one to another among these. He understood Jesus Christ not as a person but as the meaningful symbol of a decisive event in the historic process, the definitive event of *kairos,* "the fullness of time" in the midst of mere chronological sequence. Tillich's interpretation of history was a strikingly post-Hegelian one that offered itself as a Christian alternative to Marxism. Not only the Christ event but other events, such as the proletarian revolution, could be viewed in its light as timely (*en kairo*) or unpropitious, depending finally on a pragmatic assessment of actual historic factors present in the given situation—an assessment which Niebuhr managed with lighter theological tools.[31]

Tillich, who had been an active member of the German Social Democratic Party, found the American situation so different that, on Niebuhr's advice, he kept clear of politics and gave his attention to the broader sweep of world history. As time went on, his religious socialism was all but swallowed up by an increasing preoccupation with ontology, existential psychology, and systematic theology. Although from time to time he engaged in polemics with his American contemporaries, he never sank roots in the American tradition, remaining throughout his life a theological and philosophical alien. The world of his mind was a German one, and though many Americans entered it, they did so on his terms. A final observation on his and Niebuhr's socialism: At this time Niebuhr described himself as unabashedly Marxist, although in fact he was much closer to the undoctrinaire, pragmatic socialism of Walter Reuther and other stalwarts of the emerging Congress of Industrial Organizations (CIO)[32] than to the typical revolutionary rhetoric of the period. Tillich, on the other hand, was a non-Marxist who had been accustomed to relating himself to a labor movement that was then officially committed to a Marxist interpretation and goals.

The older Social Gospel did not lack advocates, nor did pacifism new or old. Shailer Mathews weathered the storm, but relevance was not the strong point of his *Christianity and Social Process* (1934). The pacifist McConnell contributed *Christianity and Coercion* (1933) to the FOR majority position and *Christian Materialism* (1936) to the labor struggle, but neither was more than a game try. More searching was Ernest

---

[31] See Paul Tillich, *The Interpretation of History* (New York: Scribner, 1936).

[32] It is perhaps more than a coincidence that Detroit's socialists, active in organizing the auto workers, displayed a breadth of social vision and a sense of relevance to American conditions not unlike Niebuhr's—in contrast to the alternatives of merely seeking immediate gains or reaching for the world. See Irving Howe and B. J. Widick, *The UAW and Walter Reuther* (New York: Random House, 1949).

Fremont Tittle's *Christians in an Unchristian Society* (1939). Perhaps the nearest liberal counterpart to Edwin Lewis's blast was Edwin McNeill Poteat's *The Social Manifesto of Jesus* (1935), a book that typified the sentimental moralizing that provoked Niebuhr's ire. Charles Clayton Morrison's *The Social Gospel and the Christian Cultus* (1933) offered a critique of normative Christianity from a similarly uncritically idealistic standpoint. From within the ecumenical movement itself came one of the decade's most popular pacifist books, *Religion Renounces War* (1934) by Walter W. Van Kirk, later a founder of the World Council of Churches. By any criteria, it attested the prevalent antiwar sentiment that was at its peak when Van Kirk wrote, but in this was its weakness. Its whole case rested on revulsion to World War I; once that mood passed, it became nothing but a relic. Popular magazines of the day, such as *Liberty* and *Collier's,* featured the findings of the U. S. Senate munitions investigations and plumped for a series of Neutrality Acts. Another church official, F. Ernest Johnson of the Federal Council, in *The Social Gospel Reexamined* (1940), offered a defense that was virtually a surrender—not on the peace issue but on the scope of social reconstruction generally. Sherwood Eddy, formerly one of the FOR's most prominent public speakers and a close friend of Niebuhr's, attempted to outflank Niebuhr in *Revolutionary Christianity* (1939), which combined urgency for peace with urgency for a more drastic social remedy than the New Deal offered. Few, if any, of these men were merely posturing. They spoke from commitments reflecting tangible involvement, from picket lines to founding such institutions as the Highlander Folk School in Tennessee.

To these must be added A. J. Muste. After a decade as an independent Marxist-Leninist political leader, Muste entered into an alliance with Leon Trotsky's anti-Stalinist international, only to learn that the alliance was merely a tactic whereby Trotsky won Muste's followers away from him. He returned from a meeting with Trotsky deeply disillusioned and soon thereafter returned to the FOR and the church, bringing with him not only revolutionary zeal but a keen intellect and a gift for hard-hitting polemics. Whether the issues were religious, social, or political, Muste could be counted on to acquit himself well in argument. His *Non-Violence in an Aggressive World* (1939) argued cogently for the effectiveness of strike action, Gandhian noncooperation, and other forms of mass action as alternatives to military force. A new aspect was Muste's demand that the church transform itself into a pacifist mass movement. He proposed this course of action as both the church's true mission and the only way out of the social crisis. In an article written soon after his break with Trotsky, he wrote that "if the church, or any substantial minority in it, will take seriously the gospel of the Lord whom it professes to serve and apply it persistently and in love, we can in all soberness and calm assert that never since the early Christian centuries has such a door been opened as now when, for the first time since that epoch, mankind is struggling to achieve a world civilization and waits . . . for a leadership possessed of dynamic and power adequate for such a task."[33] In short, pacifism was workable, morally mandatory for the church, and desperately needed by the world; all that was needed was a nation led by a church filled with dedicated pacifists. This kind of reasoning accorded with the mood of crisis and *kairos,* and it rebuked the church for "fatal apostasy" on a level other than that stressed by Lewis. Like every other pacifist proposal, however, Muste's realism foundered and became suppositious when the time came to count the recruits. Whatever the inadequacies of his program of action on the eve of World War II, however, he confirmed the intellectual thrust of pacifism in a symbiosis with Niebuhrian thought. Reared as a Dutch Calvinist, in half a century Muste absorbed the vocabularies of liberal theology, Quaker mysticism, Trotskyism and much else. Although he differed with Niebuhr, Barth, and Brunner diametrically on key assumptions, he readily invaded their worlds of discourse. It would be too much to say that he took the FOR with him, but such was his intellectual bent that, together with other

---

[33] A. J. Muste, "Return to Pacifism," *The Christian Century,* December 2, 1936, p. 1606.

factors already at work, he helped bring to an end the super-annuated and enfeebled Social Gospel.

Between March 1939, when Hitler forced Czechoslovakia to surrender to German control, and December 1941, when Japan attacked Pearl Harbor, the entire spectrum of Protestant social thought underwent a succession of changes that by 1942 had resulted in a fairly distinct polarization. Social pacifists like Muste found themselves closely allied with those whose paci-fism rested solely on individual scruples. Most of the more pragmatic social pacifists, such as Sherwood Eddy, who had defended economic sanctions in the 1935 debate, aligned them-selves more or less with Niebuhr. Isolationists, formerly allies of pacifism, became patriotic supporters of the nation at war, tacit allies of Niebuhr. *Radical Religion* was renamed *Chris-tianity and Society,* and its editors abandoned socialist partisan politics for the New Deal. Yet the New Deal was, in effect, over. In the emerging rhetoric of the actual war, the enemy ceased to be "fascism" and became "the aggressor." To put it a little too simply, the clash of democratic socialism with Nazi totalitarianism was transformed into a less explicitly ideolog-ical struggle between the democratic Allies and the Rome-Berlin-Tokyo Axis. Thus conceived, it was a defense of the American way of life against all comers, and former ideological disputants joined hands. National unity in the international struggle became normative for the theological community, moderating the drive for social change and drawing the un-social into the "war effort" with them.

It was Barth who was chiefly responsible for an upsurge of interest in Kierkegaard. Among the minor anomalies of the time is the fact that the first Kierkegaard book to appear in English, *Purity of Heart* (1938), was translated not by Lowrie but by a Quaker pacifist, Douglas V. Steere. Men like Steere and Rufus Jones, with their emphasis on spirituality and mysti-cism, offered a distinctive concept of immanence that set them off from most liberals, pacifist or otherwise, and in the FOR they were the major countervailing influence to social pacifism —an influence that Muste eventually incorporated into his multi-faceted outlook. Kierkegaard's call to a radical personal commitment could certainly be harmonized with Quaker pacifism. But this was only part of his assault on the vapid pieties of a conventionalized cultural Protestantism. And *Purity of Heart* was accompanied by *Philosophical Fragments* and books by Haecker, Geismar, and E. L. Allen on Kierkegaard's life and thought. H. Richard Niebuhr reviewed them all in *Yale Divinity News* in 1938; Princeton became a veritable bastion of Kierkegaardian thought; his influence became more broadly pervasive than that of any single non-orthodox theologian, providing them all with a new-found common ancestor. Kierkegaard also provided a link with a larger Europe than that of Switzerland and Germany—an intellectual community ranging from the Catholicism of Unamune and Maritain to the Russian Orthodoxy of Berdyaev, each with its own religious philosophy to leaven the Calvinist foundations of the neo-orthodox, but also to some extent giving Niebuhr, Barth, and Brunner the appearance of closer unity than would otherwise have been the case.

The Kierkegaardian note of commitment was sounded with relevance by a young German theologian from the Confessing Church, whose *Nachfolge* (Discipleship, 1937) contrasted "costly" with "cheap" grace. The author, Dietrich Bonhoeffer, had served as pastor of a German congregation in London and was well known in the ecumenical youth movement. Niebuhr first met him when he visited New York in 1931, and he was there again in 1939. Bonhoeffer could have remained at Union Seminary and was urged to do so, but chose to return to the German church struggle. His writings were known only to those who could read German, an increasing but still limited number.

Both he and Kierkegaard would receive greater attention later. For various reasons the war halted new translations and dimmed the continuing focus on works of German origin. For one thing, it broke contact with those who remained in Germany and cast a shadow over those like Bultmann, Gogarten, Heidegger, and Jaspers, whose stance toward Nazism was ambiguous, indifferent, or suspect. At least nominally, neo-orthodoxy took on an indigenous character, with Niebuhr cast in two interlocking roles: his own and that of surrogate for Barth et al. Remoteness enhanced Barth's stature and canonized his works. The war thus tended to diminish the pace of neo-Reformation theological development in the United States and to renew the flow of other currents. Barth and Brunner were not published again in English translation till after the war, but their available books received continuing attention, although perhaps, less than before. From Tillich, although he was in New York throughout the war years, no new book came until 1948. Whatever the reason, the volume of new theological work declined and a hiatus ensued.

By far the most outstanding book of the early forties was Reinhold Niebuhr's Gifford Lectures, *The Nature and Destiny of Man* (1941–1943), and during the war years he gained a reputation unparalleled by any other American religious thinker of the century. Many erstwhile pacifists and theological liberals rallied to his viewpoint, chastened by the actual coming of war. More than a few did so uncritically, and still others simply exchanged liberal conformity for another, more conservative kind, marching past Niebuhr to the more traditional verities. Niebuhr himself drew closer to the neo-Calvinist position, drawn there by the exigencies of war—this was taking place even before Hitler's invasion of Poland. Some of those who had made common cause with him earlier now reconsidered. Walter Marshall Horton, early in 1939, felt the trend of neo-orthodoxy and sought a middle way between it and the liberalism he had abandoned[34]—in effect, a renewal of the pragmatic freedom of critical Christian realism within the context of the church. Some of Niebuhr's closest associates felt likewise and enunciated a variation which they styled "neo-liberalism." This was the emphasis of John Bennett's *Christian Realism* (1941), which however did not hinder Bennett from joining with Niebuhr in founding a new journal that year, *Christianity and Crisis*. It was not so much the seed of a new round of controversy as a differentiation along the new spec-

---

[34] See Walter Marshall Horton, "Between Liberalism and the New Orthodoxy," *The Christian Century* LVI (May 17, 1939).

trum. Niebuhr was linked to the "right" with Barth's dialectical critique of all relative values, and to the "left" with Bennett's social pragmatism. Bennett's position at that time could be described as undialectical, exempting the church from scrutiny as one institution among others and attempting to view it as transcending society. On one level, this was Barth's view—the church as the Body of Christ—but his dialectic saw it in tension with the normative church of "religion." Niebuhr's dialectic was vaster, both transcendently and pragmatically, though it was sometimes obscured by its very complexities or by particular emphases. His identification of sin as essentially pride and self-interest, for example, was lucid enough, and more cautionary than pessimistic, but in the ears of his listeners he too often echoed what they thought was Calvin's or Barth's image of man as totally depraved. Niebuhr's cautionary view of man's sinful nature was yet to have its own excesses during the Cold War, but these were more a matter of application than of method.

After Pearl Harbor, Niebuhr abandoned both socialism and Marxism, transmuting their already pragmatized concerns into political liberalism and a commitment to the welfare state that the New Deal had preserved under wartime prosperity. More than fifteen million workers now belonged to unions; throughout the forties the urgency of their struggle gave way to the general defense of democratic values, first against the Axis powers and fascism, then against Stalinism. Niebuhr's influence continued to prevail widely during this decade and into the fifties, by which time other voices had begun to be heard as well, the religious thought alongside his own held for the most part to the emergent spectrum. Typical of the general neo-orthodox tone were the writings of John Knox, a Union Seminary colleague, whose *The Man Christ Jesus* (1941) was one answer to Lewis's call for a new Christology. Walter Marshall Horton's *Our Eternal Contemporary* (1942) was a capable neo-liberal effort that also began to show the influence of Kierkegaard. Another manifestation of neo-liberalism, or more accurately of the whole spectrum, was Van Dusen's symposium, *The Christian Answer* (1945), which was keyed to the vaguely hopeful mood that greeted the war's end. Theodore O. Wedel's *The Coming Great Church* (1945) expanded upon the ecumenical accents of Van Dusen's book, looking toward the creation of the World Council of Churches. Explicitly or implicitly, the church was a dominant motif in many books and articles; others adumbrated classical doctrines—redemption, the trinity, resurrection—with subdued socio-ethical focus or none at all. The humanity of Jesus and the idea of the church as a brotherhood were fiercely out of fashion. Protestantism became "the churches of the Reformation heritage," with Christ as Lord and Savior; the church was where the Word was proclaimed, ostensibly with sharp fidelity to creedal authority. Theologically, the minister's role was not so much to lead or to counsel but to preach, sticking close to a text chosen for its doctrinal bearing and working out its exegesis and exposition.

Philosophy was not dead, but it was relegated to a subservient position, such as the philosophy of history as an adjunct to revelation, which was taken to be the only valid norm for theology. The biblical God, it was insisted, was Lord of creation and of history, not of nature; to develop a natural theology, a philosophy of religion, or a rational or empirical understanding of God were outside the tradition of the Reformation and were therefore discountenanced by the neo-orthodox.

Yet it was from that quarter that an alternative idea of a "new Reformation" came—not a renewal or a return of Calvinism but a deepening of the enterprise already in progress before the Depression, at Chicago. With the installation of a new president, Robert M. Hutchins, in 1929, the university was slated for sweeping changes that set it still further apart from other institutions of higher learning. In the fields of religion and philosophy significant change was felt within the continuities noted earlier, just as Henry Nelson Wieman and Charles Hartshorne began their careers there. By the mid-thirties, with the retirement of Mathews and Ames, a transition had taken place. For these reasons, Wieman and Hartshorne were able to develop their thought in comparative isolation from the mainstream of theological controversy, notwithstanding a certain trend there, too, toward European influences. The latter, typified by the non-Catholic neo-Thomism of Mortimer J. Adler, were in a sense comparable to the neo-orthodox trend elsewhere, but they had little if any influence on these men. At Harvard meanwhile, Perry Miller and Ralph Barton Perry carried on studies that would eventuate in the former's *The New England Mind* (1939) and the latter's *Puritanism and Democracy* (1944), but of greater importance for Chicago was Alfred North Whitehead's arrival at Harvard in 1924. Of the ten books by Whitehead that appeared between 1926 and 1954, several contain one or more chapters on religion, symbolism, and related subjects, informed by but not confined to a Christian perspective. Whitehead's *Process and Reality*, his crowning philosophical achievement, was published in 1929 and had pronounced effect on Hartshorne's thought, not to mention its broader repercussions, chiefly at a later date.

It was in the following book, *Adventures of Ideas*, that Whitehead proposed a "new reformation" for theology. The Protestant Reformation, he said, was a "complete failure, in no way improving Catholic theology,"[35] because neither the Reformation nor Catholic thought had grown forward from the three successive stages which comprise Christianity's revelation. The first is not, as one would expect, the Old Testament; for Whitehead it is Plato's conception of "the divine element in the world . . . as a persuasive agency and not as a coercive agency."[36] The second phase, "which forms the driving power of the religion, is primarily an exhibition in life of moral intuition,"[37] "its revelation in act of that which Plato divined in theory."[38] The third phase is that of the early Christian theologians, whose great achievement was an improvement upon Plato's understanding of immanence rather than to Plato's doctrine of the derivative or imitative image. In so

---

[35] Alfred North Whitehead, *Adventures of Ideas* (New York: Macmillan, 1933), p. 212.
[36] *Ibid*, p. 213.
[37] *Ibid*.
[38] *Ibid*, p. 214.

doing, says Whitehead, they discovered the direction Plato's metaphysics should have taken if it was to account for God's persuasive agency. But here the theologians blundered; instead of pursuing the metaphysical inquiry into the nature of God, they merely sublimated into philosophical terms the figure of an Egyptian despot. "In the final metaphysical sublimation, [God] became the one absolute, omnipotent, omniscient source of all being, for his own existence requiring no relation to anything beyond himself."[39] Thus they ended up with the same kind of gulf Plato had and foreclosed the possibility of developing the doctrine of immanence as an interpretation of the unity that may be observed among the world's diversities. The task to which theology should address itself, said Whitehead, was to undertake a new reformation that would take that interpretation as its foundation—not simply a revision of the traditional conception of God. To do so, Whitehead, argued, would not be merely an innovation keyed to contemporary needs but a correction that would conserve the unique power of the revelation in Christ.

Liberal theology since the Enlightenment had "confined itself to the suggestion of minor, vapid reasons why people should continue to go to church in the traditional fashion,"[40] while neglecting the momentous task of rationally accounting for the rise of civilization "in a world which superficially is founded on the clashings of senseless compulsion,"[41] "to show how the world is founded on something beyond mere transient fact"[42] and to account for that which is enduring and undying in the finite and perishing lives of men.

The idea of a personal God, for Whitehead, is not a direct intuition but a rational interpretation of an intuition provided by religious experience. The insight behind that idea is the real revelaton, a sense of a "character of permanent rightness,"[43] which inspires reverence. If it is a valid insight, it will

---

[39] *Ibid,* p. 217.
[40] *Ibid,* p. 218.
[41] *Ibid.*
[42] *Ibid,* p. 221.
[43] Whitehead, *Religion in the Making* (New York: Macmillan, 1926), p. 61.

reward philosophical inquiry beyond the apparent facts of experience. Science has disclosed that reality is not static; there is no ultimate level of reality or being that may be regarded as timelessly eternal. That which endures must somehow be found within the process of time and change. Moreover, the cosmic process is not mechanical but organic, which is to say that it is characterized by creativity, by the evolution and emergence of new things. If God is eternal, it is not as the fixed pivot on which everything else turns but rather as an actuality at the heart of ongoing cosmic process, as a principle of order and direction.

Creation is not a once-for-all occurrence in the remote past; rather, Whitehead prefers to speak of creativity, that which continuously brings order and value—not out of nothingness, but in the infinite multiplicity of processes within the total process. In terms of such a metaphysic, God must be a living reality, not simply a prime mover who once set things in motion but both "primordial" and "consequent." God is the continuously operating principle of selection in the cosmic process of which biological evolution and human history are subprocesses, or, as Whitehead terms it, the "principle of concretion," in this sense not so much creating the world as sustaining it, rescuing it from chaos. This is why Whitehead says that God "does not create the world, he saves it.[44] This is also why God is love rather than mere structural order. Whitehead was particularly struck by the fact of "tenderness" and its survival and growth—a fact hardly compatible with God conceived as prime mover or moral tyrant. "Love neither rules nor is unmoved; also it is a little oblivious as to morals. It does not look to the future; for it finds its own reward in the immediate present."[45] It is "the tender elements in the world"—the lilies of the field—that suggest to Whitehead not only the ultimacy of love but a metaphysical theory predicated on the mutual interplay between love and the world. The complexity of his theory is an explication of that mutual interplay. Elements of Whitehead's thought might be traceable through Coleridge

---

[44] Whitehead, *Process and Reality* (New York: Macmillan, 1929), p. 526.
[45] *Ibid*, p. 521

to Schelling and earlier antecedents, accounting for certain resemblances between his conception of God and Tillich's. But where Tillich sought to mediate between traditional theology and modern thought, correlating the symbols of faith with secular ideas, Whitehead's "new reformation" begins with a much more fully developed understanding of process than Schelling's or Tillich's and, like James, he is readier to reduce the Christian faith to its indispensable rudiments. In addition, Whitehead's pioneering work in mathematical logic helped him to break out of traditional ways of understanding both knowledge and nature. If one recalls the influence of Peirce on Royce and James, it will be apparent how Whitehead's most telling influence would be felt by men schooled in their world of thought, whether at Harvard or Chicago or more indirectly.

The early writings of Whitehead, from *The Organisation of Thought* (1916) to *The Concept of Nature* (1919), had wide general effect in fostering an empirical religious realism in conjunction with other currents of thought. Henry Nelson Wieman, Robert L. Calhoun of Yale, Walter Marshall Horton, and D. C. Macintosh were among those brought together on this basis. Wieman, in particular, synthesized Whiteheadian thought with value theory and other elements, and by the end of the 1930s his synthesis had taken definite shape, retaining a processive concept of God as the source of value and creativity but emphasizing structures of growth and health among human beings. Wieman represents a kind of renovation of naturalism closer to Dewey than to Tillich but on a spectrum between the two. Charles Hartshorne, in contrast, represents a more direct expression of the type of new reformation Whitehead called for and a more consistent response to Whitehead's whole approach, particularly his cosmology, metaphysics, and logic.[46] But where Whitehead speaks of "tenderness," Hartshorne develops "sensitivity" as a characteristic of relationship. God, far from being exalted and aloof, is the very power

---

[46] For an excellent brief discussion of Whitehead and Hartshorne, see John E. Smith, "Philosophy of Religion and Process Philosophy," in Paul Ramsey, ed., *Religion* (Englewood Cliffs: Prentice-Hall, 1965), pp. 430–448.

that sustains and redeems. "Love, defined as social awareness, taken literally, is God."[47]

A common characteristic of Whitehead, Wieman, and Hartshorne is their concern for civilization. Whitehead's is expressed as a detached overview of the centuries—humane, liberal, stressing not so much the processes of society as the educational values likely to keep "social progress" going. Both of the Americans are more explicitly involved with the nature of the good society or how to make American democracy work. But by comparison with the mainstream of social Christianity or with the realism of Niebuhr and Bennett they appear as general theorists rather than men seeking to address actual problems.

If, however, we were to compare Whitehead and Barth, we would find a more clearly impassable gulf between them than between, say, Wieman and H. Richard Niebuhr. Despite the latter's avowed confessionalism, it is coupled with a pragmatism and secularity that are close to the spirit of William James and to Wieman's usage of revelation as that which renders experience intelligible. To Niebuhr, "the reason which is correlate with revelation is practical reason, or the reason of self rather than of impersonal mind."[48] As Bernard Loomer has pointed out, there is no basic incompatibility between process philosophy and Niebuhr's understanding of revelation.[49] The disjunction between them is rather a matter of emphases magnified in the polarizing tensions of divergent schools of thought. At a later time, less given to polemics, biblical and philosophical theology would discover in each other alternative and complementary approaches rather than conflicting claims. At the time of their initial acceleration, each had to assert its distinctive strengths in opposition to a liberal establishment. The Whiteheadians did it by a route that

---

[47] Charles Hartshorne, *The Divine Relativity* (Yale University Press, 1948), p. 36.
[48] H. Richard Niebuhr, *The Meaning of Revelation* (New York: Macmillan, 1941), p. 94.
[49] See Bernard Loomer, "Neo-Naturalism and Neo-Orthodoxy," *Journal of Religion,* XXVIII (April 1948), pp. 79–91.

seemed super-liberal, while the others seemed anti-liberal. Both may be more accurately viewed as post-liberal.

Virtually unique among the religious thinkers of the 1940s was Nels F. S. Ferré. A student of Brightman and Whitehead, he combined their understanding of process with the neo-orthodoxy of Gustaf Aulén and Anders Nygren. "We must," said Ferré, "combine theologically the absolutes of Christian faith with the relativities of the human reason."[50] Another way of stating the matter is to acknowledge the two great traditions of Western civilization. The one emphasizes transcendence, a rigorous ethic of righteousness and asceticism; it finds expression in Hebraicism, Calvinism, Puritanism. The other stresses immanence, "fullness of life, aesthetic enjoyment, freedom of expression. The Renaissance and the romantic period are historical examples of this spirit."[51] Ferré's *Faith and Reason* (1946) remains a cogent and large-minded exploration of the nature of science, philosophy, and religion, drawing upon a wide range of resources in each field, from James and Whitehead to Kierkegaard and Berdyaev.[52]

TOWARD THE POST-MODERN ERA

Although *Faith and Reason* was warmly received by Reinhold Niebuhr, its author was soon widely rumored to be heretical. In less than a decade, he resolved the ambiguities of his position by embracing what he called "classical Christianity," a kind of neo-orthodoxy centered in the Nicene Creed rather than in Reformed doctrines. In the Centennial Lectures at Louisville Presbyterian Seminary, 1955, he proposed a Christology of incarnation and *agape* based on biblical exegesis and the theology of the early church, with barely a passing nod to

---

[50] Nels F. S. Ferré, *The Christian Fellowship* (New York: Harper, 1940), p. 125.
[51] *Ibid*, p. 126.
[52] Nels F. S. Ferré, *Faith and Reason* (New York: Harper, 1946). See also Ferré, *Reason in Religion* (New York: Nelson, 1963).

process thought, which now assumed only an incidental role. With the publication of these lectures amplified as *Christ and the Christian* (1958), his transition from philosopher of religion to churchly theologian was virtually complete. His move was paralleled by that of Daniel Day Williams, a moderate Whiteheadian who by the early 1950s was celebrating the onset of a "theological renaissance" arising from the general victory of neo-orthodoxy.

The immediate postwar period rapidly modulated into a new phase of world crisis. The end of World War II itself was problematical. The hopeful founding of the United Nations was shadowed by America's use of the atomic bomb at Hiroshima and Nagasaki and by a series of Communist takeovers which, as Winston Churchill stated barely six months after the war's end, clamped an Iron Curtain over eastern Europe. Soon the Cold War between the West and the Soviet bloc was under way, with harsh consequences for American culture and religious thought. As early as 1947, the Stalinist cultural purges in the Soviet bloc were to find their American counterparts in "loyalty" investigations and the blacklisting of ten Hollywood directors and writers. Those few Protestant liberals like Henry F. Ward, who clung to their wishful illusions about the USSR, were thoroughly discredited. What was worse, however, pacifists like A. J. Muste, who had no such illusions but sought ways of reconciling the great powers, were smeared as "Communist sympathizers." Political liberals and Christian realists, committed from Pearl Harbor onward to a united national struggle against Axis totalitarianism, now had to choose between the establishment and dissent in a different kind of atmosphere. Reinhold Niebuhr's *Christianity and Power Politics* (1948) appeared in a year marked by the Communist seizure of Czechoslovakia and the Berlin blockade and airlift, and *Christian Realism and Political Problems* (1954) came in the wake of the Korean War, at a time when Senator Joseph R. McCarthy was still able to gain a hearing for sweeping charges of treason against respected American leaders. It was an agonizing time, characterized by conformity and suspicion, and even the best of the establishment liberals found it hard to temper their support for the Cold War with sufficient prophetic criticism. Niebuhr and his associates tended to narrow their range of vision, at least partly earning the sardonic epithet, "theologians of the State Department." Whatever its validity or lack of validity, neo-orthodoxy became the normative religious outlook of the educated Protestant of the 1950s.

The era of the Cold War was also the era of a new, disillusioned, secular philosophy, the tragic humanistic existentalism of Jean-Paul Sartre and Albert Camus. From another quarter, former Communists testified to the collapse of their utopian vision in Arthur Koestler's symposium, *The God That Failed* (1950). In an age of alienation, mass culture, and material affluence, shadowed by the nuclear weapons race and the hydrogen bomb, a religious revival arose. Whether church membership actually increased in proportion to population growth is debatable,[53] but expenditures for the building of new church edifices rose steadily from $26 million in 1945 to a peak of over one billion dollars in 1960. Church attendance soared, and alongside such obvious religious best sellers as Norman Vincent Peale's *The Power of Positive Thinking* (1952) there appeared a smaller but substantial readership for Paul Tillich's *The Courage to Be* (1952). This, however, was no longer the Tillich of *The Socialist Decision* but of a personal, existential affirmation mediating between secular perspectives and a generally neo-orthodox concept of faith and transcendence. Both Peale and Tillich gained readers because they offered remedies for individual anxiety. Peale's remedy promised an easy way to success; Tillich's offered a way to self-acceptance and meaningful existence on a firmer basis of integrity.

The 1950s were also characterized by important denominational mergers such as the United Presbyterian Church in the U.S.A. and the formation of the United Church of Christ, both

---

[53] See Winthrop S. Hudson, "Are the Churches Really Booming?", *The Christian Century*, LXXII (1955), pp. 1494–1496, and Benson Y. Landis, "Trends in Church Membership in the United States," *The Annals of the American Academy of Political and Social Sciences*, vol. 332 (November 1960), pp. 1–8.

in 1958, while large crowds flocked to hear conservative evangelist Billy Graham preach literal hellfire and invite "decisions for Christ." Religion gained renewed popularity and respectability such as it had not seen since the early 1920s. The general response to its intellectual expression was without exact precedent; the nearest equivalent would be the Progressive Era. Theologians such as Tillich, Niebuhr, and Barth were featured in such magazines as *Time* and *The Saturday Evening Post* and were studied by small groups of laymen in many local churches. In striking contrast to earlier periodic religious revivals in American history, this one was "formless and unstructured, manifesting itself in many different ways and reinforcing all religious faiths quite indiscriminately."[54] Moreover, thanks to a general acceptance of the neo-orthodox distinction between "religion" and "faith," there was a strong impulse among church historians and other Protestant intellectuals to discount mere numerical success and to seek a more deeply authentic result. There was, to be sure, a superficial kind of neo-orthodox "style"—form without substance—but even amid its conventions and pieties it was hard to be merely fashionable when the style involved a Kierkegaard or a Barth, a Tillich or Bonhoeffer.

Daniel Day Williams, summarizing the prevalent neo-orthodoxy in the early 1950s, outlined the essential articles of faith as follows. Only the one true and transcendent God is holy "above all the splendid and yet corruptible values of our civilization."[55] It is because the values of civilization are not holy that they do not save us. The story of Jesus discloses that man is the bearer of this holy God's image. "Man is made for God. Man can despoil his holy destiny", but "God makes possible a new life for sinful men" through forgiveness.[56] "The meaning of the new life is personal existence in faith, in humility and in

---

54 Winthrop S. Hudson, *Religion in America* (New York: Scribner, 1965), p. 383. See also William Peters, "The Growing Doubts About Our Religious Revival," *Redbook*, November 1957, and Martin E. Marty, *The New Shape of American Religion* (New York: Harper, 1959).
55 Daniel Day Williams, *What Present-Day Theologians Are Thinking* (New York: Harper, 1952; rev. 1959), p. 18.
56 *Ibid*, p. 21, p. 23.

love. . . . To be 'in Christ' is to live as one of his 'congregation.' "[57] In a dozen pages, Williams takes note of four groups of theologians who provide alternatives to Karl Barth's "exclusive biblicism." Both there and in discussions of ethics, Christology, and the doctrines of God and the church, cursory attention is given to American theologians, but they are greatly overshadowed by Barth. On the whole, one gets the impression that serious theology is mainly the province of Europeans, including the British. The impression is not altogether inaccurate as a statement of the general climate in American theological circles of the 1950s and early 1960s, whose roots in the American past had been all but destroyed. A generation of younger theologians reaching maturity in the years after World War II confronted a world in which, with few and dwindling exceptions, American seminaries seemed little more than colonial outposts of the great centers of learning at Basel, Zürich, Marburg, Göttingen, Heidelberg, and St. Andrews. Even such Americans as the Niebuhrs tended to be assessed in terms of European theology and philosophy, and their American roots were discounted as a kind of adolescence.

Some of the historical factors responsible for this trend have already been suggested. American politics were internationalized by the Cold War, and Europe in that period underwent a major intellectual upheaval in the wake of the traumatic Hitler years. The founding of the World Council of Churches at Amsterdam in 1948 and the building of its headquarters in Geneva, the rise of Evangelical Academies in West Germany— these and other developments riveted attention on the European scene. Karl Barth's monumental *Church Dogmatics* came to be regarded as unquestionably the greatest contribution to Protestant thought since Luther and Calvin, a view which carried with it a hunger for the sense of tradition that only European Christendom could give. With this, in the context of the ecumenical church, went an even larger sense of tradition, still European, which could provide common ground for the divergent Reformation and post-Reformation churches

----

[57] *Ibid*, p. 24.

and those of the worldwide Anglican communion, not to mention Roman Catholicism and Eastern Orthodoxy. Barthian and similar concepts of the church and faith were congenial to the ecumenical dialog. Two centuries of American religious thought, from the Enlightenment to the dawn of neo-orthodoxy, were dismissed as "essentially erroneous"[58], a statement which could only imply that the whole history of American Protestant thought since Jonathan Edwards was to be regretted.

The words are Paul Tillich's, and in the 1950s his influence surpassed that of any American theologian, including the Niebuhrs. Notwithstanding his differences with Barth or his long residence in the United States, he remained an emissary of European thought. Throughout his writings, his passing references to Americans are patronizing. If Dewey had an insight, Marx had it earlier and better; Hartshorne is reducible to Schelling; Kierkegaard anticipated Niebuhr; and so forth.[59] It is symptomatic of the climate of Europeanization that Tillich, upon his retirement from Union Seminary in 1955, was appointed to a special professorship at Harvard and to another at Chicago in 1962. Also symptomatic was a general rise in the standards of theological education, enlarging greatly the number of first-rate seminaries and university religion departments with a predominantly European orientation.

By the middle and late 1950s, such distinguished Americans as James Robinson and Carl Michalson were making important contributions to international theological discussion from an almost wholly European intellectual context. To a very large extent, this meant a narrowing of theological focus and an alienation from American traditions and problems. Much of the theological writing of the period was arid and derivative, but it was by no means all shallow or misconstrued. What-

---

[58] Paul Tillich, "The Present Theological Situation in the Light of the Continental European Development," *Theology Today,* VI (October 1949), p. 299.

[59] See, for example, Paul Tillich, *Perspectives on 19th and 20th Century Protestant Theology* (New York: Harper & Row, 1967). This posthumous book, based on lectures given in 1962–63, is entirely devoted to German thought.

ever its deficiencies and distortions, the general character of neo-orthodoxy, whether European or American, provided a firm matrix for serious, illusionless thinking about the nature and condition of man. If it restricted the range of vision, much of the thinking within that range was nevertheless hardheaded. The distinctive stresses of both Niebuhr and Barth, not necessarily in their response to immediate events but certainly in their doctrinal groundwork, militated against any notion that the religious revival portended the triumph of Christendom. On the contrary, neo-orthodoxy was typically better attuned to resisting the claims of "religion" and of secular culture than to meeting them in a positive way. It was, after all, in resistance that Barth's strongly transcendent God had emerged, making the Confessing Church a bastion against Hitlerism. It was in opposition to the bland normativeness of liberal Protestantism that Kierkegaard's notion of the solitary "knight of faith" had arisen. And for reasons already discussed, every type of social Christianity had been sublimated into something much less ambitious than the Social Gospel—defense of a moderate welfare state against Communist totalitarianism.

Between 1955 and 1958 a number of important historical and theological events occurred—the end of the McCarthy period, a significant thaw in the Cold War, the accession of Pope John XXIII. The year 1956 began with the epochal bus boycott led by Martin Luther King in Montgomery, Alabama—a struggle led by Christian ministers and motivated in Christian terms. Its immediate impact on the theological community was slight until four years later, but in many ways it already portended an "Americanizing" trend. In 1956, too, Karl Barth delivered a lecture, "Die Menschlichkeit Gottes" ("The Humanity of God"), which was widely read in pamphlet form before it was translated into English in 1960. In it, Barth proposed "a change of direction in the thinking of evangelical theology"[60]—a revision in the direction of that immanentist outlook against which he had earlier reacted so vehemently.

-----

[60] Karth Barth, *The Humanity of God* (Richmond: John Knox Press, 1960), p. 37.

The roots of the change in Barth's thinking need not concern us, but this change was not an isolated development. As early as 1948, in his volume of sermons, *The Shaking of the Foundations,* Tillich had begun to raise anew the question of the immanence of God; and in that same year Dietrich Bonhoeffer's *Nachfolge* appeared in translation as *The Cost of Discipleship,* followed in 1954 by his prison writings, under the title *Prisoner for God,* which suggests the ambiguity of the theological renaissance within the religious revival. In 1956 Ronald Gregor Smith's *The New Man* was published, adding impetus to the growing interest in the legendary Bonhoeffer. It would be an oversimplification to say that a major shift took place in 1956, for it is more evident in retrospect, but it would be fair to suggest that some of the events which came to the surface in 1960 and after are traceable to the mid-1950s. At least figuratively, the dissolution of neo-orthodoxy began to take place then, ostensibly at the crest of its influence.

During the heyday of neo-orthodoxy, church historians produced new studies of America's religious past, often with little or no attention to its intellectual manifestations. By the late 1950s, however, foreshadowed by the studies of Perry Miller and by such pathfinding books as H. Shelton Smith's *Changing Conceptions of Original Sin* (1955), studies in American religious history were increasingly taking account of theological currents. However, it was not until well into the 1960s that such major figures as Bushnell and Rauschenbusch were "rediscovered" outside the precincts of such specialized journals as *Church History.* The point is that such moves as were made, at first, toward a recovery of the American tradition in religious thought came not from theologians but almost as a by-product of another kind of scholarly endeavor. Most of the younger American theologians played no part in this development, and indeed they were scarcely touched by it until it had reached full fruition.

It was fashionable and respectable to be religious in the 1950s, as it had not been for several decades. If the Cold War scuttled most forms of social idealism and made anything smacking of Marxism suspect, it by no means eliminated the individual's quest for a meaningful personal orientation. College students, through literature and philosophy courses, discovered Maritain, Buber, Augustine, Thomas Aquinas, T. S. Eliot, Dostoevsky, Kierkegaard, Pascal, Gerard Manley Hopkins. Some began by seeking security and comfort, but many found themselves embarked on a quest for depth and honesty. "This search," noted one observer, "typically results in an *unbelieving religion*, a religion without God."[61] For each individual who was drawn into the life of the church there were many others who shunned its genteel social patterns. There were some who bypassed Christianity for a secular existentialism or for Zen Buddhism or other Eastern religious disciplines, but there were also those who responded to an untraditional interpretation of faith, such as Tillich's conception of religion as "ultimate concern" or "the dimension of depth." Within the churches, too, young adults moved out of the orbit of neo-orthodoxy. In discussion groups keyed to ecumenical themes of church renewal or responding to the nascent civil rights movement or their own inner impulse for personal meaning in an impersonal world, new realms of discourse took shape in which Tillich, Bonhoeffer, and Camus were major figures.

The Protestant neo-orthodox decade was also a decade in which a new intellectual current reached fruition among Roman Catholics in the United States, with a new generation of educated laymen probing and challenging their church's traditions. The accession of Pope John XXIII, with his irenic, ecumenical spirit and his call for *aggiornamento*, gave great encouragement to the liberal Catholics and broadened the scope of the Protestant ecumenical thrust. In the 1960s the Reformation of Calvin, Luther and Knox receded in importance as a normative starting point for Protestant thought. Robert McAfee Brown's *The Spirit of Protestantism* (1961) was not so much a celebration of the 16th-century struggle as it was an account of the factors of renewal to be found in contemporary ecumenical Protestantism. Typically, its few spo-

[61] Roy Finch, "The Return of Nerve: Religion and the New Generation," *Liberation*, May 1957, p. 12.

radic references to American religious thinkers other than the Niebuhrs are overshadowed by references to British and Continental theologians.

In the United States 63 percent of the population were church members in 1958. The greatest growth among the Protestant churches in the course of the twentieth century had been in conservative denominations—the Southern Baptist Convention and the Lutheran Church—Missouri Synod—which played no part in either the ecumenical movement or the development of American theology. Compared with the nineteenth century, the American religious complexion was vastly altered. Demographically, former bastions of Congregationalism had become strongholds of Catholicism. Yet the Pilgrim-pioneer tradition somehow persisted and made its claims upon Lutherans and Catholics. It sought its correctives chiefly from kindred Calvinist sources. In another dimension, too, the Yankee impulse toward science and democracy called forth related impulses from the world—not because of any Anglo-Saxon ethnic superiority but for innately pragmatic reasons. However stated, the drift of development followed a course roughly patterned on the American, or if not directly on the American course, on others related to it, such as the Swiss and the Dutch. The democratization of the Catholic Church is a case in point, as is the response to the work of Pierre Teilhard de Chardin, whose *Le Milieu Divin* was published in 1957 after years of suppression, augmenting trends manifested eighty years earlier in American religious thought. Teilhard by no means derived his cosmic Christ from John Fiske, nor need any great originality be claimed for Fiske to suggest the significance of an "American" pattern. Somehow that pattern worked; Christian allegiances and even church affiliations survived, and were perhaps enhanced by, the free flow of ideas and free, disestablished churches. It was, in the long run, these elements in the European experience that elicited the most enduring response from the Americans—not the European variety of church establishment but its exceptions in the independent Confessing Church and the Evangelical Academies; not the well-adjusted proper bourgeois churchman but the resistance fighter.

Many crisscrossing and interacting forces, on a world scale, were pressing toward major changes in the realm of religious thought and the style of Christian life, and we have perhaps already exceeded our scope without fully taking account of them. If we were primarily concerned with British developments, we would have to examine the interplay of the New Left and its secular emphasis on "commitment" rather than ideology with the Campaign for Nuclear Disarmament; the authors of *New Essays in Philosophical Theology* (1955) and specific trends in church renewal, journalism, and religious thought. If we did, we would find reasons for a growing interest in Dietrich Bonhoeffer there. If we studied the situation of a Germany divided between Communism and the West, we would find Bonhoeffer's writings playing a remarkable part in theology on both sides of the boundary, especially in the East. These and other events must be acknowledged lest we depict the American scene as solely determinative; and among additional events are the advent of a new phase of technology featuring cybernation, television, moon rockets, contraceptive pills, etc., and the arrival of a new generation of youth to whom these rather than Depression and war are normal features of life.

What stood out for young American theologians in all of this were the sit-ins and freedom rides that swept through the South in 1960–1961. Those who were involved looked to Bonhoeffer's *The Cost of Discipleship* for spiritual sustenance, and their experiences with jail produced a demand for a paperback edition of his prison letters, which appeared in 1962. Unlike the former book, *Letters and Papers From Prison* (as it was retitled from *Prisoner for God*)[62] formulated, however sketchily, a radical revision of Christian thought for a secular society.

---

[62] The German title was *Widerstand und Ergebung* (Resistance and Submission"). Bonhoeffer was executed in April 1945 for conspiring in an attempt to assassinate Adolf Hitler. His "radical" prison letters were written in 1944, after he had been behind bars for a year. For the essential passages, see "Last Letters From a Nazi Prison" in William Robert Miller, ed., *The New Christianity* (New York: Delacorte Press, 1967), pp. 271–295. See also Mary Bosanquet, *The Life and Death of Dietrich Bonhoeffer* (New York: Harper & Row, 1969).

One of the most dramatic responses to Bonhoeffer in this context came from William Hamilton, a professor at Colgate-Rochester Divinity School and the author of several books in a Barthian vein. His *The New Essence of Christianity* (1961) closed the door on neo-orthodoxy and with vigor and clarity expounded at length Bonhoeffer's concepts of "religionless Christianity" and of Jesus Christ as "the man for others" in a "world come of age" in which the explanatory God of earlier times was notably absent. Simultaneously a former student of Barth's, Gabriel Vahanian of Syracuse University, in *The Death of God* (1961), asserted that for contemporary culture, God is indeed dead and the present era is a post-Christian one. In a later volume, *No Other God* (1966), Vahanian clarified his position, a defense of Calvinist transcendence and of the undying God of faith as distinct from the idols of culture, but meanwhile the "death of God" slogan became a rallying cry for a cluster of theologies of radical immanence that proclaimed a sharp break with neo-orthodoxy.

If the years 1955–1958 represent the erosion of neo-Reformation faith and the rise of a more elastic and diffuse religious sensibility, the entire decade that followed was marked by successive accelerations of change, many-sided yet having a general cohesion broadly resembling nothing so much as the religious philosophy of Edward Scribner Ames. Such a statement must be immediately qualified, for the technology, culture, philosophy, psychology, and other relevant forces of the 1960s were by no means the same as those of Ames' day. Nevertheless, what came after neo-orthodoxy was a reassertion of the key motifs that had preceded it—literary and linguistic questions, secular and social emphases, an empirical and pragmatic attunement to present realities, a dissatisfaction with the limits of a dogmatically conceived biblical revelation, a need to re-examine religious symbols in relation to the larger scope of human knowledge, a shift in the understanding of the church from community of faith to functionally relevant organization. For the most part, rediscovery of these themes as rooted in early 20th-century American religious thought was belated, a consequence rather than a cause of the theological revolution

of the 1960s. The discontinuity is probably even more important than the larger continuity, for it underscores the essential
validity of the earlier currents as meeting the requirements of
a new age. The inadequacies that engendered the neo-orthodox reaction arose from the provisional and transitional character of the earlier phase. By the late 1950s it had become clear
that the present age is even newer than it was earlier regarded
and that a theology committed to the God of Calvin or Luther
or Thomas Aquinas did not succeed in transcending the
ephemeral; it did not achieve a perennial perspective but made
Christianity an anachronism. That older world and its God
were operatively dead. Barth's retreat from absolute transcendence was an attempt to recognize this fact. Bonhoeffer's
stab toward theological reconstruction, fragmentary as it was,
was even more dramatic—a hectic groping from amid the
debris following the collision between the pieties of the past
and the realities of the present.

John Bennett, in 1958, announced, "It's Time to Go Beyond
Neo-Orthodoxy" (*Advance*, May 9, 1958). But he and Niebuhr
and their circle had continuously held to a position beyond that
of their Barthian allies, more pragmatic and relevant to secular
society; for them it was a matter of reconsidering priorities.
In the decade to follow, they occupied a moderate and stabiliz-
ing position adjacent to the radical turbulence which occupied
the center of attention. Those who experienced that turbulence
and made of it a theological revolution were men whose own
experience more closely resembled Bonhoeffer's in their sudden
realization of secularity. Paul van Buren and Gabriel Vahanian
were students of Barth's. Perhaps for this reason they were
more aware of the subtleties and anomalies of Barth's thought.
The Barthianism of William Hamilton's *The Christian Man*
(1955) was more typical of generic neo-orthodoxy, hence more
consistent and readier to serve as a fulcrum for the dramatic
reversal to come. Because of its roots in German thought,
American neo-orthodoxy would subsequently turn to Hegel
and Nietzsche for explication and, indeed, for the formulation
of the death-of-God theme that reached its crescendo in 1966
with the publication of Hamilton's and Altizer's *Radical The-*

ology and the Death of God, which was followed by a score of books and numerous articles even as the movement dissolved into broader currents.

Among Europeans, even the later Barth of *God Here and Now* (1964) moved significantly from the "Barthian" position of absolute transcendence toward a more immanental stance, and many American theologians who did not go so far as Hamilton and Altizer found themselves occupying a "post-Barthian" position, to some extent establishing ties with other German theological currents, but also moving independently. One feature that was common to the whole theological spectrum of the 1960s was a renewed emphasis on Christology, which reawakened in many thinkers an interest in Jonathan Edwards, Horace Bushnell, and some currents of liberal modernism.

Related to the general shift of thought between the late 1950s and the early 1960s was a revolutionizing cluster of technological and social developments, which had considerable impact on American culture. Television, still an infant at the end of World War II, had become the key mass medium of communication by 1960, with 85 million sets in use in the United States that year. Cities mushroomed into metropolitan complexes, while hundreds of miles were condensed into a few hours with the rise of air transport on a massive scale. Automation and cybernation had subtle and far-reaching effects on people's lives; fewer workers produced goods, while increasing numbers operated computers; a revolution in business and industry embraced many aspects, not the least of which for the average individual was the proliferation of revolving credit, and with it a substantive change in the American ethos regarding thrift and the use of money. Even more palpable was the advent of the contraceptive pill and the rapid rise of the "new morality"—primarily in relation to sexual behavior, thought and expression. By the late 1960s, a new sensuality and sensibility had virtually supplanted that which had altered only gradually during the preceding decades. Finally, perhaps the most publicly noticeable development was the civil rights movement, which erupted with the sit-ins in 1960 and had many subsequent reverberations, including a new militancy among black Americans and the proliferation of student revolts toward the end of the decade. None of these is an isolated phenomenon. The women's liberation movement, which came to the fore on the threshold of the 1970s, clearly owes something of its origin to the new morality and the student protest movement. The full effect of the multiple revolution cannot be assessed here, and its accelerative pace demolishes any attempt at detail or historical perspective, but it is clear that the sixties were a decade of unprecedented transformations, giving rise to changes in the shape and direction of religious thought that make it risky even to discern broad trends.

The theology of secularity, the theology of hope, the Marxist-Christian dialogue, themes of sensitivity and encounter, of celebration and social revolution, have rapidly succeeded or blended with one another since 1965. At the same time, parallel developments in American Catholic thought virtually rendered the ecumenical or "interfaith" dialogues of the 1950s irrelevant, for parallels quickly became convergences. By the end of 1969, publishers of both Catholic and Protestant books found that the market for their backlists had collapsed—including many books that tepidly attempted to bridge the gulf between traditional theology and contemporary cultural trends. Yet there were signs of renewed interest in the writings and emphases of earlier writers. Bernard E. Meland's *Realities of Faith* (1962) and *The Secularization of Modern Cultures* (1966) attest the durability and relevance of the Chicago tradition of process and pragmatism, and such younger writers as Paul van Buren and W. Richard Comstock have found new relevance in William James.[63] The Catholic philosopher, Michael Novak, in one of the decades' most singularly perceptive and perhaps prophetic essays, asserts that honesty demands a move

---

[63] See Paul van Buren, "Bonhoeffer's Paradox: Living With God Without God," *Union Seminary Quarterly Review*, XXIII (Fall 1967) and W. Richard Comstock, "William James and the Logic of Religious Belief," *The Journal of Religion*, XLVII, 3 (July 1967).

beyond theology to autobiography, for "the person is the message." One cannot help being reminded of Edward Scribner Ames when Novak writes, "Christians whose Christ pointed so resolutely to a communal bond between men as the empirical sign of God's presence should not be surprised if, as history unfolds, many other markers point to that same direction."[64]

Six decades have passed since Josiah Royce sought to determine what was vital in Christianity. Whether tomorrow's answers issue in Christianity's renewal or, as some propose, its transformation into something else, the protestant theological development, which the present volume seeks to document, has shown a persistent vigor in its American form, and it comprises a heritage not so much to be celebrated as, in characteristic American fashion, put to use wherever it still proves workable. Of its validity and relevance nothing more need be said.

Liberalism constitutes a prevalent feature of contemporary American Protestant thought. Henry Churchill King stands as a representative of its broad mainstream, socially concerned but moderate, generally approving the culture of his time. Josiah Strong, with a moralistic messianic vision of America as redeemer-nation, is a theologically less incisive member of this group, as is Woodrow Wilson, who most clearly represents the identification of faith and culture in a synthesis of moral idealism and the nation's religious identity. Harry Emerson Fosdick epitomizes the modernist version of liberalism in its clash with fundamentalism over evolution and biblical interpretation. Rufus Jones testifies both on behalf of liberalism under attack from neo-orthodoxy and on behalf of the distinctive spirituality of Quakerism.

Edgar S. Brightman, Henry N. Wieman, and Martin Luther King each stand for currents of liberalism. Brightman's contri-

---

[64] Michael Novak, "The New Relativism in American Theology," in Donald R. Cutler, ed., *The Religious Situation 1968* (Boston: Beacon Press, 1968) p. 228.

bution is a personalism that incorporates idealism and theism; Wieman's is theistic but empirical; King's is partly eclectic, close to Brightman's personalism but also encompassing Rauschenbusch, Niebuhr, and others, as well as distinctive features arising from ethnic and personal experience.

Josiah Royce is ostensibly an absolute idealist, a fact that links him with Brightman, but he is so seminal a figure that he resists categories. There is a pragmatic element that links him with James and others and a stress on community that relates him to social Christianity.

Still within the liberal ambience, if not the theological mainstream, yet perhaps more attuned to the depths of the American ethos, we find the pragmatism of William James and its theologically humanistic adumbration in Edward S. Ames, both of whom in their empiricism contribute to the thought of Wieman.

Walter Rauschenbusch is in some sense Roycean, and like Fosdick he is a liberal interpreter of the Bible. Yet he is at once more evangelical and, in his social outlook, more revolutionary than any of the liberals. Usually considered a spokesman of the Social Gospel, he takes a more socialist stand than the typical civic reformer.

Reinhold Niebuhr embraces the pragmatism of James, the social concern of Rauschenbusch, and the dialectic of Royce, transcending them all in a dialectical pragmatism that has more often been called Christian realism or, somewhat misleadingly, neo-orthodoxy. It is the Niebuhrian rather than the Jamesian pragmatism that we find in Martin Luther King.

Walter Lowrie may most conveniently be termed neo-orthodox, since he appears here simply as a spokesman for that general trend. Like Niebuhr, he qualifies as a post-liberal, but his affinities are more thoroughly with the German crisis theology. H. Richard Niebuhr, while a sympathetic interpreter of the latter and often styled neo-orthodox, sought his roots not so much in Barth's Calvin as in Jonathan Edwards. Inasmuch as James Gustafson carries forward the distinctive perspective of H. Richard Niebuhr, he too both represents and transcends neo-orthodoxy. Both men, in their later writings especially,

prefigure the Christological and secular emphases that superseded neo-orthodoxy.

Peter Berger, Carl Michalson, Paul van Buren, and to some
extent Thomas Altizer are men whose theological bearings
were initially those of Barthian neo-orthodoxy. Berger appears
here as sociologist and critic of the secular theologies of the
late 1960s; his own theological label is therefore secondary.
Michalson is seen in transition from neo-orthodoxy to an
incipient radicalism. Van Buren represents an extreme form
of secular theology, distinctively related to analytic philosophy
and engaging in a radical renewal of Christology. Altizer
comes to an apocalyptic and revolutionary vision of Jesus by
a comparably radical approach through altogether different
avenues, chiefly history of religion.

Charles Hartshorne is loosely related to the liberal theists,
Brightman, and Wieman, and in a sense Royce. Certainly he
shares with them and with James a concern for process. But
his primary philosophical root is the process metaphysics of
Alfred North Whitehead, out of which he developed his own
dipolar theism. John Cobb synthesizes a variety of trends that
align him with such post-Barthians as Michalson and van
Buren, but his primary synthesis is the theological expression
of process thought, which links him with Whitehead, Hartshorne, and Wieman.

W. Richard Comstock counts William James as a key influence, along with Santayana and Tillich. These influences,
together with interests in the death of God and in Marxism,
decidedly place him among the radicals of the late 1960s,
probably closer to Altizer than to van Buren, although distinct
from both in his engagement with contemporary culture.

The labels and groupings used above are necessarily approximate and somewhat provisional. To the extent that any
thinker is original, he will elude comparison with others, yet
the student needs some such guidelines as an aid to understanding the rise, fall and re-emergence of trends that may be
more readily felt than baldly stated. A number of scholars have
worked out typologies that have varying degrees of structure
and usefulness. They vary in scope as well, some embracing

many but not all of the Americans within a much larger framework of European and American thought, others giving a different group in a limited American context. I have drawn upon several in devising my own rough typology.[65]

---

[65] See the Bibliographical Essay for works on typology by the following authors, each of which has some usefulness. By far the most systematic is Burr, secondly Macquarrie. Ahlstrom and Hammar provide rougher sketches. See also Joseph Haroutunian, "Theology and American Experience," *op. cit.*, and Langdon Gilkey, "Sources of Protestant Theology in America," *Daedalus*, XCVI, 1 (Winter 1967).

Bibliographical Essay

No truly comprehensive bibliography of twentieth-century American Protestant thought exists at the present time. Perhaps the nearest is Nelson R. Burr, *A Critical Bibliography of Religion in America*, 2 vols. (Princeton University Press, 1961). However, theology and philosophy of religion form only one segment of Burr's enterprise, and of this the twentieth century portion is rather cursory. It has provided, however, a basic source to which a number of further titles have been added in the following selective compilation.

There is also no survey volume that covers our subject and period, but there are several worth mentioning, varying in usefulness and comprehensiveness. John Macquarrie, *Religious Thought in the 20th Century* (New York: Macmillan, 1951), gives very brief sketches of perhaps half the men included in this anthology. Older yet highly serviceable is Henry Nelson Wieman and Bernard E. Meland, *American Philosophies of Religion* (Chicago: Willett, Clark, 1936), which discusses the Niebuhrs, Royce, Jones, Brightman, Ames, Wieman, and a number of thinkers more briefly mentioned here. Ames, Wieman, and others again feature in Douglas Clyde Macintosh, *The Problem of Religious Knowledge* (New York: Harper, 1940). Charles Hartshorne and William L. Reese, eds., *Philosophers Speak of God* (University of Chicago Press, 1953) is particularly valuable for its chapters on Royce, James, Brightman, Hartshorne, and Wieman. Paul Ramsey, ed., *Religion*

(Englewood Cliffs: Prentice-Hall, 1964) contains an especially illuminating survey, "Philosophy of Religion", by John E. Smith, that succeeds in capturing the American contribution with swift incisive summaries of James, Royce, Wieman, Brightman, Jones, Niebuhr, Hartshorne, and others. The section titled "Theology" by Claude Welch in the same volume is also worth consulting but is more attuned to European developments. James Ward Smith and Leland Jamison, *The Shaping of American Religion* (Princeton University Press, 1961) contains chapters by Sydney E. Ahlstrom and Daniel Day Williams that provide valuable background. Likewise Ahlstrom, ed., *Theology in America* (Indianapolis: Bobbs-Merrill, 1967) includes a brief glimpse of the modern period as part of a survey-anthology spanning more than three centuries and includes selections by James, Royce, Rauschenbusch, and H. R. Niebuhr. Martin E. Marty and Dean Peerman, eds., *A Handbook of Christian Theologians* (Cleveland: World, 1965) contains cogent and meaty chapters on Rauschenbusch by Robert T. Handy, on Macintosh by Herbert R. Reinelt, on Reinhold Niebuhr by Hans Hofmann, and on H. R. Niebuhr by Clyde A. Holbrook. Vergilius Ferm, ed., *Contemporary American Theology* (New York: Round Table Press, 1932), containing intellectual autobiographies of figures then prominent, is dated but retains some usefulness. Herbert W. Schneider, *A History of American Philosophy* (Columbia University Press, 1946) and Joseph L. Blau, *Men and Movements in American Philosophy* (Englewood Cliffs: Prentice-Hall, 1952) are both helpful background works. See also the relevant entries in Lefferts A. Loetscher, ed., *The Twentieth Century Encyclopedia of Religious Knowledge* (Grand Rapids: Baker Book House, 1955).

The following is an attempt to correlate the sections of this book with a literature that sometimes fits our time slots and sometimes does not. Other factors being equal, a book or article spanning more than one period will be included under the period of origin or of maturation, as may seem appropriate. To aid the reader, we have cued the larger such topics, e.g., pragmatism, as subentries. Needless to say, no attempt has been made to list even the principal books of the major thinkers. For these, consult the individual headnotes.

1. THE PROGRESSIVE ERA

John Wright Buckham, *Progressive Religious Thought in America* (Boston: Houghton, Mifflin, 1919) and Frank Hugh Foster, *The Modern Movement in American Theology* (New York: Revell, 1939) are both primarily background works devoting major attention to the decades following the Civil War, with rather minor treatment of the 1900s. Gerald Birney Smith, *Current Christian Thinking* (University of Chicago Press, 1928) and G. B. Smith, ed., *Religious Thought in the Last Quarter Century* (University of Chicago Press, 1927) are better focused on the period. Kenneth Cauthen, *The Impact of American Religious Liberalism* (New York: Harper, 1962) tends to be over-schematized but has the benefit of historical perspective and critical acumen in discussing outstanding liberal theologians of this period and later. For excellent studies of James and Royce, see John E. Smith, *The Spirit of American Philosophy* (Oxford University Press, 1963), and George Herbert Mead, "The Philosophies of Royce, James and Dewey in Their American Setting," *International Journal of Ethics*, XL.

SOCIAL GOSPEL. Oddly, there is no comprehensive study that concentrates on the whole spectrum of social Christianity in this period. See, however, Charles Howard Hopkins, *The Rise of the Social Gospel in American Protestantism* (Yale University Press, 1940); Willem A. Visser 't Hooft, *The Background of the Social Gospel* (Haarlem: Willink, 1928); Robert T. Handy, ed., *The Social Gospel in America* (Oxford University Press, 1966); and Vernon Parker Bodein, *The Social Gospel of Walter Rauschenbusch* (Yale University Press, 1944). For the later period, see Donald B. Meyer, *The Protestant Search for Political Realism, 1919–1941* (University of California Press, 1960); Robert Moats Miller, *American Protestantism and Social*

Issues, 1919–1939 (University of North Carolina Press, 1959); and Paul A. Carter, *The Decline and Revival of the Social Gospel, 1920–1940* (Cornell University Press, 1954).

JAMES AND PRAGMATISM. The 1960s produced four books that emphasize the religio-ethical aspect of James's thought: John K. Roth, *Freedom and the Moral Life* (Philadelphia: Westminster, 1969); Roth, ed., *The Moral Philosophy of William James* (New York: Crowell, 1969); Bernard P. Brennan, *The Ethics of William James* (New York: Bookman, 1961); John Wild, *The Radical Empiricism of William James* (Garden City: Doubleday, 1969). See also Arthur O. Lovejoy, "Pragmatism and Theology," *American Journal of Theology*, XII (January 1908), and Paul K. Conkin, *Puritans and Pragmatists* (New York: Dodd, Mead, 1969), which places James and Peirce in the company of Jonathan Edwards and other predecessors.

2. THE OPTIMISTIC DECADE

Most of the relevant literature is subsumed under other sections. See especially G. B. Smith, both volumes cited under paragraph 1; Cauthen, and Lloyd J. Averill, *American Theology in the Liberal Tradition* (Philadelphia: Westminster, 1967); Eugene W. Lyman, *The Meaning and Truth of Religion* (1933).

PERSONALISM. For guidelines, see Cauthen; also Cobb and Williams, cited below. For a sense of the continuities and changes of this school of thought, compare Borden Parker Bowne, *Personalism* (Boston, 1908) and Edgar S. Brightman, ed., *Personalism in Theology* (Boston University Press, 1943).

THE "CHICAGO SCHOOL." By far the best survey is Bernard E. Meland, "Introduction: The Empirical Tradition in Theology at Chicago," in Meland, ed., *The Future of Empirical Theology* (University of Chicago Press, 1969), pp. 1–62. For a brief, somewhat rough-hewn survey with a good bibliography, see Charles Harvey Arnold, *Near the Edge of Battle* (University of Chicago: The Divinity School Assn., 1966). Also Darnell

Rucker, *The Chicago Pragmatists* (University of Minnesota Press, 1969). See also A. C. McGiffert Jr., "The Chicago School of Theology" in Vergilius Ferm, ed., *Encyclopedia of Religion* (New York: Philosophical Library, 1945) and Bernard E. Meland's article of the same title in Loetscher, ed., *Twentieth Century Encyclopedia of Religious Knowledge,* cited above. Also, James Alfred Martin, *Empirical Philosophies of Religion* (Columbia University Press, 1945); Bernard E. Meland, ed., *The Future of Empirical Theology* (University of Chicago Press, 1969); Robert W. Bretall, ed., *The Empirical Theology of Henry Nelson Wieman* (New York: Macmillan, 1963).

3. YEARS OF CRISIS

On Walter Lowrie, see Alexander C. Zabriskie, ed., *Doctor Lowrie of Princeton* (New York: Seabury, 1957). On H. Richard Niebuhr, see Paul Ramsey, ed., *Faith and Ethics* (New York: Harper, 1957) and Albert R. Jonsen, S. J., *Responsibility in Modern Religious Ethics* (Washington: Corpus, 1968). Also, Harry Emerson Fosdick, ed., *Rufus Jones Speaks to Our Time* (New York: Macmillan, 1961). On Hartshorne, see Eugene Peters, *The Creative Advance* (St. Louis: Bethany Press, 1966); also William L. Reese and Eugene Freeman, eds., *Process and Divinity* (LaSalle: Open Court, 1964). On Wieman, see Bretall, ed., *The Empirical Theology of Henry Nelson Wieman,* cited above.

For interpretations of the background of the theological controversies of the period, see Edmund B. Chaffee, *The Protestant Churches and the Industrial Crisis* (New York: Macmillan, 1933); Carl S. Patton, "The American Theological Scene: Fifty Years in Retrospect," *Journal of Religion,* XVI (1936); Sydney E. Ahlstrom, "Continental Influence On American Christian Thought Since World War I," *Church History,* XXVII (1958); W. Norman Pittenger, "Changing Emphases in American Theology," *Religion in Life,* XII, 3 (Summer 1943); Walter Marshall Horton, "Between Liberalism and the New Orthodoxy,"

The Christian Century (May 17, 1939); Edwin A. Lewis, "From Philosophy to Revelation," *The Christian Century* (June 14, 1939); A. C. McGiffert, "The Future of Liberal Christianity in America," *Journal of Religion*, XV, 2 (April 1935). Henry Sloane Coffin, *Religion Yesterday and Today* (Nashville: Abingdon, 1940) presents a critical review of liberal theology, while David E. Roberts and Henry Pitney Van Dusen, eds., *Liberal Theology, an Appraisal* (New York: Scribner, 1942) is a symposium in behalf of neo-liberalism. See also Bernard M. Loomer's conciliatory essay, "Neo-naturalism and Neo-orthodoxy," *Journal of Religion*, XXVIII (1948).

George Hammar, *Christian Realism in American Theology* (Uppsala, 1940) offers a European perspective that often misses the American accents but includes interesting studies of the early Reinhold Niebuhr, Van Dusen, and Walter Marshall Horton. Edwin Ewart Aubrey, *Present Theological Tendencies* (New York: Harper, 1936) includes interesting chapters on the crisis of culture, modernism, the dialectical theology, neo-Thomism, and the question of naturalism and supernaturalism —clearly in the neo-orthodox vein. See also Aubrey, "The Promise of American Theology," *Christendom* (1938). A rather more balanced presentation is to be found in Walter Marshall Horton, *Theology in Transition* (New York: Harper, 1943). See also Randolph Crump Miller, "Religious Realism in America," *The Modern Churchman* (1937).

David Wesley Soper, *Major Voices in American Theology* (Philadelphia: Westminster, 1953) contains intellectual portraits of the Niebuhrs, Edwin Lewis, Nels F. S. Ferré, Paul Tillich, and Robert L. Calhoun. See also the volumes edited by Ferm and by Wieman and Meland, cited at the beginning of this bibliographical essay. Daniel Day Williams, *What Present-Day Theologians Are Thinking* (New York: Harper, 1952, rev. 1959) gives disproportionate attention to European theologians, as does Roger Hazelton, *New Accents in Contemporary Theology* (New York: Harper, 1960). John B. Cobb, *Living Options in Protestant Theology* (Philadelphia: Westminster, 1962) is more scholarly and gives greater attention to American thinkers.

4. BRIDGING THE DECADES

Charles W. Kegley and Robert W. Bretall, eds., *Reinhold Niebuhr* (New York: Macmillan, 1956) is the best single volume on Niebuhr, including views by liberals and fundamentalists as well as by his colleagues and co-thinkers. Also included is a serviceable bibliography. More extensive is D. B. Robertson, ed., *Reinhold Niebuhr's Works: A Bibliography* (Berea: The Berea College Press, 1954). Among articles and books published since these bibliographies, see: D. B. Robertson, ed., *Love and Justice: Selections From the Shorter Writings* (Philadelphia: Westminster, 1957); Robertson, ed., *Essays in Applied Christianity* (New York: Meridian, 1959); Harry R. Davis and Robert C. Good, *Reinhold Niebuhr On Politics* (New York: Scribner, 1960); Ronald H. Stone, ed., *Faith and Politics* (New York: Braziller, 1968); *Pious and Secular America* (New York: Scribner, 1958); *The Structure of Nations and Empires* (New York: Scribner, 1959); *Man's Nature and His Communities* (New York: Scribner, 1965); Gordon Harland, *The Thought of Reinhold Niebuhr* (New York: Oxford, 1960). Also, "The Problem of the Modern Church: Triviality," *Christianity and Crisis*, XXII (December 10, 1962); "The Christian Witness in a Secular Age," *The Christian Century*, LXX (July 22, 1953); "Liberalism: Illusions and Realities," *The New Republic*, CXXXIII, 27 (July 4, 1955); "Lessons of the Detroit Experience," *The Christian Century*, LXXXII (April 21, 1965). And see the symposium, "Christian Realism," *Christianity and Crisis*, XXVIII, 14 (August 5, 1968). Other titles may be found in the footnotes to the headnote of the Niebuhr section.

5. TOWARD THE POST-MODERN ERA

The recentness of this period makes for a spotty, unbalanced, and brief bibliography. Several of the writers represented here remain unduly neglected, while others have received disproportionate attention. A decade hence, just the reverse may be the case—if indeed these selections are not then overshadowed by newcomers to the scene. Perhaps the most important single work considering the impact of Altizer and the radical theology is Langdon Gilkey, *Naming the Whirlwind* (Indianapolis: Bobbs-Merrill, 1969). See also Charles N. Bent, S. J., *The Death of God Movement* (New York: Paulist Press, 1967); John C. Cooper, *Radical Christianity and Its Sources* (Philadelphia: Westminster, 1968); Thomas C. Ogletree), *The Death of God Controversy* (Nashville: Abingdon, 1966); William Robert Miller, ed., *The New Christianity* (New York: Delacorte, 1967); Miller, *Goodbye, Jehovah* (New York: Walker, 1969). For King, see William Robert Miller, *Martin Luther King Jr.* (New York: Weybright and Talley, 1968); David Lewis, *King: A Critical Biography* (New York: Praeger, 1970); C. Eric Lincoln, ed., *Martin Luther King Jr.* (New York: Hill and Wang, 1970); and Coretta Scott King, *My Life With Martin Luther King* (New York: Holt, 1969). For Van Buren, see Ogletree and Bent, above.

PART ONE

THE PROGRESSIVE ERA, 1900–1917

1

HENRY CHURCHILL KING

Theologian of Laissez-Faire Liberalism

Henry Churchill King (1858–1934) is perhaps no more outstanding as a theologian than a dozen others who epitomize the
liberal outlook of his generation, among whom were Lyman
Abbott, Borden Parker Bowne, William Adams Brown, George
A. Gordon, and William Newton Clarke. His literary contributions to theology consist chiefly of two books, *Reconstruction in
Theology* (1901) and *Theology and the Social Consciousness*
(1902); his other works are in the areas of philosophy, psychology, and education.

King was born in Hillsdale, Michigan, some ten miles north
of the Ohio border, a small college town established by settlers
from New England. He received his college education there
and at Oberlin College, and was a tutor in Latin and mathematics while a student at Oberlin's Graduate School of Theology. After further studies at Harvard, he became associate
professor of mathematics at Oberlin in 1884, transferring to
philosophy six years later. He studied at the University of Berlin under Hermann Lotze in 1893–1894, became professor of
theology at Oberlin in 1897 and president of the college in
1902.

Like many of his contemporaries, King was influenced by
German scholarship, particularly the personalist philosophy of
Lotze and the theology of Albrecht Ritschl, a New Testament
scholar who sought to "reconceive" the Christian faith by correlating its essential components with the demands of a modern world view. The quest for the "essence" or "essentials" of
Christianity may be traced back to Lessing and Coleridge or

centered on Ludwig Feuerbach,[1] but it was pre-eminently Ritschl who offered the reinterpretation most congenial to middle-class Protestantism.

It has become an ingrained oversimplification, however, to regard King and the others as "American Ritschlians," a label that begs the question of what specifically American conditions would make Ritschl so attractive to American theologians, and what conditions occasioned departures from his emphases. Karl Barth calls Ritschl "the very epitome of the national-liberal German bourgeois of the age of Bismarck,"[2] a period of technological and industrial growth accompanied by the expansion of Prussia, which culminated in the consolidation of the German Empire in 1870, followed by colonial expansion. The industrialization of America and Germany ran roughly parallel, and there is an at least faintly similar pattern in the expansion of America, with the Northeast cast in the role of Prussia and Pittsburgh and the Midwest in the role of the Ruhr and the Rheinland. More to the point, both countries underwent a similar trend of urbanization and the rise of an industrial middle class. Just as Calvin and John Cotton expounded a theological outlook that corresponded to an ethos favorable to the socio-economic situation of the pre-industrial bourgeois, so the liberal theology of King and Ritschl both were attuned to that type of personality which assumed median leadership in the era of railroads and factories, "the strong, active, morally disciplined individual"[3] with a certain stake in social mobility and political freedom.

It is just such a state of affairs for which King's "the atmosphere of our times" is a euphemism. To make progress happen, there must be freedom of inquiry, freedom to explore, theorize, invent, innovate. In Germany, these ventures—in sci-

---

[1] See William Robert Miller, ed., *The New Christianity* (New York: Delacorte, 1967), pp. 77–104.

[2] Karl Barth, *From Rousseau to Ritschl* (London: SCM Press, 1959), p. 392.

[3] Paul Tillich, *Perspectives on 19th and 20th Century Protestant Theology* (New York: Harper & Row, 1967), p. 218. See also Tillich, "The World Situation," in Henry P. Van Dusen, ed., *The Christian Answer* (New York: Scribner, 1948).

ence, for example in chemistry—were efficiently organized and coordinated. In America they were left to solitary geniuses and entrepreneurs. The Ritschlian theology is much more a part of a coordinated enterprise involving the system of universities and the state-supported church. Even if the university and the church carried equal weight for King and Ritschl, they would differ insofar as the American churches were pluralistic and voluntaristic. It is interesting to note that the church plays a much more important role in Ritschl's theology than in King's, which is more directly concerned with the individual and with society. Both King and Rauschenbusch were influenced by Ritschl, but both reflect a social concern not found in Ritschl.

Receptivity to new knowledge, erosion of the boundary between the sacred and the secular or between the divine and the human—these are features common to the new era. The reductionism or "rationalistic essentialism" that identifies religion as the handmaiden of ethics, and salvation as the victory of the human spirit or mind or will over nature, the neglect of ontology and epistemology—these are characteristic of Ritschl and his school in Germany; but King would have had to be virtually illiterate to have avoided them. Rather, for men of King's generation, Ritschl provided the support of biblical-historical scholarship for trends already well under way in America through the widely read essays of Emerson. Despite his determined attack on historic Pietism, Ritschl remains much more within its grasp in his quest for Christian perfection and in his implicit equation of justification with admittance to the Kingdom of God through the agency of the church.

There is no denying the discernible parallels and coincidences, if not outright influence, not only from Ritschl but from Lotze, whose influence on Ritschl, King, and others was both seminal and far-reaching. Indeed, the whole tradition of German idealism from Kant to Hegel comes to a focus in Lotze's personalism, combining the sense of the Kantian moral imperative with the Hegelian notion of historical process as revealing values and evolving toward Christianity as the "absolute religion." For Lotze, Christianity stands or falls on a judgment of its value as the religion which enables man to overcome the forces of nature and actualize the spiritual potentialities inherent in man. In other words, Christianity commends itself as a means to man's self-fulfillment. Jesus is the bearer of grace not by virtue of an objective event but as the archetype of perfected humanity whose own decisive value judgment is his recognition that God's goal and humanity's *true* goal are one and the same.

King's book, *Reconstruction in Theology*, embraces most of these themes, as does his essay of the same title which appeared a year earlier in *The American Journal of Theology*. The essay has the peculiar merit of being the book in miniature, and it is both sufficiently rounded and sufficiently typical to represent the views of most American liberal theologians at the turn of the century. There is no essay that summarizes, say, Brown's *The Essence of Christianity*, and a chapter from that book or another would not bring together all the elements found in King's essay.

Among the American accents to be noted are King's insistence on "the central importance of action" and on the "practical" lordship of Christ. The recurrent stress on "progress in revelation" and the enlargement of man's conception of God, the idea of theological meaning deriving from process and of personhood as a stage in emergent evolution, are themes that typify a broad epochal trend, but the respect for science which accompanies them, King's readiness to "accept the facts," bears the stamp of American empiricism. Ritschl devoted an entire tome to an attack on metaphysics (*Theologie und Metaphysik*, 1881), while King confidently disposes of "the God of the gaps" in a few sentences. Such differences of emphasis are not unimportant, for they point to divergences of tradition and development that should not be overlooked. When King speaks of religion as supplying practical "principles for life, a method of living," he speaks from a context in which Puritan virtues are already an honorific norm for the American character and only require adaptation to new conditions. The grounds for optimism seem firm; success is assured. The German optimism is circumscribed by historical conditions that did not in fact apply to King's America—by a prevalent authoritarianism imbedded in the class structure of German society and in Lutheran theology's accommodation to it. Hence Ritschl's liberalism was at once more cautious and more embattled. In retrospect, King's virtues were often his faults, which is to say that he too was a creature of his time and place—the America of a flourishing middle class on the threshold of a period of unprecedented reform in which no problem seemed insoluble to men of character, initiative, and right religion. It was only necessary to reformulate theology in such a way as to keep it serviceable for a successful modern society.

RECONSTRUCTION IN THEOLOGY*

Reconstruction in any living thing is constant, but it may still have its marked stages. To affirm, therefore, that there is need of reconstruction in theology is not at all to overlook the fact that such reconstruction has been constantly going on, that there have been many formulations by individual men more or less satisfactory; but it is simply to say that there is much to indicate that we have reached a point where our great inherited historical statements are quite generally felt to be inadequate, and where conditions, long at work, are so culminating and combining as to give promise of a somewhat marked stage in the development of theology.

Nor does the recognition of the need of reconstruction in Christian theology reflect a feeling of dissatisfaction with the Christian *religion*. On the contrary, the need of reconstruction is perhaps felt most strongly by those who have themselves gained a new sense of the absoluteness of the Christian religion, and call the old theological statements in question, because these statements make this absoluteness so little manifest.

---

* From *The American Journal of Theology*, III, 295 (April 1899), pp. 295–323.

Obviously here the dissatisfaction is not with the Christian religion, but with our intellectual expression of its meaning. And it ought not to surprise or trouble us that this intellectual expression must change from time to time with other intellectual changes.

There is abundant evidence that the need of reconstruction in theology is widely recognized, but a single judicious testimony must suffice. In his recent *History of Christian Doctrine*, speaking simply as a historian, Professor Fisher says:[1] "It is plain to keen observers that, in the later days, both within and without what may be called the pale of Calvinism, there is a certain relaxing of confidence in the previously accepted solutions of some of the gravest theological problems. This appears among many whose attachment to the core of the essential truths formulated in the past does not wane, whose substantial orthodoxy, as well as piety, is not often, if it be at all, questioned, and who have no sympathy with agnosticism, in the technical sense of the word."

As is implied in this statement of Professor Fisher's, the reasons for this feeling of need of reconstruction—to state it summarily—are neither a rationalistic spirit in the church, nor the reaction on the church of what is called the anti-religious or anti-Christian spirit of the age. It may be distinctly denied that that spirit is especially characteristic of this age. But the reasons are to be found in a deepening of the Christian spirit itself, and the *influence of the new intellectual, moral, and spiritual world* in which we live, and upon which this spirit has been working. Just as the acceptance of the principle of the correlation of forces called for a rewriting of physics—a "new physics," or the theory of evolution for the rewriting of biology—a "new biology," so, in the same sense, the acceptance of certain great convictions of our own day calls for a rewriting of theology—a new theology. Not that in any of these cases the great underlying facts have changed, but our conception of them and of their relations has changed. These dominating convictions of our age from a universal permeating atmo-

---

[1] p. 551

sphere, which inevitably affects in some way all schools of theology.

What makes this new atmosphere, this new world? What are the convictions increasingly shared by all our generation, whose influence on theology is indubitable and inevitable? It may be worth while, at the risk of rehearsing some familiar facts, to get a clear view of precisely those convictions that make our modern life.

I. THE NEW WORLD

Even a cursory glance discloses many phenomena fairly peculiar to our age, and we are coming to an increasing understanding of the great undercurrents which produce these phenomena. We belong to the modern period, to the nineteenth century, and to the last quarter of the nineteenth century. We inherit all the influences and problems of the past. Historians in all fields recognize the modern period as throughout revolutionary, critical, protestant, but protestant for the sake of reconstruction. This distinguishing characteristic of the new age has been defined as "that enlightenment, destroying in order to reconstruct, which sought to break the dominion of all prejudice, and to undermine every ill-founded belief."[2]

A. IN RELIGION.—The protest began in religion, and was a protest, as Erdmann puts it, on the one hand, against everything in which the church had become secularized, paganized, Judaized; on the other hand, a protest "against everything in which the church had opposed itself to the rational and justifiable interests of the world."[3] Positively the protest meant, as the whole world knows, insistence, in the first place, upon justification by faith and the priesthood of all believers, and, in the second place, the recognition of the rights of property, marriage, and the state. The appeal made in support of these positions to Scripture and primitive Christianity against the authority of councils and ecclesiastical tradition could end logically only in a defense of entire freedom of conscience and

---

[2] LOTZE, *Microcosmus*, Vol. II, p. 286.
[3] *History of Philosophy*, Vol. II, pp. 3, 4.

freedom of investigation. This is the only consistent Protestant position.

B. IN THE STATE.—Revolution in the state ends in the practical universal recognition of both absolute natural right and historic legitimate right, as Lotze names them. In this recognition of the double duty of the state—on the one hand, the duty of keeping faith with the past, of preserving some living community with those gone, the conservative tendency, the recognition of historical right; on the other hand, the duty of fidelity to the interests of the present, of revolt against the "dead hand," the radical tendency, the recognition of absolute natural-right—in this double recognition lie inclosed all the modern problems of sociology and social evolution.

C. INTELLECTUAL.—In the intellectual sphere the same revolutionary and protestant spirit is to be seen.

1. *Modern philosophy* in its rebound from scholastic dogmatism begins with Descartes's "methodical doubt"—the deliberate questioning of everything that could be questioned—and early made its chief investigations in the theory of knowledge, and throughout the period this question has been prominent, if not foremost. That its great subject is man—the whole man—and neither God nor the world, means that it finds its key only in itself, and not in any external source or authority. Our own century begins with the *Critical Philosophy* of Kant that was intended by its theory of knowledge to make philosophical dogmatism forever impossible. Kant's problems were all problems of mediation and remain essentially the present problems of philosophy, though they are much differently conceived, since the great systems of Fichte, Schleiermacher, Schelling, and Hegel lie between us and Kant. These problems may all be summed up in the problem of bringing into unity the mechanical and ideal views of the world. The last few years have seen the remarkable growth of the newer psychology, the increasing influence of the idea of evolution and the accompanying historical bent of philosophy, and the hardly yet understood complete collapse of materialism as a philosophical theory. The philosophical world is utterly different from that of the Reformation.

2. *In science.*—To the modern period, too, practically belongs the very birth of natural science, in the sense of exact investigation with deliberate experiment and repeated testing. This development of modern science, it has been pointed out, has implied three things: an immensely increased respect for experience, emphasis on the universality of law, and a threefold restriction on the part of science to experience, to a mathematical, not a speculative, development of its data, and to phenomena. That is, modern science distinctly disclaims to be either *a priori*, speculative, or ultimate.

Modern science has besides greatly affected the thought and imagination of men in its immense extension of the world in space and the discernment of its laws through astronomy, and in a similar extension of the world in time and the discernment of its laws through both astronomy and geology.

To these influences science has added to the thought of the age a sense of the unity of the world which is fairly overpowering. Extensively, spectrum analysis has been made to testify to uniformity of materials; gravitation and magnetism to uniformity of forces. Intensively, the principle of the conservation of energy is held to prove the unity of all forces, and the theory of evolution aims to include all phenomena under the unity of one method. Practically, scientific inventions have made our earth a unity, in a way not only to affect our imagination, but to change in a marked manner almost all the problems of our time. No man can conceive even superficially the changes involved in the rise of modern science and not feel how impossible it is for men of this generation to occupy precisely the point of view of not more than fifty years ago, even in their theological statements.

3. *In historical criticism.*—In the field of historical criticism our characterization of the intellectual changes which have taken place must be confined to those which bear specially on our theme. "Edwin Hatch," a recent reviewer says, "rejoiced to hear 'the solemn tramp of the science of history marching in our day almost for the first time into the domain of Christian theology.'" The historical sense is itself almost a product of this century (for it practically begins with Herder), and it

meant real and great changes, in the first place, in *biblical interpretation;* since interpretation now seeks to give full weight to the intellectual, moral, and religious atmosphere of the time. And to this conviction the immense increase of the last fifty years in the literature of the historical criticism of the Bible bears unmistakable witness. It was inevitable that the same historical spirit should recognize differences not only between Old Testament and New Testament times, but differences as well within these periods, and differences also in the point of view of different classes and individuals in the same period. This brought into being the whole new science of *biblical theology,* in which all rejoice, but which, in any strict construction of it, is less than fifty years old.[4] To the same historical movement, coupled with literary analysis and carried into the individual books, belongs the so-called *higher criticism* of the Old Testament. In its recent really influential form it is scarcely more than thirty years old, since it virtually dates from Graf (1866).[5] But far the most important result of historical criticism for theology has been what Fairbairn calls "the recovery of the historical Christ." It is the unique and greatest service of Principal Fairbairn's epoch-making book on *The Place of Christ in Modern Theology* that it makes so clear the place that Christ occupies in the thought of our generation. "Our day," he says, "has also been marked by a return to the sources of a quite specific character—it has been more distinctly than any other a return to the historical Christ . . . .— to him as the person who created alike the evangelists and the apostles, by whom he is described and interpreted."[6]

Let one bring together now, for a moment, in thought the intellectual changes in philosophy, in science, and in historical criticism of the last seventy years, and he must agree with John Fiske that "in their mental habits, in their methods of inquiry, and in the data at their command, the men of the present day who have fully kept pace with the scientific movement

---

[4] *Cf.* OEHLER, *Theology of the Old Testament,* pp. 32 ff.
[5] *Cf.* BRIGGS, *The Higher Criticism of the Hexateuch,* pp. 90 ff. See also PFLEIDERER, *The Development of Theology,* pp. 258 ff.
[6] *The Place of Christ in Modern Theology,* p. 187.

are separated from the men whose education ended in 1830 by an immeasurably wider gulf than has ever before divided one progressive generation of men from their predecessors."[7] If the man of today, therefore, is really alive to the movements of his own time, it is simply impossible that he should use most naturally and easily the language of the older generation in expressing his deepest convictions on any theme.

D. MORAL AND SPIRITUAL.—Side by side with the revolution in religion, in the state, and in the intellectual sphere, and influenced by these, there have taken place in the modern period similar changes in the general moral and spiritual convictions. Is it possible to state with some clearness and precision, and yet with the utmost brevity and without argument, the greatest of these fundamental moral and spiritual convictions of our day?—(1) From modern humanism, the special influence, most of all of Christianity, but also of political and social evolution, of philosophy, and the newer psychology, has come a greatly heightened sense of the *value and sacredness of the individual person* in his entirety. Sensitiveness as to the personal throughout is stronger, as it ought to be, than in any preceding period, and under it may be brought almost every other moral characteristic of our age.—(2) From the whole spirit of the modern period, but especially from Protestantism, and the influence of philosophy and of science, has come, we may hope, finally full recognition of *freedom of conscience* and *freedom of investigation*. These principles are distinctly moral, though applied in the intellectual sphere.—(3) The influence of natural science, moreover, has been effective in bringing into clear consciousness Christianity's latent *recognition of law, conditions, and time* in the moral and spiritual life, as truly as in any other sphere.—(4) The idealistic trend in philosophy, so strongly asserted by Paulsen and evidenced by the collapse of materialism, and the teleological view of evolution, added to the constant pressure of the Christian spirit, have made two closely connected convictions increasingly dominant: that, in the order of the universe, *the mechanical is means only,* and

---

[7] *The Idea of God*, p. 56.

that the *unity of the ethical life is found in love.* Even where
not distinctly affirmed, but perhaps even questioned, it is
believed that these two convictions are really present as fundamental assumptions in the reasoning of our time.—(5) Out of
Protestantism in its original criticism of Catholicism, out of
philosophy in its emphasis on man as *both* microcosmus and
microtheos, and out of science with its implied trend toward
the doctrine of divine immanence, has grown the *denial of the
separation of the sacred and the secular.*—(6) From the growing sense of the worth of personality, helped particularly by
the immensely deepened knowledge of "the other half," and
the great influence of the analogy of the organism in the
history of thought, has developed the *social conscience* of our
time—the definite avowal that we are all members one of
another.—(7) The new psychology, too, the latest conspicuous
intellectual movement of our day, has not only confirmed the
other tendencies already named, but has also added one distinctive contribution of rapidly growing influence—*the central
importance of action.* Body and mind, we are made for action.
Nor is this a rebound to a new extreme. The natural terminus
of all experiences, bodily and mental, is action. For the very
sake, therefore, of thought and feeling, one must act. The
emphasis on action is, indeed, a protest against mere intellectualism or romanticism, but it is at the same time an insistence on the unity of man, and on the *whole* man.—(8) And
historical criticism has not only strengthened the emphasis on
the historical, the concrete, and personal, but has brought into
the very foreground the greatest of all spiritual influences, *the
practical Lordship of Christ.* "This is not," it has been well said,
"an individual or incidental thing, but represents the tide and
passion of the time; is, as it were, the sum and essence of the
living historical, philosophical, and religious spirit."[8]

These, then, we may believe, if we have succeeded in correctly discerning the trend of the modern age, are the fundamental moral and spiritual convictions of our time: reverence
for personality, freedom of conscience, and freedom of investi-

---

[8] FAIRBAIRN, *op. cit.,* p. 188.

gation; law in the spiritual world, yet the subordination of the mechanical, and the unity of the ethical life in love; no separation of the sacred and secular; the social conscience, the central importance of action, the recognition of Christ as the supreme person.

They are not wholly new—of course not, and they have not grown up in a night, as their sources plainly show; but their present emphasis *is* relatively new, and on the farther side of these convictions lies, not our world, but another. And an age in whose life and thought they are working like yeast simply cannot express itself adequately in the terms of statements made when these convictions were not so felt, and it would be no real service to the church if it could, for it belongs to the very nature of spiritual truth that each age must be its own interpreter in spiritual things.

II. THE INEVITABLE INFLUENCE
OF THIS NEW WORLD ON THEOLOGY

Now, it is this new world in which we think and live that is the one great source of our dissatisfaction with the older statements in theology. These ruling ideas of our time are constantly at work. We all accept them more or less fully in themselves, and they are certain to prevail increasingly, and their ultimate influence in theology is simply inevitable, and ought to be. What, now, do they mean for theology?

In attempting to indicate some of the ways in which it seems that the atmosphere of our time (so far as it is right) is certain to affect theological statements, one can only bear honest testimony as to the direction in which progress seems to lie for our own generation. In a time of transition like the present it is impossible for any man to speak with frankness and definiteness on theological themes and command the assent of all, or perhaps the full assent of any. But truth comes, not through the silence of all, but by each declaring honestly and earnestly his best. Honest, thoughtful testimony, charitably and reverently borne, is the greatest need of the immediate present, if we are ever to come to that better intellectual expression of Christianity for which all wait.

A. MAINLY INTELLECTUAL INFLUENCES.–1. In the first place, the Protestant principle of *freedom of investigation* means the full recognition of the legitimacy, value, and authority of literary, historical, and scientific investigation in its own sphere —that of the tracing of causal connections. It means that theology refuses to settle *a priori* how God *must* have acted in any case in nature or in revelation, but turns over to humble, patient, scientific inquiry to determine how he *did* and *does* act. All questions, thus, of natural or mechanical *process* by which things came to be what they now are are unreservedly committed to scientific investigation. This means, *e.g.,* that all questions as to the conditions of the appearance of life, of man, of conscience, and all questions of the method of God's historical self-revelation, all questions of the authorship, age, and unity of the Scriptures, are to be freely and fearlessly investigated in a strictly scientific way. Scientific investigation can only make more clear to us exactly how God did proceed. And this, if we are really in earnest in our desire to understand God, we ought to be glad to know. If tomorrow men were able to trace in the laboratory the precise steps by which the living arises from the non-living, or if in some historical seminar the exact source and composition of Isaiah could be demonstratively made out, no ideal or religious interest would be in any manner affected, except that we should simply understand a little more fully the method God took in a case in which the mode of his action is to us now quite obscure. Our only anxiety can be that the investigators be really competent, and particularly in the investigation of moral and religious problems competence requires personal experience in the sphere investigated. It is, therefore, the poorest possible policy for the church to warn off its own scholars from these investigations. Moreover, the only answer to erroneous criticism is better criticism, not the forbidding of criticism. And the latter, we may be sure, is no service to the church, by whomsoever advocated. As Julius Müller long ago said: "Wounds which have been inflicted on humanity by knowledge can be healed only by knowledge." This is the one sure road to peace. Of these scientific investigations theology simply takes the results.

It is itself strictly an interpretative science, and it reserves to itself the right to interpret the results of scientific inquiry. It leaves absolutely to science the tracing of the causal connections; it claims for itself the ideal interpretation. The process belongs to science, the meaning to theology.

2. *Its relation to natural science.*—Of the purely intellectual influences on theology in our day that of natural science is particularly strong. We cannot, therefore, avoid, in the second place, the question of the relation of natural science to theology. What does the influence of natural science mean for theology?

It is well to notice at the very start that it is easy to overestimate the importance of this relation and the extent of this influence; and both are often overestimated, I believe, today. Professor James puts the matter in his usual vigorous fashion, when he says: "The aspiration to be scientific is such an idol of the tribe to the present generation, is so sucked in with his mother's milk by every one of us, that we find it hard to conceive of a creature who should not feel it, and harder still to treat it freely as the altogether peculiar and one-sided subjective interest which it is."[9] Nevertheless, the immense progress and rightful influence of natural science in our own generation force upon theology (in its wider sense) the problem of the mediation of the mechanical and ideal views of the world. Of the ultimate solution of the problem Christian theology can have no doubt, for it is involved in the central faith in a *God of love*. And, meanwhile, it addresses itself without misgivings to the adjustment of its relation to natural science.

(1) It accepts, in the first place, *science's own restrictions of itself* to experience, to the tracing of purely causal connections, and to phenomena. This restriction necessarily excludes all questions of ultimate origin and destiny. The scientific question is one of *process* merely. And, as no one thinks of seeing God at work like a man in the changes of nature, the process would seem the same to the observer, whether he thought it purely mechanical or wholly due to God.

---

[9] *Psychology*, Vol. II, p. 640.

(2) Secondly, it accepts unreservedly science's main contention of the *universality of law,* that mechanism is absolutely
universal in extent, though it requires that the principle shall
be exactly defined. It asks, *i.e.,* that it shall be noted that the
principle is *universality* of law, not, as much talk would seem
to imply, *uniformity* of law. There has been an amazing hazi-
ness concerning this simple point. The true scientific contention is, not that laws are always and everywhere the same, but
that there is always law. With this guarding of the principle
theology may well not only accept, but itself vigorously affirm
on ideal grounds, the universality of law. Religion has as great
an interest as science in asserting a sphere of law. For a sphere
of law is necessary in order to have any growth in *knowledge*
through experience, since, if there were no law, nothing
learned today would be of any value tomorrow. Nor could
there be any growth in *power* without law, for all power of
accomplishment depends wholly on knowledge of the laws of
the forces with which we deal. Growth in *character,* moreover,
is similarly conditioned. A sphere of law, therefore, is the only
possible sphere for a progressive being, and it is precisely his
progressiveness—his capacity of indefinite growth—that
mainly distinguishes man intellectually from the lower animals;
and with man all ideal interests come in. It is to be further
noticed that a sphere of law is necessary to give any significance to *freedom* itself, the condition of character; for choices
look to ends, and there can be no accomplishment of an end
without law. For another reason, too, religion can brook no
lawless world; for to allow such a world would make God
play fast and loose with his creatures. In order to have faith in
the fidelity and trustworthiness of God himself, therefore, there
must be law. In its own distinct sphere of the moral and
spiritual life, moreover, theology distinctly welcomes the idea
of law. Drummond, more than any other man, has brought
this home to the religious consciousness of our generation, and
it is his greatest contribution—*not* that there is the *same* law
for the natural and spiritual world (as he at first affirmed), but
that there *is* law; that there are definite conditions to be fulfilled for any spiritual attainment, that these conditions may be

known, and that when fulfilled you may count on the results. Theology has much to gain in clearness and precision of statement, and in power of appeal, in development of this line of thought.

The whole ideal contention and the interest of theology, therefore, is not at all against law, against mechanism; it must rather, with science, insist upon law; it *is* that mechanism in means only, and means must not be mistaken for ends nor dominate ends. Exactly here lies the religious interest in *miracle*. The insistence on miracle for the religious man means the insistence on a living God, and the insistence that, though mechanism is absolutely universal in extent, nevertheless, as Lotze says, "it is completely subordinate in significance." We are not to make a god of mechanism, it declares, nor put mechanism above God. The universality of law, therefore, is to theology only the perfect consistency in the modes of activity of God in carrying out his immutable purpose of love. Hence, God will always act according to law—that is, in perfect consistency with his unchanging purpose of love; but his action may not always be formulable under any of the laws of nature known to us. "*All's* love, yet *all's* law."

(3) In the third place, in the relation of theology to natural science, theology accepts from natural science the *theory of evolution* as a general statement of the method of God's working, and renews in consequence its own older emphasis upon the immanence of God.

Here, too, it wishes only that there should be real precision of thought as to what the evolution theory is. It has a suspicion that, as in many another case, difficulty comes only because the principle is not carried completely through. The trouble in evolution is that we are only *half* evolutionists. Theology is interested only to insist that evolution means real evolution—a succession of stages with new phenomena and new laws (and this the law of cyclical movement itself asserts), and that it *does not stop with the animal series*, but includes the human stage. It insists, therefore, that evolution does not mean the putting of everything on a dead level, especially not a degrading of everything to the lowest level, but that when the new appears it is really *new*—it has not appeared before. It may be assumed, as in the development of the individual, that the process is ever so gradual, and that the power is there ready to appear when the conditions for its appearance are completed; but when the new power appears—life, self-consciousness, moral responsibility, or what not—it is really new. It had not appeared before. Courtney[10] maintained the whole ideal contention more fully, perhaps, than he knew, when he wrote fifteen years ago: "I *was* an anthropoid ape once, a mollusc, an ascidian, a bit of protoplasm; but, whether by chance or providence, I am not now. When I was an ape, I thought as an ape, I acted as an ape, I lived as an ape; but when I became a man, I put away apish things. Man's moral nature is what it is, not what it was."

If, then, that conception of evolution is maintained which its own definition and laws require, theology finds no religious or ideal consideration that need hinder it in accepting the most absolute and radical form of the evolution theory without any thought of intervention at any point in the process. It feels no interest in insisting upon certain unbridged gaps in the series as essential at all to a religious view of the world. The most absolute evolution theory, so long as it is scientific at all, can be only a description of the process by which God has worked, of the method which he has employed. Theology is perfectly ready to accept the facts, whatever they may be. As it has been well said: "Whichever way of creation God may have chosen, in none can the dependence of the universe on him become slacker, in none be drawn closer."[11]

And more than this is true. Not only is the religious interest here not opposed to the scientific; in one important particular it is identical with it. For its own sake, theology can remain satisfied no longer with the old, inconsistent view of a virtual independence of the world in the larger part of it, and of direct dependence on God at certain points only, where we cannot yet trace the process of God's working. It is quite unwilling to

---

[10] *Studies in Philosophy,* chap. vi.
[11] Lotze, *op. cit.,* Vol. I, p. 374.

say God is only where we cannot understand him. It is quite unwilling to admit that increasing knowledge of God's working is progressive elimination of God from the universe. It is quite unwilling to take its stand on gaps or base its arguments for God on ignorance. It believes in *God*—in a God upon whom the whole universe, in every least atom of it, and in every humblest spirit of it, is absolutely dependent. Of that dependence it is certain, and no study of the *method* of it can make it less certain.

Theology rejoices, then, in the larger view evolution seems to give of the method, plan, and aim of God in the universe; in the great extension and strengthening of the design argument; in the harmony it brings into the divine methods, and in the enlarged conception of God in his immanence in the world.

Outside of these general gains which the evolution theory seems to bring, and in which most would probably agree, exactly what does the detailed application of evolution to theological and ethical problems mean? Is there not much confusion of thought here that seems often to end only in juggling with phrases, both on the side of the mechanical philosopher and on the side of the religious apologist?

If the *entire* evolution series, including man, with his moral and spiritual nature, is meant, then the later stages will be recognized, according to the law of cyclical movement, as higher, and as having their own peculiar phenomena and laws, and interpreted accordingly, but with due regard to the lower stages.

If the *purely animal organic evolution* is meant, then the analogy is taken wholly from the realm *below* man; and, however suggestive, must obviously, on the principle of evolution itself, prove inadequate for an interpretation of the intellectual, moral, and spiritual life of man, and must finally break down, as it does even in the hands of so skilful and sympathetic an interpreter as Drummond. The analogy of organic evolution is only the farthest possible extension of the very fruitful analogy of the organism that has been so influential in the history of thought from Paul to Shaftesbury and Kant, and down to modern ethics and sociology. It is the most adequate analogy that nature furnishes us, and it is *useful* to apply it as fully as possible in order to discern the essential harmony of the laws in all the stages, and to see that the natural world is from the same hand as the moral; but, after all is said, it is still only an analogy from nature, and quite inadequate to set forth all the life of the spirit in itself and its personal relations. We are spirits, not organisms, and society is a society of persons, not an organism. The theory of the evolution of the animal series, fully accepted, therefore, in its most radical form, is still no universal solvent of ethical and theological questions where personal relations replace organic. It is a perversion of the evolution theory in its real entirety to attempt to bring all the higher stages under the laws of the lower. Yet this is what the application of evolution to theology and ethics seems to mean to many. The inadequacy of the method is seen from the way in which many of the most serious difficulties have to be solved by bringing in considerations entirely apart from evolution. Although, therefore, the writer shares with the enthusiastic advocates of evolution in theology the freest acceptance of evolution in its fullest form, he does not have their confidence in its wonder-working power in theology. It is true that the attempt to state the entire ethical or sociological problem in biological terms—in terms of life—of organic evolution, is very fascinating and sounds very scientific; but in truth its success is its failure, for it can succeed only by forgetting the essential nature of that with which it is dealing —spirit, not physical life. Guardedly used, the analogy is helpful, but adequate it never is. On the human stage of evolution we have reached persons and personal relations, and the laws are those of personal relations. God will deal with us on this stage in accordance with the principle of evolution, if he deals with us as persons and enters into personal relations with us. And this Christianity has always believed. The application of evolution here will simply mean, therefore, that in these personal relations with men God's self-revelation at every stage will be adapted to men's capacities to receive, and will progress as rapidly as possible; that the complete revelation in Christ comes as soon as there are men who can use it with value and preserve it for a progressive evaluation by those who follow. We have no call to show that in these personal relations of men with men, or of God with men, all that occurs can be brought under the laws that hold on the lower stages. It is vain, therefore, to look for revolutionary results in the statement of individual theological doctrines from the theory of evolution in its narrower scope. Helpful analogies and suggestive points of view we shall have, but scarcely more. But the legitimate application of evolution in its entirety is a thing to be welcomed, not feared. All God's ways are harmonious.

3. *As necessarily affected by historical criticism.*—Of the mainly intellectual influences on theology, the most important must be that of historical criticism. Christianity is preëminently a historical religion, and such persistent and painstaking historical researches as those of the last sixty years must help us to more accurate and illuminating statements. Theology can be certain that the assured results of patient investigation (it is quite too early to dogmatize as to details in higher criticism, if we can ever do so), because they will show us more perfectly the method that God actually did take in his revelation of himself to men, will bring, not disaster, but great enrichment to theology. His ways are higher than our ways, and his thoughts than our thoughts. Some of the adjustments required will in the time of transition no doubt seem difficult and even threatening; but it is certain that, so far as we are able actually to find God's way—and this is the sole final result of historical criticism—it will be *better* than our way. And the time is not far distant, we may believe, when we shall enumerate the blessings of critical investigation, including the higher criticism. We shall rejoice in the better understanding of God involved in the more vivid setting forth of his persistent, patient, loving adaptation to men; we shall, indeed, have lost a uniform authoritative lawbook, but we shall have gained instead a living revelation of a living God in living men, rich and throbbing as life itself; we shall be grateful that the phenomena of the Bible disclosed by patient study *compelled* us to a restatement of the doctrine of inspiration that eliminated from it

the mechanical, and brought it into full accord with the working of God in our own hearts as promised by Christ—never God alone, and never man alone, but always God and man, in a personal coöperation that means character and love. We shall come to see with some surprise that a view of inspiration as really moral and spiritual, with its natural implications, has practically removed all our own difficulties concerning the Bible and disposed of the main attacks upon it, at the same time.

Positively for theology these implications of the changed view of inspiration, which the results of historical criticism require, include, in the first place, a much fuller recognition of the principle of *progress in revelation,* that this involves inevitably the relative imperfection of the earlier stages and makes Christ the absolute standard in the Bible as well as out of it. Theology never had any need to affirm any other principle than this, but it has certainly not yet fully adjusted itself to this fact.

Further, this study of the Bible itself has brought out into striking light its one great *purpose* in absolute agreement with Paul's own clear statement[12]—that it is neither science nor history, but solely and simply a record of the historical self-revelation of God to a single people and so to all men. This means that, even in books called historical, its writers are not interested in strict scientific history at all, any more than in some other books they are interested in pure natural science. Nature and history both concerned them only as revelations of God. A complete account of either lies quite outside their task. They select only those features that can be turned to religious account. They make no attempt to trace all the causal connections; they *do* seek to show what both nature and, especially, history *mean* for religion—how God reveals himself in them. Because they concentrated themselves upon this one task, they are the world's teachers in neither science, nor history, nor law, nor art, nor philosophy—but we all sit at their feet in religion. Even the historical writers, especially in the

---

[12] Tim. 2: 16–17.

Old Testament, are, therefore, properly prophets, preaching from historical texts, and the Jews rightly called them so.

In the third place, this more careful biblical study is making clear, what a really spiritual view of inspiration would lead us to expect, that, with all its wonderful unity of development, there is no mechanical unity in the Bible or even the New Testament, but that the different writers show *individual reflections* of a religious experience more or less common to them. In the New Testament this gives individual reflections of Christ. It is in this very way that we are able to approach any adequate conception of the real significance of Christ, and of that larger unity which comes from him and not from the single expression of even his greatest disciple. No one view, no single expression, can suffice. The work of Christ is deeper and broader than any single statement of it, even in Scripture. The recognition of this fact has promise, not only of a reasonable freedom for theology, but of large growth as well, and of a better appreciation of the richness of the New Testament testimony itself.

B. MORAL AND SPIRITUAL INFLUENCES.—When we turn from the mainly intellectual influences on theology to those distinctly moral and spiritual, we may perhaps group them all under the two heads of the deepening sense of the value and sacredness of the person, and the growing recognition of Christ as the supreme person.

1. *The inevitable influence on theology of the sense of the value and sacredness of personality.*—The greatest outcome of an advancing civilization is the deepening sense of the value of the individual person. This is the very flower and test of civilization. If it be true, as was said, that the sensitiveness as to the personal throughout is stronger in our age than in any preceding, this is certain in time to influence theology profoundly. It affects at once our view of inspiration and our whole doctrine of the spirit in its hidden working, and throws light on the providence of God, on the meaning of prayer, and on the obscurity of spiritual truth; as well as affects the tone of the presentation of every doctrine.

(1) Out of it grows at once the obligation of love, and of a

love that not only includes all persons, but that is such a love
as to include all virtues. It means, therefore, a true humanism,
but no sentimentalism, for it looks only to the complete character. This *unity of the ethical life in love* is the first clear step
in an ultimate philosophy; it is the most important inheritance
left us by Edwards; it is soundly biblical; and it is constantly
gaining ground. But it is still fully recognized by few in theology. The old dualism of justice and love, or holiness and love,
still works confusion in both ethics and theology. It is still too
largely felt that there is division in God, that nature, law, and
grace root in different purposes, instead of all working to the
same end. Even those who have meant wholly to accept the
all-embracing character of love have seldom carried it fearlessly out for God and for man at all times and in all conditions. But to carry entirely through this principle of the unity
of the ethical life in love is the only logical consequence of the
present sense of the value of the person. "Not that we love
God, but that he loved us." "Every one that loveth is begotten
of God and knoweth God."

And it is the very sense of the sacredness and value of the
person which has brought about the "reduction of the area of
Calvinism" of which Fisher speaks. It is simply impossible to
hold to arbitrary decrees in the old sense in the face of this
conviction. The reaction, also, by elaborate argument and
labored exegesis against the universal fatherhood of God, that
all men as men are the children of God, is for a like reason
simply hopeless. The conviction of the fatherhood of God has
grown directly out of the representation of God by Christ, and
its connection with the root cannot be severed by ever so elaborate an argument.

(2) The deepening sense of the worth of the person means,
in the second place, *the recognition of the whole man.* The
whole man is expressed only in personal relations. Theology
accepts heartily psychology's new assertion of the unity of
man, and seeks to take account of the entire spirit. It believes
with modern philosophy that man is the key to all problems,
but only the whole man. If I do not mistake the drift of modern thinking, it is in essential agreement with Lotze's main

contention, "that the nature of things does not consist in thoughts, and that thinking is not able to grasp it; yet perhaps the whole mind experiences in other forms of its action and passion the essential meaning of all being and action, thought subsequently serving it as an instrument, by which that which is thus experienced is brought into the connection which its nature requires, and is experienced in more intensity as the mind is master of this connection."[13] This is no underrating of the intellectual, but an insistence that man is more than intellect, and, therefore, that an adequate philosophy, no less than an adequate theology, must take account of all the data —emotional and volitional as well as intellectual; æsthetic, ethical, and religious as well as mechanical. It is a revolt against a misnamed rationalism that knows only intellect, in favor of a genuine rationalism that knows the whole man. It believes, therefore, with Armstrong's putting of Seth's position, that "the language of morality or religion, the language which speaks of God in terms of our own highest experience, is really *truer* than purely metaphysical language concerning God *can be*. 'Religion and higher poetry . . . carry us nearer to the meaning of the world than the formulæ of an abstract metaphysics.'"

(3) In the third place, this emphasis on the personal means for theology *the exclusion of the mechanical* (as contrasted with the spiritual) everywhere. It is noticeable that all agree essentially in this aim of excluding the mechanical, though they do not agree as to what is mechanical. It is this spirit that makes it so certain that the attempt to press the analogy of the lower evolution is wrong. It is this that leads strong conservatives like Frank, liberals like Pfleiderer, and Ritschlians like Herrmann, all alike, to emphasize the importance of the inner spiritual evidence to Christianity. This movement logically requires of theology that it do not stop until it interpret all its strictly theological problems in terms of personal relation. The relations are nowhere more intensely personal. Theology will yet put more meaning than it ever has put into Christ's

---

[13] *Op. cit.*, Vol. II, pp. 359, 360.

declaration: "This is life eternal, that they should *know thee* the only true God, and him whom thou didst send, even Jesus Christ." Deepening acquaintance with God is the one all-embracing problem of the Christian life; every step of it is a personal relation; and its laws are the laws of friendship. This steady and certain movement away from the mechanical to the personal is the inner ground of dissatisfaction with all natural, legal, and governmental analogies, applied, *e. g.*, to the doctrine of the atonement. The deep significance of Dr. Trumbull's exhaustive survey in his remarkable books on *The Blood Covenant* and *The Threshold Covenant* is that he traces back so clearly analogies that have been otherwise interpreted to the closest personal relations. And yet the more or less mechanical analogies will pass away as only subordinately helpful, not because they are attacked from without, but because, in the deepening sense of the intensely personal nature of the relations involved, the basis of their appeal will have broken down within. They will be set aside, not because they make too much of the work of Christ in his life or death, but because they make too little of it; because they leave our relation to him still too external and mechanical, and fail to bring it home to us as a moral reality. The more personal view believes that more truly and really than any other it can say: "He was wounded for our transgressions; he was bruised for our iniquities; the chastisement of our peace was upon him; and with his stripes we are healed."

This interpretation of all strictly theological problems in terms of personal relations will bring great gain to theology in both simplicity and unity; it will make theology *seem* to many less scientific, because it will have dropped much technical language which has no longer any proper application; but it will have *deepened* in the same proportion the perception of the real spiritual problems, and will lean more on psychology and ethics, and less on metaphysics and jurisprudence.

(4) The denial of the separation between sacred and secular things, which also grows out of the sense of the sacredness of personality, looks to the inevitable *rejection of all sacramentalism* as necessarily mechanical. It knows no sacred things,

but only sacred persons. The sacredness of things and places and times is wholly borrowed from persons. And between things no line is to be drawn of sacred and secular. "All things are yours," and all are means only, but all may be made means. There is to be war on the worldly spirit, but not on the world. We are to be in the world, though not of the world. It is by no means unimportant to a theology that intends to keep itself free from mere mechanism and superstition to see clearly two sides of the truth: that the most holy things are so only because they minister to the spirit of a living person, and that *all* things are to be so used as to give this ministration. If one chooses to say so, this is to make all things sacramental; but this is the death of the older sacramentalism which lives on the assertion of the sole virtue of certain things. Just now the doctrine of the incarnation is being widely used to put new life into sacramentalism; but it is only the sound of the word, not its true meaning, which gives the view any support. The revelation of God in Christ is beyond all else personal, and only personal; it is no mere toying with the flesh of humanity. The church is no institution, but, as Fairbairn says, "the church is the *people* of God; wherever they are he is, and the church through him in them."[14]

(5) The *intense quickening of the social conscience*, too, which also is born of the sense of the worth of the person, cannot help deepening our insight into another side of biblical and Christian teaching. This is for theology simply the clear recognition of the large place given to the kingdom of God in the teaching of Christ. The astonishment is that, even apart from the explicit teaching as to the kingdom, with Christ's statement of the great commandment before men, any other view could have been held. Flight from the world, and flight from human relations, were no legitimate growth from the spirit of Christ. In any case it would seem that we can never again forget that "we are members one of another." And few principles have so many vital applications in theology. As certain as that the great commandment is love and that the

---

[14] *Op. cit.*, p. 530.

great means to character is association, so certain is it that we are necessary one to another. As certain as that each has his own individual outlook on the divine, so certain is it that we need to share each other's visions. The principle sheds its light on the problem of evil, and on the meaning of intercessory prayer, and on many another dark place in our thinking. Only through it is the full greatness of the human spirit seen, and the largeness of the life open to it, for it implies the divine friendship as well. All this is true, and much more. But we must not make here another false application of the analogy of the organism. To press, as many are now doing, the analogy of the organism is really to repudiate that out of which the whole development of the social conscience has come—the sense of the value of the individual person.

(6) Every one of these considerations drawn from emphasis on the personal implies an *increasing emphasis on the ethical* that affects theology at every point. The very definition of religion is changed. The separation of the ethical and religious is becoming impossible. The reality of the moral life of man seems to us now one of the main foundations of a religious view. And we can conceive no salvation that does not include character. We believe that the ethical is *always* involved in every genuine religious experience. As Herrmann puts it: "Neither in what is opposed to duty, nor in what is indifferent to it, can we meet with God, or do we desire to do so."[15] We are compelled, therefore, to a reinterpretation of the Reformation formula. We see with Paul in faith a real personal relation, but one that is the germ of *real* righteousness. To deny all worth to faith, any activity on the part of man, is simply to deny that that has taken place which it is the whole aim of redemption to bring about—the voluntary choosing to be a child of God, of like character with him. A thoroughly ethical conception of salvation affects theological statements in unlooked-for-ways, and to an extent impossible even to indicate. It is no denial of a real forgiveness of sins, but it makes sin not less but more serious. On the other hand, it puts an abso-

---

[15] *Communion with God,* p. 106.

lute bar to the older Calvinism of salvation by divine decree, supposing that that made conceivable the idea of character at all. The atonement, too, can get its full meaning only as it is conceived as ethical *throughout*.

(7) And if theology accepts the guidance, not only of ethics, but also of psychology, with what Paulsen calls its "voluntaristic trend," it must be *practical*. Certainly in religion—giving principles for life, a method of living—if anywhere, judgment by consequences ought to apply. Moreover, all doctrine is originally only the thought expression of experience or its supposed implications, and has, therefore, a solely practical source. And all doctrine must have meaning for life. It must be seen to bear on life; something must follow from it for attitude and conduct. This is the very ground of distinction between other truth and moral and spiritual truth. The latter is always an appeal to character. If it is not so, we may be very sure it is not correctly stated. The New England theologians, therefore, rightly sought a theology that could be *preached*. So far as theology is a science of practical religion, the test is genuine and needed, but it would cut severely much that goes under the name of theology.

2. *The influence on theology of the recognition of Christ as the supreme person.*—All these deeper moral convictions of our time which we have been considering lead naturally to the recognition of Christ as the supreme person, and therefore the supreme fact of history, and the supreme revelation of God, and this recognition in turn strengthens all the other convictions. This growing convergence of the thought of the world toward Christ is far the greatest fact of our time. At the end of every path there looms up before us this one great towering figure. The simple truth is that we stand face to face with the historical Christ, as it has been said, "in a sense and to a degree unknown to the church since the apostolic age." It is a most significant fact that every single great life of Christ since the gospels is the product of but little more than the last sixty years. Every ray of light, historical, critical, philosophic, ethical, religious, has been concentrated upon him. No such study was ever given to any theme. It would be criminal thought-

lessness that could make that fact without effect in theology. Better to know Christ is certainly to be able to speak more adequately about him. And it would be our shame, not the glory of the Fathers, if in spite of the deepening knowledge of Christ, we were content to speak precisely as they spoke. We would much better try to speak as we believe they would speak now. The very movement itself makes it certain, however, that this is not to make Christ less, but more.

(1) The recovery of the historical Christ, this growing recognition of his supremacy, means for theology, then, in the first place, that it accepts Christ in truth as the *supreme* revelation of God, its one great source of the knowledge of God's character and purpose. With this fact it is in dead earnest. It does not deny that there are other sources, but it holds them to be distinctly subordinate. Christ and only Christ is adequate to give the Christian conception of God. It welcomes gladly all other light, and it knows that the mind must do its best to bring into unity all its possessions, but natural theology is for it supplementary rather than basic, subordinate to, not coördinate with, Christ. It seeks with all earnestness approximation to *Christ's* theology. It erects no altar to an unknown God; it takes refuge in neither scholasticism nor mysticism. It knows one God, the God revealed in Christ, and it accepts with confidence the affirmation of Christ: "He that hath seen me hath seen the Father; how sayest thou, show us the Father?"

The cry "Back to Christ" means for theology that Christ is really supreme, in the Bible and out of it. And it believes that any reaction against the cry so interpreted is doomed to failure. Theology must recognize the indispensable value of the apostolic testimony to Christ, but it must reserve the right (and it is vain to deny it) by legitimate historical criticism to appeal from the reflection of Christ to the Christ reflected. That Christ is Lord ought to be no divisive cry for any disciple of Christ.

(2) And of the character of the God who reveals himself in Christ theology can have no doubt. It sees God *in Christ;* it knows and seeks no better name for him than Christ's own constantly repeated name, Father. And when it seeks to inter-

pret that name by Christ's own spirit in life and death, it seems for the first time really to know what love and what sin are. God is no longer onlooker, nor even sovereign merely; but Father, holy and loving, who because he hates sin and knows its awfulness, and yet loves with surpassing love his child, suffers in the sin of his child. It is no sentimentalism. The more the Father loves the child, the more he hates the sin of the child, and must use every means to put the sin away. On the other hand, the revelation of the Father alone brings his sin adequately to the man himself. It puts his sin in the light of the suffering love of God, of what it costs the Father's heart, and brings home so the shame of it and the guilt of it as no punishment could possibly do. Christ's conception of God as Father, as Fairbairn justly says, must be taken as the really ruling conception, determining all else in theology.

(3) Historical criticism has brought us also into the very presence of the *man* Jesus, and has renewed for us, therefore, the gospel's own emphasis on the humanity of Christ, almost forgotten by the church in spite of both gospels and creeds. But it is most significant that it is directly through this study of the humanity of Jesus that his lordship and divinity have become so plain. It is no Unitarian drift which the age has disclosed, and yet it accepts the emphasis on Christ's humanity. The religious need of the humanity of Christ is very great, for otherwise his whole life is unreal, and has no true relation to our life, and he could give to us no perfect revelation of the perfect filial relation to God. But more than this is true. It is supremely in the *character* of Christ that God stands fully revealed, and this character must be real—the real character of the man Jesus. His true humanity is, therefore, essential to the revelation of his divinity. The two stand in closest relation. Not God *and* man, but God revealed because true man.

(4) But there is one inference widely drawn from this newly awakened belief in the divinity of Christ, against which, it seems to the writer, earnest and honest protest should be made. The evangelical church knows well, with van Dyke,[16]

---

[16] *The Gospel for an Age of Doubt*, p. 110.

that "the unveiling of the Father in Christ was and continued to be, and still is, the palladium of Christianity;" and no age has had a more thorough and intelligent conviction of the lordship and divinity of Christ than ours. This conviction is the deepest and most inspiring influence in theology today; but this conviction is grounded on straightforward historical study of the character of Christ, not on metaphysical speculation. It can be no service to the church, it would seem, under this fresh and independent conviction to react toward a really metaphysical tritheism, affirming social relations and love within the Godhead, in the immanent trinity. The attempt has been widely approved, but I cannot doubt that, so far as it becomes a living faith, it means tritheism pure and simple, and will surely bring its own punishment. This, at least, is true: nothing calls for more absolute and complete personality than love and social relations. To affirm social relations, therefore, in the Godhead is to assert absolute tritheism. And no possible manipulation of the terms can avoid it. The analysis of self-consciousness, also, taken from Hegel—to put it flatly —helps not at all to a real trinity and proves nothing. It is far better that we should admit that we simply do not understand the eternal trinity than that by explanations that do not explain we should be driven to ascribe three persons to God in the only sense in which we can understand person, and not be able to say that God is one person in any sense we can understand. This new tritheism seems to me far less defensible than even the oldest credal statements of the trinity, for those were at least scrupulously careful to insist that the distinctions in the Godhead were not personal, but that God was in truth one. We are likely to find the biblical doctrine of the trinity more satisfying both intellectually and religiously than any later abstractly wrought out statements. We believe in one God, our Father, concretely and supremely revealed and brought nigh with absolute and abiding assurance in Christ, and making himself known in the hearts of all who will receive him, in the most intimate, constant, and powerful, but not obtrusive, friendship possible to man, giving thus the supreme conditions of both character and happiness.

Moreover, the religious need of the strict unity of God is very great. I want to know that God himself, the infinite source of all, is my Father; that he, not some second being, loves me. And this is the very significance of Christ that *God* is in him, speaks and works through him. This seems to be Christ's constant testimony, and the one view that includes both sides of John's representation of him. It is the whole meaning of Christ that he reveals God himself, that we may see God's love in his love. Less than this seems still to leave us far from the gospel, as Luther felt, and underestimates the significance of Christ. "He that hath seen me *hath* seen the Father." Unitarianism emphasizes the *humanity* of Christ to preserve the unity of God, the true view emphasizes the *divinity* of Christ to preserve the unity.

(5) But it is the greatest glory of this new sense of the historical Christ that, whether we are able adequately or in agreement to phrase his relation to us or to God, the fact stands out with increasing clearness for all men that simply coming into his presence we find the key to the meaning of life, we find ourselves, we find God. Not apologetically, therefore, not with misgiving, but in glad confidence, we own him Lord. In our intellectual formulations of his person we may not satisfy one another. But "no man can say Jesus is Lord, but in the Holy Spirit." It is hardly possible to mistake, *e. g.*, the note of personal confession and joy in these words of Adolf Harnack: "When God and everything that is sacred threatens to disappear in darkness, or our doom is pronounced; when the mighty forces of inexorable nature seem to overwhelm us, and the bounds of good and evil to dissolve; when, weak and weary, we despair of finding God at all in this dismal world— it is then that the personality of Christ may save us."[17]

When theology tries now honestly to take account of these great convictions of our own age, it only attempts more adequately to conceive the great abiding truths of Christianity, and make them real to *this* generation. It seeks to be more *Christian*—closer to the very spirit and teaching of Christ, its

---

[17] *Christianity and History,* p. 47.

supreme authority; more *personal* and reverent of personality—
insisting on the whole man and the personal relations which
are essential in every moral and spiritual problem; more *biblical*—with unfaltering faith in the historical revelation of God,
and owning the priceless value of the reflections of Christ in
his own generation, it means to give a weight to biblical statements in theology that has not yet been given; more *historical*
—for it wishes humbly to know the actual way that God has
taken, not its own imaginings; more *practical*—for it looks
only to life, the highest life; more *ethical*—for it knows that to
be a child of God is to be of like character with God; more
social—for it remembers the great commandment:—Christian,
personal, biblical, historical, practical, ethical, social, and, once
again and supremely, Christian. "Other foundation can no man
lay than that which is laid, which is Jesus Christ." "And this
is life eternal that they should *know* thee, the only true God,
and him whom thou didst send, even Jesus Christ."

2

JOSIAH STRONG

Neo-Puritan Moralist of American Empire

Josiah Strong (1847-1916) was not a towering intellect, but in his day his influence greatly exceeded that of many who counted as more original or more profound. For no one so well typifies the inner contradictions of the "Pilgrims' pride," that amalgam of simple moralism, smug prudery, ethnocentrism (not to say white racism), and social idealism, which was to run badly aground with the onset of the Depression. It was against such views as Strong's that the pragmatic realism of Reinhold Niebuhr was sharpened—and to a considerable extent Strong's views were normative.

Descended from the Pilgrim elder John Strong, who settled in Dorchester, Mass., in 1630, Josiah Strong was born in Illinois and reared in Ohio. He began his career as a Congregational minister in Cheyenne, Wyoming, in 1871. After two years in that recently organized territory, he returned to his alma mater, Western Reserve College, to serve as chaplain, after which he served as pastor of churches in Sandusky and Cincinnati. From 1881 to 1884 he was midwestern secretary of the Congregational Home Mission Society. In this capacity he began writing his first book, *Our Country*, which sold 175,-000 copies soon after it was published in 1885. One result of the book's success was Strong's appointment as secretary of the American Evangelical Alliance, a post he resigned in 1898 to found the League for Social Service. Eventually he was to play a leading role in the founding of the Federal Council of Churches.

In *Our Country*, Strong asserted that "the Anglo-Saxon, as the great representative of these two ideas . . . civil liberty . . .

and pure *spiritual* Christianity . . . is divinely commissioned to be, in a peculiar sense, his brother's keeper." He denounced slums and "despotic capitalism," while seeing a threat to older American values in the waves of Jewish, Catholic, and Orthodox immigrants from Eastern Europe, Italy, and the Balkans. Of his own stock, he said, "This race of unequaled energy, with all the majesty of numbers and wealth behind it—the representatives, let us hope, of the largest liberty, the purest Christianity, the highest civilization—having developed peculiarly aggressive traits calculated to impress its institutions upon mankind, will spread itself over the earth." Other peoples Strong regarded as inferior; they were "only the precursors of a superior race, voices in the wilderness crying: 'Prepare ye the way of the Lord!'"[1]

Strong's virulent jingoism was scarcely atypical in American Protestant thought, nor was its Spencerian flavor. However prejudicial, it was wedded to a passionate optimism rooted in the liberal theology of Horace Bushnell and a no less passionate sense of urgency. If the church became "the controlling conscience of the social organism," as Strong believed it must, the working man would receive justice, the socialist movement would diminish, and there would be the dawn of a "new era" of responsible capitalism. In short, Strong delineated with evangelistic fervor the alternatives of social perdition and social salvation, identifying the latter with an application of Puritan. discipline and self-restraint to the conditions of an emergent urban-industrial society. In his second book, *The New Era* (1893) and in subsequent writings, Strong asserted that Jesus' teachings centered in the Kingdom of God as an ideal society. The church must rise above denominational squabbles and generate the requisite concern for human wel-

---

[1] Josiah Strong, *Our Country* (New York: Baker & Taylor, 1885), p. 222. The benignity of Strong's racism is indicated by the fact that he did not regard anyone as genetically inferior. He even extols the English for their racially hybrid origins. Inferior peoples could be elevated through missionary tutelage and acquire all the values and merits held by the tutor race. What Strong wants is not subjugation but a melting pot in which everyone is moulded to the Anglo-Saxon image—as in fact white American missionaries attempted to do.

fare to establish, extend, and purify the Kingdom here and now—in America and from America to the rest of the world.

The Next Great Awakening (1902) was by no means Strong's most important book. His discussion of "The Social Laws of Jesus", which is reproduced here, is an abbreviated version of three chapters from a previous book. Strong's is far from the best or most definite statement of the Social Gospel, yet it demands attention, for his baldly simple moralism was perhaps more characteristic than the views of Gladden or Rauschenbusch. In large part it is the wide prevalence of such thinking as Strong's that made the Social Gospel so vulnerable to attack by such Christian realists as the Niebuhr brothers. The purported "social laws" of service, sacrifice, and love rest on a narrow, intimidatingly rigid, and curiously literalistic reading of selected New Testament passages. It is hard to see what Strong's views owe to the Great Awakening of Jonathan Edwards. They hark back, rather, to the paradox of theocratic voluntarism with which Strong's Pilgrim forebears were imbued. More to the point, they help to explain how, with great moral fervor and a paucity of insight, American Protestantism handicapped itself from the start in dealing with the problems of a complex technological society. The persistence of such thinking in the America of the 1970s continues to impede the solution of those problems. Josiah Strong is little remembered nowadays, unless as an active participant in the founding of the Federal Council of Churches or, with an aura of nobility, for a quixotic idealism that is now passé. Yet Strong and the admiration that adheres to his uncritically recalled ideas remain, without paradox, pillars of the churches' virtuous inadequacy in our time. The very conception of service, sacrifice, and love expounded in the following extract continues to serve as the rationale for most church agencies and as the ideology of the layman in business and politics—lofty ideals of personal character, self-imposed by every believer, somehow add up to a good society. If we encounter difficulty in attaining these ideals, the solution is to try harder and believe more firmly in the possibility of success. Jesus laid down the rules, and if we believe in him we had better measure up to them. Although

professedly social, it is a moralism that envisions a social result
without having any conception of social dynamics or interaction, any idea of the structure of personality or community,
or of the ironics of history. Here we see the fruition of that
romantic perfectionism which was already widespread when
Strong was born. Strong assumes, for example, that it is humanly possible (by mysterious divine aid) to be totally selfless
and morally perfect. He does not consider how easily some
Christians mistake the intention for the fact, particularly when
evaluating their own character and conduct; hence he has
no critical safeguard against self-righteousness. In the end,
Strong's theology turns out to be not so much Kingdom-centered
as self-centered. Service is the self "doing good," enacting or
emanating virtue rather than sharing or reciprocating. Sacrifice is the self "giving up" intransitively, for its own moral
benefit. Love, in effect, is reduced to the combination of these
—self-denial and self-giving. There are blessed donors and
presumably benighted recipients whom the donors bless and
uplift, but because Strong has shorn Jesus' teaching from its
context in the Palestinian community, his vision of the Kingdom is devoid of mutuality. The individual, like "our country,"
proves his superiority by his selfless mission to lesser breeds,
not by establishing a brotherhood of equals that includes all.
Just as "our" turns out to mean "we Anglo-Saxons'," so "Christian" turns out to have a certain clubbishness and a certain
eminently benign WASPishness, not to say imperialism.

THE SOCIAL LAWS OF JESUS*

The rediscovery of the kingdom of God has been accompanied
by the rediscovery of the social teachings of Jesus.

Some fourteen or fifteen years ago there was a meeting of
New York clergymen who were especially interested in social
problems, and who have been leaders in the readjustment of

---

* From Josiah Strong, *The Next Great Awakening.*

Christian thought and work, which is now in progress. There were about a dozen present, and among them were men of national and international reputation and influence. One of the leaders expressed his perplexity and regret that he could not find in the teachings of Jesus any social laws! And what is still more surprising, the statement passed unchallenged, so completely had leaders of Christian thought lost sight of the social aspects of Christianity. Since then a shelf full of books has been written on the social teachings of Jesus.

When civilization was individualistic, men went to the New Testament for light on the problems of the individual, and found what they sought. When industry ceased to be individualistic and became collective it wrought a corresponding change in civilization. With this social revolution came the consciousness of social needs and the recognition of social problems; and when men went to the Bible for light on these problems, new light broke forth from the Word of God.

A social organization implies organizing principles, and a kingdom implies laws. Jesus laid hold of three fundamental social principles, and promulgated them as the fundamental laws of the kingdom of God, viz., SERVICE, SACRIFICE and LOVE.[1]

THE LAW OF SERVICE.

So comprehensive is this law that its span includes both the spiritual and the natural world. The obedience yielded to it by nature is unconscious and of course unmoral. It is a prophecy of a higher service which may be rendered or refused by conscious man. Wherever there is human association there is service of some sort. Roman civilization was based on the compulsory service of the slave. Our modern, industrial civilization is based on the compensated service of the employee.

This principle of service, illustrated in nature and in human

---

[1] For a fuller discussion of these laws, see my *The Times and Young Men*, (1901), where a chapter is devoted to each. It is there shown that these laws belong to the natural as well as to the spiritual world, or that they are at least foreshadowed in nature; and that these universal laws, binding on both the spiritual and the physical, are doubly binding on man, in whom the spiritual and the physical meet.

society, Jesus laid hold of, ennobled, Christianized, and made one of the fundamental laws of the world society which he established. In service, as in all else that he required of his disciples, he himself afforded the supreme example. Though he thought it not robbery to be equal with God, he made himself of no reputation, and took upon him the form of a servant (Phil. ii. 6, 7). He said to his disciples: "I am among you as he that serveth" (Luke xxii. 27). "The Son of man came not to be ministered unto, but to minister" (Matt. xx. 28). "The disciple is not above his master, nor the servant above his lord" (Matt. x. 24). "As my Father hath sent me, even so send I you" (Jno. xx. 21). He was sent to minister; he sent forth his disciples to minister. And he taught that the final principle of judgment, to be applied to all nations, was that of ministration. In the picture which he gives of the last great court, men are acquitted or condemned according as they had served or failed to serve.

Jesus did not look on service as a disagreeable necessity which all should endure alike, or according to the ability of each, nor did he teach that it was to be rendered for compensation. It was, instead, to be regarded as a privilege. He found servitude a badge of dishonor; he made it the badge of distinction. "Whosoever will be chief among you, let him be your servant" (Matt. xx. 27). In the kingdom which Jesus set up, he who ranks all others is not he who knows most, nor he who prays most, nor he who enjoys the greatest ecstasies, nor he who is most served, but he who serves most. This distinction marks the law of service not as incidental, but fundamental in the kingdom of God.

It is important to make a clear distinction between commercial service and Christian service. In every civilized society there are a thousand services, an exchange of which is effected through the common medium of money, which represents them all. A fundamental law of commerce is that of demand and supply. Goods may be offered for sale which cost much time, skill and money, but if they are not wanted they have no commercial value. Another fundamental law of commerce is that of exchange—value for value. Markets may be glutted with the necessaries of life, and men may be perishing for lack of them, but, no matter how great men's need may be, if they have nothing to offer in exchange, business stagnates. These two laws of the commercial world fix attention, not on the motive of the service, but on the service itself and its proposed compensation. Motive and need are of no consequence except as they may affect the quality of the service or the demand for it. The essential thing is the act or the article which is offered for exchange.

Jesus, on the contrary, fixes attention, not on the act, but on the motive of the act. He devotes a large part of the Sermon on the Mount to showing that in the kingdom of God the essence of obedience and disobedience is to be found in the spirit, motive and purpose (Matt. v. 20–48, vi. 1–18).

"He also serves who only stands and waits."

Commercial service aims to supply a demand; Christian service aims to meet a need. The former may be selfish; the latter is unselfish. The usual object of commercial service is gain; the object of Christian service is usefulness, and its natural reward is a larger opportunity to serve and an increased ability for service, together with the satisfaction of having served.

When a man is working simply for his wages or his salary, and he loses the same, his loss is complete. But if he is working to serve and fails to get his wage, his loss, however important it may be, is only incidental after all; his real object has been accomplished and that is his real reward. In like manner, if a man is working for influence or fame, and fails to receive the recognition to which his services entitle him, he suffers defeat and disappointment. But if his object is to serve, he may congratulate himself on his success, though others wear his laurels, and he remains unhonored and unknown. They get the shell, and he the kernel. Their award is external and may be lost any day; while his is internal and eternal.

Of course I do not mean to imply that it is unchristian to receive compensation for service; but I do mean to say that the compensation should not be the predominant motive. Whether one serves for the sake of the kingdom or for the sake of the compensation makes all the difference between the Christian spirit and the commercial spirit. The Christian spirit receives, but in order that it may give; the commercial spirit gives, but in order that it may receive.

The Apostle Peter wrote: "As every man hath received the gift, even so minister the same one to another, as good stewards of the manifold grace of God" (I. Pet. iv. 10). The spirit of service recognizes every good gift that is bestowed on us by God's manifold grace, as coming under the law of stewardship. Our substance, our time, our powers, our opportunities are all entrusted to us for service. Life itself is a sacred trust. It has come to us from out the long past with its unspeakably precious store, garnered from every generation back to the beginning of life. What this treasure has cost in time cannot be reckoned; what it has cost in suffering cannot be conceived. This treasure is all that is contained in the wonderful word heredity. It has not been slowly and painfully gathered throughout the ages that we might squander it on our pleasures. We are its trustees for future generations, and are bound to hand on to them this precious legacy, not only unimpaired but enriched. The future of humanity depends on the way in which each generation fulfills this trust. The whole life of every disciple of Christ is to be spent, like that of his Master, in the service of the kingdom, and in hastening its full coming in the earth. Such service implies self-abnegation; hence the second great law of the kingdom.

THE LAW OF SACRIFICE.

This law is all-comprehending; it includes the entire man. Jesus said: "If any man will come after me, let him deny himself and take up his cross daily and follow me" (Luke ix. 23). It is one thing for a man to *deny* himself, and a very different thing for a man to deny *himself*. No one wins success of any sort without some measure of self-denial. The champion of the prize-ring has denied himself many things; and has sacrificed his intellectual and spiritual growth to his physical development. But this is not Christian self-sacrifice. Nor is the sacrifice of every natural inclination and the crucifixion of every noble desire in order to acquire wealth any more Christian. Again, a man may sacrifice body and soul to gratify his passion for knowledge or art. He is not so mean as the miser, nor so low as the prize-fighter, but his self-denial is no more Christian than theirs. In each case, one part of the man has been denied for the sake of another part. He has not denied *himself*, but only a fraction of himself. It is self-abnegation of which Christ is speaking. It is the death of self-will which he demands. This is made clear by the context. Whoever would be a follower of Christ must accept the cross. "That is one of the great words of the New Testament, but it has been belittled in common usage. We talk about our 'crosses,' meaning thereby anything that crosses our inclination. But the word never means anything so meager as that in the Bible. It never occurs there in the plural. It always means one thing, as the word 'gallows' means one thing, and that is *death*."[2] When under Roman rule a man was sentenced to crucifixion he was compelled to bear his cross to the appointed place of death. To "take one's cross" meant to start for the place of execution. Let him "take up his cross and follow me." Follow him where? To Golgotha, whither he bore his cross, there to be crucified with him. The man who knows nothing of Golgotha knows nothing of Christian discipleship. If he refuses to bear his cross to Calvary, he forsakes the path which Christ trod. If he "saves his life" by avoiding the cross, he loses it; it is only by losing his life that he finds it (Luke ix. 24). If he would live, he must die. It is only as he dies to self that he enters into the kingdom of God by the new birth. Only when self-will is surrendered is sin surrendered, for self-will is the very essence of sin. A man may give up many *sins* without giving up *sin*. The former is reformation; the latter is conversion. Giving up *sins* means new habits; giving up *sin* means a new life.

It is the will which determines character. The will is the essential man; so that the surrender of the will is the sur-

---

2 "The Times and Young Men," p. 80.

render of self, and nothing else is. A man may give his millions without giving himself. But

> "The gift without the giver is bare."

There is nothing so hard for human nature as to preserve its integrity in dealing with God. We attempt to compromise. We offer him a part—a part of our time, a part of our endeavors, a part of our love, a part of our substance, and usually a very small part. If a man gives a tenth, he is considered a shining example of benevolence. But if God has a claim on one-tenth, he has precisely the same claim on the remaining nine-tenths. He did not one-tenth create us and we nine-tenths create ourselves. If he has any claim on us, he has all claim on us.

> "Next to sincerity, remember still,
>   Thou must resolve upon *integrity;*
> God will have *all* thou hast; thy mind, thy will,
>   Thy thoughts, thy words, thy works."[3]

Some people have a "self-denial week" every year. They are only one fifty-second part right. Every week ought to be a "self-denial week." Christ taught that there ought to be three hundred and sixty-five self-denial days every year. "If any man will come after me, let him deny himself and take up his cross *daily* and follow me" (Luke ix. 23). He who follows Christ only one week in the year is not fit for the kingdom of God, for he turns back. The whole man is to be given to the service of the kingdom all the time. Nothing less is honest; nothing less is acceptable to God. He will not have any portion of a divided heart. In fact, when only a part is offered, no part is really given. When only a part is offered, it is offered for a consideration; and that is trading, not giving. If I give in order to get, I am not giving at all, I am investing. That is commercialism, not Christianity. Jesus does not say that he who loses his life with a view to gaining it shall save it. Not "Whosoever shall lose his life for" his own sake, but for "*my* sake, the same shall save it" (Luke ix. 24).

In sacrifice as in service, the essential thing is not the act

---

[3] George Herbert.

but the spirit. The spirit of sacrifice gives all, and longs for more to fill the measure of the world's sore need—gives all of self and all of substance. The consecration of all substance does not mean getting rid of all substance, any more than the consecration of life means the getting rid of life. It means the devotion of both to the service of the kingdom. All claim to ownership is renounced. The use of time and of substance and of powers is now simply a question of administration. Thus the law of Christian sacrifice, like that of Christian service, leads us to Christian stewardship.

It must not be supposed that insistence on the completeness of the sacrifice is in any respect arbitrary. It is in entire harmony with the universe of God. The oneness of the physical universe is perfect. There are no disorderly stars, no treasonable suns nor systems; no atoms rebel against the laws of their nature. There is perfect obedience, perfect order, perfect harmony; and this is the "music of the spheres," which began when the morning stars first sang together and all the sons of God shouted for joy.

But in all this perfect obedience there is no moral beauty. Suns and systems cannot disobey. God, therefore, created wills. There can be no moral beauty without the obedience of wills which are free to disobey. Thus with the possibility of moral harmony came the possibility of moral discord, which is introduced by self-will. If a thousand men live each for himself, they have a thousand different ends in view, a thousand conflicting interests, a thousand different wills, a thousand different centers; and as each life moves toward its own center it moves away from all the others. Thus selfishness is the great disintegrating force in the universe, and the cause of discord. Only when these thousand wills all have the same supreme object (that is, only when self-will has been crucified) can there be perfect organization around one center, and then there is perfect moral harmony.

The oneness of the universe is possible because its parts are interrelated and interdependent. Inorganic matter gives itself to the organic, the mould gives itself to the vegetable, the vegetable to the animal, the animal to man, man to God, and

God is ever giving himself to the objects of his creation. Thus the divine order reveals a vast endless chain of receiving and giving, each link receiving service and sacrifice that it may give service and sacrifice. Of course unconscious matter and unintelligent life can give only unconsciously, as the stars obey. But it is the high prerogative of conscious and intelligent man, like God himself, to offer conscious and intelligent service and sacrifice. When man is thus in glad harmony with the laws of his own nature and of the universe, he receives according to his need that he may give according to his ability; receives food that he may give strength, receives knowledge that he may give it forth as power.

Every man is daily made the world's debtor by a thousand ministrations from his fellows and from the ranks of nature below him. And if one receives, not that he may give, but only that he may enjoy; if he accepts the thousands of vegetable and animal lives sacrificed for him; if he benefits by the toil of his fellow men, which represents time and strength and life itself; if he appropriates all these, and, instead of transforming all into noble service and sacrifice for the common good, consumes them all on his mean little self, he dies a pauper, in debt to the universe. The streams of service and sacrifice, which emptied into his life, were diverted from blessing the world, and perverted to pampering him; and, like rivers lost in the desert, they failed to fertilize his life.

Moreover, by refusing to give, he robbed himself as well as the world, for, under spiritual laws, to keep is to lose, and to give is to acquire. It was those who had surrendered all things to whom Paul said: "All things are yours." There is a divine and miraculous mathematics by which subtraction adds and division multiplies.

Because "it is more blessed to give than to receive," the more precious the gift, the more blessed the giving. And because self is most precious, the giving of self is the highest blessedness of which we are capable. When God demands surrender which is absolute and entire, he is not confiscating a life, "as though he needed anything." He would be something less than benevolent, if he demanded less. He requires us to give that we may know the blessedness of coming into harmony with himself and with the laws of the universe; and he requires us to give all that we may know the highest possible blessedness.

Again, so comprehensive is this law of sacrifice that it includes not only the entire man, but the entire race. It knows no exceptions. God makes no class legislation. "If ANY man will come after me"; that includes rich and poor alike; the terms are all-inclusive. And not only must all sacrifice, but the measure of sacrifice is the same for all. God does not ask of any two the same *gift*, because to no two are his gifts the same; but he does require of every man the same *sacrifice*. To missionary and to millionaire, to prince and to peasant, the word is the same; "Whosoever he be of you that forsaketh not ALL THAT HE HATH, he cannot be my disciple" (Luke xiv. 33).

This law of self-sacrifice, made to embrace all human beings, is the noblest tribute ever paid to human nature. It would seem that among all peoples and in all ages there have been a few capable of the noblest self-sacrifice, willing to accept death for others; and such heroes have been honored as almost divine. Their luster shines down from a height deemed unattainable by ordinary mortals. But Jesus believed that the refuse of the race—the publicans and sinners, the thieves and prostitutes—were capable of this high heroism, capable of utter self-giving for his sake; and in no generation from that day to this has his sublime confidence been disappointed.

Selfish human nature in its most degraded representatives is surely capable of entering the kingdom of unselfishness. But how? Can self overcome self or flee from self?

> "All others are outside myself,
> I lock the door and bar them out,
> The turmoil, tedium, gad-about.

> "I lock my door upon myself,
> And bar them out, but who shall wall
> Self from myself, most loathed of all?

> "If I could set aside myself,
> And start with lightened heart upon
> The road by all men overgone!

> "God harden me against myself,
>   This coward with pathetic voice,
>   Who craves for ease, and rest, and joys.

> "Myself arch-traitor to myself,
>   My hollowest friend, my deadliest foe,
>   My clog, whatever road I go."[4]

There is but one antidote for selfishness; and this brings us to the third great social law of Jesus,

THE LAW OF LOVE.

We have seen that service and sacrifice which are not unselfish are not Christian. In like manner there may be love which is not Christian, because it is not disinterested. There is a natural love, the evolution of which began with the struggle for the life of others, and its flower, as seen in family affection and in patriotism, is the most exquisite and noble product of nature, but there is an element of selfishness in it, which is quite obvious.

Disinterested love is divine; that is the love that God is. When that enters the heart, new life, divine life, eternal life enters it. Like all life, it is not evolved, but transmitted; and like all higher life, it comes from above. Dead matter is no longer believed to possess "all the power and potency of life." When inorganic matter becomes organic, it is because vegetable life has come down to it and lifted it over the chasm between life and death, which, of itself, it was powerless to cross. The process is inscrutable, but the fact is indisputable.

In like manner, the man spiritually dead becomes spiritually alive. The process is equally inscrutable, but the fact is equally indisputable. Not only do the phenomena of spiritual life appear where they had been absent, but there is the additional evidence afforded by the testimony of consciousness. The new life has not been evolved; it began with a new birth, which, as Jesus said, must needs come "from above" (Jno. iii. 3).

We may trace matter from the inorganic form up through the vegetable and animal kingdoms to man; and it is to be

---

[4] Christina Rossetti.

observed that in each instance promotion is conditioned on a certain preparation, before life can come down to it and assimilate it, thus lifting it up to a higher kingdom, and making it subject to higher laws. As the grass must die to itself before it can live in the ox, and the ox must die to himself before he can live in the man, so man must die to himself before he can enter into a higher life, even the life of God.

I think it has been made evident in the preceding discussion that selfishness is the great enemy of the kingdom of God, the chief obstacle to the realization of an ideal world. We have seen that men must come under the laws of disinterested service and of unselfish sacrifice, if they are to enter into the kingdom of God; and to the natural man this seems impossible, and *is* impossible so long as he remains unregenerate. If you ask inorganic matter to bud and blossom and bring forth fruit, you ask an impossibility, so long as it remains inorganic. It cannot obey the laws of the vegetable kingdom until it rises into that kingdom. But after it has begun to live, obedience to the laws of life becomes as wholly natural as it was before wholly impossible.

The selfish man cannot render disinterested service and make unselfish sacrifice; and he very likely scoffs at the idea of any one's doing so. He will have to be born from above before he can "*see* the kingdom of God" (Jno. iii. 3). But after he has died to self and risen into the new life of that kingdom, what was before impossible and inconceivable to him now becomes as natural and as beautiful as the unfolding of a flower.

Men cannot be moved without motives. The heart abhors a vacuum; the only way to empty it is to fill it. If citizens of the kingdom of God do not serve and sacrifice for a selfish consideration, then they must do it for some other: and this other motive is furnished by disinterested love. That is the new and divine life, which lifts them into the new and divine kingdom, and makes them capable of obeying its laws. Thus, Christian love makes possible Christian service and Christian sacrifice. Indeed, they are only Christian love in action, its natural method of expression.

When a service is rendered for love, with a distinct consciousness of that motive, the more difficult or disagreeable or costly the service or sacrifice, the fuller and more perfect is the expression of love, and the greater, therefore, is the satisfaction. Love loves a hard task. It never chaffers; it gives all and longs for more to give. Thus Nathan Hale, when looking into the face of Death, exclaimed: "I regret that I have but one life to give for my country." And I venture to think that such men as Paul and Xavier and Judson and Livingstone would willingly have given up immortality itself, if thereby they could have saved those for whom they gladly gave their lives. They lived lives of glorious sacrifice because they lived lives of glorious love.

Here we catch a glimpse of the true glory of God. We sometimes think of the divine glory as appealing to the senses, as if it were an effulgence which dazzles the eye, or as if it were the glory of knowledge, and of power, and of immensity, transcending comprehension and staggering imagination. But there is a more excellent glory, of which Jesus is the brightness (Heb. i. 3). When certain Greeks desired to see him, he said: "The hour is come, that the Son of man should be glorified." The expectant disciples probably looked for some stupendous manifestation of power. Perhaps their Master would now assume regal authority and manifest kingly glory. The hour for which they had so long waited had at last come. And the eager disciples hear these words: "Verily, verily, I say unto you, Except a corn of wheat fall into the ground and die, it abideth alone; but if it die, it bringeth forth much fruit." He is speaking of being glorified and he is speaking of death. "He that loveth his life, shall lose it; and he that hateth his life in this world, shall keep it unto life eternal." Then as he sees close at hand the great hour for which he came into the world —the hour of his agony—his soul is troubled, and he prays: "Father, glorify thy name. Then came there a voice from heaven, saying, I have both glorified it, and will glorify it again." And with the assurance that the supreme hour of trial should glorify God, he exultantly exclaims: "Now shall the prince of this world be cast out. And I, if I be lifted up from the earth, will draw all men unto me. This he said, signifying what death he should die" (Jno. xii. 23–33). Glory, death! Glory, the cross!

The disciples' conception of his glory was very different. When the ambitious James and John desired to share it, they asked that they might sit one on either side of his throne when he should occupy it (Mark x. 35–38). And Jesus tells them they do not know that when they ask to share his glory they are asking to share his cup of death and to be baptized with his bloody baptism of agony.

At the Last Supper, Jesus said to Judas, "That thou doest, do quickly": and he went immediately out to make the bargain of betrayal. "Therefore, when he was gone out, Jesus said, Now is the Son of man glorified, and God is glorified in him" (Jno. xiii. 27–32).

No prophet ever wrought such mighty works as Jesus, but it is not his miracles of power which fix the attention of a wondering world to-day. He spake as never man spake, but it is not his more than human wisdom which attracts men to-day. It is the Christ "lifted up," who draws men. It is the cross which is the perpetual miracle of wisdom and of power—the wisdom of God to pour light into the black pit of human selfishness, and the power of God to lift men out of it.

The cross was not simply the supreme incident of Christ's life. In that wonderful high-priestly prayer, only a few hours before his crucifixion, he prayed: "And now, O Father, glorify thou me, . . . with the glory which I had with thee before the world was" (Jno. xvii. 5). He was not asking for the glory of the Transfiguration, when his face shone as the sun, and his raiment was white as the light (Matt. xvii. 2). He was asking for the eternal glory which he had before the world was. And this prayer was granted. He was given the glory of the "LAMB, *slain from the foundation of the world.*" That was the glory which he had had with the Father. That is the essential, the eternal glory of God—the glory of self-giving; and self-giving is the uttermost glory of God, because it is the most perfect manifestation of himself, because it is the uttermost expression of love.

During the reign of the Commune in Paris, the Roman

Catholic archbishop was thrown into prison and condemned to death. In this little cell there was a narrow window in the shape of a cross. At the top of it he wrote, in pencil, "Height," at the bottom, "Depth," at the end of one arm, "Length," at the end of the other, "Breadth." It is the cross which measures the height and depth and length and breadth of the love of God, and that is the secret of its glory and of its power.

"Love thy neighbor as thyself" was an old commandment, as old as Deuteronomy. Jesus said to his disciples: "A new commandment I give unto you, That ye love one another, *as I have loved you*" (Jno. xiii. 34). He loved them enough to die for them. The Golden Rule may well be the law of a normal society. But society to-day is abnormal, it is diseased, it is sick with selfishness; and its one sufficient remedy is a sacrificial love.

Can men, common men, exercise such a love? In his prayer Jesus said: "And the glory which thou gavest me I have given them" (Jno. xvii. 22). The glory of self-sacrifice, which was given to Christ, he gives to his disciples, because he inspires them with his love. So that the mean, the ignorant, the bestial and besotted become capable of sacrificial love, because of the identifying power of love that makes them one with Christ (Jno. xvii. 22, 23).

Loving is self-giving; love gives itself to its object; hence mutual love is, as it were, the exchange of two selves, the identification of two lives. In former times, when friendship was narrower and more intense than it is now, men sometimes exchanged names, and ever after each was known by the name of the other, as if their very selves had been exchanged.

There is something like this between Christ and us. He called himself the "Son of man" that we might call ourselves "sons of God." He became human that we might become divine. And when this exchange is perfected, it is the perfection of joy and blessedness, because it is the perfection of love.[5]

---

[5] Bushnell points out the fact that in the New Testament the word which signifies *love* is radically one with the word which signifies *joy*.

In marriage, the wife takes the husband's name, not for convenient identification, but rather to express identity. Their interests have now become the same, and more or less completely she lives his life. In like manner, unless we bear the name of Christ unworthily, we are called "Christians," because (more or less imperfectly, yet in some real sense) we are living his life, have the same supreme purpose, and gladly serve and sacrifice to hasten the coming of the kingdom.

When a man gives himself to God and lets God give himself to him, God's life enters into him, and he begins to enter into God's life, which is a life of service and of sacrificial love; and so far as men become one with God, they become one with each other. Thus love is seen to be the supreme social law, the great organizing, integrating power, precisely as its opposite, selfishness, is the great disorganizing, disintegrating, anti-social power.

And it is as certain that moral order will ultimately triumph over moral chaos in the world as it is certain that divine love is mightier than human selfishness.

3

JOSIAH ROYCE

Dialectician of the Spirit

Josiah Royce (1855–1916) has too often been neatly categorized as a proponent of absolute idealism, a label which does
little justice either to the breadth of his vision or to the concreteness of his major themes. Indeed, the great value of his
philosophy, according to Gabriel Marcel, is that it "marks a
kind of transition between absolute idealism and existentialist
thought."[1] Like Schelling, Royce had the misfortune of being
too rapidly superseded by another school of thought but, also
like Schelling, he offers seminal insights, which a later generation would rediscover.

Royce was born in a California mining town, of English
parents who went there during the Gold Rush of 1849. Successive moves from one such town to another and the patriotic
fervor over statehood and the Civil War combined to sensitize
the boy to the mystery and meaning of communal loyalty. It
may be conjectured that such factors also helped to set his
course on a philosophic quest for absolutes, including an
absolute concept of the state. But just as the biographical
genesis of his outlook differed radically from Hegel's, so did
its philosophical content. Where Hegel was rarefied and ab-
struse, Royce supplied concrete specifics; where Hegel glorified the Prussian monarchy, Royce asserted the values of
American democracy in a dialectical understanding of the individual and the community.

Royce was one of the first graduates of the University of
California at Berkeley, where he received his B.A. in 1875; and

---

[1] Gabriel Marcel, *Royce's Metaphysics* (Chicago: Regnery, 1956), p. xii.

this means, too, that he was among the first religious thinkers in America educated at a university that had no churchly endowment. After further studies, including two years in Germany under Lotze and Windelband, he received his doctorate from Johns Hopkins in 1878. Four years later, through the influence of one of his former teachers, William James, he joined the faculty of Harvard University, where he remained for the rest of his life.

His intellectual activity was prodigious, far exceeding the scope of his writings. His Harvard colleagues and students knew the brilliance of his lectures on Hegel's *Phenomenology of the Spirit,* and scientific specialists were often impressed with his grasp of their subjects. His later writings, reflecting close study of mathematics with Charles S. Peirce, have been said to anticipate Whitehead's and Russell's epochal *Principia Mathematica* in some respects. One of his ten major books is his *Outlines of Psychology* (1908); another, *The Spirit of Modern Philosophy* (1892), remains one of the best surveys by any author and affords a good example of the range of Royce's erudition. But from *The Religious Aspect of Philosophy* (1885) to *The Problem of Christianity* (1913), his predominant theme is philosophical theology. Indeed, his bachelor's thesis, written at the age of twenty, was a study of Aeschylus's *Prometheus Bound* from the perspective of Greek theology. The religious question was the starting point of his life work.

Like Peirce and James, Royce had a Christian upbringing but had no vested interest in its continuance, no compelling sense of obligation to a church. He was not a minister and had no stake in any theological doctrine or tradition. He chose Christianity of his own accord and interpreted it in his own way, irenically and ecumenically and without polemics, serenely disregarding questions of heresy and orthodoxy. The difference between his thinking and that of such church-related contemporaries as Henry C. King is noteworthy in this regard, for the implicit secularity of Royce's situation enabled him to regard Christianity as optional, hence to view it as a serious possibility, to set aside anything in it that was outworn. His primary commitment was to life, not to "making Christianity work" or refurbishing the gospel for modern man. Accordingly, he perhaps succeeded in a profounder achievement than refurbishing, and came closer to performing the task of reconstruction, at a level of greater depth, that the liberals attempted. Somewhat like William Blake, Royce is the "forgotten ancestor" of theological currents, that only began to have their impact in the decades following World War II.[2]

No brief selection can encompass the rich implications of Royce's theology, but "What Is Vital in Christianity" manages to embrace its cardinal points in simple terms. To attempt to reduce his statement still further is not to ignore the ramifications but to suggest why the latter have the force that they do, and invite the reader to embark on a larger exploration. Lessing, in a witty essay, reduced Johannine theology to the simple injunction, "Love one another." In much the same way, one might reduce Royce to the statement that man discovers himself through a community of interpretation and fulfills himself through loyalty to that same community. "Community" itself is a problematical term, which remains to be defined, but provisionally it can be said to be a group of persons joined together in a common cause, sharing a purpose; to the extent that it is valid it is inclusive, ultimately embracing all of mankind in a totality of reconciliation—what Blake called "the Great Humanity Divine." The divine, in terms common to Blake and Royce, is a function of the community itself, of the relationships it embodies. Genuine faith is more than belief; it is fidelity or loyalty between the individual and the community. This is not a simple structural matter. The structure is perfect only as an ideal Absolute; its empirical manifestations are defective and in dialectical flux which contains error and evil. Royce sees Jesus' suffering and sacrificial death as redemptive because they—"the work of Christ"—so affirm loyalty to the community that they overcome and restore the

---

2 See William Robert Miller, ed., *The New Christianity* (New York: Delacorte, 1967), p. 8. A more remote ancestor, Meister Eckhardt, may be seen as a common influence in Blake, Royce, and Paul Tillich. Note the use Royce makes of Eckhardt in his essay in the following pages.

brokenness of the community, which is the sin of disloyalty. This is no once-for-all historic event but an eternal paradigm of a recurrent phase in an ongoing process of life. Loyalty is voluntary devotion, service rendered freely, for "the only way to be practically autonomous is to be freely loyal."[3] A key reason for disloyalty and its evils is conflict between lesser and greater loyalties, the betrayal of the universal community for the sake of a smaller, exclusive group. It is the work of Christ to develop a continuum of loyalties that forms a harmonious unity. Closely allied to this task is the development of knowledge and understanding; and this is a continuous dialectical process of interpretation. This is a subtle but crucial point, which Marcel has summarized succinctly: "Interpretation is essentially social, as opposed to perception, which lives in a deserted world where there is neither man nor God. Interpretation alone makes a spiritual community possible."[4] It is also essential to the individual, who exists and understands himself in process of interpretation. For Royce this process is "triadic" —one's present self interprets his past to the future self which he is becoming. Even in the act of reflection this process goes on; insight is not received but is created in this triadic rhythm of the mind. But this inner life is only a kind of adjunct to the larger creative interaction of the community; the basic triad consists of A interpreting B to C. It is from such interpretation that meaning occurs—not in the sense of an exact concurrence but of an ambience of discourse which transcends and unites those who are engaged in the process.[5] In its full panoply, Royce's theory possesses extraordinary cogency and elasticity, mediating the legacy of the past to a future which remains open to experience and experiment. It is not designed as a special theory to deal with the questions posed by the Bible or the church, but it is equipped to deal with them and to do

---

[3] Royce, *The Philosophy of Loyalty,* p. 95.
[4] Marcel, *op. cit.,* p. 122. See also Royce, *The Problem of Christianity,* vol. II, p. 151.
[5] Meaning, for Royce, signifies intention or purpose ("internal meaning") as well as descriptive or "external" meaning.

so in terms that do not presuppose their special validity. Whatever its weaknesses, Royce's interpretation of Christianity has relevance for the human condition, predicated on certain universalities of human experience that can be empirically examined and rationally understood. And its relevance is not purchased at the cost of discarding or making light of important theological concepts but rather it illuminates them—sin, redemption, the Christian life. Royce's weakness, in common with idealist philosophy in general, is his ostensible strength—his deliberate remoteness from the actualities of application, his lack of pragmatic bite.

WHAT IS VITAL IN CHRISTIANITY?*

I do not venture to meet this company as one qualified to preach, nor yet as an authority in matters which are technically theological. My contribution is intended to present some thoughts that have interested me as a student of philosophy. I hope that one or another of these thoughts may aid others in formulating their own opinions, and in defining their own religious interests, whether these interests and opinions are or are not in agreement with mine.

My treatment of the question, What is vital in Christianity? will involve a study of three different special questions, which I propose to discuss in order, as follows:

1. What sort of faith or of practice is it that can be called vital to any religion? That is, By what criteria, in the case of any religion, can that which is vital be distinguished from that which is not vital?

2. In the light of the criteria established by answering this first question, what are to be distinguished as the vital elements of Christianity?

3. What permanent value, and in particular what value for

---

* Three addresses given at the Phillips Brooks House, Harvard University, March 18 and 25 and April 1, 1909. Published in *Harvard Theological Review*, II, 4 (October 1909), pp. 408–445.

us today, have those ideas and practices and religious attitudes which we should hold to be vital for Christianity?

I

The term vital, as here used, obviously involves a certain metaphor. That is vital for a living organism without which that organism cannot live. So breathing is a vital affair for us all. That is vital for an organic type which is so characteristic of that type that, were such vital features changed, the type in question, if not altogether destroyed, would be changed into what is essentially another type. Thus the contrast between gill-breathing and lung-breathing appears to be vital for the organic types in question. When we treat the social and mental life which is characteristic of a religion as if it were the life of an organism, or of a type or group of organisms, we use the word vital in accordance with the analogies thus indicated.

If, with such a meaning of the word vital, we turn to the religions that exist among men, we find that any religion presents itself to an observer as a more or less connected group, (1) of religious practices, such as prayers, ceremonies, festivals, rituals, and other observances, and (2) of religious ideas, the ideas taking the form of traditions, legends, and beliefs about the gods or about spirits. On the higher levels, the religious ideas are embodied in sacred books, and some of them are emphasized in formal professions of faith. They also come, upon these higher levels, into a certain union with other factors of spiritual life which we are hereafter to discuss.

Our first question is, naturally, What is the more vital about a religion, its religious practices, or its religious ideas, beliefs, and spiritual attitudes?

As soon as we attempt to answer this question, our procedure is somewhat different, according as we dwell upon the simpler and more primitive, or on the other hand upon the higher and more reflective and differentiated forms or aspects of religion.

In primitive religions, and in the religious lives of many of the more simple-minded and less reflective people of almost any faith, however civilized, the religious practices seem in general to be more important, and more vital for the whole structure of the religious life, than are the conscious beliefs which accompany the practices. I say this is true of primitive religions in general. It is also true for many of the simple-minded followers even of very lofty religions. This rule is well known to the students of the history of religion in our day, and can easily be illustrated from some of the most familiar aspects of religious life. But it is a rule which, as I frankly confess, has frequently been ignored or misunderstood by philosophers, as well as by others who have been led to approach religions for the sake of studying the opinions of those who hold them. In various religious ideas people may be very far apart, at the same moment when their religious practices are in close harmony. In the world at large, including both the civilized and the uncivilized, we may say that the followers of a cult are, in general, people who accept as binding the practices of that cult. But the followers of the same cult may accompany the acceptance of the cult with decidedly different interpretations of the reason why these practices are required of them, and of the supernatural world which is supposed to be interested in the practices.

In primitive religions this rule is exemplified by facts which many anthropologists have expressed by saying that, on the whole, in the order of evolution, religious practices normally precede at least the more definite religious beliefs. Men come to believe as they do regarding the nature of some super-natural being largely in consequence of the fact that they have first come to follow some course of conduct not for any con-scious reason at all but merely from some instinctive tendency which by accident has determined this or that special expres-sion. When the men come to observe this custom of theirs, and to consider why they act thus, some special religious belief often arises as a sort of secondary explanation of their practice. And this belief may vary without essentially altering either the practice or the religion. The pigeons in our college-yard cluster about the benevolent student or visitor who feeds them. This clustering is the result of instinct and of their training in seeking food. The pigeons presumably have no conscious ideas or theories about the true nature of the man who feeds them. Of course, they are somehow aware of this presence, and of what he does, but they surely have only the most rudimentary and indefinite germs of ideas about what he is. But if the pigeons were to come to consciousness somewhat after the fashion of primitive men, very probably they would regard this way of getting food as a sort of religious function and would begin to worship the visitor as a kind of god. If they did so, what idea about this god would be to them vital? Would their beliefs show that they first reasoned abstractly from effect to cause, and said, "He must be a being both powerful and benevolent, for otherwise his feeding of us in this way could not be explained"? Of course, if the pigeons developed into theologians or philosophers, they might reason thus. But if they came to self-consciousness as primitive men generally do, they would more probably say at first: "Behold, do we not cluster about him and beg from him and coo to him; and do we not get our food by doing thus? He is, then, a being whom it is essentially worth while to treat in this way. He responds to our cooing and our clustering. Thus we compel him to feed us. Therefore he is a worshipful being. And this is what we mean by a god, namely, some one whom it is practically useful to conciliate and compel by such forms of worship as we practice."

If one passes from this feigned instance to the facts of early religious life, one easily observes illustrations of a similar process, both in children and in the more primitive religions of men. A child may be taught to say his prayers. His early ideas of God as a giver of good things, or as a being to be propitiated, are then likely to be secondary to such behavior. The prayers he often says long before he sees why. His elders, at least when they follow the older traditions of religious instruction, begin by requiring of him the practice of saying prayers; and then they gradually initiate the child into the ruling ideas of what the practice means. But for such a stage of religious consciousness the prayer is more vital than the interpretation. In primitive religions taboo and ritual alike precede, at least in many cases, those explanations of the taboos and of the ritual practices which inquirers get in answer to questions about the present beliefs of the people concerned. As religion grows, practices easily pass over from one religion to another, and through every such transition seem to preserve, or even to increase, their sacredness; but they get in the end, in each new religion into which they enter, a new explanation in terms of opinions, themselves producing, so to speak, the new ideas required to fit them to each change of setting. In this process the practices taken over may come to seem vital to the people concerned, as the Mass does to Catholics. But the custom may have preceded the idea. The Christmas and Easter festivals are well-known and classic examples of this process. Christianity did not initiate them. It assimilated them. But it then explained why it did so by saying that it was celebrating the birth and resurrection of Christ.

It is no part of my task to develop at length a general theory about this frequent primacy of religious practice over the definite formulation of religious belief. The illustrations of the process are, however, numerous. Even on the higher levels of religious development, where the inner life comes to be emphasized, the matter indeed becomes highly complicated, but still, wherever there is an established church, the term "dissenter" often means in popular use a person who will not attend this church, or who will not conform to its practices, much more consciously and decidedly than it means a person whose private ideas about religious topics differ from those of the people with whom he is willing to worship, or whose rules he is willing to obey.

Nevertheless, upon these higher levels a part of the religious requirement very generally comes to be a demand for some sort of orthodoxy. And therefore, upon this level, conformity of practice is indeed no longer enough. However the simple-minded emphasize practice, the religious body itself requires not only the right practice, but also the acceptance of a profession of faith. And on this higher level, and in the opinion of those concerned with the higher aspect of their religion, this acceptance must now be not only a formal act but a sincere one. Here, then, in the life of the higher religions, belief tends to come into a position of primacy which results in a very notable contrast between the higher and the simpler forms and aspects of religious life. When religions take these higher forms, belief is at least officially emphasized as quite equivalent in importance to practice. For those who view matters thus, "He that believeth not shall be damned," an unbeliever is, as such, a foe of the religion in question, and of its gods and of its worshippers. As an infidel he is a miscreant, an enemy not only of the true faith but perhaps of mankind. In consequence, religious persecution and religious wars may come to seem, at least for a time, inevitable means of defending the faith. And those who outgrow, or who never pass through, this stage of warlike propaganda and of persecution may still insist that for them it is faith rather than practice which is the vital element of their religion. To what heights such a view of the religious life may attain, the Pauline epistles bear witness "Through grace are ye saved." And grace comes by faith, or in the form of faith.

II

So far, then, we have two great phases or stages of religious life. On the one stage it is religious practice, as such, that is for the people concerned the more vital thing. Their belief is relatively secondary to their practice, and may considerably vary while the practice remains the unvarying, and, for them, vital feature. On the other and no doubt higher, because more self-conscious, stage it is faith that assumes the conscious primacy. And on this second stage, if you believe not rightly, you have no part in the religion in question. That these two stages or phases of the life of religion are in practice closely intermingled, everybody knows. The primitive and the lofty are, in the religious life of civilized men, very near together. The resulting entanglements furnish endlessly numerous problems for the religious life. For in all the higher faiths those who emphasize the inner life make much of faith as a personal disposition. And this emphasis, contending as it does with the more primitive and simple-minded tendency to lay stress upon the primacy of religious practice, has often led to revolt against existing formalism, against ritual requirements, and so to reforms, to heresies, to sects, or to new world-religions. Christianity itself, viewed as a world-religion, was the outgrowth of an emphasis upon a certain faith, to which its new practices were to be, and were, secondary. On the other hand, the appeal that every religion makes to the masses of mankind is most readily interpreted in terms of practice. Thus the baptism of a whole tribe or nation, at the command of their chief, has been sometimes accounted conversion. A formal profession of a creed in such cases has indeed become an essential part of the requirements of the religion in question. But this profession itself can be regarded, and often is regarded by whole masses of the people concerned, as a ceremony to be performed obediently, and no doubt willingly, rather than as an expression of any highly conscious inner conviction. In consequence, an individual worshipper may come to repeat the creed as a more or less magic charm, to ward off the demons who are known not to like to hear it; or, again, the individual may rise and say the creed simply because the whole congregation at a certain point of the service has to do so.

In particular, since the creeds of the higher faiths relate to what are regarded as mysteries, while the creed must be repeated by all the faithful, the required belief in the creed is often not understood to imply any clear or wise or even intelligent ideas about what the creed really intends to teach. Even in emphasizing belief, then, one may thus interpret it mainly in terms of a willing obedience. The savage converted to the Roman Catholic Church is indeed taught not only to obey, but to profess belief, and as far as possible to get some sort of genuine inner belief. But he is regularly told that for his imperfect stage of insight it is enough if he is fully ready to say, "I believe what the church believes, both as far as I understand what the church believes and also as far as I do not understand what the church believes." And it is in this spirit that he must repeat the creed of the church. But his ideas about God and the world may meanwhile be as crude as his ignorance determines. He is still viewed as a Christian, if he is minded to accept the God of the church of the Christians, even though he still thinks of God as sometimes a visible and "magnified and non-natural" man, a corporeal presence sitting in the heavens, while the scholastic theologian who has converted him thinks of God as wholly incorporeal, as not situated *in loco* at all, as not even existent in time, but only in eternity, and as spiritual substance, whose nature, whose perfection, whose omniscience, and so on, are the topics of most elaborate definition.

Thus, even when faith in a creed becomes an essential part of the requirements of a religion, one often meets, upon a much higher level, that primacy of the practical over the theoretical side of religion which the child's prayers, and the transplanted festivals, and the conceivable religion of the pigeons illustrate. The faithful convert and his scholastic teacher agree much more in religious practices than in conscious religious ideas.

Meanwhile this very situation itself is regarded by all concerned as by no means satisfactory. And those followers of the higher faiths who take the inner life more seriously, are never content with this acceptance of what seems to them merely external formalism. For them faith, whether it is accompanied with a clear understanding or not, means something essentially interior and deep and soul-transforming. Hence they continually insist that no one can satisfy God who does not rightly view God. And thus the conflict between the primacy of the practical and of the right faith constantly tends to assume new forms in the life of all the higher religions. The conflict concerns the question whether right practice or right belief is the more vital element in religion. Well-known formulae, constantly repeated in religious instruction, profess to solve the problem once for all. But it remains a problem whose solution, if any solution at all is reached, has to be worked out afresh in the religious experience of each individual.

III

Some of you, to whom one of the best-known solutions of the problem is indeed familiar enough, will no doubt have listened to this statement of the conflict between the primacy of religious practice and the primacy of religious belief with a growing impatience. What right-minded and really pious person does not know, you will say, that there is only one way to overcome this opposition, and that is by remembering that true religion is never an affair either of mere practice, apart from inner sincerity, or of theoretically orthodox opinions, apart from other inner experiences and interests? Who does not know, you will say, that true religion is an affair of the whole man, not of deeds alone, nor of the intellect alone, but of the entire spiritual attitude,—of emotion and of trust,—of devotion and of motive,—of conduct guided by an inner light, and of conviction due to a personal contact with religious truth? Who does not know that about this all the best Christian teachers, whether Catholic or Protestant, are agreed? Who does not know that the Roman Catholic theologian who converts the savage regards his own personal salvation as due, in case he wins it, not to the theoretical accuracy of his theological formulations, but to the direct working of divine grace, which alone can prepare the soul for that vision of God which can never be attained by mere reasonings, but can be won only through the miraculous gift of insight prepared for the blessed in heaven? Who has not learned that in the opinion of enlightened Christians the divine grace can for this very reason be as truly present in the humble and ignorant soul of the savage convert as in that of his learned and priestly confessor? Who, then, need confound true faith with the power to formulate the mysteries of the faith, except in so far, indeed, as one trustingly accepts whatever one can understand of the teachings of the church? It is indeed, you will insist, grace that saves, and through faith. But the saving faith, you will continue, is, at least in the present life, nothing theoretical. It is itself a gift of God. And it is essentially a spiritual attitude,— at once practical and such as to involve whatever grade of true knowledge is suited to all the present stage of the soul in question. Herein, as some of you will say, the most enlightened and the most pious teachers of various religions, and certainly of very various forms of Christianity, are agreed. What is vital in the highest religion is neither the mere practice as external, nor the mere opinion as an internal formulation. It is the union of the two. It is the reaction of the whole spirit in the presence of an experience of the highest realities of human life and of the universe.

If any of you at this point assert this to be the solution of the problem as to what is vital in religion, if you insist that such spiritual gifts as the Pauline charity, and such emotional experiences as those of conversion, and of the ascent of the soul to God in prayer, and such moral sincerity as is the soul of all good works, are regarded by our best teachers as the really vital elements in religion,—you are insisting upon a solution of our problem which indeed belongs to a third, and no doubt to a very lofty phase of the religious consciousness. And it is just this third phase or level of the religious consciousness that I am to try to study in these conferences. But were such a statement in itself enough to show every one of us precisely what this vital feature of the higher religions is, and just how it can be secured by every man, and just how our modern world, with all its doubts and its problems, is related to the solution just proposed, I should indeed have no task in these lectures but to repeat the well-known formula, to apply it briefly to the case of Christianity, and to leave the rest to your own personal experience.

IV

But as a fact, and as most of you know by personal experience, the well-known proposal of a solution thus stated is to most of us rather the formulation of a new problem than the end of the whole matter. If this higher unity of faith and practice, of grace and right-mindedness, of the right conduct and the clear insight, of the knowledge of what is real and the feeling for the deepest values of life,—if all this is indeed the goal of the highest religions, and if it constitutes what their best teachers regard as vital, how far are many of us at the present day from seeing our way towards adapting any such solution to our own cases! For us, the modern world is full of suggestions of doubt regarding the articles of the traditional creeds. The moral problems of our time, full of new perplexities, confuse us with regard to what ought to be done. Our spiritual life is too complex to be any longer easily unified, or to be unified merely in the ways useful for earlier generations. Our individualism is too highly conscious to be easily won over to a mood of absorption in any one universal ideal. Our sciences are too complicated to make it easy for us to conceive the world either as a unity, or as spiritual. The church is, for most of us, no longer one visible institution with a single authoritative constitution, but a variety of social organizations, each with its own traditions and values. The spirit of Christianity, which even at the outset Paul found so hard to formulate and to reduce to unity, can no longer be formulated by us precisely in his terms. Hence some of us seek for some still simpler, because more primitive, type of Christianity. But when we look behind Paul for the genuinely primitive Christianity, we meet with further problems, one or two of which we are soon to formulate more precisely in this discussion. In brief, however vital for a religion may be its power to unify the whole man, outer and inner, practical and intellectual, ignorant and wise, emotional and critical, the situation of our time is such that this unification is no longer so presented to us by any one body of religious teaching, that we can simply accept it from tradition (since in the modern world we must both act and think as individuals for ourselves), nor that we can easily learn it from our own experience, since in these days our experience is no longer as full of the religiously inspiring elements as was the experience of the times of Jonathan Edwards, or of the Reformation, or of the founders of the great mediaeval religious orders, or of the early Christian church. If this unity of the spiritual life is to be reconquered, we must indeed take account of the old solutions, but we must give to them new forms, and adopt new ways, suited to the ideas and to the whole spirit of the modern world. Hence the proposed solution that I just rehearsed is simply the statement of the common programme of all the highest religions of humanity. But how to interpret this programme in terms which will make it of live and permanent meaning for the modern world,—this is precisely the religious problem of today.

To sum up, then, our answer of the first of my three problems, namely, What form of faith or of practice can be called vital to any religion? I reply: In the case of any one of the more primitive religions it is, in general, the religious practices that are the most vital features of that religion, and these practices, in general, are vital in proportion as they are necessary to the social life of the tribe or nation amongst which they flourish, so that, when these vital practices die out, the nation in question either dwindles, or is conquered, or passes over into some new form of social order. Secondly, in the higher religions, because of the emphasis that they lay upon the inner life, and especially in the world-religions such as Buddhism, Mohammedanism, and Christianity, belief tends to become a more and more vital feature of the religions in question, and the beliefs—such as monotheism, or the acceptance of a prophet, or of a longer or shorter formulated creed—are vital to such a religion in ways and to degrees which the preachers and the missionaries, the religious wars and the sectarian conflicts of these faiths illustrate,—vital in proportion as the men concerned are ready to labor or to die for these beliefs, or to impose them upon other men, or to insist that no one shall be admitted to the religious community who does not accept them.

But thirdly, as soon as religious beliefs are thus emphasized as over against religious practices, the religious practices are not, thereby, in general set aside or even discouraged. On the contrary, they generally grow more numerous, and often more imposing. And consequently, in the minds of the more ignorant, or of the less earnest, of the faithful appears throughout the life of these higher religions a constant tendency to revert to the more primitive type of religion, or else never, in fact, to rise above that type. Hence, even in the religions wherein conformity is understood to imply a sincere orthodoxy, the primacy of ritual or of other practice over against faith and the inner life constantly tends to hold its own. There arises in such religions the well-known conflict of inner and outer, of faith and merely external works. This conflict remains a constant source of transformations, of heresies, and of reforms, in all these higher religions, and is in fact an irrepressible conflict so long as human nature is what it is. For a great mass of the so-called faithful, it is the conformity of practice that thus remains vital. But the teachers of the religion assert that the faith is vital.

And now, fourthly, the higher religions, especially as represented in their highest type of teachings, are deeply concerned in overcoming and in reducing to unity this conflict of formal observance with genuine faith, wherever the conflict arises. The proposed solution which is most familiar, most promising, if it can be won, and most difficult to be won, is the solution which consists in asserting and of showing, if possible, in life, that what is most vital to religion is not practice apart from faith, nor faith apart from practice, but a complete spiritual reaction of the entire man,—a reaction which, if possible, shall unite a right belief in the unseen world of the faith with the inner perfection and blessedness that ought to result from the indwelling of the truth in the soul, and with that power to do good works and to conform to the external religious requirements which is to be expected from one whose soul is at peace and lives in the light. In a word, what this solution supposes to be most vital to the highest religion is the union of faith and works through a completed spirituality.

Meanwhile, as we have also seen, just our age is especially beset with the problem: How can such a solution be any longer an object of reasonable hope, when the faiths have become uncertain, the practices largely antiquated, our life and our duty so problematic, and our environment so uninspiring to our religious interests? So much, then, for the first of our three problems.

V

It is now our task to consider the second of our questions. How does this problem regarding what is vital to a religion appear when we turn to the special case of Christianity?

Our review of the sorts of elements which are found vital upon the various levels of the religious consciousness will have prepared you to look at once for what is most vital about Christianity upon the third and highest of the three levels that

I have enumerated. It is true that in the minds of great masses of the less enlightened and less devoted population of the Christian world certain religious practices have always been regarded as constituting the most vital features of their religion. These practices are especially those which for the people in question imply the obedient acceptance of the sacraments of the church. Of course for such, faith is indeed a condition for the efficacy of the sacraments. But faith expresses itself especially through and in one's relation to these sacraments. Such emphasis upon religious practices is inevitable, so long as human nature is what it is. But Christianity is obviously, upon all of its higher levels, essentially a religion of the inner life; and for all those in any body of Christians who are either more devout or more enlightened the problem of the church has always included, along with other things, the problem of finding and formulating the true faith; and such faith is, to such people, vital to their religion. In consequence of its vast successes in conquering, after a fashion, its own regions of the world, Christianity has had to undertake upon a very large scale, and over a long series of centuries, the task of adapting itself to the needs of peoples who were in very various, and often in very primitive, conditions of culture. Hence, in formulating its faith and practice, it has had full experience of the conflict between those who in a relatively childlike and primitive way regard religious practice as the primal evidence and expression of the possession of the true religion, and those who, on the contrary, insist primarily upon right belief and a rightly guided inner life as a necessary condition for such conduct as can be pleasing to God. Where, as in the case of the Roman Catholic Church, the effort to reconcile these two motives has the longest traditional expression, that is, where the most elaborate official definition of the saving faith has been deliberately joined with the most precise requirements regarding religious practice, the conflict of motives here in question has been only the more notable as a factor in the history of the church,— however completely for an individual believer this very conflict may appear to have been solved. In the Catholic doctrine of the sacraments, in the theory of the conditions

upon which their validity depends, and of their effects upon
the process of salvation, the most primitive of religious tendencies stand side by side with the loftiest spiritual interests in
glaring contrast. On the one hand the doctrine of the sacraments appeals to primitive tendencies, because certain purely
magically influences and incantations are in question. The
repetition of certain formulae and deeds acts as an irresistible
miraculous charm. On the other hand the life of the spirit is
furthered through the administration of these same sacraments
by some of the deepest and most spiritual of influences, and
by some of the most elevated forms of inner life which the
consciousness of man has ever conceived. That there is an
actual conflict of motives involved in this union of primitive
magic with spiritual cultivation, the church in question has
repeatedly found, when the greater schisms relating to the
validity or to the interpretation of her sacraments have rent
the unity of her body, and when, sometimes within her own
fold, the mystics have quarrelled with the formalists, and both
with the modernists, of any period in which the religious life
of the church was at all intense.

Most of you will agree, I suppose, as to the sort of solution
of such conflicts between the higher and lower aspects of
Christianity which is to be sought, in case there is to be any
hope of a solution. You will probably be disposed to say:
What is vital in Christianity, if Christianity is permanently to
retain its vitality at all in our modern world, must be defined
primarily neither in terms of mere religious practice nor yet
in terms of merely intellectual formulation, but in terms of
that unity of will and intellect that may be expressed in the
spiritual disposition of the whole man. You will say, What is
vital in Christianity must be, if anything, the Christian interpretation of human life, and the life lived in the light of this
interpretation. Such a life, you will insist, can never be identified by its formal religious practices, however important, or
even indispensable, some of you may believe this or that religious practice to be. Nor can one reduce what is vital in Christianity merely to a formulated set of opinions, since, as the
well-known word has it, the devils also believe, and tremble,

and, as some of you may be disposed benevolently to add, the philosophers also believe, and lecture. No, you will say, the Christian life includes practices, which may need to be visible and formal; it includes beliefs, which may have to be discussed and formulated; but Christianity is, first of all, an interpretation of life,—an interpretation that is nothing if not practical, and also nothing if not guided from within by a deep spiritual interest and a genuine religious experience.

So far we shall find it easy to agree regarding the principles of our inquiry. Yet, as the foregoing review of the historical conflicts of religion has shown us, we thus merely formulate our problem. We stand at the outset of what we want to do.

What is that interpretation of life which is vital to Christianity? How must a Christian undertake to solve his problem of his own personal salvation? How shall he view the problem of the salvation of mankind? What is that spiritual attitude which is essential to the Christian religion? Thus our second problem now formulates itself.

VI

Amongst the countless efforts to answer these questions there are two which in these discussions we especially need to face. The two answers thus proposed differ decidedly from each other. Each is capable of leading to various further and more special formulations of opinion about the contents of the Christian religion.

The first answer may be stated as follows: What is vital about Christianity is simply the spiritual attitude and the doctrine of Christ, as he himself taught this doctrine and this attitude in the body of his authentic sayings and parables, and as he lived all this out in his own life. All in Christianity that goes beyond this,—all that came to the consciousness of the church after Christ's own teaching had been uttered and finished, either is simply a paraphrase, an explanation, or an application of the original doctrine of Christ, or else is not vital, —is more or less unessential, mythical, or at the very least external. Grasp the spirit of Christ's own teaching, interpret life as he interpreted it, and live out this interpretation of life as completely as you can, imitating him—and then you are in essence a Christian. Fail to comprehend the spirit of Christ, or to live out his interpretation of life, and you in so far fail to possess what is vital about Christianity. This, I say, is the first of the two answers that we must consider. It is an answer well known to most of you, and an emphasis upon this answer characterizes some of the most important religious movements of our own time.

The second answer is as follows: What is vital about Christianity depends upon regarding the mission and the life of Christ as an organic part of a divine plan for the redemption and salvation of man. While the doctrine of Christ, as his sayings record this doctrine, is indeed an essential part of this mission, one cannot rightly understand, above all one cannot apply, the teachings of Christ, one cannot live out the Christian interpretation of life, unless one first learns to view the person of Christ in its true relation to God, and the work of Christ as an entirely unique revelation and expression of God's will. The work of Christ, however, culminated in his death. Hence, as the historic church has always maintained, it is the cross of Christ that is the symbol of whatever is most vital about Christianity. As for the person of Christ as his life revealed it,—what is vital in Christianity depends upon conceiving this personality in essentially superhuman terms. The prologue to the Fourth Gospel deliberately undertakes to state what for the author of that Gospel is vital in Christianity. This prologue does so by means of the familiar doctrine of the eternal Word that was the beginning, that was with God and was God, and that in Christ was made flesh and dwelt amongst men. Abandon this doctrine and you give up what is vital in Christianity. Moreover, the work of Christ was essential to the whole relation of his own teachings to the life of men. Human nature being what it is, the teaching that Christ's sayings record cannot enter into the genuine life of any one who has not first been transformed into a new man by means of an essentially superhuman and divine power of grace. It was the work of Christ to open the way whereby this divine grace became and still becomes efficacious. The needed transformation of human nature, the change of life which according to Christ's sayings is necessary as a condition for entering the kingdom of heaven, this is made possible through the effects of the life and death of Christ. This life and death were events whereby man's redemption was made possible, whereby the atonement for sin was accomplished. In brief, what is vital to Christianity includes an acceptance of the two cardinal doctrines of the incarnation and the atonement. For only in case these doctrines are accepted is it possible to interpret life in the essentially Christian way, and to live out this interpretation.

Here are two distinct and, on the whole, opposed answers to the question, What is vital in Christianity? I hope that you will see that each of these answers is an effort to rise above the levels wherein either religious practice or intellectual belief is over-emphasized. It is useless for the partisan of the Christianity of the prologue to the Fourth Gospel to accuse his modern opponent of a willingness to degrade Christ to the level of a mere teacher of morals, and Christianity to a mere practice of good works. It is equally useless for one who insists upon the sufficiency of the gospel of Christ simply as Christ's recorded sayings teach it, to accuse his opponent of an intention to make true religion wholly dependent upon the acceptance of certain metaphysical opinions regarding the superhuman nature of Christ. No, the opposition between these two views regarding what is vital in Christianity is an opposition that appears on the highest levels of the religious consciousness. It is not that one view says "Christ taught these and these moral doctrines, and the practice of these teachings constitutes all that is vital in Christianity." It is not that the opposing view says: "Christ was the eternal Word made flesh, and a mere belief in this fact and in the doctrine of the atoning death is the vital feature of Christianity." No, both of these two views attempt to be views upon the third level of the religious consciousness,—views about the whole interpretation of the higher life, and of its relation to God and to the salvation of man. So far, neither view, as its leading defenders now hold it, can accuse the other of lapsing into those more primitive views of religion which I have summarized in the earlier part of this paper. And I have dwelt so long upon a preliminary view of the relations between faith and practice in the history of religion, because I wanted to clear the way for a study of our problem on its genuinely highest level, so that we shall henceforth be clear of certain old and uninspiring devices of controversy. Both parties are really trying to express what is vital in the Christian conception of life. Both view Christianity as a faith which gives sense to life, and also as a mode of life which is centred about a faith. The true dispute arises upon the highest levels. The question is simply this: Is the gospel which Christ preached, that is, the teaching recorded in the authentic sayings and parables, intelligible, acceptable, vital, in case you take it by itself? Or, does Christianity lose its vitality in case you cannot give a true sense to those doctrines of the incarnation and the atonement which the traditional Christian world has so long held and so deeply loved? And furthermore, can you, in the light of modern insight, give any longer a reasonable sense to the traditional doctrines of the atonement and the incarnation? In other words: Is Christianity essentially a religion of redemption, in the sense in which tradition defined redemption? Or is Christianity simply that religion of the love of God and the love of man which the sayings and the parables so richly illustrate?

However much, upon its lower levels, Christianity may have used and included the motives of primitive religion, this our present question is not reducible to the terms of the relatively lower conflict between a religion of creed and a religion of practice. The issue now defined concerns the highest interests of religious life.

In favor of the traditional view that the essence of Christianity consists, first, in the doctrine of the superhuman person and the redemptive work of Christ, and, secondly, in the interpretative life that rests upon this doctrine, stands the whole authority, such as it is, of the needs and religious experience of the church of Christian history. The church early found, or at least felt, that it could not live at all without thus interpreting the person and work of Christ.

Against such an account of what is vital in Christianity stands today for many of us the fact that the doctrine in question seems to be, at least in the main, unknown to the historic Christ, in so far as we can learn what he taught, while both the evidence for the traditional doctrine and the interpretation of it have rested during Christian history upon reports which our whole modern view of the universe disposes many of us to regard as legendary, and upon a theology which many of us can no longer accept as literally true. Whether such objections are finally valid, we must later consider. I mention the objections here because they are familiar, and because in our day they lead many to turn from the tangles of tradition with a thankful joy and relief to the hopeful task of trying to study, to apply, and to live the pure Gospel of Christ as he taught it in that body of sayings which, as many insist, need no legends to make them intelligible, and no metaphysics to make them sacred.

Yet, as a student of philosophy, coming in no partisan spirit, I must insist that this reduction of what is vital in Christianity to the so-called pure Gospel of Christ, as he preached it and as it is recorded in the body of the presumably authentic sayings and parables, is profoundly unsatisfactory. The main argument for doubting that this so-called pure Gospel of Christ contains the whole of what is vital in Christianity rests upon the same considerations that led the historical church to try in its own way to interpret, and hence to supplement, this gospel by reports that may have been indeed full of the legendary, by metaphysical ideas that may indeed have been deeply imperfect, but by a deep instinctive sense of genuine religious values which, after all, was indispensable for later humanity,—a sense of religious values which was a true sense. For one thing, Christ can hardly be supposed to have regarded his most authentically reported religious sayings as containing the whole of his message, or as embodying the whole of his mission. For, if he had so viewed the matter, the Messianic tragedy in which his life-work culminated would have been needless and unintelligible. For the rest, the doctrine that he taught is, as it stands, essentially incomplete. It is not a

rounded whole. It looks beyond itself for a completion, which
the master himself unquestionably conceived in terms of the
approaching end of the world, and which the church later
conceived in terms of what has become indeed vital for
Christianity.

As modern men, then, we stand between opposed views.
Each view has to meet hostile arguments. Each can make a
case in favor of its value as a statement of the essence of Christianity. On the one hand the Christ of the historically authentic sayings,—whose gospel is, after all, not to be understood
except as part of a much vaster religious process; on the other
hand the Christ of legend, whom it is impossible for us modern men longer to conceive as the former ages of the church
often conceived him. Can we choose between the two? Which
stands for what is vital in Christianity? And, if we succeed in
defining this vital element, what can it mean to us today, and
in the light of our modern world?

Thus we have defined our problems. Our next task is to face
them as openly, as truthfully, and as carefully as our opportunity permits.

VII

Let us, then, briefly consider the first of the two views which
have been set over against one another.

The teachings of Christ which are preserved to us do indeed
form a body of doctrine that one can survey and study without forming any final opinion about the historical character of
the narratives with which these teachings are accompanied in
the three Synoptic Gospels. The early church preserved the
sayings, recorded them, no doubt, in various forms, but learned
to regard one or two of the bodies of recorded sayings as especially important and authentic. The documents in which
these earliest records were contained are lost to us; but our
gospels, especially those of Matthew, Mark, and Luke, preserve the earlier tradition in a way that can be tested by the
agreements in the reported sayings as they appear in the different gospels. It is of course true that some of the authentic
teachings of Christ concern matters in regard to which other

teachers of his own people had already reached insights that tended towards his own. But nobody can doubt that the sayings, taken as a whole, embody a new and profoundly individual teaching, and are what they pretend to be; namely, at least a partial presentation of an interpretation of life,—an interpretation that was deliberately intended by the teacher to revolutionize the hearts and lives of those to whom the sayings were addressed. Since a recorded doctrine simply taken in itself, and apart from any narrative, is an unquestionable fact, and since a new and individual doctrine is a fact that can be explained only as the work of a person, it is plain that, whatever you think of the narrative portions of the gospels, your estimate of Christ's reported teachings may be freed at once from any of the perplexities that perhaps beset you as to how much you can find out about his life. So much at least he was; namely, the teacher of this doctrine. As to his life, it is indeed important to know that he taught the doctrine as one who fully meant it, that while he taught it he so lived it out as to win the entire confidence of those who were nearest to him, that he was ready to die for it, and for whatever else he believed to be the cause that he served, and that when the time came he did die for his cause. So much of the gospel narrative is with all reasonable certainty to be regarded as historical.

So far, then, one has to regard the teaching of Christ as a perfectly definite object for historical study and personal imitation, and as, in its main outlines, an accessible tradition. It is impossible to be sure of our tradition as regards each individual saying. But the main body of the doctrine stands before us as a connected whole, and it is in its wholeness that we are interested in comprehending its meaning.

Now there is also doubt, I have said, that this doctrine is intended as at least a part of an interpretation of life. For the explicit purpose of the teacher is to transform the inner life of his hearers, and thus to bring about, through this transformation, a reform of their individual outer life. It is, furthermore, sure that, while the teaching in question includes a moral ideal, it is no merely moral teaching, but is full of a profoundly religious interest. For the transformation of the inner life which is in question has to do with the whole relation of the individual man to God. And there are especially two main theses of the teacher which do indeed explicitly relate to the realm of the superhuman and divine world, and which therefore do concern what we may call religious metaphysics. That is, these theses are assertions about a reality that does not belong to the physical realm, and that is not confined to the realities which we contemplate when we consider merely ethical truth as such. The first of these religious theses relates to the nature of God. It is usually summarized as the doctrine of the Fatherhood of God. In its fuller statement it involves that account of the divine love for the individual man which is so characteristic and repeated a feature of the authentic sayings. The other thesis is what we now call a judgement of value. It is the assertion of the infinite worth of each individual person,—an assertion richly illustrated in the parables, and used as the basis of the ethical teaching of Christ, since the value that God sets upon your brother is the deepest reason assigned to show why your own life should be one of love towards your brother.

VIII

So much for the barest suggestion of a teaching which you all know, and which I have not here further to expound. Our present question is simply this: Is this the whole of what is vital to Christianity? Or is there something vital which is not contained in these recorded sayings, so far as they relate to the matters just summarily mentioned?

The answer to this question is suggested by certain very well-known facts. First, these sayings are, in the master's mind, only part of a programme which, as the event showed, related not only to the individual soul and its salvation, but to the reform of the whole existing and visible social order. Or, expressed in our modern terms, the teacher contemplated a social revolution, as well as the before-mentioned universal religious reformation of each individual life. He was led, at least towards the end of his career, to interpret his mission as that of the Messiah of his people. That the coming social revolution was conceived by him in divine and miraculous terms, that it was to be completed by the final judgment of all men, that the coming kingdom was to be not of this world, in the sense in which the Roman Empire was of this world, but was to rest upon the directly visible triumph of God's will through the miraculous appearance of the chosen messenger who should execute this will,—all this regarding the conception which was in Christ's mind seems clear. But however the coming revolution was conceived, it was to be a violent and supernatural revolution of the external social order, and it was to appear openly to all men upon earth. The meek, the poor, were to inherit the earth; the mighty were to be cast down; the kingdoms of this world were to pass away; and the divine sovereignty was to take its visible place as the controller of all things.

Now it is no part of my present task to endeavor to state any theory as to why the master viewed his kingdom of heaven, in part at least, in this way. You may interpret the doctrine as the church has for ages done, as a doctrine relating to the far-off future end of all human affairs and to the supernatural mission of Christ as both Saviour and Judge of the world; or you may view the revolutionary purposes of the master as I myself actually do, simply as his personal interpretation of the Messianic traditions of his people and of the social needs of his time and of the then common but mistaken expectation of the near end of the world. In any case, if this doctrine, however brought about or interpreted, was for the master a vital part of his teaching, then you have to view the resulting interpretation of life accordingly. I need not say, however, that whoever today can still find a place for the Messianic hopes and for the doctrine of the last judgment in his own interpretation of Christianity, has once for all made up his mind to regard a doctrine, —and a deeply problematic doctrine,—a profoundly metaphysical doctrine about the person and work of Christ, and about the divine plan for the salvation of man,—as a vital part of his own Christianity.

And now, in this same connection, we can point out that, if the whole doctrine of Christ had indeed consisted for him in regarding the coming of the kingdom of heaven as identical with the inner transformation of each man by the spirit of divine love, then that direct and open opposition to the existing social authorities of his people which led to the Messianic tragedy, would have been for the master simply needless. Christ chose this plan of open and social opposition for reasons of his own. We may interpret these reasons as the historical church has done, or we may view the matter otherwise, as I myself do. In any case, Christ's view of what was vital in Christianity certainly included, but also just as certainly went beyond, the mere preaching of the kingdom of heaven that is within you.

But one may still say, as many say who want to return to a purely primitive Christianity: Can *we* not choose to regard the religious doctrine of the parables and of the sayings, apart from the Messianic hopes and the anticipated social revolution, as for us vital and sufficient? Can we not decline to attempt to solve the Messianic mystery? Is it not for us enough to know simply that the master did indeed die for his faith, leaving his doctrine concerning the spiritual kingdom, concerning God the Father, and concerning man the beloved brother, as his final legacy to future generations? This legacy was of permanent value. Is it not enough for us?

I reply: To think thus is obviously to view Christ's doctrine as he himself did not view it. He certainly meant the kingdom of heaven to include the inner transformation of each soul by the divine love. But he also certainly conceived even this spiritual transformation in terms of some sort of Messianic mission, which was related to a miraculous coming transformation of human society. In the service of this Messianic social cause he died. And now even in Christ's interpretation of the inner and spiritual life of the individual man there are aspects which you cannot understand unless you view them in the light of the Messianic expectation. I refer to the master's doctrine upon that side of it which emphasizes the passive non-resistance of the individual man, in waiting for God's judgment. This side of Christ's doctrine has been frequently interpreted as requiring an extreme form of self-abnegation. It is this aspect of the doctrine which glorifies poverty as in itself an important aid to piety. In this sense too the master sometimes counsels a certain indifference to ordinary human social relations. In this same spirit his sayings so frequently illustrate the spirit of love by the mention of acts that involve the merely immediate relief of suffering, rather than by dwelling upon those more difficult and often more laborious forms of love which his own life indeed exemplified, and which take the form of the lifelong service of a super-personal social cause.

I would not for a moment wish to over-emphasize the meaning of these negative and ascetic aspects of the sayings. Christ's ethical doctrine was unquestionably as much a positive individualism as it was a doctrine of love. It was also as genuinely a stern doctrine as it was a humane one. Nobody understands it who reduces it to mere self-abnegation, or to non-resistance, or to any form of merely sentimental amiability. Nevertheless,—it was taught, it included sayings and illustrations which have often been interpreted in the sense of pure asceticism, in the sense of simple non-resistance, in the sense of an unworldliness that seems opposed to the establishment and the prizing of definite human ties,—yes, even in the sense of an anarchical contempt for the forms of any present worldly social order. In brief, the doctrine contains a deep and paradoxical opposition between its central assertion of the infinite value of love and of every individual human soul on the one hand, and those of its special teachings on the other hand, which seem to express a negative attitude towards all our natural efforts to assert and to sustain the values of life by means of definite social cooperation, such as we can by ourselves devise. Now the solution of this paradox seems plain when we remember the abnormal social conditions of those whom Christ was teaching, and interpret his message in the light of his Messianic social mission with its coming miraculous change of all human relations. But in that case an important part of the sayings must be viewed as possessing a meaning which is simply relative to the place, to the people, to the time, and to those Messianic hopes of an early end of the existing social order,—hopes which we know to have been mistakenly cherished by the early church.

I conclude then, so far, that a simple return to a purely primitive Christianity as a body of doctrine complete in itself, directly and fully expressed in the sayings of Christ, and applicable, without notable supplement, to all times, and to our own day,—is an incomplete and therefore inadequate religious ideal. The spiritual kingdom of heaven, the transformation of the inner life which the sayings teach, is indeed a genuine part,—yes, a vital part,—of Christianity. But it is by no means the whole of what is vital to Christianity.

I turn to the second of the answers to our main question. According to this answer, Christianity is a redemptive religion. What is most vital to Christianity is contained in whatever is essential and permanent about the doctrines of the incarnation and the atonement. Now this is the answer which, as you will by this time see, I myself regard as capable of an interpretation that will turn it into a correct answer to our question. In answering thus, I do not for a moment call in question the just-mentioned fact that the original teaching of the master regarding the kingdom of heaven is indeed a vital part of the whole of Christianity. But I do assert that this so-called purely primitive Christianity is not so vital, is not so central, is not so essential to mature Christianity as are the doctrines of the incarnation and the atonement when these are rightly interpreted. In the light of these doctrines alone can the work of the master be seen in its most genuine significance.

Yet, as has been already pointed out, the literal acceptance of this answer to our question, as many still interpret the answer, seems to be beset by serious difficulties. These difficulties are now easily summarized. The historical Christ of the sayings and the parables, little as we certainly know regarding his life, is still a definite and, in the main, an accessible object of study and of interpretation, just because, whatever else he was, he was the teacher of this recorded interpretation of life,—whether or not you regard that recorded interpretation as a fully complete and rounded whole. But the Christ

whom the traditional doctrines of the atonement and of the
incarnation present to us appears in the minds of most of us
as the Christ of the legends of the early church,—a being
whose nature and whose reported supernatural mission seem
to be involved in doubtful mysteries—mysteries both theological and historical. Now I am not here to tell you in detail
why the modern mind has come to be unwilling to accept, as
literal reports of historical facts, certain well-known legends.
I am not here to discuss that unwillingness upon its merits. It
is enough for my present purpose to say first that the unwillingness exists, and, secondly, that, as a fact, I myself believe it to be a perfectly reasonable unwillingness. But I say
this not at all because I suppose that modern insight has
driven out of the reasonable world the reality of spiritual truth.
The world of history is indeed a world full of the doubtful.
And the whole world of phenomena in which you and I daily
move about is a realm of mysteries. Nature and man, as we
daily know them, and also daily misunderstand them, are not
what they seem to us to be. The world of our usual human
experience is but a beggarly fragment of the truth, and, if we
take too seriously the bits of wisdom that it enables us to
collect by the observation of special facts and of natural laws,
it becomes a sort of curtain to hide from us the genuine realm
of spiritual realities in the midst of which we all the while
live. Moreover, it is one office of all higher religion to supplement these our fragments of experience and ordinary notions
of the natural order, by a truer, if still imperfect, interpretation of the spiritual realities that are beyond our present vision.
That is, it is the business of religion to lift, however little, the
curtain, to inspire us, not by mere dreams of ideal life, but by
enlightening glimpses of the genuine truth which, if we were
perfect, we should indeed see, not, as now, through a glass
darkly, but face to face.

All this I hold to be true. And yet I fully share the modern
unwillingness to accept legends as literally true. For it is not
by first repeating the tale of mere marvels, of miracles,—by
dwelling upon legends, and then by taking the accounts in
question as literally true historical reports,—it is not thus

that we at present, in our modern life, can best help ourselves
to find our way to the higher world. These miraculous reports
are best understood when we indeed first dwell upon them
lovingly and meditatively, but thereupon learn to view them
as symbols, as the products of the deep and endlessly instructive religious imagination,—and thereby learn to interpret the
actually definite, and to my mind unquestionably superhuman
and eternal, truth that these legends express, but express by
figures,—in the form of a parable, an image, a narrative, a tale
of some special happening. The tale is not literally true. But
its deeper meaning may be absolutely true. In brief, I accept
the opinion that it is the office of religion to interpret truths
which are in themselves perfectly definite, eternal, and literal,
but to interpret them to us by means of a symbolism which is
the product of the constructive imagination of the great ages
in which the religions which first voiced these truths grew up.
There are some truths which our complicated natures best
reach first through instinct and intuition, through parable and
legend. Only when we have first reached them in this way,
can most of us learn to introduce the practical and indeed
saving application of these truths into our lives by living out
the spirit of these parables. But then at last we may also hope,
in the fulness of our own time, to comprehend these truths
by a clearer insight into the nature of that eternal world which
is indeed about and above us all, and which is the true source
of our common life and light.

I am of course saying all this not as one having authority.
I am simply indicating how students of philosophy who are of
the type that I follow, are accustomed to view these things. In
this spirit I will now ask you to look for a moment at the doctrines of the Incarnation and of the Atonement in some of
their deeper aspects. It is a gain thus to view the doctrines,
whether or no you accept literally the well-known miraculous
tale.

There has always existed in the Christian church a tradition
tending to emphasize the conception that the supernatural
work of Christ, which the church conceived in the form of the
doctrines of the incarnation and the atonement, was not a work

accomplished once for all at a certain historical point of time, but remains somehow an abiding work, or, perhaps, that it ought to be viewed as a timeless fact, which never merely happened, but which is such as to determine anew in every age the relation of the faithful to God. Of course, the church has often condemned as heretical one or another form of these opinions. Nevertheless, such opinions have in fact entered into the formation of the official dogmas. An instance is the influence that such an interpretation had upon the historic doctrine of the Mass and of the real presence,—a doctrine which, as I have suggested, combines in one some of the most primitive of religious motives with some of the deepest religious ideas that men have ever possessed. In other less official forms, which frequently approached, or crossed, the boundaries of technical heresy, some of the mediaeval mystics, fully believing in their own view of their faith, and innocent of any modern doubts about miracles, were accustomed in their tracts and sermons always and directly to interpret every part of the gospel narrative, including the miracles, as the expression of a vast and timeless whole of spiritual facts, whereof the narratives are merely symbols. In the sermons of Meister Eckhart, the great early German mystic, this way of preaching Christian doctrine is a regular part of his appeal to the people. I am myself in my philosophy no mystic, but I often wish that in our own days there were more who preached what is indeed vital in Christianity in somewhat the fashion of Eckhart. Let me venture upon one or two examples.

Eckhart begins as follows a sermon on the text, "Who is he that is born king of the Jews" (Matthew 2 2): "Mark you," he says, "mark you concerning this birth, where it take place. I say, as I have often said: This eternal birth takes place in the soul, and takes place there precisely as it takes place in the eternal world,—no more, no less. This birth happens in the essence, in the very foundation, of the soul." "All other creatures," he continues, "are God's footstool. But the soul is his image. This image must be adorned and fulfilled through this birth of God in the soul." The birth, the incarnation, of God occurs then, so Eckhart continues, in every soul, and eternally.

But, as he hereupon asks: Is not this then also true of sinners, if this incarnation of God is thus everlasting and universal? Wherein lies then the difference between saint and sinner? What special advantage has the Christian from this doctrine of the incarnation? Eckhart instantly answers: Sin is simply due to the blindness of the soul to the eternal presence of the incarnate God. And that is what is meant by the passage: "The light shineth in the darkness, and the darkness comprehendeth it not."

Or again, Eckhart expounds in a sermon the statement that Christ came "in the fulness of time"; that is, as people usually and literally interpret the matter, Christ came when the human race was historically prepared for his coming. But Eckhart is careless concerning this historical and literal interpretation of the passage in question, although he doubtless also believes it. For him the true meaning of the passage is wholly spiritual. When, he asks in substance, is the day fulfilled? At the end of the day. When is a task fulfilled? When the task is over. When, therefore, is the fulness of time reached? Whenever a man is in his soul ready to be done with time; that is, when in contemplation he dwells only upon and in the eternal. Then alone, when the soul forgets time, and dwells upon God who is above time, then, and then only, does Christ really come. For Christ's coming means simply our becoming aware of what Eckhart calls the eternal birth; that is, the eternal relation of the real soul to the real God.

It is hard, in our times, to get any sort of hearing for such really deeper interpretations of what is indeed vital in Christianity. A charming, but essentially trivial, religious psychology today invites some of us to view religious experience simply as a chance play-at-hide-and-seek with certain so-called subliminal mental forces and processes, whose crudely capricious crises and catastrophes shall have expressed themselves in that feverish agitation that some take to be the essence of all. Meanwhile there are those who today try to keep religion alive mainly as a more or less medicinal influence, a sort of disinfectant or anodyne, that may perhaps still prove its value to a doubting world by curing dyspepsia, or by removing nervous worries. Over against such modern tendencies,—humane, but still, as interpretations of the true essence of religion, essentially trivial,—there are those who see no hope except in holding fast by a literal acceptance of tradition. There are, finally, those who undertake the task, lofty indeed, but still, as I think, hopeless,—the task of restoring what they call a purely primitive Christianity. Now I am no disciple of Eckhart; but I am sure that whatever is vital in Christianity concerns in fact the relation of the real individual human person to the real God. To the minds of the people whose religious tradition we have inherited this relation first came through the symbolic interpretation that the early church gave to the life of the master. It is this symbolic interpretation which is the historical legacy of the church. It is the genuine and eternal truth that lies behind this symbol which constitutes what is indeed vital to Christianity. I personally regard the supernatural narratives in which the church embodied its faith simply as symbols, the product indeed of no man's effort to deceive, but of the religious imagination of the great constructive age of the early church. I also hold that the truth which lies behind these symbols is capable of a perfectly rational statement, that this statement lies in the direction which Eckhart, mistaken as he often was, has indicated to us. The truth in question is independent of the legends. It relates to eternal spiritual facts. I maintain also that those who, in various ages of the church, and in various ways, have tried to define and to insist upon what they have called the "Essential Christ," as distinguished from the historical Christ, have been nearing in various degrees the comprehension of what is vital in Christianity.

X

What is true must be capable of expression apart from legends. What is eternally true may indeed come to our human knowledge through any event that happens to bring the truth in question to our notice; but, once learned, this truth may be seen to be independent of the historical events, whatever they were, which brought about our own insight. And the truth about the incarnation and the atonement seems to me to be statable in terms which I must next briefly indicate.

First, God, as our philosophy ought to conceive him, is indeed a spirit and a person; but he is not a being who exists in separation from the world, simply as its external creator. He expresses himself in the world; and the world is simply his own life, as he consciously lives it out. To use an inadequate figure, God expresses himself in the world as an artist expresses himself in the poems and the characters, in the music or in the other artistic creations, that arise within the artist's consciousness and that for him and in him consciously embody his will. Or again, God is this entire world, viewed, so to speak, from above and in its wholeness as an infinitely complex life which in an endless series of temporal processes embodies a single divine idea. You can indeed distinguish, and should distinguish, between the world as our common sense, properly but fragmentarily, has to view it and as our sciences study it,—between this phenomenal world, I say, and God, who is infinitely more than any finite system of natural facts or of human lives can express. But this distinction between God and world means no separation. Our world is the fragmentary phenomenon that we see. God is the conscious meaning that expresses itself in and through the totality of all phenomena. The world taken as a mass of happenings in time, of events, of natural processes, of single lives, is nowhere, and at no time, any complete expression of the divine will. But the entire world, of which our known world is a fragment,—the totality of what is, past, present, and future, the totality of what is physical and of what is mental, of what is temporal and of what is enduring,—this entire world is present at once to the eternal divine consciousness as a single whole, and this whole is what the absolute chooses as his own expression, and is what he is conscious of choosing as his own life. In this entire world God sees himself lived out. This world, when taken in its wholeness, is at once the object of the divine knowledge and the deed wherein is embodied the divine will. Like the Logos of the Fourth Gospel, this entire world is not only with God, but is God.

As you see, I state this doctrine, for the moment, quite summarily and dogmatically. Only an extensive and elaborate philosophical discussion could show you why I hold this doctrine to be true. Most of you, however, have heard of some such doctrine as the theory of the Divine Immanence. Some of you are aware that such an interpretation of the nature of God constitutes what is called philosophical Idealism. I am not here defending, nor even expounding, this doctrine. I believe, however, that this is the view of the divine nature which the church has always more or less intuitively felt to be true, and has tried to express, despite the fact that my own formulation of this doctrine includes some features which in the course of the past history of dogma have been upon occasion formally condemned as heresy by various church-authorities. But for my part I had rather be a heretic, and appreciate the vital meaning of what the church has always tried to teach, than accept this or that traditional formulation, but be unable to grasp its religiously significant spirit.

Dogmatically, then, I state what, indeed, if there were time, I ought to expound and to defend on purely rational grounds. God and his world are one. And this unity is not a dead natural fact. It is the unity of a conscious life, in which, in the course of infinite time, a divine plan, an endlessly complex and yet perfectly definite spiritual idea, gets expressed in the lives of countless finite beings and yet with the unity of a single universal life.

Whoever hears this doctrine stated, asks, however, at once a question,—the deepest, and also the most tragic question of our present poor human existence: Why, then, if the world is the divine life embodied, is there so much evil in it,—so much darkness, ignorance, misery, disappointment, warfare, hatred, disease, death?—in brief, why is the world as we know it full of the unreasonable? Are all these gloomy facts but illusions, bad dreams of our finite existence,—facts unknown to the very God who is, and who knows, all truth? No,—that cannot be the answer; for then the question would recur: Why are these our endlessly tragic illusions permitted? Why are we allowed by the world-plan to be so unreasonable as to dream these bad dreams which fill our finite life, and which in a way constitute this finite life? And that question would then be precisely equivalent to the former question, and just as hard to solve. In brief, the problem of evil is the great problem that stands between our ordinary finite view and experience of life on the one hand and our consciousness of the reasonableness and the unity of the divine life on the other hand.

Has this problem of evil any solution? I believe that it has a solution, and that this solution has long since been in substance grasped and figured forth in symbolic forms by the higher religious consciousness of our race. This solution, not abstractly stated, but intuitively grasped, has also expressed itself in the lives of the wisest and best of the moral heroes of all races and nations of men. The value of suffering, the good that is at the heart of evil, lies in the spiritual triumphs that the endurance and the overcoming of evil can bring to those who learn the hard, the deep but glorious, lesson of life. And of all the spiritual triumphs that the presence of evil makes possible, the noblest, is that which is won when a man is ready, not merely to bear the ills of fortune tranquilly if they come, as the Stoic moralists required their followers to do, but when one is willing to suffer vicariously, freely, devotedly, ills that he might have avoided, but that the cause to which he is loyal, and the errors and sins that he himself did not commit, call upon him to suffer in order that the world may be brought nearer to its destined union with the divine. In brief, as the mystics themselves often have said, sorrow,—wisely encountered and freely borne,—is one of the most precious privileges of the spiritual life. There is a certain lofty peace in triumphing over sorrow, which brings us to a consciousness of whatever is divine in life, in a way that mere joy, untroubled and unwon, can never make known to us. Perfect through suffering,—that is the universal, the absolutely necessary law of the higher spiritual life. It is a law that holds for God and for man, for those amongst men who have already become enlightened through learning the true lessons of their own sorrows, and for those who full of hope still look forward to a life from which they in the main anticipate joy and wordly success, and who have yet to learn that the highest good of life is to come to them through whatever willing endurance of hardness they, as good soldiers of their chosen loyal service, shall learn to choose or to endure as their offering to their sacred cause. This doctrine that I now state to you is indeed no ascetic doctrine. It does not for a moment imply that joy is a sin, or an evil symptom. What it does assert is that as long as the joys and successes which you seek are expected and sought by you simply as good fortune, which you try to win through mere cleverness—through mere technical skill in the arts of controlling fortune,—so long, I say, as this is your view of life, you know neither God's purpose nor the truth about man's destiny. Our always poor and defective skill in controlling fortune is indeed a valuable part of our reasonableness, since it is the natural basis upon which a higher spiritual life may be built. Hence the word, "Young men, be strong," and the common-sense injunction, "Be skilful, be practical," are good counsel. And so health, and physical prowess, and inner cheerfulness, are indeed wisely viewed as natural foundations for a higher life. But the higher life itself begins only when your health and your strength and your skill and your good cheer appear to you merely as talents, few or many, which you propose to devote, to surrender, to the divine order, to whatever ideal cause most inspires your loyalty, and gives sense and divine dignity to your life,—talents, I say, that you intend to return to your master with usury. And the work of the higher life consists, not in winning good fortune, but in transmuting all the transient values of fortune into eternal values. This you best do when you learn by experience how your worst fortune may be glorified through wise resolve, and through the grace that comes from your conscious union with the divine, into something far better than any good fortune could give to you; namely, into a knowledge of how God himself endures evil, and triumphs over it, and lifts it out of itself, and wins it over to the service of good.

The true and highest values of the spiritual world consist, I say, in the triumph over suffering, over sorrow, and over unreasonableness, and the triumph over these things may appear

in our human lives in three forms: First, as mere personal fortitude,—as the stoical virtues in their simplest expression. The
stoical virtues are the most elementary stage of the higher
spiritual life. Fortitude is indeed required of every conscious
agent who has control over himself at all. And fortitude, even
in this simplest form as manly and strenuous endurance,
teaches you eternal values that you can never learn unless you
first meet with positive ills of fortune, and then force yourself
to bear them in the loyal service of your cause. Willing endurance of suffering and grief is the price that you have to pay
for conscious fidelity to any cause that is vast enough to be
worthy of the loyalty of a lifetime. And thus no moral agent
can be made perfect except through suffering borne in the
service of his cause. Secondly, the triumph over suffering appears in the higher form of that conscious union with the
divine plan which occurs when you learn that love, and loyalty, and the idealizing of life, and the most precious and
sacred of all human relationships, are raised to their highest
levels, are glorified, only when we not merely learn in our own
personal case to suffer, to sorrow, to endure, and be spiritually
strong, but when we learn to do these things together with
our own brethren. For the comradeship of those who willingly
not merely practise fortitude as a private virtue but as brethren in sorrow is a deeper, a sweeter, a more blessed comradeship than ever is that of the lovers who have not yet been
tried so as by fire. Then the deepest trials of life come to you
and your friend together, and when, after the poor human
heart has indeed endured what for the time it is able to bear of
anguish, it finds its little moment of rest, and when you are
able once more to clasp the dear hand that would help if
it could, and to look afresh into your friend's eyes and to see
there the light of love as you could never see it before,—
then, even in the darkness of this world, you catch some faint
far-off glimpse of how the spirit may yet triumph despite all,
and of why sorrow may reveal to us, as we sorrow and endure
together, what we should never have known of life, and of
love, and of each other, and of the high places of the spirit,
if this cup had been permitted to pass from us. But thirdly, and

best, the triumph of the spirit over suffering is revealed to us not merely when we endure, when we learn through sorrow to prize our brethren more, and when we learn to see new powers in them and even in our poor selves, powers such as only sorrow could bring to light,—but when we also turn back from such experiences to real life again, remembering that sorrow's greatest lesson is the duty of offering ourselves more than ever to the practical service of some divine cause in this world. When one is stung to the heart and seemingly wholly overcome by the wounds of fortune, it sometimes chances that he learns after a while to arise from his agony, with the word: "Well then, if, whether by my own fault or without it, I must descend into hell, I will remember that in this place of sorrow there are the other souls in torment, seeking light; I will help them to awake and arise. As I enter I will open the gates of hell that they may go forth." Whatever happens to me, I say, this is a possible result of sorrow. I have known those men and women who could learn such a lesson from sorrow and who could practise it. These are the ones who, coming up through great tribulation, show us the highest glimpse that we have in this life of the triumph of the spirit over sorrow. But these are the ones who are willing to suffer vicariously, to give their lives as a ransom for many. These tell us what atonement means.

Well, these are, after all, but glimpses of truth. But they show us why the same law holds for all the highest spiritual life. They show us that God too must sorrow in order that he may triumph.

Now the true doctrine of the Incarnation and of the Atonement is, in its essence, simply the conception of God's nature which this solution of the problem of evil requires. First, God expresses himself in this world of finitude, incarnates himself in this realm of human imperfection, but does so in order that through finitude and imperfection, and sorrow and temporal loss, he may win in the eternal world (that is, precisely, in the conscious unity of his whole life) his spiritual triumph over evil. In this triumph consists his highest good, and ours. It is God's true and eternal triumph that speaks to us through the well-known word: "In this world ye shall have tribulation. But fear not; I have overcome the world." Mark, I do not say that we, just as we naturally are, are already the true and complete incarnation of God. No, it is in overcoming evil, in rising above our natural unreasonableness, in looking towards the divine unity, that we seek what Eckhart so well expressed when he said, Let God be born in the soul. Hence the doctrine of the incarnation is no doctrine of the natural divinity of man. It is the doctrine which teaches that the world-will desires our unity with the universal purpose, that God will be born in us and through our consent, that the whole meaning of our life is that it shall transmute transient and temporal values into eternal meanings. Humanity becomes conscious God incarnate only in so far as humanity looks godwards; that is, in the direction of the whole unity of the rational spiritual life.

And now, secondly, the true doctrine of the atonement seems to me simply this: We, as we temporally and transiently are, are destined to win our union with the divine only through learning to triumph over our own evil, over the griefs of fortune, over the unreasonableness and the sin that now beset us. This conquest we never accomplish alone. As the mother that bore you suffered, so the world suffers for you and through and in you until you win your peace in union with the divine will. Upon such suffering you actually depend for your natural existence, for the toleration which your imperfect self constantly demands from the world, for the help that your helplessness so often needs. When you sorrow, then, remember that God sorrows,—sorrows in you, since in all your finitude you still are part of his life; sorrows for you, since it is the intent of the divine spirit, in the plan of its reasonable world, that you should not remain what you now are; and sorrows, too, in waiting for your higher fulfilment, since indeed the whole universe needs your spiritual triumph for the sake of its completion.

On the other hand, this doctrine of the atonement means that there is never any completed spiritual triumph over sorrow which is not accompanied with the willingness to suffer vicariously; that is, with the will not merely to endure bravely, but to force one's very sorrow to be an aid to the common cause of all mankind, to give one's life as a ransom for one's cause, to use one's bitterest and most crushing grief as a means towards the raising of all life to the divine level. It is not enough to endure. Your duty is to make your grief a source of blessing. Thus only can sorrow bring you into conscious touch with the universal life.

Now all this teaching is old. The church began to learn its own version of this solution of the problem of evil when first it sorrowed over its lost master; when first it began to say: "It was needful that Christ should suffer"; when first in vision and in legend it began to conceive its glorified Lord. When later it said, "In the God-man Christ God suffered, once for all and in the flesh, to save us; in him alone the Word became flesh and dwelt among us," the forms of its religious imagination were transient, but the truth of which these forms were the symbol was everlasting. And we sum up this truth in two theses: First, God wins perfection through expressing himself in a finite life and triumphing over and through its very finitude. And secondly, Our sorrow is God's sorrow. God means to express himself by winning us through the very triumph over evil to unity with the perfect life, and therefore our fulfilment, like our existence, is due to the sorrow and the triumph of God himself. These two theses express, I believe, what is vital in Christianity.

4

WILLIAM JAMES

Psychologist of Belief

William James (1842–1910) is most frequently characterized by the terms "pragmatist" and "pluralist." These he was indeed—and with that patrician, civic-minded, and genially progressive individualism that sometimes accompanies inherited wealth. His religious thought is decidedly that of the individual, whether reflected in his philosophy or in his psychological theories and studies.

James was the grandson and namesake of a prosperous Irish Presbyterian immigrant who settled in Albany, New York. A stern and frugal Calvinist, the elder William James died in 1832, leaving an estate valued at $3 million. His son Henry studied at Princeton Theological Seminary, but soon after he was graduated and ordained, he became "permanently alienated from the church,"[1] and chose to devote his abundant leisure to the study of philosophy and religion. He became strongly attracted, in particular, to the social ideas of the communitarian, Charles Fourier, and to the religious thought of Emmanuel Swedenborg. Among his closest companions during the 1840s were Ralph Waldo Emerson and Henry David Thoreau.

Thus the young William James was nurtured in a setting of complete financial security, intellectual liberality, and religious vibrancy. Yet his formative years were also marked by much travel; by the time he was eighteen he had spent five years in England, Germany, and Switzerland. He studied painting

---

[1] Ralph Barton Perry, *The Thought and Character of William James* (Boston: Little, Brown, 1935), Vol. I, p. 11.

before deciding on a scientific career that successively took him to Brazil in 1865–1866 with Louis Agassiz's expedition and to German universities in 1867–1868, returning to Harvard in 1869 for his M. D. degree. Four years later, James was an instructor in anatomy and physiology at Harvard, switching in 1875 to psychology and adding philosophy in 1879.

This biographical matrix goes a long way toward explaining some of the contours of James's religious thought—its piecemeal, unsystematic character, its semi-eclectic blend of many influences, both cosmopolitan and distinctively American. In a sense, he perpetuated his father's lifelong "belief in believing," his conviction that "the deepest truth has to be lived and can never be adequately thought."[2] James's radical empiricism identified reality itself with man's experience, and it understood that experience as much in terms of the relations between things as in things *per se* or their actions. John E. Smith has summarized some of the key features of James's philosophy: "Experience starts, in James's famous phrase, as 'a booming, buzzing confusion,' a welter of items encountered, feelings, tendencies, reactions, anticipations, and so forth . . ."[3] Although both James and Smith are speaking in general terms, the description might well be applied to the "nervous collapse" James underwent at the age of 28. The breakdown was in large part brought on by the death of a dear friend, Mary Temple—or rather by James's closeness to the process of her dying, from tuberculosis, over a period of more than a year. James' coinage of the term "the sick soul" arose in just that crucible of Mary's and his own respective illnesses.[4]

Thus for James the self is no passive spectator but a participant who must find out what to do. James's three basic ideas of purpose, effort, and the will to believe represent facets of his pragmatism and, by the same token, of his critique of rationalism. "Our conduct," summarizes Smith, "cannot be re-

---

[2] *Ibid,* p. 146.
[3] John E. Smith, *The Spirit of American Philosophy* (New York: Oxford, 1963), p. 49.
[4] See Gay Wilson Allen, *William James* (New York: Viking, 1967), pp. 161 ff.

garded as fully human unless it is informed by ideas believed in with sufficient passion and sincerity to make them into wellsprings of action."[5] And such beliefs express, ultimately, the individual's dominant purpose in life. When James referred to the "cash value" of an idea, he sometimes had in mind only the feasibility or relevance of a proposed course of immediate action, but in his more profound assertions of his type of pragmatism, says Smith, "he meant the success or failure of the self as a whole in the quest for self-understanding and a purposeful life."[6]

If his background, training, and experience sensitized James to his quest for purpose, Charles Sanders Peirce's notion of "pragmaticism" was a crucial factor in the mature expression of James's outlook. Primarily a scientist and logician, Peirce came from a solid Puritan background. Like many others of his and James's generation, he sought to adjust basic Christian affirmations to the requirements of a scientific worldview. "In our day," wrote Peirce in 1878, "belief . . . depends more and more on the observation of facts."[7] In another paper published earlier that year, Peirce first identified belief with habit. It is "thought at rest," in other words the starting place for "thought in action"—"the *final* upshot of thinking is the exercise of volition." True belief is "the result of investigation carried sufficiently far," and truth itself is the reality disclosed by convergent lines of inquiry. Facticity and scientific method are the touchstones. Reality is operational, not *a priori*. Metaphysics, to Peirce, is "more curious than useful"[8]; in general he prefers to steer clear of it, and of the traditional rhetoric of theology as well. One finds in his work more than a few sporadic references to God, fate, Christianity, but no attempt to systemize them. His conception of God is not unlike Schelling's—panentheistic, dipolar, emphasizing growth, be-

[5] Smith, *The Spirit of American Philosophy*, p. 56.
[6] *Ibid*, p. 61.
[7] Charles Sanders Peirce, "The Order of Nature," *Popular Science Monthly*, XIII (June 1878), p. 203.
[8] Peirce, "How to Make Our Ideas Clear," *Popular Science Monthly*, XIII (January 1878), in Philip P. Wiener, ed., *Charles S. Peirce: Selected Writings* (New York: Dover, 1966), p. 121, pp. 131–5.

coming and potentiality.[9] James's classic essay "The Will to Believe" (1896) owes much to Peirce's discussion of belief, but its drift is different, inasmuch as James was both psychologically and philosophically more immersed in problems of volition and of religious belief. James focuses in particular upon beliefs which make a difference—those which involve a real and urgent choice, an option which is "live," "momentous" and "forced" (i.e., inescapable). For a belief or concept to be true, it must be instrumental to some worthwhile human purpose. James carries the pragmatic argument farther than Peirce, inveighing against the totalistic "block universe" of Aquinas, Spinoza and Royce and insisting that such reliable knowledge as man possesses is partial, piecemeal and provisional. Human experience, says James, does not point to a single perspective but to a variety of them, and each individual's perspective is conditioned by his temperament—human nature itself is not uniform. James's concept of a "limited" God, *primus inter pares,* is a corollary of this experiential pluralism.

In his *Varieties of Religious Experience,* James examines "experiences which have a meaning for our life"[10]—experiences that show the "cash value" of a whole range of theological concepts such as sin, guilt, and atonement. Salvation, for example, is shown to be a way in which believers experience the power of unifying their fragmented, divided selves. James was not lacking in tolerant, broadly progressive socio-political opinions, but they were at best marginal to his philosophy, and *Varieties* is altogether lacking in the interpersonal, communal, or social dimensions of religious experience; it is limited to the personal and individual.[11] Individualism was a strong component of the American intellectual and religious traditions

---

9 See for example, Peirce, "Evolutionary Love," *The Monist,* III (1893).
10 *Loc. cit.,* p. 509.
11 See C. Wright Mills, *Sociology and Pragmatism* 1943 (New York: Oxford, 1966), pp. 215–276. James' essay, "The Moral Equivalent of War," attests his humane, anti-war outlook. He was also highly critical of United States policy in the Spanish-American War—but here too his individualism is evident. See Mills, pp. 263–268. For a sustained study of James' ethical thought, see John K. Roth, *Freedom and the Moral Life* (Philadelphia: Westminster, 1969).

that formed James's views, and in him, by virtue of his patrician philosophical detachment, it culminates in a wholly nonsectarian and humanistic type of theism, embracing many individual religious experiences as valid and establishing operational—basically psychological—common denominators among them. Orthodoxy, already under fire, need no longer serve as the criterion for religious seriousness; nor can religious beliefs or experiences be dismissed out of hand as irrational or pathological if they can be observed to meet human needs. Like Anselm and Schleiermacher, James vindicates faith in terms calculated to appease doubt, but he carries the enterprise further, mediating between idealism and materialism, between dogmatism and skepticism, between tradition and modernity. Finally, James's pragmatism offers a *modus vivendi* between the claims of empirical fact or science and the demonstrable human propensity to purposive belief.

At every turn, James's philosophical and religious outlook is infused with his psychological observations. In *Varieties,* he speaks of the "sick soul" who sees life as hindered by sin, meaningless, impotence. This sense of malaise is alleviated by a feeling of being in contact with "higher powers," leading to a belief that the individual's own "higher part is coterminous and continuous with a *more* of the same quality, which is operative in the universe outside of him, and which he can . . . get on board of and save himself when all his lower being has gone to pieces in the wreck."[12] This higher or larger power, said James, "need not be infinite, it need not be solitary. It might conceivably be only a larger and more godlike self, of which the present self would be but the mutilated expression . . ."[13] Here we may detect an echo of Ludwig Feuerbach's Christocentric humanism, but the explicit figure of Christ is

---

[12] *Varieties of Religious Experience,* p. 515. Donald B. Meyer points out that James identified the "Sick Soul" with Calvinism and the "healthy minded" with Christian Science, and that in so doing, James finds Calvinism more realistic, hence a healthier perspective than the shallow optimism of the latter despite his labels. See Meyer, *The Positive Thinkers* (Garden City: Doubleday, 1965), pp. 317–321.

[13] *Ibid,* p. 499.

conspicuously absent from James's considerations. In his *Principles of Psychology* (1890), James stressed the continuity of living experience, which forms a "stream of consciousness" rather than a chain or series of ideas. Discrete concepts are products of abstract thinking; they provide convenient diagrams of reality, but reality itself is homogeneous and perpetually in flux. It is for this reason that James tends to be vague about God or any particular statement about "higher powers," and chooses to speak in terms relative to the experience itself. At the same time, he does not limit the validity of belief to its therapeutic efficacy, nor does he regard it as merely subjective.

A *Pluralistic Universe* comprises the Hibbert Lectures given at Manchester College, Oxford, in May 1908. It is the final and perhaps the best synopsis of James's world view and general philosophical outlook. Rejecting the dialectical method of Hegel and other absolute idealists, James asserts his own conception of a "superhuman consciousness" along lines similar to the thought of Gustav Theodor Fechner, who held that God must be a being who continually surpasses himself, hence cannot be all-embracing.[14] In brief, James re-asserts and expands a point noted above from the *Varieties*, that we are not pragmatically entitled to say that anything (e.g., God) includes or dominates everything else; hence if God is in the universe he must be less than the whole. In the following selection, which is the concluding Hibbert lecture, these themes are woven together to argue for the view that the universe is by no means a settled affair but a plurality of streams of reality, crisscrossing, blending, evolving, always unfinished. The order of such a universe is not fixed and immutable but is highly relative, just as is the religious experience of each man in each age and circumstance. In short, whatever its defects, this is James's final defense of freedom and individualism on a cosmic

---

14 See Fechner, *Zend-Avesta* (Leipzig: Leopold Vess, 1922). Key selections will be found in Charles Hartshorne and William L. Reese, *Philosophers Speak of God* (University of Chicago Press, 1953), pp. 243–257. Fechner's influence on James is at least partly due to the fact that he was one of the founders of experimental psychology; "his chief contribution . . . consisted in a kind of psychology of deity." *Ibid*, p. 255.

scale, his testament of theistic humanism. If it is a dethrone-
ment of the absolute, it may also be regarded as the inauguration of an authentic mode of self-transcendence for free men
—not an abandonment of faith but the sketching of its true
frontier and the risks this implies. In this vision, man looks
beyond his finite self and finds God not infinitely remote but
close at hand, at the growing edge of life.

PLURALISM AND RELIGIOUS EXPERIENCE*

At the close of my last lecture I referred to the existence of
religious experiences of a specific nature. I must now explain
just what I mean by such a claim. Briefly the facts I have in
mind may all be described as experiences of an unexpected
life succeeding upon death. By this I don't mean immortality,
or the death of the body. I mean the deathlike termination of
certain mental processes within the individual's experience,
processes that run to failure, and in some individuals, at least,
eventuate in despair. Just as romantic love seems a comparatively recent literary invention, so these experiences of a life
that supervenes upon despair seem to have played no great
part in official theology till Luther's time; and possibly the
best way to indicate their character will be to point to a certain contrast between the inner life of ourselves and of the
ancient Greeks and Romans.

Mr. Chesterton, I think, says somewhere, that the Greeks
and Romans, in all that concerned their moral life, were an
extraordinarily solemn set of folks. The Athenians thought that
the very gods must admire the rectitude of Phocion and Aris-
tides; and those gentlemen themselves were apparently of
much the same opinion. Cato's veracity was so impeccable
that the extremest incredulity a Roman could express of anything was to say, 'I would not believe it even if Cato had told

* From William James, *A Pluralistic Universe* (New York: Longmans,
Green, 1909.) The title of this selection has been supplied by the editor.
In the original it is titled "Lecture VIII: Conclusions."—*Ed.*

me.' Good was good, and bad was bad, for these people. Hypocrisy, which church-Christianity brought in, hardly existed; the naturalistic system held firm; its values showed no hollowness and brooked no irony. The individual, if virtuous enough, could meet all possible requirements. The pagan pride had never crumbled. Luther was the first moralist who broke with any effectiveness through the crust of all this naturalistic self-sufficiency, thinking (and possibly he was right) that Saint Paul had done it already. Religious experience of the lutheran type brings all our naturalistic standards to bankruptcy. You are strong only by being weak, it shows. You cannot live on pride or self-sufficingness. There is a light in which all the naturally founded and currently accepted distinctions, excellences, and safeguards of our characters appear as utter childishness. Sincerely to give up one's conceit or hope of being good in one's own right is the only door to the universe's deeper reaches.

These deeper reaches are familiar to evangelical Christianity and to what is nowadays becoming known as 'mind-cure' religion or 'new thought.' The phenomenon is that of new ranges of life succeeding on our most despairing moments. There are resources in us that naturalism with its literal and legal virtues never recks of, possibilities that take our breath away, of another kind of happiness and power, based on giving up our own will and letting something higher work for us, and these seem to show a world wider than either physics or philistine ethics can imagine. Here is a world in which all is well, in *spite* of certain forms of death, indeed *because* of certain forms of death—death of hope, death of strength, death of responsibility, of fear and worry, competency and desert, death of everything that paganism, naturalism, and legalism pin their faith on and tie their trust to.

Reason, operating on our other experiences, even our psychological experiences, would never have inferred these specifically religious experiences in advance of their actual coming. She could not suspect their existence, for they are discontinuous with the 'natural' experiences they succeed upon and invert their values. But as they actually come and are

given, creation widens to the view of their recipients. They
suggest that our natural experience, our strictly moralistic and
prudential experience, may be only a fragment of real human
experience. They soften nature's outlines and open out the
strangest possibilities and perspectives.

This is why it seems to me that the logical understanding,
working in abstraction from such specifically religious experiences, will always omit something, and fail to reach completely
adequate conclusions. Death and failure, it will always say,
are death and failure simply, and can nevermore be one with
life; so religious experience, peculiarly so called, needs, in my
opinion, to be carefully considered and interpreted by every
one who aspires to reason out a more complete philosophy.

The sort of belief that religious experience of this type
naturally engenders in those who have it is fully in accord
with Fechner's theories. To quote words which I have used
elsewhere, the believer finds that the tenderer parts of his
personal life are continuous with a *more* of the same quality
which is operative in the universe outside of him and which
he can keep in working touch with, and in a fashion get on
board of and save himself, when all his lower being has gone
to pieces in the wreck. In a word, the believer is continuous,
to his own consciousness, at any rate, with a wider self from
which saving experiences flow in. Those who have such experiences distinctly enough and often enough to live in the
light of them remain quite unmoved by criticism, from whatever quarter it may come, be it academic or scientific, or be it
merely the voice of logical common sense. They have had
their vision and they *know*—that is enough—that we inhabit
an invisible spiritual environment from which help comes, our
soul being mysteriously one with a larger soul whose instruments we are.

One may therefore plead, I think, that Fechner's ideas are
not without direct empirical verification. There is at any rate
one side of life which would be easily explicable if those ideas
were true, but of which there appears no clear explanation so
long as we assume either with naturalism that human consciousness is the highest consciousness there is, or with dualis-

tic theism that there is a higher mind in the cosmos, but that it is discontinuous with our own. It has always been a matter of surprise with me that philosophers of the absolute should have shown so little interest in this department of life, and so seldom put its phenomena in evidence, even when it seemed obvious that personal experience of some kind must have made their confidence in their own vision so strong. The logician's bias has always been too much with them. They have preferred the thinner to the thicker method, dialectical abstraction being so much more dignified and academic than the confused and unwholesome facts of personal biography.

In spite of rationalism's disdain for the particular, the personal, and the unwholesome, the drift of all the evidence we have seems to me to sweep us very strongly towards the belief in some form of superhuman life with which we may, unknown to ourselves, be co-conscious. We may be in the universe as dogs and cats are in our libraries, seeing the books and hearing the conversation, but having no inkling of the meaning of it all. The intellectualist objections to this fall away when the authority of intellectualist logic is undermined by criticism, and then the positive empirical evidence remains. The analogies with ordinary psychology and with the facts of pathology, with those of psychical research, so called, and with those of religious experience, establish, when taken together, a decidedly *formidable* probability in favor of a general view of the world almost identical with Fechner's. The outlines of the superhuman consciousness thus made probable must remain, however, very vague, and the number of functionally distinct 'selves' it comports and carries has to be left entirely problematic. It may be polytheistically or it may be monotheistically conceived of. Fechner, with his distinct earth-soul functioning as our guardian angel, seems to me clearly polytheistic; but the word 'polytheism' usually gives offence, so perhaps it is better not to use it. Only one thing is certain, and that is the result of our criticism of the absolute: the only way to escape from the paradoxes and perplexities that a consistently thought-out monistic universe suffers from as from a species of autointoxication—the mystery of the 'fall' namely, of reality lapsing into appearance, truth into error, perfection into imperfection; of evil, in short; the mystery of universal determinism, of the block-universe eternal and without a history, etc.;—the only way of escape, I say, from all this is to be frankly pluralistic and assume that the superhuman consciousness, however vast it may be, has itself an external environment, and consequently is finite. Present day monism carefully repudiates complicity with spinozistic monism. In that, it explains, the many get dissolved in the one and lost, whereas in the improved idealistic form they get preserved in all their manyness as the one's eternal object. The absolute itself is thus represented by absolutists as having a pluralistic object. But if even the absolute has to have a pluralistic vision, why should we ourselves hesitate to be pluralists on our own sole account? Why should we envelop our many with the 'one' that brings so much poison in its train?

The line of least resistance, then, as it seems to me, both in theology and in philosophy, is to accept, along with the superhuman consciousness, the notion that it is not all-embracing, the notion, in other words, that there is a God, but that he is finite, either in power or in knowledge, or in both at once. These, I need hardly tell you, are the terms in which common men have usually carried on their active commerce with God; and the monistic perfections that make the notion of him so paradoxical practically and morally are the colder addition of remote professorial minds operating *in distans* upon conceptual substitutes for him alone.

Why cannot 'experience' and 'reason' meet on this common ground? Why cannot they compromise? May not the godlessness usually but needlessly associated with the philosophy of immediate experience give way to a theism now seen to follow directly from that experience more widely taken? and may not rationalism, satisfied with seeing her *a priori* proofs of God so effectively replaced by empirical evidence, abate something of her absolutist claims? Let God but have the least infinitesimal *other* of any kind beside him, and empiricism and rationalism might strike hands in a lasting treaty of peace. Both might then leave abstract thinness behind them, and seek together, as scientific men seek, by using all the analogies and data within reach, to build up the most probable approximate idea of what the divine consciousness concretely may be like. I venture to beg the younger Oxford idealists to consider seriously this alternative. Few men are as qualified by their intellectual gifts to reap the harvests that seem certain to any one who, like Fechner and Bergson, will leave the thinner for the thicker path.

Compromise and mediation are inseparable from the pluralistic philosophy. Only monistic dogmatism can say of any of its hypotheses, 'It is either that or nothing; take it or leave it just as it stands.' The type of monism prevalent at Oxford has kept this steep and brittle attitude, partly through the proverbial academic preference for thin and elegant logical solutions, partly from a mistaken notion that the only solidly grounded basis for religion was along those lines. If Oxford men could be ignorant of anything, it might almost seem that they had remained ignorant of the great empirical movement towards a pluralistic panpsychic view of the universe, into which our own generation has been drawn, and which threatens to short-circuit their methods entirely and become their religious rival unless they are willing to make themselves its allies. Yet, wedded as they seem to be to the logical machinery and technical apparatus of absolutism, I cannot but believe that their fidelity to the religious ideal in general is deeper still. Especially do I find it hard to believe that the more clerical adherents of the school would hold so fast to its particular machinery if only they could be made to think that religion could be secured in some other way. Let empiricism once become associated with religion, as hitherto, through some strange misunderstanding, it has been associated with irreligion, and I believe that a new era of religion as well as of philosophy will be ready to begin. That great awakening of a new popular interest in philosophy, which is so striking a phenomenon at the present day in all countries, is undoubtedly due in part to religious demands. As the authority of past tradition tends more and more to crumble, men naturally turn a wistful ear to the authority of reason or to the evidence of present fact. They will assuredly not be disappointed if they open their minds to what the thicker and more radical empiricism has to say. I fully believe that such an empiricism is a more natural ally than dialectics ever were, or can be, of the religious life. It is true that superstitions and wild-growing over-beliefs of all sorts will undoubtedly begin to abound if the notion of higher consciousnesses enveloping ours, of fechnerian earth-souls and the like, grows orthodox and fashionable; still more will they superabound if science ever puts her approving stamp on the phenomena of which Frederic Myers so earnestly advocated the scientific recognition, the phenomena of psychic research so-called—and I myself firmly believe that most of these phenomena are rooted in reality. But ought one seriously to allow such a timid consideration as that to deter one from following the evident path of greatest religious promise? Since when, in this mixed world, was any good thing given us in purest outline and isolation? One of the chief characteristics of life is life's redundancy. The sole condition of our having anything, no matter what, is that we should have so much of it, that we are fortunate if we do not grow sick of the sight and sound of it altogether. Everything is smothered in the litter that is fated to accompany it. Without too much you cannot have enough, of anything. Lots of inferior books, lots of bad statues, lots of dull speeches, of tenth-rate men and women, as a condition of the few precious specimens in either kind being realized! The gold-dust comes to birth with the quartz-sand all around it, and this is as much a condition of religion as of any other excellent possession. There must be extrication; there must be competition for survival; but the clay matrix and the noble gem must first come into being unsifted. Once extricated, the gem can be examined separately, conceptualized, defined, and insulated. But this process of extrication cannot be shortcircuited—or if it is, you get the thin inferior abstractions which we have seen, either the hollow unreal god of scholastic theology, or the unintelligible pantheistic monster, instead of the more living divine reality with which it appears certain that empirical methods tend to connect men in imagination.

Arrived at this point, I ask you to go back to my first lecture and remember, if you can, what I quoted there from your own Professor Jacks—what he said about the philosopher himself being taken up into the universe which he is accounting for. This is the fechnerian as well as the hegelian view, and thus our end rejoins harmoniously our beginning. Philosophies are intimate parts of the universe, they express something of its own thought of itself. A philosophy may indeed be a most momentous reaction of the universe upon itself. It may, as I said, possess and handle itself differently in consequence of us philosophers, with our theories, being here; it may trust itself or mistrust itself the more, and, by doing the one or the other, deserve more the trust or the mistrust. What mistrusts itself deserves mistrust.

This is the philosophy of humanism in the widest sense. Our philosophies swell the current of being, add their character to it. They are part of all that we have met, of all that makes us be. As a French philosopher says, 'Nous sommes du réel dans le réel.' Our thoughts determine our acts, and our acts redetermine the previous nature of the world.

Thus does foreignness get banished from our world, and far more so when we take the system of it pluralistically than when we take it monistically. We are indeed internal parts of God and not external creations, on any possible reading of the panpsychic system. Yet because God is not the absolute, but is himself a part when the system is conceived pluralistically, his functions can be taken as not wholly dissimilar to those of the other smaller parts,—as similar to our functions consequently.

Having an environment, being in time, and working out a history just like ourselves, he escapes from the foreignness from all that is human, of the static timeless perfect absolute.

Remember that one of our troubles with that was its essential foreignness and monstrosity—there really is no other word for it than that. Its having the all-inclusive form gave to it an essentially heterogeneous *nature* from ourselves. And this great difference between absolutism and pluralism demands no difference in the universe's material content—it follows from a difference in the form alone. The all-form or monistic form makes the foreignness result, the each-form or pluralistic form leaves the intimacy undisturbed.

No matter what the content of the universe may be, if you only allow that it is *many* everywhere and always, that *nothing* real escapes from having an environment; so far from defeating its rationality, as the absolutists so unanimously pretend, you leave it in possession of the maximum amount of rationality practically attainable by our minds. Your relations with it, intellectual, emotional, and active, remain fluent and congruous with your own nature's chief demands.

It would be a pity if the word 'rationality' were allowed to give us trouble here. It is one of those eulogistic words that both sides claim—for almost no one is willing to advertise his philosophy as a system of irrationality. But like most of the words which people used eulogistically, the word 'rational' carries too many meanings. The most objective one is that of the older logic—the connexion between two things is rational when you can infer one from the other, mortal from Socrates, *e. g.;* and you can do that only when they have a quality in common. But this kind of rationality is just that logic of identity which all disciples of Hegel find insufficient. They supersede it by the higher rationality of negation and contradiction and make the notion vague again. Then you get the æsthetic or teleologic kinds of rationality, saying that whatever fits in any way, whatever is beautiful or good, whatever is purposive or gratifies desire, is rational in so far forth. Then again, according to Hegel, whatever is 'real' is rational. I myself said awhile ago that whatever lets loose any action which we are fond of exerting seems rational. It would be better to give up the word 'rational' altogether than to get into a merely verbal fight about who has the best right to keep it.

Perhaps the words 'foreignness' and 'intimacy,' which I put forward in my first lecture, express the contrast I insist on better than the words 'rationality' and 'irrationality'—let us stick to them, then. I now say that the notion of the 'one' breeds foreignness and that of the 'many' intimacy, for reasons which I have urged at only too great length, and with which, whether they convince you or not, I may suppose that you are now well acquainted. But what at bottom is meant by calling the universe many or by calling it one?

Pragmatically interpreted, pluralism or the doctrine that it is many means only that the sundry parts of reality *may be externally related.* Everything you can think of, however vast or inclusive, has on the pluralistic view a genuinely 'external' environment of some sort or amount. Things are 'with' one another in many ways, but nothing includes everything, or dominates over everything. The word 'and' trails along after every sentence. Something always escapes. 'Ever not quite' has to be said of the best attempts made anywhere in the universe at attaining all-inclusiveness. The pluralistic world is thus more like a federal republic than like an empire or a kingdom. However much may be collected, however much may report itself as present at any effective centre of consciousness or action, something else is self-governed and absent and unreduced to unity.

Monism, on the other hand, insists that when you come down to reality as such, to the reality of realities, everything is present to *everything* else in one vast instantaneous co-implicated completeness—nothing can in *any* sense, functional or substantial, be really absent from anything else, all things interpenetrate and telescope together in the great total conflux.

For pluralism, all that we are required to admit as the constitution of reality is what we ourselves find empirically realized in every minimum of finite life. Briefly it is this, that nothing real is absolutely simple, that every smallest bit of experience is a *multum in parvo* plurally related, that each relation is one aspect, character, or function, way of its being taken, or way of its taking something else; and that a bit of reality when actively engaged in one of these relations is not *by that very fact* engaged in all the other relations simultaneously. The relations are not *all* what the French call *solidaires* with one another. Without losing its identity a thing can either take up or drop another thing, like the log I spoke of, which by taking up new carriers and dropping old ones can travel anywhere with a light escort.

For monism, on the contrary, everything, whether we realize it or not, drags the whole universe along with itself and drops nothing. The log starts and arrives with all its carriers supporting it. If a thing were once disconnected, it could never be connected again, according to monism. The pragmatic difference between the two systems is thus a definite one. It is just thus, that if *a* is once out of sight of *b* or out of touch with it, or, more briefly, 'out' of it at all, then, according to monism, it must always remain so, they can never get together; whereas pluralism admits that on another occasion they may work together, or in some way be connected again. Monism allows for no such things as 'other occasions' in reality—in *real* or absolute reality, that is.

The difference I try to describe amounts, you see, to nothing more than the difference between what I formerly called the each-form and the all-form of reality. Pluralism lets things really exist in the each-form or distributively. Monism thinks that the all-form or collective-unit form is the only form that is rational. The all-form allows of no taking up and dropping of connexions, for in the all the parts are essentially and eternally co-implicated. In the each-form, on the contrary, a thing may be connected by intermediary things, with a thing with which it has no immediate or essential connexion. It is thus at all times in many possible connexions which are not necessarily actualized at the moment. They depend on which actual path of intermediation it may functionally strike into: the word 'or' names a genuine reality. Thus, as I speak here, I may look ahead *or* to the right *or* to the left, and in either case the intervening space and air and ether enable me to see the faces of a different portion of this audience. My being here is independent of any one set of these faces.

If the each-form be the eternal form of reality no less than it is the form of temporal appearance, we still have a coherent world, and not an incarnate incoherence, as is charged by so many absolutists. Our 'multiverse' still makes a 'universe'; for every part, tho it may not be in actual or immediate connexion, is nevertheless in some possible or mediated connexion, with every other part however remote, through the fact that each part hangs together with its very next neighbors in inextricable interfusion. The type of union, it is true, is different here from the monistic type of *all-einheit*. It is not a universal co-implication, or integration of all things *durcheinander*. It is what I call the strung-along type, the type of continuity, contiguity, or concatenation. If you prefer greek words, you may call it the synechistic type. At all events, you see that it forms a definitely conceivable alternative to the through-and-through unity of all things at once, which is the type opposed to it by monism. You see also that it stands or falls with the notion I have taken such pains to defend, of the through-and-through union of adjacent minima of experience, of the confluence of every passing moment of concretely felt experience with its immediately next neighbors. The recognition of this fact of coalescence of next with next in concrete experience, so that all the insulating cuts we make there are artificial products of the conceptualizing faculty, is what distinguishes the empiricism which I call 'radical,' from the bugaboo empiricism of the traditional rationalist critics, which (rightly or wrongly) is accused of chopping up experience into atomistic sensations, incapable of union with one another until a purely intellectual principle has swooped down upon them from on high and folded them in its own conjunctive categories.

Here, then, you have the plain alternative, and the full mystery of the difference between pluralism and monism, as clearly as I can set it forth on this occasion. It packs up into a nutshell:—Is the manyness in oneness that indubitably characterizes the world we inhabit, a property only of the absolute whole of things, so that you must postulate that one-enormous-whole indivisibly as the *prius* of there being any many at all—in other words, start with the rationalistic block-universe, entire, unmitigated, and complete?—or can the finite elements have their own aboriginal forms of manyness in oneness, and where they have no immediate oneness still be continued into one another by intermediary terms—each one of these terms being one with its next neighbors, and yet the total 'oneness' never getting absolutely complete?

The alternative is definite. It seems to me, moreover, that the two horns of it make pragmatically different ethical appeals—at least they *may* do so, to certain individuals. But if you consider the pluralistic horn to be intrinsically irrational, self-contradictory, and absurd, I can now say no more in its defense. Having done what I could in my earlier lectures to break the edge of the intellectualistic *reductiones ad absurdum,* I must leave the issue in your hands. Whatever I may say, each of you will be sure to take pluralism or leave it, just as your own sense of rationality moves and inclines. The only thing I emphatically insist upon is that it is fully co-ordinate hypothesis with monism. This world *may,* in the last resort, be a block-universe; but on the other hand it *may* be a universe only strung-along, not rounded in and closed. Reality *may* exist distributively just as it sensibly seems to, after all. On that possibility I do insist.

One's general vision of the probable usually decides such alternatives. They illustrate what I once wrote of as the 'will to believe.' In some of my lectures at Harvard I have spoken of what I call the 'faith-ladder,' as something quite different from the *sorites* of the logic-books, yet seeming to have an analogous form. I think you will quickly recognize in yourselves, as I describe it, the mental process to which I give this name.

A conception of the world arises in you somehow, no matter how. Is it true or not? you ask.

It *might* be true somewhere, you say, for it is not self-contradictory.

It *may* be true, you continue, even here and now.

It is *fit* to be true, it would be *well if it were true,* it *ought* to be true, you presently feel.

It *must* be true, something persuasive in you whispers next; and then—as a final reuslt—

It shall be *held for true,* you decide; it *shall be* as if true, for *you.*

And your acting thus may in certain special cases be a means of making it securely true in the end.

Not one step in this process is logical, yet it is the way in which monists and pluralists alike espouse and hold fast to their visions. It is life exceeding logic, it is the practical reason for which the theoretic reason finds arguments after the conclusion is once there. In just this way do some of us hold to the unfinished pluralistic universe; in just this way do others hold to the timeless universe eternally complete.

Meanwhile the incompleteness of the pluralistic universe, thus assumed and held to as the most probable hypothesis, is also represented by the pluralistic philosophy as being self-reparative through us, as getting its disconnections remedied in part by our behavior. 'We use what we are and have, to know; and what we know, to be and have still more.' Thus do philosophy and reality, theory and action, work in the same circle indefinitely.

I have now finished these poor lectures, and as you look back on them, they doubtless seem rambling and inconclusive enough. My only hope is that they may possibly have proved suggestive; and if indeed they have been suggestive of one point of method, I am almost willing to let other suggestions go. That point is that *it is high time for the basis of discussion in these questions to be broadened and thickened up*. It is for that that I have brought in Fechner and Bergson, and descriptive psychology and religious experiences, and have ventured even to hint at psychical research and other wild beasts of the philosophic desert. Owing possibly to the fact that Plato and Aristotle, with their intellectualism, are the basis of philosophic study here, the Oxford brand of transcendentalism seems to me to have confined itself too exclusively to thin logical considerations, that would hold good in all conceivable worlds, worlds of an empirical constitution entirely different from ours. It is as if the actual peculiarities of the world that is were entirely irrelevant to the content of truth. But they cannot be irrelevant; and the philosophy of the future must imitate the sciences in taking them more and more elaborately into account. I urge some of the younger members of this learned audience to lay this hint to heart. If you can do so effectively, making still more concrete advances upon the path which Fechner and Bergson have so enticingly opened up, if you can gather philosophic conclusions of any kind, monistic or pluralistic, from the *particulars of life,* I will say, as I now do say, with the cheerfullest of hearts, 'Ring out, ring out my mournful rhymes, but ring the fuller minstrel in.'

5

WALTER RAUSCHENBUSCH
Prophet of Social Christianity

Walter Rauschenbusch (1861–1918) is by all odds the most profound and durable of the many writers who expounded the Social Gospel in early 20th-century America. He was at once a synthesizer of the various strands of progressive social thought then current, as typified by Strong, Gladden, Scudder, Ely, Sheldon, Herron, Bliss, and a score of others, and a strong original intellect who planted in this well-tilled soil his own large conception which identified the biblical Kingdom of God with the ideals of social and industrial democracy.

He was born in Rochester, New York, the son of Karl August Rauschenbusch, a pietistic Lutheran missionary who had left his native Westphalia in 1846. The sixth in an unbroken line of Lutheran pastors, the elder Rauschenbusch became a Baptist in the new world. As a faculty member of the German Department of Rochester Theological Seminary from 1858 until his retirement in 1890, he specialized in the study of the Anabaptist movement.

Young Walter's formative years were almost evenly divided between America and Europe. At the age of four he was sent to school in Germany for four years, returning to his native land virtually an immigrant. In the summer of 1870 he had a deeply moving personal religious experience and was baptized on confession of faith. Although he later gained wide knowledge of the world and of history and theology, he retained the saintly innocence of his pietistic upbringing, both morally and spiritually.

In the fall of 1879, Rauschenbusch returned to Germany for

another four years, graduating from the Gütersloh Gymnasium with honors in classical studies and with a firm grasp of Hebrew, Greek, Latin, and French. By the age of 25, he had completed his studies at Rochester Seminary, whereupon he applied for a post as a foreign missionary. His way was blocked, however, by denominational conservatives who found his view of the Old Testament unsound, apparently a result of his exposure to the theological liberalism of Schleiermacher, Ritschl and Harnack.

As an alternative, the idealistic young minister accepted the pastorate of Second German Baptist Church on West 45th Street, New York City. It was not a slum church, but it was located on the fringe of Hell's Kitchen. The year was 1886, in which the American Federation of Labor was founded. Josiah Strong's *Our Country* had appeared the year before, but Henry George's *Progress and Poverty* came to Rauschenbusch's attention first and seemed to suggest the direction in which to seek answers to the urban misery the young pastor observed. For the next eleven years, he wrestled with the day-to-day problems of his parish and of the nearby slums, at first equipped with little more than a sense of compassionate discipleship but groping for deeper understanding.

These were years of gestation not only for Rauschenbusch's approach to the problems of urban, industrial America, but for social Christianity as a whole and for secular movements. Populism, Edward Bellamy's "Nationalism," the Marxism of Daniel De Leon and other varieties of political radicalism were proliferating. Some of these currents found a religious outlet in the Society of Christian Socialists, founded in 1889 by W. D. P. Bliss, which published *The Dawn*, the first periodical devoted to social Christianity in the United States. In that year, Rauschenbusch joined with other Baptist ministers to launch *For the Right*, a paper that expressed sympathy for socialism in its first issue.

"In 1891," Rauschenbusch later recalled, "I spent a year of study in Germany, partly on the teachings of Jesus and partly on sociology . . . . Christ's conception of the Kingdom of God came to me as a new revelation."[1] He also visited England and was greatly impressed with the growing cooperation movement there. It was probably as an outgrowth of this trip, and of his continuing work in New York, that he wrote his first book, *The Righteousness of the Kingdom*. In it, he spoke of Jesus as a successor to the Old Testament prophets and stated, "Christianity is in its nature revolutionary."[2] The book was, however, not published during its author's lifetime—and remained undiscovered for nearly half a century afterward.

Soon after his return from Europe, he joined with Samuel Zane Batten and others in founding the Brotherhood of the Kingdom, a fellowship patterned after the Friars Minor of Francesco d'Assissi. Study and frequent discussions within the Brotherhood were of lasting value, shaping and clarifying Rauschenbusch's social and theological perspectives. His full participation, however, was hindered by the onset of deafness after an illness in 1888. This tended to isolate him and to concentrate his attention on the written word.

In 1897, Rauschenbusch returned to Rochester to teach, and he remained there for the rest of his life. He continued, however, to absorb the ongoing currents of social and religious thought, writing numerous articles before his first published book, *Christianity and the Social Crisis*, appeared in 1907. It is often remarked that this book met with instant acclaim, establishing Rauschenbusch "at once as the recognized leader of the social-gospel movement."[3] The significance of this claim cannot be denied, but it requires some explanation.

The inauguration of Theodore Roosevelt as President in 1901 opened a new era. Two months earlier (July 1901), the Socialist Party of America was formed, uniting many of the earlier currents of dissent. In the years that followed, the polit-

---

[1] Walter Rauschenbusch, *Christianizing the Social Order* (New York: Macmillan, 1912), p. 93.
[2] Walter Rauschenbusch, *The Righteousness of the Kingdom*, edited by Max L. Stackhouse (Nashville: Abingdon, 1968).
[3] Charles Howard Hopkins, *The Rise of the Social Gospel in American Protestantism* (Yale University Press, 1940), p. 218.

ical center of gravity veered sharply to the left. Whether expressed in demands for social revolution or Rooseveltian trust-busting, there was a sharp acceleration of social consciousness. Perhaps the clearest index was the rapid growth of the Socialist Party in membership and votes. "Onward and upward" was one slogan that actual events seemed to justify. In 1903 *The Christian Socialist* was founded, rapidly growing to a circulation of 20,000, of whom ten percent were clergymen. In 1906 the Christian Socialist Fellowship was established. Although Rauschenbusch never joined it or the Socialist Party, his articles often appeared in the magazine. During the Socialists' heyday, the first dozen years of the century, the social service agencies of the major Protestant denominations were founded, beginning with the Presbyterians in 1903. And during the same period direct steps were taken to effect interdenominational cooperation, with social Christians playing a major role. The Inter-Church Conference on Federation was formed in 1905, and in 1906 it issued a statement on the church and organized labor. This was the instrumentality that prepared the official founding of the Federal Council of Churches in 1908.

The term "Social Gospel" was inherited from a previous decade. It was a phrase coined by the utopian Christian Commonwealth Colony, an experimental community in Georgia, which was disbanded in 1900 after five years of attempting to apply the social principles of Leo Tolstoy. The community was first inspired by George D. Herron's paper *The Kingdom,* and in turn founded a 36-page monthly, *The Social Gospel,* which was widely read and to which Rauschenbusch and many other distinguished writers contributed.

If ever there was a line of demarcation between the centuries, clearly there was a strong one between the demise of the Commonwealth Colony and the early electoral successes of the Socialist Party.[4] It should be noted that the latter was no

---

[4] In 1911, thirty-three towns and cities had Socialist administrations, including Milwaukee, Berkeley, Butte, and Flint, Michigan. See David A. Shannon, *The Socialist Party of America* (New York: Macmillan, 1955), p. 5.

doctrinaire sect during this period, but a relatively broad-based political organization embracing a variety of factions and viewpoints, and only later on would these harden into left and right wings. As for the Christian Socialists, they leaned to a moderate position, and while they did not lack for spokesmen, propagandists, and literature, the latter rarely rose above the level of the sermon or tract. They were virtually starved for a book like *Christianity and the Social Crisis*—a factually and theologically sturdy presentation of the vital issues of the day, written in terms that could be easily understood. The book was this and more. It was persuasive; its vision was at once boldly prophetic and general, even in a sense moderate. By comparison, the writings of Strong, Washington Gladden, and Herron belong to the earlier epoch. Rauschenbusch was more attuned to his times, at once closer to the spirit of the Christian Socialists and to that of the churches. His greatest achievement, perhaps, was that he synthesized the best thinking of each, encompassing also the emergent perspective of the new social sciences and the uninflated spirituality of his Pietist forebearers. Not the least of the influences he absorbed was that of Royce's *Philosophy of Loyalty*.

There is great optimism in Rauschenbusch's outlook, and this undoubtedly was one of his attractions, for he mirrored the hopes of many who were witnessing the implementation of needed reforms in the social order. This optimistic belief in progress was rooted in fact as well as in the philosophical matrix shared by virtually all liberal American theologians since the 1890s—the acceptance of Darwinian evolution, the immanentist view of God and its corollary, the presence of God's Kingdom. But Rauschenbusch, more than any other, tempered and qualified these emphases. The Christian Socialists, he felt, too readily identified the Kingdom of God with the Marxists' classless society, and too often neglected what he considered the key factors of human initiative and Christian faith.

Like Strong and others like him, Rauschenbusch saw in industrialism a catastrophic force, which destroyed the past and ushered in a new era, posing an unprecedented social crisis fraught with danger and promise. The essential Christian task, he wrote, was "to transform human society into the Kingdom of God by regenerating all human relations and reconstituting them in accordance with the will of God."[5] In the light of this crisis, sin and salvation must be reinterpreted in a profoundly social dimension, and the chief danger stems from the sin of organized selfishness in the form of private property, a survival from the dead past which jeopardizes true Christianity. Jesus was important not as the Son of God but as a prototype of the new man for the new age. A decade earlier, Lyman Abbott had said, "what Jesus was, humanity is becoming."[6] Rauschenbusch shared the widely held view of evolution as spiritual progress, but he did not see it as inevitable. It required human decision and action. Jesus showed the way, expressed man's potentiality and responsibility, explained that love was the key to God's relation to man and man's relation to man. Industrialism now for the first time made possible the salvation of humanity, and the rise of democracy, a secular parallel to the doctrine of brotherly love, was a decisive step toward social salvation and the coming of the Kingdom. The individual, Rauschenbusch maintained, must save himself by saving his society. He envisioned the masses of the common people extending the principles of democracy into the socioeconomic order and establishing a cooperative commonwealth. To motivate and inspire this effort, a religious revival was needed. Asceticism, dogmatism and ceremonialism had no place in such a revival, however; it was to be rather a "social awakening"—a spiritual and ethical renewal centered on "the fundamental convictions of Jesus" regarding the value of life and human solidarity.[7] He credited his typical reader with sound moral instincts and an elementary grasp of "Christ's law of love and the golden rule;" it was his task to probe

---

[5] Walter Rauschenbusch, *Christianity and the Social Crisis* (New York, 1907), p. xi.
[6] Lyman Abbott, *Theology of an Evolutionist* (Boston, 1897), p. 73.
[7] See Rauschenbusch, *The Social Principles of Jesus* (New York: The Woman's Press, 1916). This was Rauschenbusch's most popular book; 20,000 copies were distributed in its first year by the International YMCA.

further "in the direction toward which Jesus led" and "to bring to a point what we all vaguely know."[8]

The year 1912 marked the high tide of American socialism and the acceleration of progressive reform from its Republican to its Democratic phase. In that year the Federal Council of Churches issued its "Social Creed." The Christian Socialist Fellowship was gradually declining as social Christianity began to permeate the churches. The Social Gospel, in one form or another, was becoming normative. In that year Rauschenbusch's *Christianizing the Social Order* was published, which reflected the temper of the times. By implication, at least, Rauschenbusch concluded that the churches and America generally had risen to the challenge of the social crisis, and he now laid out the course of historic progress in broad stages. The Protestant Reformation, the Enlightenment, and democracy all represented great strides forward. "The largest and hardest part of the work of Christianizing the social order has been done."[9] Indeed, all that remained was to Christianize the economic order by overcoming man's antisocial competitive urge for material gain, and the currents of history were clearly working for Christianity against capitalism. The labor movement, said Rauschenbusch, gave the first full historic expression of the ethics of the cooperative commonwealth. At this juncture we see a decisive shift in Rauschenbusch's thought, a move away from the revolutionary socialist notion of class struggle. He simply applauds the contribution of organized labor to the evolving ethos of the American middle class. Compromising with the pragmatic progressivism of the mainstream of American political thought, he now felt that industry should be socialized only in those sectors where it had become monopolistic, such as the railroads and basic utilities.

Rauschenbusch died of cancer in July 1918. Four months earlier, he wrote: "I leave my love to those of my friends whose souls have never grown dark against me. I forgive the others and hate no man . . . . Since 1914 the world is full of

---

[8] *Ibid*, Introduction
[9] Rauschenbusch, *Christianizing the Social Order, op. cit.*, p. 124.

hate, and I cannot expect to be happy again in my lifetime."
With relatives on both sides of the battle lines and with his
fellow-citizens yielding to a savage jingoism against all things
German, Rauschenbusch was filled with anguish by World
War I. The previous year, his last book was published: *A
Theology for the Social Gospel,* which attempted to provide
a more theological undergirding for social Christianity. With
his other two major books, it forms a legacy that is of more
than passing historical interest. It is in *Christianizing the Social
Order,* however, that his mature outlook is most characteristically expressed. Its title became virtually a slogan for the social perspective of ecumenical American Protestantism. The
following extract requires no comment. It is, however, clear
evidence that the personal piety of this social prophet was an
essential ingredient in his prescription for social change, attest-
ing eloquently to the nature of the religious revival he felt
must occur if genuine social salvation was to be made possible.
With its emphasis on a truly spiritual "good will" combined
with "scientific good sense," it is a statement that comes from
the wellspring of the American character.

SOCIAL CHRISTIANITY AND PERSONAL RELIGION*

We who know personal religion by experience know that there
is nothing on earth to compare with the moral force exerted
by it. It has demonstrated its social efficiency in our own lives.
It was personal religion which first set us our tasks of service
in youth, and which now holds us to them when our body
droops and our spirit flags. Religion can turn diffident, humble
men like Shaftesbury into invincible champions of the poor.
All social movements would gain immensely in enthusiasm,
persuasiveness, and wisdom, if the hearts of their advocates
were cleansed and warmed by religious faith. Even those who

---

* From Walter Rauschenbusch, *Christianizing the Social Order* (New
York: Macmillan, 1912).

know religious power only by observation on others will concede that.

But will the reënforcement work the other way, also? Religion strengthens the social spirit; will the social spirit strengthen personal religion? When a minister gets hot about child labor and wage slavery, is he not apt to get cold about prayer meetings and evangelistic efforts? When young women become interested in social work, do they not often lose their taste for the culture of the spiritual life and the peace of religious meditation? A hot breakfast is an event devoutly to be desired, but is it wise to chop up your precious old set of colonial furniture to cook the breakfast? Would the reënforcement of the social spirit be worth while if we lost our personal religion in the process?

If this is indeed the alternative, we are in a tragic situation, compelled to choose between social righteousness and communion with God.

Personal religion has a supreme value for its own sake, not merely as a feeder of social morality, but as the highest unfolding of life itself, as the blossoming of our spiritual nature. Spiritual regeneration is the most important fact in any life history. A living experience of God is the crowning knowledge attainable to a human mind. Each one of us needs the redemptive power of religion for his own sake, for on the tiny stage of the human soul all the vast world tragedy of good and evil is reënacted. In the best social order that is conceivable men will still smolder with lust and ambition, and be lashed by hate and jealousy as with the whip of a slave driver. No material comfort and plenty can satisfy the restless soul in us and give us peace with ourselves. All who have made test of it agree that religion alone holds the key to the ultimate meaning of life, and each of us must find his way into the inner mysteries alone. The day will come when all life on this planet will be extinct, and what meaning will our social evolution have had if that is all? Religion is eternal life in the midst of time and transcending time. The explanations of religion have often been the worst possible, God knows, but the fact of religion is the biggest thing there is.

If, therefore, our personal religious life is likely to be sapped by our devotion to social work, it would be a calamity second to none. But is it really likely that this will happen? The great aim underlying the whole social movement is the creation of a free, just, and brotherly social order. This is the greatest moral task conceivable. Its accomplishment is the manifest will of God for this generation. Every Christian motive is calling us to it. If it is left undone, millions of lives will be condemned to a deepening moral degradation and to spiritual starvation. Does it look probable that we shall lose our contact with God if we plunge too deeply into this work? Does it stand to reason that we shall go astray from Jesus Christ if we engage in the unequal conflict with organized wrong? What kind of "spirituality" is it which is likely to get hurt by being put to work for justice and our fellow-men?

Some of the anxiety about personal religion is due to a subtle lack of faith in religion. Men think it is a fragile thing that will break up and vanish when the customs and formulas which have hitherto incased and protected it are broken and cast aside. Most of us have known religion under one form, and we suppose it can have no other. But religion is the life of God in the soul of man, and is God really so fragile? Will the tongue of fire sputter and go out unless we shelter it under a bushel? Let the winds of God roar through it, and watch it! Religion unites a great variability of form with an amazing constancy of power. The Protestant Reformation changed the entire outward complexion of religion in the nations of northern Europe. All the most characteristic forms in which Christianity had expressed itself and by which its strength had hitherto been gauged were swept away. No pope, no priest, no monk, no mass, no confessional, no rosary, no saints, no images, no processions, no pilgrimages, no indulgences! It was a clean sweep. What was left of religion? Religion itself! At least your Puritans and Huguenots seemed to think they had personal religion; more, in fact, than ever before. Catholics thought it was the destruction of personal religion; really it was the rise of a new type of religion. In the same way the social Christianity of to-day is not a dilution of personal religion, but a new form of experimental Christianity, and its religious testimony will have to be heard henceforth when "the varieties of religious experience" are described.[1]

Nevertheless, conservative Christian men are not frightened by their own imaginings when they fear that the progress of the social interest will mean a receding of personal religion. They usually have definite cases in mind in which that seemed to be the effect, and it is well worth while to examine these more closely.

In the first place, personal religion collapses with some individuals, because in their case it had long been growing hollow and thin. Not all who begin the study of music or poetry in youth remain lovers of art and literature to the end, and not all who begin a religious life in the ardor of youth keep up its emotional intimacy as life goes on. Take any group of one hundred religious people, laymen or ministers, and it is a safe guess that in a considerable fraction of them the fire of vital religion is merely flickering in the ashes. As long as their life goes on in the accustomed way, they maintain their religious connections and expressions, and do so sincerely, but if they move to another part of the country, or if a new interest turns their minds forcibly in some other direction, the frayed bond parts and they turn from their Church and religion. If it is the social interest which attracts them, it may seem to them and others that this has extinguished their devotional life. In reality there was little personal religion to lose, and that little would probably have been lost in some other way. This would cover the inner history of some ministers as well as of church members.

In other cases we must recognize that men become apathetic about church activities in which they have been interested, because they have found something better. The Hebrew prophets turned in anger from the sacrificial doings of their people; Jesus turned away from the long prayers of the Phar-

---

[1] My friend Elie Gounelle has a fine discussion on this in his book, "Pourquoi sommes-nous chrétiens sociaux?" p. 29 (Librairie Fischbacher, Paris). A remarkable little book.

isees, who were the most pious people of his day; the Reformers repudiated many of the most devout activities of medieval
Catholicism. Wherever there is a new awakening of spiritual
life, there is a discarding of old religious forms, and it is to the
interest of personal religion that there should be. Is there
nothing petty, useless, and insipid in the Catholic or Protestant
church life of our day from which a soul awakened to larger
purposes ought really to turn away? Is it reprehensible if
some drop out of a dress parade when they hear the sound
of actual fighting just across the hills?

It is also true that in this tremendous awakening and unsettlement some turn away in haste from things which have
lasting value. Few men and few movements have such poise
that they never overshoot the mark. When the Reformation
turned its back on medieval superstition, it also smashed the
painted windows of the cathedrals and almost banished art
and music from its services. When mystics feel the compelling
power of the inner word of God, they are apt to slight the
written word. So when religious souls who have been shut
away from social ideals and interests and pent up within a
fine but contracted religious habitation get the new outlook
of the social awakening, it sweeps them away with new
enthusiasms. Their life rushes in to fill the empty spaces. Their
mind is busy with a religious comprehension of a hundred new
facts and problems, and the old questions of personal religion
drop out of sight. In such cases we can safely trust to experience to restore the equilibrium. In a number of my younger
friends the balancing is now going on. As they work their way
in life and realize the real needs of men and the real values of
life, they get a new comprehension of the power and precious-
ness of personal and intimate religion, and they turn back to
the old truths of Christianity with a fresh relish and a firmer
accent of conviction. We shall see that rediscovery in thousands within a few years. No doubt they are to blame for their
temporary one-sidedness, but their blame will have to be
shared by generations of religious individualists whose own
persistent one-sidedness had distorted the rounded perfection
of Christianity and caused the present excessive reaction.

The question takes a wider meaning when we turn to the alienation of entire classes from religion. There is no doubt that in all the industrialized nations of Europe, and in our own country, the working classes are dropping out of connection with their churches and synagogues, and to a large extent are transferring their devotion to social movements, so that it looks as if the social interest displaced religion. But here, too, we must remember that solid masses of the population of continental Europe have never had much vital religion to lose. Their religion was taught by rote and performed by rote. It was gregarious and not personal. Detailed investigations have been made of the religious thought world of the peasantry or industrial population of limited districts, and the result always is that the centuries of indoctrination by the Church have left only a very thin crust of fertile religious conviction and experience behind. This is not strange for whenever any spontaneous and democratic religion has arisen among the people, the established churches have done their best to wet-blanket and suppress it, and they have succeeded finely. When these people cut loose from their churches, they may not be getting much farther away from God. Usually these unchurched people still have a strong native instinct for religion, and when the vital issues and convictions of their own life are lifted into the purer light of Jesus Christ and set on fire by religious faith, they respond.

A new factor enters the situation when we encounter the influence of "scientific socialism." It is true, the party platform declares that "religion is a private affair." The saving of souls is the only industry that socialism distinctly relegates to private enterprise. If that meant simply separation of Church and State, Americans could heartily assent. If it meant that the Socialist Party proposes to be the political organization of the working class for the attainment of economic ends and to be neutral in all other questions, it would be prudent tactics. But in practice it means more. The socialism of continental Europe, taking it by and large, is actively hostile, not only to bad forms of organized religion, but to religion itself. Churchmen feel that a man is lost to religion when he joins the Socialist Party, and socialist leaders feel that a socialist who is still an active Christian is only half baked. When French and German socialists learn that men trained in the democracy and vitality of the free churches of England and America combine genuine piety and ardent devotion to the Socialist Party, it comes to them as a shock of surprise. In May, 1910, about 260 delegates of the English "Brotherhoods" visited Lille in France and were received by the French trades-unionists and socialists with parades and public meetings. The crowds on the streets did not know what to make of it when they saw the English-men marching under the red flag of socialism and yet bearing banners with the inscriptions: "We represent 500,000 English workmen;" "We proclaim the Fatherhood of God and the Brotherhood of Man;" "Jesus Christ leads and inspires us." What were these men, Christians or socialists? They could not be both. The Frenchmen lost all their bearings when they heard Keir Hardie, the veteran English labor leader and socialist, repudiating clericalism, but glorifying the Gospel and the spirit of Christ, and declaring that it was Christianity which had made a socialist of him.

The antireligious attitude of continental socialism is com-prehensible enough if we study its historical causes dispassion-ately. Its most active ingredient is anticlericalism. I surmise that if some of us Americans had been in the shoes of these foreign workingmen and had seen the priest from their angle of vision, we should be anticlerical too. But in the old churches religion, the Church, and the priest mean the same thing; you must accept all or reject all. Men do not discriminate when they are hot with ancient wrongs.

Another ingredient in socialist unbelief is modern science and skepticism. Socialists share their irreligion with other radicals. They are unbelievers, not simply because they are socialists, but because they are children of their time. Great masses of upper-class and middle-class people in Europe are just as skeptical and materialistic, though they show no touch of red. Socialists have no monopoly of unbelief.

But in addition to this, materialistic philosophy does come to socialists embodied in their own literature as part of socialist "science." The socialist faith was formulated by its intellectual leaders at a time when naturalism and materialism was the popular philosophy of the intellectuals, and these elements were woven into the dogma of the new movement. Great movements always perpetuate the ideas current at the time when they are in their fluid and formative stage. For instance, some of the dogmas of the Christian Church are still formulated in the terminology of philosophy that was current in the third and fourth centuries. Calvin worked out a system of thought that is stamped with his powerful personality and with the peculiarities of his age. But after it had once become the dogmatic fighting faith of great organized bodies, it was all handed on as God's own truth. Socialism is the most solid and militant organization since Calvinism, and it is just as dogmatic. Thus we have the tragic fact that the most idealistic mass movement of modern times was committed at the outset to a materialistic philosophy with which it had no essential connection, and every individual who comes under its influence and control is liable to be assimilated to its type of thought in religion as well as in economics.[2]

Those who fear the influence of the social interest on personal religion are not, therefore, wholly wrong. In any power-

---

[2] While I was writing these pages I received a letter from a socialist who had read "Christianity and the Social Crisis." "Speaking for the proletarian class, I shall say that we all, who have gone far enough in the study of socialism to become revolutionary, regard the so-called Christian churches as our bitterest enemies. It is an axiom among us that any man who comes into our party must drop his religion (by that, of course, I mean churchianity) before he can become a valuable member of the socialist party. And he always does. I did. It is a fact that most of us are atheists, not because we want to be, but because the churches are always on the side of our enemies. They preach against us. As a consequence, the hardest person to wake up is the workingman who has been chloroformed by the church in the interest of the master class. . . . Personally I do not want to see the churches take your advice. Keep them out of our movement. We have built it so far with blood and tears without their help. I believe in God. I do not know whether I believe in immortality. I would like to, and so would all my comrades. I am by nature religious. Worship is a necessity of the human heart and I am lost without something to cling to." This letter in its mixture of anger and longing doubtless expresses the attitude of a great number.

ful spiritual movement, even the best, there are yeasty, unsettling forces which may do good in the long run, but harm in the short run. Atheistic socialism may influence the religious life of great classes as deforestation affects a mountain side.

On the other hand, where the new social spirit combines harmoniously with the inherited Christian life, a new type of personal religion is produced which has at least as good a right to existence as any other type. Jesus was not a theological Christian, nor a churchman, nor an emotionalist, nor an ascetic, nor a contemplative mystic. A mature social Christian comes closer to the likeness of Jesus Christ than any other type.

In religious individualism, even in its sweetest forms, there was a subtle twist of self-seeking which vitiated its Christlikeness. Thomas a Kempis' "Imitation of Christ" and Bunyan's "Pilgrim's Progress" are classical expressions of personal religion, the one Roman Catholic and monastic, the other Protestant and Puritan. In both piety is self-centered. In both we are taught to seek the highest good of the soul by turning away from the world of men. Doubtless the religion of the monastery and of the Puritan community was far more social and human than the theory might indicate. Bunyan seems to have felt by instinct that it was not quite right to have Christian leave his wife and children and neighbors behind to get rid of his burden and reach the heavenly city. So he wrote a sequel to his immortal story in which the rest of the family with several friends set out on the same pilgrimage. This second part is less thrilling, but more wholesomely Christian. There is family life, love-making, and marriage on the way. A social group coöperate in salvation. Bunyan was feeling his way toward social Christianity.

Evangelicalism prides itself on its emphasis on sin and the need of conversion, yet some of the men trained in its teachings do not seem to know the devil when they meet him on the street. The most devastating sins of our age do not look like sins to them. They may have been converted from the world, but they contentedly make their money in the common ways of the world. Social Christianity involves a more trenchant kind of conversion and more effective means of grace. It may teach a more lenient theory of sin, but it gives a far keener eye for the lurking places of concrete and profitable sins. A man who gets the spiritual ideals of social Christianity is really set at odds with "the world" and enlisted in a lifelong fight with organized evil. But no man who casts out devils is against Christ. To fight evil involves a constant affirmation of holiness and hardens the muscles of Christian character better than any religious gymnasium work. To very many Christians of the old type the cross of Christ meant only an expedient in the scheme of redemption, not a law of life for themselves. A man can be an exponent of "the higher life" and never suffer any persecution whatever from the powers that control our sin-ridden social life. On the other hand, if any man takes social Christianity at all seriously, he will certainly encounter opposition and be bruised somehow. Such an experience will throw him back on the comforts of God and make his prayers more than words. When he bears on his own body and soul the marks of the Lord Jesus, the cross will be more than a doctrine to him. It will be a bond uniting him with Christ in a fellowship of redemptive love.

The personal religion created by social Christianity will stand one practical test of true religion which exceeds in value most of the proofs offered by theology: it creates a larger life and the power of growth. Dead religion narrows our freedom, contracts our horizon, limits our sympathies, and dwarfs our stature. Live religion brings a sense of emancipation, the exhilaration of spiritual health, a tenderer affection for all living things, widening thoughts and aims, and a sure conviction of the reality and righteousness of God. Devotion to the Reign of God on earth will do that for a man, and will do it continuously. A self-centered religion reaches the dead line soon. Men get to know the whole scheme of salvation, and henceforth they march up the hill only to march down again. On the contrary, when a man's prime object is not his soul, but the Kingdom of God, he has set his hands to a task that will never end and will always expand. It will make ever larger demands on his intellect, his sympathy, and his practical efficiency. It will work him to the last ounce of his strength. But it will keep him growing.

It is charged that those who become interested in "social work" lose interest in "personal work." Doubtless there is truth in that, and it is a regrettable one-sidedness. It is only fair to remember, however, that they share this loss of interest with the entire American Church. Evangelism itself had long become so one-sided, mechanical, and superficial in its gospel and methods that the present apathy can be explained only as a reaction from it. Precisely those who have themselves gone through its experiences are now reluctant to submit young people to it. The social gospel will gradually develop its own evangelistic methods and its own personal appeals. What was called "personal work" was often not personal at all, but a wholesale regimentation of souls. It offered the same prescription, the same formula of doctrine, the same spiritual exercises and emotions for all. Those who add the new social intelligence to the old religious love of man's soul will take every man in his own social place and his own human connections, will try to understand his peculiar sin and failure from his own point of view, and see by what means salvation can effectively be brought to him. Such an evangelism would be more truly personal than the old; it would have more sense of the individuality of each man. As Robert A. Woods finely says, "It calls each man by his own name."

Christianity must offer every man a full salvation. The individualistic gospel never did this. Its evangelism never recognized more than a fractional part of the saving forces at work in God's world. Salvation was often whittled down to a mere doctrinal proposition; assent to that, and you were saved. Social Christianity holds to all the real values in the old methods, but rounds them out to meet all the needs of human life.

Salvation is always a social process. It comes by human contact. The word must become flesh if it is to save. Some man or woman, or some group of people, in whom the saving love of Jesus Christ has found a new incarnation, lays hold of an enfeebled, blinded human atom and infuses new hope and courage and insight, new warmth of love and strength of will, and there is a new breathing of the soul and an opening of the inner eye. Salvation has begun. That man or group of men was a fragment of the Kingdom of God in humanity; God dwelt in them and therefore power could go out from them. When a lost soul is infolded in a new society, a true humanity, then there is a chance of salvation.[3] No matter what set of opinions they hold, such men and women have been one of the most precious assets of our American life, and a social theorist who scoffs at them is blind with dogmatic prejudice.

When the Church insisted that it is the indispensable organ of salvation, it insisted on the social factor in redemption. The Church stands for the assimilating power exerted by the social group over its members. The same influence which a semi-criminal gang exerts over a boy for evil is exerted by the Church for good. The advice in the Gospel to win an offending brother back by pleading with him first alone, then drawing two or three others into it, and finally bringing the matter before the Church, shows a keen insight into the powers of the social group over its members. More and more units of power are switched on until the current is overpowering.[4]

In a small and simple country or village community the Church could follow a man in all his relations. In our modern society the social contact of the Church covers only a small part of life, and the question is whether the influence it exerts on the saved man is strong and continuous enough to keep him saved. Suppose a poor "bum" leaves the Salvation Army barracks with a new light of hope in his eyes. He passes out on the streets among saloons and gambling dens, among sights and sounds and smells that call to his passions, among men and women who are not part of the saving Kingdom of God, but of the carnivorous kingdom of the devil. So the poor fellow backslides. Suppose a millionaire has been at a meeting where

---

[3] Begbie's "Twice-Born Men," which has been a summons to personal work, proves throughout that salvation comes by social contact with religious groups.
[4] Matt. xviii. 15–20.

he has caught a vision of a new order of business, in which men are not boozy with profits, but in which such as he might be brothers to all. Next morning stocks are tumbling on 'Change, and profit is calling to him. So the poor fellow backslides. The churches do save men, but so many of them do not stay saved. Even in very active churches an enormous percentage of members are in the long run swept back so that all can see the failure, and if love of money and the hardness of social pride were properly reckoned as a religious collapse, the percentage of waste would be still greater.[5] The social organism of the Church becomes increasingly unable in modern life to supply the social forces of salvation single-handed. It may save, but its salvation is neither complete nor durable.

Sin is a social force. It runs from man to man along the lines of social contact. Its impact on the individual becomes most overwhelming when sin is most completely socialized. Salvation, too, is a social force. It is exerted by groups that are charged with divine will and love. It becomes durable and complete in the measure in which the individual is built into a social organism that is ruled by justice, cleanness, and love. A full salvation demands a Christian social order which will serve as the spiritual environment of the individual. In the little catechism which Luther wrote for the common people he has a charmingly true reply to the question: "What is 'our daily bread'?" He says: "All that belongs to the nourishment and need of our body, meat and drink, clothes and shoes, house and home, field and cattle, money and property, a good wife and good children, good servants and good rulers, good government, good weather, peace, health, education, honor, good friends, trusty neighbors, and such like." Yes, especially "such like." In the same way "salvation" involves a saved environment. For a baby it means the breast and heart and love of a mother, and a father who can keep the mother in proper

---

[5] The General Conference of the Methodist Church and the General Assembly of the Presbyterian Church in 1912 confronted the tremendous losses by the "dropping" of members as one of the most serious questions of church life.

condition. For a workingman salvation includes a happy home, clean neighbors, a steady job, eight hours a day, a boss that treats him as a man, a labor union that is well led, the sense of doing his own best work and not being used up to give others money to burn, faith in God and in the final triumph and present power of the right, a sense of being part of a movement that is lifting his class and all mankind, "and such like." Therefore the conception of salvation which is contained in the word "the Kingdom of God" is a truer and completer conception than that which is contained in the word "justification by faith," as surely as the whole is better than a part.

I set out with the proposition that social Christianity, which makes the Reign of God on earth its object, is a distinct type of personal religion, and that in its best manifestations it involves the possibility of a purer spirituality, a keener recognition of sin, more durable powers of growth, a more personal evangelism, and a more all-around salvation than the individualistic type of religion which makes the salvation of the soul its object. I want to add that this new type of religion is especially adapted to win and inspire modern men.[6]

It must be plain to any thoughtful observer that immense numbers of men are turning away from traditional religion, not because they have lapsed into sin, but because they have become modernized in their knowledge and points of view. Religion itself is an eternal need of humanity, but any given form of religion may become antiquated and inadequate, leaving the youngest and livest minds unsatisfied, or even repelling where it ought to attract. The real religious leaders of this generation must face the problem how they can give to modern men the inestimable boon of experiencing God as a joy and a

---

[6] In the following pages I am deeply indebted to the inaugural address of Leonhard Ragaz, "Zur gegenwärtigen Umgestaltung des Christentums," published in *Neue Wege,* Basel, October, 1909. Professor Ragaz is one of the most brilliant preachers of Switzerland, professor of systematic theology in the University of Zurich, together with Kutter one of the most eminent leaders of Christian Socialism in Switzerland, and altogether one of the finest examples of the new type of Social Christianity that I have met.

power, and of living in him as their fathers did. I claim that social Christianity is by all tokens the great highway by which this present generation can come to God.

For one thing, it puts an end to most of the old conflicts between religion and science. The building of the Kingdom of God on earth requires surprisingly little dogma and speculative theology, and a tremendous quantity of holy will and scientific good sense. It does not set up a series of propositions which need constant modernizing and which repel the most active intellects, but it summons all to help in transforming the world into a reign of righteousness, and men of good will are not very far apart on that. That kind of religion has no quarrel with science. It needs science to interpret the universe which Christianity wants to transform. Social Christianity sets up fewer obstacles for the intellect and puts far heavier tasks on the will, and all that is sound in modern life will accept that change with profound relief.

Social Christianity would also remove one other obstacle which bars even more men out of religion than the scientific difficulties of belief. The most effective argument against religion to-day is that religion has been "against the people." The people are coming to their own at last. For a century and a half at least they have been on the upgrade, climbing with inexpressible toil and suffering toward freedom, equality, and brotherhood. The spirit of Christ has been their most powerful ally, but the official Church, taking Christendom as a whole, has thrown the bulk of its great resources to the side of those who are in possession, and against those who were in such deadly need of its aid. This is the great scandal which will not down. Scientific doubt may alienate thousands, but the resentment against the Church for going over to the enemy has alienated entire nations. Nothing would so expiate that guilt and win back the lost respect for religion, as determined coöperation on the part of the Church in creating a social order in which the just aspirations of the working class will be satisfied. Those Christian men who are the outstanding and bold friends of the people's cause are to-day the most effective apologists to Christianity.

The Christian demand for the Kingdom of God on earth responds to the passionate desire for liberty which pervades and inspires the modern world. That desire is really a longing for redemption. Just as an individual may long to be free from vicious habits that enslave him and rob him of his manhood and self-respect, so great social classes now want freedom from the social unfreedom and degradation which denies their human worth and submerges their higher nature in coarseness, ignorance, and animal brutality. The theological word "redemption" originally meant the ransoming of slaves and prisoners. Christ is the great emancipator. Every advance in true Christianity has meant a broadening path for liberty. The highest Christian quality is love; but love is supreme freedom, a state in which even moral compulsion ceases because goodness has become spontaneous. This world-wide desire for freedom is the breath of God in the soul of humanity. Men instinctively know it as such, and they hate a Church that would rob them of it. Social Christianity would rally that desire in the name of the Kingdom of God, and help the people to a consciousness that they are really moved by religion when they love freedom. On the other hand, by its strong emphasis on social solidarity and the law of service, it will counteract that exaggerated assertion of individual rights and that selfish soul-culture which dog the steps of Freedom.

Every individual reconstructs his comprehension of life and duty, of the world and of God, as he passes from one period of his development to the next. If he fails to do so, his religion will lose its grasp and control. In the same way humanity must reconstruct its moral and religious synthesis whenever it passes from one era to another. When all other departments of life and thought are silently changing, it is impossible for religion to remain unaffected. Other-wordly religion was the full expression of the highest aspirations of ancient and medieval life. Contemporary philosophy supported it. The Ptolemaic astronomy made it easy to conceive of a heaven localized above the starry firmament, which was only a few miles up. But to-day the whole *Weltanschauung* which supported those religious conceptions has melted away irretrievably. Copernican astronomy, the conviction of the universal and majestic reign of law, the evolutionary conception of the history of the earth and of the race, have made the religious ideas that were the natural denizens of the old world of thought seem like antique survivals to-day, as if a company of Athenians should walk down Broadway in their ancient dress. When Christianity invaded the ancient world, it was a modernist religion contemptuously elbowing aside the worn-out superstitions of heathenism, and the live intellects seized it as an adequate expression of their religious consciousness. To-day the livest intellects have the greatest difficulty in maintaining their connection with it. Many of its defenders are querulously lamenting the growth of unbelief. They stand on a narrowing island amid a growing flood, saving what they can of the wreckage of faith. Is religion dying? Is the giant faith of Christianity tottering to its grave?

Religion is not dying. It is only molting its feathers, as every winged thing must at times. A new springtide is coming. Even now the air is full of mating calls and love songs. Soon there will be a nest in every tree.

As the modern world is finding itself, religion is returning to it in new ways. Philosophy in its most modern forms is tending toward an idealistic conception of the universe, even when it calls itself materialistic. It realizes spirit behind all reality. The new psychology is full of the powers and mysteries of the soul. It is no slight achievement of faith to think of God immanent in the whole vast universe, but those who accomplish that act of faith feel him very near and mysteriously present, pulsating in their own souls in every yearning for truth and love and right. Life once more becomes miraculous; for every event in which we realize God and our soul is a miracle. All history becomes the unfolding of the purpose of the immanent God who is working in the race toward the commonwealth of spiritual liberty and righteousness. History is the sacred workshop of God. There is a presentiment abroad in modern thought that humanity is on the verge of a profound change, and that feeling heralds the fact. We feel that all this wonderful liberation of redemptive energy is working out a true and divine order in which our race will rise to a new level of existence. But such a higher order can rise out of the present only if superior spiritual forces build and weave it. Thousands of young minds who thought a few years ago that they had turned their back on religion forever are full of awe and a sense of mystery as they watch the actualities of life in this process of unbuilding.[7] By coöperating with God in his work they are realizing God. Religion is insuppressible.

It is true that the social enthusiasm is an unsettling force which may unbalance for a time, break old religious habits and connections, and establish new contacts that are a permanent danger to personal religion. But the way to meet this danger is not to fence out the new social spirit, but to let it fuse with the old religious faith and create a new total that will be completer and more Christian than the old religious individualism at its best. Such a combination brings a triumphant enlargement of life which proves its own value and which none would give up again who has once experienced it. There is so much religion even in nonreligious social work that some who had lost their conscious religion irretrievably have found it again by this new avenue. God has met them while they were at work with him in social redemption, and they have a religion again and a call to a divine ministry. Faith in a new social order is so powerful a breeder of religion that great bodies of men who in theory scorn and repudiate the name of religion, in practice show evidence of possessing some of the most powerful instincts and motives of religion.[8] One of the most valuable achievements in the domain of personal

---

[7] This line of thought was worked out more fully by me in a sermon preached before the National Conference of Charities and Corrections, 1912, and in a little book, "Unto Me," published by the Pilgrim Press, Boston, 1912.

[8] This is the message of the brilliant book of Kutter of Zürich, "Sie müssen," which has been edited in English by Rufus W. Weeks, and published by the Coöperative Printing Company, Chicago. Richard Heath has summed up all the teachings of Kutter in "Social Democracy: Does it Mean Darkness or Light?" Letchworth, England, 1910.

religion which is now open to any man is to build up a rounded and harmonious Christian personality in which all the sweetness and intensity of the old religious life shall combine with the breadth, intelligence, and fighting vigor of the social spirit. Every such individuality will reproduce itself in others who are less mature, and so multiply this new species of the genus "Christian."

6

WOODROW WILSON

Progressive Calvinist Statesman

Thomas Woodrow Wilson (1856–1924) provides us with indispensable illumination of that broadly progressive trend of American thought that typified the early twentieth century and led head-on to disillusion and the collapse of the Social Gospel. Pragmatism and perfectionism, traceable to Pilgrim roots, represented the polarities of Wilson's thought, both in the arena of national and international politics and in the religious sentiments which underlay Wilson's moral idealism. Like Strong, he conceived of America as a missionary nation. Unlike Strong, he wielded political power and sought through it to instruct and improve the world. He looked to the future as "the most glorious time" and thus typified the optimism of the age—a vaster, more ebullient kind than that of the twenties. The polarities in Wilson's thought, which were in large measure endorsed by the American people,[1] are well expressed in Ralph Gabriel's words: "Wilson, although as President he established the most important administrative agencies which made possible the pragmatic approach to national planning, lived in a world of eternal values in which progress is a journey toward moral perfection . . ."[2]

Wilson was the son of Scotch-Irish Ohioans who moved to Staunton, Virginia, just three years before he was born. He

---

[1] Wilson never received a majority of the votes in either the 1912 or 1916 election, but, in 1912 at least, the substantial votes for the Progressive and the Socialist candidates may be counted as affirmation of the same general trend or reform.

[2] Ralph Henry Gabriel, *The Course of American Democratic Thought* (2nd ed.; New York; Ronald Press Co., 1956), p. 365.

was only a year old when, in 1857, twenty-one Southern presbyteries seceded from the nationwide Presbyterian Church. The Southern Presbyterian Assembly first convened in the home of his father, Joseph Wilson, a minister who served as its permanent clerk for 37 years. Most of the boy's childhood was spent in Augusta, Georgia, where the horrors of the Civil War effaced his Midwestern background and confirmed his identity as a Southerner. The intense Calvinist piety of his home life was augmented by his father's many-sided involvement in the life of the church, which included four years as a professor at Columbia Theological Seminary in South Carolina. He was also strongly influenced by his maternal uncle, James Woodrow, who was both a New School Presbyterian minister and a scientist, trained at Heidelberg, who headed the Confederate chemical laboratories during the Civil War. James Woodrow was later president of the University of South Carolina and the author of an article on Darwinism and the Bible which brought him under attack for heresy in 1884.

Woodrow Wilson received his undergraduate schooling at Presbyterian institutions—Davidson College and Princeton University. Although he became a teacher of jurisprudence and political science rather than of theology, he brought to his vocation a firm sense of moral rectitude and a passion for the orderly reform of institutions. He taught at Bryn Mawr, Johns Hopkins, and Wesleyan, and then for a dozen years at Princeton until 1902, when he was elected the university's first president who was not a clergyman.

A brilliant and forceful speaker, Wilson's power "was derived from the passionate persistency with which he adhered . . . to [the] ideal of acting on principle. . . . All that language of rhetorical idealism—truth, righteousness, service, faith . . . —were in some sense a gospel with Wilson, and it was the realization of this that arrested the attention of the public."[3] At Princeton he conceived plans for organizational reform and fought for them with more tenacity than tact. The defeat of

---

[3] Edmund Wilson, *The Shores of Light* (New York: Farrar, Straus, 1952), p. 302. The two Wilsons are not related.

his largely admirable plans was mainly due to his insistence on relying solely on the plans' merits; it was beneath his dignity to resort to strategies of persuasion to win over his opponents.

In 1910 Wilson accepted the Democratic nomination for the governorship of New Jersey from a political machine which hoped to use him to combat Republican Progressivism. Much to the bosses' discomfiture, however, he asserted his own principles of reform. He became a candidate for the Presidency of the United States two years later. His victory was aided greatly by the split between regular Republicans and Roosevelt Progressives in the 1912 election.

Wilson's presidency, perhaps more than any before or since, was marked not only by idealistic intentions but by a sense of religious mission and a rigid adherence to principle. A leading biographer referred to Wilson's policy toward Mexico, China, and the Caribbean as "missionary diplomacy"[4]—a term that aptly suggests the application of Josiah Strong's vision of America's destiny as moral arbiter to the world. The crusading zeal of the war "to make the world safe for democracy" is of a piece with it. Kindred in spirit though opposite in policy, was Wilson's neutralism expressed in the idea of a nation "too proud to fight." On the domestic front, Wilson recouped and extended the reforms of Rooseveltian progressivism. His idea of the New Freedom was imbued with a Calvinistic sense of righteousness coupled with a white Southern ethos that, on at least one occasion, caused him to dismiss Negro demands for fair employment practices as "insulting."[5] Nor could he abide dissent. Both in his insistence on American neutrality and in his prosecution of the war, he interpreted his policy in narrowly moralistic terms. In the latter event this left no latitude for solicitude toward conscientious objectors. The very dis-

---

[4] See Arthur S. Link, *Woodrow Wilson and the Progressive Era* (New York: Harper, 1954).

[5] See John Hope Franklin, *From Slavery to Freedom* (2nd ed.; New York: Knopf, 1967), p. 454. Richard Hofstadter points out that Theodore Roosevelt was a moralist, too, but that his were the "hairy-chested Darwinian virtues." See Hofstadter, *The Age of Reform* (New York: Knopf, 1955), p. 274n.

interestedness of his high sense of purpose wrecked the Progressive era in 1917 and assured the recoil of public opinion to isolationist "normalcy" afterward. The applied science of mechanized warfare using high explosives and poison gas wreaked havoc with the notion of science as benign *per se,* and Americans understandably recoiled from the brutal reality into which the Wilsonian idealism had led them.

Many of the reasons for both Wilson's success and failure, and with it for the failure of his era's naïve Social Gospel, may be found in his religious addresses—not because they are original or profound but because they mirror the beliefs of the average American citizen. Those included here date from 1909, before he entered political life, and from 1914–15, reflecting respectively the weight of office and of the overseas war. The differences between Wilson's simple bootstrap Christianity and Rauschenbusch's more complex optimism are self-evident, and they invite comparison. All the essential features of the Social Gospel are to be found here in strongly acculturated form—the power of example, the force of character and moral goodness, the call to follow Christ, the confidence in moral progress. These virtues are rhetorically splendiferous but actually very attenuated by way of the institutions and operative values through which the world was to be saved. It would have required a more penetrating, critical mind to ask whether, even at their best, the Wilson administration, the Young Men's Christian Association, or the local minister were adequate for the task. For Wilson it often seemed that not Christ but Christian America was the hope of the world. Too many of his countrymen were prepared to believe in Wilson's assertion, during the debate over the Versailles Treaty, that "America . . . is the only idealistic Nation in the world."[6] It accorded, too, with the YMCA's avowed aim of Christianizing the world in this generation, an aim which asked rather less of Americans' generosity.

In the following pages, Wilson refers neither to the Kingdom

---

[6] *The Public Papers of Woodrow Wilson* (New York: 1925–1927), vol. 6, p. 52.

of God nor to his New Democracy, but implicitly he equated the two, just as he confused his own moral scruples with the will of God, and the myth of America's innocence with its salvation. Wilson's easy optimism and misbelief in the inexhaustible and selfless generosity of Americans (because they were supposed to be "good Christians") are a far cry from the more tempered idealism of his Calvinist forebears. It is the Halfway Covenant diluted and stretched to national proportions, with the ranks of the elect enlarged to include every loyal American. The rigors of the New England theology have given way to a mere recital of the virtues of the Pilgrim heritage, now ascribed to every conventional right-thinking person.

Wilson never recovered from the collapse he suffered in 1919, after the refusal of the United States to join the League of Nations. By the time he died in 1924, the pacifist and isolationist reaction to the war had taken hold. The optimism that continued was a revision of his own—no less fatuous, perhaps, and retaining the typically American "bootstrap" emphases, but by the same token more individualistic and self-centered, less public-spirited in any broad sense of seeking to improve society or the world.

THE MINISTER AND THE COMMUNITY*

There are two ideals between which the Church, first and last, has oscillated in respect to the position that a minister ought to hold in the community. The one is the ideal which expects the minister to hold himself aloof from the ordinary transactions of life, and to devote himself exclusively, and I was about to say almost ostentatiously, to the things which are spiritual. This is the ideal which has led to asceticism, to practices of the Church which have absolutely shut the priesthood off from the life of the community, which have forced

---

* Address published as a leaflet. New York: The International Committee of Young Men's Christian Association, 1909.

upon them an unnatural way of living and an unnatural separation from the ordinary interests of the world.

Then there is the opposite idea—that the minister ought to
be part of everything in a community that makes for its betterment, its improvement, its amelioration, its reformation—that
he should take a deep interest in everything that affects the
life of the community and be at particular pains to live as
other men live, and not in any way show himself separate
from the world, not in any way, that, at any rate externally,
changes the current and method of his life. Certain men in our
own generation have taken the position that, though they
wish to preach the Gospel and influence men to come to Christ,
they will have a greater influence if they do not accept the
ordination of the Church, but remain laymen. It is their impression that a layman can preach straighter to the hearts of
laymen than ministers can. There is something of the idea
creeping in in various quarters, that the lay instrumentalities
find the straightest roads to the hearts of men, and that the
ministerial instrumentality is tainted a little by the professionalism which is in it; that the advice of the professional spiritual
adviser is less cogent than the advice of the amateur spiritual
adviser. This is the extreme form of this view.

Let us acknowledge at the outset that in our time we have
been trying to unfrock the ministerial profession, literally and
metaphorically. We are afraid of the frock, we are afraid of
the sign, we are afraid of the touch of professionalism. It is a
characteristic of our time that we wish to combine all things
without differentiation in one single thing that we call life, and
the consequence is that we do not know what we would be at.
The consequence is that no man sees distinctly enough the
particular road that he is trying to tread, the particular function which he is trying to perform in society. He says, "I must
be a man," by which he means an added general force in
society and not a specialized force in society; by which he
means that he must disperse his powers and not concentrate
them. And yet the difficulty of modern times is this very
dispersion of professional energy, this obliteration of the lines
that run and should run between one calling and another. The

soldier is proud of his uniform and of the straps over his arms and shoulders, the marks of his rank; and every man who counts for as much of direct force as the soldier counts for ought to be proud of the things that distinguish his calling. I trust that no man will go into the ministry with the hope that he can conceal himself in the crowd, so that no man may know that he is a minister. I hope that he may plan his life so that nobody may ever associate with him without knowing that he is a minister.

How are we going to do this? By resuming the costume, by resuming the ritual, by resuming the aloofness and separateness from the world? That would be better than nothing. It is true, whether we like the fact or not, that the Roman Catholic priesthood, when its members have really remembered their consecration and lived true to it, have made a deeper impression upon the communities they lived in than the Protestant clergy, because they were men whom to look upon was to recall the fact that they were commissioned out of the unseen, that they did not live as other men lived, that they did devote themselves to something separate and apart; that it was intended that when they came into a company of men, those men should be reminded that here was a commissioner who was not a commissioner of the world; and when these men have been true to that standard they have been incomparable forces in the world.

The Protestant minister has too much forgotten the ideals of this separate priesthood. What is it that the minister should try to do? It seems to me that the minister should try to remind his fellow-men in everything that he does and in everything that he says, that eternity is not future, but present; that there is in every transaction of life a line that connects it with eternity, and that our lives are but the visible aspect of the experience of our spirits upon the earth; that we are living here as spirits; that our whole conduct is to be influenced by things that are invisible, of which we must be constantly reminded lest our eyes should be gluttonously filled with the things that are visible; that we should be reminded that there lurks everywhere, not ungraciously and with forbidding mien, but graciously and with salvation on its countenance, the image and the memory of Christ, going a little journey through the earth to remind men of the fatherhood of God, of the brotherhood of men, of the journey that all spirits are taking to the land that is unseen and to which they are all to come.

It is very interesting to note how miscellaneous the Church of our day has become in its objects and endeavors. It is interesting to note how central it regards its kitchen in the basement, the bowling alley attached to the church, the billiard table where youngsters may amuse themselves, the gymnasium—the things that naturally associate themselves with what we call the institutional work of the Church. Did you ever ask yourself what an institution is? An institution is merely a way of doing some particular thing. Now, I am not now making any objection to entertainments, fairs, and amusements, but I do want to call your attention to the fact that the persons whom we lead to do these things are not often reminded of why it is that we ask them to do them there, at the church. I have been in some churches where, when these things were going on, the minute the minister came into the room, you somehow got the impression that you had been reminded of something. The walls of the room were no longer as solid as they were; you saw bigger spaces; the mind seemed to go back to dreams that had seemed vague before you at your mother's knee, and that gentle figure there seemed to say: "It is delightful that we should so disport ourselves, but we are spirits. We know each other only as we know each other spiritually, and only as these things bind us together in an eternal brotherhood is it worth while to be here." I have been at other such gatherings when the entrance of the minister did not suggest anything of the kind—when only another human being had come into the room—a human being who had no more suggestion of the eternal about him than the youngest person present, a man who did not carry in his mien and attitude and speech any message whatever, whose personality was not radiant with anything.

Now, it does not take a great man to radiate a pure spirit, because the most modest gifts can be associated with very deep and real religious experiences, and the spirit may speak when the tongue is tied. I have myself witnessed the history of a pastor whose preaching was impossible but whose life, divine; and in twenty years there was built up a power out of that church, out of what I might call that speechless church, which did not radiate from the most eloquent pulpit in the other churches of the place; where eloquence seemed empty alongside of radiant godliness; where the spirit seemed to have a thousand tongues and the mind only one; where the doctrine was more expounded by the daily life of the one pastor than by all the expositions of the others. If you can combine the two, if your life can display the secret and otherwise not readily understood principles of the Gospel and your sermons expound the life exemplified, then you have something irresistible for the regeneration and revolution of a community; but as compared with each other, the reminder of the life is worth a thousand times the suggestion of the pulpit.

Is not that the supreme lesson of the life of Christ? I have sometimes thought that we would be unspeakably enriched if we had known some of the incidents of the days that Christ lived on the earth which were quite distinct and separate from His teaching—the ordinary, now unregarded incidents of His day. For I am sure that there we should have had an example infinitely fruitful for our own guidance, and should have been conscious that in everything that He said, every little thing that He did, there was a divine suggestion, a suggestion of divinity which was not a rebuke to humanity, but which heartened and revealed all that was best of itself, seemed like a sweet air out of some unattained country, like a light coming from some source that other men could not uncover; and that it must have been infinitely gracious to have Him lodge in the house. There must have seemed an atmosphere lingering there which made it impossible to forget that time was part of eternity.

Now the world is not going to be saved except the minister model himself on Christ. The world is not going to be evangelized unless the minister distinguish himself from the community. The Church is not going to recover its authority

among men until its ministers display their credentials in their
lives, by showing that the thought that is in them is always the
thought that makes for salvation; that they will not teach the
things that are impure; that they will not play with the things
that are dangerous; that they are not reformers, but ministers
of Christ. Did you ever notice that Christ was not a reformer?
Not that He would have frowned upon a reformer, but He was
not a reformer. He was not organizing men to do what is necessary to be done in order to reconstruct and better human life.
He was supplying the whole motive force of that and everything else. It is just as much of a reform to go into a household
where there is not the sweetness of Christian feeling and introduce it there by contagion, as it is to sit on a platform at a
public meeting intended to set forward some missionary enterprise.

I remember—for I have had the unspeakable joy of having
been born and bred in a minister's family—I remember one
occasion which made a very profound impression upon me
when I was a lad, in a company of gentlemen where my father
was present, and where I happened to be, unobserved. One of
the gentlemen in a moment of excitement uttered an oath, and
then, his eye resting upon my father, he said with evident
sincerity: "Dr. Wilson, I beg your pardon; I did not notice that
you were present." "Oh," said my father, "you mistake, sir; it is
not to me you owe the apology." I doubt if any other one remark ever entered quite so straight to the quick in me as that
did, the consciousness that my father, taken by surprise, was at
once so conscious that he was not the person offended, that he
should so naturally call the attention of the man who had
uttered the oath to what was the simple fact; that the offense
was not to him but to his Master. It was exactly as if a disrespectful word had been spoken of the President of the
United States in the presence of an ambassador of the United
States, the apology would be due not to him but to his Government. And if ministers could always so contrive it that in their
presence the presence of God was manifest, the whole problem
of the ministry would be solved and evangelization would be
irresistible.

There is only one way by which fire is spread and that is by contact. The thing to be ignited must touch the fire, and unless the fire burns in you, nobody will be lighted by contact with you. No amount of studious knowledge of the subject-matter or of the methods of your profession will do you the least degree of service unless it is on fire, and has communicated its fire to your very heart and substance.

Let every man, therefore, who goes into the ministry set himself apart; let every man who goes into the ministry go into it with a determination that nobody shall fail to know that he is a minister of the Gospel. It can be graciously done, without austerity, without rebuke, without offensiveness; it can be done by the simple method merely of being conscious yourself that you are the minister of God. For what a man is conscious of believing, he communicates to those who consort with him; what a man is known to stand for, he transmits to those who are in his presence though he speak never a word. And this consciousness of his will be the consciousness of every company he moves in, a sweet consciousness that will make his presence very gracious and everything he does acceptable to those with whom he consorts—not shutting him off from the ordinary relationships of life, but irradiating those relationships, making them the means of spreading the consciousness he has of what he is.

When I hear some of the things which young men say to me by way of putting the arguments to themselves for going into the ministry, I think that they are talking of another profession. Their motive is to do something, when it should be to be something. You do not have to *be* anything in particular to be a lawyer. I have been a lawyer and I know. You do not have to *be* anything in particular, except a kind-hearted man, perhaps, to be a physician; you do not have to *be* anything, nor to undergo any strong spiritual change in order to be a merchant. The only profession which consists in *being* something is the ministry of our Lord and Saviour—and it does not consist of anything else. It is manifested in other things, but it does not consist of anything else. And that conception of the minister which rubs all the marks of it off and mixes him in the crowd so that you cannot pick him out, is a process of eliminating the ministry itself.

Now, it is all very easy to say these things; it is impossible to do these things except by the influence and power of the Holy Spirit. If I could do the various things the right method of doing which I understand, I should be a most useful person. I know that we all should in some measure be ministers of Christ, and a man does not like to say the things that I have said and remember how little he has used his own profession to express that ministry. But, because we are imperfect, is it not the more necessary to know what the ideal is, to see it clearly, to see it steadily enough not to lose sight of it? If you lost the vision where would you go? If you did not know what you would be at, how would you ever find the way again? If you did not know what it was that you were embarking in, how could you make sure that you had found the right course of life? And the beauty of the Gospel is that it is a Gospel which leaves us, not the barren hope that in our own strength we can be useful, but the splendid, fruitful hope that there is One who if we but reply upon Him can inform us with these things and make our spirits to be the true spirits of God.

MILITANT CHRISTIANITY*

I feel almost as if I were a truant, being away from Washington to-day, but I thought that perhaps if I were absent the Congress would have the more leisure to adjourn. I do not ordinarily open my office at Washington on Saturday. Being a schoolmaster, I am accustomed to a Saturday holiday, and I thought I could not better spend a holiday than by showing at least something of the true direction of my affections; for by long association with the men who have worked for this organization I can say that it has enlisted my deep affection.

---

* Address to a YMCA celebration in Pittsburgh, October 24, 1914. From the White House files.

I am interested in it for various reasons. First of all, because it is an association of young men. I have had a good deal to do with young men in my time, and I have formed an impression of them which I believe to be contrary to the general impression. They are generally thought to be arch radicals. As a matter of fact, they are the most conservative people I have ever dealt with. Go to a college community and try to change the least custom of that little world and find out the conservatives will rush at you. Moreover, young men are embarrassed by having inherited their fathers' opinions. I have often said that the use of a university is to make young gentlemen as unlike their fathers as possible. I do not say that with the least disrespect for the fathers; but every man who is old enough to have a son in college is old enough to have become very seriously immersed in some particular business and is almost certain to have caught the point of view of that particular business. And it is very useful to his son to be taken out of that narrow circle, conducted to some high place where he may see the general map of the world and of the interests of mankind, and there be shown how big the world is and how much of it his father may happen to have forgotten. It would be worth while for men, middle-aged and old, to detach themselves more frequently from the things that command their daily attention and to think of the sweeping tides of humanity.

Therefore I am interested in this association, because it is intended to bring young men together before any crust has formed over them, before they have been hardened to any particular occupation, before they have caught an inveterate point of view; while they still have a searchlight that they can swing and see what it reveals of all the circumstances of the hidden world.

I am the more interested in it because it is an association of young men who are Christians. I wonder if we attach sufficient importance to Christianity as a mere instrumentality in the life of mankind. For one, I am not fond of thinking of Christianity as the means of saving *individual* souls. I have always been very impatient of processes and institutions which said that their purpose was to put every man in the way of developing his character. My advice is: Do not think about your character. If you will think about what you ought to do for other people, your character will take care of itself. Character is a by-product, and any man who devotes himself to its cultivation in his own case will become a selfish prig. The only way your powers can become great is by exerting them outside the circle of your own narrow, special, selfish interests. And that is the reason of Christianity. Christ came into the world to save others, not to save himself; and no man is a true Christian who does not think constantly of how he can lift his brother, how he can assist his friend, how he can enlighten mankind, how he can make virtue the rule of conduct in the circle in which he lives. An association merely of young men might be an association that had its energies put forth in every direction, but an association of Christian young men is an association meant to put its shoulders under the world and lift it, so that other men may feel that they have companions in bearing the weight and heat of the day; that other men may know that there are those who care for them, who would go into places of difficulty and danger to rescue them, who regard themselves as their brother's keeper.

And, then, I am glad that it is an association. Every word of its title means an element of strength. Young men are strong. Christian young men are the strongest kind of young men, and when they associate themselves together they have the incomparable strength of organization. The Young Men's Christian Association once excited, perhaps it is not too much to say, the hostility of the organized churches of the Christian world, because the movement looked as if it were so nonsectarian, as if it were so outside the ecclesiastical field, that perhaps it was an effort to draw young men away from the churches and to substitute this organization for the great bodies of Christian people who joined themselves in the Christian denominations. But after a while it appeared that it was a great instrumentality that belonged to all the churches; that it was a common instrument for sending the light of Christianity out into the world in its most practical form, drawing young men who were strangers into places where they could have companionship that stimulated them and suggestions that kept them straight and occupations that amused them without vicious practice; and then, by surrounding themselves with an atmosphere of purity and of simplicity of life, catch something of a glimpse of the great ideal which Christ lifted when He was elevated upon the cross.

I remember hearing a very wise man say once, a man grown old in the service of a great church, that he had never taught his son religion dogmatically at any time; that he and the boy's mother had agreed that if the atmosphere of that home did not make a Christian of the boy, nothing that they could say would make a Christian of him. They knew that Christianity was catching, and if they did not have it, it would not be communicated. If they did have it, it would penetrate while the boy slept, almost; while he was unconscious of the sweet influences that were about him, while he reckoned nothing of instruction, but merely breathed into his lungs the wholesome air of a Christian home. That is the principle of the Young Men's Christian Association—to make a place where the atmosphere makes great ideals contagious. That is the reason that I said, though I had forgotten that I said it, what is quoted on the outer page of the program—that you can test a modern community by the degree of its interest in its Young Men's Christian Association. You can test whether it knows what roads it wants to travel or not. You can test whether it is deeply interested in the spiritual and essential prosperity of its rising generation. I know of no test that can be more conclusively put to a community than that.

I want to suggest to the young men of this association that it is the duty of young men not only to combine for the things that are good, but to combine in a militant spirit. There is a fine passage in one of Milton's prose writings which I am sorry to say I can not quote, but the meaning of which I can give you, and it is worth hearing. He says that he has no patience with a cloistered virtue that does not go out and seek its adversary. Ah, how tired I am of the men who are merely on the defensive, who hedge themselves in, who perhaps enlarge the hedge enough to include their little family circle and ward off all the evil influences of the world from that loved and hallowed group. How tired I am of the men whose virtue is selfish because it is merely self-protective! And how much I wish that men by the hundred thousand might volunteer to go out and seek an adversary and subdue him!

I have had the fortune to take part in affairs of a considerable variety of sorts, and I have to hate as few persons as possible, but there is an exquisite combination of contempt and hate that I have for a particular kind of person, and that is the moral coward. I wish we could give all our cowards a perpetual vacation. Let them go off and sit on the side lines and see us play the game; and put them off the field if they interfere with the game. They do nothing but harm, and they do it by that most subtle and fatal thing of all, that of taking the momentum and the spirit and the forward dash out of things. A man who is virtuous and a coward has no marketable virtue about him. The virtue, I repeat, which is merely self-defensive is not serviceable even, I suspect, to himself. For how a man can swallow and not taste bad when he is a coward and thinking only of himself I can not imagine.

Be militant! Be an organization that is going to do things! If you can find older men who will give you countenance and acceptable leadership, follow them; but if you can not, organize separately and dispense with them. There are only two sorts of men worth associating with when something is to be done. Those are young men and men who never grow old. Now, if you find men who have grown old, about whom the crust has hardened, whose hinges are stiff, whose minds always have their eye over the shoulder thinking of things as they *were* done, do not have anything to do with them. It would not be Christian to exclude them from your organization, but merely use them to pad the roll. If you can find older men who will lead you acceptably and keep you in countenance, I am bound as an older man to advise you to follow them. But suit yourselves. Do not follow people that stand still. Just remind them that this is not a statical proposition; it is a movement, and if they can not get a move on them they are not serviceable.

Life, gentlemen—the life of society, the life of the world—has constantly to be fed from the bottom. It has to be fed by those great sources of strength which are constantly rising in new generations. Red blood has to be pumped into it. New fiber has to be supplied. That is the reason I have always said that I believe in popular institutions. If you can guess beforehand whom your rulers are going to be, you can guess with a very great certainty that most of them will not be fit to rule. The beauty of popular institutions is that you do not know where the man is going to come from, and you do not care so he is the right man. You do not know whether he will come from the avenue or from the alley. You do not know whether he will come from the city or the farm. You do not know whether you will ever have heard that name before or not. Therefore you do not limit at any point your supply of new strength. You do not say it has got to come through the blood of a particular family or through the processes of a particular training, or by any thing except the native impulse and genius of the man himself. The humblest hovel, therefore, may produce you your greatest man. A very humble hovel did produce you one of your greatest men. That is the process of life, this constant surging up of the new strength of unnamed, unrecognized, uncatalogued men who are just getting into the running, who are just coming up from the masses of the unrecognized multitude. You do not know when you will see above the level masses of the crowd some great stature lifted head and shoulders above the rest, shouldering its way, not violently but gently, to the front and saying, "Here am I; follow me." And his voice will be your voice, his thought will be your thought, and you will follow him as if you were following the best things in yourselves.

When I think of an association of Christian young men I wonder that it has not already turned the world upside down. I wonder, not that it has done so much, for it has done a great deal, but that it has done so little; and I can only conjecture that it does not realize its own strength. I can only imagine that it has not yet got its pace. I wish I could believe, and I do believe, that at 70 it is just reaching its majority, and that from this time on a dream greater even than George Williams ever dreamed will be realized in the great accumulating momentum of Christian men throughout the world. For, gentlemen, this is an age in which the principles of men who utter public opinion dominate the world. It makes no difference what is done for the time being. After the struggle is over the jury will sit, and nobody can corrupt that jury.

At one time I tried to write history. I did not know enough to write it, but I knew from experience how hard it was to find an historian out, and I trusted I would not be found out. I used to have this comfortable thought as I saw men struggling in the public arena. I used to think to myself, "This is all very well and interesting. You probably assess yourself in such and such a way. Those who are your partisans assess you thus and so. Those who are your opponents urge a different verdict. But it does not make very much difference, because after you are dead and gone some quiet historian will sit in a secluded room and tell mankind for the rest of time just what to think about you, and his verdict, not the verdict of your partisans and not the verdict of your opponents, will be the verdict of posterity." I say that I used to say that to myself. It very largely was not so. And yet it was true in this sense: If the historian really speaks the judgment of the succeeding generation, then he really speaks the judgment also of the generations that succeed it, and his assessment, made without the passion of the time, made without partisan feeling in the matter—in other circumstances, when the air is cool—is the judgment of mankind upon your actions.

Now, is it not very important that we who shall constitute a portion of the jury should get our best judgments to work and base them upon Christian forbearance and Christian principles, upon the idea that it is impossible by sophistication to establish that a thing that is wrong is right? And yet, while we are going to judge with the absolute standard of righteousness, we are going to judge with Christian feeling, being men of a like sort ourselves, suffering the same temptations, having the same weaknesses, knowing the same passions; and while we do not condemn, we are going to seek to say and to live the truth. What I am hoping for is that these 70 years have just been a running start, and that now there will be a great rush of Christian principle upon the strongholds of evil and of wrong in the world. Those strongholds are not as strong as they look. Almost every vicious man is afraid of society, and if you once open the door where he is, he will run. All you have to do is to fight, not with cannon but with light.

May I illustrate it in this way? The Government of the United States has just succeeded in concluding a large number of treaties with the leading nations of the world, the sum and substance of which is this, that whenever any trouble arises the light shall shine on it for a year before anything is done; and my prediction is that after the light has shone on it for a year it will not be necessary to do anything; that after we know what happened, then we will know who was right and who was wrong. I believe that light is the greatest sanitary influence in the world. That, I suppose, is scientific commonplace, because if you want to make a place wholesome the best instrument you can use is the sun; to let his rays in, let him search out all the miasma that may lurk there. So with moral light: It is the most wholesome and rectifying, as well as the most revealing thing in the world, provided it be genuine moral light; not the light of inquisitiveness, not the light of the man who likes to turn up ugly things, not the light of the man who disturbs what is corrupt for the mere sake of the sensation that he creates by disturbing it, but the moral light, the light of the man who discloses it in order that all the sweet influences of the world may go in and make it better.

That, in my judgment, is what the Young Men's Christian Association can do. It can point out to its members the things that are wrong. It can guide the feet of those who are going astray; and when its members have realized the power of the Christian principle, then they will not be men if they do not unite to see that the rest of the world experiences the same emancipation and reaches the same happiness of release.

I believe in the Young Men's Christian Association because I believe in the progress of moral ideas in the world; and I do not know that I am sure of anything else. When you are after something and have formulated it and have done the very best thing you know how to do you have got to be sure for the time being that that is the thing to do. But you are a fool if in the back of your head you do not know it is possible that you are mistaken. All that you can claim is that that is the thing as you see it now and that you can not stand still; that you must push forward the things that are right. It may turn out that you made mistakes, but what you do know is your direction, and you are sure you are moving in that way. I was once a college reformer, until discouraged, and I remember a classmate of mine saying, "Why, man, can't you let anything alone?" I said, "I let everything alone that you can show me is not itself moving in the wrong direction, but I am not going to let those things alone that I see are going downhill"; and I borrowed this illustration from an ingenious writer. He says, "If you have a post that is painted white and want to keep it white, you can not let it alone; and if anybody says to you, 'Why don't you let that post alone?' you will say, 'Because I want it to stay white, and therefore I have got to paint it at least every second year.'" There isn't anything in this world that will not change if you absolutely let it alone, and therefore you have constantly to be attending to it to see that it is being taken care of in the right way and that, if it is part of the motive force of the world, it is moving in the right direction.

That means that eternal vigilance is the price, not only of liberty, but of a great many other things. It is the price of everything that is good. It is the price of one's own soul. It is the price of the souls of the people you love; and when it comes down to the final reckoning you have a standard that is immutable. What shall a man give in exchange for his own soul? Will he sell that? Will he consent to see another man sell his soul? Will he consent to see the conditions of his community such that men's souls are debauched and trodden underfoot in the mire? What shall he give in exchange for his own soul, or any other man's soul? And since the world, the world of affairs, the world of society, is nothing less and nothing more than all of us put together, it is a great enterprise for the salvation of the soul in this world as well as in the next. There is a text in Scripture that has always interested me profoundly. It says godliness is profitable in this life as well as in the life that is to come; and if you do not start it in this life, it will not reach the life that is to come. Your measurements, your directions, your whole momentum, have to be established before you reach the next world. This world is intended as the place in which we shall show that we know how to grow in the stature of manliness and of righteousness.

I have come here to bid Godspeed to the great work of the Young Men's Christian Association. I love to think of the gathering force of such things as this in the generations to come. If a man had to measure the accomplishments of society, the progress of reform, the speed of the world's betterment, by the few little things that happened in his own life, by the trifling things that he can contribute to accomplish, he would indeed feel that the cost was much greater than the result. But no man can look at the past of the history of this world without seeing a vision of the future of the history of this world; and when you think of the accumulated moral forces that have made one age better than another age in the progress of mankind, then you can open your eyes to the vision. You can see that age by age, though with a blind struggle in the dust of the road, though often mistaking the path and losing its way in the mire, mankind is yet—sometimes with bloody hands and battered knees—nevertheless struggling step after step up the slow stages to the day when he shall live in the full light which shines upon the uplands, where all the light that illumines mankind shines direct from the face of God.

A NEW KIND OF CHURCH LIFE*

I feel an unaffected diffidence in coming into this conference without having participated in its deliberations. I wish that I might have been here to learn the many things that I am sure

---

* An address to the Federal Council of Churches, Columbus, Ohio, December 10, 1915. Published in the Congressional Record, 64th Congress, 1st Session, vol. 53, pp. 15751–15753.

have been learned by those who have attended these conferences. I feel confident that nothing that I say about the rural
church will be new to you. I am here simply because I wished
to show my profound interest in the subject which you have
been considering and not because I thought I had anything
original to contribute to your thought.

I think that as we have witnessed the processes of our civilization in recent years we have more and more realized how
our cities were tending to draw the vitality from the country-
side, how much less our life centered upon country districts
and how much more upon crowded cities. There was a time
when America was characteristically rural, when practically all
her strength was drawn from quiet countrysides, where life
ran upon established lines and where men and women and
children were familiar with each other in a long-established
neighborliness; but our rural districts are not now just what
they used to be and have partaken in recent years of something of the fluidity that has characterized our general life. So
that we have again and again been called upon from one point
of view or another to study the revitalization of the country-
side. There was a time, no longer ago than the youth of my
own father, for example, when pastors found some of their
most vital work in the country churches. I remember my dear
father used to ride from church to church in a thickly popu-
lated country region and minister to several churches with a
sense of ministering to the most vital interests of the part of
the country in which he lived.

After all, the most vitalizing thing in the world is Christianity. The world has advanced, advanced in what we regard
as real civilization, not by material but by spiritual means, and
one nation is distinguished from another nation by its ideals,
not by its possessions; by what it believes in, by what it lives
by, by what it intends, by the visions which its young men
dream and the achievements which its mature men attempt.
So that each nation when it writes its poetry or writes its mem-
oirs, exalts the character of its people and of those who spring
from the loins of its people.

There is an old antithesis upon which I do not care to dwell, because there is not a great deal to be got from dwelling on it, between life and doctrine. Here is no real antithesis. A man lives as he believes he ought to live or as he believes that it is to his advantage to live. He lives upon a doctrine, upon a principle, upon an idea—sometimes a very low principle, sometimes a very exalted principle. I used to be told when I was a youth that some of the old casuists reduced all sin to egotism, and I have thought as I watched the career of some individuals that the analysis had some vital point to it. An egotist is a man who has got the whole perspective of life wrong. He conceives of himself as the center of affairs. He conceives of himself as the center of affairs even as affects the providence of God. He has not related himself to the great forces which dominate him with the rest of us, and therefore has set up a little kingdom all his own in which he reigns with unhonored sovereignty. So there are some men who set up the principle of individual advantage as the principle, the doctrine, of their life, and live by that, and live generally a life that leads to all sorts of shipwreck. Whatever our doctrine be, our life is conformed to it.

But what I want to speak of is not the contrast between doctrine and life, but the translation of doctrine into life. After all, Christianity is not important to us because it is a valid body of conceptions regarding God and man, but because it is a vital body of conceptions which can be translated into life for us, life in this world and a life still greater in the next. Except as Christianity changes and inspires life, it has failed of its mission. That is what Christ came into the world for, to save our spirits, and you cannot have your spirit altered without having your life altered.

When I think of the rural church, therefore, I wonder how far the rural church is vitalizing the lives of the communities in which it exists. We have had a great deal to say recently, and it has been very profitably said, about the school as a social center, by which is meant the schoolhouse as a social center; about making the house which in the daytime is used for the children a place which their parents may use in the evenings and at other disengaged times for the meetings of the community, where they will be privileged to come together and talk about anything that is of community interest and talk about it with the utmost freedom. Some people have been opposed to it because there are some things that they do not want talked about. Some boards of education have been opposed to it because they realized that it might not be well for the board of education to be talked about. Talk is a very dangerous thing, community comparisons of views are a very dangerous thing, to the men who are doing wrong, but I, for my part, believe in making the schoolhouse the social center, the place that the community can use for any kind of coordinating that it wants to do in its life. But I believe that where the school is inadequate, and even where it is adequate, the most vital social center should be the church itself, and that not by way of organizing the church for social service—that is not my topic to-night; that is another topic—but of making the community realize that that congregation, and particularly that pastor, is interested in everything that is important for that community, and that the members of that church are ready to co-operate and the pastor ready to lend his time and his energy to the kind of organization which is necessary outside the church, as well as within it, for the benefit of the community.

It seems to me that the country pastor has an unparalleled opportunity to be a country leader, to make everybody realize that he, as the representative of Christ, believes himself related to everything human, to everything human that has as its object the uplift and instruction and inspiration of the community or the betterment of any of its conditions; and that if any pastor will make it felt throughout the community that that is his spirit, that his interest, and that he is ready to draw his elders or his deacons or his vestrymen along with him as active agents in the betterment of the community, the church will begin to have a dominating influence in the community such as it has lost for the time being and we must find it means to regain.

For example, in a farming community one of the things that the Department of Agriculture at Washington is trying to do is to show the farmers of the country the easiest and best methods of co-operation with regard to marketing their crops —helping in their effort to learn how to handle their crops in a co-operative fashion so that they can get the best service from the railroads; to learn how to find the prevailing market prices in the accessible market so as to know where it will be best and most profitable to send their farm products; and to draw them together into co-operative association with these objects in view. The church ought to lend its hand in that. The pastor ought to say, "If you want somebody to look after this for you, I will give part of my time and I will find other men in my congregation who will help you in the work and help you without charging you anything for it. We want you to realize that this church is interested in the lives of the people of this community and that it will lend itself to any legitimate project that advances the life and interest of this community."

Let the rural church find that road and then discover, as it will discover, that men begin to swing their thoughts to those deeper meanings of the church in which we wish to draw their attention; that this is a spiritual brotherhood; that the pastor and his associates are interested in them because they are interested in the souls of men and the prosperity of men as it lies deep in their hearts. There are a great many ways by which leadership can be exercised. The church has too much depended upon individual example. "So let your light shine before men" has been interpreted to mean, "Put your individual self on a candlestick and shine." Now, the trouble is that some people cannot find a candlestick, but the greater trouble is that they are very poor candles and the light is very dim. It does not dispel much of the darkness for me individually to sit on top of a candlestick, but if I can lend such little contribution of spiritual force as I have to my neighbor and to my comrade and to my friend, and we can draw a circle of friends together and unite our spiritual forces, then we have something more than example: we have co-operation.

Co-operation, ladies and gentlemen, is the vital principle of social life; not organization merely. I think I know something about organization. I can make an organization, but it is one thing to have an organization and another thing to fill it with life. And then it is a very important matter what sort of life you fill it with. If the object of the organization is what the object of some business organizations is and the object of many political organizations is, to absorb the life of the community and run the community for its own benefit, then there is nothing beneficial in it. But if the object of the organization is to afford a mechanism by which the whole community can co-operatively use its life, then there is a great deal in it. An organization without the spirit of co-operation is dead and may be dangerous. The vital principle is co-operation, and organization is secondary. I have been a member of one or two churches that were admirably organized and they were accomplishing nothing. You know some people dearly love organization. They dearly love to sit in a chair and preside. They pride themselves upon their knowledge of parliamentary practice. They love to concoct and write minutes. They love to appoint committees. They boast of the number of committees that their organization has and they like the power and the social influence of distributing their friends among the committees, and then when the committees are formed there is nothing to commit to them.

This is a Nation which loves to go through the motions of public meeting whether there is anything particularly important to consider or not. It is an interesting thing to me how the American is born knowing how to conduct a public meeting. I remember that when I was a lad I belonged to an organization which at that time seemed to me very important, which was known as the Lightfoot Baseball Club. Our clubroom was a corner, an unoccupied corner, of the loft of my father's barn, the part that the hay had not encroached upon, and I distinctly remember how we used to conduct orderly meetings of the club in that corner of the loft. I had never seen a public meeting and I do not believe any of the other lads with whom I was associated had ever seen a public meeting, but we somehow knew how to conduct one. We knew how to make motions and second them; we knew that a motion could not have more than two amendments offered at the same time; and we knew the order in which the amendments had to be put, the second amendment before the first. How we knew it I do not know. We were born that way, I suppose. But nothing very important happened at those meetings, and I have been present at some church organization meetings at which nothing more important happened than happened with the Lightfoot Baseball Club. I remember distinctly that my delight and interest was in the meetings, not in what they were for; just the sense of belonging to an organization and doing something with the organization, it did not very much matter what. Some churches are organized that way. They are exceedingly active about nothing. Now, why not lend that organizing instinct, that acting instinct, to the real things that are happening in the community, whether they have anything to do with the church or not?

We look back to the time of the early settlements in this country and remember that in old New England the church and the school were the two sources of the life of the community. Everything centered in them. Everything emanated from them. The school fed the church and the church ran the community. It sometimes did not run it very liberally, and I for my part would not wish to see any church run any community, but I do wish to see every church assist the community in which it is established to run itself, to show that the spirit of Christianity is the spirit of assistance, of counsel, of vitalization, of intense interest in everything that affects the lives of men and women and children. So that I am hoping that the outcome of these conferences, of all that we say and do about this very important matter, may be to remind the church that it is put into this world not only to serve the individual soul but to serve society also. And it has got to go to work on society with a greater sense of the exigency of the thing than in the case of the individual, because you have got to save society in this world, not in the next. I hope that our society is not going to exist in the next. It needs amendment in several particulars, I venture to say, and I hope that the society in the next world will be amended in those particulars—I will not mention them. But we have nothing to do with society in the next world. We may have something to do with the individual soul in the next world by getting it started straight for the next world, but we have got nothing to do with the organization of society in the next world. We have got to save society, so far as it is saved by the instrumentality of Christianity in this world. It is a job, therefore, that you have got to undertake immediately and work at all the time, and it is the business of the church.

Legislation can not save society. Legislation can not even rectify society. The law that will work is merely the summing up in legislative form of the moral judgment that the community has already reached. Law records how far society has got, and there have got to be instrumentalities preceeding the law that get society up to that point where it will be ready to record. Try the experiment. Enact a law that is the moral judgment of a very small minority of the community, and it will not work. Most people will not understand it, and if they do understand they will resent it, and whether they understand it and resent it or not they will not obey it. Law is a record of achievement. It is not a process of regeneration. Our wills have to be regenerated, and our purposes rectified before we are in a position to enact laws that record those moral achievements. And that is the business, primarily, it seems to me, of the Christian.

There are a great many arguments about Christianity. There are a great many things which we spiritually assert which we can not prove in the ordinary, scientific sense of the word "prove"; but there are some things which we can show. The proof of Christianity is written in the biography of the saints, and by the saints I do not mean the technical saints, those whom the church or the world has picked out to label "saints," for they are not very numerous, but the people whose lives, whose individual lives, have been transformed by Christianity. It is the only force in the world that I have ever heard of that does actually transform the life, and the proof of that transformation is to be found all over the Christian world and is multiplied and repeated as Christianity gains fresh territory in the heathen world. Men begin suddenly to erect great spiritual standards over the little personal standards which they theretofore professed and will walk smiling to the stake in order that their souls may be true to themselves. There is nothing else that does that. There is something that is analogous to it, and that is patriotism. Men will go into the fire of battle and freely give their lives for something greater than themselves, their duty to their country; and there is a pretty fine analogy between patriotism and Christianity. It is the devotion of the spirit to something greater and nobler than itself. These are the transforming influences. All the transforming influences in the world are unselfish. There is not a single selfish force in the world that is not untouched with sinister power, and the church is the only embodiment of the things that are entirely unselfish, the principles of self-sacrifice and devotion. Surely this is the instrumentality by which rural communities may be transformed and led to the things that are great; and surely there is nothing in the rural community in which the rural church ought not to be the leader and of which it ought not to be the vital actual center.

That is the simple message that I came to utter tonight, and, as I began saying, I dare say it is no message; I dare say it has been repeatedly said in this conference; I merely wanted to add my testimony to the validity and power of that conception. Because, ladies and gentlemen, we are in the world to do something more than look after ourselves.

The reason that I am proud to be an American is because America was given birth to by such conceptions as these; that its object in the world, its only reason for existence as a Government, was to show men the paths of liberty and of mutual serviceability, to lift the common man out of the paths, out of the sloughs of discouragement and even despair; set his feet upon firm ground; tell him, "Here is the high road upon which you are as much entitled to walk as we are, and, we will see that there is a free field and no favor, and that as your moral qualities are and your physical powers so will your success be. We will not let any man make you afraid, and we will not let any man do you an injustice."

Those are the ideals of America. We have not always lived up to them. No community has always lived up to them, but we are dignified by the fact that those are the things we live for and sail by; America is great in the world, not as she is a successful Government merely, but as she is the successful embodiment of a great ideal of unselfish citizenship. That is what makes the world feel America draw it like a lodestone. That is the reason why the ships that cross the sea have so many hopeful eyes lifted from their humbler quarters toward the shores of the new world. That is the reason why men, after they have been for a little while in America and go back for a visit to the old country, have a new light in their faces—the light that has kindled there in the country where they have seen some of their objects fulfilled. That is the light that shines from America. God grant that it may always shine and that in many a humble hearth, in quiet country churches, the flames may be lighted by which this great light is kept alive.

7

HARRY EMERSON FOSDICK

Biblical Modernist

Harry Emerson Fosdick (1878–1969) was for two or three decades one of America's most popular preachers and the author of several widely read books for the layman, such as *On Being a Real Person* (1943). His popularity, however, rested on something more solid than public demand or pulpit manners, and his intellectual eminence as a proponent of theological modernism secures his place in the history of American Protestantism.

Fosdick was born in Buffalo, New York, the son and grandson of teachers. His grandfather, an Episcopalian, had settled in Western New York during pioneer days and became a Baptist, a strong advocate of temperance, and a staunch opponent of slavery who maintained a station on the Underground Railroad, helping fugitive blacks escape to Canada in pre-Civil War times.

In his senior year at Colgate College Harry Emerson Fosdick decided to train for the ministry. After receiving his B. A. in 1900, he enrolled at Colgate Divinity School and found congenial William Newton Clarke's emphasis on the vitality of religious experience. The following year he transferred to Union Theological Seminary, plunging into slum mission work and other activities that overtaxed his resources and precipitated a severe nervous breakdown, from which he emerged with a strong conviction of the reality of God and the effectiveness of prayer. Taking his B. D. in 1904, he served as pastor of First Baptist Church in Montclair, New Jersey, commuting to New York for the next decade. He first studied for his M. A. at Columbia University (1908) and then taught practical theology at Union Seminary, becoming Jessup Professor in 1915 and adjunct professor in 1934. He served overseas with the YMCA during World War I and as a result became a lifelong pacifist. This decision harmonized with his other interests and formed part of a larger bond with two men whose writings were especially influential, Rauschenbusch and Rufus Jones.

Never a strong denominationalist, Fosdick combined his seminary duties with the pastorate of First Presbyterian Church, New York City, from 1919 until 1925, when fundamentalists forced his resignation. In a retrospect of fifty years, his sermons preached there seem models of moderation, but in these days fearful conservatives were accusing the Federal Council of Churches of harboring "radical and bolshevik elements."[1] It was the Scopes trial in Dayton, Tennessee, which brought the matter to a head. The trial took place in July 1925, some months after Tennessee adopted a law prohibiting the teaching of evolutionary theories that conflicted with a literal interpretation of Genesis. In the trial, the state was represented by William Jennings Bryan, an ardent fundamentalist, and in the months leading up to it the issues were hotly contested, with Fosdick rising to the occasion and assailing Bryan's "wild anachronisms" as doing "gross injustice to the Bible."[2] One result of Fosdick's ouster was that a number of liberal-minded Baptists, led by multimillionaire John D. Rockefeller Jr., undertook to build and endow the maintenance of the interdenominational Riverside Church. The imposing edifice was completed in 1931; but Fosdick first served as minister of its predecessor, the Park Avenue Baptist Church, from 1926. In 1946 he retired to emeritus status, and he also retired from Union Seminary.

Orthodoxy was never a live option for Fosdick; the choice that confronted him from his youth onward was between

---

[1] From a statement published by the Employers' Association of Pittsburgh, quoted in Fosdick's sermon, "Progressive Christianity," May 8, 1921. The sermon appears in a pamphlet by Harry Emerson Fosdick and Sherwood Eddy, *Science and Religion: Evolution and the Bible* (New York: George H. Doran, 1925), p. 15.

[2] "Evolution and Mr. Bryan," *The New York Times*, March 12, 1925; in *ibid*, pp. 28, 30.

liberal Christian faith and no faith at all. His views were not strikingly different from those of his teacher and senior colleague at Union, William Adams Brown, but he presented him with fresh lucidity and with a cogency designed to meet the fundamentalist challenge. *Christianity and Progress* (1922) originated as the Cole Lectures at Vanderbilt University. In it, as in *The Modern Use of the Bible* (1924) and subsequent books, Fosdick set out to discern man's basic "abiding experiences" among the "changing categories" or thought forms of the Bible. Like Rauschenbusch, Fosdick maintained a serious awareness of the realities of human nature, including its sinfulness. He accepted evolution unequivocally as a scientific fact of life and rejected supernaturalism in favor of a biblical theism predicated on the infinite value of personality. In its main points, Fosdick's theology stands squarely in the liberal mainstream, finding no discontinuity between the divine and the human. Personality is dynamic, embracing conflicting drives and impulses. Man's central thrust is toward the good, toward moral perfection. This spiritual tendency is hindered by man's natural inclinations. The task of religion is to supply ideals and examples to motivate man to realize his best potentialities, which are limitless. Here Fosdick adds a distinctively twentieth-century dimension—the insights of psychotherapy. Fosdick's own nervous breakdown, more than anything else, made his search for a meaningful faith vital to him and determined the shape of his ministry, with its emphasis on personal counseling. This in turn led him to the study of psychology and to an operative realism and sensitivity in dealing with deep-seated human distress. The guilt and anxiety of those who came to him spiritually troubled, and the neurotic devices whereby they avoided facing the facts about themselves, pointed to something deeper than a simple moral problem. For Fosdick, it pointed to a psychological interpretation of original sin. As he understood it, "humanity's sinful nature is not something which you and I alone make up by individual deeds of wrong, but . . . it is an inherited mortgage and handicap on the whole human family."[3]

---

[3] Harry Emerson Fosdick, *Christianity and Progress* (Westwood, N. J.: Revell, 1922), p. 176.

Salvation is the victory over this handicap by a transformation of character, a renewal of the individual's moral self—in short, by the integration of the powers of the self around a new, healthy, purposive center. Jesus Christ represents the model of the integrated self, the "real person" that each man can become; hence it is pre-eminently Jesus who can offer the way of salvation and mediate forgiveness, creating trust, confidence, and enduring change from within each person. Kenneth Cauthen has called Fosdick "a modern Pelagian," for unlike the orthodox view, his concept of sin is ultimately optimistic; it is a disorder of the self that can be healed, not a basic corruption of man's nature.[4] Similarly, Fosdick follows the Ritschlian tradition in defining a God who apparently is totally immanent. "Wherever goodness, beauty, truth, love, are—there is the divine."[5] To the extent that a man embodies these characteristics, he is relatively divine. Jesus is unique because he embodies them fully. In *The Modern Use of the Bible,* Fosdick places Jesus at the upper terminus of a succession of figures who increasingly manifested the ideal, and he finds, in good Ritschlian fashion, that Jesus as a moral person merits the respective titles of Messiah and Logos because, so to speak, he measured up to the highest possible degree to a divine image of moral behavior, revealing the highest ideals in his teaching and demonstrating his adherence to them by his acceptance of the cross. Basically lacking in Fosdick is an awareness of irony and paradox. His God is too readily reducible to simple categories of human good, and despite his psychological acuity regarding individual problems and neuroses, the image of man that shades over into a divine image is a shortsighted one, circumscribed by the orbit of Fosdick's own middle-class culture. Nevertheless, no less a student of paradox than Reinhold Niebuhr credited Fosdick with a major contribution, challenging "theological obscurantism" and affirming "the message of biblical faith in such a way as to prove its relevance

---

[4] See Kenneth Cauthen, *The Impact of American Religious Liberalism* (New York: Harper & Row, 1962), p. 79.
[5] Harry Emerson Fosdick, *The Hope of the World* (New York: Harper, 1933), p. 103.

to the experience of modern man."[6] Fosdick's exposition of "progressive Christianity" in the following selection is important for its frank avowal of the need for flexibility and historical perspective in the reinterpretation of Christianity for modern man. To a considerable degree he succeeds in bridging the gap from the experience of biblical times to that of the present, thus presenting Christianity as a living faith rather than either a set of orthodox dogmas or a system of liberal principles.

PROGRESSIVE CHRISTIANITY*

Among the influences which have forced well-instructed minds first to accept and then to glory in the progressive nature of Christianity, the first place must be given to the history of religion itself. The study of religion's ancient records in ritual, monument and book, and of primitive faiths still existing among us in all stages of development, has made clear the general course which man's religious life has traveled from very childish beginnings until now. From early animism in its manifold expressions, through polytheism, kathenotheism, henotheism, to monotheism, and so out into loftier possibilities of conceiving the divine nature and purpose—the main road which man has traveled in his religious development now is traceable. Nor is there any place where it is more easily traceable than in our own Hebrew-Christian tradition. One of the fine results of the historical study of the Scriptures is the possibility which now exists of arranging the manuscripts of

---

* From Harry Emerson Fosdick, *Christianity and Progress* (Westwood, N.J.: Fleming H. Revell Co., 1922, pp. 144–165.
[6] Reinhold Niebuhr, "Fosdick: Theologian and Preacher," *The Christian Century*, LXX, 22 (June 3, 1953), p. 658. An article written by Niebuhr in 1928, "How Adventurous is Dr. Fosdick?" offered a less generous estimate. See also Donald Meyer, *The Positive Thinkers* (Garden City: Doubleday, 1965), p. 214: "Like most liberal Protestant pastors [Fosdick] had only a sketchy sense of modern industry, and like most of them responded nervously to new, more obvious, less accustomed organizations of power."

the Bible in approximately chronological order and then tracing through them the unfolding growth of the faiths and hopes
which come to their flower in the Gospel of Christ. Consider,
for example, the exhilarating story of the developing conception of Jehovah's character from the time he was worshiped as
a mountain-god in the desert until he became known as the
"God and Father of our Lord Jesus Christ."

We are explicitly told that the history of Jehovah's relationship with Israel began at Sinai and that before that time the
Hebrew fathers had never even heard his name.[1] There on a
mountain-top in the Sinaitic wilderness dwelt this new-found
god, so anthropomorphically conceived that he could hide
Moses in a rock's cleft from which the prophet could not see
Jehovah's face but could see his back.[2] He was a god of battle
and the name of an old book about him still remains to us,
"The book of the Wars of Jehovah."[3]

> "Jehovah is a man of war:
> Jehovah is his name"[4]—

so his people at first rejoiced in him and gloried in his power
when he thundered and lightened on Sinai. Few stories in man's
spiritual history are so interesting as the record of the way in
which this mountain-god, for the first time, so far as we know, in
Semitic history, left his settled shrine, traveled with his people
in the holy Ark, became acclimated in Canaan, and, gradually
absorbing the functions of the old baals of the land, extended
his sovereignty over the whole of Palestine.

To be sure, even then he still was thought of, as all ancient
gods were thought of, as geographically limited to the country
whose god he was. Milcolm and Chemosh were real gods too,
ruling in Philistia and Moab as Jehovah did in Canaan. This is
the meaning of Jephthah's protest to a hostile chieftain: "Wilt
not thou possess that which Chemosh thy god giveth thee to
possess?"[5] This is the meaning of David's protest when he is

---

[1] Exodus 6:3; Chap. 19.
[2] Exodus 33:22–23.
[3] Numbers 21:14.
[4] Exodus 15:3.
[5] Judges 11:24.

driven out to the Philistine cities: "They have driven me out this day that I should not cleave unto the inheritance of Jehovah, saying, Go, serve other gods."[6] This is the meaning of Naaman's desire to have two mules' burden of Jehovah's land on which to worship Jehovah in Damascus.[7] Jehovah could be worshiped only on Jehovah's land. But ever as the day of fuller understanding dawned, the sovereignity of Jehovah widened and his power usurped the place and function of all other gods. Amos saw him using the nations as his pawns; Isaiah heard him whistling to the nations as a shepherd to his dogs; Jeremiah heard him cry, "Can any hide himself in secret places so that I shall not see him? . . . Do not I fill heaven and earth?"[8]; until at last we sweep out, through the exile and all the heightening of faith and clarifying of thought that came with it, into the Great Isaiah's 40th chapter on the universal and absolute sovereignty of God, into the Priestly narrative of creation, where God makes all things with a word, into psalms which cry,

> "For all the gods of the people are idols;
> But Jehovah made the heavens."[9]

Moreover, as Jehovah's sovereignty thus is enlarged until he is the God of all creation, his character too is deepened and exalted in the understanding of his people. That noblest succession of moral teachers in ancient history, the Hebrew prophets, developed a conception of the nature of God in terms of righteousness, so broad in its outreach, so high in its quality, that as one mounts through Amos' fifth chapter and Isaiah's first chapter and Jeremiah's seventh chapter, he finds himself, like Moses on Nebo's top, looking over into the Promised Land of the New Testament. There this development flowers out under the influence of Jesus. God's righteousness is interpreted, not in terms of justice only, but of compassionate, sacrificial love; his Fatherhood embraces not

---

[6] I Samuel 26:19.
[7] II Kings 5:17.
[8] Jeremiah 23:24.
[9] Psalm 96:5.

only all mankind but each individual, lifting him out of obscurity in the mass into infinite worthfulness and hope. And more than this development of idea, the New Testament gives us a new picture of God in the personality of Jesus, and we see the light of the knowledge of God's glory in his face.

Moreover, this development, so plainly recorded in Scripture, was not unconsciously achieved by the drift of circumstance; it represents the ardent desire of forward-looking men, inspired by the Spirit. The Master, himself, was consciously pleading for a progressive movement in the religious life and thinking of his day. A static religion was the last thing he ever dreamed of or wanted. No one was more reverent than he toward his people's past; his thought and his speech were saturated with the beauty of his race's heritage; yet consider his words as again and again they fell from his lips: "It was said to them of old time . . . but I say unto you." His life was rooted in the past but it was not imprisoned there; it grew up out of the past, not destroying but fulfilling it. He had in him the spirit of the prophets, who once had spoken to his people in words of fire; but old forms that he thought had been outgrown he brushed aside. He would not have his Gospel a patch on an old garment, he said, nor would he put it like new wine into old wineskins. He appealed from the oral traditions of the elders to the written law; within the written law he distinguished between ceremonial and ethical elements, making the former of small or no account, the latter all-important; and then within the written ethical law he waived provisions that seemed to him outmoded by time. Even when he bade farewell to his disciples, he did not talk to them as if what he himself had said were a finished system: "I have yet many things to say unto you, but ye cannot bear them now. Howbeit when he, the Spirit of truth, is come, he shall guide you into all the truth."

In Paul's hands the work which Jesus began went on. He dared an adventurous move that makes much of our modern progressiveness look like child's play: he lifted the Christian churches out of the narrow, religious exclusiveness of the Hebrew synagogue. He dared to wage battle for the new idea that Christianity was not a Jewish sect but a universal religion. He withstood to his face Peter, still trammeled in the narrowness of his Jewish thinking, and he founded churches across the Roman Empire where was neither Jew nor Greek, barbarian, Scythian, male nor female, bond nor free, but all were one man in Christ Jesus.

Even more thrilling were those later days when in Ephesus the writer of the Fourth Gospel faced a Hellenistic audience, to whom the forms of thought in which Jesus hitherto had been interpreted were utterly unreal. The first creed about Jesus proclaimed that he was the Messiah, but Messiah was a Jewish term and to the folk of Ephesus it had no vital meaning. John could not go on calling the Master that and that alone, when he had hungry souls before him who needed the Master but to whom Jewish terms had no significance. One thing those folk of Ephesus did understand, the idea of the Logos. They had heard of that from the many faiths whose pure or syncretized forms made the religious background of their time. They knew about the Logos from Zoroastrianism, where beside Ahura Mazdah stood Vohu Manah, the Mind of God; from Stoicism, at the basis of whose philosophy lay the idea of the Logos; from Alexandrian Hellenism, by means of which a Jew like Philo had endeavoured to marry Greek philosophy and Hebrew orthodoxy. And the writer of the Fourth Gospel used that new form of thought in which to present to his people the personality of our Lord. "In the beginning was the Logos, and the Logos was with God, and the Logos was God"—so begins the Fourth Gospel's prologue, in words that every intelligent person in Ephesus could understand and was familiar with, and that initial sermon in the book, for it is a sermon, not philosophy, moves on in forms of thought which the people knew about and habitually used, until the hidden purpose comes to light: "The Logos became flesh and dwelt among us (and we beheld his glory, glory as of the only begotten from the Father), full of grace and truth." John was presenting his Lord to the people of his time in terms that the people could understand.

Even within the New Testament, therefore, there is no static

creed. For, like a flowing river, the Church's thought of her
Lord shaped itself to the intellectual banks of the generation
through which it moved, even while, by its construction and
erosion, it transfigured them. Nor did this movement cease
with New Testament days. From the Johannine idea of the
Logos to the Nicene Creed, where our Lord is set in the framework of Greek metaphysics, the development is just as clear
as from the category of Jewish Messiah to the categories of
the Fourth Gospel. And if, in our generation, a conservative
scholar like the late Dr. Sanday pleaded for the necessity of a
new Christology, it was not because he was primarily zealous
for a novel philosophy, but because like John of old in Ephesus
he was zealous to present Christ to his own generation in terms
that his own generation could comprehend.[10]

IV

Undoubtedly such an outlook upon the fluid nature of the
Christian movement will demand readjustment in the religious
thinking of many people. They miss the old ideas about
revelation. This new progressiveness seems to them to be
merely the story of man's discovery, finding God, here a little
and there a little, as he has found the truths of astronomy. But
God's revelation of himself is just as real when it is conceived
in progressive as when it is conceived in static terms. Men
once thought of God's creation of the world in terms of fiat—
it was done on the instant; and when evolution was propounded men cried that the progressive method shut God out.
We see now how false that fear was. The creative activity of
God never was so nobly conceived as it has been since we
have known the story of his slow unfolding of the universe.
We have a grander picture in our minds than even the psalmist
had, when we say after him, "The heavens declare the glory
of God." So men who have been accustomed to think of revelation in static terms, now that the long leisureliness of man's
developing spiritual insight is apparent, fear that this does
away with revelation. But in God's unfolding education of his

---

[10] William Sanday: Christologies Ancient and Modern.

people recorded in the Scriptures revelation is at its noblest. No man ever found God except when God was seeking to be found. Discovery is the under side of the process; the upper side is revelation.

Indeed, this conception of progressive revelation does not shut out finality. In scientific thought, which continually moves and grows, expands and changes, truths are discovered once for all. The work of Copernicus is in a real sense final. This earth does move; it is not stationary; and the universe is not geocentric. That discovery is final. Many developments start from that, but the truth itself is settled once for all. So, in the spiritual history of man, final revelations come. They will not have to be made over again and they will not have to be given up. Progress does not shut out finality; it only makes each new finality a point of departure for a new adventure, not a terminus ad quem for a conclusive stop. That God was in Christ reconciling the world unto himself is for the Christian a finality, but, from the day the first disciples saw its truth until now, the intellectual formulations in which it has been set and the mental categories by which it has been interpreted have changed with the changes of each age's thought.

While at first, then, a progressive Christianity may seem to plunge us into unsettlement, the more one studies it the less he would wish it otherwise. Who would accept a snapshot taken at any point on the road of Christian development as the final and perfect form of Christianity? Robert Louis Stevenson has drawn for us a picture of a man trying with cords and pegs to stake out the shadow of an oak tree, expecting that when he had marked its boundaries the shadow would stay within the limits of the pegs. Yet all the while the mighty globe was turning around in space. He could not keep a tree's shadow static on a moving earth. Nevertheless, multitudes of people in their endeavour to build up an infallibly settled creed have tried just such a hopeless task. They forget that while a revelation *from* God might conceivably be final and complete, religion deals with a revelation *of* God. God, the infinite and eternal, from everlasting to everlasting, the source and crown and destiny of all the universe—shall a man whose

days are as grass rise up to say that he has made a statement
about him which will not need to be revised? Rather, our
prayer should be that the thought of God, the meaning of God,
the glory of God, the plans and purpose of God may expand
in our comprehension until we, who now see in a mirror,
darkly, may see face to face. "Le Dieu défini est le Dieu fini."

This mistaken endeavour, in the interest of stability, to make
a vital movement static is not confined to religion. Those of us
who love Wagner remember the lesson of Die Meistersinger.
Down in Nuremberg they had standardized and conventionalized music. They had set it down in rules and men like Beckmesser could not imagine that there was any music permissible
outside the regulations. Then came Walter von Stolzing. Music
to him was not a conventionality but a passion—not a rule,
but a life—and, when he sang, his melodies reached heights of
beauty that Beckmesser's rules did not provide for. It was
Walter von Stolzing who sang the Prize Song, and as the
hearts of the people were stirred in answer to its spontaneous
melody, until all the population of Nuremberg were singing its
accumulating harmonies, poor Beckmesser on his blackboard
jotted down the rules which were being broken. Beckmesser
represents a static conception of life which endeavours to
freeze progress at a given point and call it infallible. But
Beckmesser is wrong. You cannot take things like music and
religion and set them down in final rules and regulations. They
are life, and you have to let them grow and flower and expand
and reveal evermore the latent splendour at their heart.

V

Obviously, the point where this progressive conception of
Christianity comes into conflict with many widely accepted
ideas is the abandonment which it involves of an external and
inerrant authority in matters of religion. The marvel is that
that idea of authority, which is one of the historic curses of
religion, should be regarded by so many as one of the vital
necessities of the faith. The fact is that religion by its very
nature is one of the realms to which external authority is least
applicable. In science people commonly suppose that they do

not take truth on any one's authority; they prove it. In business they do not accept methods on authority; they work them out. In statesmanship they no longer believe in the divine right of kings nor do they accept infallible dicta handed down from above. But they think that religion is delivered to them by authority and that they believe what they do believe because a divine Church or a divine Book or a divine Man told them.

In this common mode of thinking, popular ideas have the truth turned upside down. The fact is that science, not religion, is the realm where most of all we use external authority. They tell us that there are millions of solar systems scattered through the fields of space. Is that true? How do we know? We never counted them. We know only what the authorities say. They tell us that the next great problem in science is breaking up the atom to discover the incalculable resources of power there waiting to be harnessed by our skill. Is that true? Most of us do not understand what an atom is, and what it means to break one up passes the farthest reach of our imaginations; all we know is what the authorities say. They tell us that electricity is a mode of motion in ether. Is that true? Most of us have no first hand knowledge about electricity. The motorman calls it "juice" and that means as much to us as to call it a mode of motion in ether; we must rely on the authorities. They tell us that sometime we are going to talk through wireless telephones across thousands of miles, so that no man need ever be out of vocal communication with his family and friends. Is that true? It seems to us an incredible miracle, but we suppose that it is so, as the authorities say. In a word, the idea that we do not use authority in science is absurd. Science is precisely the place where nine hundred and ninety-nine men out of a thousand use authority the most. The chemistry, biology, geology, astronomy which the authorities teach is the only science which most of us possess.

There is another realm, however, where we never think of taking such an attitude. They tell us that friendship is beautiful. Is that true? Would we ever think of saying that we do not know, ourselves, but that we rely on the authorities? Far better to say that our experience with friendship has been unhappy and that we personally question its utility! That, at least, would have an accent of personal, original experience in it. For here we are facing a realm where we never can enter at all until we enter, each man for himself.

Two realms exist, therefore, in each of which first-hand experience is desirable, but in only one of which it is absolutely indispensable. We can live on what the authorities in physics say, but there are no proxies for the soul. Love, friendship, delight in music and in nature, parental affection—these things are like eating and breathing; no one can do them for us; we must enter the experience for ourselves. Religion, too, belongs in this last realm. The one vital thing in religion is first-hand, personal experience. Religion is the most intimate, inward, incommunicable fellowship of the human soul. In the words of Plotinus, religion is "the flight of the alone to the Alone." You never know God at all until you know him for yourself. The only God you ever will know is the God you do know for yourself.

This does not mean, of course, that there are no authorities in religion. There are authorities in everything, but the function of an authority in religion, as in every other vital realm, is not to take the place of our eyes, seeing in our stead and inerrantly declaring to us what it sees; the function of an authority is to bring to us the insight of the world's accumulated wisdom and the revelations of God's seers, and so to open our eyes that we may see, each man for himself. So an authority in literature does not say to his students: The Merchant of Venice is a great drama; you may accept my judgment on that—I know. Upon the contrary, he opens their eyes; he makes them see; he makes their hearts sensitive so that the genius which made Shylock and Portia live captivates and subdues them, until like the Samaritans they say, "Now we believe, not because of thy speaking: for we have heard for ourselves, and know." That is the only use of authority in a vital realm. It can lead up to the threshold of a great experience where we must enter, each man for himself, and that service to the spiritual life is the Bible's inestimable gift.

At the beginning, Christianity was just such a first-hand experience as we have described. The Christian fellowship consisted of a group of men keeping company with Jesus and learning how to live. They had no creeds to recite when they met together; what they believed was still an unstereotyped passion in their hearts. They had no sacraments to distinguish their faith—baptism had been a Jewish rite and even the Lord's Supper was an informal use of bread and wine, the common elements of their daily meal. They had no organizations to join; they never dreamed that the Christian Gospel would build a church outside the synagogue. Christianity in the beginning was an intensely personal experience.

Then the Master went away and the tremendous forces of human life and history laid hold on the movement which so vitally he had begun. His followers began building churches. Just as the·Wesleyans had to leave the Church of England, not because they wanted to, but because the Anglicans would not keep them, so the Christians, not because they planned to, but because the synagogue was not large enough to hold them, had to leave the synagogue. They began building creeds; they had to. Every one of the first Christian creeds was written in sheer self-defense. If we had been Christians in those first centuries, when a powerful movement was under way called Gnosticism, which denied that God, the Father Almighty, had made both the heaven and the earth, which said that God had made heaven indeed but that a demigod had made the world, and which denied that Jesus had been born in the flesh and in the flesh had died, we would have done what the first Christians did: we would have defined in a creed what it was the Christians did believe as against that wild conglomeration of Oriental mythology that Gnosticism was, and we would have shouted the creed as a war cry against the Gnostics. That is what the so-called Apostles' Creed was—the first Christian battle chant, a militant proclamation of the historic faith against the heretics; and every one of its declarations met with a head-on collision some claim of Gnosticism. Then, too, the early Christians drew up rituals; they had to. We cannot keep any spiritual thing in human life, even the spirit of courtesy, as a disembodied wraith. We ritualize it—we bow, we take off our hats, we shake hands, we rise when a lady enters. We have innumerable ways of expressing politeness in a ritual. Neither could they have kept so deep and beautiful a thing as the Christian life without such expression.

So historic Christianity grew, organized, creedalized, ritualized. And ever as it grew, a peril grew with it, for there were multitudes of people who joined these organizations, recited these creeds, observed these rituals, took all the secondary and derived elements of Christianity, but often forgot that vital thing which all this was meant in the first place to express: a first-hand, personal experience of God in Christ. That alone is vital in Christianity; all the rest is once or twice or thrice removed from life. For Christianity is not a creed, nor an organization, nor a ritual. These are important but they are secondary. They are the leaves, not the roots; they are the wires, not the message. Christianity itself is a life.

If, however, Christianity is thus a life, we cannot stereotype its expressions in set and final forms. If it is a life in fellowship with the living God, it will think new thoughts, build new organizations, expand into new symbolic expressions. We cannot at any given time write "finis" after its development. We can no more "keep the faith" by stopping its growth than we can keep a son by insisting on his being forever a child. The progressiveness of Christianity is not simply its response to a progressive age; the progressiveness of Christianity springs from its own inherent vitality. So far is this from being regrettable, that a modern Christian rejoices in it and gladly recognizes not only that he is thinking thoughts and undertaking enterprises which his fathers would not have understood, but also that his children after him will differ quite as much in teaching and practice from the modernity of to-day. It has been the fashion to regard this changeableness with wistful regret. So Wordsworth sings in his sonnet on Mutability:

> "Truth fails not; but her outward forms that
>   bear
> The longest date do melt like frosty rime,
> That in the morning whitened hill and plain

> And is no more; drop like the tower sublime
> Of yesterday, which royally did wear
> Its crown of weeds, but could not even sus-
>   tain
> Some casual shout that broke the silent air,
> Or the unimaginable touch of Time."

Such wistfulness, however, while a natural sentiment, is not true to the best Christian thought of our day. He who believes in the living God, while he will be far from calling all change progress, and while he will, according to his judgment, withstand perverse changes with all his might, will also regard the cessation of change as the greatest calamity that could befall religion. Stagnation in thought or enterprise means death for Christianity as certainly as it does for any other vital movement. Stagnation, not change, is Christianity's most deadly enemy, for this is a progressive world, and in a progressive world no doom is more certain than that which awaits whatever is belated, obscurantist and reactionary.

8

EDWARD SCRIBNER AMES

Christian Humanist

Edward Scribner Ames (1870–1958) occupies a distinctive place in the development of what came to be called empirical theology, a characteristically American, nonspeculative, nonmetaphysical type of Christian thought. In a sense, Ames forms a link between William James and Henry Nelson Wieman. Too often, he is brushed off as merely a member of the "Chicago school" rather than credited with being among its founders, a fact which in itself makes Ames worth considering.

A descendant of William Ames, author of *The Marrow of Theology* (16?), Edward Scribner Ames was the son of Lucius Bowles Ames, who departed from the stern Calvinist principles and became a minister of the Disciples of Christ. Soon after the Civil War, Lucius Ames left Vermont for the West. Edward was born in Eau Claire, Wisconsin, and spent his boyhood in Michigan and Illinois before the family settled in Davenport, Iowa. Evangelical simplicity was the keynote of home life, with morning prayers and frequent evening hymn sings; and such frivolities as dime novels were cheerfully forbidden. It was a frugal home, too; his father's salary was $600 a year, and sometimes it was paid in flour or coffee instead of cash.

Ames worked his way through college, receiving his B.A. from Drake University in Des Moines in 1889. He was ordained a Disciples minister the following year. At Drake he had used textbooks written by Yale professors and had great respect for its "great traditions of scholarship and of New England culture and religious leadership."[1] His graduate year

---

[1] *Beyond Theology: The Autobiography of Edward Scribner Ames* (University of Chicago Press, 1959), p. 27. As between Harvard and Yale, Ames then preferred the latter's "more conservative Congregational tradition."

at Drake, combined with pastoral experience and high grades, gained him admission to the senior class at Yale Divinity School, from which he received his B.D. in 1892. He also managed to take a course in the philosophy of religion in the University's philosophy department. For that course he had to write a paper based on Otto Pfleiderer's *The Philosophy of Religion on the Basis of Its History* (E.T., 1888). The section titled "The Historical Development of Religious Consciousness" flung wide open for him the gates to a new and challenging world of thought and shook his belief in Christianity as "unique and supreme by virtue of its supernatural origin," (*Beyond Theology*, p. 30). In 1891 Ames read William James's recently published *Principles of Psychology*, that "great revolutionary work [which] opened new doors to the understanding of the human mind,"[2] and in 1892, after a visit to Pike's Peak, he traveled to Harvard with a view to enrolling for study with James. James, however, was in Europe for the academic year. He talked with Royce but found his metaphysical bent uncongenial. Returning to Yale, he gained much from the study of Kant and Schopenhauer, and mined the vein opened by Pfleiderer, but James continued to eclipse them all in influence.

Meanwhile an uncle, Sanford Scribner, was active in carrying out John D. Rockefeller's plan for a great university in Chicago. William Rainey Harper of Yale Divinity School had been chosen as its first president and had converted Morgan Park Baptist Seminary into an interdenominational school attached to the new university. Harper offered Ames a fellowship in philosophy and invited him to set up a Disciples Divinity House as an adjunct to the University of Chicago Divinity School. He prepared his doctoral dissertation under James H. Tufts and George Herbert Mead, and first met John Dewey when he took his oral examination in 1895. Ames received the first Ph.D. degree conferred by the University of Chicago.

In Tufts' seminar on John Locke he gained new insight into the sources of James's and Dewey's pragmatism, finding the

---

[2] *Ibid.*

Lockean empiricism mediated by John Stuart Mill. He discovered much evidence of Locke's rationalism in the religious thought of Alexander Campbell,[3] founder of the Disciples, and from 1895–1896 he taught a course on this in the Disciples Divinity House, while teaching elementary psychology in the University, using James's *Principles* as his text, and preaching regularly at a mission church in Evanston.

Ames accepted a professorship at Butler College in 1897 but returned to Chicago three years later as pastor of Hyde Park Church, a position he held until 1940. He resumed teaching in the philosophy department and was its chairman when he retired in 1935. In 1905, just two years after the publication of *The Varieties of Religious Experience,* he began teaching the first course in the psychology of religion offered at an American university. Among his earliest major articles are "Theology From the Standpoint of Functional Psychology"[4] and "The Psychological Basis of Religion."[5] His first book, *The Psychology of Religious Experience* (1910), remained for many years the standard text in its field, holding its place despite the inroads of Freudian thought which eventually eclipsed it.

Ames was a pioneer of demythologizing, but in a style and on a basis quite different from that of the German school of Strauss, Baur, Weiss, and Bultmann. At a time when Bultmann was Weiss' student at Marburg, Ames was writing *The Divinity of Christ* (1911), which presents an empirical view of Jesus and accounts for such miracles as the virgin birth in terms of the context of beliefs already present in Jesus' world.

At the same time that Karl Barth was opening the way to a theology that came to be called neo-orthodox, Ames published *The New Orthodoxy* (1918), by which he meant something quite different—a "new orthodoxy of method and spirit" conforming to scientific research and theory. Martin Luther, he

---

[3] The Lockean influence on Campbell has been challenged by recent scholars, but this does not alter the fact that Ames held the view he did. See S. Morris Eames, *The Philosophy of Alexander Campbell* (New Brunswick: Rutgers, 1966).

[4] In *The American Journal of Theology,* X (April 1906), pp. 219–232.

[5] In *The Monist,* XX (1910), pp. 242–262.

pointed out, was in his time no slave to canonical orthodoxy. Luther had termed the Letter of James "an epistle of straw" and consigned it to an appendix, along with Hebrews, Revelation and Jude. It was only with the widespread publication of Bibles in the nineteenth century and their distribution among men of limited education, that belief in its inerrancy arose. In contrast to dogmatic theology, Ames conceived biblical studies as humanistic, in much the same sense that literature and philosophy are classed as "humanities" rather than exact sciences. The collection of books which form the Bible is like the corpus of, say, Elizabethan literature, "the great names of which are Spenser, Shakespeare and Bacon. The lesser lights are Ben Jonson, Marlowe, Beaumont and Fletcher, with others like Lodge and Sidney and numerous anonymous authors making up the chorus and background."[6] Taken together, they comprise the literature of an epoch, some parts of which are merely typical of the age, while a *Hamlet* or a *Doctor Faustus* in varying degree transcends it. The way in which parts of the Bible transcend the biblical era is different in degree but not in kind. "They are the records of the moral and religious aspirations and ideals of all humanity."[7] Not unlike Shailer Mathews, he argues that "the Bible, like other vital books, grows by constant reinterpretation."[8] This, indeed, is the key to the greatness of Jean Calvin, who "made the Bible a new book to his generation by a radically different type of interpretation."[9]

Ames disliked the word "theology." In a sermon preached in 1902, "A Personal Confession of Faith," he spoke of a "religious ideology" subject to revision as are both the sciences and the humanities. He understood heaven or salvation to be "participation in the divine life," meaning "the realization of the natural powers of the soul"—by no means an automatic or easy achievement—and "hell is the failure to attain this realiza-

---

[6] Edward Scribner Ames, *The New Orthodoxy* (University of Chicago Press, 1918), p. 68.
[7] *Ibid*, p. 69.
[8] *Ibid*.
[9] *Ibid*, p. 71.

tion of one's powers."[10] The church and its ordinances (baptism, marriage, etc.) are essential but not infallible instruments of salvation. "Many people are saved without them, and many people are lost in spite of having observed them."[11] Kenneth Latourette likens Ames to John Haynes Holmes: "Ames, like Holmes, sought an interpretation of religion which would unify all religious people, both those who were in and those who were outside existing churches, and endeavored to utilize differences in 'the cooperative quest for truer ideas and finer attitudes.' "[12] A neo-orthodox critic states that "his idea of God is entirely humanistic and pragmatic. God to Ames is only a symbol of 'reality idealized."[13] One would scarcely guess from either of these statements that Ames spent half a century in the active ministry, or that his keen awareness of the pragmatic values of religion was accompanied by a large and vital faith centering in Jesus and concerned with what he called "the inside of things."

Religion, said Ames, "sensitizes [man] to the mystery and strangeness of ordinary things, invites him to look beneath their surface, and habituates him to the poetry in the plain facts of life. It is somewhat disconcerting that religion does not more often develop this normal, rewarding mystical experience. It might well be cultivated in place of many hard doctrinal arguments and fervid moralizations. Most of the sayings of Jesus have this mystical quality."[14] Another quality was "his ability to see things in their relations, to show that the simplest deeds bear religious meaning when the artificial distinctions between departments of life are removed."[15]

Ames saw, as did few of his contemporaries within the religious community, the depth of the changes wrought by the

---

[10] *Beyond Theology,* p. 76.

[11] *Ibid,* p. 76.

[12] Kenneth Scott Latourette, *Christianity in a Revolutionary Age,* V: *The 20th Century Outside Europe* (New York: Harper, 1962), p. 87.

[13] George Hammar, *Christian Realism in Contemporary American Theology* (Uppsala: Lundeqvist, 1940), p. 39. Others, too, speak of Ames as "drifting toward humanism."

[14] *Beyond Theology,* pp. 94 f.

[15] *Ibid,* p. 185.

industrial revolution—not only the ethical implications of the "impersonal relations" and "less of the old face-to-face relations of small groups"[16] but in his acknowledgement that "Christianity is entering upon the profoundest transformation it has experienced since it came in contact with Greek thought in the second century."[17] This is not to say that Ames was a lonely prophet, for in a broad sense such views were shared by many liberal theologians, especially at Chicago. Yet something more than a difference of tone and accent is involved. Perhaps it is the concatenation of these themes and their focusing in a clearly American perspective with its pluralism and experimentalism and democratic faith. He was, indeed, a certain kind of humanist; for as a pastor he was aware of the problem of "getting religious people to believe in themselves, to throw off the long-standing idea that man is evil and that he has a deep-seated natural disposition to choose the worse rather than the better part."[18] "The problem is to live in such a way that life is good and satisfying in spite of all its pain and defeat . . . . Religious faith does not require us to believe that the world is wholly good, but it does, it seems to me, require that we recognize that there are values in life and that they can be increased."[19] Schopenhauer, he said, tempered his optimism with realism. Yet optimism remained in the ascendancy. Ames's own life was a testimony to the "onward and upward" trend of historic progress. He admired William James' pacifism but accepted America's entry into World War I with calm resignation. His conception of the social gospel was "fair dealing" aid to social welfare agencies and trust in the democratic process. "Here in America, for the first time," he asserted, "Christianity has come under the influence of a democratic society."[20] He believed that this fact constituted an experiment of great moment, and he looked for positive results as he participated in it.

---

[16] *Ibid,* p. 109.
[17] *Ibid.,* p. 77, as quoted from a sermon of 1902.
[18] *Ibid,* p. 117.
[19] *Ibid,* p. 40.
[20] *Ibid,* p. 82.

Ames' last major book, *Religion,* appeared in 1929. It is interesting that he refers to the stove called "New Perfection No. 62," as he does in the 1922 essay reproduced in the following pages—and again in his autobiography. In *Religion,* he also speaks of God as "reality idealized." But let us see the phrase in its context:

> The religious view of the world, in its emotional intensity and affectionate appraisal, naturally employs vivid and intimate personal symbols of the most perfect and absolute kind. In religious appreciation, God is Reality idealized and glorified with the attributes of complete and flawless personality.[21]

Just like the stove! One of the points that can hardly be missed in Ames is the psychologist's awareness of the imprecision of religious language and the pragmatist's willingness to accept the different vocabularies in which the word "God" appears. At one point he comes close to anticipating the early Hartshorne in speaking of God philosophically as "concrete universal." At another point, he states that God is reality manifesting order, intelligence, and love "in the daily and commonplace experience of living"[22]—a version of the "practical absolute" which he discusses in his 1922 essay. As Hartshorne has pointed out, Ames is inconsistent in his metaphysics.[23] Ames might well reply, however, that his usage is metaphorical, not metaphysical; that in the end God is understood in the wholeness of experience, which in its nature is imprecise. Accordingly, some element of poetic license enters into the interpretation, from which the psychological dimension of "will to believe" and similar factors cannot be expunged. Reinhold Niebuhr would go on to develop the darker side of this consideration, probing at "wishful belief" and hidden, complex motives. Ames recognized the presence in life of "much brute force, sheer impulse, blind activity"[24]; his psychology was not ignorant of these. But he gave them insufficient attention, and this fact rather

---

[21] Ames, *Religion* (New York: Holt, 1929), p. 161.
[22] *Ibid,* p. 156.
[23] See Charles Hartshorne & William L. Reese, *Philosophers Speak of God* (University of Chicago Press, 1953), p. 384.
[24] *Religion, op. cit.,* p. 156.

than any inherent failure of his viewpoint accounts for his
subsequent eclipse.

RELIGIOUS VALUES AND THE
PRACTICAL ABSOLUTE*

One of the striking facts in the studies of the psychology of
religion which have appeared since the beginning of this century is the measure of agreement as to the nature of religion.
It is commonly supposed that religion is the subject about
which there is the greatest divergence of opinion and that
these differences emerge most violently when the attempt is
made to formulate exact definitions. It may therefore be taken
as an evidence of the substantial contribution which the science of psychology has made that we are now in possession of
a working denomination of religion. This definition centers
upon the concept of values. In Höffding's phrase it is the conservation of values. For Coe it is the determination and the
effort to realize the highest social values. In the recent Philosophy of Religion by W. K. Wright it is "the endeavor to secure
the conservation of socially recognized values through specific
actions." All of these definitions show the marked tendency of
psychology away from the old faculty theories and away from
the standpoints of intellectualism stressing belief, and of feeling which made religion primarily a matter of emotion. The
agreement lies in the application of the functional or behav-
ioristic point of view. Religion is thus regarded as an active
striving toward the realization of desired ends or felt values.
That these ends are ideal and social in character may also be
included in the agreement. Religion is therefore conceived as
a practical interest as contrasted with science and philosophy
which are reflective. This paper undertakes to deal with these
values of religion in respect to two questions: First, specifi-

* From *The International Journal of Ethics*, XXXII, 4 (July 1922), pp.
347–365. Reprint by permission of the University of Chicago Press.

cally, what are they? Second, why are they accompanied by such a sense of validity in the active effort to realize them?

I

In stating what are the values of religion, it may be said at the outset that religion has no values of its own. The values of religion are also other kinds of values at the same time,—economic, political, social or æsthetic. This, of course, is not peculiar to religious values. Moral values are not exclusively matters of ethics. All moral problems are at the same moment problems of business, of political science, of eugenics or art. It is needless to say here, though the neglect of the fact constantly leads to difficulty, that the phenomena with which any specific science deals are also, from other points of view, the legitimate material of various scientific and practical interests. Religion, then, should be understood to find the values which it cherishes, in the stream of actual, concrete experience.

It may be assumed also, though less casually, that these values of religion, imply an order of values of differing degrees of importance in all human societies where religion is found. James observed that the individual's consciousness is, in normal experience, "figurate." So accustomed is the mind to working with patterns and meanings that it is restless and irritated when confronted with materials which do not fall into some appreciable order. When attention is directed to them it is disconcerting if the objects along the roadside at dusk do not take their places readily in the familiar classification as trees, or men or animals. If a teacher puts random lines and figures on the blackboard before a class of students they will seek for a meaning, an intelligible arrangement. Even in dreams some semblance of the form and structure of waking mental life appears. Not only does man respond to the environment with this organizing, systematizing activity of apperception but he also displays characteristic emotional reactions in reference to the objects and situations with which he has vital experience. In the hunting stage, when the savage is driven by meat hunger, it is not difficult to appreciate the fact that the sight of the bear or deer should elicit intense emotional excitement; or that the cry of an enemy warrior should stir him with fear and rage; or that the call of his mate in distress should rouse him to frantic effort.

The studies of many tribes in relatively low stages of cultural development disclose interest-patterns and scales of values of a very definite character. Among the natives of Central Australia the food interest is dominant. Generosity in sharing food is a prime virtue. Infanticide is common but is apparently due to the difficulty of nourishing the infant and an unweaned older child at the same time. Marriage relations also hold a very important place and within their complex system the marriage relation is strictly observed. Their sense of obligation and their fortitude under suffering appear conspicuously in the observance of their food and initiation ceremonials. The regard shown for the sacred places and the *Churinga*, or sacred objects of these ceremonials, further indicates the most important concerns of their interest. For the head-hunters of Borneo, life reaches the apex of its ecstasy and meaning in capturing heads from neighboring tribes. It is said that "they find therein the complete expression of their ideals of life, of their highest conceptions of value." It is not difficult to realize how a code of approved conduct and a scale of manly qualities could develop out of that supreme and dangerous interest. For the Todas, life organizes around the care of the buffaloes and the habits involved in that occupation determine the relative importance of personal qualities and conduct. The Shinto religion exalts two characteristics of the Japanese, cleanliness and joyousness. "In Shinto," King observes, actual personal dirt is worse than moral guilt. "To be dirty is to be disrespectful to the gods." The festivals of Shinto are very merry and, so to speak, seriously promote light-heartedness. For example, in one of the festivals, when the offerings are brought in procession before the shrine, the village chief calls out in a loud voice, "According to our annual custom, let us laugh."

While, then, the interest-patterns of various peoples differ very widely the important thing is that where there is any tension or struggle whatever, there comes to be an organiza-

tion of ends, of conduct and of values. The highest of these
values are the foci of the ceremonials and they are determining factors in moulding the conceptions of the gods. To say
then that religion is the "consciousness of the highest social
values" is to employ a formula which is applicable to all organized societies, however they may differ from one another
in the particular values they cherish or however their values
may change by addition or loss, by enlargement or deteriora-
tion. The only qualification of this formulation of religion in
terms of the highest social values which seems to be required
is in the case of religions extended beyond the culture in
which they were indigenous, or in the case of religions which
have become static and unresponsive to the growing life and
the new social values of an expanding civilization. The zeal of
missionary propaganda has shown instances of the artificial
imposition of the ideals of one religious tradition upon the
mores of another people, and the rapid expansion of Greek
reflective thought made it impossible for the religion of an
earlier age to assimilate the new conceptions and the new
evaluations of life. But where the customs and institutions of
a people unfold under the influence of a settled habitat and
through the processes of normal development there emerges
a scale of values, often modified from age to age but presenting in the upper ranges those values which are the chief concerns of religion. This was impressively true of the Egyptian
people who through a vast historic existence and many different dynasties held in the foreground a dominating interest
in the future life.

The existence of a hierarchy of social values in the earlier
stages of human life is, from the instances cited, sufficiently
illustrated for the present purpose. With all the diversity
noted, a general principle of explanation commends itself.
This principle is the influence of the environment, physical
and social. The values have been those which evolved in the
process of securing a living from such animals, fruits and
products of the soil as were available; in the accidental fix-
ation of attention upon accompanying phenomena of the chase
or warfare or social relations or natural events; and in the in-

fluence of conspicious persons, such as chiefs, kings, and medicine men. These earlier stages are under the sway of custom
and the value scales which develop are relatively unconscious
and wholly uncriticized.

A radical difference appears when the rule of custom begins
to be felt to be inadequate and the questioning intelligence is
called forth. This critical process in its beginnings was most
acute and most complete among the Greeks. Plato's Dialogues
are the glowing record of that achievement. The same process
in different terms and with a different emphasis occurred
among the Hebrews, and the writings of the great prophets
Amos and Hosea, Isaiah and Jeremiah preserve that history.
Confucius and Buddha performed a similar task for the cultures of their inheritance. In all of these there is a common
work performed. It is the deliverance of the human spirit from
the bondage of blind custom and the assertion of a conscious,
selective determination of values in the interest of a more
rational and a nobler human existence. That birth of reason
did not at once abolish all superstition, magic, and abject obedience to custom. But it did open a new conception of the
world and of human institutions. From that day to this it has
offered to educated men a world view, and has stimulated increasing numbers of people to pursue larger ideals and to devote themselves to the realization of more clearly conceived
values. Not the least important of the results has been a critical survey of the traditional cultures of all tribes and peoples.
It is now possible to see how naïvely and how unconsciously
those cultures grew up out of the conditions and accidental
circumstances of tribal existence. It is also possible to make
new estimates of these customs in terms of the new standpoint
of more critical reflection.

I am aware that some of the most diligent students of the
folkways do not attach importance to any criticism which
may be passed upon the mores in the light of such comparative studies. Professor Sumner was so impressed by the diversities of the folkways and by the force of use and wont in
modern societies that he seems to have thought that every
standard of judging social values could be nothing but the

opposition of one set of conventions against another. Perhaps
he meant rather to say that the problem is so complex and our
methods for dealing with it so little developed that any solution is at the present time quite hopeless. In reference to the
attempts or the hopes of statesmen and social philosophers
in the direction of manipulating institutions and mores "as an
architect or engineer would obtain data and apply his devices
to a task in his art," Sumner thinks a fallacy is included which
is radical and mischievous beyond measure. "We have as yet,"
he says, "no calculus for the variable elements which enter
into social problems and no analysis which can unravel their
complications. The discussions always reveal the dominion of
the prepossessions in the minds of the disputants which are in
the mores. We know that an observer of nature always has to
know his own personal equation. The mores are a social equation. When the mores are the thing studied in one's own society, there is an operation like begging the question. Moreover,
the convictions which are in the mores are 'faiths.' They are
not affected by scientific facts or demonstration. We 'believe
in' democracy, as we have been brought up in it, or we do
not. If we do, we accept its mythology. The reason is because
we have grown up in it, are familiar with it, and like it. Argument would not touch this faith."[1]

One is tempted to turn his own words upon the author and
say that this is just Professor Sumner's prejudice about the
futility of criticism and the marshalling of facts. It might be
thought to be the attitude of a mind so wearied by ruminating
among conflicting and contradictory mores that it was overwhelmed and paralyzed and helpless to do anything but to
succumb to the detached view of its own inquiry and to refuse
to make any judgment whatsoever. "What man of us gets out
of his adopted attitude,"[2] he exclaims. Yet in another passage
he insists upon the critical attitude as the only guarantee
against delusion and deception and the only means of finding
out whether propositions correspond to reality.[3]

---

[1] *Folkways,* pp. 97 f.
[2] *Ibid,* p. 98.
[3] p. 633.

At least I may assume that most academic persons accept the latter position as the truer and recognize a very great debt to the modern students of the mores for the wealth of information and the amount of disillusionment they have furnished. Two results of the application of scientific criticism to human experience would generally be admitted. One is the addition of a new dimension, as it were, to human life. Those who participate in the self-analysis and social analysis which present knowledge makes possible feel that such knowledge is itself a value. Human history, in any adequate sense of the term, has only recently begun to be written. But the mind furnished with even a high-school course in ancient and modern history is released from its narrow limits of present time and place and from the bondage of a merely provincial outlook. Similar emancipation is afforded by the study of literature and science. There is therefore a great difference between the mind of the wisest man of the Arunta tribe of central Australia as described by Spencer and Gillen, and the mind of a sixteen-year-old boy just finishing a high-school course. The latter may have no greater native talent and he may lack certain kinds of personal prowess and resourcefulness but he is so far superior in his understanding of nature, of his own inheritance, and of himself, his body and mind and surroundings, that he is like a being of a different order. However much he is trained in the customs of his people he is also greatly emancipated and has at hand the means of still greater freedom. A society whose individuals are enlightened persons of that kind sets up a conscious and a consciously criticized process of education for its members.

A second result of the application of scientific criticism is the new emphasis upon the value of human life itself. Many a custom-ruled society has paid more deference to animals and trees and stones than to human beings. But in all the peoples where reflective morality has appeared, in theory at least, man and his social relations have had first consideration. This was particularly true of the Greeks and Hebrews. The central problem of the greatest of the Greek philosophies was that of the development of man, of his mind that he might know what is good and find it, of his powers in the arts that he might create and enjoy beauty, of his sense of justice that he might live harmoniously and happily with his fellows. A human life guided by reason, brave, temperate and just, was the ideal of all schools of thought. That ideal wrought into a profound philosophical statement, embodied in enduring literature and sculpture, has been an inspiration to all succeeding culture in the western world.

The Hebrew prophets remained closer to the religious traditions of their race, but they insisted on complete liberation from those things which did not contribute to individual and social righteousness. Jeremiah rejected the old conception of social solidarity, in which the children are bound by the sins of the fathers, and conceived the individual himself to be responsible for his deeds. Like Hosea, he renounced animal sacrifice and exalted personal righteousness. Isaiah championed the cause of the poor and the oppressed and looked for deliverance through a king of justice and wisdom. Through the idea of a covenant relation man was raised to a new dignity and made to share in the moral code which he voluntarily accepted. The faith of the heart and the effort of active will were the means of attaining the fullest measure of life. Thus Hebrew religion, like Greek ethics, transcended the inherited mores by a new conscious attitude which rejected the external authority of tradition and magnified those ideals of conduct which were approved in the experience of the individual and the common life.

From this development of reflective thought sprang new ideas of a universal society and the projection of inclusive political organizations. The military campaigns of Alexander the Great represented the endeavor to organize the known world into a single state. The Stoic philosophers acted upon the conception of a universal kinship of human beings and announced themselves as no longer merely citizens of Greece but citizens of the world. Their assertion of a common rational life for all mankind clearly marked the conscious attainment of a new standpoint which in principle relegated the old tribal loyalties and customs to a lower order of existence. The Roman Empire created the external structure of political unity and Christianity became the spiritual sponsor for its realization in the soul of the individual. It is unimportant here to determine which influence contributed most to the common end but certain it is that the human world, as a conscious, universal reality came into being in the age which produced the Stoic philosophy, the Christian religion and the Roman Empire. The difficulties in the way of the practical fulfillment of the demands which such a comprehensive social and spiritual order imposed were indeed vast. They are only to be appreciated by an intimate knowledge of the struggles which the succeeding centuries witnessed,—struggles in councils of church and state, on battle fields, and in cloistered retreats of scholars and saints. It is not strange that man was compelled through a millennium and more to think of his universal life as belonging in heaven while his troubled, confused experience of change and imperfection was bound up with this present world. But the significant fact is that he possessed the universal at all and that he clung to it as the very substance of his life.

The Renaissance was the birthday of the universal in the concrete experience of this mundane sphere. At first it was announced only in terms of physical science, in the conceptions of natural law, and of the uniformity of nature. Bacon and Hobbes and Descartes did not admit that they were setting up a rival to the celestial universal. Their world of science was so novel and seemingly so different from the world of scholastic faith that they did not themselves realize the conflict they were preparing for their successors. By various dualisms and compromises men still held to the celestial verities of permanence and order while working out the laws and hypotheses of the earthly sciences in wider fields and by fruitful discoveries. At length the old essences and entities and occult forces were discarded, the divine right of kings was challenged, and the light of reason outshone the light of supernatural revelation. But still nature remained, governments attained new stability, and illuminating spiritual ideals commanded allegiance.

What I am concerned to point out is that a new scale of values came with this reflective life, a scale of values which is characteristic of the reflective life wherever it is developed, and which stands in sharp contrast to all customary-tribal value systems. It is true that tribal customs still survive in modern life but in so far as they have not stood the test of reflective assessment, they are just survivals and belong to the primitive world. It seems therefore that those who have been so diligent in setting forth the variations of primitive customs might have been more instructive and less confusing if they had remarked the difference between the custom-ruled life of our remote ancestors, including our "contemporary ancestors," and the life of those whose culture comprises, however dimly, the philosophical and scientific inheritance.

As a statement of the scale of values of civilized society I quote a passage from James' well-known description of the hierarchy of the selves. He says, "A tolerably unanimous opinion ranges the various selves which men may seek in an hierarchial scale according to their worth. A certain amount of bodily selfishness is required as a basis for all the other selves. But too much sensuality is despised, or at best condoned on account of the other qualities of the individual. The wider material selves are regarded as higher than the immediate body. He is esteemed a poor creature who is unable to forego a little meat and drink and warmth and sleep for the sake of getting on in the world. The social self as a whole, again, ranks higher than the material self as a whole. We must care more for our honor, our friends, our human ties, than for a sound skin or wealth. And the spiritual self is so supremely precious that, rather than lose it, a man ought to be willing to give up friends and good fame, and property, and life itself."[4] In other passages he identifies this spiritual self with the widest possible ideal social self. The counterpart of that conception is a social order in which the individuals seek mutually to build up that type of character. Hence social sympathy, mutual aid, co-operation for the attainment of the common good is the

---

[4] *Psychology*, Vol. I, p. 314.

great ideal of the modern world and becomes the central aim
of religion.

Christianity, from the first, centered attention upon the value
of the human soul but it could not regard the natural order of
society as consistent with, or conducive to, a spiritual existence. It therefore learned to endure this present temporary,
physical state and to prepare the soul for a heavenly realm of
pure and changeless bliss. Very slowly did the humanism of
the Renaissance affect this view of the individual. For a long
time the changes wrought by science and industry and social
reorganization were thought to pertain only to outward, material conditions, and consequently to create only stronger
earthly bonds about the soul. But gradually the antagonism of
body and soul relaxed under the genial influence of the new
learning and the physical came to be regarded as at least a
condition of mental and spiritual vitality. Medicine and hygiene at last won a decisive victory. Religion generously
founded hospitals and clinics not merely under the claim of
"good works" but also as means to health of soul. In every
direction as science and secular life yielded practical advantages religion more and more freely supported their claims.
Religion has become the champion of better government, better education and better art. Instead of being complacently
obedient to the powers that be, she has often helped to turn
them out of office and put in others. Instead of despising the
wisdom of this world she has endowed it in numerous colleges
and universities. New appreciation of the fine arts, of poetry
and the drama, of music and the dance, of play and recreation
has developed. Nor are these tendencies due to mere unconscious drifting away from old habits. They are cultivated on
principle, with the conviction that the full rounded development of all the natural powers of human life is the supreme
good. No longer does this development relate to some hidden
essence, or latent force, or occult power of personality. It does
not proceed by mysterious rites but rather by cultivating a
sane and responsive life in the midst of vital social relations.
Religion has learned to direct attention to the ideal of democracy, recognizing that this ideal fundamentally involves the

qualities of neighborliness and genuine respect and love of
fellow man. Just what these attitudes demand in any age and
especially in an industrial and urban society like ours is not
easy to determine. To find out what these claims of understanding sympathy are, becomes as urgent a need of religion
as of social settlements and bureaus of charity.

Therefore along with this social idealism of democracy
there is demanded the scientific spirit of inquiry and experi-
mentation. It is in this connection that religion is undergoing
the greatest readjustment. Having been accustomed, like politics and family life, to respect the authority of established
routine, it is difficult to accept the spirit of free inquiry, to
undertake novel, social experiments. But this method is gaining favor everywhere by the results it shows. Religious people
are told that they should test prophets by their fruits and that
wisdom is justified of her children. That encourages the use of
experiment. Through it man comes to rely more upon himself
and gains in power and responsibility. That makes for growth
in character. Religious leaders are beginning to appreciate
these new values of the social-scientific spirit. They see that
all external authority, whether of custom, or of institutions, or
of a revelation from heaven, hinders the creative spirit and the
development of a responsible will in man. It is in the interest
of this intelligent, responsible freedom for all the members of
society that religion attaches positive value to the fact that it
has no infallibility left,—no infallible Bible, no infallible Pope
or Council, no infallible creed or conscience or reason or person. Strangely enough the attainment of that conclusion has
already become the starting point of new and vital movements
in religion, movements which sincerely and reverently make
the values of a democratic-scientific social order the genuine
and dominant values of a new religious faith and hope. Neither
Catholic nor Protestant Christianity has ever consistently accepted the implications of a real democratic-scientific social
order. It is highly improbable that either will ever be able to
do so. Therefore Christianity faces a new epoch, an epoch
which requires that she identify herself completely in spirit
and purpose with the highest values of modern democracy and

science. What that involves cannot be known in advance. One cannot know beforehand what love to one's neighbor will entail. He can only find out as the days unfold their experiences. Therefore democracy is always a venturesome and interesting experiment. Freeing slaves and giving votes to women are no more the end of certain processes than they are the beginning of others. Neither does the scientific inventor know what the effect of his invention will be. Certainly that was true for the inventors of the gas engine which made possible the automobile and the airplane, with astonishing effects upon social and industrial life.

II

The second question of this discussion is, Why are the values of religion accompanied by such a sense of validity in the active effort to realize them? This question is peculiarly pertinent in reference to such values as have just been discussed. The explanation of the seeming validity of established customary values is that it arises from familiarity and long repetition. Such values, through long use, have accumulated sanctions and authority. But is this the whole story? Is there not something else in the nature of practical conduct which is even more important in accounting for the sense of the validity of religious values?

The point referred to is the nature of the practical judgment at the moment of action. The definition of religion as a practical endeavor to realize values implies that it is primarily a matter of action, an affair of overt deeds. In this respect it is sharply contrasted with the reflective attitude of philosophy. Now it is characteristic of overt action that it requires the definite selection of an end or plan. Since only one plan can be followed at one time, the one chosen must be carried out as if it were the only possible one and as having, at least at the moment of action, absolute worth and validity. If a person cannot bring himself to choose one line of action with such definiteness and exclusiveness then he either does not act at all or acts without force and effectiveness. He wabbles and hesitates and vacillates. He does not make the clear-cutting, forward thrust of successful action. The man of affairs, the captain of industry, becomes habituated to quick decisions and to prompt and vigorous action. He is said to have a firm will, to be a man of strength, and force of character. His manner takes on the attitude of settled conviction. His words are few and terse but fateful. He tends to be an absolutist. At the other extreme is the man of reflective habits. His tendency is to analyze, to deliberate, to balance contrasting views, to see the other side of every question. He develops a Hamlet-like hesitation. In every situation he is given to questioning whether it is better to be or not to be, to act or not to act. So long as he refrains from action he may enjoy the contemplation of the alternatives, of the numerous possibilities which play through his thought. The approach of the movement when he must act is repellent because in order to launch himself into the objective deed he must abandon all but one of his cherished potentialities. This line of inquiry has led me to the conception of the *practical absolute,* the absolute of the moment of action and the absolute of predominantly practical modes of life. While looking through the writings of the logicians with this conception in mind I came upon the following passage in an article by Dewey treating of different stages of logical thought. He says: "The nearer we get to the needs of action the greater absoluteness must attach to ideas. The necessities of action do not wait our convenience. Emergencies continually present themselves where the fixity required for successful activity cannot be attained through the medium of investigation. The only alternative to vacillation, confusion, and futility of action is ascription to the ideas of a positive and secured character, not in strict logic belonging to them."[5] Bosanquet also remarks that "the only really categorical, concrete, moral judgment is that which determines what the course of action is, by adopting which we can be equal to the occasion; and the predicate of this judgment is a course of action."[6]

---

[5] Dewey: Some Stages of Logical Thought; *Philosophical Review,* Volume IX, Number 5, September,1900.
[6] Bosanquet: *The Psychology of the Moral Self,* p. 113.

These observations may throw light upon the fixed character of the religious values of early society and may also furnish a suggestion as to the way in which new elements in the development of modern culture, especially the method of modern science, achieve the sense of absolute value. As is now well known the life of primitive man was one of action more than of reflection. Such reflection as he experienced was rather of the nature of reverie, of day-dreaming and fancy. This flow of imagery was largely bound down to the patterns and events of the more strenuous and thrilling moments of action, as in the chase or battle. Hence the mental life, either in times of leisure or stress, had little opportunity to become released from the absoluteness and fixity of action. Durkheim has undertaken to show how the unconscious "collective representations" of primitive man became the rigid framework of the conceptual life, the categories of space, time, causality and the rest, and that these categories were the counterpart of the habits of action, binding customs, generated by the necessities of man's struggle for existence. This suggests a deeper reason for the authority of religious attitudes than those explanations which refer its absoluteness to its natural conservatism or to the fact that it is a product of custom or of revelation.

This deeper reason lies in the nature of religion as a life of action. It has always been marked by the struggle to meet emergencies, to make safe the food supply, or the marriage relation and childbirth, to ward off evils in times of crises, in illness and death and war. Religion reflects the desperate conflict man has had to adjust himself to his world,—the world of physical nature and even more to the world of his troubled imaginings. He has had to battle demons and ghosts, devils and sprites and relentless furies in a thousand shapes. Or the struggle may be represented from the other side of the shield as the urgent effort to attain relief, to enjoy happiness, to gain paradise, to found a city which has foundations, to build an eternal kingdom. Religion is ever waging a warfare, conducting a campaign, striving for fuller life. Even its contemplative life has followed this pattern. It has dreamed of victory after battle and of those who have come up through great tribulation into triumph and peace. It has therefore lived constantly by the use of the absolutes of action. And these absolutes have been of the most absolute kind because the values for which the actions were precipitated were felt to be of the profoundest importance.

From this point of view it may be possible to gain a better understanding of the conflict between science and religion in our modern world. Science has invaded the precincts of religion, too often in its narrower conception of itself merely as a critic, a detached reflective investigator, instead of coming in its larger function of helping to find and to realize whatever practical and vital ends man's nature craves. In its narrower rôle it has been irritating and confusing to the practical spirit of religion. In its larger function it is felt by all enlightened religionists to be a friendly and most useful ally. This is not to minimize the chastening effects of the application of science to religion. In its friendliest mood science is a strenuous physician and surgeon producing a powerful catharsis and amputating limbs and removing organs decadent and useless, or infected by superstition. Not a few have thought the patient never could survive the treatment. Because religion has been so bound up and permeated by the magic and tribal custom in which it was born it has been the conviction of many who knew its beginnings best that the coming of science would be its death. But events do not justify that prediction.

It is, however, a vital question as to how religion is to adjust itself to science. The other distinguishing characteristic of our time, the democratic ideal, seems to lie much closer to religion as we know it, for democracy is a practical endeavor, and it seeks to realize the development of the individual which is already enshrined as the highest value of religion. One approach for the hospitable reception of science by religion is through the practical advantages which science already offers for carrying out the democratic and practical religious program of good will and social amelioration. Medical science has been appropriated in that way. Educational sciences have also found their place in religious schools. Technical and applied sciences of many kinds have been used freely. The difficulties have arisen at those points where the method of science has led to general conceptions which conflict fundamentally with the prevailing religious philosophies. Notable examples are found in geology and its effect on biblical cosmology, in biology and its theory of evolution, and in historical criticism and its implications for the doctrine of revelation. But a difficulty, deeper than all these, lies in the method itself, for science cannot be content simply to help in fulfilling the ends which religion sets up. It will insist in passing criticism on the ends themselves. This means that if religion is to be thorough in appropriating and furthering, as its own values, the highest values of society, it must accept unreservedly the value of science both in its method and in its results. Applying this principle to the ideal of democracy it means that religion cannot satisfy the demands of the situation by imposing a preconceived type of society as the final goal for which we are to strive. Democracy is a genuine adventure of faith and we cannot know where we are going until we arrive. Science helps to survey the situation before the experiment is made. It presents, on the basis of past experience, and by the prognostications of trained imagination, the various possible lines of action and their probable outcome. But it is compelled to yield all of its possibilities but one at the moment the experiment is put into action. And it must allow that one to be acted upon with all the wholeness of heart and sense of absoluteness which efficient action requires. After the plan has been tried, or as its successive steps occur, science may make new observations and prepare for further specific action and so on in a continuous process of growing experience.

In this way science has won over various fields of experience in recent years. One knows the physician is not infallible but trusts him nevertheless. Oil and mining investments are known to lack perfect security yet the man who invests in them parts with his money at the moment of purchase with as much finality as perfect knowledge could warrant. Manufacturers put out their latest product as the "acme" or the "perfecto" or the "ideal" and when they discover some means of improvement they advertise a new model and without embarrassment proclaim it as perfection. The extent to which this use of a practical absolute may be carried is illustrated by a well known type of oil stove for cooking purposes which bravely bears in conspicuous letters across its front this legend: "New Perfection, Number 62."

There are indications that religion may eventually reach such an attitude where the practical absolute of action will be accompanied by a process of reflective reconstruction in the direction of an expansive social ideal. In the past, religion has often accepted, though grudgingly, modifications of its values in response to the growing life of society. But the modifications have been ascribed to other influences than reflective thought. Thereby men have excused themselves from the responsibility of the situation. They have at times held to the doctrine of progressive revelation but too often have conceived the process of revelation as ending at some point in the past, and providing no method of dealing with new conditions in the living present. In those religious systems which have announced new revelations from heaven in times of crisis, there has been no reliable means of understanding the revelation nor of determining whether it was applicable to the case in hand. And there were often conflicting revelations for the same perplexity. The scientific method of meeting human problems is radically different. It claims no infallibility, but does actually take hold of the concrete difficulty and endeavors to find a working solution in the light of all the facts. In our society this method is already yielding results so encouraging and so full of promise that the projects of expert social engineers are beginning to be thought of as guides to new social values which are genuinely religious. When facing the emergencies of the vast, insistent demands of some great social problem, like the war, or the famine in Russia, a plan of action matured in the light of all available experience and human sympathy, approves itself to all right minded men as absolutely the thing to do. It is the practical absolute. It proclaims the sure way of salvation and discloses beyond doubt what must be taken as the categorical imperative of the divine will.

9

EDGAR SHEFFIELD BRIGHTMAN

Theistic Personalist

Edgar Sheffield Brightman (1884–1953) was Borden Parker
Bowne's successor at Boston University. Accordingly, he is
often rightly regarded as an exponent of the "Boston school"
of idealistic personalism, a distinctly Methodist variety of the
theological liberalism of Lotze and Ritschl. A careful and detailed analysis of Brightman's thought and its development
would reveal a number of vital interactions foreshadowed by
the formative encounter between Methodist perfectionism and
Jamesian pragmatism. In the total scope of Brightman's
philosophical theology this interaction emerges as that between
faith and reason. There are affinities between the personalism
of Bowne and Brightman and that of a number of European
thinkers such as Berdyaev, Maritain, Mounier, Scheler, and
Nicolai Hartmann. Like the latter two, Brightman emphasizes
the concept of value; perhaps because of this he, too, has fallen
out of fashion during a period which has given greater emphasis to history and to existential concerns. On the other hand,
Brightman's affinities with Whitehead and Hartshorne and his
palpable influence on such men as Nels F. S. Ferré and Martin
Luther King suggest that his legacy may prove to be of value
for future generations, once it is adequately appraised.

Born in a Methodist parsonage in Holbrook, Mass., Edgar
Brightman was the son, grandson, and great grandson of ministers. He grew up as a Methodist in the stronghold of Congregationalism, and by the age of ten young Edgar had read
much of Adam Clarke's *Commentary on the Old and New
Testament* (1826), a monumental exposition of Wesleyan per-

fectionism.[1] At the camp meeting in Yarmouth, his interest in religion was decisively spurred by the preaching of James Mudge, a former missionary to India and author of *Growth in Holiness Toward Perfection* (1895). What impressed Brightman most in Mudge was his stress on the sovereignty of God, but sidelights on Hindu mysticism also piqued his curiosity. It was a high school principal in Whitman, Mass., however, who effected Brightman's intellectual liberation through the teaching of mathematics and Greek. Among other things, this man, Dudley L. Whitmarsh, also conducted scientific experiments in psychic phenomena.

As an undergraduate at Brown, Brightman habitually carried in his pocket a copy of the *Enchridion* of Epictetus. He read Plato in Greek and was successively enthralled by Berkeley, Nietzsche, Kant, and Schopenhauer, but his "first real allegiance" was to the idealism of Josiah Royce, an influence which endured for about a year after his graduation in 1906. Brightman's senior year was marked by a serious accident at a Christmas party in his father's church (Brightman was badly burned), and by his father's death three months later. These and other experiences of fortuitous tragedy subsequently led him to embrace James's concept of a limited God, and to build upon this notion a dualistic, implicity dialectical metaphysic of good and evil. In this area Brightman's thought, as it later developed, most closely resembles Berdyaev. For Berdyaev, the creative act represents the liberating victory of spirit over the "heaviness" of matter, of necessity, of the world.[2] For Brightman, "God's good will is forever shaping The Given to his purposes"[3]; value is sovereign over disvalue, and the movement of life is toward eternal perfection—not simply but in

---

[1] See John L. Peters, *Christian Perfection and American Methodism* (Nashville: Abingdon, 1956), pp. 103–106. For details of Brightman's life, see Janette E. Newhall, "Edgar Sheffield Brightman: A Biographical Sketch," *Philosophical Forum*, XII (1954), and E. S. Brightman, "Religion As Truth," in Vergilius Ferm, ed., *Contemporary American Theology*, I (New York: Round Table Press, 1932), pp. 53–81.
[2] See Nikolai Berdyaev, *The Meaning of the Creative Act* (London: Gollancz, 1955), *passim*.
[3] Brightman, "Religion As Truth," *op. cit.*, p. 77.

interaction with a "cosmic drag" which hinders and restrains even God.

During two years as instructor in Greek and philosophy at Brown, Brightman earned his M.A. with enough credits left over to enable him to take an S.T.B. at Boston after two years there. His relationship with Bowne was not close (they spoke on only three occasions), and he later felt it necessary to correct Bowne's personalism with "more James and more Hegel" as well as Darwin, but the personalist concept itself became central to his thinking and freed him from an earlier disposition toward determinism. From that earlier disposition, however, he retained a respect for logic, which set him at odds with Bowne as well as with Lotze and James. The sole criterion of truth, he would argue, is logical coherence; but "the logic of coherence is the living whole," arising from and interpreting the data of experience.

In 1910, the year of Bowne's death, Brightman went to Germany on a fellowship. For two semesters he studied at Berlin under Harnack, Deissmann, Münsterberg, and others, and for one semester he was at Marburg, where Wilhelm Herrmann was his principal mentor, advising him on his doctoral dissertation, "The Criterion of Truth in Albrecht Ritschl's Theology." He received his Ph.D. from Boston University in 1912, by which time he had joined the faculty of Nebraska Wesleyan University. He was married that year to a young lady he had met in Berlin. The birth of a son in 1914 was followed by tragedy as his wife succumbed to a facial cancer in 1915. Soon thereafter, Brightman began a new life at Wesleyan University in Middletown, Conn., where he married again in 1918. Despite the deep personal anguish that World War I brought him, Brightman served as an ROTC officer and gave pep talks to promote the war effort. He later became a deeply convinced pacifist.

In 1919, Brightman returned to Boston University as professor of philosophy. Six years later he was installed as the first Borden Parker Bowne Professor of Philosophy. In the same year his first two major books appeared, as well as a minor one —*An Introduction to Philosophy, Religious Values* and *Immortality in Post-Kantian Idealism.* Of his subsequent books, prob-

ably the most important are *The Problem of God* (1930) and
Person and Reality (posthumously edited by Peter A. Bertocci,
1958).[4] For a definitive statement of Brightman's philosophical
theology and metaphysic, respectively, the latter two volumes
are indispensable. Yet the selection from *Religious Values* that
comprises the following pages is of particular interest, not only
because it exhibits the general structure of his later thought,
but because, to an even greater degree, it brings out the empirical and human concerns from which his more abstract
system proceeded. Brightman's dialectic is an attenuated one;
it is more logical than dynamic, closer to the formal contrasts
of the later Hegelians than to the bold and audacious opposi-
tions found in Berdyaev. It is almost as if he wishes to mediate
between the extremes with an Aristotelian or Confucian mean,
yet is forced by both reason and experience to confront anomalies—as he does here in adjudicating values and disvalues.
The latter do not figure merely as drawbacks, which are outweighed by the positive values; they exert a limiting force or
even an undercutting or jeopardizing force that implies the
need of committed effort on behalf of values to assure their
ultimate triumph. Transposed to a theological context later in
the same book and again in *The Problem of God,* all values
are seen as the fruit of divine activity, functions of God's purpose made real through creative effort—an effort which struggles against disvalue and experiences it as evil and tragedy.
Growth through conflict and suffering, for Brightman, is of the
nature of persons, no less of the Divine Person than of those
created in his image.

Whether he has succeeded or not, Brightman offers a highly
cogent modern alternative to Thomistic personalism and,
within the context of liberal theology and idealist metaphysics,
he makes an important contribution to the critical study of
religious truth, combining a renewed and deepened under-

---

[4] For a summary and critique of *The Problem of God,* see Charles Hartshorne and William L. Reese, *Philosophers Speak of God* (University of
Chicago Press, 1953), pp. 358–364. For a discussion of *Person and Reality,*
see John B. Cobb, *Living Options in Protestant Theology* (Philadelphia:
Westminster, 1962), pp. 83–88.

standing of the classical Christian doctrine of the personal
God with more universal, transreligious conceptions of cosmic
reality. Equally important, he redeemed the perfectionist spirit
of Methodism from the excesses of moralism and gave it a
new, critical basis in an ultimate but tempered optimism.

THE HUMAN VALUES OF RELIGION*

1. The Problem of the Chapter

We have now reached the point where we may begin the specific study of religious values. All value is the conscious experience of persons, and the study of religious values must begin
with the empirical facts. These facts are to be found in the
fields that are studied by history and psychology. At a later
point (Chapter VII) an attempt will be made to describe the
psychological factors that enter into the heart of religious experience, namely, worship. In this and the two succeeding
chapters the aim will be to define and then to interpret philosophically the values of religion as they are revealed by the
larger facts of its history. The special problem of this chapter,
then, will be to inquire what contributions religion has made
historically to the value of human life. For the purposes of this
chapter we shall not ask whether these human values are
"apparent" or "real," mere "value-claims" or "true" values.

We shall leave behind every apologetic motive together
with every question or doubt; dogma, doctrine, and theology
will be left defenseless and uncriticized. Not theory, but historical fact; not proof, but life itself, will concern us. If any
belief be as true or as false as you please, in this chapter
we are indifferent to that fact. Without probing nicely into
questions of the logical cogency of anyone's creed, we shall
concern ourselves only with the question about the value of
religion in the life of man. What does religion do for human

---

* From Edgar Sheffield Brightman, *Religious Values* (New York: Abingdon Press, 1925), pp. 78–101.

life? Does it make life better or worse? Does it help or hinder the attainment of the other goods of life? In short, What are the human values of religion?

2. Definitions of Religion and Value for the Purposes of this Chapter

When we hear the word "religion," we naturally think of our own religion, that in which we have received our early training, or to which we have come by our more mature experience and reflection. But if we were to define everything that religion means to us, we might have difficulty in persuading others to recognize every factor in our conception as essential to religion; so that a merely individualistic definition will not do. We must seek one in which our religion is included, but which also finds room for what is truly religious in every religious experience or belief. The attempt to reach a valid general definition of religion is one that cannot be abandoned. Despite the obvious necessity of postponing a final definition to the end of one's investigation, a working definition is always needed at the outset, if we are to know where the field of our study is located.

The task of finding such a working definition is complicated by the fact that the word "religion" may mean either a mode of life or a scientific concept used to describe that life. Now, the religious mode of life might well exist, whether in primitive man or in our neighbors, without the use of a scientific concept of religion or even without the willingness to say, "I am religious." With reference to the scientific concept itself no agreement obtains. Pages 339 to 361 of Professor Leuba's *A Psychological Study of Religion* are filled with a collection of more than two score of definitions, to which might be added many more.

We may be able in this confusion to agree on at least one essential trait of a good definition of religion. It must represent religion as something living and developing, and not as static and unchanging; it must, then, be a law of life. If you look for any traits which appear, in unchanged form, in the religion of the Bushmen of Australia, of Socrates, of Saint Paul, of Spinoza, and of ex-President Eliot, you will deserve to look in vain, because you will have forgotten that the essence of religion must be found in some law of life rather than in any dead uniformity. A sound definition will not be a Platonic idea, but an Aristotelian entelechy: not an abstract concept, but a functional principle.

Elsewhere the present writer has suggested that historical religion, whatever its differences, always expresses at least one common function or attitude. "Religion," his proposed historical definition runs, "is the total attitude of man toward what he considers to be superhuman and worthy of worship, or devotion, or propitiation, or at least of reverence."[1]

Attitudes toward our fellow human beings, then, are not (contrary to numerous current views) to be regarded as religious unless they spring from a deeper attitude toward a superhuman being of some sort; and attitudes toward the superhuman are not religious unless the superhuman power or powers be deemed worthy of worship, that is, be in some sense a source of value. In primitive thought this value is very crudely conceived as "mana"; to-day, a Rudolph Otto interprets it as "das Heilige" ("the Holy"). Yet a common function is performed by both of these beliefs, namely, a reverence for values and a faith in their conservation.

W. G. Everett, therefore, is near to the heart of the matter when he suggests that the experiences of religion "have as their center of interest the cosmic fortune of values."[2] It is true that the Bushmen of Australia have very little interest in "the cosmic fortune of values." This element, then, must be regarded not as an actual factor always present, but as a limit which any life called religious is approaching or tends to approach.

The other element in our topic, that of value, still awaits definition. It has just reminded us of its existence by appearing in the expression "the cosmic fortune of values."

---

[1] *An Introduction to Philosophy,* p. 318. In our discussion we shall usually refer to "the superhuman" as God.

[2] *Moral Values* (New York: Henry Holt and Company, 1918), p. 382.

For the purpose of this chapter the term "value" is less in need of further definition than the term "religion." Whatever the psychologists or the metaphysicians may finally have to say about value, everyone will doubtless agree that by a value he means something that he prizes, something worthful, precious, desirable: something that meets our need, something that fulfills our ideal of what ought to be. Whatever for its own sake we thus prize is called an intrinsic value; whatever is only a means to the attainment of intrinsic value is instrumental.

It must be recognized that this distinction raises problems such as that as to whether there are many intrinsic values (as pluralism holds) or whether all reduce to one, such as the organic whole of personality, or of society, or of the universe. But, for our purposes, we may assume a practical and at least relative difference between the fact that we prize religion for its own sake and the fact that it ministers to the attainment of other values. We should note that the term used to denote the contrary of value is disvalue or evil. Whatever is unworthy, or hinders the attainment of what is worthful, is, either intrinsically or instrumentally, disvalue. If we are to deal fairly with the theme of the "Human Values of Religion," it is necessary to consider also its possible disvalues. To this aspect of the subject we shall turn for a while.

3. THE HUMAN DISVALUES OF RELIGION

The critics of religion have always been alive to its defects, and none of its friends, however ardent, could maintain that the presence of religion in life is always wholly good both in itself and in its consequences. It might well be agreed that this would be true of a proper attitude toward the true religion. But in our present study we are interested in actual religious life as it appears in history, not in the ideal of propriety and truth. Let us proceed to enumerate some of the elements of disvalue that may be found to exist in historical religion.

During the previous generation Nietzsche made famous the charge that religion, or at least Christianity, was essentially slavish and hence bad. It is doubtless true that religion

tends to accentuate the dependence of man on the superhuman, and the infinite superiority of the cosmic powers to
the human individual. It is also true that Judaism, Buddhism,
and Christianity, in particular, inculcate the virtues of love
for all and pity for the weak and suffering. Nor can it be denied that these very virtues in excess sometimes breed a false
humility, a substitution of the tender emotion for strength of
character, and more sympathy with inferiority than desire for
excellence. The great products of the religious spirit, it is true,
makes Nietzsche's charge of slavishness ridiculous, if it be intended to designate an essential trait of Christianity or of religion in general. But in the sense that a slavish spirit is a disvalue sometimes arising from religion the charge is not without
foundation.

Again, it is said that religion breeds effeminacy, that it appeals to women and children, but it lacks masculinity. Insofar
as it attracts men, they are said to be effeminate types or to
be rendered effeminate by religion. True it is that the rôle of
feeling in many religious experiences characterizes those experiences as predominantly passive rather than active, and,
insofar, as feminine rather than masculine (according to the
traditional view of sex differences which is by no means
proved). Nor can it be denied that in contemporary American
religion the distinctively religious aspects of church life are
often cultivated more devotedly by women than by men, and
that men who move in a religious society where they are
largely in the minority, more or less unconsciously resort to a
kind of screen of effeminacy as an instinctive protective coloration. Even pastors occasionally succumb to this subtle influence. There is, then, a real evil here; although any impartial
survey will make clear that effeminacy is no universal or
necessary trait of great religious personalities. It is sentimental
misrepresentation, and not historical fact, that has pictured
Jesus in such a light. Every great religion makes a profound
appeal to the powers of intellect and achievement, and so to
what is regarded as the essentially masculine. The disvalue of
effeminacy is a fact, but it is surely not inherent in religion, nor
a necessary concomitant of it.

Many great religious reformers, like Buddha, the Hebrew prophets, and Jesus, have attacked another evil tendency which keeps recurring in religion: the tendency to formalism, to an overemphasis of external rites and forms, which, carried to an extreme, passes from noble and significant ritual, through excessive ceremonialism into thoroughgoing externalism and idolatry, which substitutes the act for the spirit and the thing for the god. We shall not here seek to appraise the just claims of ritual in worship. We are only concerned to point out the manifest contradiction that excessive formalism introduces into religion. In purely formal acts, thought and feeling have vanished, the sense of relation to the superhuman is forgotten, and values are ignored. Here is a disvalue, springing from one aspect of religion itself, which tends to destroy real religion; to take it from the spirit and deliver it over to mere motor habit.

Another evil of religion, in some respects allied to formalism, yet different from it, is conservatism or traditionalism. Conservatism tends to perpetuate a tendency to formalism once established; it is not, however, necessarily formalistic, and seemingly tends to function to preserve religion rather than to bore from within as does formalism. Why, then, it may be asked, is conservatism not a value? Does it not preserve the sacred treasures of the past? Does it not cherish religion against destructive foes? Is it not humanity's guarantee against anarchy and barbarism in every field? In view of these challenges, he would be rash who would pronounce conservatism wholly evil. It belongs in the class of the mixed, to which Plato not infrequently made appeal. For along with the elements of worth which must be recognized there are also elements of a very different sort. If the spirit of conservatism attain full control, it will function to maintain the entire *status quo* unchanged. Beliefs, types of experience, and practices are to continue as they have been and shall be, world without end. The infinite has been sufficiently revealed, and the proper emotional and active attitudes toward the infinite completely categorized long ago. What is there for men to do but to continue in the enjoyment of the blessings bestowed upon them by the past? Conservatism so magnifies the function of preservation of the best in the past as to lay its dead hand upon the present and deny it the right to live and grow. It becomes intolerance and wages a quasi-holy war against every tradition or form of life that differs, if only by a hair's breadth, from its own. The spirit thus engendered is far from that recommended by the ethical teachings of religion itself. Extreme conservatism, then, like formalism, amounts to a self-destruction of religion; but since it can point to so rich and many-sided a heritage from the past, the dangers of conservatism are much more subtle and slow-working than those of formalism.

If we find in religion all elements of human nature, we may regard the evils thus far mentioned as arising from the excess of some one element: slavishness and effeminacy, for example, from an excess of feeling, formalism from an excess of standardized action, and conservatism from all elements, it is true, but especially from an excessive respect for the intellectual achievements of the past. Since these forms of disvalue characterize religion itself as more or less evil where they prevail, we may regard them as intrinsic disvalues of religion. But we also find instrumental disvalues in religion; factors in it which operate to hamper or to destroy other values in life, such as the scientific, the philosophical, and even the values of moral progress. In calling attention to this fact we do not forget the services of religion to culture and to science. The point is, however, clearly to be made that despite those great services there has also been the other side of the shield; and even today very large numbers of the religious, both leaders and followers, are suspicious of or openly hostile to æsthetic and scientific activities or to any reform that means change in approved conventions.

4. Limits of the Human Value of Religion

It is not to be supposed that an exhaustive list of the ills that man owes to religion has been presented. The catalogue has been incomplete; it does not pretend to *a priori* necessity like the Kantian table of categories. It aims only to make clear that religion as it exists is not wholly valuable. As a further precaution, it should be noted that religion, even at its best, with these evils suppressed or eliminated, is not all of life, although it is related to all of life. As much injustice may be done to any cause by expecting too much of it as by belittling its true value. In order to avoid doing this injustice to religion it should be remarked that religion cannot (or should not) pretend to impart intelligence to the unintelligent, nor to solve economic problems, nor to guarantee human freedom from bodily ills. When one expects these results one may well depart from religion with a false estimate of what religion has actually accomplished in human history.

Religion, we have said, will not impart intelligence. A religious awakening may impart a new stimulus and zest to the intellectual life, or may vitalize dormant powers of mind. The great leaders of the Christian Church from Saint Paul to Saint Augustine, Luther, Calvin, Wesley, Cardinal Newman, Phillips Brooks, and Albert Schweitzer, have been mighty men of valor in the realm of thought. But all great religions have made their appeal also to the common man, however unintellectual and untrained he may be. Christianity, as Harnack is fond of pointing out, was something which the serving-maids of Ephesus could appropriate. There is indeed a certain minimum of intelligence below which religion is impossible; a mind must be able in some measure to grasp a few fundamental ideas about God and man and human conduct, that is, about "man's place in the cosmos," if religion is to take root in that mind at all. But observation of the individual differences among men indicates that there are wide variations in their native capacity. There is no reason to believe that religion creates new capacity, or supplies deficiencies in education. A religious experience, however satisfying, or a religious belief, however firmly and reverently held, does not of itself endow its bearer with any special insight into questions of scientific or historical fact. However true it be that the facts of religious history may never be appreciatively interpreted by a historian to whom religion is not real, it is also true that the religious must be supplemented by the scientific and historical spirit before it is competent to pronounce on questions of scientific and historical fact.

In the present age it is worth while to emphasize the fact that religion does not solve economic problems. Such problems are the burning ones of to-day; how much fiercer to-morrow's conflagration will be who knows? Has religion, then, no message for the social need? Most assuredly it has. It calls society to consider its Maker, to face the meaning of life, and to seek for true and permanent value, that which is eternal. The religious spirit, when true to itself, is the soul of every undertaking; nothing human will be foreign to it. It drives men on toward an ideal solution of every problem; is the pervading stimulus of the whole of life. It drives on, but it does not build the roads on which to travel. It creates the vision of a divine plan in life, but it does not furnish the tools and instruments for building a mansion here below in harmony with the divine idea. Religious idealism is, in this world, impractical and futile, unless it joins hands with scientific knowledge of conditions and means. Hence it is that the social and economic ideas of religious personalities are often fantastic and unreal. The soul of the new order must indeed come from religion, but the body must come from the sociologists and economists. Only in the union and appropriate functioning of soul and body will the organism live and grow. Religion needs science.

Finally, it was said that religion does not guarantee freedom from bodily ills. There will at once occur to the mind of the reader numerous objections to this statement. Has not religion often taught that a complete conquest of the body was possible? Is not its ministry often a ministry of the healing of disease? Have not history and modern instances abundantly proved its power over sickness and suffering? While all this is true, it must be admitted that for one person who has sought and found in religion healing for disease, there are many others, just as genuinely religious, who have continued to suffer; and in the end, all die, the just and unjust alike.

Whatever physical well-being religion may bring—and it is no doubt a greater force for bodily health than most men know —such a result is incidental, a byproduct. It is a grateful shade cast by the tree on certain weary travelers in the hot season; it is not the very root and life of the tree. Religion is the total relation of the life to that Power which is called God; and the man who desires health as his prime aim, and God only on condition of his gaining health, does not comprehend the spirit of religion. The religious soul desires God unconditionally; this means the unconditional faith that what is supremely valuable will never be destroyed; it does not mean the unconditional guarantee of physical life and health.

In our attempt to understand the human values of religion we have thus far considered the evils, the disvalues, to which religion gives rise or may give rise, and have pointed out some of the things that religion may not justly be expected to do for men. Although doubtless the most precious possession of human life, it is not an Aladdin's lamp, nor, in itself, a panacea for all ills. With the recognition of the abuses and limitations of religion, we have advanced one stage in our journey toward the understanding of the human values of religion.

5. How Religion Meets the Ills of Life

The remainder of our journey will be concerned with the search for positive values. Since it is the human values of religion in which we are interested, we may well approach our problem from the standpoint of the nature of human life in general, then proceeding to inquire what religion is worth to it, rather than confining ourselves to the religious aspects of life. The former method is much more broad in its scope, and lends promise of a fairer final estimate of the place of religion in life as a whole. It cannot, of course, be completely carried out within the limits of a single chapter; but it may be applied to some extent.

If one surveys life with the thought of its value in mind, one is struck first of all by the ills from which life suffers, which seem to frustrate and even to destroy higher aims and purposes; and then by the needs of life, its fundamental longings and aspirations. We may fairly test the human value of religion by considering how it deals with life's ills and its needs.

Of the ills of life the most widespread and universally experienced is the fact of suffering. About this fact religion by its very nature is most profoundly concerned. If it is interested in the cosmic fortune of values, every item of experience that hinders or renders impossible the fullest attainment of value becomes a problem. Suffering not only appears to do this, but it is in itself a disvalue, an evil. The Judæan prophet who describes the fall of man in Genesis does so in order to account for the suffering of woman in childbirth and of man in the hard tasks of agriculture. The four noble truths of Buddhism are "the existence of sorrow, the cause of suffering, the cessation of sorrow, and the eightfold path that leads to the cessation of sorrow." The author of the epistle ascribed to James defines pure religion as this, "to visit the fatherless and widows in their affliction and to keep oneself unspotted from the world."

Pain, suffering, sorrow, affliction—what does religion do with these tragic facts? It seeks to reduce suffering, yet recognizes that there seems to be an irreducible element of suffering in life, and it sees the problem of suffering in a world where God and value of the practical attitude which religion takes toward each of these aspects.

Most great religions to a greater or less degree are touched with pity for a suffering world, and seek to feed the hungry and relieve the distressed. The human value of all such palliative measures is so obvious that it needs no special discussion. But religion recognizes that its humanitarian function is not the last or deepest word regarding suffering. For, strive as we will, perfect medicine and sociology as we may, it appears that suffering can never entirely be removed from human life.

Where religion is brought face to face with suffering as an irreducible fact, it is not and cannot be dumb. To the problem it has given different answers. It has said that this suffering was a punishment for sin, or a means of discipline and grace, or mere illusion and error, or a burden which God will give strength to bear, or an obstacle which a steadfast will may overcome and disregard, or a reminder that this world is not all. Religious faith may speak in many tongues about suffering, but what it says, being translated, has always one and the same meaning. This is the meaning: suffering is not the brute mystery that it seems to be; it serves some purpose, even though we know not what; it will be overcome, even though we know not how. Religion, then, meets the suffering of the individual with faith, a faith that comes to concrete and practical expression in various forms, but always as an act of implicit trust. What other resource than this in the face of suffering is not presently exhausted and baffled? Does not religion, based on faith in the Eternal, give to life its only indestructible refuge in hours of agony, and rescue it from despair or suicide?

The last word of religion, then, is God. The mere hope or trust that the problem of suffering has a solution would not long sustain the spirit were it not for the confidence that the solution of the mystery is in the hands of the supreme Power in the universe. This confidence immeasurably strengthens and fortifies the soul. Whether the belief in God is true or not does not now concern us; we are now interested only in observing that it adds substance and force to the religious conquest of suffering.

Intimately connected with suffering is death, the mysterious, which releases man from suffering by destroying life itself. It is a solution of our first problem which only creates a greater. Suffering usually leaves it possible for the sufferer to appreciate some of the values of life; death makes all meaning and value impossible. Blank nothing is left; or so it seems. Death appears to be the negation of religion, for what can be "the cosmic fortune of values" when human persons, the most precious of all values, are snuffed out like a candle? But it is precisely the acuteness of this challenge that drives men to religion. Schopenhauer's classic essay "On Man's Need of Metaphysics" is based on the thesis that it is the fact of death which gives the strongest impulse to philosophical reflection and to religious belief.

Religion, in the presence of death, may assert itself by one of two attitudes: that is, either by the assertion that the fate of the right cause is assured, even though the individual perishes, or by the faith that human personality survives bodily death. So long as religion is religion it must refuse to accept the fact of death as final.

Many finely attuned spirits are inspired to high living by the first of the two attitudes mentioned. I and we may perish, but the truly good, for which our life was lived, shall never die. Bernard Bosanquet has said, "Wherever a man is so carried beyond himself, whether for any other being or for a cause or for a nation, that his personal fate seems to him as nothing in comparison of the happiness or the triumph of the other, there you have the universal basis and structure of religion."[3] These beautiful words express the idea which underlies the attitude that we are now considering. The individual may be so utterly devoted to his cause that he will gladly lay down his life in all literalness if but the cause live on.

For some the religious conquest of death is thus achieved. But for most this conception is profoundly unsatisfactory. To them it is not clear what the cause is that will continue to endure after the last human being has vanished and left no conscious trace behind. The denial of personal immortality appears to most religious believers equivalent to the denial of ultimate value in life. Faith in immortal life is an all but universal trait of religions. In the higher forms it is an expression of the belief that all personality must survive because it is the most valuable fact in the universe, on which the real existence of all other values depends.

Whichever of these two attitudes toward death religion may assume, it means to proclaim its conviction that there is something in man's life which death cannot slay. There are, it is true, wide differences of opinion to-day as to the actual effect on twentieth-century life of this belief in personal immortality. It may be admitted that with many the faith is but a weak and powerless shadow, and that with many others it is a morbid and unwholesome force, destroying perspective, blunting the sense of value, bewitching judgment, and obsessing the entire life. It may walk the streets of the New Jerusalem in fancy, rather than cleaning the streets of the earthly Jerusalem. But despite these serious evils, it is clear that the value of the religious attitude toward death far outweighs its disvalue. It

---

[3] *What Religion Is* (London: Macmillan & Co., 1920), p. 5.

gives each believing soul the faith that his life has before it an endless road of possibility and service; it adds to the dignity of the moral law the serious reflection that we and all whom we affect are forever going to keep meeting again in our own persons the consequences of all our acts; it gives hope when death speaks only of despair. In defying death religion at once comforts with the thought of hope and compels attention to the actual eternity of moral values in an immortal society. Such thoughts of eternity, when held by a restrained faith that is not too eager to fill in imaginative details, imparts sacredness and elevation to human life. Religion thus fortifies the self-respect of man and consecrates his social obligations.

When religion emerges from its most primitive forms it confronts an ill of man's own making which becomes one of its acutest problems. I refer to sin. A Babylonian poem begins with the words,

> "I advanced in life, I attained to the allotted span;
> Wherever I turned, there was evil, evil.
> Oppression is increased, uprightness I see not.
> I cried unto God, but he showed not his face.
> I prayed to my goddess, but she raised not her head."

Moral evil must become a problem for religion, because it is hostility to the values with the conservation of which religion is concerned. Sin implies the voluntary cutting off of the individual from the whole; the setting up of a realm of narrower special interest separated from the whole. The sinner thus is unwilling to face all the facts, to confront the context and implications of his choice. He is complacent in the denial and contradiction of his own noblest aspirations.

Religion meets this ill first of all by intensifying it, by dwelling on its heinous character, for religion is never willing to regard sin merely as the misfortune of a divided self; it summons the sinner to a cosmic bar and appeals to him to contemplate a divided universe resulting from his sin; the unity of his own soul, the social structure of life, and the harmony between man and the universe have all been rent asunder. Religion views sin as a cosmic tragedy. But religion, as soon as it recognizes the existence of sin, offers some way of escape. By sacrifice or penance or repentance, or by some combination of these or other means, religion provides to the sinner some way of doing his part toward healing the breach which his act has wrought, and assures him that God has already done his part and that the Almighty will then receive him once more. Thus religion makes it possible to remold nearer to the heart's desire the world which sin had shattered to bits. It restores to life as a whole the meaning which sin had destroyed or denied.

Another ill of life is ignorance, itself a prolific source of yet further ills. It is quite true that nothing can dispel ignorance save knowledge, and that any weakening or impairment of the mind's zeal in the search for knowledge would be a calamity to the race. As history shows, religion has sometimes operated as such a weakening force. But in the nature of religion it is difficult to discern any reason for this hostility. Religion, when performing its own function, does not seek to dispel ignorance by the folly of competing against science on its own ground. It does, however, have two characteristic ways of dealing with the fact of ignorance. On the one hand, it offers objects of faith which lie beyond demonstrable knowledge, but which present themselves, notwithstanding, as revelations of truth. It would be the height of presumption to pretend that by the way of scientific or philosophic speculation it is possible cogently to prove God, or immortality, or the cosmic supremacy of values. Since Kant such an enterprise has been foredoomed to failure. But religious life and experience give to the mind items of religious, as distinct from scientific, knowledge that do not dispel our scientific ignorance, but still give humanity the faith that our ignorance does not shut us off utterly from the truly real. "Religion," says Professor Hocking, "is the present attainment in a single experience of those objects which in the course of nature are reached only at the end of infinite progression."[4] Thus does religion sustain man in the infinite task of overcoming his own ignorance.

In another fashion too does religion cope with human

---

[4] *The Meaning of God in Human Experience* (Yale University Press, 1912), p. 31.

ignorance. In the midst of his trials Job is upheld by the
thought, "He knoweth the way that I take" (Job 23. 10). Indeed, one of the chief traits of the idea of God in all developed
religions is that he is the one who knows all, who understands
all, in whom is the key to every mystery, the solution to every
riddle. The religious soul may be ignorant, perplexed, doubtful, but so long as it is still able to say, "He knows," it can
still receive the comforts of religion. For Josiah Royce it was
this reflection that constituted the essence of prayer. The
underlying faith that there is meaning in all things, though
we know not that meaning nor can surmise what it may be,
is one of the most potent values which religion imparts to
human life.

In considering the relation of religion to the ills of life we
shall mention but one more instance, namely, limitation and
weakness. In a sense this sums up all other ills; man's happiness, his physical existence, his good will, his knowledge, all
are limited. He is puny, fragile, and powerless. For the Neo-
platonists the original sin consisted precisely in this fact, that
man willed himself to be finite, a separate individual, more or
less dissevered from the one universe which should be an unbroken whole. Neoplatonism offers to the individual the
possibility of reabsorption into the One by mystical ecstasy.
Other religions, now in one fashion, now in another, assert
that man by himself is indeed finite and impotent. But they
agree that man need not continue "by himself," for very near
and accessible to weak and finite man is the infinite power of
the universe. Different religious standpoints interpret in different ways the nature of this nearness and accessibility: all
agree that man is not left alone, since the resources of an infinite universe are friendly to him. Thus does religion meet this
ill too, as it has confronted and conquered the other ills of life
that we have considered.

6. How Religion Fulfills Human Needs

Nor is religion merely a good physician to cure the ills of
life; she is also a counselor in health, showing man how to
meet the deepest needs of his life.

Of the relation of religion to the physical and economic basis of life we have already spoken. It remains to consider the higher values. We shall limit the discussion to three of the most profound needs of the human spirit: the need for unity, for purpose, and for permanence.

Our natural life, at first, is a chaos; the infant's blooming, buzzing confusion, made famous by James, continues for most of us in our higher selves far beyond the limits of infancy. If our thoughts and impulses be compared to persons, our life is often a raging mob; it needs to be a disciplined army, or, better, a town meeting with a regularly elected chairman, observing parliamentary law. If they be compared to musical instruments, it is shrieking discord; it should be a symphony.

Other interests than the religious, it is true, also aim at unity in human life, notably the philosophical. But the intellectual unification of human life at which philosophy aims is clearly an ideal goal, not an actual attainment. The religious synthesis is also, in a sense, an ideal; who is perfectly religious, who has exhausted the depth of communion with God? Nevertheless, there is a sense in which religion gives an actual unity to life that no other type of human experience can approximate. Religion is all-inclusive: it sets all our thoughts, feelings, and volitions in their relation to God, not merely as an ideal goal of life, but as a real and eternal Power, a Presence ever present. A unity in life may be orderly and systematic, like a complete card catalogue index in an office, or like the plans of a General Staff in wartime; or it may be powerful, like the will of a Napoleon; or it may be passionate, like devotion to the beauty of music or painting or a beloved person. Yet none of these offers any such complete unification of life as does religion, which seeks the harmony of the whole personality with the whole God. For this same reason religion, when she is true to herself, cannot ignore nor deny any of the other less inclusive interests of life. When she has done so she has lacked in comprehension of her own essential function.

Consider, further, how religion meets the need of life for purpose. Easy enough it is to have purposes; to have a unified purpose is not so simple. For what shall we live? America first?

Certainly our country has the right to expect the unique allegiance of all its citizens; but as the supreme purpose of life "America first" has no advantage over "*Weltmacht oder Untergang.*" Or shall the service of humanity utterly engross and satisfy us? Doubtless many who do not name the name of God are doing profoundly religious work in their service to humanity. But Bernard Bosanquet, in one of his recent writings, has remarked that when he hears one saying that he desires to serve, he is prompted to ask, "What on earth has he to offer to others?"[5] That is, humanity in the long run will not be best served unless its real needs are met. If religion is a real part of life, it is supreme; and only the purpose to serve God is in the long run inclusive enough adequately to sustain the server or to benefit the served.

Human life also needs something permanent, something on which it can depend. The evanescence of the worldly hope men set their hearts upon has ever been the theme of poet and philosopher. Men long for that which will not perish, and which will give meaning to the fleeting moments of our life. Our days are like a series of bubbles, shining and radiant, then bursting as soon as blown. It is religion that points man to the eternal in the world of change and gives him a solid anchorage. A life thus established has nothing to fear from change, for in the midst of time and circumstance it is at peace with the unchanging. To quote Bernard Bosanquet again, by faith "we rise into another world while remaining here"[6] "To be rooted and grounded in the faith" is an expression sometimes used to mean that one has a certain store of unchangeable dogmatic prejudices; it should mean that one has confidence in a God of unchangeable power and goodness.

7. Transition to the Next Chapter

In this chapter we have sought to describe the values which men have experienced in historical religion. We have also

---

[5] Bosanquet, *Some Suggestions in Ethics* (London: Macmillan & Co., 1919), p. 3.
[6] *What Religion Is,* p. 9.

faced its disvalues and limitations, and have found that they are real enough, yet not essential to religion, while it is clear that they are far outweighed by the contribution which religion makes to assuaging the ills and satisfying the needs of human life.

It is, however, important to remember the standpoint which has controlled this entire discussion: we agreed, that is, to leave out of account the question whether religious beliefs are true or not. This question is still on our hands, and, now that we have seen more clearly how potent religion is, it has become all the more pressing. Religion has this potency, we have assumed, whether it be true or not; and our discussion has implied that widely varying and mutually contradictory forms of religion may serve the values of life. Buddhism and Theosophy, Judaism and Christian Science and Mohammedanism, each may bring its faithful into a satisfying relation to the Infinite. But not all the beliefs of all these faiths can be true, for they conflict. Does it then (as many to-day appear to be saying) make no difference whether your religion is true or not, so long as it helps you? Is the only important trait of a religion the fact that it makes you happy, or well, or calm or socially-minded? Is the real existence of God, or of the future life, an unimportant and obscure question of a pedantic theology, and do the human values of religion remain untouched, whatever we may think about the truth of our beliefs?

Professor Pratt's important book[7] on religious psychology suggests that the current attitude toward these questions is wrong. In discussing prayer, he points out that "the subjective value of prayer is chiefly due to the belief that prayer has values which are *not* subjective. No, if the subjective value of prayer be all the value it has, we wise psychologists of religion had best keep the fact to ourselves, otherwise the game will soon be up and we shall have no religion left to psychologize about. We shall have killed the goose that laid our golden egg." What is true of prayer would appear to be equally true

---

[7] *The Religious Consciousness* (New York: The Macmillan Company, 1920). The passage in the text is quoted from p. 336.

of our belief in God and the cosmic fortune of values; if we believe that our beliefs are not true, it is futile to pretend that we believe at all. Religion would then become a silly game of psychological self-deception. If we are to have any religion at all, it must at least seem to us to be more than a comforting fiction. If we are to retain the human values of religion, it is only on condition that we see a reference in them to something that is not merely human and that is true no matter what we think. The subject of our next chapter will, therefore, be the more-than-human values of religion.

PART THREE

YEARS OF CRISIS, 1930–1950

10

WALTER LOWRIE

Catalyst of Neo-Orthodoxy

Walter Lowrie (1868–1959) is best remembered as the trans-lator of thirteen volumes of the works of Søren Kierkegaard, undertaken during the years 1939–1944, and the author of both a longer and a shorter biography of the Danish existentialist. The son of an Episcopal priest, Lowrie was born in Phila-delphia and received his university and theological training at Princeton as well as in Germany. Ordained to the Episcopal priesthood, he served as canon of Trinity Cathedral in Trenton, New Jersey. Beginning with his *Doctrine of St. John*, 1899, he was the author of a score of volumes reflecting a generally conservative and churchly theological orientation. Yet he can-not easily be categorized. At the age of seventy-eight he dis-played his versatility by writing a study of the religious thought of the psychologist Fechner (*The Religion of a Scientist*) and *Art in the Early Church*.

Along with Douglas Horton, Walter Marshall, and H. Rich-ard Niebuhr, Lowrie was among the first Americans to respond to the new European developments in theology associated with such names as Barth, Brunner, Bultmann and Gogarten, the so-called dialectical theology, or theology of the Word, or crisis theology. It was the existentialist aspect of this theology that was to come to the fore in Lowrie's thought, leading him to the study of Kierkegaard. That aspect is also evident in *Our Concern With the Theology of Crisis* (1932), the first full-scale attack on theological liberalism launched by an American in terms of the new European theology. The selection that fol-lows speaks for itself; it is the introductory lecture from the series that comprises that book. A decade after its publication, this book was largely neglected. By then, theological students whose German was inadequate could bypass Lowrie and go directly to proliferating translations of Barth, Brunner and others, the prime representatives of what came to be known as neo-orthodoxy. In the process a certain amount of distortion and blurring occurred, and the distinctively American types of realism tended to be confused with "Barthianism." Much of the root of this confusion may be seen in the following pages, and much of it may seem pardonable in its historical context.

THE THEOLOGY OF CRISIS*

I call this chapter "Introductory"; but by that title I would not prompt you to adopt a supine attitude, patiently expecting to hear only preliminary observations. Preliminary observations about Barth and other members of his school, about his religious pilgrimage and the writings which register his attainment, about Kierkegaard, Dostoevski and others through whom he traces his spiritual lineage, and about the philosophical and theological situation in Germany which is the background against which you must view his work—all this you may need to hear, if you have not read any of the numerous introductions to Barthianism. But obviously, in these few lectures, we have no time for so slow an approach. Whatever of this sort imperatively needs to be said, must be interjected incidentally in the course of the discussion. The purely preliminary matter I can eliminate without regret because I am not intent upon describing with the detachment of an historian all the phases of Barthian theology which actually are observable and which are relevant to the German environment; but rather am I desirous of determining the character it must assume in our environment, if it is to be assimilated at all. I

---

* From Walter A. Lowrie, *Our Concern With the Theology of Crisis* (Boston: Meador Publishing Co., 1932), pp. 25–54. Lowrie's title for this chapter was "Lecture One: Introductory"; I have supplied the present one.—ED.

desire first of all to make you feel the need of it, and then the necessity. "Necessity," when it is understood as absolute, leaves us no longer in the attitude of a spectator, enquiring if it be possible or impossible. The alternative, Christian or not Christian? signifies, Life or death? I might say ever so much about the Theology of Crisis, and yet be saying nothing to the point, if I were not seeking first of all to make you recognize it as your crisis. If I do not present it as a crisis, I am not presenting it at all. For that is the essence of it. Of all that Barth derived from Kierkegaard, that which became most central to his thinking was the crisis involved in the absolute alternative, "Either—Or"—the solemn choice which is presented to us, not once for all, but again and again, and sometimes in circumstances so trivial that we can easily ignore its eternal significance. Under the same influence, and as his rendering of the same thought, Ibsen puts into the mouth of his hero Brand the motto, "All or Nothing." Unamuno rightly interprets this as the alternative of life or death, and like Kierkegaard he dwells upon the "anguish" of man in the face of this dilemma. Martin Heidegger, the philosopher now most acclaimed in Germany, generalizes Kierkegaard's "Idea of Anguish" to make it serve (under the name of *Sorge*—care) as explanation of the substance of all created being. Under the influence of Kierkegaard his ontology reflects the Biblical scheme of man's fall and redemption. The individual is "gefallen an das Man" (*i.e.* lost in the opinions of the impersonal generality), and to become himself again (or indeed for the first time) he must make the critical "Decision."[1] In accepting the invitation to deliver

---

[1] Having remarked upon the immense influence of Sören Kierkegaard upon some of the most significant leaders of modern thought, it may be necessary to remind you that he was a litterateur, aesthetic critic, a philosopher, a psychologist, a moralist, a theologian and an anticlerical who flourished (ironical word!) in Denmark about the middle of the last century, till, overwhelmed by the ridicule of the people and the obduracy of the clergy, he died in his forty-second year as he was carrying home the last money he had in the bank. His influence began to be felt in Europe soon after the beginning of this century, when his works were being translated one by one into German. Barth gave great impetus to this vogue. And now all of his published works are to be had in German, as well as some of his private papers, making twenty volumes in all—"a literature within a litera-

these lectures I proposed to devote them to either of two
themes: Karl Barth, or Sören Kierkegaard. The latter is evidently our greater need, but it is still an unfelt want—a long
unfelt want, which perhaps must be filled before it is felt. Kierkegaard's influence, as I have hinted, is not only deep but wide.
Very properly we might speak of his School. We must recognize that it *comprises* the School of Barth, that it has as good
a claim to be called the School of Crisis, and no less appropriately might be called a School of Dialectical Theology. This
consideration justifies me in considering here, along with
Barth, remoter members of the School of Kierkegaard. It may
even serve as an excuse for quoting appreciatively many a
word of Nietzsche's, who, because of a striking similarity of
mind, has been called "a pagan Kierkegaard." Barth generously
acknowledges his debt to Kierkegaard; but how immense it is,
and how pervading, from first to last, one will not understand
without reading this master.

This that I have been saying may appear to be preliminary,
and I shall linger upon it no longer. For I am in haste to introduce you *into* the Theology of Crisis. In this lecture we shall
plunge deeply into it.

But before we start straight for the goal I require you (like
carrier pigeons when they are released) to circle around in
order to discover where we are at (to use a strong though
vulgar idiom) and get the right orientation. That is to say, I
ask you now to consider what actually are the doctrines most
surely believed among us and most widely acceptable. And to
fix your reflection upon this query I presume to propose a

---

ture," as Kierkegaard liked to say of his work—and about it has grown up
a literature of comment which is equal in volume. In English, we insular
people (I refer especially to this continent of North America) have nothing
of Kierkegaard's except a brochure containing *Selections* translated by S. M.
Hollander, published as a Bulletin of the University of Texas, No. 2326,
in date of July 8, 1823; and we have no comment upon him that I know
of except an article by Swansen in the Philosophical Review which ap-
praises him merely as a philosopher. The South American continent is less
insular. I am told that three of Kierkegaard's works have been translated
into Spanish and published in the Argentine Republic. The book by Unamuno which I have referred to is entitled *Del sentimiento tragico de la
vida.* It is to be had also in English, *The Tragic Sense of Life.*

common creed. I express it persuasively, as a preacher would do with the aim of winning the assent of his hearers—or I had better say, of winning their approbation, since I am assuming that already all have been converted to these doctrines.

If in what I am about say you detect a note of irony, you ought not to resent it in this place, for it is an example of the method followed by Barth and Kierkegaard. From Socrates Kierkegaard learned not only dialectic but irony. And if it seem presumptuous of me to assume that a creed which I compose might serve as a common creed for Protestant Christendom—and then to presume to criticise it in every detail—you are to understand that I do not do this superciliously. There is hardly an article of this creed which does not represent my belief at one time or another during the last forty-two years since I matriculated as a student of theology. Who among us has escaped the influence of the nineteenth century? I reflect grimly that the creed of Lausanne or that of the great missionary conference at Jerusalem would have served the present purpose almost as well—if I did not shrink from criticising in the name of Barth documents which are accounted so sacred. It is a matter of course that any creed which depends today upon the suffrages of a representative gathering of Protestants must at least be vaguely enough expressed to admit of a Modernist interpretation.

(1) Of all the religions of mankind, Christianity, we are sure, is the highest; (2) for we regard it as the climax of a long evolutionary process, (3) in which the people of Israel, because they were a race especially gifted for religion, played a conspicuous part, while above this high level of human attainment towered (4) the Founder of our religion, (5) a religious genius so unique that men may well hesitate to deny that (6) in some sense he was divine. (7) We acclaim him as the Master, in appreciation of the fact that his (8) religious consciousness, as manifested in precept and example, is in some degree normative for us—in spite of the fact that the movement to which he gave (9) impetus has resulted in clearer conceptions of the divine and of the human than was possible at the beginning. We still envisage the moral task in the figurative terms

which Jesus proposed, as a (10) "building up of the kingdom of God," which we understand as (11) the realization of a perfect human society, having no doubt that (12) man is equal to such a task, (13) because man is inherently a child of God and therefore essentially good. We cannot ignore the fact that this great end is (14) more remote than Jesus seems to have conceived, and that the chief obstacle is something that used to be called sin. But we are confident that (15) at the long last the evolutionary process will eliminate (16) this organic defect of our brute inheritance. And if ever we reflect how great a dose of resignation is required of us in laboring for a utopia in which we shall personally have no part, we are consoled by the Christian belief in (17) the immortality of the soul, which we associate with the "kingdom of heaven." (18) By this faith in the continuity of the here and the hereafter, of time and eternity, we have (19) robbed death of its terror, and even of its apparent significance. Jesus purified religion by teaching us to see (20) that God is our Father, and therefore can be approached without fear and without the sense of awe-ful distance. (21) For God is essentially near, immanent in his world, and therefore discoverable in it—(22) but especially in the depths of the human heart, in a more or less mystical experience. (23) Experience is therefore the foundation of faith, (24) though Jesus of Nazareth as an historical person, in whom we see realized the (25) ideal of humanity, is none the less necessary to give a note of (26) authority to our intuitions. (27) Therein lies the supreme value of the Gospels. But a unique religious value attaches to the whole Bible: to the (28) Old Testament, because it is a record of the most significant evolution of the religious idea (what may be called by analogy the vertebrate line of development); and (29) to the New Testament, because it is the record of the experience of the first generations of Christians, which we cannot but regard as the classical experience, (30) since the disciples who in line were nearest to the initial thrust must have experienced it more vividly, though they naturally could not understand its signifi-cance so adequately as we who view it from a position im-mensely more remote.

In this creed I count thirty fundamental propositions. Though perhaps not all of them are expressed as one or another of you would prefer, I believe it would be difficult to formulate a creed which today would be more generally acceptable in Protestant Christendom. If such be the fact, it will seem as if I were adopting the clumsiest and most uningratiating way of recommending the Barthian Theology when I say that it asserts the polar opposite of all this which we most surely believe—that it can be summarily understood as the contradiction, point by point, of all of our thirty propositions. That, you may judge, is enough to condemn it without a further hearing. But pray suspend this judgment while you reflect that this creed, if it indeed be our creed, is precisely the faith which confessedly we have so much difficulty in maintaining and recommending, which encounters so many objections, and is assailed by so many doubts. We might be grateful, I should suppose, to anyone who would rid us of the weak perplexities that have so long baffled us—even if at the same time he confronts us with new and sterner difficulties. With you I might argue—assuming that the majority will confess to being Pragmatists—that our present creed cannot be true, seeing that as this present time it notoriously does not "work," is evidently *not* "the faith which overcometh the world."

Be patient with me while I recite the creed again—incorporating with it now the doubts and queries which the preacher might be supposed to pencil upon the margin of his manuscript, though he would not propound them to the congregation he is seeking to edify.

(1) Religion! Who can altogether disguise from himself what a questionable thing it is? Especially if one is familiar with the innumerable religions of mankind, from the basest to the highest, and reflects at times upon the quality of his own religiousness. "Human—all-too-human!" And if Christianity could be shown to be supreme in *this* category, how infinitely far *that* is from its absolute claim to be "the Way"! (2) Christianity as the climax of evolution would have seemed a flat anticlimax to the men of the Bible, to whom the Word of God was as fire from heaven. (3) The very "relative absoluteness" of

our claim is demonstrated when we derive it from the religious genius of the Hebrews. Quite apart from the fact that this alleged genius for religion seems exceedingly questionable when we consider what the Prophets said about this people, what their historians relate, and what the religious depravity of the Semitic peoples most nearly akin to them lead us to surmise. (4) It may not occur to the preacher to question the propriety of speaking of Jesus as the Founder of our religion, unless he has read Christoph Blumhardt's indignant repudiation of this title; (5) but it is clear that we have an elegant instance of "absolute relativism" in the attempt to base the unique claim of Jesus to be the Christ upon the observation that as a religious genius he surpassed even the Prophets of his gifted race. (6) When we assert that for this reason he should be regarded as divine, we mean (at the most) that he was a man who *became* God. (7) When we call Jesus "the Master," the people may be satisfied with the ambiguity of the title, and because of its use in the Gospels it may seem to them to be justified. But we preachers know that it means nothing else but *rabbi,* and unambiguously implies that we value Jesus most of all for his teaching, and that we need only *that* to enable us to save ourselves. The title by which he was known "in the days of his flesh"—in the time of his incognito, as Kierkegaard and Barth like to say—was no longer appropriate when by his resurrection from the dead he was made known as both Lord and Christ. From that moment until our day the Church never spoke of him as *rabbi, didaskalos, magister,* or teacher, but as *Mara, Kyrios, Dominus,* Lord. When we say "Master" it is an ominous indication of a change of faith. (8) We cannot speak of the "religious consciousness" of Jesus as the source of his inspiration without putting him altogether on a level with ourselves. For man has been defined as a religious animal—"incurably religious." It is much more significant that Jesus, religious man as he was, was so irreligious as the Evangelists take pains to represent him. (9) We unconsciously desert the standpoint from which we have viewed Jesus as a teacher when, using a physical analogy, we represent his influence upon history in terms of cause and effect. Although at this point the preacher is not likely to note any caveat on the margin, the Barthians here register an indignant protest. (10) The preacher will still continue to exhort his people to coöperate in "building up the kingdom of God," and to add pathos to the appeal he may remind them that "God has no hands but our hands"; yet he himself knows (or is in a position to learn) that the Scripture nowhere implies that man is expected to build, or to help to build the Kingdom of God. (11) And that this kingdom is equivalent to social reform, culture, civilization, progress, which is a notion we learned from Ritschl, we can now no longer teach with a good conscience, seeing that even such scholars as do not understand it eschatologically are agreed that Jesus had in mind no secular interests when he proclaimed the coming of the kingdom of God. The kingdom simply "comes," and man "enters" it . . . or fails to enter.

But to listen to more of this (to nineteen more queries and doubts and denials!) would be tedious to the hearer, and only for the sake of the reader (who can skip if he will), and to show completely the fragility of our creed, do I continue to register the doubts which assail us point by point.

(12) That man is equal to the task of realizing even the ideal of a perfect human society is an illusion which no people in Europe has shared with us since the war, and which we hardly can hold any longer with steady conviction. (13) That man is essentially good (or even "too good to be damned," as Dr. Holmes ironically put it) can be believed only with heroic obstinacy. Jesus "knew what is in man," and no one has given a more somber account of "the things that proceed out of the heart of man" (Mark 7:21–23). Nietzsche, with his indignant cry that "man is a thing which must be surpassed," echoes the complaint of the ancient Prophets—and the glad expectation of the Apostles of our Lord. (14) We cannot without grave disquietude reflect upon the fact that this kingdom which seemed "near" to Jesus seems still very far away to us . . . after two thousand years. (15) And though it is natural for us to think of the development of the "kingdom" in evolutionary terms, it is plain that the men of the Bible were acquainted

with no such category. (16) For that same reason, if for no
other, they could not explain sin away as a vestigial defect or
a mere "not yet." (17) When we come to the doctrine of the
immortality of the soul, it may be presumed that the preacher
will know enough philosophy to write on the margin the
significant name "Plato!" But will he know enough about the
Bible to recognize that this is *not* a Scriptural doctrine? and
that it is *not* equivalent to the "resurrection of the dead"?
(18) Or that it *could* have no place in the Scriptures for the
reason that the men of the Bible did not at all share our notion
of continuity as between this world and the next, between time
and eternity. (19) We all, like good Christian Scientists, skim
triumphantly over the grim fact of death, and do not like to
hear anyone speak of corpses, or coffins, or biers, or graves, or
burials. It is not in the *Monitor* alone we read of a man who
has "passed" and whose "rites" will be held. "Crucified, dead
and buried," is the tremendous lapidary formula of the Apostles'
Creed! To the men of the Bible, because of their realism, death
was too awe-full a fact to be slurred over; and it was most
tremendous to the men of the New Testament because of the
faith (or shall we call it "the beautiful risk"?) that beyond that
brink was Life! "Where there are no graves there are no
resurrections," is a saying of Nietzsche's. Wherefore St. John
does not think of hiding from us how Jesus was moved at the
tomb of Lazarus, and the other Evangelists do not scruple to
let us see the shuddering horror with which he faced his own
death. This has often been compared with the serenity of
Socrates; and those who do not know that death, "the last
enemy," is more significant to the Christian, than to other men
may think that Jesus did not meet his end like a "Christian."
But death is significant also with reference to this present life
of which it is the end. It is not, as we like to think, merely an
event which some day we shall encounter; but because it is
the only event we can certainly count on, it defines what we
are in every moment. And this perception is not distinctive of
Evangelical piety: it is sober common sense, such as we find
in the Epicurean Ecclesiastes, and commonly among the
Greeks, who by the picture of a human skeleton illustrated the

Delphic saying adopted by Socrates, "Know thyself." To one who will deign to take notice of death it is at once *tremendum* and *fascinans*—to use Otto's expressions. "What after all is the *numinous*," says Bultmann, "but death itself?" In refusing to notice it we drive madly by a divine signal which is meant to save our life—God's signal, Stop!

(20) That Jesus brought God nearer to us, in teaching us to call him Father, is truth—but it is true only when we hold it in dialectical tension with the other truth that God is infinitely exalted. We must not for a moment forget that he is the "Father *in heaven*." Even the Son addressed him as "Holy Father," and holiness means at least "distance"— "unapproachable and full of Glory." Jesus, we may say in dialectical terms is "the nearness in that distance" (I use an expression of Barth's). But even in the nearness of Jesus we must recognize the distance. (21) Today nothing is so much taken for granted as God's *immanence* in the world which he has created—the absolute nearness of the Creator—and the belief that he is clearly discoverable in the things which he has made. And yet the preacher might be moved to write a *Caveat!* on the margin of this proposition, if he reflects that precisely here is the field where the fearful battle is waged between science and religion.

Against the remaining propositions of our creed (items 22 to 30) I should expect to see no marginal notes or queries. For with regard to the value of religious experience (and the "Christian experience" most of all) we are as yet troubled by no doubts. We have all become Methodists—without our knowing it we have all become disciples of Schleiermacher, "the father of modern theology." The notion that upon individual experience is founded the faith of the individual, that upon collective experience is founded the theology of the Church, that the Gospels reflect the religious experience of Jesus, and that the New Testament as a whole derives its authority solely from the fact that it registers the experience of the first generation of Christians—all these positions are now common to Liberals, Anglo-Catholics and Evangelicals. It is notorious that the mystic finds God (and all that he needs to know about him) in the depths of his own consciousness (or unconsciousness)—and how many more there are who believe they could find him there, if only they cared to take the pains! This is the only place where our creed seems unshaken and unshakable. Therefore it is at this place Barth and his School (who are not inclined to punch the air or break down open doors) enter their most vigorous protest. By the same token, this is the place where you will be most inclined to resent their protest.—Unless you have already been led to consider in what jeopardy we put the faith when we found it upon experience, and how helplessly we have delivered ourselves into the hands of the psychologists.

In this tedious enumeration I have mentioned most of our favorite beliefs and many of the Barthian protests against them. Barthian protests, and yet not *distinctively* Barthian; for anyone could make them, and many had been making them, point by point—but querulously, as doubts, and without perceiving any wholeness in the protest. Therefore they had not the power, nor even the intention, to overthrow: they merely undermined, but *that* they did thoroughly. Here is the naturalistic explanation of the fact that these so solid seeming walls of Jericho fell down flat at the first blast of Barth's trumpet. The foundations had already disintegrated. The significant thing is that Barth did not tap the wall suspiciously here and there, but made men perceive the wholeness of his protest, almost before he was aware of it himself. He made us perceive that in every article of our creed—in our exaltation of religion, of Christian experience, of mysticism, of the kingdom of God as a social Utopia, and of Jesus as the ideal of humanity—we were not thinking of God but of man. Not long ago an anonymous clerical writer in the *Atlantic Monthly* bewailed the fact that the preacher is no longer able to pronounce the name of God in a way that arouses a feeling of the numinous, a sense of aweful reverence. Barth explains this when he calls our attention to the fact that while we thought we were speaking about God we were merely "saying Man with a loud voice." We could not ignore this, as we had ignored the querimonious doubts of this man or the other about our creed; for in this we heard a resolute "No!" God's "No!" A divine and salutory signal to *stop!*

At the first, while he was writing his *Romans,* Barth conceived that he was doing nothing more than write marginal notes—but "marginal notes to *all* theology." He saw the distinction of his theology in the fact that it was a "corrective." And this point of view he does not relinquish even now when he is writing his *"Dogmatics,"* which he does not presume to call a theology, still less a systematic theology. Very significant is the fact that over the Introduction to this work he writes this inscription:

WHAT WE CALL DOGMATICS IS PAINSTAKING EFFORT AFTER THE KNOWLEDGE OF THE LEGITIMATE CONTENT OF CHRISTIAN DISCOURSE ABOUT GOD AND MAN.

In the first paragraph he makes plain what that means.

"There is such as thing as Christian dogmatics because there is such a thing as Christian speech. There was Christian speech before there was Christian dogmatics, and when there is no more Christian speech, then no more Christian dogmatics. Dogmatics is an explicit concern about Christian speech, which existed before dogmatics, and apart from it still occurs. This is not, as in homiletics, a concern about its rhetorical effectiveness; and not, as in apologetics, concern about its inherent power to convince the hearers by reason of its appropriateness to their ways of thinking and feeling; but simply and only a concern about the *legitimacy* of its contents—one might also say the suitableness of its contents, meaning the inward suitableness, suitableness in relation to that about which Christian speech speaks. That is assuredly a subject about which questions can be raised. There is not only such a thing as perfect and less perfect Christian speech, not only inherently evident and less evident; there is also speech which is legitimate and illegitimate, real and unreal, speech which serves the truth and speech which serves error, edifying and destructive speech. There is no Christian speech, whether it be uttered in the name of the Church or of the individual, which does not have to meet the test of this question about the legitimacy of its

content. And this question is the question of dogmatics. Because this question is justified, there has always been, since
first there was Christian speech, such a thing (though not
exactly with this name) as Christian dogmatics, concern with
regard to the knowledge of the legitimate content of Christian
speech. And because this question will be justified so long as
there are Christian speakers, just so long must dogmatics follow Christian speech like its shadow—as a reminder that even
Christian speech is not spoken from heaven but on earth.
Dogmatics does not inspire Christian speech. It does not
create its content or even its form. It simply assumes it as a
fact, form and content and all. But wherever without its assistance Christian discourse is held, it asks whether and in how
far, with reference to the point at issue, all is well and wisely
said. It seeks a universally valid answer to the question, under
what conditions one *could* wisely speak about God. When we
say Christian speech we naturally do not mean all and every
sort of speech that Christians might use, but particular speech
about that which makes Christians Christian, about the Christianly understood relationship between God and man. Dogmatics rests upon the assumption that this speech is by no
means infallibly released, but rather that in this matter truth
and error are to be distinguished, right and wrong, legitimate
and illegitimate, real and unreal. It rests upon the assumption
that *criticism* and the query about a *norm* applicable to the
phenomenon of Christian speech is not only permissible but is
required by the very nature of this phenomenon. It therefore
does not measure Christian speech by a rule that is foreign
to its nature. But it confronts it with its own measuring rod,
reminds it of its own immanent logic, it discovers what this
speech evidently means, what it must mean if it understands
itself aright, when it really would be what it is called, namely,
Christian speech. At least it seeks to do all this, is painstaking
about it. For dogmatics after all, like the Christian speech
which it examines, is human and not divine. Yet human task
as it is, it proceeds upon the assumption that Christian speech
can and must be taken seriously, taken at its word, that even
in its human illegitimacy it at least aims at a legitimate con-

tent, that reality (within the bounds of the humanly possible) is even in this field an attainable and a necessary aim, and that it is worth while, where Christian discourse is held, to take pains to insure that it shall be Christianly spoken."

This passage shows that Barth, though he speaks now in more measured terms as a theological professor, is still chiefly concerned with theology as a corrective, so that even his dogmatics is predominantly critical and polemical, and never in the strictest sense systematic. But this, as we shall see later, is only what we must expect of the Dialectical Theology, if it is to remain truly dialectical.

The quotation I have made is longer than it need be to prove that point. But it is significant in other respects, and I am glad to introduce it here because it relieves me for a moment of the necessity of describing Barthianism in my own terms. You will understand that this necessity means the necessity of being brief. I would linger a moment here to remark that this definition of dogmatics is well calculated to persuade those who are inclined to slight theology that it is an exceedingly necessary discipline, even though it is a long unfelt want which it fills. And never more necessary than in our day and place, seeing that the speech of our preachers is now hardly tempered by self-criticism, and is chastened by no effective criticism from without.

It is natural that, in the first shock of surprise which was occasioned by Barth's *Romans,* his attitude should have been thought to be predominantly negative. Speaking of himself at that time he says that he was like a man groping his way in the dark up the winding stair of a belfry and snatching for support at a rope—which to his dismay proved to be the bell-rope. He was as much astonished as anyone else at the unexpected clanging of the church bell. Commenting on this figure, I would remark upon the significance of the fact that it was the *church* bell that rang so unexpectedly. It reminded men how far they had wandered from the Church, without meaning to, and without knowing it. The familiar sound of the church bell—though they had not heard it for so long a time—carried associations of authority, and also of comfort. For that reason

Barth's protest was perceived to be not merely negative. That is to say, Barth's protest would not have been truly heard at all, if it had been heard merely as his all-too-human protest against the human errors of the current theology, and not heard also as God's "No." And God's "No" men cannot bear to hear, if they do not hear in it also God's "Yes."

In the light of this context I say again that all the queries and doubts I so tediously enumerated a while ago, though substantially they are such criticisms as Barth has made, do not yet give us an idea what Barthianism is as a whole, and cannot even be said to be a part of it. For this reason first of all, that they are expressions of doubt and not of faith. For I am assuming that the marginal notes of the average preacher are question marks attached to his own sermon, are consequently only doubts about his faith, and are not in the proper sense of the word negations. A strong negation, a round No, is always supported by some faith. And it is proper to apply here St. Paul's saying, "Whatsoever is not of faith is sin." In Barth's protest, because it was an absolute negation, the divine "No" was heard—and in it the divine "Yes" was audible as a reminiscence of the old theology not yet quite forgotten.

In all this, however, we can barely detect a trace of the dialectic which characterizes the Barthian School so essentially that it justifies their favorite title, Dialectical Theology. For there is no dialectic in the denial of sheer falsehood. And, above, it was to the falsehoods of our common creed I drew attention, without lingering to consider how much of truth there may be in it. Dialectic emerges in the tension between truth and truth—between two truths which are really or apparently opposite, or at least not obviously concordant. Dialectic, therefore, expresses itself in paradox—of necessity, and not as a whim. I cannot lead you further till you get some idea of what the Dialectical School means by dialectic. For though this word denotes a method, it must be understood as a method essential to the School of Crisis—which would cease to be what it is, if it should cease to be dialectical. This suggests a danger which is not imaginary. For the dialectical method is not one which everybody can handle or likes to handle. It is a gift, a disposition. Barth would not have learned it from Kierkegaard, the great master of dialectic, unless he himself had had a preëminent disposition for it. Even now, in the character of a dogmatist, he does not abate the rigorous consistency of this method. He continues to turn a deaf ear to the many appeals that he adopt finally a positive *position,* clearly defined against all other possible positions. He replies that his "position" is like that of a bird in flight. Or by a more pedestrian figure he describes himself as a "viator"—always on the march, or, by an Alpine analogy, as a climber on the knife edge of an arête, shrinking from the abyss on either side, and unable to keep his balance except by going on. This does not mean that he goes on triumphantly, leaving behind him the firm positions which he has acquired. For these "positions" remain just as precarious for one who comes after him. I have used just now Kierkegaard's phrase which scornfully describes Hegel's dialectical method: "He then goes on!" Having established, that is to say, one secure position after another (each one serving in turn as a base for the next hop, skip and a jump), "he then goes on" (with his thesis, antithesis and synthesis) to explain the whole of existence. Barth's early critics lifted up hands of horror at the mere mention of such a word as dialectic—for in Germany Hegel is no longer held in high honor. They ought to have observed, however, this very essential difference, that Barth does not go on . . . to the synthesis. He learned his dialectical method, not from Hegel, but from Kierkegaard—who believed in his turn that he had learned it from Socrates. Even if this opinion of Kierkegaard's may be open to doubt, his method is not thereby invalidated. It is the dialectical method, however, more than any inherent obscurity, that accounts for the impression that Barth's teaching is hard to understand. Many people are not capable of believing that the paradox is all he ventures to offer them, that instead of going on triumphantly to resolve by a synthesis the paradoxical thesis and antithesis, he stops short and contents himself with the wholeness which is divined but is not perceived in a balanced pair of opposite truths. Or rather, because the balance is unstable, he does not "stop," but moves almost instantaneously from the

one to the other in the "dialectical moment." There are many
who cannot content themselves with that attitude, which is
not a stable "position." Not all the members of the Dialectical
School are equally dialectical. Brunner, it seems to me, is not
so dialectically inclined as Barth. He is disposed to take unequivocal and firm positions, both positively and negatively.
Perhaps it is for that reason interpreters of the Barthian theology prefer to quote him rather than Barth or Gogarten, and
perhaps it is for that reason I quote him here. It is manifestly
difficult to describe a theology which takes no positions. And
perhaps that is a reason why Paul Tillich holds aloof. But for
that there is also another reason—namely, the fact that Tillich
is impatient to go on to *practical* conclusions, to *Gestaltung*
and *Verwirklichung* (*i.e.* to a practical re*form*ation of society
by putting genuine Christian ideals into effect). His impatience
finds a sympathetic echo in our activistic civilization. Some
berate Barth because, having begun as a socialist of the school
of Ragaz, he now is content to be simply a theologian. Many
more will feel that this time in which we live cries loudly for
formative effort and the practical realization of ideals. For in
this chaotic time our life lacks form, it lacks "style." That is the
railing accusation of Oswald Spengler, and it is true. I am not
indisposed to admit that we may justly detect here a limitation of Karl Barth. In this respect he is not like Kierkegaard,
who died fighting for realizations. And yet it is a limitation I
do not resent. Man kann nur etwas nicht alles werden. And in
this time of transition a theologian may be counted excusable
if he does not presume to know *what* form can and must be
impressed upon society—or upon the Church. *Between the
Times* (*Zwischen den Zeiten*) is the significant title the Barthian
School has chosen for its bimonthly review. Partly this has
reference to the time just before us and the better time soon
to come. We really are living in a transitional period; and
much as it needs form-giving (*Gestaltung*), it is not so obvious
how this is to be given. But "Between the Times" certainly
has also a much larger significance, for it refers to eternity at
both ends of time, the *arche* and the *telos,* the Beginning and
the End. Between them lies *all* time. For time is finite. And

one who understands how time is conditioned by the End will not be tempted to build Towers of Babel, but will go about his form-giving and realization of ideals with a chastened spirit. Barth does not presume to restrain us from the pursuit of such activities. Practically, I find in his doctrine incitement to do and to dare (just as Albert Schweitzer's eschatology prompts one to "live dangerously"), although in the same dialectical moment one is convinced that "all is vanity." "Therefore strive!" would be Kierkegaard's conclusion. *That* is dialectic! Schweitzer's phrase, "interim ethics," which originated with Johannes Weiss, has met with general reprobation—I cannot get it through my stupid head *why*. And I have reason to fear that I shall not commend the Barthian theology when I call it *interim theology*. But that is what a theology must be which knows itself to be "between the Times"—that is to say, under the sign of finitude, which admonishes us that it is not possible for man to know or think or say anything direct and positive and unequivocal about God, but only indirectly, reflectedly, refractively (like "a straight staff bent in the pool")—

> Thus making Him broken lights
> And a stifled splendor and gloom.

Precisely what the Dialectical School means by dialectic you can best understand by examples. And the most exemplary examples that occur to me are selections from the Diaries of Kierkegaard which Diem translates into German and publishes in *Zwischen den Zeiten*.[2] From this selection I choose only a few. They are examples of dialectical paradox which will not seem fantastic to you, because they deal with the familiar antithesis between man's work and God's work, Law and Gospel. Here it is more precisely the contrast between the *immitatio Christi* and divine grace. Like us, Kierkegaard puts the practical duties of discipleship *first* and conceives of the "following" of Jesus as *immitatio*. Like us, too, he is inclined to linger exclusively upon *this* term of the paradox—as if there were no paradox. But you are to note that when he puts "grace" *last* he puts it where it receives the strongest accent.

---

[2] 9 Jahrgang, 1931, Heft 1.

"I must now take good care (or I had better say, God will take good care for me) that I be not bewildered by fixing my gaze one-sidedly upon Christ as Example. That is the dialectical moment to the next, which regards Christ as Gift, as one who (according to Luther's constant distinction) was bestowed upon us. But dialectical as my nature is, in the passion of dialectics it always seems as if the opposite thought simply did not exist—and hence this (the thought of the *immitatio*) is always first and strongest."

"In the recognition of the contemporaneousness of Christ you discover that you never succeed in being like him. Not even in what you call your highest moment. For in such a moment you do not experience the appropriate tension of reality, but reflect upon it with the aloofness of a spectator. Hence it follows that you profitably learn to flee to faith and grace. The Example is that which makes endless demands upon you, and you feel terribly the unlikeness—then you flee *to* the Example, and he will have mercy upon you. Thus the Example is he who most sternly and endlessly condemns you —and at the same time it is he who has mercy upon you."

In this connection it occurs to me to translate one of Rückert's *Strung Pearls*, the first line of which he borrows from the Koran:—

> From God there is no flight but only to him.
> Against a father's sternness no revolt avails,
> The child's sole refuge is within his arms,

"The following of Jesus—though it be prosecuted with the most strenuous effort—should only be like a jest, something childish, if by it we think to accomplish something serious, that is, before God and in the direction of merit—the Atonement is the serious thing. But it is horrible that men, 'because there is such a thing as grace,' will use it as an excuse for making no effort."

This is an appropriate place to interject a saying of Kierkegaard's which is found in his *Philosophical Fragments:*

"To abbreviate the hours of sleep by night, and to buy up every hour of the day, without sparing oneself—and then to understand that all this is jest . . . that is earnestness indeed!"

"Only in this way can man be supported in effort. In order to gain courage to strive one must rest in the blessed assurance that all is already decided, that he has already conquered—in faith and through faith."

And here finally is a paragraph which is especially instructive to us and is much more than a formal paradigm of dialectical method.

"Only with respect to that which is on the same level with ourselves can there be any question of merit—as with respect to the fulfillment of a 'claim' upon us. But 'grace' has placed itself endlessly high above you, and therefore it makes meritoriousness impossible. Hence 'grace' is on the one hand the expression of God's endless love, but at the same time and in the highest degree it is an expression of majesty which indicates God's infinite sublimity. In view of the distance of 'grace' you are endlessly further from God than you are put by the distance of the Law and its claim upon you (though in another respect you are endlessly nearer—that is, when you take refuge in his love which is hidden under 'grace'). For with respect to the Law and its claims upon you, it is as if God stooped to contend with you; and on the other hand you might imagine it possible for you to achieve the fulfillment of the Law. But with respect to the distance of 'grace' God has placed you once for all at an endless distance—in order that he might have mercy upon you. At the same time that God in Christ came infinitely nearer to men, in 'grace,' he assured for himself therewith an infinitely more majestic expression for the *distance* —that is, for the name of 'grace.'"

I am well aware that I have not expounded the Barthian theology seductively. I cannot present it truly and clearly except as "foolishness" and as a "stumbling-block." That is what the Gospel is today, as much as it was at the beginning—except as we have deformed it to suit the present taste. I have sought importunately to press it upon you as *your* crisis,—to wrench you out of the superior and secure position of a spectator. Accordingly I have not represented Barth's protest as directed against the theology of Schleiermacher, Ritschl, Otto and other Germans, but as applying precisely and directly to the principal tenets of our modernistic theology. To be sure, it would be well for you to realize that our modern Liberalism was "made in Germany," and that we have contributed to it not one original thought. For then you might look expectantly to Germany for the cure of it. There where the virus has worked longest and most virulently you might hope to find the defensive antitoxin. For the situation of Christianity in Germany is evidently more perilous than here. And for that reason may perhaps be accounted more hopeful—as when a sickness has reached its crisis. (This is one of the implications of the title "School of Crisis.") For until man has reached the end of his tether, and in his extremity is compelled to hear the divine *Stop!* God has no opportunity. In a book published only in French Unamuno envisages even "the death pangs of Christianity" (*L'agonie du Christianisme*) as God's opportunity. But he has been taught by Kierkegaard to think chiefly in terms of the individual. *Agonia* is his rendering of Kierkegaard's "Anguish."[3] And he has small hopes of a man until he has come, not with a "cold doubt" but in fear and trembling, *desperado,* to the brink of the abyss. Kierkegaard describes paradoxically even that moment when a man heeds God's voice as a "comforted despair." Heidegger, for the purposes of metaphysical argument, as I have said, generalizes Kierkegaard's notion of anguish and speaks only of *Sorge*—anxious care. But in the end he is more terrible than his master when he writes (with italics and with heavy-faced type) of the moment of *decision* in which man is delivered from his *perdition in the world* and becomes himself, by the passionate, illusionless, factual, self-conscious and anguished *openness to death* (*Freiheit zum Tode*) as his utmost and most intrinsic human possibility.[4]

I return now nearer to the surface when I remark that you cannot be expected to embrace with enthusiasm a dialectical

---

[3] *Der Begriff der Angst* is the title of one of Kierkegaard's most powerful works.
[4] *Sein und Zeit*, p. 266 *et passim*. Here I have rendered freely a passage which as a whole could not be understood out of its context.

method, which is confessedly "broken" thinking (argument in broken lines) so long as you are confident that it is perfectly possible for man in time to speak adequately and directly about eternity and about God, and so long as boundless credulity ascribes to Science the power to explain all the problems of existence, even the deepest—or at the least to prove that there is nothing very deep. In Germany not only, but everywhere on the Continent of Europe men have ceased to hold science in extravagant reverence. They are even questioning whether the very foundations of the natural sciences are securely laid. The Darwinian theory of biological evolution is universally discarded. And where an evolutionary philosophy exists, optimism has been eliminated from it. In all these respects their situation is more hopeful than ours. In Germany especially, we can easily perceive how great an advantage it is to such men as Barth that they have no pragmatic philosophy to contend with, and no behaviorist psychology. With the "deep psychology" of Freud and Jung and Adler they can come to terms, and still more easily with the deeper introspective psychology sponsored by the Phenomenological School. Though Barth is chary of accepting any philosophy as an ally of theology (considering that the philosophers have and must have a very different aim), he reaps no small advantage from the fact that Heidegger speaks the language of Kierkegaard.

In none of these respects are we so fortunate. I have said that the situation of Christianity in Germany is evidently more perilous than here. Perhaps it would be more true to say that it is more evidently perilous. That, it seems, is what Barth thinks. For though he recognizes (with a comforted despair) that Christianity everywhere shows signs of dissolution, he remarks that only in America are we intent upon seeing to it that it dies *beautifully*—"preparing for it a euthanasia." Not long ago, when on Thanksgiving Day I was escorting a Methodist minister to my pulpit, I was moved to say to him brusquely, "*You* are no better than we are." "True," he replied, "we too are building million dollar churches." But building churches on the installment plan is not the only way we show our zeal to prepare for Christianity its euthanasia.

In America our plight is not *essentially* different from the plight of the Protestant churches in Germany—only we do not perceive it so clearly. We can boast of more evident signs of ecclesiastical stability; but it would be wise for us to recognize that what we most boast of, whether they be ritual embellishments or triumphs of social service, might be described in Ruskin's phrase as "parasitical sublimities," in comparison with the essential notes of Christianity. Even here our ebullient optimism and our blind belief in the inevitability of progress has lately been checked by a shock which seems trivial to the European. When we are financially "broke" we are in a position to understand what Barth means by "brokenness." He does not use this word *only* of the broken line of dialectical thought, to indicate that *straight* thinking about God and eternity is not a human possibility, and indeed that we can know nothing about God except as he has revealed himself. He uses it more commonly to denote our moral bankruptcy—not the bare fact of it, but a conscious recognition of it. It means the brokenness of spirit which the Psalmist had in mind. The flesh is always under condemnation: "They who are in the flesh cannot please God." The question is whether we recognize how fragile we are, and how problematical, how questionable is everything that we can boast of—even when we have become Christians "according to the flesh." For in fact it is the Christians especially, if not exclusively, who in this sense are "broken" and know it. Mindful of a phrase already quoted from Kierkegaard, we might call this brokenness of ours a comforted brokenness. At all events, we must reflect that, if Christians should claim to be unbroken, then in this whole world there are no "broken spirits"—no men at all whom God will not despise.

In this lecture I have briefly referred to almost all the themes which are distinctive to the Barthian theology. In the following lectures we shall have time to consider more fully only a few of the principal topics. I have made it clear that Barth's protest is chiefly against Liberal Theology, in its positive as well as in its negative aspects. Against its positive aspects most of all. For you hardly need to be told that it is not aimed against the results of Biblical criticism—however negative they may seem to be. An obscurantist theology could gain no ascendancy in Germany. It is aimed, as you doubtless have heard with surprise, also against orthodoxy. And you may be puzzled to know what that can mean, when you are told in the same breath that Barthianism is a return to the theology of the Reformation. Evidently it is not simply a return, a reactionary return, to the Protestant orthodoxy of the seventeenth century. It could not be that, because it is dialectical. What it protests against in Protestant orthodoxy and in every other orthodoxy is the assumption that man can say anything directly, positively and unparadoxically about God, can occupy assured positions —"and then go on." But that is also its complaint against Liberal Theology in its most positive aspects. Nothing is more *unbroken* than the confidence of the Liberal that he possesses the truth. Liberalism is only apparently a system of doubt. It deals, in fact, coldly with many doubts; but it does not suffer to emerge the one hot and devastating doubt which impugns our faith in . . . Man. So the Barthian School wages war on the right hand and on the left. Yet there is a very great difference in the pathos of these two protests. It coldly declines to ally itself with orthodoxy—but hotly it attacks the positive Liberalism, in which it discovers a zeal to exalt man . . . at the expense of God. But evidently it is against pietism also, the sole warm remnant of Evangelicalism, which exalts its questionable experiences and problematical goodness into a proof of the existence of God.

It is not surprising that the Barthian theology is not welcomed in the United States. The Fundamentalists cannot thole it because it refuses to attach any great religious importance to Biblical criticism. And what else have we here but Liberalism and Catholicism? For Liberalism is not confined to the large and self-confident school which cuts athwart all denominational lines, but it has deeply impregnated the old Evangelical parties in all the Churches, and Anglo-Catholicism is by no means free from its influence. It still predominates in the pew *and* in the pulpit. *But* I perceive now, on my return from a residence of many years in Europe, that it no longer sits in the highest places. Not in such places, I mean, as Union Seminary, or the Harvard Theological School, or our own Divinity School in Cambridge. For the watchmen in those high places have seen what has happened in the homeland of Liberal Theology, where the most outstanding Liberal leaders (Prof. Troeltsch at the head of them) have conceded that Liberalism, though it is the only form in which Christianity can be held today by enlightened men, is *not* Christianity. That concession puts an end to a vast deal of hypocrisy; and it ushers in a new era, in which Radicalism must increase at the expense of Liberalism, because it has stolen the glamour from it. The Liberals may be just as liberal as ever, but in the eyes of the Radicals they are conservatives. To religious Liberalism the same thing has happened that has overwhelmed political Liberalism. It is no longer at the head of the column. It has been forced back to a middle position where it cannot but be suspected of compromise.

11

H. RICHARD NIEBUHR

Radical Confessionalist

Helmut Richard Niebuhr (1894–1962), though less prolific and less known to the general public than his brother Reinhold, was quite likely the most influential American theologian of his generation. His *Christ and Culture* enjoys an international stature, and at least two other books of his have become classics in the study of America's religious history. The full scope of his concerns includes theology, ethics, social analysis, and the interpretation of history.

Like his brother Reinhold, H. Richard Niebuhr was born during his family's brief residence in Wright City, Missouri, but spent his childhood in St. Charles, a larger town on the Missouri River near St. Louis. He was eight when they moved to Lincoln, Illinois, a heavily German-American community of conservative, retired farmers some thirty miles northeast of Springfield. After high school there, both he and Reinhold attended Elmhurst, a small denominational proseminar near Chicago, from which Richard was graduated in 1912. From that point on, their careers diverged, with Reinhold's leading rapidly into the arena of modern industrial America and its social movements, while Richard's remained closer to the life of the church and specifically the Evangelical Synod of North America. For most of two decades, Richard Niebuhr was closely involved with the Synod's educational institutions. He received his B.D. from Eden Theological Seminary in 1915 and was ordained the following year. After three years in a St. Louis pastorate he became a professor at Eden. His first real departure from that milieu came in 1922 when he went to Yale for his Ph.D., having earned an M.A. at Washington University in 1917. His doctoral dissertation was on "Ernst Troeltsch's Philosophy of Religion." In 1924 he was appointed president of Elmhurst and embarked on a major program of upgrading his alma mater's academic standards. It was under his administration that the proseminar became a degree-awarding college. In 1927 he returned to Eden Seminary as dean, and here he wrote his first book, still a classic in its field—*The Social Sources of Denominationalism* (1929), a brilliant application of Troeltsch's sociological perspective to the history of the American churches.

In 1931, after a year in Europe, H. Richard Niebuhr joined the faculty of Yale University as associate professor of Christian ethics. He was by then already well-versed in the varieties of Protestant theology that for a decade had been emanating from Switzerland and Germany, and his translation of Paul Tillich's *The Religious Situation* (1932) contributed much toward broadening its impact on American religious thought. In his contribution to Douglas Clyde Macintosh's symposium, *Religious Realism* (1931), Niebuhr emphasized Tillich's "faith realism" or "belief-ful realism" as a needed corrective to the American empirical tendency "to define God in terms of his utilizable relations to the neglect of his uniquely divine or holy character."[1] This same concern unites the two essays by Niebuhr from 1929 and 1936 that comprise the selections that follow—a concern like that of Karl Barth for an objective and transcendent notion of God. Yet in contrast with Barth, Niebuhr remains in the tradition of Troeltsch and Tillich in recognizing that man's grasp of the absolute is relativized by socio-historical factors. Part of the theologian's task is to uncover those factors and to become aware of the biases inherent in a given tradition or viewpoint. Niebuhr welcomed the German criticism of American optimism and rationalism, but he was also mindful of the German bias toward pessimism and dogmatism, and he sought to develop a critical perspective surmounting both of these tendencies. "There is no greater

---

[1] H. Richard Niebuhr, "Religious Realism and the Twentieth Century," in D. C. Macintosh, ed., *Religious Realism* (New York: Macmillan, 1931), p. 421.

barrier to understanding," he wrote, "than the assumption that the standpoint which we happen to occupy is a universal one, while that of the object of our criticism is relative."[2] One begins with faith as given and confessed, and one seeks out its continuities and transformations within the empirical processes of history. Faith is not knowledge but a point of view, a hypothesis which is not merely adopted arbitrarily but is a product of history as remembered experience, the inner experience of the community that shares in that faith. In *The Kingdom of God in America* (1935), Niebuhr set out to augment his study of denominationalism by looking for the idea of the Kingdom as a persistent unifying pattern, but what he found was rather a pattern of development and variation of this theme, from the Kingdom as a symbol of transcendent divine sovereignty through the immanentist Kingdom of Christ to the idea of the coming Kingdom on Earth and its secularization. Nowhere, not even in Barth, is there to be found a more trenchant indictment of the shallowness of liberal, middle-class Christianity:

> The romantic conception of the kingdom of God involved no discontinuities, no crises, no tragedies or sacrifices, no loss of all things, no cross and resurrection. In ethics it reconciled the interests of the individual with those of society by means of faith in a natural identity of interests or in the benevolent, altruistic character of man.[3]

Or, as expressed in this often quoted sentence, "A God without wrath brought men without sin into a kingdom without judgment through the ministrations of a Christ without a cross."[4]

Perhaps no single work has done more to spark the re-evaluation of the theology of Jonathan Edwards. Of five books cited by Reinhold Niebuhr as formative of his own outlook, *The Kingdom of God in America* is the only one by an American—his brother.[5] This book before any other sounds the keynote

---

[2] H. Richard Niebuhr, *The Kingdom of God in America* (New York: Harper, 1935), p. 13.
[3] *Ibid*, p. 191.
[4] *Ibid*, p. 193.
[5] The others were by Troeltsch, Augustine, Temple, and Barth. See "Ex Libris," *The Christian Century*, LXXIX, 24 (June 13, 1962), p. 754.

of neo-orthodoxy, not only with an American accent but with probing relevance for America's religious history, for it is the sovereign God of Edwards to which Richard Niebuhr was led rather than that of Calvin or Luther or Barth. For all his ready rapport with European theology, and despite his ties to a denomination rooted in the German Reformation, Richard Niebuhr, scarcely less than his brother, emerges as distinctively American, consciously relating himself to the main current of American religious development. It was undoubtedly from Troeltsch that he learned empathy for the past as remembered experience or *Nachempfindung*, but he applied this empathy first of all to the American past. He felt indebted to Barth, too, as a major influence, particularly for Barth's insistence that only God is absolute; but far from following out Barth's program of dogmatics, he combined the Barthian emphasis with the Troeltschian, and these in turn with several others—Royce, Buber, F. D. Maurice in particular. With Royce, he understood God pragmatically defined as a focus of loyalty and commitment. The validity of radical monotheism, for Niebuhr, arose from man's need for integrity, for a single central commitment that integrates all lesser loyalties and finds its focus in that which transcends them. Only a truly sovereign God, he argued, could provide that unity of purpose that gives meaning to life and saves man from the self-deception of idolatry. In *The Meaning of Revelation* (1941) he maintains that the historic Christian faith meets the demand for a revelation that illumines the full range of human experience. Centering in God's action in Christ, this revelation binds all human history together. The pragmatic clincher is the claim that the same revelation has relevance to present events and their meaning. Niebuhr never speaks as a modern man in search of a religion, but as a person born into and responding to the Christian community, which in Royce's sense is a community of interpretation. Having, so to speak, inherited this faith, his task is to understand its general shape and structure, the variations to which it gives rise, the sources of its strength.

In *Christ and Culture* (1951), Niebuhr examines the radical perfectionism of Tolstoy ("Christ Against Culture"), the liberal accommodation of Ritschl ("Culture-Protestantism" or "The

Christ of Culture"), the Thomistic synthesis of "Christ Above Culture," the dualism of Paul, Marcion, and Luther ("Christ and Culture in Paradox"), and the perspective closest to his own, "Christ the Transformer of Culture," featuring the ideas of the Gospel of John, Augustine, Jonathan Edwards, and F. D. Maurice. Each of these approaches has its merits and its difficulties. Niebuhr not only weighs each of them with care; once he has taken his own stand he acknowledges that it, like the others, is at best only partial and relative. One takes one's position within the church, but "no single man or group or historical time is the church," and "the world of culture—man's achievement—exists within the world of grace—God's kingdom."[6] Faith, finally, is not reasoned inference but decision and affirmation, choice of a loyalty which is larger than any degree of knowledge and which transcends differences of opinion and method. God is not incomprehensible, but even as revealed through Christ there is an inescapable pluralism of human understanding which introduces a subjective element into one's choice. This Niebuhr calls "objective relativism," for God is "independent of human desire and the consciousness of need, but not independent of the human constitution and its actual need."[7] Man in history is like the fish in water; his very existence relativizes his efforts to attain a universal perspective, but it is in the nature of man to aspire to such a perspective, to seek a higher objectivity, to see himself "in the eyes of God." The transforming power in the Edwardsian idea of conversion or in the Augustinian idea of regeneration is finally the power of Christ manifested through faith. Its results are seen, for example, in the rise of democracy—but the latter remains relative and to some extent precarious, for cultural or historic achievements remain contingent upon God's grace. The human task is a never-ending one, to bring human culture and the human self into right and responsible relation to the true God. It is not a simple, cut-and-dried assignment or a matter of

---

[6] H. Richard Niebuhr, *Christ and Culture* (New York: Harper, 1951), p. 256.

[7] H. Richard Niebuhr, "Value-Theory and Theology" in Bixler, Calhoun & Niebuhr, eds., *The Nature of Religious Experience: Essays in Honor of Douglas Clyde Macintosh* (New York: Harper, 1937), p. 113.

finding the right formula once for all; it is rather a matter of steering a course in the currents of history.

The central purpose of the church, for H. Richard Niebuhr, is the "increase among men of the love of God and neighbor"[8]; to love truly is to affirm oneself and the other in a context of the "conviction that there is faithfulness at the heart of things: unity, reason, form and meaning in the plurality of being." It is such conviction that is man's love to God, and only in its light can the church's proximate goals have any validity:

> It is loyalty to the idea of God when the actuality of God is mystery; it is the affirmation of a universe and the devoted will to maintain a universal community at whatever cost to the self. It is the patriotism of the universal commonwealth, the kingdom of God, as a commonwealth of justice and love, the reality of which is sure to become evident.[9]

The occasion for those lines was an intensive, 15-month study of theological education at more than ninety seminaries in the United States and Canada, directed by H. Richard Niebuhr. But the guidelines for the inquiry and the reflections arising from it were the product of a lifelong enterprise of historical interpretation and theological definition—a scholarly quest for that "universal commonwealth" of free and responsible human beings which is true democracy because it lets God be God and permits nothing less to be absolutized. In *Radical Monotheism and Western Culture* (1960) Niebuhr restated the theme of the sovereignty of God as providing the center of value for the relativities of human civilization, and in his last book, *The Responsible Self* (1963), he laid the groundwork for an ethic predicated neither on theology nor on radical obedience but on responsibility—"for the ethics of responsibility the *fitting* action, the one that fits into a total interaction as response and as anticipation of further response, is alone conducive to the good and alone is right."[10] The synthesis toward

---

8 H. Richard Niebuhr, *The Purpose of the Church and Its Ministry* (New York: Harper, 1956), p. 31.

9 *Ibid*, p. 37.

10 H. Richard Niebuhr, *The Responsible Self* (New York: Harper, 1963), p. 61.

which Niebuhr was moving was both biblical and pragmatic. Although he took account of every major Western ethical thinker, he explicitly set aside the excessive biblicism of Barth, Bonhoeffer, and other Europeans and examined the Bible anew in the light of George Herbert Mead's social psychology. He made no claim for the superiority of his view or indeed of any Christian type of ethics as against other types. He offered his theory, rather, as one viable viewpoint compatible with the historic ethos of the Christian community in which he took his stand. In this, as in the rest of his life work, he was addressing himself to a task of self-understanding that was deeply human- istic because it looked beyond the normatively human to God as the only absolute criterion of what makes man human, and because for him the task was given, not imposed, just as the church itself was voluntary, a community freely covenanted in loyalty. For H. Richard Niebuhr such desiderata as the good society and the good individual could only be arrived at through historical interpretation. For him, biblical monotheism provided the cornerstone of such interpretation. The sense of a vital tradition and its insights made his contribution to that enterprise one of lasting value. He built no system, but in his dealing with facts he demonstrated a method and offered perspectives that transcend his own time.

MORAL RELATIVISM AND THE CHRISTIAN ETHIC*

The theory that morality in its principles and precepts is quite dependent on the social conditions and public opinion of any given time and place is an ancient doctrine which has achieved new significance today because of the extent of its influence on the democratic mass. Moral relativism seems to be the

---

* This comprises in its entirety a pamphlet, *Moral Relativism and the Christian Ethic,* in the series *Theological Education and the World Mission of the Church* (Madison, N. J.: Drew Theological Seminary, 1929), pp. 3–11.

inevitable product of every age in which the stale cake of custom has been broken by new experiences; hence it has appeared in the wake of great wars of migrations, colonizations and of improvements in the means of communication. It is itself a relative phenomenon—no less a fashion, surely, and no less a product of public opinion than the absolutisms it condemns.

Yet to accuse moral relativism of being itself a relative doctrine is not so much to answer as to illustrate its contention. Its rise as a theory is the reflection of its development as a fact in the actual history of morals. Historically relativism appears as one movement in that inevitable rhythm between innovation and conservation, between emancipation and discipline which is the characteristic of all organic and spiritual life, and, perhaps, the necessary dialectic of progress. In theory it arises as the complement and antithesis of absolutism and as the fruit of that empiricism which must ever be opposed to an equally necessary rationalism in the polar interaction in which creative thinking moves.

Its value lies in its evident truth; its error in its equally evident failure to comprehend the whole truth—a statement which with equal right may be made of absolutist ethics also. Relativism is really not so much a theory as a report of experience. It is strongly entrenched in modern times not only because of the justification it supplies to the strongly individualistic and naturalistic motives of conduct newly released from the bonds of Catholic and Puritan discipline, and not only because of the casual experience of varying systems of morality which the new communication has brought to the masses, but also because of the descriptive accounts of morality offered by the social sciences. That there is a fashion in morals, that economic and social conditions are responsible for considerable variation in what men honor as good or right, that the standards which we apply at any time to the ethical measurement of past periods are themselves highly relative to our own situation, all of these facts have been made patent by disinterested inquiry into social codes. And social psychology has gone beyond its sister sciences in showing that not only the content but also the form of conscience may be something less than an absolute datum—a derivative from the social life rather than a category of practical reason.

Nor is it possible to safeguard the ethics of Christianity against the disintegrating action of this "acid of modernity." The farther historical research is pushed, the more closely the relation of the church and the religious ethic of any period to the remaining elements in the culture is scrutinized, the more relative the content of its moral teaching is revealed to be. Industrialism and the social gospel, Capitalism and Puritanism, Feudalism and Catholic ethics, have arisen in close interaction and have mutually conditioned each other. The history of the term "Kingdom of God" as an ethical ideal shows the profound modification of the content of Christian ethics by social situations. Not even the ethic of Jesus seems to be free from such relativity, for was it not propounded against the background of revolutionary political conditions or of an eschatological world-view? Was it not shot through and through with ideals and counsels pertinent enough within the simple economy of agricultural Galilee but not so evidently designed for the complex conditions of social life in an impersonal industrial civilization? And what shall be said of the Christian ethic in general as opposed to the ethics of non-Christian religions? It appears to be relative to the whole Western culture which it has nurtured but by whose various non-religious interests it has also been modified and interpreted. The representatives of Christianity, furthermore, seem unable to take an unbiased position in comparing their ethical system with that of other religions. The very standards to which they must appeal in comparing the ethical codes of Buddhism or Mohammedanism with their own are standards which have grown out of Christianity and so are themselves relative. Whether the common standard which is to serve as a yardstick for the comparative measurement of Eastern and Christian ethics is the Christian ideal of love or some humanistic pattern of social welfare or some philosophical determination of the essence of the moral life—the standard is in every case a product, directly or indirectly, of Christianity.

Kantian and positivistic ethics alike are the products of a rationalism, which, despite its claims to universalism, is a definitely Western rationalism, and one which has been formed to a great extent by the influence of Western religion. The source of the idea of progress, Western rather than human as it is, was Hebrew prophecy, and the values of personality which seem so evident to even the non-religious West, may owe their parentage to Christianity more than to human experience in general.

II

Faced with the practical problems which these considerations force upon him what honest and truth-loving position can the Christian, as missionary, teacher, preacher, or parent take? He may, knowing how great are the values which he has found in his faith and how imperative is its moral counsel, be tempted to assert dogmatically the absolute superiority of his religious and ethical heritage, contending that Christianity is revelation while all other religions are merely human aspirations and that the Christian ethic is absolute while all other moral systems are relative. Accepting such a position, however, he will need to be content if other religions make a similar claim, and he will with difficulty defend his inevitable selection from all that has passed for Christianity against the charge that this selection is itself relative. In the end, as in the beginning, his position will rest upon a pure dogmatism. Such dogmatism will gain converts at home and abroad, for confident assertion is always psychologically effective on a great number of people whatever be its intellectual and moral disabilities. It may be an expression of faith and its repristination in modern theology is to be welcomed insofar as it is such an expression. Yet it remains a dogmatism which meets the problems of relativism, whether in the sphere of religion or of ethics, only by denying them.

A second way of meeting the problem is that chosen by Christian rationalism which seeks for the absolute within the relative by distinguishing the rational from the empirical or from the traditional and thereupon proceeding to define the relation of Christian ethics to this rational absolute, whether the latter be defined as the categorical imperative, happiness or social welfare. Such a procedure has great value in furnishing a critical principle for the examination of that large mass of ethical precepts which constitutes the Christian ethic of any period and in providing for the systematic development of this content. But it does not escape the suspicion of relativism, as we have seen, and, furthermore, it is likely, as in the parallel case of "natural and revealed theology," to diminish the content of the Christian morality by neglecting those elements which do not agree with the rationalist principle.

There are elements of value in both of these ways of dealing with the problem of relativism, but these elements will need to be included in a more empirical and broader attitude toward the subject than they alone provide for. The theory and the practical attitude of Christian ethics face to face with the facts and the temptations of relativism will need to embody within themselves not only the relative truth of moral relativism but also the truth-elements in these absolutisms.

III

In the first place it seems necessary that Christian ethics should recognize the truth of relativism by resisting the temptation of making an absolute principle, valid for all times and places, out of such insights into principle as come to it under the pressure of new conditions. Furthermore, the truth in relativism makes it necessary to undertake the task of criticizing all our current interpretations of the Christian ethic in order that the purely cultural and Western influences may be distinguished from the original Christian content. Historical inquiry furnishes the best method for the accomplishment of this task. The distinction between the original and the accretions can never be completely made, for all our selections and interpretations must be made from the point of view of our own time; yet the critical task may be partly successful and it will enable the Christian missionary and teacher to present Christianity apart from its unholy alliance with civilization.

Such critical processes, however, only raise, they do not

answer, the ultimate question raised by relativism—the question whether there is present within the acknowledgedly relative code of any particular period an absolute element. The historical method tends to regard the teaching of Jesus as representing this absolute element, yet the charge of relativism may be made against this teaching also as is done by the eschatological school. If relativism is conceded at one point must it not be conceded all the way? If it is recognized that some elements in a moral code are due to purely temporary social conditions, must it not be acknowledged that all morality is relative? To argue in this fashion is to worship that "Demon of the Absolute" which ever leads philosophy and theology to their nemesis.

The Christian ethic, which has always been proclaimed as the absolute ethics of the will of God, not relative to Jew or Greek, is under no compulsion to give up the claims which it has made to unswerving loyalty and universal validity because it must be formulated in relative terminology and applied to changing conditions. To say that there are relative elements in the Christian ethic, even in the New Testament formulation, is not to say that the Christian ethic is relative. The absolute within the relative comes to appearance at two points—in the absolute obligation of an individual or a society to follow its highest insights, and in the element of revelation of ultimate reality.

One might conceivably concede that the Christian ethic is not universally valid, that the failure of a Mohammedan or an atheist to recognize its claims may be justifiable from his point of view. Even such a concession would not impair the obligation of the Christian to obey that will of God which, from his point of view, lays absolute obligation upon him. The obligation of the Christian to follow the Christian ethics does not arise, first of all, from the fact that Christianity is the universally valid religion but from the fact that he is a Christian, whether as the result of religious experience or as a result of his commitment to Christianity by an act of faith. His best insight and his greatest good are not made less valid for him by the fact that others fail to share his point of view. He is, indeed, as an honest man, compelled to criticize his partialities and to recognize his limitations, but his obligation to follow what he has found true remains undiminished. There is a fateful and an obligatory element present in the very point of view which an individual or a society occupies not by choice but by fate. One who is born into a Christian society must needs share something of the Christian point of view. In a very real sense of the term "Christ is his fate." The viewpoint which is imposed upon him by his birth at this point of history and under these particular conditions is not only a limitation but also an opportunity for discovery, not only a confinement to a relative insight but also an obligation to make the best of his insight. The absolute within the relative appears in this wise in no different fashion to societies and cultures than it does to individuals.

Yet Christianity is not confined to this last attempt to fortify by argument its experience of an absolute element within the relative. It has the right to claim that its experience of the will of God is not only obligatory in form but also in content; that its claim to absoluteness does not rest only upon the character of human experience but also on the character of reality; that goodness does not depend upon human judgment but on the pattern of existence, or the will of God. The discovery of the absolute within the relative is the discovery of the real within the apparent, of the permanent character in changing relations. The discovery of this pattern of ultimate goodness has been the practical interest of that long process of trial and error which is set forth in the ethical experiments of all ages and races. The differences between these experiments give rise to the theory and practice of relativism, but the similarities are just as striking and testify to the absolute element present in the ethical life of man. The supreme intuition and revelation of that absolute element, the Christian maintains, is given in the life and teaching of Jesus. The verification of that revelation is to be sought in the experience of those individuals and societies whose lives are governed by this insight, and in the deductions to be drawn from the moral experiences of humanity outside of Christianity. The large agreements which exist between the empirical ethics of modern times and the ethics of the great world-religions on the one hand and the Christian teaching on the other, point to a common underlying factor, the "will of God," to which men must needs adjust themselves for the attainment of their highest blessing.

All attempts to define this absolute factor will necessarily be incomplete, and all definitions will perforce be partly relative; but incomplete experience of the absolutely good is not experience of the incompletely good, nor is relatively true definition of moral reality a definition of a relatively moral reality.

Finally, of course, it is true that such conviction of the actuality of the holy, moral, loving will of God involves a large measure of faith. Verification remains incomplete. For Jesus upon the cross the only verification was a final daring act of trust; Paul staked everything on the verification offered by the resurrection of Christ. We are not free from the same necessity of trust in the actuality of God's love. But the trust is not blind trust; it is supported by the moral experience of the race. And in it at least and alone our moral and religious relativism must yield to the affirmation of the absolute.

THE ATTACK UPON THE SOCIAL GOSPEL*

The question of the Social Gospel is explicitly or implicitly involved in a great deal of the contemporary theological and religious discussion. To exponents of the "application of Christianity" to social problems the new movements—neo-Protestant or Barthian, neo-Evangelical or Buchmanite and neo-Catholic or Anglo-Catholic—appear to be retreats from the battlefield of social life back to the line of individualistic and other-worldly Christianity. They believe that those who are influenced by these movements intend to give up the endeavor to influence group behavior as impossible in a world lost in sin or to devote themselves to the cultivation of a

* From *Religion in Life*, V, 1 (Spring 1936), 176–181. Copyright renewal 1964 by Abingdon Press.

spiritual life in quietist isolation from a confusing civilization. Representatives of the post-liberal movements, on the other hand, are inclined to speak of the Social Gospel as though it were the epitome of all those humanistic, melioristic and anti-revolutionary tendencies in modernist religion against which they protest. They think of the Social Gospel as a message of self-help, as an optimistic faith that men can enter the kingdom of God without profound revolution, as the expression of cultural Protestantism which is more interested in civilization and its improvement than in God's judgment and love. Very important issues are at stake and it will not do to attempt a superficial synthesis of ideas which are antithetical, yet it seems to the present writer that the issues are still confused and that the debate may become more fruitful if certain distinctions are made. Above all else it seems that the issue of the objective should be distinguished from the issue of the means. The first question is whether the individual or society is the proper object of Christianity's mission; the second, whether the Church is to employ direct or indirect means.

I

The Social Gospel is characterized by the conviction that social units of every sort are the primary human realities to which the Church ought to address itself, or that, in dealing with individuals, not the isolated soul but the social individual —the citizen, class-member, race-member—should be regarded as the being who is in need of redemption. In this respect it is the heir of sociological science rather than of liberal philosophy. It rejects the doctrine of eighteenth- and nineteenth-century liberalism which proclaimed with Bentham that "the community is a fictitious body" and which regarded all societies as based upon contracts into which independent individuals entered for the sake of promoting common interests. However true this liberalism may have been of a period in which new societies were being established, the Social Gospel has noted that it is not true of our time. Now, at least, society appears to precede the individual, to mold his character, to determine his interests, to bestow rights upon him. The individual is what he is by virtue of the place in society which he occupies; or, if this is too extreme a statement, the interaction between society and individual is such that an interpretation which always makes the individual the first term is manifestly wrong. The Social Gospel has seen sin and righteousness as characteristics of group life; it has noted that vicarious suffering is laid upon group for group rather than upon individual for individual; it has seen the problem of salvation as a social problem and it has worked for the conversion or "change" of societies rather than of individuals who, no matter how much they may be changed, yet remain bound by common social evils and participants in common social sin.

This social interest of the Social Gospel is as pertinent to our time as the individualist gospel was to the eighteenth and early nineteenth centuries. In that earlier period Christianity confronted individuals who had been emancipated from political, ecclesiastical and economic bonds, who had sometimes also— as in the case of the American frontiers—been freed from the restraint which popular mores had imposed upon them. These emancipated individuals not only became perilous to one another but were in danger of losing significance from lives which had become ends-in-themselves. The bases of a new common life needed to be laid; the individual needed to be related to a source of meaning which transcended his particular desires and his selfhood; he needed to be given an inner discipline which would direct his new freedom; those who had become victims of the free egotism of others needed to be rescued from despair and its consequences. How well Evangelicalism (Methodism, Pietism, the American revival movement) met these problems, how splendidly it succeeded in supplying inner discipline in place of vanished external restraints, how effectively it related lives to a transcendent God, how genuinely it gave new faith, courage and zest to suppressed individuals—these facts are frequently overlooked by men who regard the whole individualistic movement as an error which might have been avoided, or who note that the Evangelical answer no longer suffices in an age which poses a different problem. But it is possible to give all due credit to the effectiveness of the individualistic gospel without maintaining that it is adequate for our day.

It is true that every person has interests, problems and responsibilities as a self which is directly related to God; no full presentation of the gospel can ever leave these out of account. Yet it seems evident that in our time the doom and the salvation, the creation, sin and redemption with which men are concerned are social rather than individual in character. The emancipated individuals of our day are the societies, the races and classes which have made themselves laws to themselves; which commit crimes against other classes, races and nations and believe they will go unpunished; which suffer injustice and suppression as groups; which are faced with the problem of their own futility and emptiness. It is in this area that the reality of sin and hell, and the necessity of salvation have become most apparent. In that sense the modern situation is more like that of the Hebrew nation in the time of the prophets than like that of eighteenth-century individuals. The question of personal salvation is important but, as in the whole of Hebrew history, it is secondary to the question of social salvation. It is true that in this situation much can be done for men as independent individuals, and the Oxford Group movement has demonstrated something of the possibilities. But insofar as this movement deals with persons as the primary factors and tends to overlook the fact that the amount of honesty, purity and love which persons can exercise while they participate in the dishonesties, impurities and hatefulness of capitalism, nationalism is very limited, it will continue to be regarded with many reservations not only by exponents of the Social Gospel but by all who see the problem of society as the problem of the day. But it may be that this movement will not remain as individualistic as it now appears to be, while there is nothing in either neo-Protestantism or in neo-Catholicism which is inimical to the social approach. On the contrary the exponents of these movements may claim with considerable right that their return to sixteenth- and thirteenth-century modes of thought is due precisely to the necessity of overcoming the individualism of the more recent past. After all, both Catholics and Protestants were interested in the conversion of societies, in the ordering of social life, in the fate not only of men but of humanity. It is certainly true that both neo-Protestants and neo-Catholics have a far more social conception of the Church than many even of those who represent the Social Gospel in its liberal form, for whom the Church remains too often a contract society. And both of these groups with their orthodox conceptions of original sin, of historic revelation, of general judgment and of the salvation of mankind are operating with ideas which have direct relevance to men's existence as members of mankind and its societies. Doubtless these ideas will need to be rethought, but there is nothing individualistic about them, and those who believe that in them the solution to the human problem is to be found not only can but must participate in the social direction of the Social Gospel.

II

It is at the point of the second issue that the real divergence of the day is to be sought. The Social Gospel has been directed not only toward the changing of social entities but it has largely sought to accomplish this end by indirect means, and by way of self-help. The means which it has employed are indirect from the religious point of view. It has used political and economic means to gain the end. Its exponents have sought to influence legislatures to enact laws, schools to teach attitudes, political parties to adopt programs. Or it has sought to work through the labor movement, using economic means for the purpose of changing society. It has worked for international peace by trying to influence governments to adopt treaties or by writing to congressmen with requests to vote for that law. Such measures are doubtless good in their place but as used by the church they represent the strategy of indirect action. They are not only efforts to get some other organization to do something about the intolerable situation but also presuppose the convictions that religion as such has no direct bearing on social life, that prophetic and Christian analysis of the situation with corresponding direct religious action are unimportant and that the analysis of society in terms of its political and economic arrangements is fundamental.

In the second place the strategy of the Social Gospel has largely been a strategy of self-salvation, or of salvation by works. It has tended to speak of social salvation as something which men could accomplish for themselves if only they adopted the right social ideal, found adequate motivation for achieving it and accepted the correct technical means. The social ideal has been regarded as the product of men's independent ethical insight, the knowledge of correct means as the product of social science, and religion has been looked to for the motivation. God, in this theory, becomes a means to an end; he is there for the sake of achieving a human ideal and he does not do even this directly but only through the inspiration which he offers to those who worship him. The failure of this whole scheme of social salvation has driven many Social Gospel advocates to look for non-religious motivation in the self-interest of classes or races, in which case even the last vestige of a religious strategy has been given up.

It is against this indirect, self-help strategy, rather than against the social objective of the Social Gospel, that the major protest of the day is being made. There are significant differences, of course, between neo-Protestant and neo-Catholic movements, but they seem to agree in this: that whatever place be given to the indirect strategy the primary attack of Christianity upon the social situation or the social individual must be direct, not via governments and economic units, but via the Church or the word of God. They agree in the second place in regarding salvation, whether social or individual, as a divine process, not as something man can achieve by moralistic means.

From the neo-Protestant point of view the strategy of the Social Gospel rests upon a false analysis of the social situation, and the false strategy results from this false analysis. A true analysis will see that our social injustice and misery cannot be dealt with unless their sources in a false faith are dealt with. So long as the faith of man remains "capitalistic," that is, a faith in the security which can be given economically, so long the profit-system and the system of private property cannot be budged. So long as any sort of this-worldly security remains the object of confidence our nationalisms and mammonisms will flourish. Both just and unjust live by faith, though by different kinds of faith, and our social no less than our individual lives are an expression of these faiths. From the neo-Protestant point of view repentance for the *sins* of social life is not enough; there needs to be repentance for the *sin*, for the false faith, for the idolatry which issues in all these sins. Men will be ready for no radically new life until they have really become aware of the falsity of the faith upon which their old life is based. But an attack upon faith requires the direct action of the Church rather than indirect action.

In the second place neo-Protestantism's analysis of the situation in which social groups live runs counter to the analysis upon which the doctrine of self-salvation is based. The Social Gospel is related to the neo-Protestant movement somewhat as Utopian Socialism is related to Marxism. Utopianism also believed in the saving power of the ideal, motivated by sympathy and love of the good. Whatever the quarrels may be between "deterministic" and "synergistic" Marxians they all recognize the priority of the historic process to which the party must adjust itself; Marxism salvation at least is not self-salvation. In another sphere, with a far more profound analysis of the total situation than Marxism offers, neo-Protestantism would base its strategy on the priority of God—not as a human ideal, or the object of worship, but as the moving force in history—who alone brings in His kingdom and to whose ways the party of the Kingdom of God on earth must adjust itself. But strangely enough the Social Gospel, when it recognizes the inadequacy of Utopianism, tends to accept Marxist rather than Christian determinism as offering the correct analysis.

The strategy toward which neo-Protestantism is feeling its way is not only the direct strategy which attacks false faith and proclaims true faith, or the strategy of action corresponding to the way of God in history as revealed in the event Jesus

Christ, but for both of these reasons it is also a revolutionary strategy, which regards the death of the old life as inevitable and as necessary before a new beginning can be made.

Our interest here, however, is not that of trying to set forth the strategy of an orthodox Christianity which is thoroughly alive to the problem of the day. The development of this strategy still lies in the future. The question is rather whether such a strategy does not need to be developed. The issue between the Social Gospel and the new movements lies here, not at the point of social versus individual salvation.

The present situation may be compared to that which existed at the beginning of the eighteenth century. The rationalist effort to deal with the problem of emancipated individual life in terms of moral self-salvation and by means of indirect and melioristic action through education and reason failed. Then came the direct, revolutionary Evangelical approach based upon a theory of salvation in which—whatever the differences between Calvinists and Arminians—the adjustment of human ways to the way of God as revealed in Jesus Christ was demanded. The new movements in Christianity, it seems to the present writer, must not be interpreted as reactions to Evangelical individualism, but as efforts to discover in our own day the social equivalent of the Evangelical strategy.

12

RUFUS M. JONES

Guardian of the Inner Light

Rufus M. Jones (1863–1948) stands apart from most of the religious thinkers of his time, though he is perhaps closest to William James in his concern for the nature of individual religious experience and in the psychological dimension of his *The Nature and Authority of Conscience* (1920). He was a scholar of vast historical and philosophical erudition, and his central focus was on the vitality of mystical awareness.

Born and raised on a farm near South China, Maine, young Rufus was steeped in Quaker piety from his earliest years. The Bible formed virtually his only childhood literature, and biblical events and characters were vividly real to him. In most respects, rural Maine was as much a pioneer setting as was the West; Kennebec County was a Quaker enclave as isolated as those in Ohio and Indiana. Attendance at the weekly meeting meant a three-mile wagon ride through the woods. The boy's uncle, Eli Jones, was South China's leading citizen, a superb preacher widely traveled in England and Europe. Through his inspiration and influence, Rufus Jones was enabled to attend Friends Boarding School in Providence and subsequently Haverford College, a Quaker school which then had an enrollment of eighty students.

At Haverford he read Emerson's essay, "The Over-Soul," a spark that ignited the hoarded kindling of his spiritual upbringing, expanding his conception of the mystical Inner Light and leading him to the study of Plato, Plotinus, Proclus, Jakob Boehme, George Fox, and oriental mysticism. In many respects, he counted Josiah Royce as a towering influence—particularly through Royce's essays on Eckhardt and George Fox in *Studies of Good and Evil.* The idea of a God "up there" had never been part of his tutelage; now Emerson and the others added depth to his understanding of God as Divine Presence—a depth of scholarly comprehension corresponding to the experiential depth which he already had. He graduated from Haverford in 1885 and a year later went to Europe, where he readily mastered French and German. Subsequent studies at Heidelberg, Oxford, and Harvard equipped him for a lifelong scholarly task. He taught philosophy at Haverford from 1893 to 1934, remaining as emeritus professor until his death in 1948. In 1905 a grant from Joseph Rountree, an English Quaker, enabled him to embark on sixteen years of study in the history of mysticism and Quarkerism. Among the many fruits of this enterprise are his *Studies in Mystical Religion* (1909), *The Quakers in the American Colonies* (1911), and *Spiritual Reformers of the Sixteenth and Seventeenth Centuries* (1914). His published writings exceed fifty volumes, of which a dozen represent pioneering scholarship in their field and were regarded as authoritative until very recently, when new research has opened some of his findings to question.[1]

Scholarship aside, probably no man since John Woolman has exerted such wide influence within the Society of Friends, nor did so much to renew and rekindle its ethic. Torn by the same divisions that split other American denominations, Quakerism was fragmented and in decline in Jones' youth. Habits of plain speech and dress had become anachronistic oddities rather than the marks of simplicity they once were, and the Friends' historic peace testimony was badly bruised by conflicts of conscience that led many to take up arms against the Indians on the frontier and to combat the forces of slavery in the Civil War. As editor of *Friends Review* and its successor, *The American Friend*, from 1893 to 1912, Jones mediated among the factions with irenic dedication. When America entered World War I, he was largely responsible for orga-

---

[1] On the whole, however, they have endured. The only references to Jones, for example, in George Huntston Williams, *The Radical Reformation* (Philadelphia: Westminster, 1962), cite him as the best source for details of several spiritual sects.

nizing the American Friends Service Committee, channeling
the energies of conscientious objectors into ambulance and
relief work. In 1938, at the age of 75, he led an AFSC delega-
tion to Gestapo headquarters in Berlin to try to aid persecuted
Jews. He also founded the Wider Quaker Fellowship as a
means of sharing the values of his tradition without proon
proselytizing among other denominations. In sum, the legacy of his
life, work, and thought forms a whole, and his religious philosophy of the spirit represents not a separate compartment
but the experiential wellspring of his external activities. When
he discusses the soul or the "inner life," he does not speak
only as a scholar, nor at all as a man withdrawn from the
world.

In late colonial, America Quakerism was numerically on a
par with Episcopalians, Baptists and Presbyterians. Today
there are fewer Quakers than there are Mennonites. Regardless of numbers, however, Quakerism has exerted a unique
influence from a sector that forms a kindred root beside the
Calvinist and Arminian ones, dating from the Cromwellian
era and extending into the present. It is not surprising, then,
if the solitary witness of Rufus Jones and a few others has
had palpable influence on the thought of such men as Harry
Emerson Fosdick and Charles Hartshorne.

In his Ayer Lectures for 1936, given at Colgate-Rochester
Divinity School, Rufus Jones spanned a considerable range of
concerns under the broad heading, *The Testimony of the Soul.*
In one lecture, "Soul-Force," he takes as a point of departure
a conversation he had with Mahatma Gandhi in 1926. In the
space of twenty-three printed pages he adumbrates that conversation with observations drawn from Francis of Assisi,
Goethe, the Gospel of John, Coleridge, Suzuki, Lincoln, Cle-
ment of Alexandria, and Descartes, with asides to depth psychology, Hinduism, and Greek etymology, all in an easy
conversational manner, as Jones probes the relationships between knowledge, truth, action, and growth, explaining Gandhi's spiritual power finally as the energizing of a "center of
repose." Each lecture, in its own way, is a kind of intellec-

tual *tour de force* abounding in both insight and sidelights
that open up avenues for further reflection.

The selection that follows is more straightforward than the
other lectures. It is chosen less for its typicality than because
it addresses itself to themes reflected in the mainstream of
American Protestant thought at the time of its writing. Among
other things, it testifies to the existence of an alternative,
within the general spectrum of liberal theology, to both the
modernism of Mathews and the Christian realism of Niebuhr.
Or rather, like the historic relation of Quakerism to the Protestant mainstream, Jones stands not so much opposed as simply
adjacent to those viewpoints which vied for leadership. He
offers not a different program for the period of crisis but a
simple testimony to the primacy of the inner life, a perspective that sees itself as tributary rather than normative.

---

*THE INNER LIFE AND THE SOCIAL ORDER**

Some time ago in the Chapel of the University of Chicago,
Charles Clayton Morrison, Editor of the *Christian Century*,
preached a challenging sermon at the Pastors' Institute in that
city. He began his sermon with the statement that Christianity
now stands at the crisis of its entire history. That crisis, he
asserted, has emerged out of the fact that Christianity is now
shifting the centre of its gravity from the inner life to the
social community. The speaker contended that, in the past,
religion has derived its vitality from the private experience of
individual men and women; it is now discovering the religious
resources that have lain hidden in the wide field of the social
order. In the past the religious transactions which were believed to take place in the inner life between God and the
soul were transactions "in an ethical vacuum." Religion of this
former type was occupied with the subjectivities of the inner

---

* From Rufus M. Jones, *The Testimony of the Soul* (New York: The Macmillan Co., 1936), pp. 32–48.

life, it was busy with "its abstractions and fantasies and ideologies," and was unable to pass over from the inner life "into the burly world outside."

A religious experience, he held, which originates in the inner life tends to become a private luxury and lacks the disposition to take control and direction of the world. The shift of the centre of gravity now taking place, he said, is away from *the primacy of the inner life* as the field of a valid and creative religion over to *the primacy of a social vision,* out of which a real inner life may spring. "The present crisis then in Christianity," he declared, "arises from the necessity of finding the foundations of religion in the world of human society conceived as the Kingdom of God."

There can, I think, be little question that Christianity today is facing a momentous crisis, though I am too familiar with the numerous crises of its past history to accept without further debate the conclusion that it is *the* crisis *par excellence.* In any case I am profoundly convinced that the above diagnosis of the cause and occasion for this present crisis is an adequate one. The situation in the religious world is far too complex to be squeezed down to a single shift of the centre of gravity. We are still in the swirl of the mighty currents of the incompleted Renaissance, and the entire basis of the significance, the validity and the authority of religion has for some time now been undergoing an acid test. We have outgrown to a large extent the doll stage of religious life with its enjoyment of pictorial imagery, magic, and the dim magnificence of mythology and superstitious creations. We have left behind, with the discarded Ptolemaic astronomy, the vivid conceptions of a sky-dome heaven and a literal subterranean hell.

It is not easy to overestimate the mental effect which has been occasioned by the loss of this vivid pictorial imagery through which most persons for two thousand years have formed for themselves "the scenery and circumstance of the newly parted soul." Much that was real and vital in religious thought only a little while ago now seems to us like intolerable babyism, and it has dropped away forever from our minds, as our baby clothes have done from our bodies. But these discarded ideas which our growing knowledge has pushed off were the slow growth of the racial life of the world. They formed the psychological climate of many generations. They had become comfortable with long habit, and they furnished a cultural atmosphere of faith that made it easy to breathe and act as though religion were a normal, natural function of life.

We of modern times have been stripped of the comfortable clothing which our ancestors found so convenient. That cultural atmosphere of theirs does not fit our minds. A mighty transition has passed over the world and left it forever altered. And we happen to be living at a time when the old order is dead and the new order is not yet quite born. We have shed the literal, the pictorial, the mythological imagery of religious life and we have not yet created a spiritual cultural atmosphere in which we breathe and live with natural ease as our forebears did.

We have not, furthermore, quite succeeded in passing over from external authorities, imposed from without, to inward compulsions, which work as silently and yet as powerfully as do those invisible forces which hold the earth in its journey around the sun. The Renaissance, now more than five hundred years in extent, will not be over and finished until these *new birth processes* have come to fruition and man has found those springs of life and faith which fit his new stages of intellectual growth. Among the changes of attitude that will mark the new birth of religion there will certainly be an immensely increased emphasis on the redemption of society as the true organ of the Kingdom of God, but that will be only one feature, however important a feature, of a newly created religious faith which fits the world-order of the new time.

My next observation in reference to the sermon under consideration is that there never has been any genuine religion of the inner life which operated in "an ethical vacuum," except possibly in the primitive stages of religion and ethics. Religion and ethics have always developed together in the closest intimacy of interaction. They probably, however, do not have the same psychological origin. One does not spring out of the other. There is no use arguing which has the primacy, which is Jacob and which is Esau, for they are in their own nature quite unique and *sui generis* attitudes, as irreducible into terms of anything else as in the appreciation of beauty.

Religion in its original unique form is the soul's attitude, response and adjustment, in the presence of what are felt to be supreme of a transcendent order. Ethics in its essential meaning has to do with that strange attitude which we express by the words, "I ought," and with the *right* adjustment of life within a society of men and women. They are alike in the fact that both have their ground in man's fundamental capacity to expand life in ideal directions and to live out beyond what is presented to the senses of fact. There would be no use of *ought* if one could be satisfied with *what is,* and there would be no awe and wonder, no "numinous" state of mind, if we were mere calm spectators of passing phenomena. They both attach to that sphere of life in us that has been called "imaginative dominion over experience."

Religion springs out of our faith, which often amounts to discovery, that there is a divine Overworld with which we have dealings, while ethics moves in the horizontal sphere of human society, but always at the same time implies a faith, amounting often a compelling vision, that actions that *ought to be done* will enlarge the scope of both individual and social life. There can be no significant ethics without ideal vision of a life that *ought* to be. They both have to do with a *beyond,* in one case with an eternal world which already is as it ought to be; in the other case with an imperfect temporal world which can be made by human effort more nearly like what ought to be.

The story of the sublimation of religion under the influence of the growth and historical process of ethical ideals is the story of one of the most impressive achievements which man has yet made on the earth. In its primitive stage the element of fear in religion was very great. It was never true, as the Roman poet Lucretius thought, that "fear created the gods," but it is a fact that man in his childhood was much more impressed with the *power* of unseen beings above him than with their goodness or their friendliness and their intention to bless and help. Religion in its primitive form, as Bergson has put it, was the cradle in which the race in its infancy rocked itself to sleep from its fears and terrors.

Little by little in the slow stages of expanding social life man discovered the immense significance of human love and the worth of moral goodness, both in itself and in its creative social effects. It gradually dawned upon him, that what had seemed at first like sternness or anger in men's dealings with one another was often only a way of training and discipline for the making of a better person. It is an immemorial discovery of patterns that young and immature lives cannot be guided into the formation of wisdom and stability of character alone by soft and easy methods. There must be agencies of restraint in the great business of moral guidance. Men came, through such experiences, to see, even if only dimly, that the strongest and most effective persons were, after all, the persons who had been trained by severe discipline. Through his ethical discoveries of the social significance of love, the worth of goodness and the value of discipline in the sphere of his own life, man began to refashion his thoughts and ideals of the beings above him who controlled and guided his destiny. He saw them now through the imaginative ethical forms of what was the highest and best that he knew in his own world of experience.

The most momentous step in the process of sublimation came through the insight that human life continues after death in another sphere and that the divine beings above are moral guardians of those higher issues of destiny. That *insight* throws back much light upon the transcendent quality of man's mind, even in the early dawning stages of life, and it is, of course, a nice question how far the original insight had its birth in the sphere of what may be called religious experience, and how far it was the outgrowth of ethical ideals of an animistic type. We do not need to stop and debate that question now. It is clear enough in any case that when once the insight was reached ethical ideals from that time on worked powerfully upon religious conceptions. The divine beings were thought of not merely as embodiments of capricious power but as the keepers of the issues of life and death.

It was an epoch in the life of the race when the faith was born that the moral gains of life are conserved and, under the guardianship of divine beings, determine man's future destiny. When that discovery was made the long process of casting out *fear* with *love* was well under way. I have presented here the higher constructive aspect of this insight of the conservation of personality and have omitted to speak of the burden and drag which utilitarian conceptions of the future life have often been to human progress. As I write this I have just seen a shaft of light break through the clouds and make one glorious spot of radiance on the sea, while all the rest of the surrounding sea lay dark in shadow. So it has often been with man's noblest insights. A shaft of illumination throws a sudden gleam of light, revealing in a flash man's divine possibilities, while the main stream of life runs on untouched by the glory.

Not less powerfully has religion influenced the development of the ethical life of man. There has always been interaction, osmosis, between these two supreme values of life. If ethics with its ideals has sublimated religion, religion at the same time has brought steadiness, fortification and an *élan* of marching power to man's ethical life. It is quite impossible to conceive what our life would have been if it had been deprived of the faiths which religion has brought to birth in us. We make our risky ventures for ideal ends with very little empirical evidence that they will lead to triumph. Anybody who engages in moral battles is as familiar with defeats as he is with victories. Frustration is one of the most common experiences of life. What we care for most as a goal to be attained often seems to be at the mercy of a trivial or capricious happening. If we had no assurances except those which our senses and our memories give us, we should have a feeble armor for the supreme battles of life to which we feel summoned.

Religion whenever it has been at its best has brought the steadiness of a wider reference. We can bear the tragedy of present frustration or of momentary defeat if we have inward assurance enough that eternal forces are allied with us for the cause that is *good*. Religion has in the main brought this vision of expectation. It has contributed the faith that the deepest nature of things is morally grounded and is there behind the lonely fighter for what is right. It has brought confidence to man that the eternal Heart of the universe backs his moral endeavors and that in the long run—the run is sometimes very long—in the long run what ought to be is what will be.

Religious faith at its highest has brought the conviction that our God Himself is an Emmanuel God and has entered the darkly colored stream of history, partakes of the sorrows and tragedies of the temporal order and treads the winepress with us even when it is reddest, and that we are never alone when we are striving upward. It fortifies us with the hope that we can in some sense become organs of His divine purpose and be revealing places for His will to break into manifestation. In fact, too, religion furnishes to ethics its richest and most adequate goal of life. It heartens us with the belief that we are most completely ourselves when we are nearest in spirit and character to the pattern of life which the Christian religion presents and that we are most truly at the goal of human life when we approximate most closely to the nature of the God whom we worship.

In the light of this constant interaction between religion and ethics, I maintain that it is an historically untenable position to claim that an inner religious experience is "bound to exist without reference to the public social world outside." It is quite possible that theological conceptions—what Dr. Morrison loves to call "ideologies"—may come to be ends in themselves, in fact they have no doubt frequently come to be ends in themselves and have lulled the smug and satisfied soul to rest with the existing social *status quo*—"the mess we's in" —but I seriously doubt whether *vital inward religion* has ever done it.

I mean by "vital inward religion" an actual personal contact with the central eternal Stream of Life. He says that "the first Christians derived their inner experience from their social vision." I believe that is a misreading of the facts. What happened in the first instance was a fresh discovery of God, a breaking in of Eternity into the life of men—"we have beheld His glory," they say, and forthwith all the ethical values of life were altered. These men did not originate the idea of the Kingdom of God, nor did their Master himself originate it, it was the slow growth of centuries, but their new vision of God and the throbbing experience of His life in their lives recast the entire meaning of the Kingdom and brought to them a burning passion for its coming as a realm of love and brotherhood—"righteousness, peace and joy in the holy Spirit."

Dr. Morrison has much to say of the social sterility of "evangelicalism," in which, as he says, the doctrine of the new birth holds a central place. But here once more he is talking about a congealed system and not about a vital inward experience. One of the most dynamic things the modern world has seen was that same evangelical movement in the days when it *moved*, with its original high *caloric*. It came like a vernal equinox into the morally dull and static life of the eighteenth century. It turned water to wine, it brought prodigals home, it raised life out of death. It produced miracles of transformation. But the most remarkable thing about it was the freshly inspired social impulse which it produced. It reformed prisons, it stopped the slave trade, it freed slaves. It made its converts uncomfortable over wrong social conditions. It sent missionaries to create hospitals and to conquer ignorance in almost every land on the globe. It was always as much outward as it was inward, though its creative spring was assuredly a birth of new life from the central Source of Life.

It is surely an exaggeration to say, as was said in this sermon, that "after nineteen centuries of Christianity's presence in the world the brutalities of the secular social system have not been radically mitigated." If the writer of that sentence could make an excursion into almost any previous century of the nineteen past ones he would pine to return to the one in which he lives. And the contrast that would strike him most as he came back would be the fact that nearly everybody in the former centuries took the "brutalities" as a matter of course, as a settled feature of a "wrecked and fallen world," as a *datum* of foreordination, whereas almost no inwardly alive Christian feels that way today in reference to the secular social system. Something new has happened. *We* are determined to remake the social world and we *expect* to remake it. That is a fact of major importance.

I have spent most of my life studying mystical religion and its exponents. It reveals in its long history a large amount of physical abnormality, a good-sized element of doubtful metaphysical theory, and more than one likes to see of "gullibility." But there remains over and above the liabilities a great central nucleus of extraordinary religious experience through which men and women have found themselves raised to an irresistible consciousness of contact with God. They have felt through that experience as though the Ocean of Eternal Life had surged into the tiny inlet of their being. This experience of rising into the Eternal Life has again and again brought with it a marvelous increase of vitality and power for the individual to live by. To use William James' phrase it has turned them into "human dynamos." It does not of course take them out of the social and intellectual environment of their time and give them supernaturally the outlook, the ideals and the social patterns of epochs not yet born. Even St. Francis with all his social passion struggled on with thirteenth-century economic and social ideas. But what does happen, what has happened, to these persons whose inner life has been vivified and quickened, is that they begin at once to feel a passion for the enrichment and enlargement of the lives of others. They say with almost one accord that no vision of God is adequate which remains private and is not translated into life and action. The true test of an inner vision, they all insist, is the impact it gives toward pushing back the skirts of darkness and making the area of the Kingdom of God wider.

It is true that "the kingdoms of this world are still the kingdoms of *this world.*" But as soon as one studies the history of Christianity minutely he discovers that the main-line stream of Christianity through the centuries has not been concerned with Christ's ethics, has hardly been aware indeed that he brought a new ethic. The gaze has been fixed on a supernatural Being from another world whose mission here was to bring a way of *redemption* and to found a mysterious Church as the authoritative instrument of it.

The hymn which I used to sing with enthusiasm in my early Christian experience,

> *Hallelujah! 'tis done*
> *I believe in the Son;*
> *I am saved by the blood*
> *Of the crucified One,*

expresses quite accurately what Christianity has in general meant to men. The focus of attention has been on a supernatural nativity, a crucifixion of agony and death and a supernatural resurrection and ascension. The theology of the Church has been built around those doctrines, the art of the Church has glorified those features of its faith. One looked in vain and listened in vain until recent times in the historic Church for the proclamation of a way of life which involves the practice of the Galilean gospel. It has been in the main the mystic and the heretic who have endeavored to *restore* primitive Christianity as a way of life among men. The social gospel is for most persons a new discovery. Furthermore the affiliation of the Church with the State has of course always tended to secularize Christianity and to make the Sermon on the Mount seem to be an utterly foreign, if not a fantastic, group of ideas. We are very young in the faith that Christianity is something to be *done*, not something to be recited, or used as a scheme to insure heavenly joy. Give us a little more time!

It should be added, I think, that there is no magic in that phrase "social gospel." It is no easy matter to settle offhand precisely what was the ethics of Jesus. It is one of the most acute problems of New Testament scholarship. But even if it were as plain and clear as is the ethics of John Dewey we should still be confronted with grave difficulties. It is never possible to pick up an ethical system and lift it out of its temporal setting and local habitat and put it down unaltered upon a world of new complexities and wholly altered civilization. What has to be done if Christ's ethics is to be effective is to reincarnate the spirit that was in the founder of this way of life, to recapture his faith in God and man and to live in the dominion and power of a love like his.

My final trouble with the sermon in question lies in its insistence on the *primacy of social vision* in the sphere of religion. We are, it tells us, to put the social vision first and then to get an inner life to match it. "The quest for God is to be in the collective life of mankind." There are two difficulties here. The first difficulty is that first, last and always religion is bound to be an individual person's experience, or appreciation, or attitude, or discovery. We are dealing with "a grin without any face" until religion *personalizes* into the concrete. We cannot talk of beauty in the collective life of mankind, for whenever beauty is actually felt it is felt by somebody in particular. No crowding of heads together ever fuses experiences into a composite experience which exists over and above the persons who own the heads. There is no known contrivance by which we can get away from "inner experience." To the end of time, so long as we remain persons, religion will begin as an inner experience in somebody's soul. It will not be the operation of an entity called a "group mind." We are of course powerfully affected by our relations to a group and there is no such existing reality as "an isolated individual," but the moment we ask for the origin and basis of conscious experience we are invariably sent to a concrete mind, which is *somebody's mind,* and what he experiences will be "an inner experience" within himself.

The other difficulty is the insuperable one of making society —the collective life of man—an adequate locus for the quest of God. Society, the collective life of mankind, is an empirical affair which goes on in time, begins and ends, is now better and now worse, or, I hope, the reverse; but in any case, it is a temporal process which is not self-explanatory nor intelligible in its own right. Human society in itself, however perfected, is not, and cannot be, a worshipful totality, not even in a totalitarian state. Like stars and mountains and sunsets—human history, human yearnings and human tragedies and triumphs give us clues and suggestions and intimations in our quest for

God, but the God we seek is not a temporal object of the empirical order, nor a sum total of many objects added together.

What we shall do, what we are doing, will be that we shall make our inner life richer through better philosophies of life, through more clarified knowledge of history, through a much closer approach to the actual Christ who lived and loved and suffered and triumphed, through a more vital apprehension of His way of life as a way of living, and through the cultivation of a greater sensitiveness of soul to the environing Spirit in which we are. We shall pass from a religion of abstract creeds and repeated rituals and external performances to a religion of life. Its primacy will always be within, but its sphere of life and action will be in the world of men, and its goal, as Christ's was, will be that of changing the kingdoms of this world into the Kingdom of God.

13

CHARLES HARTSHORNE

Metaphysician of Dipolar Theism

Charles Hartshorne (1897–   ) is generally regarded as the foremost exponent of a theology akin to the process philosophy of Alfred North Whitehead. Indeed, the Hartshorne Festschrift, *Process and Divinity*, comprises essays related specifically to Whitehead as well as Hartshorne, and its very title is cousin to that of Whitehead's magnum opus, *Process and Reality.* Hartshorne's originality certainly transcends this undeniable influence and has its own prior roots, notably in American experience and thought. His world of discourse and his legacy, however, are vast in their embrace, and his full impact has only recently begun to be felt both in the United States and abroad.

Hartshorne was born in Kittanning, thirty miles up the Allegheny River from Pittsburgh. His father was a low-church Episcopal clergyman of liberal views. "My mother," says Hartshorne, "was a truly, rather angelically pious, charming Christian, daughter of a saintly, much beloved, scholarly clergyman."[1] Neither at home nor at boarding school, where Hartshorne spent four years prior to college, was he subjected to any conflict between science and religion. His father believed that "love was the whole content of Christian ethics"; he had nothing to say about hell and "did not use terms like immutability, absoluteness or infinity of God." The boarding school headmaster, also a liberal Episcopal clergyman, taught

---

[1] Quotations unless otherwise attributed are from an autobiographical letter to the editor of this volume, upon which the account given here is largely based.—Ed.

science and "presented evolution positively and as religiously inspiring."

Soon after he enrolled at Haverford College in 1915, his interest in metaphysics began to take shape, whetted by Coleridge's *Aids to Reflection* and the essays of Emerson and Matthew Arnold, whose concept of God as "the Eternal" was a seed from which a profounder notion grew. Perhaps more than incidentally, these authors also fed two interests of Hartshorne's besides metaphysics—ornithology and aesthetics.[2] His first academic encounter with metaphysics, however, came through the study of Royce's *The Problem of Christianity* in Rufus Jones' course in the history of Christian doctrine during the spring term at Haverford in 1917. America's entry into World War I interrupted Hartshorne's schooling, but during two years as an orderly in an army hospital in France he read *The Confession of St. Augustine,* James' *Varieties of Religious Experience,* H. G. Wells' metaphysical novels, *Mr. Britling Sees It Through* and *The Bishop,* and Amiel's *Journal.* From these varied influences grew a number of convictions with which Hartshorne entered Harvard as a junior in 1919:

> They were: 1) psychicalism, reality is *given* only in terms of feeling, not of mere dead matter (Croce uses this phenomenological argument, and so do Peirce and Whitehead, but I knew nothing of this then), hence the concept of "mere matter" is only verbal, corresponding to nothing knowable; 2) the unity of sentient individuals, hence of all reality, in an inclusive or divine life.
>
> The basis of the vague psychicalistic monism which I once for all adopted, leaving clarification for later, lay in the analysis of the way an individual's purposes overlap those of others.

---

[2] These interests form an important subcurrent in the development of Hartshorne's theological perspective, which unfortunately is beyond the scope of this essay. Parallel with his philosophical studies, Hartshorne has made scientific studies of birdsong. He finds in birdsong both an evolutionary predecessor and early influence on human music. Such evidence of interconnection between human and nonhuman beings as to experience, feeling, and consciousness suggests the inadequacy of a merely humanistic metapyhsic. See Hartshorne, "Freedom, Individuality and Beauty in Nature," *Snowy Egret,* XXIV, 2 (Autumn 1960). Emerson's essay, "Nature," and Whitehead's *The Concept of Nature* have played a part in this aspect of Hartshorne's thought.

Perhaps Royce's discussion of community most nearly expressed this notion of unity. Hartshorne also found in Wordsworth an insight into "the way we intuitively sympathize with the 'life of things' in direct perception. Later, in Whitehead's theory of prehension as "feeling of feeling," he found articulate expression of his own surmise. As a graduate student at Harvard in 1922 he first read part of Whitehead's *The Concept of Nature*. From this and from conversations with F. S. C. Northrop, who had studied with Whitehead at Cambridge, Hartshorne came to the conclusion that "events, not things, are the most concrete units of reality." His doctoral dissertation, written in 1922–1923, makes virtually no use of Whitehead, yet developed "a rather elaborate metaphysical system not too different from what later turned out to be Whitehead's view," although it was rather primitive in comparison with the latter.

Two years of study in Europe provided Hartshorne with exposure to Husserl, Heidegger, Ebbinghaus, and Kroner. Very much like Wieman, however, he found that "none of this seemed very convincing to me (and still does not)." In contrast to Husserl, he was to find the phenomenological categories of Charles Sanders Peirce more illuminating. "They were closer to Heidegger than to Husserl, but without the oracular, pretentious obscurantism of Heidegger."

Hartshorne discovered Peirce quite by accident. When he returned to Harvard as an instructor in 1925, he was asked, in his capacity as a research assistant, to take on the assignment of compiling and editing Peirce's collected papers.

> I simply accepted the assignment, knowing next to nothing at all of Peirce. It turned out that I had by chance been pushed into a congenial world of ideas. Peirce was an epistemological realist and an ontological idealist or psychicalist, an indeterminist and creationist about both creatures and creator (with some wavering on the latter point). He strengthened the tendency I already had of looking to formal logic as the clue to metaphysical problems.

Whitehead had come to Harvard one year earlier. At the same time that Hartshorne was working on the Peirce papers, he heard the Whitehead lectures, which were subsequently published as *Religion in the Making.* Again, quite by chance, Hartshorne was asked to grade papers for Whitehead. The philosopher and his wife took a liking to the brilliant young man, and he became a frequent visitor of their home. However, it was mainly Whitehead's writings which exercised the greatest influence on Hartshorne. He found that Whitehead and Peirce agreed on "a fair number of basic points"; where they differed, he found Whitehead more cogent, as in the latter's quantum view of becoming. "The primacy of event over substance thus became the primacy of the not actually divided 'actual entity' which 'becomes rather than changes.' " Hartshorne found vivid religious intuitions in both thinkers, but Whitehead's were the less ambiguous; they harmonized with his own ideas and clarified them. Whitehead's idea of "objective immortality" struck him as "a real religious inspiration, and something like a revelation to me." Hartshorne had never been preoccupied with conventional ideas of heaven and hell, so the Whiteheadian notion of the individual's life as a contribution to the divine life which is alone immortal struck him as a valuable gain—"a sublime, positive idea of the counterbalance to death." For this and other reasons, Whitehead may be seen as the key influence causing Harthshorne to pursue a distinct line of inquiry diverging from the vaguer kind of process philosophy found in James, Bergson, Peirce, Hocking, and Fechner.

In 1928, Hartshorne went to the University of Chicago as an instructor in philosophy, subsequently becoming a full professor. He resigned in 1955, taught for seven years at Emory University and in 1963 was appointed Ashbel Smith Professor of Philosophy at the University of Texas. The two essays which follow date from 1934, the year in which Hartshorne's first book appeared—*The Philosophy and Psychology of Sensation.* This was the period in which his mature religious thought began to crystalize—the last years of the "Chicago school" that included Mathews (who retired in 1933), Ames (who retired in 1935), and Wieman, whose career in the Divinity School (1927–47) paralleled Hartshorne's. Hartshorne's social and humanistic emphases are to some extent congruent with the Chicago tradition but also represent a significant departure, as is evident in his Terry Lectures given at Yale in 1947: *The Divine Relativity: A Social Conception of God* (1948), and in *Reality As Social Process* (1953). Even earlier, Hartshorne's conception was larger than that of humanism, as his *Beyond Humanism* (1937) attests.

There is probably more that unites Hartshorne and Wieman than divides them, in the general outline of their thought; they share common emphases on immanence, creativity, experience, love, the centrality of Jesus. Their respective stress on God as "concrete" and "empirical" seems to be another link; but closer scrutiny brings out their divergence at just such a point as this. It is largely the difference between Whiteheadian realism and Deweyan pragmatism—but it is a gulf that can be too easily exaggerated, as the following sketch of some of Hartshorne's key concepts may indicate.

Hartshorne's theism is dialectical or "dipolar." Discussing the analogy between God and man, he says: "On neither side do we have simply direct, literal understanding, or wholly indirect, nonliteral understanding. Rather, on both sides, we have something literal, but inadequate, needing to be helped out by the other."[3] "Monopolar" theism is a distortion based on the misalliance of classical theology with Greek metaphysics. Wieman rejects metaphysics largely on this ground, while Hartshorne seeks to construct a new metaphysics, more adequate both to the modern understanding of man and to the biblical account of man's relation to God. For this reason, no doubt, a generation of younger theologians steeped in Barth, Bultmann, and Tillich responded so avidly to Hartshorne in the early 1960s, for he "spoke to their condition" more clearly —their condition being one which was primed for metaphysics.[4] The "death of God" theology and the quest for "secular" theology came as primarily American reactions against

---

[3] Hartshorne, "Process As Inclusive Category," *The Journal of Philosophy*, 52 (1955), p. 99.
[4] For example, see Schubert M. Ogden, "Bultmann and Hartshorne" in William L. Reese and Eugene Freeman, eds., *Process and Divinity: The Hartshorne Festschrift* (LaSalle: Open Court, 1964). The thrust of phenomenological thought, from Hegal to Heidegger, provides much of the philosophical impetus, for Ogden and others, toward Hartshorne's metaphysics, which is phenomenologically acute.

both classical metaphysics and neo-orthodox dogmatics, both of which feature an abstract, transcendent God, discontinuous with human experience.

Hartshorne's dipolar concept provides a way of understanding concrete reality as encompassing the abstract. The concrete is processive, actual, ultimately the total of "minute particulars" in their myriad interactions. The abstract, that which "is," what is fixed as "being," is so to speak only a stationary cross-section of processive reality. Or rather, the identity of any portion of concrete reality is necessarily abstract, less than real. Abstractions are indispensable to understanding; they are patterns or modes of conceptually uniting experience, of establishing continuity within change. Eternity is just such an abstract identity uniting all temporal diversity, to which the actual past is internal and the potential future is external. That is to say, time is asymmetrical; in the process in which the potential becomes actual, there is both qualitative continuity (or identity) and the possibility of discontinuity, of innovative change that can alter the meaning or direction of the abstract identity. Personality is a characteristic of relative being, both ordinary (e.g., a man) and perfect (God as "self-contrasting life"). Both God and man, in this sense, are concrete. Abstraction is characteristic of absolute being, both ordinary (e.g., honesty) and perfect (God as "self-identical essence").[5] The fallacy of classical theology, Hartshorne contends, is that it restricts itself to God as abstract, absolute, self-identical being. The "dipolarity" of God, for Hartshorne, is a dialectical relation between the latter and God as concrete reality. God has two aspects: changeless and relative, or objective and subjective. This general idea is not original with Hartshorne; it is traceable to the medieval mystics' distinction between the personal God and the impersonal God-head. Latent here is what might be called a dipolarity of love—love as divine essence and as activity; "God is love" and "love is of God." In an intricate and systematic way, Hartshorne's metaphysics elaborates the implica-

---

[5] See Hartshorne, *Reality As Social Process: Studies in Metaphysics and Religion* (Boston: Beacon, 1953), p. 116.

tions of this seeming paradox—and, what is more important, defines the role of man in it. For man is not only a participant in but a contributor to the creative process of concretion; not merely a passive vehicle but an agent of change; and reciprocally, God in his concrete aspect takes part in human suffering and joy and undergoes change.

REDEFINING GOD*

For nearly two thousand years European theology has staked its fortunes upon a certain conception of divinity. In the last decade or two a genuinely alternative type of theology has been proposed—so unobstrusively, however, that nearly all opponents of theism are still fighting the older conception, convinced that if they can dispose of it the theological question will be settled. And those who feel dissatisfied with a Godless universe suppose that it is to traditional theology that they must turn. Both parties are mistaken. Today the theistic question, like so many others, is a definitely new one. The old controversies in their old form are antiquated.

God, for all the Church writers, was the infinite, the perfect, the absolute being. All his properties were to be deduced from this absolute character. It would seem that the only alternative would be the now somewhat fashionable conception of a "finite God." This, however, is not what I have in mind. The notion of a finite God seems simply polytheism with a lamentable lack of variety. In order that the virtues of one may make amends for the defects of another, of imperfect deities we can hardly have too many. If theology is capable of rejuvenation its hope lies rather in a reëxamination of the idea of infinity or absoluteness. The new theology will define God as the infinite being, but it will not define infinity as did the Neo-Platonists and the Augustinians.

Stated summarily, the differentia of the new definition are

* From *The New Humanist,* July-August 1934, pp. 8–15.

that it is positive rather than negative, and that it is quantitative rather than merely qualitative. It limits comparison between the creator and the creatures to differences of degree. It will be admitted that relative or quantitative distinctions are characteristic of scientific thought wherever it has been successful. But it is a curious paradox that in theology it is precisely the popular rather than the technical conceptions which are the most unambiguously quantitative in meaning. The technical terms of Thomism are above all those of self-dependence (*ens a se*), immutability, simplicity, immateriality, and pure actuality (*actus purus*). Contrast these, with their relatively qualitative or negative connotations,—with such popular notions as almighty, all-knowing, maker of all things. The common basis of these latter descriptions is the quite positive and quantitative idea of all-ness or totality. The same idea is utilized in the Latin forms, omnipotent, omnipresent, etc.

There is, however, one popular adjective which seems to be of a different character. This is *eternal*. As it stands the word is negative, meaning beginningless and endless in time. But to make the idea positive we need only substitute the formula: existing at all times. Here the theological technician interposes and objects that God is not simply the forever existing being, but rather the being who is quite superior to time and change. Moreover, the timelessness or immutability of God is no merely negative concept, according to theology, for it really means the vision of *all* times in a single "now"—or *totum simul*. Yet if all times are but a single time to God, then for him is no past, present, or future, and hence no time that has any analogy to the time that we know. And consequently, when God is said to act, or to have purposes, it may be doubted whether these ideas can have meaning for us in whose experience of activity and striving toward ends the contrast between actual present enjoyment and unrealized future possibilities constitutes the essential aspect of the phenomenon. The technical doctrine of eternity is purely negative or it appears to be a self-contradiction. But, we shall be told, surely time is essentially limitation, finitude, dependence! And how could a being existing in time possess all-knowledge?

To this latter question the answer is that "knowledge of all things" must indeed be a *totum simul* with respect to the things coming under the "all" in question. These things include all that there is; but they do not include, I should suggest, future events. This is not a paradox, for future events do not, until they are present, exist; they do not fall under the "all which there is." How then can one speak of them, as I have just done? The answer, as the mediaevals would say, lies in a distinction. "Future events" exist as a general class, but this class has no wholly particular members. The future is an outline, a more or less unparticularized plan, and this unparticularity is its futurity. If we try to deny this character on the ground that God's omnipotent plans must be wholly definite, we do not preserve our concept of divinity but merely fall into a contradiction. A wholly definite plan must lack the very character by which the concept of purpose has its meaning in our experience, namely the character of incomplete definiteness by which alone anticipation falls short of achievement. If a man were aware of the exact quality of happiness which he desires, he would desire it no more, for he would have it. Complete awareness is possession in the fullest possible sense. To be sure, we are told that, for omnipotence, intent and fulfilment *are* one, but this is merely to say that omnipotence is incompatible with intent or purpose in any intelligible sense.

There is nothing defective in a vision of things as they are, and hence if the future is consistently conceivable only as the indefinite then divine foresight will not see it as definite. An objection might be that by the same reasoning the past, which for us human beings is indefinite no less than the future, should also be regarded as objectively an outline, and nothing would remain of the *totum simul*. But this consequence does not follow. We much remember that time has a "direction," that some general difference between past as such and future as such seems to be involved in it. Now if both past and future are definite, or if both are indefinite, we shall not be able to identify this difference. Suppose I remember how as a boy I conceived a certain plan, which I am now engaged in carrying out in detail. No matter how fully the past were still present to me, I should be able to distinguish between the general outline of my plan and the particular fashion in which it is being carried out. Thus no matter to what detail the past were recovered, it would still be related to the present as universal to particular, as indefinite to definite. Time is objectively asymmetrical, and that fact and not human ignorance or limitation is the ground for denying the possibility of complete foresight of the future as a set of details. (With this view contemporary physics, with its recognition of indeterminacy, need have no quarrel.) Thus an omniscient being *may* be in time. Failure to note this irrefutable truth is a cardinal oversight of European metaphysics. The classic example is Augustine (in his *Confessions*, Book XI, Section 41).

Is omnipotence likewise compatible with being in time? The omnipotence of God has been valued as a guarantee of the victory of good over evil. If, however, this means that "in God" (as Spinoza would phrase it) the exact degree of victory, the precise quantum of value, to be realized in the future is already an assured fact, so that there is no risk that future realization will be less good or more evil than it is possible for it to be, then human choice is deprived of the very cosmic significance which theology purports to give it. If choice is significant then risk is real. On the other hand, risk must have some limit, since even he who bravely "takes a chance" must at least believe that this bravery itself will ultimately have added a value to the universe though the outcome is otherwise unfavorable:

> God has said, ye shall fail and perish,
> But the thrill ye have felt tonight
> I shall keep in my heart and cherish
> When the worlds have passed in night.
> Give a cheer! For our hearts shall not give way;
> Here's to a dark tomorrow, and here's to a bright today!
> —RICHARD HOVEY.

Assurance that, at worst, our sincerely right efforts will, in the long run, however distant, produce on the average more good than our insincere or perversely motivated actions, we must have. Thus omnipotence in the form of a general providential tendency favoring the good and able to guarantee it a minimum of persistence through all future time answers to a genuine spiritual need. But for omnipotence which guarantees the exact degree and the last detail of future goods there is not only no need but also no possible place in an ethically significant world.

God, to be sure, is infinite with respect to value, i.e., he is "perfect." And if he is perfect how can anything significant be added to him? How can he grow? I answer: we must distinguish the eternal self-identity of God from his successive states in time (each of which includes all preceding but not the succeeding states). Professor Whitehead, who more than anyone else perhaps has made the new conception possible,[1] calls the former aspect the primordial, the latter the consequent, nature of God. Now each of these aspects is perfect, but each in its own way. The primordial nature is changeless and incapable of growth. Its perfection is qualitative, and may be expressed as the quality of all-penetrating love. At no time is God without interest in and benevolence toward his creatures as existent at that time. The changeless character of God is his absolute loyalty. "Without a shadow of turning," as the Bible says. To this changeless quality of value—which, be it well noted, is a general or universal quality—is added at each time the values which the *particular* creatures have for God. The sum of these values is quantitative. No other supposition seems open to Christianity, or to any view which is founded on the admission that the individual as such is valued. But in that case each new individual is a new and added value, and even though the number of individuals be already infinite, more are logically possible. Nevertheless, though each consequent nature is capable of quantitative improvement—for no other purpose does future time exist, in the sense in which it does exist—it can still in a genuine sense be called perfect. For no good exists or ever has existed which it lacks. It is the sum of all *actual* values. If it be asked why God, being perfect, is not the realization, in actual form, of all possible values, the

---

[1] My own first introduction to the great conception of an omniscient but temporal deity was not, however, in any way due to Mr. Whitehead, but to my former teacher, Professor W. E. Hocking.

answer is that this is a phrase without meaning, since it would abolish the very distinction between actual and possible.

It is worth noting that the equivalent of the distinction between primordial and consequent natures is inevitable in any theology; the question being only whether it shall be a temporal distinction. For God is always to be considered in two aspects: (1) in himself, or apart from having created just this world as it now exists, or any other particular world that might be thought of (and both medieval and contemporary logic agree that the detail of the world might have been otherwise than they are); and (2) as having in fact created the particular world in question. Thus there is God in his essential, and God in his accidental functions. The only way such distinctions can be made humanly conceivable is in terms of time; the essential being the eternal, and the accidental, the temporal or changing, aspects of the divine. The unity of God is preserved in principle in the same way as that of a human person, but here, as always, the difference is between a partial and a maximum realization of the principle. God identifies himself as the same in basic purposes through all the details of the past, and all the general traits of the future (the farther in the future the more general); whereas we finite creatures have only an extremely partial memory of even the limited time during which we have existed, and are densely ignorant of what is ordained for the future, that is to say, of the partial limits set in advance to the freedom of the creatures.

The belief that even for God the future means opportunity to realize additional values does away with the last vestige of excuse for the alliance between theism and a reactionary attitude toward social problems. A God for whom the world is a completed entity is of doubtful humanistic value.

Another problem is that of the transcendence of God and of its relation to his immanence. Pantheism destroys the distinction between God and the world; deism destroys their interrelation. Now if God and only God is eternal, then in thinking of him in this primordial aspect we cannot possibly confuse him with the mere whole of existing finite things, no one of which, and still less the totality, is eternal. On the other hand, we avoid deism as completely as does pantheism; for the consequent nature of God at a given time is just God as at that time embracing in himself the then existing creatures. Here there is immanence in all things. But the eternal factor as such infinitely transcends the non-eternal factors. "Outside" the world or "above" it, though spatial metaphors, really mean, quite as much, temporal superiority, omnipresence in time, though they also mean omnipresence in space.[2]

A favorite way of putting the question of theism is to ask whether the world is self-existent or created. The recent Humanist Manifesto states the matter in this way. But the new definition of God makes such a statement irrelevant to theism. God *is* the world in its aspects of self-existence and of totality. Now surely not everything in nature is eternal, surely something is created by the enduring powers in nature. And what are these powers? Can physics tell us of anything that can be guaranteed to exist for all eternity? No competent physicist will answer affirmatively. So that the theistic problem of the nature of the primordial and everlasting aspect of the world is simply not dealt with in the Manifesto, nor in the natural sciences. Does the other theistic problem, that of the world in its present totality (the Consequent Nature of God) fare much better in science? How do minds and physical things form one universe? Do physicists feel that they understand this? Are the psychologists untroubled by it?

There is a converse problem to that of God as the maximal aspect of existence. If the essence of the creator is completeness, and that of the creature incompleteness, then the difference between creator and creature must always conform to this formula: *whatever is at a maximum in God is present in some degree in every creature; whatever is present in some degree in every creature is maximally present in God* (excluding self-contradictions like a maximum number, or like perfect evil). This formula has never been consistently followed out. For just as there has been a tendency to say that what is present finitely in the creatures is simply absent altogether

---

[2] In a note to the editor of this volume, Hartshorne has suggested that the two preceding sentences, beginning "Here there is immanence . . ." could well be omitted. "These sentences," he says, "I now find somewhat confusing." Letter dated 28 October 1968.—ED.

from God, e.g., temporality, so there has been the converse tendency to say that what is present maximally in God is at an absolute zero in certain at least of the creatures. Thus in God is all knowledge, in an atom, as formerly interpreted, absolutely none. It was regarded as unconscious, insentient. Here primitive popular thought, with its tendency toward animism, the admission of numerous finite spirits as the agencies of natural events, even in the inorganic world, was, once more, consistently quantitative. Theology must return, as Leibniz was the first to see, to this "panpsychic" standpoint.

Again, if man is strictly determined, has a zero degree of creative choice, then God can have only a zero degree. We can never have the right to treat the gap between the finite and the perfect as though it were the gap between nothing and perfection. It is the gap between something and perfection, between "some" and "all." Hence, if God creates, then every creature is in some degree creative. Thus a theological determinism is nonsense, just as is a theology that admits of absolutely dead matter. Admissions of contemporary physicists concerning the problematic status of determinism and materialism indicate a new opportunity for a consistent theology.

The question of the evidence for the reality of an infinite being, thus redefined, is too large for consideration here. But it is obvious that this question is not the one over which the traditional battles between theists and atheists have been fought. Even though one grants that all such battles have been lost on points to the atheists, the question of theism remains as unsettled by them as though it had never been discussed.

ETHICS AND THE NEW THEOLOGY*

The relations between goodness and theistic belief have been conceived in ways that are extraordinarily various. The main European tradition is, of course, the supposition that atheism

* From *The International Journal of Ethics*, XLV, 1 (October 1934), pp. 90–101. Reprint by permission of The University of Chicago Press.

or agnosticism connotes moral disintegration. But, not only does experience present what to most of us appear to be more or less flagrant instances to the contrary, it even suggests to certain persons a very real connection between some of the most unethical aspects of modern life and belief in God. Those who profit most by social injustices have only to recall that since God's in his heaven, all must be right with the world. Those who have reasons of their own for opposing social change have only to reflect that the Orderer of all things is above time and change, and that all possible value is realized —despite the seeming evils of the world—in the eternal perfection of the Creator. Those, again, who have power of such a kind and degree as virtually to enslave their fellows point to the absolute righteousness of the Dispenser of all powers. Moreover, those who are on the other side of social inequalities tend to accept these religious apologies for their misfortunes, and to console themselves with the hope of restitution in a future life. Thus, the chief use of faith seems to be to disarm criticism of social arrangements; to promote smugness in the fortunate, and stoical resignation in those deprived of the means of life on a really human plane.

Another type of ethical objection to theism questions its compatibility with intellectual honesty, in the exacting sense which scientific progress has given to that conception. Can a mind which permits itself to accept a belief so devoid of scientific foundation as theism has been shown by Hume, Kant, and many others to be, really maintain, with respect to its other interests, the critical alertness and integrity which ethics must regard as an important duty, perhaps as the foundation of all other duties? Furthermore, how can the effort to maintain a belief so beset with obstacles fail to drain off much of the best energy of the mind which might otherwise be more profitably expended? Are not those theists who escape ethical nullity in the form of smugness rendered no less its victims in the form of anxious and exhausting absorption in metaphysical preoccupations?

These are formidable charges. True, answers to all of them have long since been proposed by theists; the result, however, has been a continually increasing dissatisfaction, among thoughtful and high-minded men and women, with theism as a postulate of ethics. If there are no better replies to the charges than these traditional answers, then the apologists of theism must accuse its persistent critics of a degree of perversity or blindness which not only renders polite discussion difficult, besides surpassing all reasonable evidence furnished by other activities of such critics, but also implies a dark future both for theism and for mankind. Either theism has largely failed in recent times only because men have deserted it, or they have deserted it in no small measure because it has failed as an answer to the ultimate problems posed by a scientific age. It is easy to scold men for abandoning a tradition; it is more rational to suspect that some part of the trouble lies in the tradition itself. Now the theistic tradition has undeniably been exposed to at least three main sources of error: the primitive beliefs, extending back to magic and idolatry, which cluster about the religious memories of mankind; the technical philosophy which European theologians inherited from the brilliant but not infallible Greeks; and the ethical and political ideals of the Roman Empire, together with those of the peoples assimilated into Christendom after the fall of Rome. The concept of revelation has discouraged purification from errors arising from the first source; the self-interest of ruling classes has barred the way to the third; and the failure of metaphysicians to discover a way to apply scientific method to their problems has, until very recently, prevented a genuine revision of the philosophical framework of theism. Since the modern mind has been primarily occupied with physical science and technology (are not the social sciences even now struggling to find and establish themselves among the accredited branches of inquiry?) this last difficulty is not surprising, and proves little against theism as such.

A doctrine whose implications show it to be of such doubtful value, even if its truth could be known, the origins of which contain so many causes of error, and the demonstration of which has encountered such appalling obstacles, as is the case with theism in its traditional form, is a doctrine which calls aloud for revision, if it is not to be dispensed with altogether. If theism cannot be improved upon *profoundly,* then I for one have little desire to see it survive. This imperative improvement concerns equally the ethical implications of theistic doctrine and its amenability to scientific analysis. In the present article the former aspect must be emphasized. But the question finally envisaged is whether or not the changes in the conception of God which ethical interests require are also those which would facilitate the construction of a scientific cosmology. If this is not so, then I should suggest that history shows the futility of any attempt, such as Kant's, to maintain theism upon a merely ethical foundation. Where even potential knowledge is admitted to be zero, faith will not endure.

Ethics today generally accepts the assumption that among alternative modes of action some are "better" than others in the sense that anyone vividly aware of the circumstances and probable consequences involved would prefer such better alternatives to their worse correlates. Now traditional theism posits among the circumstances of all acts the existence of an absolutely perfect being. It appears to follow inexorably that no act can, in its consequences, be better than any other, for in either case the outcome can be neither better nor worse than the continued or eternal reality of a value from which real subtraction and to which real addition are meaningless. The notion that through right conduct we can "serve" a deity in whom all possible value is actual is metaphysical nonsense. Love of such a god and ethical choice are mutually irrelevant. This is the paradox at the heart of medieval theism.

On the other hand, if we give up the idea of an existing perfection, we are confronted with an opposite difficulty. The probable consequences of an act which determine its ethical value are those which hold in the long run. But where shall we draw the line in this projection of an act into the future? What—to plunge to the heart of the matter—is the use of serving tomorrow's good if for all we know the final state of things, however far off in the future, may be the complete destruction of all the values which our efforts have created? Those who object that in the meantime these values will have been really enjoyed seem to me unconsciously to smuggle in an assumption contrary to the hypothesis. For if, after the hypothetical final catastrophe, it would indeed be true that values would "have been" realized, and that this would be better than if they "had not been" realized, then surely some value would have escaped the allegedly complete catastrophe, namely, a sort of anonymous reminiscent savoring of past enjoyments. This assumption may be as inevitable as the assumption that what occurs will always have occurred, or that the past is "immortal" in some sense. It is none the less true that, apart from the theistic assumption of a cosmic memory, it is an assumption which we do not in the least understand. Moreover, I cannot for a moment take seriously those who say that they regard the future reduction of all values to the status of mere reminiscences, in a universe which will have ceased to create values, as quite compatible with the nature of things. To believe is to stand ready to act in a certain way. Now no action, not even suicide, could express the belief in the possible eventual nullity of all action; I must politely decline to entertain the supposition that anyone, except in words, doubts the existence in nature of some factor which is incompatible with eventual unrelieved catastrophe, and in relation to which our acts have their long-run fundamental meaning. Some reliable tendency in nature toward the average production, even in the infinite long run, of greater value from acts which embody our best judgment than from those which do not is, so far as I can see, an inescapable implication of ethical concepts. To ignore the question of the ultimate long run, as do for instance pragmatists, seems to me to evade an important issue.

Admitting for the moment that nature contains such a tendency, how is this to be understood? The simplest, perhaps the only, answer is the theistic one. If there is in nature a purposive intelligence, benevolently inclined toward other purposive beings, and so powerful that its destruction or utter defeat is impossible, then we have the required condition. At once, however, we face the dilemma: if the cosmic intelligence is perfect, then there can be no unrealized values, and action is once more nullified; and if the intelligence is imperfect, there seems no guarantee against its ultimate defeat or destruction. Only infinite power seems safe from the development of superior power or combination of powers. Thus, both a finite and an infinite God seem to elude ethical requirements. (The latter seems to have the additional disadvantage of suggesting callousness to the evils in the world, which omnipotence implies to be preventable evils.)

There is need for perfection, that we may have a cause infinitely worthy of our devotion. For though we may make reservations about various of our causes, there must be a deeper cause that we wholly accept (even though we cannot sharply formulate it) or we are in so far not wholly ourselves in any act. Moreover, as ethics should note, this deficiency would not be our fault, if no wholly acceptable cause exists. On the other hand, there is need for imperfection that we may remake the world to some purpose. The traditional theistic course has been to accept the paradox, with more or less indirection and glossing over, as insoluble. Traditional anti-theism has denied, or as I should say, simply not noticed the (undeniable) need for perfection. But there is a third possibility. Perhaps "perfection" (or infinity) is ambiguous. Perhaps a being may be conceived as perfect in one sense and capable of increase in value in another.

Now in fact we have only to go, where theologians have too seldom betaken themselves, to experience, to find operating there an ideal of perfection which does not mean the possession once for all of all possible values. We do not say that a man's love for his friend, is, as love, defective because he must admit the presence in his friend of unrealized capacities. Yet we should never deny that the actualization of some of these capacities would provide new content for the love of which the friend is the object, nor that this new content would enrich *aesthetically* the value of the love—without for all that rendering it necessarily more complete or perfect in the *moral* sense. Adequacy, loyalty, to the given content, not the scope of the latter, constitutes perfection in the only sense in which love can, without self-contradiction, be conceived as perfect.

The content of the divine love is the world as it actually exists, and God's love may be conceived as morally perfect with respect to that content without in the least entailing that the latter is a maximum incapable of increase, or containing no element of evil, actual or potential. Owing largely to Greek influences the medieval theists overlooked the essentially ethical meaning of the divine constancy as posited by Hebrew writers. Clearly it is unalterableness of character, not of value, in the full sense of aesthetic enjoyment (with which indeed the Hebrews were all too little concerned), that is meant by "in whom is no shadow of turning."

The entire notion of deity as out of time is unethical, responds to no aspect of ethical aspiration, centrally contradicts that aspiration. Granted an eternal moral fixity in the divine love, there remains as the sting of time, precisely those genuine dangers and opportunities which give ethical choice its meaning, without that possibility of eventual complete nullification of efforts which would conflict with such meaning from an opposite angle. As for the melancholy destruction of values which has been lamented as the very essence of passage, it cannot occur except as memory is defective, and need not, therefore, occur at all if the divine memory is complete. For this there is ethical need. For in this way only can that value be preserved which we feel to inhere in a good act, even though unsuccessful in its objective, and even though no one, except the Divine, fully knows its purity in intention. On the other hand, for complete prevision of the future in all its details, there is no ethical need. General foreknowledge, corresponding to whatever degree of predeterminism exists in nature, is enough for any practically usable notion of providence; while foresight of absolute details would entirely eliminate temporal passage, and with it choice, activity, or purpose, in any intelligible senses. The ethical dimension would thus be banished altogether.

The view of perfection as in every sense complete and above time has encouraged social conservatism. It is true that this influence is illogical. For if the view mentioned implies anything concerning human action it implies much more than that reform is unimportant or objectionable. It implies that all activity in time is meaningless. Thus it cannot in any fashion serve as a guide for action. It is the same with determinism. Apologists of the latter doctrine have easily shown that it is foolish to deduce from it the appropriateness of an attitude of pessimism or laissez faire. For to adopt such an attitude is itself a choice, and no better than any other if all choice is absurd. But the question is whether the notion of choice which is wholly predetermined is a self-consistent idea. Determinism, like the timeless absolute, is irrelevant to action because it is absurd in itself. But men are often illogical, and just as many individuals, including men of genius like Ambrose Bierce and Mark Twain, have been illogically depressed, instead, as logically should have occurred, of suffering sheer paralysis of conscious activity, through their "belief" in determinism; so, likewise, many persons have been illogically rendered conservative, and yet less than completely inactive, through their adherence to the formula of a timeless deity. This formula is thus vicious by inconsequence when it is not idle through adherence to its internal self-contradictoriness or meaninglessness.

The fundamental fact seems to be that theologians have never taken really seriously the proposition that God is love. Evidence of this is on every hand. There is the doctrine of eternal damnation, which implies that the saved shall be more happy because of their consciousness that some have been shut off from all hope of salvation. There is the Thomistic assertion that in God intellect is prior to love, based on grounds which show a failure to grasp the very meaning of love as participation in the being of another, a function which for a truly spiritualistic view is nothing less than the secret of self-transcendence involved in knowing itself. There is the tolerance of theologians for the notion of dead matter in which the literal immanence of the divine as love is inconceivable. There is the general failure to make the solution of any basic problem of ontology or cosmology really turn upon the *caritas* concept. Omnipotence, for example, is not really shown to consist essentially in love, that sympathetic sharing of experience which to a spiritual philosophy is the very atmosphere of being. And though being itself is said as such to be good, we are not told that all good is feeling of feeling, i.e., love. Nor is the essence of the self seen in its—more or less imperfect—embodiment of love. Both in medieval and some more modern theistic systems of ethics the ground of right action is placed in the individual's desire for his own happiness. Self-love is made metaphysically prior to other-regarding love.

Perhaps this general tendency, of which many other aspects could be specified, to subordinate "persuasion" (in Whitehead's phrase) to compulsion, or mere knowing or mere being or mere desire, has some connection with the tendency of religious thought to issue in apologetics for social injustice. The supreme compulsion, or enslaving power, delegates "authority" to the mighty of this world. They rule by reflection of divine might, not of divine sharing and participation. Thus, God is the supreme tyrant, by which all tyranny is upheld. This is not simply intolerable ethics; it is absurd theology. It is self-contradiction at the heart of theism, which has always pretended to find in love the key to the nature of things.

There is poetic justice in the fact that many of the commonest arguments against theism turn upon the incompleteness with which theism has affirmed its essential tenet. For instance, the argument, the most worthy of respect of all, from the evil in the world. Why does not morally perfect omnipotence prevent regrettable occurrences? The most intelligible answer involves, among other considerations, these two in particular. Power over genuine individuals, and I can think of no other form of power, must choose between annihilation of them and some degree of tolerance of their free intiative. Omnipotence means all power that is consistent with this alternative, and with other consequences of the law of contradiction. It is therefore no implication of omnipotence that God is wholly responsible for the course of events. The second consideration is that if there are to be degrees of value in the world then the reality of choice on the part of finite beings will involve the possibility of passage from a greater to a lesser good, or preference of the latter to the former. This is evil. To say it will, when conscious, involve suffering is only to say that the act of disapproval, no less than that of approval, must have a quality. Also, if there is participation, suffering may be vicarious, thrust upon one, like physical evil for instance. In the construction of a hypothetical world, free from evil, either individuality, or gradations of value, or both, must be suppressed, leaving also the general paradox of good with no contrasting term bad, an up without a down, a yes without a no. To this attempted construction theologians have themselves contributed in many ways: sometimes by dallying with determinism (as predestination); sometimes by conceiving the perfect good as in no need of imperfect beings, the creator as in no need of the creation, hence of finitude and evil, so that it seems things would have been altogether without a world containing the latter; above all by failing to emphasize that, except for non-vicarious moral evil and related evils due to one's own mistaken choices, God himself endures all the evil of the world vicariously. This neglect of the meaning of the cross is due to the failure to distinguish between moral and aesthetic perfection, and is embodied in the doctrine of the impassivity of God. Hence, and owing also to the necessity of a reliable order which is not a respecter of persons, although without it no personal life is conceivable—a necessity obscured by tolerance for primitive conceptions of providence—arises the impression which atheism exploits of the callousness of the deity.

Such are some of the changes which ethics might desire in traditional theism. And now we must ask, would a theism, so revised, prove any more accessible to rational evidence than the older forms? It should at least be clear that the view of God as, on the one side, an enduring and ethical character *in* the temporal process (in Whitehead's phrase, the "primordial nature" of God) and, on the other, its ever-changing total aesthetic content (the "consequent nature"), renders him less obviously inaccessible to scientific analysis than the view of him as a perfection entirely without the character of temporal process by which reality as we experience it is universally qualified. In the most complete cosmological theory which anyone thoroughly familiar with natural science has constructed, the theory of Professor Whitehead, a temporalistic and ethical view of God emerges with considerable clearness. And if it be felt that the ethical character imputed to the primordial nature is read into the analysis by wishful thinking it must be replied that, on the contrary, it is a definite solution proposed for the otherwise unsolved problem of the validity of scientific induction, which Russell has termed "the despair of philosophy." And as to the aesthetic character imputed to the consequent nature, it is the only effective solution with which I am acquainted for the problem of the inclusion—upon the necessity of which we all agree—of qualities in nature. Whitehead's work, together with Bergson's discussion in *Les deux sources de la religion et de la morale,* and other writings by less distinguished authors, places theistic inquiry and controversy upon a new basis.[1] Attacks upon theistic doctrines which antedate in essentials the recent revolutions in logic and in conceptions of philosophic method, as though the fate of these ancient doctrines may be expected to determine the fate of theism itself, are to be regarded as examples of cultural lag. (Even systems so recent and original as that of Royce may be essentially traditional in the sense in question.)

It is very natural to suppose that if the form of theology which has persisted almost unchanged for two thousand years is unacceptable, then theology must be given up as hopeless. It is natural, but it is uncritical. Since the translation of the germinal theistic idea into terms of scientific method has barely begun, the question of theism as a question of science can hardly be regarded as settled. The very formulation of the principles of scientific method in a logic not ridiculously inadequate to the actual practice of science is (except for the long-neglected work of Peirce) an achievement of the present

---

[1] Reference may also be made here to Professor G. Watts Cunningham's carefully documented demonstration that the concept of an absolute which recent idealistic philosophies have really succeeded in validating is not that of a timeless perfection, but of a perfection compatible with infinite potentiality for further value (*The Idealistic Argument in Recent British and American Philosophy,* Part II).

century. Yet many opponents of theism think it almost sufficient to shelter themselves behind the estimate of theology
contained in the writings of Kant, although this estimate is
inextricably intertwined with mistaken conceptions of science
(more than one of the antinomies depends upon the supposed
necessity of determinism as a postulate of science) and with
the features in the definition of God which I have been suggesting are quite unnecessary to theism, indeed contradictory
of its real intention.

There remains the final question whether it is worth while
for man to confront the cosmos at large with his finite intellect
and attempt its interpretation. To this no lengthy reply is necessary. It is somewhat easy for "humanists," whose concern is
with man as distinct from the rest of nature, to forget that it is
an interest in what is not man, and a trust in human capacity
eventually to find means to understand the non-human, that
has yielded much of the value which humanists find in life. It
is not for man to declare his complete helplessness before any
problem. Granting that in the immediate future a certain degree of concentration upon economic and political reorganization is imperative, and that theology will doubtless have to pay
toll to this necessity along with astronomy, phonetics, and a
number of other studies, it remains true that for us to renounce as a race all possibility of settling the question of theism one way or the other, or to turn our backs upon the
question completely in favor of more immediate practical
concerns, would be to renounce an essential element in the
consciousness of what it is to be man. Whether this renuncia-
tion would be unattended by other and more indirect evils,
whether it has really been shown, even by the Russians, that
an adequate as well as enthusiastic ethical consciousness can
flourish in a people who have no idea whether the universe at
large and in the long run contains that which sympathizes
with men and with which men can reasonably sympathize, is
a question concerning which dogmatic pronunciations are
perhaps premature. Like the theistic question itself, it is a
fair subject for debate.

14

HENRY NELSON WIEMAN

Empirical Theorist of Creativity

Henry Nelson Wieman (1884–   ) is among the most characteristically American thinkers in the field of religion. For nearly half a century his empirical theology has held its own ground, in and out of fashion, as a serious attempt to systematize religious insights for man in a scientific, complex technological culture. Perhaps more than any other proponent of theological liberalism since William James, he has developed a pragmatic, non-metaphysical interpretation of religious experience and values, which has proved capable of meeting the challenge of both humanism and neo-orthodoxy, without accommodating itself to either.

Wieman was born in Rich Hill, Missouri, a small town near the Osage River some sixty miles south of Kansas City. The son of a Presbyterian minister, he earned his B.A. at Park College and his B.D. at San Francisco Theological Seminary, both Presbyterian institutions. His parents were not overbearingly religious, however, and did not indoctrinate him, but talks with his mother about the purpose of life early whetted his appetite for philosophy. At the age of fourteen he discovered John Fiske's *The Destiny of Man* among his father's books and was fascinated with Fiske's account of evolution. Throughout high school and most of college he thought he wanted to be a journalist, but not long after he began reading Josiah Royce in his senior year, he became enraptured with the philosophy of religion. Barely two months before he graduated from Park College in 1907, he decided to enroll in seminary—not to train for the ministry but to study religion. Accordingly, he was regarded as a maverick there—and he was. He spent a year at Jena and Heidelberg, studying under Rudolf Eucken, Wilhelm Windelband, and Ernst Troeltsch, none of whom satisfied him—and he passed up the chance to hear Harnack at Berlin.

On his return to the United States, Wieman was ordained to the Presbyterian ministry and spent some two years in a pastorate, not because he wanted to but because he was unable to find a suitable academic post. In 1915 he went to Harvard and studied for a Ph.D. under William Ernest Hocking and Ralph Barton Perry, the respective heirs of Royce and James. His two years there were enormously stimulating, particularly through Hocking's "profound insights" and Perry's clarity and precision.[1] Each in his way confirmed and deepened Wieman's empirical, pragmatic bent. Early in his career, Wieman came to the conclusion that the object of man's devotion must be the empirical reality of God rather than ideas about God, and the empirical study of God meant scientific observation and reasoning, with major attention given to mystical awareness as a source of religious insight.

From 1917 to 1927, Wieman taught philosophy at a Presbyterian school, Occidental College in Los Angeles. During these years the influence of Hocking and Perry gave way to that of Alfred North Whitehead and John Dewey, whose experimentalism is much in evidence in Wieman's first two books, *Religious Experience and Scientific Method* (1926) and *The Wrestle of Religion With Truth* (1927). Their publication soon led to his appointment as professor of the philosophy of religion at the Divinity School of the University of Chicago, where Wieman remained until his retirement in 1947. He resumed his academic career in 1949 with two years at the University of Oregon and has subsequently taught at the University of Houston.

There are tangential similarities between Wieman's and Brightman's concern with values and with God as their source.

---

[1] See Henry Nelson Wieman, "Theocentric Religion," in Vergilius Ferm, ed., *Contemporary American Theology* (New York: Round Table Press, 1932), p. 344.

Both bear the imprint of the processive thinking of Bergson and Whitehead, but where Brightman stresses the structure and growth of personality in terms of Gestalt-like wholes, Wieman stresses the processes of growth themselves. From this point, the two diverge in opposite directions, and Wieman's reconstruction of theology emerges as a more fundamental kind. For Wieman, God is not a cosmic, transcendent person but a radically immanent aspect or dimension of nature and especially of the human personality. Despite Wieman's rejection of traditional concepts, however, in key points of doctrine he is a true descendant of Jonathan Edwards. The purpose of man's search for "the source of human good" is not information for its own sake but what Edwards would have called salvation from sin. In Wieman's terms, man becomes aware that he is maladapted to the universe. What Edwards called conversion, Wieman calls the reorganizing of personality, which enables man to adapt to the hard facts of existence, thereby attaining peace, joy, and power. It is fairly certain that these and other parallels are quite inadvertent, but they seem clear enough to suggest the magnitude of Edwards' generic influence on the American Protestant ethos, or else the consistent pervasiveness of that ethos over two centuries. If any religious thinker may be regarded as wholly American, it is Wieman. At the height of the Fundamentalist controversy of the twenties, Wieman insisted that religion must provide evidence for its verification. Mere rationalization, no less than unreasoned convictions, results in nothing more than illusion:

> The religion of dreamland seems easy and lovely at first. But it leads ultimately to intolerance and the grossest superstitions, to the use of legislation, persecution and war to enforce its convictions. When one discards the persuasiveness of evidence, and fairness in reasoning together, there is no way to defend and propagate the faith save emotional contagion and violence.[2]

For Wieman, the proper role of reason is not to justify faith but simply to conceptualize and clarify the results of

---

[2] Wieman, "Religion in Dreamland," *The New Republic*, May 12, 1926, p. 378.

experience. Prayer, worship, mystical states, devotion to known values, and openness to new values—these comprise the experiment of religious living. "By their fruits you shall know them"—and Wieman's inquiry begins with the hypothesis that in life such conduct yields results, both practically and in the larger sense of providing serviceable concepts for dealing with those aspects of reality which are beyond observation. Thus Wieman's concept of God is inferred from those processes of nature that produce human good. One way of stating it is that God is "the changeless factor found in all change"[3]; but no statement about God can be exhaustive, for the reality of God exceeds man's capacity to conceptualize. There is evidence of God in certain interactions between persons—God is the total process of which these interactions are a part. God does not control the universe but represents a direction-process within it that is unitive and value-producing. Evil, by contrast, may be regarded as blocked or arrested growth, or as processes of disruption, disintegration, disharmony.

Human brotherhood is one extremely important type of organic unity, and for Wieman, Jesus is of unique significance as a highly creative experiment in living, demonstrating the experience of redemption in a definitive way. In effect, Wieman transposes Jesus out of his historico-literary setting and into the broad stream of human evolution. The existence of Jesus involves no special act of God-as-person; it is a fortuitous event arising from favorable concatenations of cosmic or historic process; and it derives its towering significance not from Jesus' personality but from the principles which his life disclosed. Thus it *is* a revelation, but on empirical grounds, and ultimately validated by the actual lives transformed by it. In much of liberal theology, the "principles of Jesus" have been made normative and the concept of God subordinate to Jesus. What is strikingly different in Wieman is the absence of Christocentrism and the insistence on an empirical equivalent of the sovereignty of God, in and beyond human life. As the

---

[3] Wieman, "Faith and Knowledge," *Christendom,* Autumn 1936, p. 772.

following essay shows, for Wieman the functional principles disclosed through the Christian revelation are by no means reducible to moral rules. They embrace the key points of doctrine quite frankly, but each time in relation to God as creative process. Wieman's use of such traditional terms as sin and resurrection here represents a departure from his earlier vocabulary—a concession which bears witness to the impact of Barth, Brunner, and Tillich, not on the content of Wieman's thought but on the community of theological discourse.

Wieman's response to the years of economic crisis and war is worth noting. If Niebuhr was a prophet, Wieman was a visionary. He had little to say that was of immediate relevance; he lacked Niebuhr's sense of institutions and historical possibilities and ironies. But he saw the need for a faith adequate to the kind of social order that could withstand the onslaught of a Hitler or Stalin—a saving faith in a creative God rather than a humanistic *summum bonum*, a faith capable of sustaining a democratic community in "a situation in which new forms of interaction are developing between human beings."[4] Perhaps more explicitly than others, Wieman makes it clear that his empirical theism is not an attempt to construct a new faith but to achieve a reformulation of Christian faith—"the old faith by which our fathers lived."[5] The goal, then as now, is a working faith which can sustain a way of life shared by a community of free men.

The full value of Wieman's legacy has barely begun to be assessed. When the task is undertaken and his verbal and conceptual idiosyncrasies are set aside, he may well appear to a later generation one of the truly outstanding pioneers of Christian thought. Schleiermacher, at the beginning of the democratic era, redefined faith as man's "feeling of absolute dependence." In our time, this is patently hard for mature men to accept as a normal condition of existence. It is the genius of Wieman, however, to restate the essential truth in terms that go beyond the restrictive parent-child imagery.

---

4 Wieman, *Now We Must Choose* (New York: Macmillan, 1941), p. 206.
5 *Ibid*, p. 208.

Man participates in the divine process much as a farmer participates in the growth of crops—he is inescapably dependent upon it; he is powerless to cause it; but his understanding and practical intelligence are nonetheless vital to the furtherance of that process as it affects his life. Both agriculture and religion are possible with blind, rudimentary faith, but reliable knowledge and insight can enrich the harvest. Implicit here is a reasoned faith in the capacity of free men to act upon the best that they know, and to use their freedom to further their knowledge. To depend upon God in this way is to refuse to succumb to the authority of unreason. It is to understand, better than Schleiermacher did, *why* we not only feel but *are* dependent, and in what way. It is to recognize that, after all, the true God is the living God—in a profounder way than our ancestors imagined.

WHAT IS MOST IMPORTANT IN CHRISTIANITY?*

We are not asking what is essential Christianity as over against the accidental husk. Much less are we interested in what, if anything, is held in common by all Christians, for the most common is rarely if ever the most excellent. Least of all are we trying to point out something in Christianity which can be found nowhere else. We are seeking what is most important in our faith even though this most important feature might appear outside Christianity, as well as inside, and even though it might be displayed very rarely in Christian history and in the lives of only a few Christian people, and even though many might say that it is not inclusive of what is essential. On the other hand this most important element might be found nowhere save in the regions where Christianity has reached. It might be a deep undercurrent running through all Christian history and it might be what some would call essential Christianity. The point is that these are subordinate

* From *Religion in the Making,* I, 2 (November 1940), pp. 149–166.

questions which do not concern us here. We only want to know what is most important in our religious heritage and must not predetermine or pervert our evaluation by these other questions.

We shall not take space to discuss all the different views that have been held concerning what is most important and then range our own along with them and show the agreements and disagreements. This would be a worthy and scholarly undertaking. But for the present we shall be content with stating as clearly as we know how what we think is most important and then let our presentation justify itself or provoke disagreement as the case may be.

We suggest at the start that the most important element in Christianity is the forgiveness of sin. A complex of events occurring in the Greco-Roman world, in which the life and death and resurrection of Jesus Christ were central, released into history and into the lives of all men who are able to receive it, a dynamic, creative process variously called the Holy Spirit or the Living Christ, or the Grace of God, whereby it became possible to overcome man's resistance to God without destroying the resisters. This is the forgiveness of sin. It is the way of grace as over against the way of the law.

Sin is anything in the conduct of human living which resists the creativity of God. When sin is unforgiven, God cannot overcome this resistance except by destroying the individual or group which does the resisting. When sin is forgiven the resistance is still present but God can overcome it without destroying the individuals or groups concerned. The one is sin unto death, the other is sin not unto death. This second is the power of God unto salvation. It is the grace of God in Christ Jesus whereby we know the power of his resurrection, the fellowship of his sufferings, being conformed unto his death.

All this will not make sense until we clarify three things: the nature of this creativity of God; the nature of man's resistance to it which is sin; the conditions which must be met in order that this creativity may overcome the resistance without destroying the resisters.

The Creativity of God

Suppose Mr. Box and Mr. Cox are brought into association with one another. If the situation is at all favorable, they will talk or make some signs. Not only that, but all manner of interactions, conscious and unconscious, will occur between them. Much of this interaction will be quite unintended, impulsive and spontaneous but unavoidable in the situation. In consequence of all this interaction the mind of each will be transformed to some degree. Each will become a participant in the life of the other. Habits, thoughts, words, impulses and feelings of Mr. Box will become supplementary to those of Mr. Cox. The same will be true of Mr. Cox in relation to Mr. Box. The behavior, feelings, and ideas of each will become a fragment of a larger whole, incomplete without the reciprocal and complementary behavior of the other. The expressions of each will enrich the life of the other, meaning by enrichment not merely pleasant feelings but greater vividness and variety of feelings, some of which may be very painful. It is important to note that our awareness of the badness of evil (which generally involves the kind of feeling we call suffering) is just as great a good as our appreciation of the goodness of what is excellent. The point is that this interaction between persons widens and deepens the appreciative consciousness. It makes us more alive, it makes life more abundant, it increases the qualitative richness of conscious experience. Greater heights and depths of positive and negative evaluation enter our experience because of such interactions. No other contact is so enriching as this of interaction between persons when it is free, spontaneous and abundant.

What we have been describing is creative of all that is distinctively human in man. All the relevant sciences would support us in this claim, particularly that science which makes this matter its peculiar field of study, namely social psychology. This kind of interaction creates and transforms progressively the human mind, human purpose and ideals, and all human values. We suffer great impoverishments and decline in all that is distinctively human when we try to con-

trol it so as to fulfill what we are now able to appreciate, because it creates and transforms our appreciations. We cannot
harness it to our own purposes because it creates and transforms our purposes. In that sense it is more than human. It is
going on in us and around us all the time, although it may
sink to a dying trickle or rise to great volume. It is so commonplace that we scarcely pay any attention to it. It is the
most wonderful thing in the world and yet is so intimately
and persistently with us that we scarcely ever take any note
of it nor of what it is doing to us.

Even enemies when brought into association interact in such
a way that the words, actions and feelings of each generate and
enrich the meanings, the feelings, the actions of the other.
Associated individuals may do everything in their power to
prevent and destroy the growth of these connections whereby
they become members one of another and may succeed in
keeping this mutuality down to the minimum. But unless
they break off all association, or utterly annihilate one another, some such interactions, transformative and creative of
the personalities and groups involved, will develop between
them despite all that they can do. Each will derive from the
other meaning, imagery and qualitative richness of feeling
which will widen and deepen his consciousness of good and
evil. This interaction will recreate the mind of both so that
they will become adjuncts of one another.

Even when great modern, industrialized nations are at war
each trying to annihilate the other, this interaction of mutual
support and enrichment cannot entirely be cut off. It is recorded that during the first world war France and Germany
could not have continued to carry on the conflict against one
another if there had not been a continuous stream of interchange by way of Luxembourg whereby one provided coal
to the other, and the second gave iron to the first. And this is
only a very small illustration of the material and spiritual
reciprocation which goes on all the while between nations
engaged in mortal combat whereby more abundant life for
each and both is created, even when each uses this enriched
and magnified life to destroy life faster than creativity can
create it.

Certainly this creative interaction between persons and nations, between groups and sensitive organisms of every kind, is by no means so full and free as it should be. Perhaps nowhere in all the vast expanse of human and subhuman living do we find so tragic and awful a contrast between what might be and what actually is, as we find here between the amount of creative interaction which does occur and what might. Men, and all living things for that matter, are so torpid! They are so fearful of one another, and with good cause! They are so vain and self-centered, so preoccupied with the impression they are making that they cannot interact with the freedom and fullness that yields abundant life! They are so envious and so jealous! They are so dull, so fixated, so stupid in ways that could be remedied! We are so secretive and so covered with protective armor plate, that creative interaction is kept down to the minimum. The fixative, protective and malignant patterns of behaviors which dominate all living seem at times to crush the life out of creativity. And yet, when one is observant and thinks about it, it is amazing how much of this kind of interaction is able to break through all the obstructive and destructive armament of life.

Let us state the nature of this creative interaction or creativity in general and comprehensive terms and present it in such a way that it becomes open to daily observation. It is the growth of connections between sensitive organisms, all the way from cells and plant spores to human personalities and groups, which transforms the participant individuals so that they interact in mutual support and mutual enrichment. The enrichment, of course, does not begin until the sensitive organisms become conscious, for we mean by enrichment increase in the vividness and variety of all the feelings which make up the qualities of conscious experience.

This growth of connections which enriches life is subject to three kinds of obstructions or perversions. They might be called the fixative, the protective and the malignant perversions. We see all three most strikingly today in the growth of connections between sovereign states. We see them in the psychoses of human personality. The most common example of malignant growth in the biological organism is cancer.

But individual personalities, groups and whole cultures have no absolute value. They should rise or fall, come and go, live and die, according as may best serve the increase of creative interaction between individuals and groups. We are not suggesting that any human individual, class or other group is competent to judge when any other should be sacrificed. We are only saying that such sacrifice is right and good when creativity is thereby advanced.

Creative interaction is the one and only absolute good against which all others must be measured because it is the generative source of all value. It is the creative origin of all richness of experience as well as of personality and society. It is precisely this creative interaction which, for example, transforms the biochemical organism of the human infant into a human personality. It is the creative work of God in the world.

Nothing is truly good, no matter how much I desire it, unless it contributes to, and is an expression of, this interaction between cells, organisms, personalities and groups, whereby mutual support and enrichment are magnified. Anything and everything becomes evil when it obstructs the growth of connections which sustain and stimulate such interaction. If, for example, I cling to good health with such tenacity and persistence that it prevents me from moving freely and fully into all connections which sustain and enrich life, I not only destroy my good health in the end, but whatever health I have becomes destructive of other goods. On the other hand, if I sustain and promote my health only as it contributes to creative interaction between cells, organisms, personalities and groups, it is a great and growing good. The same can be said of wealth, popularity, beauty, truth and every other alleged good. All specific values are in reality good only as they are expressions and forms of the growth of these connections, and only when enjoyed and promoted as expressions of creativity. They are good only as they are held subject to the working of that interaction between individuals and groups which sustains, generates and enriches the appreciative consciousness of each.

Even the continued existence of the individual is good only as long as it can undergo the transformations required by this enriching interaction between itself and others. When the individual can on longer undergo the transformations of creativity by reason of physiological or psychological or social inertia or decay or perversion, he should die, unless there is some hope that he can recover this capacity. As human personalities we are both originally and continuously generated by God's creativity. We belong ultimately and absolutely to that creativity. There is nothing else to live for save for it. There is no ground or reason for our existence except as we belong to it. We destroy our humanity and all the meaning and value of life when we break connections with it.

This creativity of God which we have been describing is not, of course, peculiar to Christianity. It is to be found at work everywhere that man exists and even beyond, wherever sensitive organisms exist. But we must understand this working of God in order to see what is the most important element in Christianity. We said that this most important component is the forgiveness of sin which means the setting up of conditions whereby it is possible for God's love to overcome man's resistance without destroying the resister. God's love is this creativity.

God's "judgment" or "wrath" is inseparable from his love. It is, indeed, the same thing but working under different conditions. God's love is the growth of connections whereby individuals and groups become mutually enriching members of a shared life. It is what we have just been describing as creativity. God's wrath is the mutual destructiveness of such individuals and groups when they are drawn closer together by these connections but resist the transformation which is required by the life of mutual enrichment within these closer bonds of interdependence. Such mutual destructiveness (the wrath of God) is an obvious fact in the world today. The closer draw the cords of love, the more destructive of one another do men become when they resist the transformation imposed by these closer connections and required in order to interact within these closer connections with mutual support and mutual enrichment. The present war is an excellent example of this.

God's forgiveness is accomplished by setting up conditions whereby it is possible to circumvent this mutual destructiveness and transform sinners despite their resistance to God's love. To see how this is accomplished by the life and death and resurrection of Christ when joined with the continuing practice of confession and repentance of sin, we must look a little closer at the nature of man's sin.

Man's Sin

Sin is any blockage to the creativity of God arising from the way man conducts his living. The most deadly sin is that which is unconscious and unintended. If one wishes to reserve the word sin for conscious and deliberate transgression, then we must invent another word to designate that evil arising out of man's way of living which is most destructive of life and of all the goods of life, in the clutch of which man is most helpless and from which he most desperately needs salvation. All this is so because it is quite obvious that when man is fully conscious of doing what is obstructive to the generative source of all good, he is well on the road to deliverance from it. It is the unconscious, unintended resistance to God's love which has on man the hold of death.

Sin is the clinging to anything, or the striving after anything, when such clinging or striving prevents one from undergoing the transformations involved in creative interaction. When connections have been formed between individuals and groups requiring such interactions, they become mutually destructive or mutually impoverishing when they resist the transformation which they must undergo to interact in the required way. Any social structure, any ideal or moral code, any institution or other order of existence, which men uphold or promote, becomes sinful just as soon as that upholding or promoting obstructs creativity, which is to say, obstructs the mutual transformations of enriching interaction. Obviously in a world like ours a vast amount of this obstructiveness to creativity is inevitable, due to the inability of individuals and groups to undergo the transformations involved in creative interaction.

The art of living plainly indicates that this creativity must be the one and only object of absolute religious commitment.

Everything else must be sought or held or relinquished according to the requirements of this. If need be one must come to love what now he hates, seek what now he dreads, fight what now he cherishes, destroy what now he upholds. No other tie can be absolute save only this commitment to creativity. This alone can be sovereign over life. For the Lord thy God is a jealous God and human life can have but one ruling devotion. No other loyalty, no other love, no desire, satisfaction, hope, fear or dread must stand against this. One must be free to move with creativity, giving up anything or taking anything. In this way only is found freedom and all the riches of value. Any other way leads to impoverishment and destruction of value. Every other way is the way of sin. Plainly our hope is not that we shall be sinless but that our sins shall be forgiven.

This necessity of making creativity sovereign in any life which would experience value abundantly, and the correlative necessity of being able to give up any specific good according as creativity may require, can be illustrated by a rather mechanical device. Suppose a lofty and spacious building from the ceiling of which is suspended a cable. At the end of the cable is a parachutist's harness in which you are strapped. The game is to swing high and wide on this cable for it represents creativity or the forming of connections between individuals whereby they are so transformed as to be mutually enriching in their behavior, their feelings, thoughts and words. To swing on the cable, however, one must have pull-ropes. So ropes extend inward from the sides of the building to where you hang suspended. Each rope has on its end a ring which you can seize and thus pull yourself this way and that. One rope represents the specific value of health, another that of wealth, another popularity, another good looks, another knowledge or education, another some specific love, another some friendship, and so on indefinitely. Now as long as one can pull on his health or his wealth or any other of these ropes, *and then let go of it*, he can swing wide and high and free. But if he holds fast to these specific values, he cannot swing with creativity. If, worst of all, he takes a cord and ties himself to health, to wealth, to popularity, to any or all of these, it is plain that he cannot swing. He can only jiggle about in one locality.

One must be able to let go of every specific good if he is going to live under the sovereign control of creativity. And the strange thing is that when one holds fast to his popularity or some particular friendship or love or specific loyalty with such persistence and tenacity that he cannot move with the ever changing formation of connections which yield enrichment, he is much more likely to lose that good to which he clings than when he is not so bound to it. Stranger still, perhaps, he cannot fully appreciate and enjoy the values of health and wealth and love and all the rest when he is overly anxious about them or considers any of them a necessary good. Only when he can let go of them, only when he can draw upon them and then release them, as may be required by the forming of connections which transform him and others, can he experience the real value in all these so called values. As a matter of fact they are not values at all except as they promote the forming of those connections which elicit interactions which sustain and enrich. When death contributes more to creativity than continued life, then death is better than life. A human personality absolutely committed to creativity and to nothing else, can in this way die with joy. We are always delivered unto death for Christ's sake, said Paul.

I must die to all specific goods in order to be born again with this one and only tie whereby I hang suspended on one cable only, free to move with creativity through all things, whether it be life or death, or things present or things to come, or any other creature. Then I can do all things through Christ which strengtheneth me, meaning that I can let go of anything or take hold of anything as creativity may require. Then nothing can separate me from the love of God, for the love of God is precisely this forming of connections between me and others and between them and me whereby we are transformed from day to day and from glory unto glory.

THE FORGIVENESS OF SIN

In order for the working of God to overcome the obstructions to creative interaction which are set up by inertia, fear and malignancy of men three things are required.

(1) Creative interaction between persons must be released from confinement to any one set of structures or order of life in the sense that it shall be able to transform or create whatever organization may be required for mutual enrichment when wider or deeper association between individuals and groups may occur. This first condition for the forgiveness of sin was partially met in the Roman Empire by the intermingling of races, the interpenetration of cultures, the interchange between diverse tribal patterns and races. In this way the individual and the group was somewhat released from the coercive and absolute control of any one order of life, which for the Jew meant the law. In this way it became possible (although by no means fully actual) that persons could interact differently from the prescribed ways of the ancestral pattern when creativity might require. It was a situation favorable to the creation of new orders and to meet the requirements of wider, freer, richer creative interaction between members within the same group or with men who under other circumstances would be considered "outsiders."

But in itself alone all this was not sufficient. A second condition was required and after that a third.

(2) The second condition which had to be met in order that sins be forgiven was that a psychological, social historical process get under way which would make creativity potent and sovereign over the lives of a few (at least) so that no hope or dream, no ideal or order of existence could exercise equal control over them. This was accomplished by the life, crucifixion and resurrection of Jesus Christ.

Jesus during his life developed in a small group a height and depth and richness of creative interaction that was unique. Perhaps he attained one of the high points in history in this respect. In any case it was something more wonderful than anything those simple peasants had ever experienced. Nevertheless it never broke free of the established patterns of their Hebrew heritage as long as Jesus lived. They continued to dream and hope that Jesus would establish a kingdom and they with him would sit upon thrones and rule the world as Hebrew tradition prescribed.

The crucifixion cracked this structure of existence and possibility, this order of dream and practice, which had been the framework within which their creative interaction had heretofore occurred. It did not destroy the control which was exercised over their lives by the law and order of Hebrew tradition, but it loosened somewhat further its absolute coerciveness and sovereignty. It did this by destroying their hope and even, for a little while, the creative interaction which they had had in fellowship with one another when Jesus was with them. With the crucifixion Jesus failed them utterly. They had hoped that he was the messiah. But he died miserably upon a cross and was wholly unable to be or to do what their Hebrew way of life prescribed for him. It was one of the most complete "blackouts," one of the most miserable "washouts," that men ever experienced. Hope and promise was so high, disillusionment so complete. Everything was gone. Nothing was left for them to live for. The hope of Israel and the marvelous creative interaction which had been theirs, all disappeared in the black-out of the crucifixion.

But after the numbness and the despair had lasted for about three days, a miracle happened. That kind of interaction which Jesus had engendered among them came back. They found themselves interacting with one another and with other people in that marvelous way which had only happened when Jesus was in their midst.

This was the resurrection. Jesus had initiated a kind of creative interaction which went beyond anything men had known before, or at any rate beyond anything these men had known before. But now, after it had seemed to be destroyed by his death, it rose again from the dead and was with them. It was not the resurrection from the grave of one hundred and sixty pounds, more or less, of the flesh and of the blood of the Nazarene. No, it was not the resurrection of the poundage of meat and bone which pertained to the man Jesus, but it was the resurrection of that height and depth and richness of creativity which only the physical presence of Jesus had heretofore been able to engender. But more than that was involved. The power of the resurrection was the power of a creativity on the way to being liberated from bondage to the law, which is to say, liberated from any limitations imposed by any structure of society, any organization of personality, any form of existence. That does not mean that there can be creative interaction apart from some social structure, some organization of society, some form of existence. But it means a creativity that can transcend any structure, organization and form by transforming what has heretofore been attained and creating structures which have never yet been experienced and doing this without known limit.

Thus the new creativity which issued into history from the crucifixion and the resurrection was a creative interaction which could break through the bounds of the law and thereby forgive sin. That is to say, it could overcome man's resistance to creativity without destroying the resisters, providing they met one further condition which is repentance, to be discussed later. It was the unlimited grace of God. It could occur not only between the circumcised but between the circumcised and the uncircumcised, which is a symbolic way of saying that it need not be confined to any one way of living, any one order of society, any one kind of people, any one set of ideals. It could occur between Jew and Gentile, Greek and Barbarian, bond and free, rich and poor, foolish and ignorant, high and low. It could be creative and transformative of every structure of existence and way of living to whatsoever measure might be required by the utmost mutual enrichment of creative interaction.

It took some time for the theory and the established practice of this new way of living to become formulated and recognized. Hence the vacillation of Peter and the controversy between Paul and the Judaizers and, for that matter, all the vacillation, compromises, regressions, fixations, heresy hunting, witch-burning and other sorry spectacles of Christian history. We repeat, what here concerns us is not what is universal among Christians but something which is the most important element in their history, no matter how rare it may be, nor how faint and discontinuous may be the thread of its historic existence.

One further thing should be said about this matter of the resurrection. When people have had a strange and wonderful experience in dealing with a certain person, the vivid recurrence of that experience, even when the person is no longer physically present, will give them a profound sense of the real presence of that one. If the experience is sufficiently vivid and unique, and if it has never heretofore occurred except in association with that one person, then its occurrence will almost inevitably create the illusion that the person involved is now physically here. In such case, some will very likely think that they see and feel and hear the face and hands, the body, wounds, and voice of this person. This is a well known characteristic of human psychology. After the experience has been retold several times by a sequence of reporters, the illusion will become like an established fact of history. But the important thing about the resurrection was not an illusion. The important thing about the resurrection was not the avoirdupois of flesh that had been crucified, but it was the resurrection of a creator free to overcome the resistance of men without destroying the men and groups who resisted. It was the power of God unto salvation.

The creativity of God had at last broken free and now issued into history by way of a continuing social process of creative interaction. It had broken free of every social structure, form of existence, system of values, goal, hope and ideal of men. It was free of these, we repeat, not in the sense that it could operate apart from some such structures, but free in the sense that it could now transform and create structures suited to its need. It was no longer confined to the law, meaning any established system of social organization and patterns of behavior. It could transcend any and all of these in the sense of creating whatever modifications it might require. Again we must repeat that such new creations can never be the work of human intelligence because human intelligence naturally is limited to that totality of ideal structures available to it at any given time, while creativity is precisely the introduction of new structures not previously available to intelligence. Such innovations come by way of creative interaction between individuals and groups. This is a common fact of experience and generally recognized by all the relevant sciences.

The creativity of God had at last broken free of the law and issued into history with power to save beyond the law through the co-working of the social situation in the Roman Empire with the life, death and resurrection of Jesus Christ. After this any man might cry: I count all things to be loss for the excellency of the knowledge of Christ Jesus my Lord, for which I have suffered the loss of all things and do count them but dung, that I may win Christ (the unlimited creativity of God) and be found in him; not having a righteousness of mine own, even that which is of the law, but the righteousness which is through faith in Christ, a righteousness from God by faith; that I may know him and the power of his resurrection and the fellowship of his suffering, being conformed unto his death.

CONFESSION AND REPENTANCE OF SIN

There is, however, a third condition which must be met before the power of God unto salvation is free to work without limit in delivering men from that sin which is unto death. It is repentance. Why it is a necessary condition becomes apparent as soon as we see what is involved.

The confession and repentance of sin means three things. It means, first, to recognize that my personality at depths far below the reach of consciousness at any given time is patterned and structured by an organization which does resist the transformations required for that fullness of creative interaction demanded by the connections I have with other people. Since I do not undergo the required transformation, I interact with them in ways that are mutually impoverishing and mutually destructive. Some of this destructiveness I see. Much of it escapes my focus of attention and my capacity for sensitive appreciation. But I know enough about life and about myself to know that it does occur. To recognize this fact about myself, and to realize the depth and tragedy of evil that is involved in it, is to confess my sin.

Confession and repentance of sin means, in the second

place, that I shall resolve repeatedly, and with all the depths of sincerity that is in me, to hold myself subject to every transformation creative interaction may require, no matter what pain, death or loss such changes may involve I do this because I know that in this I am gainer in every way along with God and everyone else who may be involved. I and all are gainers because in so far as I do yield to such transformation, and in so far as I am the responsible agent in each situation, I become the medium and the expression of that creativity which is the generative source of all the values that can ever be experienced.

Confession and repentance of sin mean in the third place that I shall search out every habit, every object of desire, fear, hope and dread, that I can at all suspect to be recalcitrant to creative interaction, and resolve that each one shall be taken from me or given to me, according as creative interaction may require. Nothing shall be mine except as I receive it from the creativity of God. Nothing shall be held back by me when the creativity of God would take it away. Everyone who practices this kind of commitment to creativity will become aware of certain desires, habits, propensities in himself that resist the transformation necessary to fruitful interaction with things and persons and groups. These specific patterns of behavior in himself he will not fight directly, for that may only make their hold upon him tenacious. But he will take them one by one and resolve that each shall be given over to the creative process of transformation as it arises in the concrete situations into which he enters day by day and hour by hour. He will seek to formulate and develop whatever habits, propensities and cherished objectives may produce in himself the kind of personality that can move freely and fully with all the transformations and fulfillments of creativity in each concrete situation as it develops.

If this interpretation of the confession and repentance of sin be correct it should be apparent, without further argumentation, that it is a third condition which must be met before the creativity of God is free to work freely and fully beyond the bounds of the law to save each sinner from that sin which is unto death.

We have tried to point out what we hold to be the most important element in Christianity. We have called it the forgiveness of sin. It is to be understood, however, not in the form of some static decree nor as a juridical pronouncement. When it is so understood, it is falsified, we think. Rather it is a dynamic reality working in history, in society and in each personality who has been touched by this dynamic, social, historical process and who meets the condition of repentance.

Let us summarize. The life, crucifixion and resurrection of Jesus Christ released the creative work of God from obstructions which had elsewhere limited its operations. The creative work of God is the transformation of individuals and groups by way of interaction so that they progressively sustain and enrich one another. Interaction may be impoverishing and destructive but creative interaction is the opposite. It generates the qualitative riches of conscious experience with all the meanings, imagery, feeling and vivifying sense data of consciousness. It releases the appreciative consciousness from bondage to special goods so that it may range more widely and deeply. Its work is obstructed and perverted by the inertia of the world and the sin of man. In order to overcome these perversions and obstructions it must have a medium through which to work in the form of a community of persons, however few they may be. This community must be made up of persons who commit themselves absolutely to the transformative working of the creativity of God. The Roman Empire, combined with the life, death and resurrection of Jesus Christ and the practice of repentance, created such a community of interacting persons. This community is not the church as an institution but it is made up of certain interacting individuals who have made this absolute commitment.

Thus the released and unlimited creativity of God reaches us through Jesus Christ. Perhaps it may be found through other religions. Perhaps not. It is not our part to pronounce judgment on that point. We only say that Christianity is the way by which it reaches us and that it is the best and greatest reality to be found in our Christian heritage.

PART FOUR

BRIDGING THE DECADES

15

REINHOLD NIEBUHR

Dialectical Pragmatist

Karl Paul Reinhold Niebuhr (1892–1971) has been variously labeled neo-orthodox, post-liberal, relativistic, and Christian realist. Yet he is a man whose life and work resist pigeon-holing, and especially polemical labels. If his outlook over half a century moved from idealism to realism, it did so in no simple progression but rather by a change in the balance of continually interacting opposites. At his most idealistic, his idealism was imbued with realism; at his most realistic, his realism was leavened with a chastened but indefatigable idealism. Niebuhr's greatness is that of a man who does not rest easy in his opinions but keeps them always under critical surveillance. Throughout his career, his thought on every level was characterized by a pragmatic approach and a dialectical method of criticism that offers the key to every problem by locating within it the opposites by which it moves. There is a sense in which Niebuhr's thought coincides with the dialectical theology of neo-orthodoxy, but its distinctive quality and its ethical edge come from a deeply rooted American concern for situations and practical applications.

Niebuhr was born in Wright City, Missouri, a small village thirty miles from St. Louis, where his father, Gustav Niebuhr, was pastor to a German-speaking congregation of the Evangelical Synod of North America. Gustav Niebuhr, son of a prosperous Westphalian landowner, had run away to America at seventeen, partly to avoid military service. In northern Illinois, he hired himself out to a German-American farmer who encouraged him to study for the ministry. Gustav Niebuhr did so at Eden Seminary, and he did it thoroughly. He preferred to read the Bible in Hebrew and Greek. A man of liberal temper, candid about his doubts, he had a great love for his adopted country and a great admiration for such statesmen as Carl Schurz, Abraham Lincoln, and Theodore Roosevelt. Each of his four children who survived infancy (a fifth died) achieved distinction. Hulda became professor of Christian Education at McCormick Theological Seminary in Chicago; Walter, a newspaper publisher and documentary film producer; Reinhold and H. Richard, major figures in religion and ethics.

In 1902, the Niebuhr family moved to Lincoln, Illinois, where Reinhold went to high school. "I was thrilled by my father's sermons," he later recalled, "and regarded him as the most interesting man in our town. So what should I do but be a minister, in his image?"[1] He studied for his B.A. at Elmhurst proseminar and began his ministerial training at Eden Seminary, where he developed a close relationship with Samuel D. Press, a German-trained theologian, who in 1908 became Eden's first full-time professor teaching in English. In April 1913, Gustav Niebuhr died of diabetes. Reinhold was now 21, and in the next few years he went through a number of changes. The first was his transfer to Yale Divinity School, where he received his B.D. in a year and his M.A. in 1915. He was strongly influenced by D. C. Macintosh, and among the books he read in those two years were William James' *The Varieties of Religious Experience* and *The Will to Believe,* William Adams Brown's *Theism,* Hocking's *The Meaning of God in Human Experience* and Royce's *The Problem of Christianity.* The subject of his B.D. thesis was "The Validity of Religious Experience and the Certainty of Religious Knowledge."

In 1915 Niebuhr went to Detroit as pastor of Bethel Evangelical Church, a small mission church of barely eighteen families of businessmen and professionals. Detroit was rapidly mushrooming as the center of the new automobile industry,

---

[1] John Cogley, "An Interview With Reinhold Niebuhr," *McCall's* XCIII, 5 (February 1966), p. 171.

and Niebuhr was there during the heyday of the first mass-production methods, witnessing the phenomenal growth of the Ford Motor Company and the early struggles of unionists to organize the auto workers. Niebuhr's congregation grew rapidly, became a self-supporting church and in 1919 abandoned the use of German in worship. The young pastor was soon drawn into civic affairs, both local and national; within a year of his arrival in Detroit he was writing articles for national magazines such as *The Atlantic*, displaying his dialectic of social realism in a penetrating essay on the antinomy of the individual conscience confronted with the collective evil of war.[2] The actual war in Europe did not pose for him the acute agony it did for Rauschenbusch, who had lived in Niebuhr's ancestral region. Niebuhr, along with most Americans, was readier to accept a struggle between democratic ideals and "the Kaiser." Nevertheless, his dual heritage made him sensitive to ambiguities that others did not experience. He opposed the war until America was in it, then supported Wilson's policy.

Niebuhr became a pacifist when he visited the Ruhr in 1923, together with Sherwood Eddy, Kirby Page, and William Scarlett. As early as 1920, he was contributing articles to *The World Tomorrow* and was a contributing editor of *The Christian Century* and a leader of the Fellowship for a Christian Social Order. Within a few years he became a member of the Socialist Party and an avowed Marxist. In 1924, at the request of Jane Addams, he served as chairman of a large Detroit rally for Robert LaFollette, part of the latter's presidential campaign on the Progressive ticket. A year earlier, he met Henry Sloane Coffin, president of Union Theological Seminary, who subsequently offered him a professorship in the philosophy of religion (later in applied Christianity). Niebuhr accepted, and in 1928 he moved to New York.

He came to New York not only as a professor of religion but as head of the FCSO, which in 1928 merged with the

---

[2] See Reinhold Niebuhr, "The Nation's Crime Against the Individual," *The Atlantic*, November 1916.

Fellowship of Reconciliation with Niebuhr soon to become
its national chairman. In 1929, when John Dewey formed the
League for Independent Political Action, Niebuhr joined its
executive committee; and the following year he was the Socialist Party's candidate for the Congressional seat of Democratic incumbent Sol Bloom. For the next decade, as founder
of the Fellowship of Socialist Christians, as a member of the
radical wing of the Socialist Party, and as a radical churchman, he was to be found at the center of the era's controversies, exerting a growing influence through books, lectures, and
articles that made both an immediate and an enduring contribution to the shaping of social Christianity, ethics and
theology, as well as secular politics. Neither the Depression,
the rise of Hitler and Stalin nor the outbreak of World War II
occasioned an abrupt reversal of his outlook, although his
position changed in response to them, proceeding out of the
ongoing dialectic of re-evaluation, which broadened and deepened his thinking over the years. The most crucial period was
that of the late 1930s, marked by two crises—his resignation
from the FOR in 1935 and from the Socialist Party in 1940.
The outbreak of the war in Europe in 1939 provoked a severe
emotional crisis marked by depression and neurasthenia, recurring through the spring of 1940. It was on the eve of the
war that Niebuhr prepared his Gifford Lectures, given at the
University of Edinburgh in 1939 and later published as *The
Nature and Destiny of Man*. In them one can already see the
intellectual foundations of his break with his Socialist comrades over the war issue. He did not retreat from the political
arena but went on to form the Union for Democratic Action,
which in 1948 became Americans for Democratic Action, with
Niebuhr as its first chairman.

Despite the crises of the late 1930s, it is easy to note the
basic integrity and continuity of Niebuhr's critical thought
from before the Depression to the brink of war and after. His
writings of 1927, before he came to New York, are indicative.
In May his "A Critique of Pacifism" appeared in *The Atlantic;*
in June, the last of three articles on Henry Ford in *The*

Christian Century; in August, "A Religion Worth Fighting For" in *The Survey Graphic,* in which Niebuhr declared, "The universe is simply not the beautiful Greek temple pictured in the philosophy of the absolutists and the monists." From his father and from men like Samuel Press, Niebuhr inherited a blend of rationalism and the spirit of the Heidelberg Catechism, a mixture not vastly different from the Calvinism of Jonathan Edwards, which was further conditioned by Macintosh's critical realism and other influences. Commenting on the *Survey Graphic* article, Arthur Schlesinger has observed that Niebuhr "shared with William James a vivid sense of the universe as open and unfinished . . . Where James called it a 'pluralistic universe,' Niebuhr would call it a 'dynamic universe'; but the sense of reality as untamed, streaming, provisional was vital to both."[3]

Niebuhr's trenchant critique of "Christian Moralism in America" (1940), with its assertion of relativism as over against absolutism, is of a piece with these earlier writings. His best-known book, *Moral Men and Immoral Societies* (1932) was written at the height of his leadership in the FOR. Neither his pacifism of 1928 nor his anti-pacifism of 1940 is that of the Greek temple or of simple moralism; the pragmatic dialectic is recurrently in evidence. It is reaffirmed on a vast scale in *The Nature and Destiny of Man,* in which Niebuhr attempts a synthesis of Renaissance and Reformation thought. The two strands do not clash head-on, as in Barth, nor do they achieve a neat harmony. The synthesis is a dynamic interplay of affirmation and critique, encompassing major religious and ethical thinkers from Augustine and Luther to Hulme and Dewey. Despite the book's systematic structure, William Lee Miller's description holds good: "Niebuhr's reasoning is not deductive and systematic but empirical and pragmatic . . . in the American style. He is always testing theoretical constructions against experience. He is primarily a critical thinker, rushing on to indicate a truth, not stopping

---

[3] Arthur M. Schlesinger Jr., *The Politics of Hope* (Boston: Houghton, Mifflin, 1963), p. 163.

to formalize it. He is quite the opposite of a dogmatist, arbitrarily applying some *a priori* scheme to the facts. He is an upsetter of dogma, challenging the complacent acceptance of uncriticized assumptions."[4]

All things considered, Niebuhr's is a more highly developed pragmatism than James'. It builds upon foundations laid by James, but it is infused with a greater degree of critical realism —a realism tested in the crucible of a more problematic and complex era—and with a closer scrutiny of a wider range of relevant facts. Above all, perhaps, Niebuhr's pragmatism is steeped in an understanding of history and of social forces as well as of individual character and experience.

The label "neo-orthodox," often applied to Niebuhr, is unfortunate and misleading. He owed nothing to Barth, Brunner, or the other European exponents of dialectical or dogmatic neo-Calvinist-Lutheran theology. He and they shared in a general reaction against liberal illusions and in opting for a tougher-minded understanding of human nature. This led them all to a serious reconsideration of classical Christian doctrines and to a kind of united theological front involving real areas of common ground, as with Barth's and Niebuhr's parallel notions of sin and of the self-deceptions of the bourgeois church. But the differences between them are equally striking. Inherent in Barth's absolute polarization of God and man, for example, was the means for determined resistance to Hitler and later for coming to terms with Communism in East Europe—but as Niebuhr observed in his Gifford Lectures, Barth's theology, by its "exclusive emphasis upon the ultimate religious fact of the sinfulness of all men," threatened "to destroy all relative moral judgments" and thus endangered those "relative moral achievements" that are possible and worth attaining. Niebuhr does not hesitate here to commend "the more Pelagian, more self-righteous and religiously less profound Anglo-Saxon world" for its greater success "in achiev-

---

[4] William Lee Miller, "The Irony of Reinhold Niebuhr," in *Piety Along the Potomac* (Boston: Houghton, Mifflin, 1964), p. 154 f.

ing a measure of political sanity and justice."[5] On a whole
series of issues involving grace, eschatology, the meaning of
history and the difference between sin and evil, Niebuhr hews
to a dynamic realism that is much closer to Jonathan Edwards
than to Barth, but also closer to empirical observations.

One never forgets for long that Niebuhr's basic commitment is to mankind, that the ultimate justification of theology
is that it enables man to understand himself and to derive
meaning from the ironies and paradoxes of his existence.
Despite his innumerable polemics, Niebuhr's aim is never
simply to defeat liberalism but rather to deepen and strengthen
it—to overcome its inadequacies through a purgative transformation, refusing to settle for simple solutions, which evade
rather than solve urgent and difficult problems. Beginning
with politics as the art of the possible, with some idea of the
problems at hand, and with a fairly clear Christian ideal of
perfection, the root question for the typical liberal was how
to make that perfection possible. Niebuhr did not reject the
ideal, but he reorganized the priorities in the light of the actual way things happen. The art of the possible means dealing
with facts, and not only those facts that can be marshaled in
favor of the ideal but especially those that wishful thinking
loses sight of. Like Fosdick, he knew that man is a creature
not only of reason but of imagination and impulse. But he
went far beyond Fosdick in his understanding of sin as an
ineradicable given of human nature—sin as self-will, as pride,
as the Nietzschean will to power. Where Fosdick and other
liberals tended to regard sin as a neurosis for which the gospel
provided therapy, and where Barth regarded sin as a fixture
of human nature to be overcome by divine initiative, Niebuhr

---

[5] Reinhold Niebuhr, *The Nature and Destiny of Man* (New York: Scribner,
1943), I, 22. In later writings, both Barth and Niebuhr moved in a
humanistic direction, relative to their stance during World War II. See,
for example, Niebuhr, *Man's Nature and His Communities* (New York:
Scribner, 1965), esp. p. 23 ff., where he writes of his "unpardonable
pedagogical error" in using the term "original sin" to designate "the persistence and universality of man's self-regard."

regarded sin as an ever-present variable in every encounter of the human self with the world—a factor to be located and measured in each situation. Expressed in secular terms, sin manifests itself as self-interest, and not only in the individual but in social groups of every kind, be they churches, corporations, socio-economic classes, nations, empires, or alliances.

History, Niebuhr saw (and he found confirmation in Marx and the social sciences), was neither a mere train of events nor the unfolding of a predestined plan. It was a struggle of conflicting interests in which material power and its accretion and dispersal were primary facts. The Kingdom of God, the perfection of Christ, divine love—these were relevant ideals, but remote from the arena of possibility. The fact that they were unattainable did not mean they were worthless; rather they stood as transcendent norms, as absolutes, as a kind of eternal horizon. One never reaches the horizon or the stars, but they are indispensable to any journey toward a real destination. In this sense, love is for Niebuhr "the law of life," not by its direct application but as an overall criterion for justice; and justice is basically an equilibrium of power. Hence the attempt to change the world through unadulterated love is founded on illusions about the nature of man, and the attempt to achieve justice without a redistribution of power is based on a misunderstanding of the nature of society.

It is interesting to note the dialectical character of Niebuhr's Christology, seen in "the paradoxical relation of a divine *agape,* which stoops to conquer, and the human *agape* which rises above history in a sacrificial act."[6] As one critic pointed out, "the assumptions of his 'symbolic Christology' . . . always tends to translate the concrete biblical pronouncements into a paradigm of things in general."[7] More profoundly, there is never a single, simple starting point in Niebuhr's thought, and this goes for his understanding of the nature of Christ. He

[6] *Ibid,* II, p. 74.
[7] J. M. Lochman, "The Problem of Realism in R. Niebuhr's Christology," *Scottish Journal of Theology,* XI (Fall 1958), p. 263. See also John C. Danforth, *Christ and Meaning: An Interpretation of Reinhold Niebuhr's Christology* (New York: Union Theological Seminary Book Service, 1958).

does not, cannot cut Christ off from humanity by regarding him as unique, for he understands faith not as propositional but psychologically as "trust in the meaning of human existence," an interpretation shaped by "endless dialogues" with his wife Ursula and brother Richard, and confirmed by his studies of the psychological works of Erik H. Erikson.[8]

The basis of Niebuhr's Christian realism is his conviction that "human nature contains both self-regarding and social impulses and that the former is stronger than the latter."[9] John Bennett, his closest colleague under the banner of Christian realism, has stated that "one could interpret Niebuhr's whole theology as the understanding of Christianity as an antidote to self-righteousness and pride."[10] Whether stated in these terms or as ego or will-to-power or aggression, the problem of man's nature leads inevitably to problems of man in social contexts involving power. Power, Niebuhr insists, is both necessary and dangerous. It cannot simply be got rid of. As he saw increasingly with the spread of fascism and the outbreak of World War II, and again in the Cold War, those who were concerned with both justice and peace had to take responsibility for the wielding of power in all its forms— economic, political, military, etc., depending on the situation and its demands. At one point, during the sit-down strikes of the auto workers, strikers were being subjected to severe beatings, and on other occasions they were fired upon by company guards. Should the workers be urged to avoid taking up arms in self-defense? This was the central issue that split the FOR in 1935. Niebuhr was no ardent proponent of street fighting, but he was pragmatically realistic enough to conclude that, if all else failed, workers must have the same rights of resistance as those expounded by Milton and other Calvinist champions of liberty. Niebuhr was then a Marxist in his critique of society but a democratic socialist, not a Soviet sym-

---

[8] Reinhold Niebuhr, "Some Things I Have Learned," *Saturday Review,* XLVIII (November 6, 1965), p. 24.

[9] Niebuhr, *Man's Nature and His Communities,* op. cit., p. 39.

[10] John C. Bennett, "The Contribution of Reinhold Niebuhr," *Union Seminary Quarterly Review,* XXIV, 1 (Fall 1968), p. 6.

pathizer, in his vision of the good society. In a later perspective he spoke of the victory of the workers' struggle for power:

> The powerless insecurity of the worker created the revolutionary climax predicted and proposed by Marxism. But when the free societies of western Europe [and America] endowed the worker with the power of collective bargaining, including the right to strike, the resulting equilibrium of power created a tolerable justice which made Marxist collectivism irrelevant . . .[11]

Niebuhr, throughout his long career, continually probed the anomalies and paradoxes of the human condition. Man's capacity for self-transcendence is at once his greatness, leading to his relation to an ultimate reality and to his ability to observe and criticize himself, and also to an almost limitless greed and destructiveness. This latter excessive egotism is dangerously magnified when it takes on the collective form of communities, nations and empires. This fact poses a formidable challenge, seeming to suggest that both power and collectivities are irredeemable. One thing is clear, that the possibilities open to man are "indeterminate," not absolute. "There are no limits to be set in history for the achievement of more universal brotherhood, for the development of more perfect and more inclusive human relations."[12] The coloration of this relativism is almost exactly that of William James' usage of the "more." Another point also keeps recurring in various forms—the loftier moral possibilities of the individual, for it is individual and not collective man who can rise above nature and history, it is he who can, on occasion, "rise to an heroic defiance of the community" or envision a better one, even a "community of mankind" in his imagination.[13] Yet even the primacy of the moral individual must be understood as indeterminate and dialectical, for the individual is not perfectible, nor is his society totally irredeemable.

The universe of Niebuhr's discourse is broad, much as that

---

[11] Reinhold Niebuhr, "Toward New Intra-Christian Endeavors," *The Christian Century*, LXXXVI, 53 (December 31, 1969), p. 1665.

[12] Niebuhr, *The Nature and Destiny of Man*, II, p. 122.

[13] Niebuhr, *The Self and the Dramas of History* (New York: Scribner, 1955), p. 37 f.

of a St. Augustine transposed to twentieth-century technopolis. But at its core is both the critical-analytical method of dialectics and faith in love. Christianity, for Niebuhr, is "an interpretation of the human situation which holds that not only is love the law of life but that self-love is a perennial factor in life."[14] Nothing is simple, least of all the most basic issues; "no neat system of coherence is able to comprehend the beauty and terror of life."[15] The symbols of religion attest to this fact; they are "tangents toward the ultimate and therefore fruits of the human imagination. These symbols create a penumbra of mystery around every realm of meaning within the bounds of verifiable knowledge."[16] But more characteristic of Niebuhr is the discernment of definable human problems within those ambiguous realms of meaning, usually with emphasis on their irony and paradox but also with concern for results, with practical applications.

What finally makes Niebuhr's thought irreducibly Christian, and in no sectarian sense, is his awareness not only of sin but also of the possibility of forgiveness. "He believes," says Bennett, "that the man who is conscious of being forgiven is capable of humility, for he knows that the best that he is comes as a gift; of honesty, for he need not keep hiding the truth from himself and others; of charity, because he knows that he is a receiver of the divine mercy."[17] One can only speculate on the biographical roots of these convictions, but there is abundant evidence that when Niebuhr spoke of love and forgiveness he spoke not only as a thinker but as a son, father, brother and husband, and one becomes aware that Bennett's statement is itself a biographical testament to the

---

[14] Henry Brandon, "A Christian View of the Future" (interview), *Harper's Magazine*, December 1960, p. 75.
[15] Niebuhr, "Some Things I Have Learned," p. 64. See also his interview in Patrick Granfield, *Theologians at Work* (New York: Macmillan, 1967), p. 68: "We have an obligation to save each other from our characteristic vices by cooperating with each other. . . . Only humble men who recognize the mystery and majesty of life are able to face the beauty and terror of life without exulting over its beauty or becoming crushed by its terror."
[16] Ibid.
[17] Bennett, "The Contribution of R. Niebuhr," p. 11.

tenderness in the heart of man. One can almost picture the boy and his father when Gustav Niebuhr's son, grown to old age, said: "There is a deep relationship between the basic trust of childhood and the more comprehensive trust of religious meaning in maturity."[18] One may appreciate, too, the deeply bonded marriage of Reinhold and Ursula Niebuhr, sustained by a love that had to endure years of physical illness, suffering, and debility, when Niebuhr, at age 77, could prescribe for both Protestants and Catholics "the task of relating eros to the agape of Christian family life" and refer to "love between husband and wife (or between parents and children) as a seed pod of a more universal love."[19] Love, grace and redemption were realities he had experienced as an individual. In the light of historical experience, both past and contemporary, he had more reason to be skeptical about the access of nations and races to these renewing forces, and he was accordingly constrained to point out the necessity of "non-Biblical instruments of calculation, chiefly a rational calculation of competing rights and interests and an empirical analysis of the structures of nature, the configurations of history and the complexities of a given situation in which a decision must be made."[20] Barth, he noted, attempted to dispense with non-Biblical factors, but "the cellars of Biblicist obscurantism" were as much a peril as anything secular and doubtless more so.

Among Niebuhr's admirers there have been those who wished to accommodate his thinking to that of Barth, and there have been those who felt that his theological preoccupations were largely extraneous to his cogently pragmatic method and perspective. The living Niebuhr and the contours of his thought would escape both kinds of admirers. In like manner, he has long eluded detractors, both from the fundamentalist right and the perfectionist left, who have reduced him to a convenient caricature. During the decade of the Cold War,

---

[18] Cogley, "Niebuhr Interview," p. 171.
[19] Niebuhr, "Intra-Christian Endeavors," pp. 1666, 1667.
[20] See Niebuhr, "The Problem of a Protestant Social Ethic," *Union Seminary Quarterly Review*, XV, 1 (November 1959), p. 11.

his endorsement of nuclear deterrence and containment earned him the unhappy reputation of "the theologian of the State Department," but his pacifist critics usually failed to note his firm endorsement of the nonviolent civil rights struggle of the 1960s and his attack on the Establishment over the Vietnam war.[21]

Just as the real Niebuhr transcends the wishful caricatures, so does his whole career rise above the successive movements with which he was actually associated during his lifetime. He can be authentically related to the Social Gospel, to neo-orthodoxy and Christian realism—and less typically but truly to William James. But his proportions resist any such labeling. He is both *sui generis* and profoundly American, like Abraham Lincoln—with all that such a statement implies of both hope and a tragic sense of life. The inherent structure and dynamics of his method, regardless of specific conclusions with which one may disagree, establish the Niebuhrian approach as a permanently viable legacy, while at the same time his ob-servations, as such, often remain insightful. As a method, the search for unexamined presuppositions, the insistence on ex-tricating ideals from illusions and discerning relative possibil-ities dialectically related to ultimate values, without confusing the two—these are among the salient features that any student of human nature will ignore at his peril. It is a method that both transcends and validates its Christian origins. If Chris-tianity is renewed, the Niebuhrian contribution to that pro-cess will likely play a significant role. Yet it offers vitality as well to any alternative outlook, secular or religious, which seeks to be effective in dealing with human problems.

The selections that follow span 35 years and provide a very approximate guide to the continuities and changes that mark Niebuhr's career. If there are any features to which I would call special attention, they are the incipient realism, the prag-

---

[21] When the sit-ins occurred in 1960, I heard him preach an extem-poraneous sermon extolling them as a splendid combination of perfection-ism and realism. What is particularly interesting—and characteristic of the real Niebuhr—is that he praised the values in both halves of the combination.—ED.

matism, and the dialectical elements in the first selection, dating from 1928—imperfect and incomplete, perhaps; perhaps even sitting cheek-by-jowl with incompatible illusions, yet present and prefiguring the more mature perspectives to come. Although he was a pacifist at that time, or perhaps *because* he was, he brought to bear needed interior criticisms of that position, thus transcending it. The second article finds him attacking Christian moralism from the viewpoint of a post-pacifist Christian realism (1940), yet once again noteworthy is his refusal to choose between simple alternatives; the moralists' switch from pacifism to belligerency is just such a move, to which Niebuhr counterposes a perspective at once relativistic, relevant and transcendent. The last two articles (1958 and 1963) combine theological acuity with Niebuhr's familiar concern with history, culture and institutions.

---

*PACIFISM AND THE USE OF FORCE**

When defining pacifism and discussing its relation to the social problems of modern society it is important to begin by disclaiming the right to express anyone's opinion except one's own. Pacifists are no more divided than other groups who try to apply general principles and ideals to the specific facts of the common life; but it is inevitable that they should hold with varying degrees of consistency to the common principles which bind them into a group. In a general way pacifists may be defined as social idealists who are profoundly critical and sceptical of the use of physical force in the solution of social problems. At the extreme left in the pacifist group are the apostles of thoroughgoing non-resistance, who refuse to avail themselves of the use of physical force in any and every situation. At the right are the more circumspect social analysts who disavow the use of force in at least one important social situation, as, for instance, armed international conflict. What

---

* From *The World Tomorrow,* May 1928, pp. 218–220.

really unites this group in spite of its varying shades of conviction is the common belief that the use of force is an evil. The consistent exponents of non-resistance would regard it as an unnecessary evil in all situations. Those who are less consistent regard it as an evil in all situations but as a necessary evil in some situations.

The writer abhors consistency as a matter of general principle because history seems to prove that absolute consistency usually betrays into some kind of absurdity. He must begin, therefore, by stating two positions which represent the two poles of his thought. One is that the use of physical violence in international life has impressed itself upon his mind as an unmitigated and unjustified evil. The other is that some form of social compulsion seems necessary and justified on occasion in all but the most ideal human societies. Between these two positions a line must be drawn somewhere, to distinguish between the use of force as a necessary and as an unnecessary evil. Different men of equal intelligence and sincerity will draw that line in different places. Perhaps some, while claiming to be critical of the use of force, will find it practically necessary in so many situations that they may hardly be counted among the pacifists. It is necessary, therefore, to draw an arbitrary line and count only those among the pacifists who express their critical attitude toward the use of force by disavowing it completely in at least one important situation. Perhaps it ought to be added that a true pacifist will prove the sincerity of his conviction by seeking the diminution of force and by experimenting with other methods of social cooperation in every social situation.

The reason armed international conflict stands in a category of its own is because history has proven its worthlessness as a method of solving social problems so vividly that it has become practically impossible to justify it on any moral grounds. It is morally so impotent and so perilous chiefly for two reasons. One is that force in an international dispute is used by the parties to a dispute and it therefore aggravates rather than solves the evils and misunderstandings which led to the dispute. If there is any possibility of force being redemptive it is an absolute prerequisite that it be exerted by an agency which is impartial and unbiased with reference to the controversy. The other reason is that the use of force in international conflict inevitably issues in the destruction of life, and, what is more, in the destruction of the lives of many who have had no share in the dispute and who are innocent of the evils which a war may be designed to eliminate.

If international conflict is outlawed on these two grounds it would follow that the use of force by some society of nations would fall in a different category. If force is under the control of an impartial tribunal it has a better chance of being redemptive, or, at least, of not being totally destructive of morals, than if it is merely the means of conflict. However, it must be observed that it is so much more difficult to create an impartial society and an impartial tribunal with reference to disputes between large groups, national and economic, than with reference to controversies between individuals, that it is much more necessary to seek the total abolition of force in overcoming group conflict than in settling the difficulties of individuals within a group. A "league to enforce peace" between nations has much less chance of succeeding than has a government to enforce peace between individuals, simply because the total number of groups which make up the league is relatively small in comparison with the number which may be engaged in a controversy that it is practically impossible to guarantee the impartiality of the groups which enforce the decision of a tribunal. Added to this is the fact that a league of nations is no more able to punish a recalcitrant nation without destroying the lives of innocent people than is a single nation. Economic pressure rather than military force may reduce this moral hazard to a certain extent and it may therefore have a higher moral justification than the latter; but it does not entirely remove the difficulty and must therefore be regarded as a dangerous expedient. Though it is a dangerous expedient it does not follow that it is an expedient that may never be justified on moral grounds.

Pacifists assume too easily, it seems to me, that all controversies are due to misunderstandings which might be solved by a greater degree of imagination. When the strong exploit the weak they produce a conflict which is not the result of ignorance but of the brutality of human nature. It may be that the strong can be convinced in time that it is not to their ultimate interest to destroy the weak. But they can hardly gain this conviction if the weak do not offer resistance to oppression in some form. It may be that this resistance need not express itself physically at all. It may express itself in the use of the "soul force" advocated by Gandhi. But even as thorough-going a spiritual idealist as Gandhi has realized that the forgiving love of the oppressed lacks redemptive force if the strong are not made to realize that alternatives to a policy of love are within reach of the oppressed. Oppressed classes, races and nations, like the industrial workers, the Negroes, India and China, are therefore under the necessity of doing more than appeal to the imagination and the sense of justice of their oppressors. Where there is a great inequality of physical advantage and physical power it is difficult to establish moral relations. Weakness invites aggression. Even the most intelligent and moral individuals are more inclined to unethical conduct with those who are unable to offer resistance to injustice than with those who can. It must be admitted than an inert China did not succeed in inviting the attention of the world to its maladies, while a rebellious China did. Even the social idealists in the western world who were not totally oblivious to the evils of western imperialism in the Orient before the nationalist movement assumed large proportions had their conscience quickened by it.

It is obviously possible to resist injustice without using physical force and certainly without using violence. In a world in which conscience and imagination have been highly sensitized the oppressed may seek relief against their oppressors and punish them for their misdeeds by indicting them before the bar of public opinion. But it seems that the world in which we live is not so spiritual that it is always possible to prompt the wrongdoer to contrition merely by appealing to his conscience and to that of the society in which he lives. It may be necessary to deprive him of some concrete advantage or inflict some obvious hurt upon him to bring him to his senses. In other words, Gandhi's boycott in India and the Chinese boycott against the English in Hongkong and the strike of the industrial worker would seem to be necessary strategies in the kind of world in which we live. It is possible to justify the use of such force without condoning violence of any kind. The distinction between violence and such other uses of force as economic boycotts is not only in degree of destruction which results from them but in the degree of redemptive force which they possess. Parents frequently find it necessary to aid the defective imagination of a child by creating painful consequences by artificial means for acts which would result in painful consequences of their own accord in the long run. But the character of the child might be ruined before it had the opportunity to test the actual consequences. On the other hand, if such punishment is administered violently it will confuse rather than clarify the moral judgments of the child. When oppressed groups resort to violence they also confuse the moral judgment of the society from which they seek justice. They give society the pretext for identifying social maladjustments with social peace and for maintaining the former in the effort to preserve the latter. In the same way the effort of society to maintain a social equilibrium by the undue use of force, particularly by the violent use of force, inevitably confuses rather than clarifies the moral judgments of its minorities and easily prompts them to violence and destruction.

If force is used, therefore, for the sake of gaining moral and social ends, it is necessary to guard its use very carefully. Every society, every individual as well, is easily tempted to overestimate the importance of force in the creation of social solidarities. Many people live under the illusion that a nation is integrated by force and that order is maintained in its life by police power. The fact is that societies are created by attitudes of mutual respect and trust; and standards of conduct within a society are created by mutual consent. Every society seems under the necessity of maintaining its integrity against and forcing its standards upon a certain anti-social minority by the use of force. It is this anti-social minority which justifies, or at least seems to justify, the use of a certain minimum amount of force. It is because every society tends to overemphasize the place of force in its social strategy that absolutists have considerable justification for the thesis that force ought to be completely abolished; for the social efficacy of force is very definitely limited and most societies have been too uncritical to discover these limitations.

The first obvious limitation is that force can be used only upon a very insignificant minority. If the great majority of a people do not choose to observe a law it is not possible to enforce it by even the most ruthless police action. If a government does not rest upon the consent of the governed every effort to maintain it by ruthlessness must ultimately result in complete disintegration, as, for instance, in the Russian revolution. If a political policy does not achieve the uncoerced acceptance of a vast majority of the population, every effort to enforce it finally proves abortive. Even when the minority which opposes a government or a governmental policy is numerically small and insignificant, its coercion is fraught with moral and social peril. A so-called anti-social minority is, for one thing, never as completely anti-social as the society which tries to coerce it imagines. A part of the minority is usually made up of social idealists who resist the moral compromises upon which the life of every society is inevitably based, not because they are too high for its attainment but because they are too low for its ideals. It has been the tragic mistake of almost every society to number its prophets among its transgressors. Thus the same coercion by which it sought to avoid social disintegration has operated to produce social stagnation. The same force which preserved its standards also destroyed the social forces by which those standards might have been gradually perfected. A high degree of imagination, which few societies have achieved, is required to distinguish between creative and the disintegrating forces in its life. It may be observed in passing that while it is in the interest of social progress to dissuade societies from undue reliance upon coercion it will probably always be necessary for creative minorities to pay a certain price in martyrdom for their achievements. All social organisms are conservative and are bound to resist not only those who try to draw them backward but those who try to pull them forward.

Even after the distinction between creative and disintegrating forces in the social minority has been made there is no clear case for the use of force upon the remaining, really "criminal" minority. Some force may be necessary in dealing with the criminal, but every undue reliance upon force obscures the defects in the life of society itself which have helped to create the criminal. A wayward child is just as much the product of a faulty pedagogy as of innate human defects. It is dangerous to follow Clarence Darrow's moral nihilism and insist that every individual is merely the product of his environment and therefore without blame; but it is obvious enough that much anti-social conduct is definitely due to maladjustments in society. That is what Jesus meant by suggesting that he who is without guilt should throw the first stone. Of the cases of criminality which remain after those for which society is responsible have been subtracted a certain proportion must be attributed to purely pathological causes. A wise society will deal with these without passion and will use force only to put their unfortunate authors in social quarantine.

What is left after all these subtractions have been made represents the real criminal minority. While physical restraint and coercion are probably necessary in dealing with this group, it is obvious that even here force has its limitations. Imagination and understanding may restore a goodly portion of this group to useful membership in society, while the uncritical use of force will merely aggravate its defects. We must arrive, then, at the conclusion that the use of force is dangerous in all social situations, harmful in most of them and redemptive only in a very few.

The validity of the pacifist position rests in a general way upon the assumption that men are intelligent and moral and that a generous attitude toward them will ultimately, if not always immediately, discover, develop and challenge what is best in them. This is a large assumption which every specific instance will not justify. The strategy of love therefore involves some risks. These risks are not as great as they are sometimes made to appear, for the simple reason that love does not only discover but it creates moral purpose. The cynic who discounts the moral potentialities of human nature seems always to verify his critical appraisal of human nature for the reason that this very scepticism lowers the moral potentialities of the individuals and groups with which he deals. On the other hand, the faith which assumes generosity in the fellowman is also verified because it tends to create what it assumes. If a nation assumes that there is no protection against the potential peril of a neighbor but the force of arms, its assumption is all too easily justified, for suspicion creates hatred. It is interesting to note in this connection how in the relations of France and Germany since the war every victory or seeming victory of the nationalists in Germany has given strength to the chauvinists of France, and vice versa; while every advantage for the forces of one nation which believe in trust has resulted in an almost immediate advantage for the trustworthy elements in the other. Hence the contest between the apostles of force and the apostles of love can never be decided purely on the basis of scientific evidence. The character of the evidence is determined to a great degree by the assumptions upon which social relations are initiated. This is the fact which gives the champions of the strategy of love the right to venture far beyond the policy which a cool and calculating sanity would dictate. It may not be true that love never fails; but it is true that love creates its own victories, and they are always greater than would seem possible from the standpoint of a merely critical observer.

CHRISTIAN MORALISM IN AMERICA*

The annual pastoral letter of the bishops of the Episcopal church declared: "War as an instrument of national policy is a hideous denial of God and His condemnation rests upon it. It is rationally unjustifiable, morally indefensible and reli-

---

* From *Radical Religion*, V, 1 (Winter 1940).

giously irreconcilable with the love of God and our neighbor.
And it is wholly incompatible with the teachings and example
of our Lord Jesus Christ. We recognize however that there are
times when, peaceful expedients having failed, we are inescapably involved in war and we sympathise with all those
whose consciences impel them to participate in armed conflict."

The Christian Century took occasion in one of its editorials
to point the glaring inconsistency between the first and the
second of the episcopal propositions. It illustrated the inconsistency by collating the two quoted sentences so that they
would read: "The Christian is sometimes inescapably involved
in a hideous denial of God and in a course which is wholly
incompatible with the example and teachings of our Lord
Jesus Christ." The Century evidently believes that it is enough
to point to the absurdity of such a sentence to persuade the
bishops and other Christians to disavow the moral relativism
of the second proposition. Thus logic is to force them into a
pure pacifism. Logic—but what about life?

We are inclined to believe that the bishops might have saved
themselves some of the unqualified adjectives of the first
proposition—that war is rationally unjustifiable, morally indefensible and religiously incompatible with the life and
teachings of Christ. Such absolute judgments make it logically
impossible to accept the reservations which are advanced in
the final proposition. But waiving the matter of logic, has the
Christian Century never had some suspicion that the absurd
proposition, that the Christian "is sometimes inevitably involved in a course of action which is a hideous denial of God
and which is wholly incompatible with the example and
teachings of Christ," is really an accurate description of the
human situation, and that warfare is only a final and not a
singular revelation of this fact? Is not the whole difficulty with
liberal Christian moralism that it regard the life and teachings
of Christ as simple moral possibilities? Sometimes, as in the
world war, it escapes the problem of the relation of the absolute demands of the Kingdom of God and the relativities of
a sinful world by imagining that a relative duty, such as the
defence of democracy, is really identical with the absolute

demands. It talks about democracy as the realization of the Kingdom of God in political life, and it engages in long exegetical exercises to prove that Jesus drove the money-changers out of the temple with a whip. Sober reflection causes a reaction to this identification of the relative and the absolute so that, the next time, Christian moralism takes a more absolute position and insists that it is impossible to square Christianity and warfare.

In the burst of hysterical self-righteousness which now consumes the energies of the American churches, it has not yet occurred to the Christian moralists that an attitude which is dictated or influenced by the neutrality of a nation in which those churches live, may be just as dubious from the standpoint of the "example and teachings of Christ" as the identification of war with the Christian ethic. They point with scorn to the churches of the belligerent countries who "have put Christ in khaki," lacking even the Christian charity to appreciate how heavily this whole tension between the Kingdom of God and the sad realities of our world weighs upon the decent Christians of other lands. But not only that; they obscure an obvious fact which Christianity ought not to obscure. That fact is that nations as well as individuals never overcome the temptation to self-righteousness completely and that they easily claim only ideal motives for their actions—when in reality the actions are prompted by a mixture of motives. Nations fight only when there is a coincidence between the defensive requirements of the nation and the ideal values to which the nation declares itself pledged. In the same way nations do not fight when this coincidence is lacking. Thus America hates fascism and has some conscience about the terrible cruelty which a religious racialism has visited upon its racial foes and victims. But American national interests are not involved in this war and consequently we do not fight the Nazis. I do not challenge the policy of neutrality, for I rather believe that it is impossible to achieve a completely disinterested national policy and that America is still suffering from having been drawn into the world war beyond the obvious necessities of national defence.

What we find difficult in the American religious situation is the failure of our religious moralists to call attention to the primary basis of American neutrality—the fact that American vital interests are not imperiled in the conflict. Instead we are told that we must remain out of the conflict because war is incompatible with the ethic of Jesus. We obviously have a slightly uneasy conscience about this rationalization; for it was only yesterday that we protested violently against Nazi tyranny and criticized Chamberlain for submitting to it. To cover our uneasy conscience we have invented the fiction that there is no difference between British imperialism and Nazi tyranny. One pacifist leader has gone so far as to declare that this cannot be a war for democracy since a nation ceases to be democratic and becomes totalitarian the moment it fights.

As a consequence of all this moralistic rationalization, a neutral nation which constantly points its finger of scorn at the belligerent nations, for having put "Christ in khaki," is actually in greater danger of covering the very relative values of a particular political position with the aura of sanctity than are the warring nations. There are, to the personal knowledge of the writer, more Christian sermons and articles being preached and written in Britain today in which the judgment of God is interpreted as a judgment upon Britain than are appearing in America. Most of our sermons adopt the simple expedient of pronouncing judgment upon the warring nations while complacently assuming that the slogan, "Keep America out of war," is a practical fulfillment of the Sermon on the Mount. This is a simple way of evading the judgment of God which stands equally over every nation and of escaping the important duty of making relative distinctions between good and evil, between truth and falsehood, between freedom and tyranny—which is, incidentally, the only kind of distinction we ever have a chance of making in history.

Our simple moral purists imagine that they can purge their souls for having identified Christianity too simply with democracy during the world war by now refusing to make any distinction between democracy and tyranny. The identification of the absolute and the relative didn't make sense during the world war, and the refusal to make relative distinctions makes no sense now. Neither does it make sense to inveigh against tyranny and to declare in the next breath that it is useless to resist tyranny because (1) you are no better than the tyrant anyway and (2) you will turn into a tyrant and gangster if you dare to resist tyrants and gangsters.

The real difficulty with a simple moralism is precisely its inability to understand that all life is involved in a contradiction to the will of God. As Christians we must have some contrite recognition of this fact; but we must also have some responsibility toward the task of achieving and preserving a relative freedom, justice and decency in a warring world. It is because Christian moralism regards the precepts of the Sermon on the Mount as simple moral possibilities that it never becomes conscious of the elements in all human existence which contradict the will of God until they break forth in overt conflict. It is then too late to elaborate a theology or strategy which does justice both to the legitimacy of relative distinctions on one level of judgment and to the illegitimacy of such distinctions on the final level of religious judgment.

Long before a war breaks out we ought to ask ourselves the question whether we are not involved in life and actions which are "incompatible with the example and teachings of Christ." There is the word: "Whoso loveth father and mother more than me is not worthy of me." Are any of us good enough to maintain that the particular love which we have for our own does not come in conflict with the love which we owe God and our fellowmen? And is not this narrow love, this alteregoism, the very root of all human conflict? Or, again, Jesus declares: "Be not anxious for your life." This commandment is just as ultimate and relevant as the commandment: "Thou shalt love thy neighbor as thyself." Anxiety is the basis of all undue self-assertion. We are anxious about our life, and we seek to make it secure; and invariably we interfere with the security of our fellowmen in trying to make our own life secure. There is no question about the validity of this law of Christ. But also there is no question that every life, even the life of the best of us, is involved in a contradiction of this commandment.

It is because the sinfulness of man leads to the destruction of brotherhood that a good part of human history is the effort to construct such relative justice as is possible within the limits of human selfishness. This effort involves resisting the proud, even though we run the danger of becoming proud in the process of resistance; of resisting the strong even though we are not free of selfishness as we resist—and may become as unjust as the strong if we should be victorious over them and ourselves become the powerful in turn. The task of securing a relative justice in the world quite obviously involves setting sin against sin. We ought never fool ourselves and imagine that we are the righteous who must destroy the sinners. But neither can we easily bow ourselves out of the responsibility of securing such justice as is possible through resisting flagrant injustice and tyranny.

If any one wants to bow himself out of that responsibility he ought at least be clear about what he is doing. He ought to say to us: "You are involved in a dangerous game. You may produce anarchy by trying to resist tyranny, or you may create tyranny by trying to overcome anarchy. I will try therefore to symbolize the more excellent way." But if he presents this more excellent and absolute way as a simple alternative to a political program, he merely makes confusion worse confounded. Usually he also detracts from the splendour of his moral example by self-righteous preachments. This at least is what modern pacifists tend to do in contrast to the best of medieval perfectionists.

No amount of perfectionist preaching has yet discovered a way by which tyranny can be destroyed without being resisted; or how it can be resisted without the risk of overt conflict; or how the forces which resist it can be purged of every self-regarding motive and be made absolutely pure champions of freedom and justice.

Our whole difficulty in American Protestantism is in having so long regarded Christianity as synonymous with the simple command to love God and our fellowmen, that we have forgotten that the Christian religion is really a great deal more than this. The Christian faith really begins in the cry of despair of St. Paul: "For the good that I would I do not: but the evil which I would not, that I do. . . . Wretched man that I am, who will deliver me from the body of this death?" In answer to this cry it declares that the divine mercy revealed in Christ is on the one hand a power which overcomes the contradiction between what we are and what we ought to be, and on the other hand a pledge of forgiveness for this sinful element which is never completely overcome short of the ultimate culmination of history. Only such a faith can disclose the actual facts of human existence. It alone can uncover the facts because it alone has answer for the facts which are disclosed. Most religion is an effort to obscure the actual situation in which we stand for the simple reason that, without an answer for this situation, we should be driven to despair by what is revealed. That is why we try to prove that other nations stand under the judgment of God, but that we do not stand there; that ignorant men stand under it, but that intelligent and wise men are safe because their intelligence has made them good; that religious "dogmatists" and "ecclesiasts" stand under judgment because they have obscured the simple commands of Jesus, but that we do not stand under judgment because we are bending our efforts to reveal these simple commands. We do anything and everything to hide the fact that every man stands under judgment because every man is involved in contradicting the law of Christ, there being a law in his members which wars against the law that is in his mind.

This "pure gospel" which we claim to have rescued from the obscurantists and dogmatists, including St. Paul, is little more than eighteenth-century rationalism and optimism, compounded with a little perfectionism, derived from the sanctificationist illusions of sectarian Christianity.

To understand American Christianity one must understand that the eighteenth-century Enlightenment has been curiously compounded with the various strains of sectarian Protestantism, in all of which the doctrine of "justification by faith" was virtually rejected in favor of a simpler doctrine which made the perfection of Christ the simple possibility of every true believer. Whatever the weaknesses of the Protestant Reformation, it saw the basic human problem more truly than either Catholic or sectarian moralism. It is for this reason that our tragic era demands a return to the Reformation—though it is to be hoped that we may be able to escape the obscurantism, Biblical literalism, and antinomianism which frequently disfigured Reformation theology. To whatever we return or advance, the insights of Christian moralism are obviously inadequate. These insights are little better than an arid secularism in which men save themselves from despair by a tentative fanaticism and fall into despair when the fanaticism is dissipated by the hard realities and bewildering complexities of human history.

It may be pointed out in closing that the radical wing of Christian liberalism is just as uncertain and vacillating on the relation of absolute to relative as the purer liberalism. Only yesterday most religious radicals were challenging pacifism because they did not see how the domestic social struggle could be solved in terms of pure love. They were certain that social justice was the consequence of a social struggle, though they were rightly not agreed in regarding social revolution as an inevitable consequence of this struggle. Today the international situation has persuaded them to change their minds. They have become pacifists again. If they merely declared that they regarded the international struggle as a conflict between rival imperialisms, they might be wrong or right; but their judgment would at least remain in the proper category of a relative political judgment. But, being religious radicals and feeling conscious of having a rather tenuous connection with the Christian faith, they are glad to be able to return to the faith and prove the intimacy of their relation with the Christian gospel. Therefore they butter their political convictions with the unction of the "Jesus way of life" and declare that they must at all costs remain true to the simple standards of Jesus. Once the war is over and the social struggle becomes urgent again, as it will and must, they will find a way of disavowing their pacifism and discovering anew that the ethic of Jesus is not immediately applicable to the social struggle. They will probably also conclude tomorrow, as they concluded yesterday, that since the ethic is not immediately applicable it is not relevant at all. Thus Christian faith is buffeted about by every wind of doctrine arising from the historical cave of the winds, and is formed and reformed in the light of every historical exigency.

If our faith and our ethic shift continually between what is believed in peace time and what is believed in war, that is fairly good proof that they are not profound enough to have disclosed the unity of the total human situation. For the human situation remains the same in peace and in war, though it may be more clearly seen in war than in peace.

THE GOSPEL IN FUTURE AMERICA*

In every age Christian believers face two problems. One is to relate the gospel to the culture of the age without losing its essential truth. That is not any easy task because the essential truth of the gospel is "the foolishness of God which is wiser than men"; that is to say, the gospel tells us something about God and ourselves which taxes our credulity and offends our self-esteem. The culture of all the ages consists of the scientific, philosophical and artistic ideas and preconceptions by which the mind of man tries to make sense out of life. Inevitably, these cultures make sense out of life too simply by having human freedom, man's sin and God's grace out of the system— leaving them out inevitably because no scientific system can possibly make room for freedom, sin and grace.

But this does not mean that the culture of an age is inevitably wrong and that the Christian faith should have no commerce with it. Inevitably when commerce is cut off, whether by a Tertullian or by a Karl Barth, in order to protect that part of the Christian revelation which offends our self-esteem, the Christian faith is also freed from the wholesome disciplines of culture; and then that which taxes our credulity—the speaking

---

* Copyright 1958 Christian Century Foundation. Reprinted by permission from the June 18, 1958 issue of *The Christian Century*, pp. 712–716.

about God and the receiving of an ultimate message which we could not have invented—degenerates into obscurantism which not only takes the credulity of the wise but offends the intellect of any intelligent man who knows that the world is governed by law.

TWO VERSIONS OF PROTESTANTISM

The problem of faith and culture in the next decades is, as usual, partly determined by the struggle of faith and culture in the immediate past and present. In the immediate past the Christian faith, at least the Protestant version of it, was divided into an obscurantist version and a "liberal" version. The former, usually termed fundamentalism, guarded the ultimate truths of the gospel but was not in sufficient contact with the disciplines of a scientific culture to prevent obscurantist corruptions of the gospel. The liberal version had the virtue of freeing the study of the Scriptures from religious taboo and thus opening the Scripture to the discipline of historical scholarship. This discipline had the religious merit of freeing the Christian faith of biblicism and of freeing the Christ, as our norm and as the revelation of our redemption, from the extraneous and various social standards which were embodied in the biblical canon. It made the Bible again into what Luther rightly apprehended to be its true function—the "cradle of Christ."

These were very great achievements; but unfortunately liberal Christianity suffered the same fate that befell patristic Christianity before Augustine: it capitulated to the errors of the contemporary culture even while it profited from its disciplines. In this case it was not to Platonism that it capitulated, but to the two great dogmas of the Enlightenment, the evolutionary conception of history and the perfectibility of man. In America this concession came with particular ease because the sectarian Christianity whose prestige grew on our frontier was informed by an evangelical Pelagianism and optimism very similar to the optimism of the Enlightenment. Thus the "Kingdom of God" was equated with the idea of progress; the Enlightenment idea of the perfectibility of man through reason became Christian Pelagianism in which piety, rather than science, guaranteed virtue; and Christ became either the symbol of the historical process or the first fruits of the Kingdom.

THE THRUST OF NEO-ORTHODOXY

The tragic realities of the 20th century destroyed this liberalism, whether in its secular or its Christian version. It was destroyed in Europe in the First World War. In America, with her wealth and seeming security from the new terrors and tumults of history, liberalism lasted until the depression and the Second World War.

Theologically, Karl Barth's *Römerbrief* was the agent of resurgence of Reformation thought, in opposition to the old liberalism. Barth's creative thrust placed all of us in his debt and established what became known as "neo-orthodoxy." The word is meaningless now, for its theological spectrum ranges from Barth himself to Tillich, whose ontology would be, from Barth's perspective, gnostic and docetic. But originally it meant a form of theology which took all the biblical concepts seriously without submitting to the prescientific world view of the old orthodoxy.

This was the situation in the beginning of the century, or roughly in the second decade of the new century upon the decline of the old liberalism. But much has changed since then, and the immediate present determines in some degree the problems we face in the future. One change has taken place in the Barthian type of orthodoxy. The epigoni, and in some degree Barth himself, have been betrayed by their sole reliance on scriptural truth in defiance of culture into an orthodoxy which is frighteningly similar to our old fundamentalism. It accepts the Bible *en bloc*, and it champions the cause of women against the age-old male supremacy without regard to the creative forces in modern culture but merely because Barth's *Dogmatics* has a chapter on the Creation in which he proves that the Old Testament's assurance "Male and female created he them" implies the equality of the sexes. Nothing is said about the help which a secular culture rendered the church in making explicit what was implicit in the Bible but not explicit in all the previous Christian ages.

The revolt against this new orthodoxy, with its new obscurantism which knew nothing of Barth's early sophisticated and imaginative definition of "myth, legend, saga and prehistory," was not long in coming. It was led by a former disciple of Barth, the learned New Testament theologian Rudolph Bultmann, whose New Testament theology, and particularly his essay in the volume *Kerygma and Myth*, became the flag of this revolt. Bultmann seemed anxious to guard the "kerygma" as the old liberalism had not guarded it; but the fruit of all his labors was that the gospel was equated with Heidegger's existentialist analysis of the human situation. This existentialism was not very different from the old liberalism, having the same or a similar Pelagianism and emphasizing the necessity of "authentic" being against the perils of "anonymous" existence. Bultmann's interest in purging the Scripture of prescientific myths was informed by a rationalism which failed to make a distinction between history and nature, between pure reason expressed in the natural sciences and "historical reason" (cf. Richard R. Niebuhr, *The Resurrection and Historical Reason*). He did not recognize that the Bible, dealing with historical experience, contained not only prescientific myths but "permanent myths" or symbols in which the meaning of existence was revealed as man in dialogue with God; and Christ clarified the mystery of the God who was the creator but also, through his mercy, the redeemer of man.

Where We Come In

The new existentialism had merely been substituted for the old optimism. The new formula is more in keeping with the mood of this century than the old liberalism; but its interpretation of the gospel subordinates the conviction of sin and the possibility of grace as pardon, and grace as power on the other side of the confession of our human predicament, to the assertion of "eternal life" (taken by Bultmann from Johannine literature) and to the affirmation of being "spiritually minded" as over against being "carnally minded" (as taken from the Pauline dualism)—both lines ostensibly in agreement with Heidegger's "authentic" existence. This is where we come in.

The first impression is that there has not been very much movement in a quarter-century. The old neo-orthodoxy has been, for all practical purposes, transmuted into the old orthodoxy, and the reaction to it is something very much like the old liberalism—not as optimistic but quite as Pelagian. Man is challenged to assert an authentic existence against the perils of nature and anonymity.

Our modern task must begin with the Reformation's rediscovery of the gospel's assurance of God's redeeming mercy in Christ. All who have accepted Christ as their judge, and in that judgment have quitted the various forms of self-deception and self-delusion, know that there is no moral way of closing the hiatus between man's righteousness and God's righteousness. The only way to peace ultimately is the assurance of pardon. But out of this religious reconciliation there must come all the adventures of commitment and responsibility, all the fruits of the love of God and neighbor by men who know that they are not good and that they cannot fool God by their strenuous virtues (or appearances of virtue), but who feel themselves committed to a life of responsibility which has no norms short of the love of Christ.

This old gospel must and can be validated to a generation which is not at all sure about the meaning of human existence and indeed seems to be particularly skeptical of the whole structure of meaning which biblical faith gives to human existence by faith in the "Almighty Creator of heaven and earth" and faith that in the whole drama of Christ's life, death and resurrection the believer has a revelation of the mystery of the divine power and love.

This revelation clarifies the relation of God's creative power to his love and clarifies the relation of the two sides of his love: his justice and his mercy. The knowledge of his justice teaches us to take the sinful rebellion of man seriously. The knowledge of his mercy saves us from despair, particularly in this age when the historic predicament of security through a nuclear stalemate becomes a vivid symbol of the whole human predicament and a reminder that "all our righteousnesses are as filthy rags," that all human virtues are fragmentary, that all appre-

hensions of truth by man are tentative and all human achievements ambiguous. To forget this fact debases the Christian
faith to the dimension of some form of fanaticism in which
men claim a too simple identity between their ends and the
divine will.

NOT SOMETHING TO BE 'PROVED'

Our task in validating the gospel is bound to be less rational
and "scientific" than in any previous age because it must be
apparent that the affirmation of a whole structure of meaning,
which not only completes but contradicts all human apprehen-
sions of meanings and ends, is not something that can be
"proved" by any science or philosophy. One can only bear
witness to the truth of the faith by a life in which humility
generates charity and prevents fanatic self-righteousness. The
succinct definition of this witness is given by Paul: "Be ye
kindly affectionate one to another forgiving one another even
as God also in Christ has forgiven you."

Any religious faith which manifests itself in hatred of the
Negro, for instance, and in a fanatic loyalty to the "southern
way of life" or the "American way of life," will display an
idolatrous element which constitutes a heresy even though the
believer claims virtue because he believes that Christ was born
of a virgin. We will not forget that it was Christ himself who
rejected this kind of belief rather than faith as trust. "This
wicked generation," he said, "seeketh a sign, but no sign will
be given unto it except the sign of Jonah."

By implication we have already moved from the problem of
validating the message of the cross of Christ in the culture
(where it is bound to be, as in every culture, a scandal, and yet
the source of wisdom and power because it shatters our self-
esteem and makes the renewal of life possible) to the validation of the gospel in our civilization. This has always been an
equally grave problem, and it has become more grievous in a
technical and nuclear age. It has always been a problem because the "love of Christ" is at the same time both the fulfillment of the law and the sum and substance of all law, and a

form of grace revealed in self-sacrifice and forgiveness which transcends all law. The problem has always been to transmute the spirit of love and express it in such laws and such a spirit of justice that the spirit of Christ will help to form wholesome communities and inspire these communities to live together in peace. We cannot serve this generation in its heightened communal problems unless we admit that the whole Christian enterprise has not been as successful in inspiring a "Christian" attitude toward the political order as the Christian faith has been in inspiring heroic martyrdom, patient suffering and loving service in individual life.

THE GOSPEL IN A NUCLEAR CIVILIZATION

In America, despite the contributions of the various versions of Protestantism to our open society, the "rule of the saints" in our New England theocracy made Puritanism odious in the memory of our people. Moreover, later Puritanism became involved in the ethos of the complacent middle classes produced by a growing industrial civilization, and complacency was accentuated by the curious alliance between the Puritan ethic of thrift, diligence and honesty and the social Darwinism, mixed with free enterprise doctrines, which quieted uneasy consciences by the assurance that these injustices were the price that must be paid for the boon of noninterference with the "Laws of Nature" which presumably would guarantee justice in the end.

From this dreadful combination of graceless Puritanism and false science the "social gospel" rescued us. But the price was an undue reliance on "love as the community-building faculty" and a consequent yearning for collectivist politics which would "exalt people not things." This involvement of the sensitive part of Protestantism in the errors of modern collectivism was an unfortunate reaction to the errors of pietistic and Calvinistic individualism. The right wing of the social gospel movement escaped these dangers by its purely moral approach to politics; that is, by Shailer Mathews' warning, "It is evangelical to give justice but it is not evangelical to get justice."

Love and the Instruments of Justice

Meanwhile our free society achieved, by strategies that neither the Christian realists nor the Christian idealists anticipated, a belated justice which the earlier industrialism lacked. The realists hoped for order and the idealists commended love. But justice was achieved by a balance of social and economic forces which would prevent sinful men from taking advantage of one another. Today, our primary task in relating the Christian faith to our technical civilization is to guide the Christian conscience in transmuting the purer impulse of love so as to use the instruments of justice for the sake of the neighbor. That means the faith must avail itself of both the calculation of rights and the equilibria of power in the ever more intricate relations of technical togetherness. If we cannot do this and insist that the religious impulse must express itself purely without calculation and rational contrivance, we may indeed prove that the Christian faith still validates itself in family relations, where fidelity is the most direct and relevant expression of the love commandment. But our faith will cease to be relevant to the main concerns of men involved in the intricate affairs of a business civilization.

The task of our generation begins where these achievements end. It consists of making moral people aware of the fact that they are not so righteous that the community can afford to dispense with various strategies which prevent self-interest from producing either injustice or tyranny. It includes the preservation of the dignity of the person in those large-scale aggregates of power in management and labor which are indispensable in a technical society but are nevertheless dangerous to the person. It consists further in something which is more natural to the religiously sensitive spirit: we must fill these structures of justice with the living reality of love in personal relations. Love as a substitute for justice is odious, but love as a supplement to justice is an absolute necessity. Furthermore, we can do something else for which the American church is peculiarly fitted. We can build Christian fellowships on the congregational level which will be asylums for persons in the anonymity of a technical and urban society—fellowships in which both their dignity and the misery of sin and death are fully understood and met by the gospel of Christ.

MORALITY FOR NATIONS

But justice in a technical age is only the first of the three great problems we face today. The second is an age-old problem—namely, the relation of the nation to the Kingdom of God; but it has become aggravated, particularly for Americans, because our nation has achieved an unwanted degree of power and responsibility which extends beyond our national destiny and covers the destiny of the "free world" and of modern mankind, for that matter. It will not do to solve this problem by the moral and moralistic observation that unless our nation ceases to be selfish it is doomed.

We have the larger and more difficult problem of relating a very powerful and very wealthy nation to an impoverished world in terms of a tolerable justice. This cannot be done by appealing to the nation to be "unselfish" but only by reminding it that what will seem generous to its self-esteem (the Marshall plan, for instance) will be judged by others to be imaginatively conceived as in our national interest. A Christian moralism which assumes that nations have the same moral capacities as individuals, that they are capable of self-sacrifice as individuals are, does not make nations unselfish. But it does run the danger of obscuring the real mixture of motives which is the highest moral achievement of nations; namely, a mixture of concern for the nation's interest and a sense of responsibility for a larger community than the nation, whether this be the Western community, the community of free nations or the community of mankind. Europeans rightly criticize us for adding to a great nation's natural pride of power the less sufferable pride of virtue. But Christian moralism aggravates this second fault when a proper application of the gospel to national and international affairs might help our people to understand that we can neither disavow our power and our responsibilities for the sake of our innocency or purity, nor exercise such great power with perfect justice. Such a spirit might make us more sufferable to our friends and allies, who must find the combination of pride of power and pride of virtue in us difficult to bear.

The moral problem of our nation is further aggravated by the fact that we have had world hegemony forced upon us at the moment in history when the free nations are locked in a tremendous contest with a utopian political movement which has distilled world tyranny from the idealistic dreams of the secular prophet Karl Marx. We are tempted to exchange the irresponsibility to which we succumbed in the days between the two world wars for an inflexible anticommunism colored with a note of hysteria which frightens our more experienced but less powerful allies. In our contest with communism the Christian faith can offer religious—more than merely moral—guidance by reminding our people that even powerful nations are creatures, that they must avoid the "illusion of omnipotence," and that providence may confront us with tasks and responsibilities which cannot be accomplished in a generation, and place us before frustrations to which this nation has never been accustomed and which are the more difficult to bear because the frustrations are greater in the days of our strength than they were in the days of our weakness.

THE IRRESPONSIBILITY OF ESCHATOLOGY

In coming to terms with our responsibilities we are unfortunately not helped by the combination of the old liberalism and the old pietism which has become the staple of modern evangelism and which assures us that we are doomed unless the nation becomes "unselfish." But even less can we expect help from the much more sophisticated theology of Barth, who helped to destroy the old liberalism, who was the religious inspiration of the resistance to nazi tyranny, but who has relapsed into his previous mood of eschatological irresponsibility. From the eschatological stratosphere, we are assured that there is little to choose between "American dollar worship" and communist despotism. In such arbitrary political judgments, mature men can find little guidance. Nor will our pride be moderated by a neutralism which plays God to the world, while we know ourselves to be men with responsibilities to our nations and civilizations. A neutralism having its geographical locus in little Switzerland and its theological locus in the knowledge of that "big event" of Jesus Christ which makes all little events and changes of systems of small moment, is no longer informed by the biblical impulse toward historical responsibilities. It has risen from the earth to a premature heaven, even though it calls that heaven the "coming Kingdom of Christ." Undiluted eschatology can be as irresponsible toward historic tasks as pure otherworldliness.

Meanwhile, we as a nation have the problem not only of relating our power to the weakness of the smaller nations but of countering the threats of tyranny in an atomic age without falling into the catastrophe of a war with hydrogen bombs. There is no simple moral solution for this ultimate moral dilemma. Religiously, it is a reminder of the ambiguity of all human virtue and the inconclusiveness of all human achievements in a day which had prepared itself for realization of the Kingdom of God upon earth. There is no single moral solution for the problem. But among the many proximate solutions there is a policy of uniting and supporting the free world with patience in bearing for a century or more burdens we have never before borne. The Christian church must help our nation to measure the depth of this predicament, for it is a perfect historic presentation of the human predicament as seen from the standpoint of the gospel. It validates the biblical estimate of our human situation and it can be faced without illusion and without despair only in terms of a faith which knows that all our meanings for life and history are fulfilled and refuted by the final meaning that Christ gives to our private and collective destinies.

THE RELIGIOUS ANSWER

The Christian faith does not give us technical knowledge about the relations of our nation to the budding nations of Africa and Asia, or tell us how to help them gain both independence and stability, or how to transmute an agrarian or pastoral economy into a technical one. It can only inspire us

to a sense of responsibility and justice in offering our strength
to conquer their weakness.

Any form of the Christian faith which gives simple answers,
involving the disavowal of responsibility for the sake of guaran-
teeing our own purity, is a part of the old liberal moralism
which has eliminated all the Pauline and gospel indications of
the depth of the human and historical dilemma for the sake of
proclaiming a new religion of historical optimism. The old
liberalism affirmed that all problems could be solved if only
Christians would take "the Jesus way of life" seriously. History
has certainly refuted the relevance of this version of the gospel,
has refuted the implied assertion that Jesus was a noble man
who died for his ideals and that we could be as noble if we
only tried hard enough. If the New Testament's proclamation
that "God was in Christ reconciling the world unto himself"
is not the gospel then the gospel is as irrelevant in this nuclear
age as it has been in any age. For in every age all human
virtues have proved inadequate, and all human achievements
more tentative and all human striving more unavailing than
moralism imagines, either to bridge the hiatus between the
divine and human righteousness or to guide us in performing
our ordinary responsibilities.

There is no moral answer to our moral dilemma. But there
is a religious answer. It reminds us that "if in this life only we
had hoped in Christ we are of all men most miserable." This
is to say that it belongs to the permanent condition of sinful
humanity that "our reach exceeds our grasp," that Christ gives
us a clue to the meaning which overarches all our meanings
and refutes them. We are bidden to undertake burdens and
responsibilities for ends and consequences that we cannot fore-
see, and to become implicated in the guilt and frustrations of
these responsibilities, which citizens of a young and innocent
nation will find particularly perplexing.

In short, the primary task of the Christian church in America in the coming years is to apply the wisdom and power of
the gospel to individual and collective human predicaments.
This task is illumined by the refutation in our experience of
both the old liberalism, which wrongly identified historical

optimism with the Christian message, and the neo-orthodox
eschatology, which makes for irresponsibility and is, therefore,
irrelevant to our pressing responsibilities.

THE CRISIS IN AMERICAN PROTESTANTISM*

It has been said that perhaps the weakness of American Protestantism reveals itself in the fact that it is "captive to the
power structure."

In a sense there is not, in an open society, a single power
structure. Such justice as we have achieved in a technical age
has been due to a tolerable equilibrium between various
power structures. We have "big business" and "big labor" and
"big government," and the government is still democratic and
functions under a two-party system. In his brilliant new book
The American Economic Republic Adolf Berle argues that
we have achieved a tolerable harmony and a consequent tolerable justice through an equilibrium of social forces.

We do not have a single power structure. But we have a
single culture. Yet the Protestant church, which has created
this individualistic culture, is no more able to exercise a critical function over its handiwork than was the Roman church
able to be critical of (or extricate itself from) the medieval
feudalism which it had created. On the other hand, the Roman
church, with its sense of the social substance of human existence, has been more creative in efforts to solve the modern
problems of technical collectivism than has Protestantism.

I

The crisis of American Protestantism derives from the fact
that it is inveterately individualistic in a collectivist age which
must deal with the moral and social problems raised by rela-

* Copyright 1963 Christian Century Foundation. Reprinted by permission from the December 4, 1963 issue of *The Christian Century*,
pp. 1498–1501.

tions between classes and races—not to speak of nations. We are individualistic. Our sense of virtue is individualistic. Has not Max Weber revealed (in *Protestantism and the Spirit of Capitalism*) that the Protestant virtues of "thrift, honesty and industry" launched the modern enterprise?

Beyond those economic virtues, however, we have had some nobler ones. We encouraged all people to love their neighbors. We made much of the fact that the New Testament admonishes us not only to love our neighbor in the sense of being responsible for his welfare, but also to sacrifice for our neighbor in the spirit of Christ. Yet in all such noble sentiments there were lacking a sense of justice and a passion to achieve just adjudication of competing rights and interests in a world of self-seeking men. We are, of course, all self-seeking: the universality of self-regard was one of the doctrines of the Reformation.

Incidentally, one of the sources of confusion in American Protestantism is the fact that Protestants in this nation derive from two reformations rather than from one. The classical Reformation was realistic; it regarded all men as actuated by self-love. The other, which the late Rufus Jones regarded as the real Reformation, was perfectionist: it saw the Christian enterprise as an effort to transmute selfish men and nations into unselfish ones. American Protestantism, whatever its origins, has exhibited more sectarian perfectionism than Reformation realism. But whether perfectionist or realist, it has been consistently individualistic in its conception of virtue and of vice.

II

Throughout the period from the close of the Civil War to the end of the century, the nation rapidly industrialized, producing the social distresses consequent upon a tremendous shift of power in the economic sphere like that which characterized the industrial period in European democracy. The social distresses produced in America, as they did in Europe, a spate of social movements and revolts: the populists, the

"Knights of Labor" and, finally, the American Federation of Labor.

But Protestantism was not moved by any of these revolts. Perhaps its complacency stemmed from the fact that the owners of modern industry were members of the white, Protestant, earlier immigration; while the workers, the "hewers of wood and drawers of water," were later arrivals, mainly Catholic and Jewish. In any case, the regnant social creed of Protestantism was, except for aspects espoused by a few heroic spirits, drawn from a moribund Calvinism which regarded wealth as the reward of virtue and poverty as the punishment for drunkenness or laziness. The more secular "social Darwinism" was a staunch ally of this Calvinism. Nothing in the distress of the impoverished workers and farmers could penetrate the complacency of the consistently bourgeois, Protestant conception of heaven.

The organization of labor, however, proceeded. But the culture was still so individualistic that the Supreme Court, reading the presuppositions of the culture into the Constitution, prevented by judicial injunction all action on behalf of labor. It was not until a worldwide depression arrived that an astute statesman, Franklin D. Roosevelt, belatedly persuaded a reluctant middle-class culture to establish the legal right to set collective power against collective power and thus establish that equilibrium of power in the economic sphere which is the necessary prerequisite of a tolerable justice in a technical age. The United States achieved this milestone in the third decade of the present century, long after European democracies had through gradual steps in social legislation laid the foundations of the welfare state.

Meanwhile, of course, there were critical and prophetic voices in American Protestantism which sought to bring Christian morality into terms of relevance with the burning issues of social justice. The social gospel emerged at the turn of the century. Walter Rauschenbusch wrote his *Christianity and the Social Crisis*. Washington Gladden, Richard Ely and a host of other Protestant leaders challenged the regnant in-

dividualism of American Protestantism. The Federal Council
of Churches adopted a "social creed" in which the rights of
the workers to organize were affirmed. Franklin Roosevelt won
his first election armed with the Protestant social creed and
Pope Leo XIII's historic encyclical *Rerum Novarum,* published
in 1871.

Despite the great contribution of the social gospel school,
it must be admitted that it never consistently analyzed the
complicated relation between power and justice. Vaguely
socialist and pacifist, it ultimately separated into two wings.
The right wing talked of "evangelical justice" which was
"given" and not "grasped." The left wing was involved in socialist and even communist speculations, and a sorry fringe
of that wing finally became enmeshed in Stalinist politics.

In short, the major issues of economic and social justice
were met and solved, and American industrial society came to
terms with its neglected collective problems without too
much aid from the Protestant churches. This judgment must
not, however, be seen as detracting from the value of those
services to the nation which many heroic spirits in the Protestant ministry have contributed through their witness.

Our nation has thus reached a tolerable solution of its
problems of economic justice because the society was "open"
enough to allow the economically weak but politically strong
(armed with the ballot) to use their power to achieve economic
as well as political gains. So a tolerable equilibrium of power
was established, an equilibrium without which justice cannot
be achieved in a world of self-seeking men, particularly when
those men act collectively.

Since the church is not a social engineer we cannot demand
from it a blueprint of the relation of justice to power. But the
Protestant church was undoubtedly both too individualistic
and too sentimental to be able to give much guidance to a
nation in the throes of industrial unrest. Above all, it failed
to acquaint the community with the deviousness of the human
heart and with the labyrinthine depth of self-deception into
which the self-seeking heart can sink. Is not the Christian
gospel a good guide to the mysteries of good and evil in the

human heart? Should it not make us aware of both the heights of true love and the depths of self-love of which man is capable?

III

The tolerable solution of the issue of economic justice has not affected the issue of racial justice. A century after their emancipation from slavery one-tenth of our population, the Negroes, the real proletarians of the American scene, still wait in vain for justice from their fellow citizens. In his classic inquiry into our racial situation published in 1948, the Swedish sociologist Gunnar Myrdal characterized the Negro's position in our Christian, democratic nation as constituting the "American dilemma." It was more than that. It was a scandal.

From the very beginning a certain degree of dishonesty entered into the relation of the idealistic young republic with the Negro. Thomas Jefferson, who wrote the brave words of the Declaration of Independence about equality and liberty being "inalienable rights," was a slaveholder. The founding fathers, who had accused King George III of profiting from the slave trade, did nothing to abolish slavery in the several states. While the Constitution allowed a certain percentage of representation for citizens "in servitude" and did not use the hated word "slavery," ironically enough slavery spread in those colonies and states in which Jeffersonian liberalism and evangelical Christianity were very strong. In fact, both were employed as ideological defenses for slavery. The Jeffersonians used the states' rights doctrines to protect their "peculiar institution." The Christians had discovered Augustine's dictum, "It is better to be a slave of man than a slave of sin." They did not acknowledge the obvious fact that slavery is the instrument of sin for the slaveowner who has arbitrary power over a fellow human being. But the fact that they defended slavery, an obvious defiance of the basic love commandment of the Christian faith, left their consciences uneasy. Therefore evangelicalism hardened into a graceless legalism in which Christians tried to prove their faith by "tithing mint, anise and cummin," by exaggerated prudery in sex behavior and extravagant sabbatarianism. The institution of slavery turned even the sweetest things sour.

The Civil War was fought on the issue of the preservation of the union, not on the issue of slavery. The Emancipation Proclamation issued by President Abraham Lincoln in order to ensure victory for the union had, in the words of a learned historian, "all the eloquence of a bill of lading." The Negro was indeed emancipated. But a decade later the Fourteenth amendment, which was supposed to give him the vote, was circumvented when, as the price for the south's support of Rutherford B. Hayes in the disputed election results of 1876, the north did not insist on enforcement of the enfranchisement. In many states even now, a century after the Civil War, the Negro must fight for the right to vote. Thus one-tenth of our population has been rendered rightless and powerless— the former because of the latter. In this world of self-seeking men the Negro, because of his powerlessness, is being defrauded of opportunity for access to housing, education and employment, as well as of every civil right in regard to which the Constitution had ensured his "equality."

Since this state of affairs has been an affront not only to democratic justice but also to Christian universalism, the Christian church should have championed the cause of these disfranchised people. The complacency of the church has, however, been as great as that of the community at large. It represents an evil in which we are all involved and which should make us sympathetic whenever we are tempted to judge the German people severely for their acquiescence in the racism espoused by the nazis. Meanwhile, the Catholic Church has been truer to the principles of Christian universalism than has Protestantism—though in making that statement one must allow for the fact that it has had no great strength in the south and that its rigor in desegregating parochial schools is a recent development.

Nothing can excuse the abject capitulation of American Protestant Christianity to perpetuation of this social injustice. Our Negro friends are right when they term the Sunday morning church hour the most segregated area of American

life. There were, of course, good reasons for the Negroes to
organize their own churches, and those churches have proved
themselves stalwart in the present crisis. But there has been
no good reason for the absence of fellowship between white
and colored churches. The church has proved to be no resource in efforts to bridge the tremendous gap that yawns between the two separate nations within a single nation.

Protestantism has not supplied a cohesive and tough Christian culture to defy the racism of the American culture. There
have, thank God, been some notable exceptions. Heroic par-
sons have lost their pulpits; many of them, though themselves
southerners, have been able to find pulpits only in northern
suburbs. The student movement has sought to do its part.
I remember with gratitude the student interracial conferences
organized three decades ago in the south by the Christian
Student Federation. In one of them a young miss confessed:
"My mamma said I would vomit if I ate a meal with a Negro.
I have had several meals with Negroes and have not vomited
at all." But we cannot deny that we have all been remiss in
cultivating a Christian universalism in the congregations, and
that frequently an extravagant congregationalism has delivered Christian people from the alleged evils of clericalism
only to place them in subjection to white citizens' councils.

Our failure in the cause of racial justice is the more shock-
ing because the issues are fairly simple. They do not involve
the technical details which had to be mastered when we confronted the issue of economic justice in a modern industrial
society. The law of love, which demands justice, has been
displayed in all its starkness—and we have failed to heed it.

IV

If we speak of the "renewal of the church" in the light of
these failings, it must become clear that renewal will not come
through the fervency of our commitment to the cause of
Christ. The portions of the country most scourged by racism
have probably had more revivals than any other part.

The simple fact is that the evangelistic tradition in American evangelicalism accentuated the failure of a highly indi-

vidualistic version of faith to come to terms with a social evil which is embedded in the mores and customs of the community. We can repent of individual derelictions and defections from general standards of decency and virtue. We can become converted. But the whole community will have to be converted from those mores and customs which defy the ultimate standards of Christian virtue. We have been too individualistic to come to terms with these social sins. The renewal of the church demanded of us now must therefore include encounter with the sins of the community.

The cause of racial justice and the position of the hapless Negro in our culture until the day of his present revolt may serve to point out the issue. The Negro revolt was sparked by an act of emancipation. The Supreme Court was the instrument of that emancipation. The Negroes appealed to the court on the ground that segregated schools violated the Bill of Rights embedded in our Constitution to ensure our citizens "equal protection of the laws." Thus a long-since forgotten right, one drawn from the social ideals of the 18th century, was used to challenge the present customs and inequalities of our culture.

While the Supreme Court ordered desegregated schools "with all deliberate speed," many states and counties have not yet heeded the court order. But the act of emancipation set up the Negro revolt, for revolutions are fed not only by resentments but also by hopes. Intervention of the law suggested that the long night of connivance with the white man's arrogance was over, for the submerged portion of our nation was thus led to protest any form of inequality, injustice or discrimination. We shall probably not experience in this century the end of this significant revolt; it will not spend itself until full justice is achieved.

Two important aspects of the Negro revolt are significant for the renewal of the churches. One is the fact that the Negro church has been renewed in the process of leading the struggle for justice. A clergyman, Martin Luther King, Jr., has become one of the leading citizens of our nation. The Negro church has had its problems; but many of them were resolved when it forgot the minutiae of creed and law and strove for essential justice for its people.

The other important aspect of the present struggle for justice is the fact that the courts used an ancient and purer standard of justice to correct a contemporary and corrupted standard. To be sure, the court had behind it the sovereign authority of the state, while the church has no such supporting authority. But within its own community it has—or ought to have—sufficient authority to use an even older tradition than that of the 18th century to correct the impurities of our present traditions. In dealing with social evils embedded in a culture, we must challenge the culture to repent and reform. Individual conversion, the mark of an individualistic evangelicalism, can deal only with the moral corruptions which violate a general standard. It has never been successful in correcting the standard. The results of heroic individual actions among both the white and the Negro population reveal that there is always room for individual responsibility and response. But these individual acts of heroism, while displaying the freedom of the individual above and beyond the standards of his culture, gain in significance when they are directed to the evils embedded in a culture. Then they display both the individual and the social dimension of our human existence.

Among the many weaknesses of the Protestant movement, surely its indifference to the social substance of human existence is the most grievous one. In an industrial civilization and in an age of nuclear terror, the renewal of the church must certainly include full awareness of the fact that we are all involved in the virtues, the vices, the guilt and the promises of our generation. In a sense it is true that we cannot be saved unless we are all saved.

PART FIVE

TOWARD THE POST-MODERN ERA, 1951–1970

16

JAMES M. GUSTAFSON

Ecumenical Ethicist

James Moody Gustafson (1925–   ) may be regarded as a traditionalist within the context of radical theology, or as a moderate in the debate over situation ethics. Yet his tradition is that of solid and careful scholarship, and it is well attuned to the actualities of the human condition in our time.

James Gustafson was born in Norway, Michigan, a small iron-ore mining town in the Menominee Range, where his father was pastor of the Swedish Mission Covenant Church and a man comparatively liberal and scholarly within the ethos of this pietistic immigrant sect. The elder Gustafson's battles against "rampant fundamentalism and revivalism," his son recalls, "formed the spiritual crisis of the family"[1] and suggested to young James the possibility of a larger perspective. A historical account of the religious backgrounds of the Swedish immigrants, which he read in his father's study, gave rise to a nascent cultural relativism and kindled an interest in sociology and history as means of liberation from an atmosphere he found increasingly restrictive.

Gustafson was scarcely five years old when the Depression descended and the mines were closed. Poverty and social injustice were much in evidence—he often heard of the mine owners' failure to provide compensation to men injured at work, and the face of unemployment was grim and real. He was thirteen when the family moved to Scranton, Kansas, another poverty-stricken rural community near Topeka. The

---

[1] Quotations, unless otherwise attributed, are from a letter by James M. Gustafson to the editor, dated 16 August 1968.

coming of World War II, however, proved to be pivotal for his life. In the fall of 1942, Gustafson enrolled as a business administration major at a denominational college in Chicago. He found its ethos "morally repressive and intellectually stifling," but among his fellow students he met a conscientious objector with whom he became friends. Their conversations sharpened his moral sensibility. He did not share his friend's stand, but it made his decision to go into the army a matter of conscientious choice rather than mere acquiescence. In 1944 he entered active duty in the U.S. Army Engineers and served in Assam and Central Burma. After his discharge in 1946, he resumed his studies as a sociology major at Northwestern University, where he read most of the works of George Herbert Mead before receiving his B. S. degree in 1948. Many of his courses had an ethical thrust—criminology, the family, race relations, sociology of religion—and his cultural relativism was nourished by anthropology. At the Federated Theological Faculty of the University of Chicago, where he decided to study for the ministry, he found further sociological terrain to cover. His most influential teacher was James Luther Adams, under whose stimulus he avidly read Ernst Troeltsch and Max Weber and wrote his B. D. thesis on Weber's methodology. Under Daniel Day Williams he was introduced to the ethical thought of Reinhold Niebuhr and the theology of Henry Nelson Wieman. "But it was the reading of H. R. Niebuhr's *The Meaning of Revelation* which was most illuminating for my theological development, coming out of the social science concerns."

Not till his last year at Chicago did Gustafson decide upon graduate studies and chose Yale. During his three years there, he served as pastor of a Congregational church in nearby Northford, an experience as vital for his understanding of the theology and sociology of the church as were the writings of P. T. Forsyth and Daniel Jenkins on the church and its ministry, which had a direct bearing on his work. Among his professors, Kenneth Underwood was a powerful influence, combining "disciplined social analysis, policy thinking, ethics and theology in a most complex and creative way." But his association with Richard Niebuhr was of incalculable importance, particularly in the year he served (1954–55) as assistant director of the Study of Theological Education in America. Following his Ph. D. (1955), he remained Niebuhr's colleague as instructor in ethics. Since 1963 he has been professor of Christian ethics in both Yale Divinity School and in the graduate faculty's department of religious studies. There his interests have ranged from the sociology of religion to social ethics and increasingly theological and philosophical ethics. Ethics can be construed in a variety of ways, and in addition to those already mentioned, Gustafson has studied papal social encyclicals, engaged in discussions with Catholic political scientists and, as a result, developed a specialized interest in the moral theology of Thomas Aquinas and of present-day moral theologians such as Bernard Häring. He has also found biology and medical technology an area of ethical concern and has written informed papers on the uses of brain research and on the question of abortion.

Gustafson is the author of two books—*Treasure in Earthen Vessels: The Church As a Human Community* (1961) and *Christ and the Moral Life* (1968). His reputation as a Christian ethical philosopher is firmly established, although only in the 1960s and particularly since about 1965 has he begun to emerge as an authoritative voice. It is still too soon to estimate his stature among other men in his field and of his generation. The following selection, dating from 1959, does not represent the highest level of his achievement. It is of interest, as one of the first and best efforts of Christian ethicists to assess the impact of the technological revolution. Its kinship to the theology and ethics of Richard Niebuhr is evident, both in its neo-orthodox concept of God and in its sensitivity to empirical fact. The validity of such an interpretation speaks for itself, and the questions it raises have retained their relevance. It is perhaps worth noting that here as elsewhere the emphases are more empirical, more sociological than would tend to be typical of Niebuhr. Although it speaks from a perspective of Christian concern, it does so with that secular accent and that sense of the present and future that distinguishes the technological era. As the article itself makes clear, the "technological society" dates back at least to the era of the Social Gospel. What is less self-evident, perhaps, is that its full revolutionary force has only begun to be felt since the decade in which this essay was written, and it has only been recognized as such in the 1960s.

CHRISTIAN ATTITUDES TOWARD A TECHNOLOGICAL SOCIETY*

A technological society is a society of disenchantment. We generally assume that disenchantment is a mark of maturity. A child's world is an enchanting world. The patterns of ice and frost on the windows on cold February mornings lead to awesome delight, and give credibility to the wonderful story of Jack Frost. They are not problems to be solved scientifically and objects to be removed by better control of temperature and humidity. Expressions of parental fondness in spontaneous marks of affection are delightfully received at their face value, not phenomena to be interpreted by concepts from depth psychology or explained by statistical correlations between such moments of affection and the lack of tension during the course of one's work in kitchen or in office. The child often delights in the novel, the unexpected, the unanswerable things that take place in the course of his day. He is in a world of enchantment: fear, wonder, awe, delight. Primitive responses are the stuff of his world. Adulthood involves disenchantment of the world. It depreciates the elements of wonder and fear, of delight and awe. Adulthood involves growing rationality.

The technological society is hard put to appreciate enchantment. The artist protests the rationalization of the world with his own forms of deeply personal expression. But men geared to the dominant motifs of a technical age have some difficulty in appreciating the childlikeness of the artist. Tech-

° From *Theology Today*, XVI, 2 (July 1959), pp. 173–187. Reprint by permission of *Theology Today*.

nical man's concerns are not directed to simplicity in observation and the profundity of more primitive expressions of
delight or fear. The forest is potential lumber, the mystery
of matter is potential energy, words and ideas are potential
means of human persuasion and manipulation. Persons are
functions, potential producers and consumers. A technological
society gets on with its business when the elements of mystery
can be reduced if not eliminated. It seeks in every possible
way to push out the limit beyond which lies the uncontroll-
able, the unpredictable, the discontinuities. The elements of
childlikeness remain for purposes of leisure; they are moments
of relaxation, of refuge from rationality. They provide the
occasional overtones that keep the melody and theme from
becoming monotonous. At worst, the world of enchantment
itself becomes something we rationally create in order to relieve ourselves from the dominant world of rationality. For the
sake of his participation in a technological society any rational
man takes a vacation, visits the Metropolitan Museum, crowds
the highways on sunny Sunday afternoons, gets a good sun
tan, reads Shakespeare and Dostoyevsky, and drinks martinis.
We can rationally induce enchantment, and rationally reduce
rationality with a good stiff drink.

I

The spirit of disenchantment and rationality is not without
its Christian origins, though other factors are also involved.
The primitive and childlike response of enchantment seems
to imply the excessive holiness of created things. Wonder and
awe are the responses of persons who seem to believe that
there is an irreducible sanctity to nature. To profane this
sanctity is to abuse it; to make the world so awesome is to
assume that somehow the deity resides in things. But we can
have a calculating attitude toward the world because, we are
informed by Christian thought, the world is not God. We can
treat the world with intellectual ruthlessness because it is the
realm of the creation, and not the place in which God resides.
The spirit of the child, and often the spirit of the artist, is
akin to that of the primitive man who believes that an un-

controllable power, *mana*, resides in birds and trees, in rocks and volcanoes. The spirit of a technological society does not deny that potency exists in these things, but the potency is devoid of the primitive aesthetic-religious significance it has for the simple mind. This is pragmatically justified, for the dreadful consequences assumed to be forthcoming in the profaning of the world do not come. But the attitude of rationality in relation to the created world is theologically justified as well; God and the world are separate. We ought not treat the world with a reverence, awe, and respect properly reserved for God.

Further, in the spirit of much of Protestant life there is an ethical impulse to rationality that has contributed to the development of the technological society. Much of classical and pietistic Protestantism has nurtured what Weber and Ernst Troeltsch have characterized as a "this-worldly asceticism." The self-denial is inward; it is denial of ostentatious display of virtue or abundance, the denial of satisfaction from worldly gain and pleasure. Yet it impels a compulsive duty to busyness, to hard work, to disciplined life in the world. As Weber has pointed out, the maxims we all remember from Benjamin Franklin, such as "early to bed and early to rise makes a man healthy, wealthy, and wise," are secularized expressions of what has been the religious duty of man in much of Protestant life. Rationality is a religious duty; the moral life is judged by the virtues that lead to achievement in a technological society. Thus the technological society is not related simply to the secular elements of our social history, but is grounded in religious elements themselves: the treatment of the world as created and not as the abode of the Creator, and the this-worldly asceticism of Protestant life.

The spirit of our technological society is the spirit of rationality. It involves the reduction of elements of mystery, with concentration on elements of predictability, calculation, and manipulation of things and persons. Knowledge has as its end not the inner joy of finding a new harmony of the spheres, but usefulness in the human control of human destiny. Economies, social organization, philanthropies, science, education, welfare governments, concentrations of economic, political, and social power—all these things are based upon the implications of rationality. The ends for which these things work, unfortunately, are not as universal as the spirit that informs them. Calculation and manipulation can serve evil masters and reasonably good ones. They can become expressions of self-interest, of the interest of the nation or a particular social segment of mankind, or presumably can be responsibly used in a more universal loyalty. But the existence of rationality, and its implications in calculation and manipulation of persons and things, informs our society and in turn is nourished by it.

Many of the specific aspects of the society in which we live manifest its spirit. Industrialization, a process beginning perhaps with the lever and culminating for us in automation, manifests man's ability to know how to use elements of nature, energy, and humanity in a productive way. Urbanization as the dominant social pattern in the industrialized world is an expression of the need for concentration of labor force, the division of labor, the complexity of processes needed in industrialization. The benefits and the ills of urban existence are both the creatures of the more fundamental spirit. The more recent concerns for a continued increase in productivity, with its consequent requirements for a revision of our assessments of what we need in order to survive, is a fruit of rationality. The whole process requires that persons be able to entice our consumer habits so that money may circulate more rapidly. Power is required to direct and correlate the processes of a technological society. Social power concentrates itself in large scale social organizations: corporations, trade unions, political parties, governments. The immediate world to which we are related is less and less raw nature of Divine creation, and more and more the culture created by men. Even the most "natural" of occupations, farming, finds a vast world created by men standing between the farmer and the soil, between the farmer and the animal. Commercial fertilizers supplement manure, milking machines remove the simple pleasure of talking to a cow while draining her milk, tractors replace horses. Man is increasingly dependent upon the world created by men; he is less and less dependent upon the immediacies of raw nature given in creation. Perhaps he is also increasingly separated from those realities which remind him that he is not his own author and does not control his own destiny. Or, perhaps in this regard technological society has simply reduced the little crises that confront man in favor of a great crisis with far greater consequences.

Technological society is a rationalized society. It proceeds on the basis of human ability to know and control the course of events. It enlarges the sphere of our dependence upon the things created by man. It feeds on human ability to calculate the factors involved in any decision and action, and to manipulate these factors so that the consequences sought and predicted by men can be achieved. It is a society that seeks to overcome contingency and create its own novelty. It sets farther off the time and place when man acknowledges his limitations, and in turn acknowledges his dependence upon the Divine.

II

How have Christians responded to the rise of a technological society? What have been the characteristics of the attitudes of sensitive religious souls to a "thingified" world? What assessments have been made of the relative goods and evils that have come into our history from man's drive toward rationality?

Christians, like sensitive humanists, have been caught in the moral ambiguities of our modern society. In the main they have not condemned social developments as absolutely demonic, nor have they welcomed them as signs of the appearing of the Kingdom of God. Indeed, with reference to modern society Christians have had to face a perennial problem in the history of their moral community. It appears that God has called us to live in a given time and place. What is given is not the creation simply of the generation of the present for whom it is provided. The forms of social organization and technology are not of the making of our generation. They are the present shape of an historical process rooted far into the history of the human race. Just as the primitive Church did not choose to come into being in the Roman Empire, and did not choose to have to hammer its convictions out in relation to Gnostic and mystery religions, so we Christians did not choose to face questions thrust upon us by our own society. Rather, we are faced with a given shape of the concrete world, and its own patterns are not always susceptible to the reshaping we might wish to do if we could begin *de novo,* creating our social world *ex nihilo.* The givenness of our society must be accepted, at least in general.

Christians have been dubious about how they ought to be related to this given society for at least two major reasons. First, its fruits appear to be both good and evil for man. Men are healthier because of technology; the distribution of food and basic materials for the preservation of life has been more just because of the abundance of things we can now produce. Technology has eased the sheer physical burdens of work so that not all man's energy is consumed by labor; many comforts and pleasures that were limited at one time to a wealthy few are now available to all. Perhaps if our society had reached a crisis in which some either-or decision about its basic goodness or its basic evil had to be made, some of our dubiousness would be removed. But there is no such crisis in the minds of most of us in the middle of American abundance, a relative degree of peace, and a modest amount of excitement. There are no clear grounds for the total rejection of modern social and technical patterns. Thus we have to wrestle with obscurity and ambiguity in our relation to them.

It is not only the presence of immediate signs of both badness and goodness, however, that causes us consternation. It is also the conviction of our faith that this modern world is in some measure ordered by God. Such a conviction is baffling when we look at contemporary events in its light. We deny that God resides in the social forms, or in nature, and thus we can treat these things with some profaneness. But we also affirm that the ordering of life is ultimately in the power of God, and that the world in which we live speaks to us of his sustaining life, and indeed of his redeeming love. Christians face the difficult question of determining at what point the technical and social order has reached such a degree of corruption that it no longer reflects God's order, but must be questioned and perhaps altered, or even destroyed.

Such a determination is more difficult because in God's grace we have been granted an inner freedom from absolute determination by the world in which we live. We are not bound to the contemporary forms of life; we are freed to live within them without their being the final locus of our fears and hopes. There is an otherworldliness in the Christian life that gives an emancipation from the immediacies of this world. Yet it impels us to act in this world, for the Lord who has given us the modern world as the place in which we are called to live impels us in both joy and in duty to be responsible to Him in this place.

Fortunately, Christians have not been satisfied simply to say that the world is full of ambiguities and, therefore, that all things are equally corrupt and equally good. There are tendencies in this direction in the ethics of Karl Barth, but Barth is by no means the dominant Christian ethicist in the Churches. Barth can say, "Trust your own understanding"; he can avoid the level of relative moral discriminations because of his singleness of vision, looking only at the goodness of God. Why is the act of the Christian good? Not because of its moral consequences with reference to the neighbor, but because God is good; because God has redeemed the world, and the Christian knows this. Moral calculation is not an important vocation for Christians; they believe in Jesus Christ. But such a point of view is possible because the Christian who expresses it is not in a systematic conversation with the multiplicity of what is given in the world.

Ambiguity is present, and Christians have wrestled with it. The social gospel movement in American Christianity, often oversimplified as an optimistic humanism, really came into being because of the disorders in an industrialized society. The inner impulse of love and grace was challenged by the external conditions of labor in Massachusetts factories, and life in industrialized and urbanized communities such as New

York and Chicago. Washington Gladden, Graham Taylor, Rauschenbusch, and others of our fathers in American Christian social movements were appalled by the human consequences of the technological society of their time. They were not swept up into the glory of its moral possibilities; rather, they were moved by the dislocations that accompanied man's increased power to bring other men under his control. The hope of increased democratization and socialization of centers of power and of the benefits of an industrial economy was tempered by the realization that such benefits would not come apart from a struggle. The movement was a call to action, not a call to allow the certain course of history, either in Spenser's or Marx's understanding of the certainty, to take its way toward the finally harmonious society on earth. Each man had to choose with whom he was to act in order to bring a greater degree of justice into American society. There were no clean white parties to join, no certain loyalties to which one could forever be committed. For some, socialism provided the proper answer; for others, the progressivism of Theodore Roosevelt; for still others, politics farther to the right. But the motif of hope for historical achievement was tempered by the motif of consternation at what man had wrought in the human dislocations of the American economy and its social order. The technological society appeared to distort man's humanity, to create hideous situations in which millworkers and immigrants lived, and to make possible the vast differentiation between the wealth of the entrepreneurs and the poverty and uncertainties of the laborers. Action was required, not theological reflection.

Out of this movement men went in various directions. Some were called to the work of ameliorating the consequences of social upheaval in settlement houses, social work, and institutional churches. Others were called to speak for the right of labor to organize, to condemn the "robber barons" and their power. Others felt that nothing less than a serious reconstruction of the whole society would be needed. The Word of the Lord seemed to them, as it did to the dissenting sectarians of seventeenth century England, to call for radical socialization of property, and a reform of almost every human institution. Technology was accepted; the ordering of it and its implications for humanity had to be rectified.

Alongside of the pioneer Christian critics of the industrial society stood those Christians who invoked the blessing of the Almighty indiscriminatingly upon the men of power and wealth. Men like Andrew Carnegie sought to find a moral basis for this success, and turned to the seemingly natural law of competition to justify it. They were met half-way by clergymen, who assured them that God was on their side. Bishop William Lawrence of Massachusetts wrote in 1901 that man could recognize two guiding principles in his life. First, that it is "his divine mission to conquer Nature, open up her resources, and harness them to his service." The second is that "in the long run, it is only to the man of morality that wealth comes," for "Godliness is in league with riches." (Quoted by Sidney Mead, "From Denominationalism to Americanism," *Journal of Religion,* Vol. 36, p. 10.) Henry Ward Beecher, in the flush of Civil War victory, spoke with assurance for the industrialized Northeastern region of our country,

> "We are to have charge of this continent. The South has been proved, and has been found wanting. She is not worthy to bear rule. She has lost the scepter of our national government. . . . And this continent is to be from this time forth governed by Northern men, with Northern ideas, and with a Northern gospel" (*Ibid.,* p. 7).

Such arrogant assurance that God was on the side of industrialization, particularly as was represented by the Protestant entrepreneurs of this region, is superseded only by the often quoted remark of one George F. Baer of the Philadelphia and Reading Railway.

> "The rights and interests of the laboring man will be protected and cared for—not by the labor agitators, but by the Christian men to whom God in His infinite wisdom has given control of the property interests of the country, and upon the successful Management of which so much depends." (*Ibid,* p. 11.)

In spite of suffering caused by the rapid social change that came with industrialization, and by the boom and bust cycle of the economy, the hand of God was upon those who gained power in the struggle for survival.

III

The heirs of the critics, and the heirs of those who saw the development of the technological society as the inexorable historical realization of the will of God, are both with us today. The critics have many concerns: they are concerned for the depersonalization that occurs when men become objects to be manipulated by other men of power. They acknowledge the element of social and economic power that is necessary for the establishment of any rectification in the social disorder. They are sensitive to the implications of a technological society of abundance in the midst of a world dominated by insufficiencies of almost every kind. Alongside of the critics are those who believe that God willed the free market system by which economy, technology, and society are to be governed. Indeed, the passionate faith in the free market system expressed by its religious defenders is far greater than the working faith of men of social power in this tin god. Alongside of those who maintain a prophetic and critical distance from the current manifestations of rationalization, acknowledging its ambiguity and seeking to be responsible within uncertainty, are those for whom competitiveness is God, and the fruits of the present society are good in so far as they manifest competition and bad in so far as competition has been tempered by the other concerns. By almost all the canons of judgment, the responsible critics are worthy of more attention. The believers in a pantheistic God, who no longer resides in nature but in the economy of a technological society, are not.

Among the critics there are important differences. Many of these are along a scale, beginning at one point with rejection of the modern society as a fit society for Christian blessing, and moving in the direction of greater acceptance of this society and its particular structures in mass communications, automation, and other institutions as the "given" within which responsible action occurs.

One pattern of criticism stems from a romantic Christian detachment. T. S. Eliot suggests in *The Idea of a Christian Society* that a Christian society can better be established on an agricultural and piscatorial economy than a modern industrial one. We often have a latent nostalgia for the country, where presumably life was ordered, secure, moral, and good. But such dreams are illusive; even fishing and farming are mechanized. There is no new place to which we can go to establish this Christian society. An important principle underlies this point of view. It is that the *natural* is Christian, and that the natural is close to nature in a double sense. Presumably the Christian and natural life can best occur when the cultural world created by man is minimized, or at least the mechanical aspects of it are minimized. Also there is a *moral* order of nature in the fabric of man and his relations to other men that can be known and can be actualized historically. The technological society seems to distort man's true nature. At least it is more difficult for man to become what he truly is in modern society than it was in some simpler society.

An acceptance of the view that the society is good which enables man to be what he essentially and truly is, does not lead to romantic-nostalgia in all its supporters. On the part of the contemporary Roman Catholic social movement an aggressive pattern of ideas and action has been formulated out of which the modern society can be bent to some extent into the image of the natural society, the society given in the moral law of nature. An example can illustrate this response of Christians to the technological society. God's order of nature brings into being human families. It requires stability within the family; basic physical and spiritual needs must be met. The family is a moral order, sacred in its own right as a creation of God. Any social forces which tend to destroy this order must be evaluated critically. Certainly an industrial society, with urbanization and all the pressures of rapid social change and mobility, makes the actualization of the true nature of the family difficult. A more stable rural society provided better conditions within which the proper relation of parents to children, families to other families, and all to the full order of nature could occur. New conditions require new directions by implication from the understanding of man's nature. An industrial family needs a living wage; it needs to have enough money so that its physical and spiritual potentialities can be realized. The wages of workers, then, must be just. But justice of wage is not measured according to productivity alone, or according to a determined proportion of the total cost of operation. Justice is measured according to what the family requires. How is such justice achieved? In part by the organization of labor so that workers can gain their rightful share. In part by state family subsidies if necessary. In part by a reorganization of the society and economy itself in which the interests of all groups will be rightfully considered. The realization of the natural will be achieved only by action on the part of Christians, and indeed the Church itself, to bend the forces of our social order to the right moral pattern that exists in life. The order is essentially good; there is an ontological order that exists and is not destroyed. The Christian response to a contemporary social order is to bring it into such a shape that it more clearly manifests the true order. This requires action.

Christian critics, Catholic and Protestant alike, have been concerned for the existence of a personal society, in which there can be a full flowering of the spiritual and aesthetic aspects of man's nature. For the Catholic a society which does not provide the conditions under which personal existence can flourish is disordered, for the spiritual aspects of man's nature are the distinctive thing about the human species. Catholics object to the "thingification" of man in Communism and nineteenth century entrepreneurial capitalism alike. They sometimes object to the use of manipulative devices to extort confessions out of men. They are ill at ease when the sheer preservation of life through labor leaves no time for religious and cultural pursuits. Protestants also view the self as something enchanting—something not to be reduced to the central nervous system and its interactions, or to a thing to be directed by centers of power in the hands of men, no matter under what auspices and by what motivation.

An extreme example of the rationalization of man sets the problem sharply. Religious men are concerned with the success of the motivation manipulators, though the success is not proved, for they wonder how far man's control of other men can go before some rebellion springs up from within. But the Dr. Dichters and the mass communicators are working with peanuts compared with the potential of research in the exploration of the brain. Dr. Jose Delgado of Yale has continued research in the control of motor activity of monkeys through the implantation of electrodes in their brains. Monkeys, at man's will, can be made to look up, extend their arms, or gag. They can enjoy a delicious banana until stimulated through an electrode, and then suddenly spit it out in disgust. Using the pain and pleasure centers of the monkey's brain, the experimenter can keep him docile, or arouse his ire. Indeed, with electronic devices Dr. Delgado has been able to experiment by remote control (*Reporter*, May 15, 1958). We have learned that many things that work on monkeys work also on man. In the hands of morally responsible physicians fine things can come about. In the hands of some one else, we invite social chaos and the degeneration of man as this earth has known him. Who controls the panel for remote control?

Christians have asked before such techniques were discovered: What is finally inviolable about man? The depersonalization has taken place in many ways. Relationships with people are segmented in character; we recognize others as the girl who sells us our cigarettes, or the man who delivers the milk. We are led to believe that people are controlling our deepest recesses of response through their use of appealing symbols and images, but we dare not become totally suspicious of being used. If we did we would be paranoid, and the whole fabric of society which rests heavily on common confidence in each other would deteriorate. "No man wants to put on nut #999 until he becomes nut #999," Kermit Eby used to say. The simple mechanization of human energy turned out to be unproductive, so Taylorism with its time and motion studies is not so much in vogue. But out of the new concern came more subtle forms of depersonalization: the ethos of organization man in which, in the name of being persons, we play life's game under rules never brought out into the open.

Christians assume something enchanting, awesome, and irreducible about man. Indeed, his moral integrity and his religious relationships are grounded in the more ineffable aspects of man. The capacity to be morally responsible, to engage in purposive action, assumes a "terminal individual" (J. N. Hartt's phrase), a being not totally conditioned by its relationships, not subject to complete cause-effect analysis, more than the sum of its relationships.

The picture of depersonalization is often overdrawn. Mass producers in factories were found to thrive on the moments of play in lunch hours, and to fit themselves into a status system in their work rooms. Family life, for all the institutions that fulfill its former functions, remains deeply personal, indeed almost exclusively personal. The "meaninglessness" that has been decried *ad nauseam* appears to be truer for many on the fringes than for those in the main stream of life. Our Marjorie Morningstars go through their existential quandaries, and settle down fairly happily in the suburbs. Overdrawn or not, depersonalization remains a concern. The Jew Buber, the Christians Brunner and Tillich, and many others see this as a great problem in our time. Maritain seeks a humanistic society in which the fulness of personal existence is possible. Tillich suggests that "the person as a person can preserve himself only by a *partial non-participation in* the objectifying structures of technical society" (J. Hutchison, *Christian Faith and Social Action,* p. 151).

For some, the concern for the personal is a flight from the technological society. Churches, out of distrust in the anonymity of existence in "mass" society, find a partial answer in the establishment of intimate cells, or small groups in the congregations. Here one can be oneself; one need not be a "role," or a function. Here grace is made real through the intimacy of personal relationships. Like all Christian responses to a technological society, this is subject to distortions from within. Coziness is no substitute for moral responsibility in human existence. Fellow-feeling is no substitute for the anxiety of having to face hard decisions and to act. Indeed, the romantic memory of the intimate warmth of the small group sometimes appears to be a reconstruction of the pleasures presumably found in the stable, quiet, rural communities, communities which were not as pleasant as we sometimes now think they were. Actually, the Church has to confront the question of what Christian community is and is not in an urban society. Some have answered that it is a personal community. It is the transplantation of the rural church into the city. Others are not so certain. Personal community may simply reinforce the class prejudices of its members, the pleasures of being secure. Indeed, it may, as in Buchmanism, become so concerned about personal sins and personal virtues that it loses touch with the rationalized society in which it lives. Perhaps, though, personal communities can be a place of renewal out of which people move with new faith and moral commitment into their stations in the world.

How much of the rationalized society does one accept as the place in which he must live and act? How much can one change this structure? Another distinction made by Weber and Troeltsch is helpful here. It is between the ethic of conscience and the ethic of cultural responsibility, or the difference between exemplary prophetism and emissary prophetism. The ethic of conscience would say that the Christian vocation is to witness to a new order of life without worrying too much about relevance and one's responsibility for the preservation of cultural values—like the preservation of democracy against Nazi or Soviet totalitarianism. The ethic of cultural values would say that what is, is partially good. The proper response is to conserve the good that exists against threats of greater evils, to make moral discriminations about the relative values of things in the present order. Some would bear prophetic witness by being examples of the possibilities of a new creation; others, by moving into the established patterns of society and identifying themselves to the extent of being able to effect some small change. The conditions, they would say, under which the Christian life must be lived are set by the world. Take it as it is, act responsibly within it, exert influence and power to change it where you can, and hope in the mercy of God that the consequences will not be too bad.

I would hazard the guess that many Christians have not accepted the existence of *any* moral question in the rationalized world. They do take it, act within it, and hope for the best. But this is different from the prophetic consciousness that impels much of the best in contemporary American Christianity. Christian prophetism accepts certain conditions under which life must be lived and action taken, but it does not accept these conditions without question. It does not accept them as *per se* the gift of God, or *per se* the rule of life. The subtlety of Christian ethics of cultural responsibility lies in its acceptance of the relativities of a social order and technology precisely *as relative*. Power exists—physical energy, economic, military and political power, the capacity to order the course of events within limitations in various realms of life including the personal. Accept the conditions, yes. But all power exists by the power of God; all power is responsible to God; all power is potentially an expression of the divine purpose. Social and personal power, in whatever its rationalized forms, is not in itself good or ultimate. It is something to which Christians must be relatively related while they are absolutely related to God, as Kierkegaard suggests (*Postscript*). There is a rightful relativity to our social structures, our technology, and our economy. Society exists for the sake of man; man and the world exist for the sake of the glory of God. Indeed, these things exist because God has ordered life in such a manner that they come into existence. But their proper existence depends upon their being rightly related to the absolute power and the absolute good, and to the welfare of man. Politics, production of goods, technical discovery, and the whole realm of things made by man are neither to be denied nor embraced without question.

The Christian prophetism we have known, for example in the life and work of Reinhold Niebuhr, has a delicate stance in relation to the world. Man is freed from domination by his society; he does not justify himself according to its norms and standards, but is justified by what God has done for man in

Jesus Christ. In his inward freedom man can accept both his own moral ambiguity and the moral ambiguity of the world in which he lives. But his inward freedom gives him freedom to act, taking responsibility without assuming absolute responsibility (which is in the hand of God). Indeed, as Luther, Calvin, Bonhoeffer, Barth, Maurice, and others have helped us to see, God calls us to witness to his power and grace in a concrete world.

The rationalized world is our world in this generation. Its physical scope now extends beyond the limits of the earth. If it is the work of the devil, the devil has created a thing that is awesome and wonderful to behold. If it is the immediate work of God, it is terribly incomplete and deformed. If it is the work of man alone, why did he not do better? How did he manage to do so well? The delight in being human is that we must wrestle with the question of what our right relation to technological society, in very specific forms, is. Our right relation is complex, for we are related not only for the world, but to God who has ordered and redeemed it and us.

17

THOMAS J. J. ALTIZER

Visionary Theologian

Thomas Jonathan Jackson Altizer (1927–   ) first came to prominence in April 1966, when *Time* Magazine published a cover story, "Is God Dead?" Soon thereafter a volume of essays by Altizer and William Hamilton appeared under the title, *Radical Theology and the Death of God.* Six months later, Hamilton organized a three-day conference at the University of Michigan, and by the following year a spate of books appeared; then the excitement subsided. The question remained.

A descendant of General Thomas Jonathan "Stonewall" Jackson, Altizer was born in Cambridge, Mass., but grew up in Stonewall's native West Virginia. From early childhood he had an abiding interest in religion which never slackened, although it took a variety of directions—Judaism, Catholicism, Marxism, Barthianism, Oriental mysticism—in addition to the indigenous evangelical Christian earnestness with which each of them has been blended.

After serving in the U. S. Army Air Force at the close of World War II, including a brief period in Japan, Altizer enrolled at the University of Chicago, receiving his B.A. in 1948. He went on to the Divinity School, intending to become an Episcopal priest, but decided against ordination and took an M.A. in theology (1951), followed by a Ph. D. in the history of religions under Joachim Wach (1955). Altizer's first mature theological commitment was to the dogmatics of Karl Barth, but he subsequently became fascinated, through Wach and Mircea Eliade, with the myths and symbols of Hinduism, Buddhism, and Gnosticism; and he found in Tillich a theology more congenial to the religious perspective of the latter. He did not move from Barth to Tillich, however, but began early to shape an outlook of his own in which Hegel, Nietzsche, and Blake played formative roles. How well the Altizerian synthesis holds together may be questioned, but it is a distinctive and original one—something more than the sum of its parts.

The theology of Karl Barth has been variously termed "dialectical theology" and "the theology of the Word." God, for Barth, is absolutely transcendent or "wholly other," yet he acts in history decisively through his revelation in Jesus Christ, "the Word made flesh." A brief quotation can hardly do justice to the richness of Barth's full statement, but here is enough to suggest why he is able to insist on the uniqueness of Christian faith and to distinguish Christianity from "religion":

> His [God's] Word remains a comforting announcement to *all* fellow men of the one Son of God, an announcement calling for repentance and faith. It is God's good Word about his good work in the midst, and for the good, of all creation. It is a Word directed to all peoples and nations of all times and places. . . . The Christ of Israel is the Savior of the world.[1]

Altizer would agree with virtually all of the above statements, but he adds that the God who for Barth is radically transcendent is dead, that the historic event of the incarnation opens a new and dynamic phase of the dialectic between God and man—or, as Altizer transposes it, between spirit and flesh, between the sacred and the profane. His first book, *Oriental Mysticism and Biblical Eschatology* (1961), examines the Christian concept of the Kingdom of God in comparison with the Buddhist concept of *nirvana* and similar ideas about man's ultimate destiny.

Throughout his writings, the death of the transcendent God looms as a pivotal datum. Man in the modern era has experienced the "loss of transcendence," the absence or eclipse of God. For Altizer, this is not only a fact of human experience, however, but a clue to a large historic and cosmic truth—that

---

[1] Karl Barth, *Evangelical Theology* (New York: Holt, 1963), p. 23. See also Barth, *The Epistle to the Romans* [1918] (Oxford University Press, 1933), pp. 341, 363–366, wherein Barth distinguishes "the eternal and absolute Word of God" from "religion," characterizing the latter as "a human work."

the Word, having become incarnate in human existence through Jesus, is now radically and irreversibly immanent. In a sense, Altizer has taken Barth's affirmation of the sovereignty of God seriously enough to insist that God's self-giving in Christ was without remainder. In his summation of this logic in *The Gospel of Christian Atheism* (1966), Altizer abandons traditional or "religious" Christianity and proclaims the full force of God's redemptive death:

> It is God who becomes Jesus and not Jesus who becomes God. The forward movement of the Incarnate Word is from God to Jesus, and the Word continues its kenotic movement and direction by moving from the historical Jesus to the universal body of humanity.[2]

The traditional "Word of faith", which continues to affirm the transcendent deity, cannot be a living or liberating faith, for it confines itself to "the repressive authority of the past."[3] True faith involves not so much remembrance as vision—apocalyptic insight into the promise and potential of the future, of that which Jesus spoke of as the Kingdom of God and which William Blake called "the Divine Humanity." Traditional or "religious" Christianity, with its dead orthodoxy and its closed revelation, does not worship the living God, says Altizer; rather, it perpetuates the sovereignty of the dead God of transcendence. It is not possible to return to the authentic faith of primitive Christianity, but it is both possible and necessary to embrace a radical Christian vision for the present epoch, which will carry forward the process begun earlier and hindered by orthodoxy. The promise of man's liberation from the external authority of the dead God of tradition can be fulfilled only through the divinization of humanity in the ongoing process of incarnation. Altizer's kenotic Christ in some ways resembles the self-fulfilled "free spirit" of Nietzsche, and in others the Jesus of Blake's *Jerusalem.* The composite image

---

[2] Thomas J. J. Altizer, *The Gospel of Christian Atheism* (Philadelphia: Westminster, 1966), p. 83. See also Thomas W. Ogletree, *The Death of God Controversy* (Nashville: Abingdon, 1966), and William Robert Miller, *Goodbye, Jehovah* (New York: Walker, 1969).
[3] Altizer, *The New Apocalypse: The Radical Christian Vision of William Blake* (Michigan State University Press, 1967), p. xv.

is of man become fully human and fully free—human rather than isolated in selfhood, free to live and to love, to achieve unrestricted community and brotherhood.

The essay that follows does not present Altizer's theology in its fullness. The idea of the death of God is there, but not yet developed; the idea of the Kingdom of God has not yet evolved into that of the Divine Humanity. But it is of interest precisely because its transitional character affords a glimpse of the genesis and direction of Altizer's thought, which may not be apparent in its more fully developed form. In this essay, as in most of his writing to date, the total absence of any visible roots in the traditions of American religious thought is strikingly evident. The closest he comes to any discussion of America is in a paper, "Theology and the Contemporary Sensibility" (1965), dealing not with the American experience but with William Blake's *America* and Herman Melville's *Moby-Dick* as these symbolically express the death of God.[4]

It is nevertheless worth noting that the death-of-God theologies as a whole and in their full variety arose in the 1960s, each as a departure from Barthianism. All of them were developed by Americans, and those most consistently radical, of whom Altizer is perhaps the leading example, moved rapidly to conclusions prefigured in earlier types of American theology—Christocentric humanism or radical immanence, a renewal of the Kingdom of God, an assertion of freedom and loyalty in contrast to obedience and external authority.[5]

In 1968, after a decade of professor of Bible and religion at Emory University in Atlanta, Altizer was appointed professor of English at the State University of New York at Stony Brook. The turbulence on many American campuses in the closing years of the decade, together with his engagement with

---

[4] In William A. Beardslee, ed., *America and the Future of Theology* (Philadelphia: Westminster, 1967), pp. 15–31. See also Charles H. Long, "The Ambiguities of Innocence," *Ibid.*, pp. 41–51, which offers the beginnings of a creative alternative.

[5] These themes, of course, are not exclusively American. See John C. Cooper, *The Roots of the Radical Theology* (Philadelphia: Westminster, 1967) and William Robert Miller, ed., *The New Christianity* (New York: Delacorte, 1967).

a different kind of student, give a sense of revolutionary urgency to Altizer's book, *The Descent into Hell*,[6] which draws heavily upon literature and politics as well as biblical thought and Eastern mysticism. He reaffirms the death of God, but carries the radical immanence forward, toward a more explicit consideration of the path leading to the fulfilment of Blake's vision of the Divine Humanity—a path of revolutionary struggle that is no simple ascent to perfection but, on the contrary, involves immersion in the crucible of risky conflict. As in *The Gospel of Christian Atheism*, with its Nietzschean references to a dialectical phase of chaos, negation, and meaninglessness, man has to "go through hell" in order to achieve self-realization as person and as community. The revolutionary student movement in America and elsewhere, in its confrontation with the established authorities, provides Altizer with a key illustration of this development, particularly the emergence of new community and new value configurations. In short, such a movement represents a social re-enactment of Jesus' crucifixion, descent, and resurrection, and is thus a source of hope, though not unproblematical.

The selection that follows predates Altizer's public emergence as a death-of-God theologian, and it is ostensibly far removed from a politically radical Christianity; yet the visionary dialectic is present and his subsequent major themes are prefigured in it. At a minimum, it represents the first, clear departure from Altizer's Barthian background, by way of the historical critique of world religions, toward radical immanence.

THE CHALLENGE OF MODERN GNOSTICISM*

Few fields of study today are in such a state of flux as is that of Gnosticism. The discovery for the first time of a genuine

* From *The Journal of Bible and Religion*, XXX (1962), pp. 18–25. Copyright by the American Academy of Religion.
[6] See Thomas J. J. Altizer, *The Descent into Hell: A Study of the Radical Reversal of the Christian Consciousness* (Philadelphia: Lippincott, 1970).

ancient Gnostic library, the renewed appreciation of the problem posed by the transition of Christianity from a primitive eschatological form to a Hellenistic mystical and sacramental form, and the realization that in numerous and startling ways ancient Gnostic motifs parallel modern man's experience of God and the world, have all contributed to the ferment in contemporary Gnostic studies. One is immediately faced with the vexing problem of whether Gnosticism embodies a universal religious reality or is no more than a particular and ancient historical episode. This article assumes that there is a modern religious phenomenon which may justly be termed Gnostic regardless of whether any genuine historical continuity exists between ancient and modern Gnosticism.

I

Ancient Gnosticism must be defined here, if only in a cursory manner. Gnosticism was a violent reaction against the world of selfconscious and rational thinking evolved by classical and Hellenistic culture and an ecstatic return to the mythical world of archaic religious sensibility. To borrow Nietzsche's categories, it was a victory of the Dionysian over the Apollonian consciousness. This accounts for the artificial quality of much Gnostic myth-making, as well as for the deeply rooted opposition of ancient Gnosticism to the whole Greek way of understanding and celebrating the world. Perhaps the most distinctive feature of Gnosticism is the violence of its opposition to the world (whether defined as the Greek *kosmos* or as the whole realm of history and civilization). The Gnostic deity can be defined as simply the polar opposite of the world. Union with this deity takes place only through a mystical form of knowledge, *gnosis,* which is realized in the believer to the extent that he progressively dissolves all awareness of the world. The soul (*pneuma*) of man is ordinarily a prisoner of the world; redemption can take place only through a shattering or dissolution of everything that binds man to the world, so that the soul may then "ascend" to the absolutely transcendent realm.

The radically world-denying spirit of ancient Gnosticism has been astutely captured by Hans Jonas:

> . . . contrary to the modern analogue, the withdrawal of the divine from the cosmos leaves the latter not as a neutral, value-indifferent, merely physical fact but as a separatistic power whose very self-positing outside God betrays a direction of *will* away from God; and its existence is the embodiment of that will. Thus awareness of the world denotes not only its being alien to God and devoid of his light but also its being a *force alienating* from God. In short, it denotes ultimately a spiritual, not merely physical, fact. . . .To Gnostic piety the true God is chiefly defined by this contraposition. As the world is that which alienates from God, so God is that which alienates and liberates from the world. God as the negation of the world has a nihilistic function with regard to all inner-worldly attachments and values.[1]

Although Jonas ignores the fact that much modern myth-making symbolizes the evil of the world—e.g., Rimbaud, Yeats, and Kafka—the truth is that all Gnosticism is essentially and profoundly world-opposing. For the Gnostic, whether ancient or modern, his true or authentic self must be wholly other than the being of this world. Accordingly, the Gnostic God is an "alien" god, if only because of the Gnostic's own alienation from the world. As Jonas says, "This God must be acosmic, because the cosmos has become the realm of that which is alien to the self."[2] Here we find a deep coincidence between the world of ancient Gnosticism and many of the most creative expressions of the modern spirit, a state of affairs which enables scholars to play the merry game of seeking out the Gnostic roots of many of our greatest modern artists and thinkers.

II

Once we conceive Gnosticism's most distinctive feature as its opposition to the world, it is extremely difficult to limit the arena of modern Gnosticism. As Nietzsche many times re-

---

[1] Hans Jonas, *The Gnostic Religion,* Boston: The Beacon Press, 1958, p. 252.
[2] *Ibid.,* p. 263.

marked, ever since Copernicus man has been falling into a mysterious *x*. And certainly ever since the seventeenth century, Western man has been shuddering before the vastness of the cosmos and its alien character. For modern man has become increasingly alienated from the reality of the world. A glance at the basic ontological categories of two seminal contemporary thinkers will illustrate this truth. One of Heidegger's most basic distinctions is that between *Dasein*, "human existence" or "human reality," and *Seiendes*, "that which is" or "existing things." The distinction is ontological in the sense that the reality of *Dasein* is in some sense other than the reality of *Seiendes*. In like manner, Sartre's whole ontology is grounded in his distinction between the two modes of being created by human consciousness and its object, the *pour-soi* ("being-for-itself") and the *en-soi* ("being-in-itself").

This same spirit is found in much modern theology. In his commentary on Romans, the early Barth, having asked, "What is *the world?*," answered, "The world is our whole existence, as it has been, and is, conditioned by sin. There has come into being a *cosmos* which, because we no longer know God, is not Creation. . . . In so far as this world is our world, it is the world into which sin has entered. In this world, on this earth, and under this heaven, there is no redemption, no direct life."[3] While few contemporary theologians would approve the notion in some quarters that the creation itself was a "fall" from God, many would agree with Bultmann's declaration that the "Christian faith in creation affirms that man is not at home in the world."[4] Significantly enough, Bultmann follows Jonas in the following statement: "In Gnosticism awareness that man is not at home in the world is radically developed, and in this man's self is revealed as something different from all existence in the world apart from human existence."[5]

---

[3] Karl Barth, *The Epistle to the Romans*, translated by Edwyn C. Hoskyns, London: Oxford University Press, 1933, pp. 168–169.

[4] Rudolph Bultmann, *Existence and Faith*, translated by Schubert M. Ogden, New York: Meridian Books, 1960, p. 213.

[5] Rudolph Bultmann, *Essays: Philosophical and Theological*, translated by James C. G. Greig, London: S. C. M. Press, 1955, pp. 146–147.

Following the demise of classical Calvinism, Protestant thought has increasingly abandoned the world and retreated to the realm of "inwardness" and subjectivity. This has left Protestantism without a cosmology. In this connection we must remember Barth's assertion that the most profound difference between Protestantism and Catholicism is the Catholic doctrine of the *analogia entis*. As Jacob Taubes has pointed out, "The dialetical method and the stress on inwardness that mark all the varieties of modern theology only testify to the fact that the Creator of heaven and earth is veiled and that the realm of physical reality is lost for religious experience."[6] But it must not be thought that modern faith is simply alienated from the realm of physical reality; Nietzsche's proclamation of the death of God has taught us that faith has now become alienated from reality itself. One of Nietzsche's most profound contemporary interpreters, Erich Heller, has noted that the "characteristic spiritual quality of that long period of history of which we are the bewildered heirs was not only the dissociation of faith from knowledge; this was a comparatively harmless episode, lasting from the seventeenth century to the age of Victoria, a mere surface repercussion of that mightier earthquake which severed faith from sensibility. It is this rift which has made it impossible for most Christians not to *feel*, or at least not to feel *also*, as true may 'truths' which are incompatible with the truth of their faith."[7] Spengler was not misguided in identifying modern Western culture as Faustian; for everything that modern man knows to be true or real has been created either by means of an abandonment or a dissolution of faith. Only a Gnostic spirit could lead to a joyous acceptance of the chasm that lies between modern science and modern faith.

Here lies the deepest problem posed by modern Gnosticism. We may at this point elaborate upon our earlier definition and identify. Gnosticism as a world-opposing, world-loathing,

---

[6] Jacob Taubes, "Dialectic and Analogy," *The Journal of Religion*, XXXIV, 2 (April, 1954), 118.

[7] Erich Heller, *The Disinherited Mind*, New York: Meridian Books, 1959, p. 157.

and world-escaping way which seeks release or redemption from the world in an acosmic state of individual and interior isolation. Ancient Gnosticism—which here followed the archaic or traditional religious way[8]—negated the world as *profane reality* in its quest for an otherworldly *sacred reality*. But modern Gnosticism—inheriting the Faustian transformation of absolute transcendence into absolute immanence, a transformation symbolically portrayed in Nietzsche's proclamation of the death of God—attempts to escape a cosmos and a history in which man has lost his human reality by searching for a non-transcendent and non-sacred state of subjective purity and existential authenticity. When Martin Buber says that the modern manifestation of *gnosis* is the "psychological doctrine which deals with mysteries without knowing the attitude of faith towards mystery,"[9] he is referring to a form of Gnosticism which has abandoned the *sacred reality* of the traditional forms of faith. Precisely at this point lies the revolution effected by modern Gnosticism—a revolution which is manifest in literature, philosophy, theology, and, indeed, throughout the whole gamut of modern life.

A clear illustration of this revolution is found in the work of the greatest modern Gnostic psychologist, C. G. Jung.[10] As is well known, Jung believed that a process of individuation occurs in the deepest levels of the "collective unconscious" which will eventually lead to an ultimate integration and redemption of humanity. This process is reflected in a series of archetypal symbols (produced in dreams, art, and religion) which gradually form together into a "mandala" symbolism. (The term "mandala" denotes the ritual or magic circle used in various forms of Hindu and Buddhist Tantrism as a *yantra* or aid to contemplation.) Jung maintains that the mandals are

---

[8] Cf. Mircea Eliade, *The Myth of the Eternal Return,* translated by Willard R. Trask, New York: Pantheon Books, 1954.

[9] Martin Buber, *Eclipse of God,* New York: Harper Torchbooks, 1957, p. 136.

[10] Cf. Thomas J. J. Altizer, "Science and Gnosis in Jung's Psychology," *The Centennial Review,* III, 3 (Summer, 1959), 304–320.

symbolic representations of that *telos* toward which all inner growth and individuation tends, and to which he gives the name of "Self." In the historical models of the mandala, the god is symbolized by a series of circles, and the goddess by a square or series of squares. However, Jung emphasizes that the symbols which occupy the center of his patients' visions of mandalas have no reference to a deity. They may refer to a star, a sun, a flower, a serpent, or a human being, but never to a god; "A modern mandala is an involuntary confession of a peculiar mental condition. There is no deity in the mandala, and there is also no submission or reconciliation to a deity. The place of the diety seems to be taken by the wholeness of man."[11] Using the symbol of "Self" to represent the indefinable, ineffable "wholeness" of man. Jung insists that as a symbol it lies deeper than the God-symbol. It is the final consummation of the individuation process, and thus is the deepest and highest symbol of ultimate reality.

On the other hand, in Eric Voegelin's attack upon modern Gnosticism,[12] the phenomenon is portrayed in such all-encompassing fashion that its specific identity is lost. Voegelin sees secularism, scientism, positivism, political totalitarianism, and the mass social movements of modern times, as so many varying forms of Gnosticism. Indeed, he goes so far as to say that the essence of modernity is the growth of Gnosticism.[13] Voegelin defines modern Gnosticism as follows:

> The attempt at immanentizing the meaning of existence is fundamentally an attempt at bringing our knowledge of transcendence into a firmer grip than the *cognitio fidei*, the cognition of faith, will afford; and Gnostic experiences offer the firmer grip insofar as they are an expanding of the soul to the point where God is drawn into the existence of man. . . . These Gnostic experiences, in the amplitude of their variety, are the core of the redivination of society, for the men who fall into these experiences divinize them-

---

[11] C. G. Jung, *Psychology and Religion,* New Haven: Yale University Press, 1938, p. 99.
[12] Eric Voegelin, *The New Science of Politics,* Chicago: The University of Chicago Press, 1952, pp. 107–132.
[13] *Ibid.,* p. 126.

selves by substituting more massive modes of participation in divinity for faith in the Christian sense.[14]

Proceeding by this means, Voegelin can find Gnosticism in the modern West as a process beginning with the democratic movements of the seventeenth century and culminating in twentieth-century Marxism. In fact, he sees Gnosticism pervading modern thought: "Gnostic speculation overcame the uncertainty of faith by receding from transcendence and endowing man and his intramundane range of action with the meaning of eschatological fulfilment."[15] In this way, all of modern thought is comprehended—from physics and mathematics to politics and theology. However, Voegelin fails to grasp the deep hostility to the world which is invariably present in true Gnosticism. Despite the violence of his attack upon Gnosticism (an attack which is itself Gnostic in its loathing of history), Voegelin ironically perceives that the death of the spirit is the price of progress; thus he speaks of the Gnostic murder of God.[16] At this point his analysis joins forces with Nietzsche— with whom it should have begun. For it was Nietzsche who grasped most profoundly the religious meaning of the historical and existential situation of modern man.

Jacob Taubes is more discriminating and of greater help than Voegelin's attack. Adopting the category "Dionysian" (a central category of Nietzsche's mature thought but not to be confused with the latter's usage of "Dionysian" in *The Birth of Tragedy*), Taubes offers a significant key to modern theology and to modern Gnosticism alike.[17] Nietzsche's category refers to an absolute form of life-affirmation and world-affirmation (portrayed conceptually through his category of Eternal Recurrence), as opposed to the radical world-denial which he associates with all forms of religious faith. However, a Dionysian form of existence becomes possible only through the death

---

[14] *Ibid.*, p. 124.
[15] *Ibid.*, p. 129.
[16] *Ibid.*, p. 131.
[17] Cf. Jacob Taubes, "On the Nature of the Theological Method: Some Reflections on the Methodological Principles of Tillich's Theology," *The Journal of Religion*, XXXIV, 1 (January, 1954), 12–25.

of God, through the collapse of every vestige of the transcendent. It is now that an affirmation of absolute immanence can be made, liberating man from all dependence upon a transcendent reality and thereby bringing him to an absolutely autonomous state of existence. (This state in its truest form Nietzsche hopefully awaited in the coming Superman, but it is already capable of defining the deepest meaning of human existence—as witness Nietzsche's category of the Will to Power.) Taubes employs the term "Dionysiac" to describe the whole movement of Protestant dialectical theology from Hegel to Tillich which has revolved about the transformation of transcendent reality into an ecstatic state of human existence: "Dionysiac theology is an 'ecstatic naturalism' that interprets all supernaturalistic symbols in immanent terms. The ecstasy does not lead to a 'beyond,' in a supernaturalistic sense, but signifies an intensity of the immanent."[18] While Taubes exaggerates the degree to which dialectical theology is Dionysian, there seems little doubt that a Dionysian transformation of transcendence into immanence lies deeply imbedded in the theological method of all the dialectical theologians (not excepting Bultmann and the early Barth, both of whom consistently translate the eschatological into the existential).[19]

The analysis thus far should indicate the enormous complexity of the problem posed by modern Gnosticism; for there is a sense in which Eric Voegelin is right: Modern Gnosticism is simply modern existence, and a catalogue of the role of Gnosticism (as here defined) in our world would involve modern life and thought in its entirety. Unquestionably the "death of God"—or the "eclipse of God"—has profoundly affected the deepest forms of contemporary man's religious life. In an article on the mysticism of Simone Weil, Susan Anima Taubes speaks of an "atheistic mysticism" which has been created amidst the twentieth-century experience of the absence of God: "Atheism, which used to be a charge leveled against

---

[18] *Ibid.*, p. 21.
[19] Cf. Thomas J. J. Altizer, "Nietzsche's Influence upon Contemporary Theology," *The Emory University Quarterly*, XVI, 3 (Fall, 1960), 152–163.

skeptics, unbelievers, or simply the indifferent, has come to mean a *religious* experience of the death of God. The godlessness of the world in all its strata and categories becomes, paradoxically and by a dialectic of negation, the signature of God and yields a mystical atheism, a theology of divine absence and nonbeing, of divine impotence, divine nonintervention, and divine indifference."[20] Simply to entertain the possibility of an atheistic mysticism is to arrive at yet another key to the dilemma of modern man's religious existence. (One only has to think of writers as diverse as Baudelaire and Kafka to realize how pervasive this theme is in modern literature.) May we then define twentieth-century Gnosticism as a search for an authentic redemption from an alien cosmos in the context of the death of God?

III

At this point it is difficult to avoid the question of the relation between Christianity and Gnosticism, or, more particularly, the relation between twentieth-century Protestantism and modern Gnosticism. We must note the extreme difficulty in distinguishing Christianity and Gnosticism when it comes to the conception of faith held by such theologians as the early Barth, Tillich, and Bultmann. (Harnack is reported to have written his book on Marcion in response to Barth's commentary on Romans). Moreover, this difficulty must inevitably obtain, if only because of modern man's deep alienation from nature and history. Any contemporary form of Protestantism will inevitably reflect the dominant modes of sensibility of its own time. Nevertheless, there remains a real difference between Christianity and Gnosticism in the modern experience and it is essential that we uncover it.

We are not forced to identify any and every deep-rooted opposition to the world as necessarily Gnostic. In our historical sophistication we have learned that there is no such thing as a naked experience of the world; we encounter the world through

---

[20] Susan Anima Taubes, "The Absent God," *The Journal of Religion*, XXV, 1 (January, 1955), 6.

the forms, traditions, ideas, styles, etc. that surround us. The point is that it live in *our* world—as opposed to *the* world—is to experience a world from which God is absent. Therefore, authentic faith today must in some sense stand apart from or oppose *our* world.

A deeper problem is posed by Taubes' criticism of dialectical theology. Must we identify as Gnostic any religious or theological transformation of a sacred and transcendent reality into a human and immanent reality? If the answer is yes, must we also identify as Gnostic any transformation of traditional forms of faith as a method of response to the "death of God" in our time? If so, does this not mean that Christianity is obliged to turn its back upon the historical destiny that confronts contemporary man? Is there no form through which Christianity can be meaningful in the modern crisis? Is its message doomed to be hopelessly irrelevant to the world of twentieth-century man? Roman Catholicism does not accept this consequence; surely Protestantism cannot retain its integrity if it refuses to accept the destiny which confronts it.

Probably Martin Buber is the only theologian who has openly called for a transformation of faith in response to God's eclipse, to God's withdrawal of himself from the creation. In urging a steadfastness of faith which refuses to disown reality, Buber insists: "That He hides Himself does not diminish the immediacy, in the immediacy he remains the Saviour and the contradiction of existence becomes for us a theophany."[21] Significantly, by "faith" Buber means *'emuna,* a peculiarly Jewish form of faith, grounded in the Covenant and the sacred history of the people of God, which in essence can never be open to a radical dissociation of the creature and the Creator. Thus Buber is able to say that it was precisely because of the nature of its faith that Judaism could never be open to genuine eschatology; and we might add that for the same reason Judaism must remain closed to the Christian idea of the radical transcendence of God. The Christian faith rests upon a radical

---

21 Martin Buber, *Two Types of Faith,* translated by Norman P. Goldhawk, London: Routledge & Kegan Paul, 1951, p. 169.

dissociation of old aeon from new aeon, of this world from the Kingdom of God. *The consequence of this is that Christianity must always be open to a situation in which God is absent from the world.*

IV

How, then, is the Christian to respond to the Gnostic challenge? Superficially, there seems little reason for him to rejoice upon meeting a world divorced of every vestige of the Spirit. And, indeed, the Christian must share—more deeply than he has—the anguish of contemporary human existence, the torment and emptiness of a humanly and religiously meaningless world. His present life must be of sufficient depth to deliver him from every temptation to project his life in the world into his vision of the Kingdom of God. Having been "thrown" into an absolutely immanent mode of being (Rilke's and Heidegger's *Dasein*), he finds nothing in the world that is open to transcendence. By encountering a world wholly devoid of the presence of grace, he moves in a sacred void emptied of every fragment of religious meaning. The drama of Western man's loss of faith has exhibited the progressive surrender of the world to unbelief, until in our time the world is bathed in the darkness of God's absence. Thus it is that the only reality the Christian can "know" is one closed to the presence of God. Faith knows that merely to exist in our world is to dwell in a state of alienation from the reality of the sacred, from the realm of the "spirit." For *our* world is most deeply antithetical to God; it is wholly other than God. In contrast to God's absolute transcendence, the world discloses its own absolute immanence.

But while it is true that the Christian will identify the world as a fallen reality, and life in the old aeon as a matter of "darkness" and sin, he must nevertheless believe that the very existence of the world—and his own existence in the world—is grounded in the will and power of God. The greatest paradox which Christian faith in our time has to accept—one that is denied by all genuine versions of Gnosticism—is that despite all its corruptions, the world—*this* world, "our" world, the scientist's "nature," the poet's *Dasein*—stands finally under the absolute sovereignty of God. From the Christian's assurance of this latter truth it follows that he is forbidden to say an absolute no to the reality of the world, or to evade his destiny or "calling" through trying to pretend that the world in which he lives does not really exist. In no way at all is Christianity required to identify itself with the world; to do so would be to betray its very nature. But it is bound to relate itself to the *moment* (the destiny or the history) which it confronts. It is so bound precisely because of its root conviction of the absolute sovereignty of God. Here is to be found the basic meaning of the Christian doctrine of creation—or, at least, this is as much of the doctrine of creation as is visible to the Christian as he confronts a wholly profane world, a world grounded in absolute immanence. To engage in a total negation of the world is Gnosticism, which here reveals itself as the polar opposite of Christianity. The Christian doctrine of creation is the absolute dividing line between that faith and Gnosticism. On the basis of this doctrine, the Christian, precisely through his life in a sacred void, can be prepared to meet a God who is truly God, a God who is wholly other than the world. The time has come for the Christian to be open to genuine transcendence.

The Christian is enabled to stand fast before a destiny which he traces ultimately to God himself. No longer can faith pretend that the vacuous existence of modern man is a product of sin alone. The believer is tempted to say that the darkness he encounters is the product of unbelief, of rebellion against God. But again, it is the Gnostic temptation that is involved. Had sin actually produced our world, it would have to be grounded in the deepest levels of creativity. How can the Christian so condemn by implication our science, our institutions, our art, our very existence? Gnosticism is ultimately grounded in a principle, found also in Indian mysticism, that the will to *be* is the root source of alienation, illusion, and suffering. Note should be taken of a most subtle, and yet most important, difference here between Christianity and Hinduism. The Hindu looks upon existence in this world as either wholly illusory, or as a fallen and "spiritless" form of being, or, at best, as the divine yet essentially meaningless "play" (*lila*) of an ultimately impersonal deity. The believer who chooses to live in our world yet cannot accept its reality, is easily led into this essentially Gnostic way of world negation. Granted that the present world offers an overwhelming challenge to faith, authentic faith cannot evade the challenge by way of either retreat or negation.

Gnosticism as a way of salvation can only proceed by evading or negating the world—a world construed of necessity as the arena of a fallen, alienated mode of existence which must be obliterated by the individual who seeks true salvation. Since the way of *gnosis* must be a radically negative way of world-denial, it is in actuality the religious way of Gnosticism which is the real subject of Nietzsche's category of resentment. Contrariwise, Christianity must be in some ultimate sense world-affirming. This in no way implies that the Christian can affirm *this* world, the old aeon, or existence in the "flesh." Authentic faith, as known to the Christian, can never apprehend "nature," or "matter," or *Dasein,* or "actuality," as autonomous being, as pure "isness." To be sure, Christian faith faces up to reality—indeed, that reality which is most spiritless and which dissolves every sign of the divine presence. But faith knows too that this very reality lives under the sovereignty of God.

V

Is the Christian to hope, then, that our darkness may yet become a theophany? More immediately, is he to will the evident destiny of our world in the hope that he is thereby doing God's will? Can he live in this world, and thus in a sense will it, without abandoning his faith, without saying a final no to God? However timidly and with whatever reservations, surely the Christian will in some genuine sense answer these questions in the affirmative. Hoelderlin has sung that the moment of greatest danger is the moment of salvation; may not the Christian hope that the eclipse which is God's judgment may yet be the moment of his deepest epiphany? Yet, insofar as he sees that the willing of his own reality, his truth, his world, is simultaneously a willing of the "death of God," how can he believe that our God-dissolving reality can in any sense be associated with God's will? Can he believe that God wills his "death" in us?

Perhaps the wheel has now come full circle. Christianity began with God's death on the cross—for if Christ is Lord, his death must in some sense have been the death of God; has it now ended with God's death in the world, with his banishment from his own creation? Myths and religions the world over have long associated redemption with the death of deity. In the Near Eastern world (which yet remains our world), immortality was always achieved through union with a dying god. Life through death is a universal religious theme; thus too, in the New Testament, repentance or regeneration is effected by means of a dying to self, to the old world, the old aeon. No world religion has so emphasized death as has Christianity. Hindu deities never die, and in Buddhism death is ultimately unreal. Christianity ought to be most open to the deepest meaning of death. The contemporary Christian must be prepared to accept a destiny which lives out the death of God, to live immersed in an actuality whose very being blots out the presence of God. Yet it cannot be accidental that the proclamation of the death of God arose originally as an anti-Christian gospel. For it is only Christianity's assertion of the absolute sovereignty of God that enables it to be open to his death. Only in this way is the believer enabled to say yes to whatever destiny confronts him. He is then prepared to accept the death of God amidst the reality that surrounds God—to accept it as God's will, as falling under God's sovereignty. In this way any ultimate no-say-ing to the world is finally consigned to its Gnostic origin.

18

JOHN B. COBB JR.

Synthesizer of Process Theology

John Boswell Cobb Jr. (1925–   ) was born the year after
Whitehead came to Harvard. He began his graduate studies
the year after Whitehead's death. In recent years he has done
more than any other theologian to develop what is summed
up in the title of one of his books—*A Christian Natural Theology Based on the Thought of Alfred North Whitehead*
(1965). Yet in reaching that point, he first established himself
as his generation's foremost interpreter of the major trends
in contemporary Protestantism—an endeavor reflecting the
scope and depth of a lifelong search, both intensely personal
and highly typical of his generation.

Born into a missionary home in Kobe, Japan, John Cobb
was "a very pious, not to say pietistic, boy."[1] His earliest ac-
quaintances were confined to other Protestant Christians, so
he rarely had occasion to doubt the fundamentals of his faith.
As he grew older, however, he became aware of distinctions
between Christianity and Buddhism—not so much in terms
of their relative merits but as seen in the element of decision.
"For a Japanese to become a Christian was a real change,
recognized as such both by him and by other Japanese." Once
he saw this, young Cobb's piety was transformed into an
intense interest "in religion in general and Christianity in
particular."

Cobb was nearly 17 when the Japanese forces attacked
Pearl Harbor. Little more than a year later, he began three

---

[1] Quotations, unless otherwise attributed, are from a letter to the editor
by John B. Cobb Jr., dated 30 October 1968.

and a half years of service in the U. S. Army, and because he had grown up in Japan he was assigned to a Japanese language program. Most of his associates had not been in Japan but had shown aptitudes for the program. In short, Cobb found himself surrounded by intellectuals, few of whom were Protestants. They tended to be either Catholics or Jews or nonbelievers from those backgrounds. He describes the encounter as his "discovery of the modern world," in which he "came to see Protestantism as a minority movement." For a time, he was strongly drawn to Catholicism, and he was greatly influenced by Aldous Huxley's Vedanta-oriented *The Perennial Philosophy*, but somehow his Protestant faith prevailed. He had considered entering the U. S. Foreign Service as a career but now decided on a "church vocation," and chose the University of Chicago as a place where he could "spend some time studying all the objections to Christian faith I could find."

At Chicago, Cobb enrolled in a three-year interdepartmental humanities program on "the analysis of ideas and the study of methods," but during the first year he experienced a shattering loss of faith and felt "vividly, almost violently, the 'death of God.'" Yet his loss of belief was such that he was impelled to enter the Divinity School, "sensing that the professors there were operating in the context of the modern world, for which the God of my piety was indeed dead, and yet thought there was something positive and worthwhile to believe." Among those professors were Bernard Loomer, Bernard Meland, and Daniel Day Williams. Wieman, though no longer at Chicago, was an indirect influence especially through Meland. Of much larger importance, however, were Cobb's studies with Richard McKeon and Charles Hartshorne. McKeon, with whom he took more work than with anyone else, impressed upon him "the plurality of relatively consistent and adequate conceptual schemes or philosophies"—one's final choice among them rests on grounds other than the philosophical. Even more decisive, however, was Cobb's study of Whitehead under Hartshorne, which "gradually restored to me the possibility of using the word 'God' with some sense of reality."

Cobb received his M.A. from the University of Chicago in 1949 and his Ph.D. in 1952. He taught philosophy and theology at Emory University in Atlanta from 1953 to 1958; since then he has been associate professor of systematic theology at the School of Theology at Clermont, California. His first two books were surveys—*Varieties of Protestantism* (1960) and *Living Options in Protestant Theology* (1962). These studies and *A Christian Natural Theology* (1965) display a first-rate mind at work, but it is only with *The Structure of Christian Existence* (1968) and *God and the World* (1969) that he has begun to develop his own constructive ideas. As the foregoing paragraphs suggest, Cobb (unlike Michalson, for example) was never a devotee of neo-orthodoxy, although he came to maturity during its heyday and is thoroughly conversant with it. His essay, "From Crisis Theology to the Post-Modern World," which follows, documents the changing theological climate from what may be regarded as the viewpoint of a forerunner, inasmuch as Cobb has seen ideas come to the fore that he has held for some time. This changing climate, however, has also affected his own thinking, loosening his grip on Whitehead and encouraging him, in *God and the World,* to draw creatively upon the thought of Wieman, whom he had previously criticized in his M.A. thesis and in *Living Options.* Nevertheless, Whitehead remains a dominant influence—increasingly for his cosmology rather than his metaphysics. Cobb is unusually attuned to the claims of science, not only in the sense of seeking to develop a religious philosophy that does not contradict science but in trying to bring to light our assumptions about what the natural sciences permit us to believe. Many religious thinkers, he says, "ignore the natural sciences consciously," but "their sense of reality is nevertheless profoundly conditioned" by such assumptions, conscious or unconscious. He has become less relativistic than he was at Chicago, but he remains "convinced of the fundamental impossibility of overcoming relativism rationally. From a purely rational point of view there is no escaping the element of decision."

It was, of course, the factor of decision that was pivotal to the crisis theology of Barth and Brunner. In a sense, then, Cobb's perspective represents something more than a simple negation of the latter. As his choice of the term "post-modern" suggests, our present world is no longer the one which "modernism" dealt with. Tomorrow's theology has to move beyond both the recent and the earlier past to a larger synthesis. One can already dimly discern the coalescence of different strands of process thought as Cobb's theology develops. It seems evident that the next decade will find in him a knowledgable voice well worth hearing. Certainly he is among the most promising theologians at the present time.

FROM CRISIS THEOLOGY TO THE POST-MODERN WORLD*

After the thunder of a great generation of theologians in the twenties and thirties of our century, the theological horizons of the sixties are painfully silent. Even the voices of the great old men are quieter now, and in any case they cannot answer the questions of a new generation. There exists a vacuum in which even the splash of a small pebble attracts widespread attention. Theologians console themselves that the time for great systems is past and the time of the essay has come. Yet the essays for the most part are trivial.

The silence of our time is especially surprising since there is no lack of highly trained and intelligent men keenly interested in constructive theological work. Why are we so inarticulate? Why must so much of our energy be devoted to studying or interpreting our past? And why are the few efforts toward dealing with our own problems so provisional?

I would suggest that the disappearance of crisis theology has led to a situation so difficult for the theologian that he is likely to exhaust himself in taking his bearings. I will attempt in what follows to focus the problem in terms of the renewed

* From *The Centennial Review*, VIII, 2 (Spring 1964), pp. 174–188.

openness of theology to culture and of the problem of historical relativism. I will then indicate in a highly personal way a
response to this crisis and a possible way ahead.

I

Roughly we may characterize the theology of the nineteenth
century as one which sought a synthesis between faith and
culture. Culture was positively appraised, and pride was taken
in the success of faith in christianizing it. Further victories
were hoped for and worked for. Dissenting voices vigorously
protested that faith lost itself in this synthesis, that Christendom is a fraud, and that only by rejecting culture can faith be
true to itself. But these voices were not heard until World
War I had proved them prophetic.

Crisis theology undertook to distinguish sharply between
faith and culture. Culture is human; faith, of God. Faith seeks
no sustenance in culture and makes no special claims to benefit
culture. It belongs to another sphere which radically transcends culture and is even, essentially, indifferent to it. In fact,
of course, the crisis theologians were far from indifferent to
the events of history and took an active and creative part in
molding them. It was they and not the remnants of nineteenth century liberalism who gave effective leadership to
resistance against Hitler. Within their own thought, the separation of faith and culture gave way, although the insistence
on the duality remained. The legacy of crisis theology is
therefore a new openness to culture, an awareness of its importance. It is *this* world in which we are called to faith, and
though the faith to which we are called is not simply the
culmination of culture, still it must learn to provide an authentic witness within it.

In this formal statement, the new recognition of the in-
escapability of taking culture seriously seems relatively in-
nocuous. The problem, however, is that the culture we are
called to take seriously is one increasingly devoid of Christian
form and substance. It is a post-Christian culture, a culture
for which God is dead. What does it mean for Christian theology to take this culture seriously?

For some, it means that we are to look in the culture for

authentic expressions of man's humanity, and to see in them new forms of unconscious and unintended expression of the Christian faith. However, this will not do. We can, of course, as historians point out that the influence of Christianity is not dead even where it is denied, but if we are to take our world seriously we must acknowledge that the existence in which it seeks a new authenticity is not that of its Christian past.

For others, it means that we are to see in modern culture the direction in which man must inevitably fall when he turns away from faith. But this will not do either. That much in the modern world does indeed express just this is beyond question. But this approach presupposes that there is an island of security in the modern world from which it is possible to view it from without and thus take warning not to follow that course. This is precisely *not* to take seriously the modern world. This is to assume that the modern world is optional, that we choose to live in it or out of it as we choose unbelief or belief.

A third alternative is to understand the modern world as asking questions which it cannot answer, questions which can be answered only by faith. But this approach also fails. The modern world does not in fact seem to be asking those questions to which the Christian gospel provides an answer. To achieve a correlation of question and answer we seem forced to destroy the integrity both of the world and of the gospel.

A fourth alternative is to take from the modern world only a new conceptuality in which faith can express itself. Surely this is acceptable and commendable as far as it goes, but it does not deal frontally with the problem of faith and culture. What is to be expressed in the conceptuality taken from the culture? Is it something which challenges the culture, which roots itself outside the culture and claims autonomy from it? Then again the modern world is not being taken with full seriousness, for the modern world denies every transcendent perspective. Then again one presupposes an island of refuge from which one may decide how and in what way to be a part of the modern world and how and in what way to transcend it.

We seem to be confronted finally by only two choices. We

may really take the modern world seriously, acknowledge that it is the only world we know, accept it, affirm it, and live it. To do so is to accept and live the death of God. On the other hand, we may refuse the modern world, distance ourselves from it, fence in our world of traditional faith, and seek to preserve it from the corrosion of the world outside. Both expedients are desperate ones. It is no wonder that theologians find it difficult to speak relevantly in such a time.

The problem for contemporary theology is acutely compounded by historical self-consciousness. Since we are accustomed and compelled to think historically, we are accustomed and compelled to think in terms of the variety of ways in which men seek understanding and fulfillment. We see that Christian faith is one among these ways, that it arose in particular circumstances in conjunction with particular beliefs and expectations, that it spread in some directions and not in others, and that it is fundamentally an historical accident that we happen to be Christians rather than, for example, Moslems.

We may, of course, argue that the historical origins of a belief have nothing to do with the responsible judgment of its truth or falsity. But if so, we must at least assume that we do have some criteria for judging. When our suggestions of such criteria in their turn are found to be products of a peculiar history, we begin to feel the ground sinking beneath our feet. We seem plunged into an infinite regress in which every possibility of normative thinking is destroyed.

If we argue that we must believe something, and then by a leap of faith choose to be Christian, we find ourselves still confronted by the most bewildering diversity. Faith does not seem to mean the same thing for Eastern Orthodoxy, for Roman Catholicism, and for Protestantism. Even within Protestantism the variety is great. Having leapt into Christianity, are we to leap into one or another form of Christianity as well? And what attitude are we to take toward those who leap in another way? Having leapt in our particular way, are we given to know that they have leapt wrongly? Or do we simply confess our own commitment and accept other commitments as equally valid?

It is clear that one of the reasons for the power of crisis theology was that it placed faith radically outside this relativism. For it faith is the gift of God and is validated in its giving. It does not have to claim superiority over unfaith or over competing religions in any other way. Nevertheless, this solution above all sounds like special pleading. Are we really prepared to say that all the religious attainments of the East are to be seen as so much vain human striving? Is not our belief that this is so clearly a function of our historical conditioning? Can we really claim that this belief is given with the gift of faith so that it too is validated by the act of God? Or if we affirm that God has given faith to all men, what can faith mean any longer? And what happens to the Biblical distinction between believers and unbelievers?

That these difficulties can be multiplied indefinitely goes without saying, and with the passing of crisis theology they have come very much to the fore. The Christian must now recognize that his faith is one among many and that it cannot be set over against all other human phenomena as that one point at which God has acted. Yet the alternative seems to be to return to that relativistic sea from which crisis theology seemed briefly to save us.

II

In the above I have called attention to the two features of the contemporary situation which seem to be most critical for the theologian. Our culture, the culture in which we do and must live, is characterized by the death of God. We cannot but understand ourselves and our beliefs historically and hence relativistically.

These two problems are intimately interconnected. The death of God is caused in part by the historicizing of all our thinking. Since we understand an idea by understanding how it arises and develops, we can no longer view the idea as having a one-to-one correlation with reality. We can talk seriously about ideas of God but are not able to speak directly to God. More broadly, we can enter imaginatively into many ways of perceiving reality, but just for that reason we cannot affirm any of them as true. Indeed, the word "true" we are forced to place in quotes, not knowing any longer what we can mean by it.

It is also the case that the death of God is a *cause* of relativism. As long as God's reality remained a fixed pole for thought, the relativity of human experience and belief could be understood as reflecting varying ways of grasping one ultimate reality. Truth was found in God's knowledge, and even though we might not claim any final criteria for identifying the content of truth, that there existed a final truth about all things was clear. With the death of God, however, truth and reality are alike relativized. They exist nowhere.

This world in which God is dead and truth and reality are without meaning is indeed our world. Yet it is not our total world. If it were, no such statement about it could be understood. If God were wholly and unequivocally dead for us, the statement that it is so would not be made. Indeed, all discourse would be at an end. Every statement assumes that it somehow transcends total relativism, that it points to some kind of reality, that it participates in some kind of truth. We do still live in a world formed by a past that remains alive even in its decay.

I do not mean to seize the point that total relativism is self-contradictory as a basis for setting relativism aside. The *affirmation* of total relativism is self-contradictory, but there is a sense in which relativism can be lived unspoken. The complete relativist would never apply the term relativism to his own thought, for he would not think in such universals. It is the reality of lived relativism, not its philosophical defense that seems to lie ahead for our world.

I do mean to say, however, that the reality of the death of God and of the concomitant relativism does not exhaust our contemporary world. If we take seriously the historical consciousness which we have already seen to play such havoc with traditional forms of faith and theology, we must also see that the death of God and the concomitant relativism are likewise a function of time and place, one way of being among others, in themselves neither absolute not final. History shows us that just at that point at which a *Zeitgeist* seems to have swept all before it, it may already be giving way in the minds of the most creative and authentic persons to something quite different, something that certainly will not repeat the past, but something which may yet recover out of the past just what seemed in greatest danger of being destroyed. Perhaps even today at the point at which all rational structure and all human meaning seems to be evaporating, new structures and new meanings may be emerging.

If this is so, and I earnestly hope that it is so, then we may escape the desperate choice indicated above between affirming the modern world and reacting against it defensively. We may refuse the modern world not by defending the past but in the name of the new world which *may* be born. We cannot of course know that it will be born. We cannot even know whether our decision for it may help it to be born. But we can affirm it, and in doing so we can repudiate the modern world in the name of the world we will to be the post-modern world.

The picture I am proposing may be sketched as follows. The *Zeitgeist* of our world is one in which God is dead and all truth and reality have collapsed in relativity. That *Zeitgeist* is working its way into ever more consistent expression in thought, art, and existence. It leads to the death of man in the sense of self-conscious, responsible, historical, individual man. Its chief obstacle to total victory is the vast deposit of centuries of Christian thought, art, and existence which, partly consciously but more largely unconsciously, is expressing itself in a still powerful humanism. This is our contemporary post-Christian situation.

If this were the total situation, I have argued above, then the theologian could only decide between throwing his lot with the new and reacting defensively against it by appealing to the authority of the past. He has learned, as many of his colleagues have not, that there is no resting place in the midway point of rationalistic or romantic humanism. But I am suggesting now that this is not the total situation. In addition to the remnants of Christendom and to the demonic powers released by the death of God, there are other thrusts here and there, thrusts which are as authentically modern as any nihilism, but which refuse nihilism in the name of truth.

These emergent claims upon the future are endlessly varied, and there is no place to stand from which one may judge the likelihood of the success of one or another. Nor is there a place to stand from which one may safely baptize one or another such thrust as Christian. Yet I believe that, ignoring the question of success and risking the danger of apostasy, the Christian thinker today must reach out for a novelty that disdains all appeal to the authority of the past and dares to think creatively and constructively in the present.

Teilhard de Chardin is a recent figure who represents such daring. The world he knew, however strange, was surely authentic, genuinely contemporary. He discounted nothing of the magnificent intellectual achievements of science. He did not appeal to the authority of the past. He took the risk of apostasy. Whether in the end his vision is durable we cannot yet know, but that it struck a responsive chord in the minds of many is clear. That it *could* point to a new world, the beginnings of a new *Zeitgeist,* cannot be denied. For my part I would far rather live in that world than in the world being fashioned by dominant modernity.

The work of Teilhard is instructive in that though it fundamentally eschews the authority of the past it affirms Jesus Christ as the center of reality. Sceptics will understandably regard this as a nostalgic remnant of inherited faith or as a concession aimed at placating the church. But I do not believe this. Whether by historic accident or by supernatural purpose, there is an absoluteness in Jesus Christ which can speak not only through the continuity of Christendom but also across the gulf of centuries and cultures. To refuse the authority of the past need not mean to ignore its truth and reality.

I mention the work of Teilhard de Chardin not to hold it up as the one great hope for the future or for the theologian. On the contrary, I find it often vague, confusing, and unsatisfactory. But it represents a mood which challenges the predominant *Zeitgeist* on its own terms, defending nothing on the ground that "it is written" or that "it is Christian," avidly open to all truth—yet still *believing*. This mood is one with which I can identify myself as theologian, as Christian, as man.

My own effort to share in the work to which this mood gives rise is directed toward thinking into the new world opened up in the philosophy of Alfred North Whitehead. To enter Whitehead's world is to experience a psychic revolution as great or greater than the Cartesian and Kantian revolutions. To experience that revolution is to enter into possibilities of thought and self-understanding at which Whitehead himself barely hinted. I believe that from within this new Whiteheadian world one can appropriate also the world of Teilhard de Chardin—as of other revolutionary thinkers of our day— with greater clarity than they themselves could achieve.

III

Although any serious exposition of Whitehead's thought is beyond the scope of this paper, it is appropriate that some indication be given of the aspects of his thought which seem relevant to this context. Whitehead himself speaks of his speculative philosophy as like a poem, mutely appealing for understanding. One cannot begin with terms and objects as defined within some other vision of reality and then state unambiguously that which Whitehead intends. This procedure is impossible wherever there is genuine novelty of sensibility and vision. Hence, all the more, a few brief paragraphs on his thought can hardly hope to be intelligible. Yet, one must try.

Whitehead alters the locus of concreteness as over against modern common sense. Especially with the decay of idealism, modernity has identified concreteness either with things presented to us in sense experience or with the sense data themselves. Whitehead declares this to be "the fallacy of misplaced concreteness." What is concrete is experience as such, just as it occurs in each particularized moment. Whitehead's "actual occasion of experience" has close affinities with the "shining present" of Brightman and the "*Dasein*" of Heidegger. To this extent, what I have called the psychic revolution demanded by Whitehead is seconded by personalistic idealism and by existentialism.

However, Brightman and Heidegger alike, although in quite different ways, limit this revolution to human (or at least animal) reality. Brightman sees the "shining present" in the context of the "illuminating absent." Heidegger sees "*Dasein*" in the midst of other "*Seiende*." For both of them, the physical world, the world of objects, remains something fundamentally other than the experience to which they rightly direct us as the starting point. Whitehead, in contrast, sees the whole physical world as itself also composed of "actual occasions of experience" and of societies of such occasions. There is and can be no object which is not itself a subject or a society of subjects. The physical is one dimension of all experiences including the human, but it is not at all the name of a realm over against that of experience. Whitehead also differs from both Brightman and Heidegger in perceiving experience as a momentary becoming and perishing rather than as a continuum of becoming.

The profoundly distinctive character of Whitehead's vision is apparent in his understanding of relations. All real relations are the re-enactment in new experiences of elements of old experiences. All causality is to be understood in this way. Through its causal efficacy the past always profoundly affects the becoming present but never determines exactly how it will become. Causal influence and free self-determination alike characterize every entity in the world.

In terms of these briefly identified principles almost all the traditional problems of thought receive new answers or new versions of old answers. Furthermore, light is shed upon the special problems of modern mathematics and physics that relates these disciplines to human existence in a quite new way. In this context, however, we can note only the relevance of Whitehead's thought for the two acute problems previously discussed—the death of God and universal relativism.

Whitehead's earlier work reflects the death of God at least by its silence. But it gradually became clear as his philosophical speculations broadened that the philosophical reasons for the death of God were repudiated by him. Hence once again the questions of being and becoming emerged in his thought in such a way as to cry out for belief in God. It is fascinating to watch the uncompleted process whereby step by step—reluctantly, it seems at times—Whitehead unfolded a doctrine of God.

Whitehead's doctrine of God has many points of contact with traditional Christian thought—more, I think, than either he or his critics generally recognize. Nevertheless, it is profoundly new. It has been transformed by modern science and mathematics, on the one hand, and by the revolutionary vision of the world as a society of societies of occasions of experiences, on the other. The understanding of God's relation to the world is further transformed by the new understanding of space-time and of relation as re-enaction and by Whitehead's special doctrine of God's providing each momentary occasion with its ideal aim. After generations in which theologians and religious philosophers have struggled to defend some one relation in which God's importance for the world can be argued, we are confronted with a new world of thought in which all manner of modes of relatedness to God are affirmed. Within the Whiteheadian context we can understand both the person-to-person encounter of modern Protestantism and the mysticisms of both East and West. We can agree with those who have seen the relation of man to God in the ethical dimension and with those who have reasoned to God from the order and directionality of nature. We can see both the reality and the all-determinativeness of grace and also the freedom and responsibility of man. But we see all this in a frame of reference that to some degree transforms the meanings of all the traditional terms and problems.

The point of the above is not to explain Whitehead's doctrine of God—that again would be impossible in a few paragraphs—but simply to stress that once one enters the strange new world of Whitehead's vision, God becomes very much alive. The understanding of the world begins and ends with him to a far greater extent than Whitehead himself made explicit in his writings. Insofar as I come existentially to experience myself in terms of the world to which Whitehead introduces us, I experience myself in God; God as in me; God as law, as love, as grace; and the whole world as grounded in him. And I experience this not as in some separation from or tension with what I know of myself physiologically and psychologically, but precisely as illuminative of the fragmentary knowledge afforded by these and all other disciplines. If Whitehead's vision should triumph in the years ahead, the "death of God" would indeed turn out after all to have been only the "eclipse of God."

The problem of the relation of Whitehead's vision to the encompassing relativism of our time is still more complex. Obviously his vision is one among many, conditioned by time, place, and circumstance, subject to interpretation biographically, psychologically, and historically. Unlike most philosophers, Whitehead's philosophy articulates itself as just such a relative undertaking and achievement. One cannot *prove* its truth; one can only display its extraordinary coherence, relevance, and adequacy. And, of course, even the acceptance of such criteria is also conditioned and relative. There is and can be no escape from the circularity of all thinking.

Yet if we take seriously also the conditionedness and relativity of relativism, we will cease to see in the relativity of a position a reason for its rejection. Furthermore, within the position we may find an explanation of how relativism is transcended that seems to account both for relativism and its transcendence more satisfactorily than can be done while one remains, or tries to remain, at the merely relativistic level. Just this is the achievement of Whitehead's thought.

For Whitehead there is no reality that is not relational. For example, one cannot talk first of what occurred at a given time and then separately of what was experienced or perceived. What occurred was just these experiences and perceptions. If we ask "what really happened," we should always be asking "what was really experienced." And all such experience was that of one subject or another. The question of what happened in general is ultimately meaningless. In this sense, the relativity of truth is absolute.

However, this relativity is limited in two ways. First, it is objectively true that such-and-such experiences occurred. Whether they occurred is not relative to *our* opinion, available evidence, or taste. The experiences of the past are objectively immortal. Also, what occurred was not limited to the human experiences. There were electronic, atomic, and cellular experiences as well, and the reality of their occurrence does not depend on human knowledge of them.

Hence there is reality to which our opinions and experiences as a whole correspond more or less well. Truth is an important relation in experience, although certainly not the only important one. Reality as known to us in a function of our interests and our instruments, but reality as it experiences itself is relative only to its own interests. We live in a very real and determinate world, a world in which all things are relative, but determinately relative.

From this perspective, we may indeed understand how human experience and belief are functions of the everchanging situation. Certainly the genesis of ideas helps us to understand them, and appropriately so. The complexity of the reality which confronts us is so vast that our ideas can never have a one-to-one relation with it. Yet our ideas do emerge out of reality in a positive relation with it. The most diverse and even apparently contradictory ideas can have some correspondence to that reality, and the ideal of a greater, more inclusive truth-relation is by no means illusory.

Furthermore, when we combine the Whiteheadian doctrine of God with his triumph over nihilistic relativism, we can see that the truth we seek is already real. There is a perspective which shares all perspectives and relates them all truthfully to each other. And that perspective is already effective for us despite the exceedingly distorted and fragmentary character of our own participation in truth.

IV

One may well object that the effort to explore a new world of thought beyond the dominant modern world is not "theology" but "philosophy." How then can one whose passion drives him in this direction characterize himself as a theologian? The answer to this returns us yet again to the problem of relativism. I know that when I most totally reject the word of the past as authority for my thinking or respond most affirmatively to ideas suggested to me by Whitehead, I am expressing the vision that has become mine as my very selfhood has been formed by my past. When I realize and acknowledge to myself the conditionedness of my being and my stance, there does emerge some degree of transcendence over that conditioning. I can affirm it or I can reject it. Even if I reject it, it still continues to operate in me, but its power over me is nevertheless broken in principle and incipiently in fact as well. If I accept it, what had operated as a blind force becomes now my own will.

I know that the selfhood I experience is formed in the church, in Christian history. What I see in others and in the world, I see through eyes given vision by a Christian past. Knowing this, I am free also to reject it. I might reject it because there are anguish and estrangement given with the Christian vision, a burden of responsibility for a world that denies Christian truth. I might reject it because I see that it is indeed an historical accident that I am grasped by this vision, that I can show no ultimate rational justification for retaining it. Or I might reject it because so much of the reality I perceive through that vision enters into me as destructive of it and as denying its authenticity.

But I do not reject it; I affirm it. It may seem that in this act I contradict all I have said about refusing the authority of the past. This would be true except that the grounds of affirmation can only be that the Christian vision forecloses nothing, conceals nothing, refuses all self-defense. It is particular, but not exclusive. The belief that this is so is itself, of course, a function of the vision. This circularity cannot be avoided. One can only seek in complete openness to expand the circle indefinitely.

Because I know that my quest for a new world is motivated by my Christian selfhood and that the new world I see is seen through Christian eyes, I must acknowledge that all my thinking is Christian thinking, whether or not it is acceptable to other Christians. I cannot claim, as philosophy seems often to want to claim, that any intelligent person should be able to see the truth of my premises and the validity of my arguments.

But why "theology?" If Christian philosophy is the open quest for truth of a self who affirms the Christianness of the vision which is his, then theology is thinking that reflects upon the giver of that selfhood. Christian selfhood experiences itself as a gift in two modes. Historically, it is a gift of a community of faith grounded in Jesus Christ. Existentially, it experiences itself as a gift of God. Theological reflection must seek to understand how these two modes of giving are connected with each other, and in the process it must reflect on such traditional topics as Jesus Christ, the Holy Spirit, the church, the Bible, as well as God. Furthermore, even if such reflection in our day is prompted by our concern for our selfhood, the reflection itself must turn away from that selfhood toward its source in such a way as to bring that selfhood also under most radical judgment.

But this specific theological reflection upon the gift of Christian selfhood is never separable from the Christian philosophical reflection upon reality as a whole and in its parts. The theological must both illustrate and illuminate the categories of philsophical reflection. Each must act as criterion for the other, and each criterion in turn is modified and reshaped by the total reflection. At every point the decision to affirm rather than to reject the starting point in Christian selfhood and vision is open for reconsideration as reflection modifies its self-understanding or casts doubt upon its adequacy.

In this approach, theology is a part of the total reflective process and is *totally vulnerable*. There is no built-in safeguard to insure that in the end there will be any place in one's world for God, or Jesus Christ, or Christian selfhood. Because I believe God *is*, and that in Jesus Christ we find what it means to know God as he is, I also believe that reflection must ultimately lead us toward rather than away from these truths. But I know also that my belief may be shattered in the process, and I cannot appeal to some protected ground of confidence when all else fails.

19

CARL MICHALSON

Transitional Theologian

Carl Michalson (1915–1965) is an outstanding representative of what may be called the uprooted generation of American religious thinkers, those who received their theological education in the 1940s and 1950s during the ascendancy of European neo-orthodoxy and its offshoots. Unlike Douglas Horton, Walter Lowrie, and others who moved from an American background into the Barthian and Kierkegaardian worlds of discourse, men of Michalson's generation encountered the latter as normative at the outset of their seminary studies, even in the United States.

Born in the hamlet of Waverly, Minnesota, Carl Michalson was the younger of two sons who became Methodist ministers and educators. After graduating from high school in Minneapolis, he studied for his B.A. at John Fletcher College (1936), and for his B.D. at the theological school of Drew University (1939), where he was strongly influenced by Lynn Harold Hough and Edwin Lewis. Lewis's *Christian Manifesto* of 1934 was among the early American affirmations of neo-orthodoxy, and at Drew he provided a compelling invitation to the theology of Brunner and Barth. Michalson also took his M.A. at Drew (1940) with a thesis contrasting the concept of human responsibility as seen in the synoptic Gospels with that of Plato's Republic.

From 1943 until his death in an airline crash in 1965, Michalson taught systematic theology at Drew, with time out for a Ph.D. from Yale (1945) with Robert Calhoun and H. Richard Niebuhr, and further studies at Basel and Tübingen (1952–53) and Strasbourg (1960–61). His doctoral dissertation examined the themes of reason and revelation in the theology of Karl Heim. His first article was titled "Barthianism and Evangelism" (*The Drew Gateway*, XVII, 4, Summer 1946), and for the two decades of his writing and teaching activity he enjoyed a growing reputation as one of America's outstanding interpreters of German theology and philosophy—the theology of the Word and the existentialism of Jaspers and Heidegger, the spiritual heirs of the Danish philosopher Kierkegaard. John D. Godsey, his colleague at Drew, has aptly described Michalson as "a missionary who has learned from Kierkegaard that 'subjectivity is truth' and that therefore the questions of man can be answered meaningfully only in the medium in which they arise, namely, history. History is a world of meaning, a specifically human world. . . . "[1] To exist, says Michalson, is to face the possibility of nonbeing, to grasp seriously one's own individual uniqueness and "to value personal authenticity more highly than scientific exactitude" or faceless objectivity.[2] Faith, for Michalson, is a subjective structuring of history:

> Jesus Christ *happened* in the midst of a people. He came as the very *act* of God. His appearance set off a chain of *events*, the church. His presence, therefore, is a hinge. Happening in time, he both connects and separates the old and the new, the past and the future.[3]

Michalson's concern is not with empirical history but with "salvation history," history viewed in a perspective of faith. Jesus inaugurates what Michalson calls the eschatological dimension of history, or eschatological existence, ending man's search for God and ushering in the Kingdom of God among men as a new age of faith, in which men, as mature sons of God, are freed from bondage to the world and are given responsibility for the world. Jesus is not God, but he manifests

---

[1] John D. Godsey, "Thinking of the Faith Historically: The Legacy of Carl Michalson," *The Drew Gateway*, XXXVI, 3 (Spring-Summer 1966), p. 82.

[2] Carl Michalson, "What Is Existentialism?" in Michalson, ed., *Christianity and the Existentialists* (New York: Scribner, 1956), p. 17.

[3] Michalson, *The Hinge of History* (New York: Scribner, 1959), p. 169.

both God's decisive word to man and the mature human response of obedient sonship. The crucifixion is only the culmination of the meaning-event of obedience, Jesus' whole life as proclaimer of man's historic responsibility.

Michalson was closely attuned to Rudolf Bultmann's demythologizing efforts, and even more to the kindred theology of Friedrich Gogarten, who finds in Christian faith the secularizaion or "de-divinization" of the world and thus the source of man's liberation from myths and idols.[4] On the whole, it may be said that Michalson was a brilliant but derivative theologian, a translator, synthesizer, and interpreter of imported ideas. Like others of his generation, he turned his back on the American tradition in favor of the European one dominated by Karl Barth. Yet as Michalson observed with regard to the Japanese theologies he saw growing out of Western neo-orthodoxy, "in the very process of folding the insights of others into one's own language, something creative occurs. For even where imitation prevails, selectivity and translation are required."[5] *The Hinge of History* (1959) is very largely a recapitulation of the thinking of Gogarten and several others. Harvey Cox's *The Secular City* (1965) also draws upon Gogarten. But each of these books, in its way, articulates an emerging set of concerns that would eventually bring into play once more some of the leading themes in American thought, such as pragmatism and situationism.

Each of several articles by Michalson would be symptomatic of European dominance in the period following World War II —"Neo-Orthodox Theology" (*The Drew Gateway*, XXI, 1, Autumn 1950), "Communicating the Gospel" (*Theology Today*, XIV, 3, October 1957) or "Kierkegaard's Theology of Faith" (*Religion in Life*, XXXII, 2, Spring 1963). The following essay, however, written shortly before Michalson's death, signifies a shift in orientation. It is not yet quite the exile's return, and some

---

[4] See Friedrich Gogarten, *Verhängnis und Hoffnung der Neuzeit* (Göttingen, 1953), p. 99.
[5] Michalson, *Japanese Contributions to Christian Theology* (Philadelphia: Westminster, 1960), p. 14.

of his remarks (e.g. on James and Dewey) betray a lack of adequate information. What is perhaps more interesting, however, is the new openness, the air of expectancy, the willingness to accept the new, even if it is chaotic and rash. With all its imperfections, including those characteristic of a survey article, it is a significant document portending the close of a hiatus in the mainstream of American theology and the opening of a new era in which the renewal of American theology may be expected to contribute to Christian thought on a world scale.

The question of maturity, of "coming of age," is more than incidental. As we have noted above, it is closely bound up with both Gogarten's and Michalson's understanding of the relation between salvation and secularity, and, from a slightly different angle, Dietrich Bonhoeffer's call for a "religionless Christianity" for man in a "mature" (*mündige*) world from which the God of metaphysical explanation is notably absent and in which man is apparently on his own.[6] The implication is more in the nature of a question than an assertion, but it is just this which may have suggested to Michalson the need for reassessment and for new departures from neo-orthodoxy —indeed for regrouping and interplay among previously divergent methods and views.

IS AMERICAN THEOLOGY COMING OF AGE?*

Probably two factors in American life are mainly responsible for the perennial immaturity of its theology. One is that we have always depended upon Europe for our theological en-

*From *The Drew Gateway,* Volume XXXVI, Number 3 (Spring-Summer, 1966), pp. 65–75.
[6] See Bonhoeffer, "Last Letters From a Nazi Prison" in William Robert Miller, ed., *The New Christianity* (New York: Delacorte, 1967), pp. 274–295. Also, Ronald Gregor Smith, *Secular Christianity* (New York: Harper, 1966), pp. 175–185; and Carl Michalson, ed., *Worldly Theology* (New York: Scribner, 1967).

richment, a kind of theological Marshall Plan in reverse. American theologians still make jokes about how the way to become a creative theologian is to learn to read German. The other factor is that we have constantly had to contend with an expanding frontier. That means that as soon as we have received theological products from overseas, we have shipped them off to the front. The rapid transfer from import to export gave no adequate time for the theological fruit to ripen on our own vines.

The relationship to Europe remains strong. In fact, thanks to increased mobility in all areas of life today—in transportation, linguistics, ecumenicity and finance—the contacts with European thought are even more ample than ever before. In our efforts to break out of this exclusively European relationship and explore the contributions of other peoples, such as the Japanese, we have discovered that they are as we, indebted to Europe.

I

The new factor, however, is that the relation is no longer one of dependence. The reasons for this are manifold. For one thing, the frontier, while it continues to be a psychological reality among us, is no longer a geographical fact. Some of our leading theological faculties now occupy the area only recently regarded as a frontier. For another thing, a new kind of resistance to the expansion of the Church has forced upon us a form of theological reflection that did not seem so urgent in earlier times. The Church itself is calling into question its customary image and is looking to its theology as well as to its sociology for insight into the nature of congregational life. The Church is finding its expression, not in the edifice, and not in numerical expansion, but in the small group movements among laymen. European churches have seen it happen in their lay academies. The Japanese have developed it in the non-church movement. In America one finds these movements arising within established congregations. For these groups the preaching service, around which the congregation typically rallies, tends to take second place to small assemblies of concerned laymen who probe their faith in depth through biblical and theological studies. One might have called the groups *ecclesiola in ecclesia,* except that these, judged by traditional standards, seem to be comprised of the faithless, those making a last desperate effort to remain in the Church, but doing so under the auspices of the Church.

A correlative shift of accent is occurring at the academic level. In America in the past, denominationally-supported theological schools, often isolated from a university setting, have been the main *loci* for theological reflection. Now non-church-related private universities are beginning to assume theological leadership through their faculties of religion. Even state universities have found a way of transcending the constitutional strictures against mixing religion and government and in many instances have gathered competent and influential theological faculties. European theologians have been known to express their pleasure at doing theology in state-supported rather than in church-supported institutions because they enjoy more intellectual freedom there. American church-related theological faculties, of course, manifest a wide variety of emphases on a spectrum ranging from control to freedom, depending on the denominational attitude toward theology. In communions where theology is somewhat cynically indulged, on the grounds that theology is no finally crucial factor in church life and in Christian piety, theologians experience a freedom bordering on indifference. The frontier mentality is residual to that permissiveness. The theology now being done under nonsectarian circumstances, however, is enjoying a freedom which goes beyond anything we have known in either Europe or America. One should add at the risk of confusing the case that many theologians deliberately choose to work within the church-related context, because they consider theology as a function of church existence. My point about the shift of theological studies to the universities is that theology is no longer for us simply a function of church existence. Questions of faith are more and more accepted in America as *bona fide* human questions, even to the extent of being granted a hearing in the humanities curricula.

One of the main evidences that this is true is the provocative theological note being discerned in America in literature and art. I do not refer so much to the standard Broadway fare, such as MacLeish's takeoff on Job, Chayevsky's Gideon or Osborne's *Luther*. Here the stage seems edifying and sometimes even permissive toward traditional prejudices. When religious groups on university campuses are unable to secure the services of Paul Tillich for their special conferences, instead of reaching for less prestigious theologians, they will often go for Edward Albee or James Baldwin. When they do settle for a theologian, they will require him to speak in a setting of modern art and will confront his contributions with performances of plays by Sartre, Ionesco, or Brecht. As a part of the orientation program at the Theological School where I teach, almost one hundred entering students attended an off-Broadway theater in New York to witness Albee's *Zoo Story* and Beckett's *Krapp's Last Tape*. On the following day the theological classes began.

Drama of this *genre* produces a more ambiguous reaction than the usual Broadway offering. Therefore, because it cannot count on large public support as entertainment for the after dinner crowd, it must be mounted in small and inexpensive theaters "off Broadway." The playwrights seem to have anticipated this necessity, even to the extent of limiting their casts to a single character (or two, if you count the tape recorder). The ambiguity of this kind of drama is that it is a direct onslaught upon the world of illusion, so that in the end it is difficult to know what is real and what is illusory. God, while rarely mentioned outside ejaculations of profanity, always seems to hover in the wings. Is He the reality who will finally overcome our last illusions, or is He the one large illusion which we will have to release before our life together can be real again? The laceration one undergoes in auditing this kind of art leaves one like a hand which has just grasped a nettle, astringently aware of one's own existence. The ambiguity remains, however. Is this awareness of one's human reality a springboard for the realization of God's existence, or is it a substitute for God and thus a rival to faith? Is it a dialectical stage on the way to God, or is it the legitimate mode God's presence can be expected to take today? That dilemma, I believe, describes the issue underlying present American theology. How are the theologians responding to it?

II

Before I outline the points of view developing in American theology which are attempting to cope with our situation, let me cite a number of features which all of them seem to share. Karl Barth and Rudolf Bultmann taught this generation of American theologians how to take their sources seriously. To be sure, Barth called history a *Hilfswissenschaft* to theology, but he found more there than most for whom history was a major science. Bultmann treated the Bible with an almost surgical penetration, yet he brought more to light of relevance for Christian existence than one was accustomed to associate with biblical scholarship. It is also often reported of Reinhold Niebuhr that while his exegesis of the Bible was not always accurate, it was always interesting. In consequence, this epoch has witnessed the appearance of large bodies of first class biblical and historical studies which seem to have gathered their momentum under the inspiration of these great teachers.

Another feature of the times is the return of 19th century theological sources. Within a span of twenty years Schleiermacher, F. D. Maurice, and Horace Bushnell have become transformed from aliens into allies. What they called experience and what was shunned in them for its anthropocentrism is now seen as the historicality of existence. What they described of the knowledge of God as a moral reality and was rejected in them as epistemological agnosticism is now being described as a faith-event with its own inherent structures of rationality. When they used theological language as if the theologian were better qualified to speak about man than about God, they were criticized for subjectivism, but now they are looked upon as the pioneers in the New Hermeneutic, where one does not speak about God but attends to the linguisticality of Being.

This juxtaposition of an American historical figure, Bushnell, alongside a German and an English figure is, in itself, a revealing phenomenon in American theology. We have long been aware that by contrast to other areas of the Church, we Americans have scarcely any history. That rather self-conscious attitude has now been dissipated. Thanks to the impetus of such studies as *The Kingdom of God in America* by H. Richard Niebuhr and Perry Miller's investigation of the role of Puritanism in the formation of the American spirit, there has emerged as a discipline in our theological faculties "American Church History" which is considerably illuminating our theological picture. As my colleague in this field, Gordon Harland, is often quoted as saying, "An unexamined history tends to operate as a fate."

Openness toward philosophy is another feature of American theology. In the United States we have probably had only one indigenous philosophy, the pragmatism of William James and its successor in John Dewey's philosophy of education, called instrumentalism. James' position is sometimes thought to have had its roots in the common sense thinking of Benjamin Franklin and Dewey's in the discussion method of the New England town meeting. Dewey's philosophy never received expression in the theological point of view, but it did inspire the religious education movement. James' pragmatism never found its way into theology. The sole philosophy, developed distinctively in America, to have been extended into a theological position is the process philosophy of Alfred North Whitehead and its current version in Charles Hartshorne. The philosophies which rival process philosophy in their bid for American theological attention are linguistic analysis, phenomenology, and existentialism. These I will take up in connection with the points of view among us today, which draw inspiration from them. I only wish to say that far from being cautious of the role of philosophy in theology, present American theology tends to let philosophy be more than a handmaiden and more even than a midwife or dialogical partner. Some would regard this as sitting too lightly to the theological frame of reference, the Bible and the history of its interpretation. Nevertheless, I believe it can be taken as a sign of theological maturity for at least two reasons. For one thing, theology is no longer exploiting philosophy for theological purposes. For another thing, theology has a realistic appraisal of its limitations and how modest its own claims are, materially speaking.

The most startling outcome of all these affiliations is the determination to express the Christian faith without supernaturalism. It has long been understood by American theologians that we must not look for a God from the wings, a *deus ex machina.* How to express this conviction without seeming to betray the existence of God and without defaulting in one's ministry to existential needs becomes a major agenda for these theologians.

The point at which the non-supernaturalist theology is in the greatest agreement is that the life of faith must be a being-for-others. To illustrate how seriously this is meant, being-for-others expresses itself more explicitly in the form of social ethics, and social ethics tends to become almost the exclusive mode in which faith is being encouraged to formulate itself. The enormity and urgency of such problems as the development of the inner city and the momentum of the civil rights movement give credence to this direction. Therefore, the *Christian Century* magazine can repeatedly criticize the American evangelist Billy Graham for his evasiveness on the integration issue, and the ministers of New York City can protest the election of Norman Vincent Peale to the presidency of the Protestant Council of that city on the grounds of his theological incompetence to deal with the subtle social issues there. Most striking of all is the noticeable waning of interest in the theology of pastoral care, so popular a decade ago. Americans are learning to live more easily with anxieties, finitude, and guilt than they can with social injustice.

In this matrix, then, what evidence is there that American theology is coming of age? What great dogmatic systems are emerging on our shelves under the auspices of our theologians? Barth has posted his *Dogmatik* and Tillich his *Systematic Theology.* Where are the American counterparts of these?

Probably the major claim to maturity in American theology is its realization that we are living "between the times." That does not mean between the time of Christ's appearance and the time of his coming again. That means what Friedrich Gogarten meant when he first coined the phrase now so famous in our century. We live between the time of the theology which no longer makes sense to us and the time of a theology which has not yet clearly dawned. Theology written in this time between the times will not only be modest, it will be confused. It will not only decline to be systematic, it will be fragmentary, rash, and even chaotic. It will not nurse on its catechism in secret, like an arcane discipline which is afraid of being misunderstood in the open forum. It will only utter short, sometimes ejaculatory sounds, sounds sometimes barely distinguishable from profanity because the words are more percussive and resonant than their meanings seem to warrant, words like "God!", "Christ!", "Love!", "Thou!", not fully knowing what they mean, but stabbing from out of all our vast endowment of theological information for the word or words which will illuminate our way into the time beyond this time between.

III

Four theological emphases in America seem most clearly representative of our situation "between the times." These are enjoying an almost "honest to God" prominence in theological conversation today.

1. One is the "process theology" of Schubert Ogden and John Cobb. This motif in American theology is relatively venerable, but it had a major liability in its earliest form. It was an unabashed naturalism. It expressed faith in completely this-wordly terms at a time when nobody was concerned about getting rid of the "God out there." The spokesman most likely to have received a hearing at that time was Daniel Day Williams. He was the first theologian to bring the process motifs into combination with other theological traditions. Shortly after World War II, at a time when there was wide dissatisfaction over both conservative and liberal trends in

theology, he showed how Christians were not limited to those alternatives. Process motifs could overcome the weaknesses in both while conserving their strengths. Mainly, liberalism was too optimistic and orthodoxy too pessimistic. Neither view had an adequate place for redemption, because the liberal did not need it and the orthodox delayed it eschatologically.

In Whitehead's view, God was transcendent in such a way as to be a part of the universe, not "out there," entering into relation with the universe from within it. The tragic character of the universe was dramatized by the knowledge that not only is God in the universe, the universe is in God, filling up his being by its decisions. Nevertheless, through the appeal of God's aggressive love to man's freedom, the tragic universe is being moved in the direction of creativity and growth. Redemption can therefore be offered without indifference to the tragedy of existence.

Ogden and Cobb have now renewed process motifs by bringing them into relation to European theology, especially Bultmann's. Ogden contends that Bultmann to be consistent ought to get rid of the last myth, the myth of the uniqueness of Christ. Faith conceived along process lines knows no unique events, only decisive events. The *logos* is universal. Furthermore, faith must be able to stand the test of truth and not confine itself, as Bultmann seems to do, to kerygmatic proclamations. The claim to the reality of God is a metaphysical claim which should be able to stand independently of any particular faith expression. The responsibility of theology is to bring faith to understanding, to verify faith as truth. One way of fulfilling this responsibility is to find the formal intellectual system which can do it. Theology, then, is taken to be the search for the right philosophy. For similar reasons, John Cobb has shown how a natural theology can be done on the Whiteheadean model.

2. "Hermeneutical theology," mainly promoted by James M. Robinson, is the major American outlet for current European thinking, but has also contributed creative elements of its own, as European works continue to acknowledge. While it is not formulated in opposition to process theology, its

distinctive motifs clearly emerge in such a contrast. In theology as hermeneutics, faith is not the kind of reality which seeks understanding, because it is itself a mode of understanding. Truth is not something that can be tested, because truth is what is brought to light in events outside of which the truth is untrue. The revealed events of faith are not simply decisive, but unique. They are historical events and in history all events are unique. The *logos,* therefore, which occurs in the Jesus of Nazareth event is not a universal. In history there are no universals. Nor is the *logos* the truth about God. In history one does not speak about God. One hears God's word in Jesus of Nazareth as the answer to the questions of the meaning of man's existence, and in that event of God's self-revelation, not God but the world is revealed.

This view is hermeneutical in the sense in which Martin Heidegger's "philosophy" has helped it to become so. In Schleiermacher and Dilthey hermeneutics had been an art of understanding, where the object of understanding was some fixed expression of human meaning, as in a text or work of art. In Heidegger, influenced as he is by phenomenological thinking, hermeneutics is a process of understanding in which the interpreter is himself both subject and object of interpretation. In a man's relation to a text it is he, the interpreter, who is understood.

The view of speech involved in this thinking is crucial. Words here do not point to things. Words, as in poems, bring a situation to light. "God"-words, then, do not require that the reality, "God," be isolated as an object in order for their truth to be validated. "God"-words illuminate situations, and their truth inheres not in the correspondence of the word with the object, but in the luminousness of the event brought to light by their expression.

This combination of emphases on "event," "speech," and "interpretation" explains why "the new quest of the historical Jesus" is central to this position. Jesus' historicity is established by recent historiography and hermeneutics not in isolation from his influences but precisely in these influences. Therefore, the familar dichotomy between Jesus and Paul is no longer entertained. In addition, Jesus' words, as in his parables, are inseparable from his deeds, because words have the historiographical function of illuminating events which might otherwise remain brute facts, with no capacity to interpret, therefore, with no real historicity. Thus one looks to Jesus' own words as interpretations of his cross and resurrection, not simply to the words of the post-resurrection Christ. The effect of this position is to locate the question of faith firmly within historical reality, to place theological conclusions in direct reliance upon the traditions stemming from the preaching of Jesus, and to confine the language about God to a mode of expression more reminiscent of poetry with its evocation of worlds, than of metaphysics with its denotation of beings.

3. "Secularizing theology" takes two quite different forms among us. One is in the work of Paul Van Buren, who takes his cue from linguistic analysis, where statements to be "meaningful" must have some empirical reference. Van Buren believes that the man of today is a "secular" man. That is, he is oriented to human, historical, empirical type realities. His *milieu* is dominantly scientific and technological. "Non-objective" realities are meaningless to him and existential language strange. If the gospel is to be made meaningful to the secular man, those aspects of the gospel which lend themselves to empirical certification must be accentuated. So, for instance, Christology is more central than theology. Christ, especially in his humanity, is a more plausible object than God. In this preference, the contrast with process theology is explicit. The cross has the theological advantage of having been "two pieces of wood joined together."

Fortunately, van Buren does not seem to carry out the empirical promise in his project. In his delineation of faith he is more cognizant of the existential meanings characteristic of the hermeneutical theology than he is of the empirical basis, except for one possibly ironical outcome. Van Buren believes there was no Christian faith prior to the resurrection of Jesus. That sets him against the "new quest" theology. On what empirical base does he place his theology then? On the base of the history that comes into existence when the preaching of

Christ is heard. That outcome has the irony of a double dis-advantage for his case: the alleged empirical base is no more empirical than existential meanings are, and the historical significance of Christianity's historical origin in the pre-resurrection Jesus has been obscured for him.

The other form of secularizing theology is expressed in Harvey Cox's work, *The Secular City*. While this is not primarily a theological work, it is a compendious and artistically conceived presentation of major trends in contemporary theology. "Secular" for Cox has the meaning it does in the work of Cornelis van Peursen and Gogarten. The secular man is not the scientific, technological man who never really bothers about the question of meaning. He is the man, as Bonhoeffer described him, who has learned to get along without God, who has answered the questions of the meaning of existence without reference to the God hypothesis. The modern city is the best illustration. Many deplore that God has left the city. Cox finds that to be the theological charm of city life: it is mature enough not to "need" God. But that outcome is not, in this view of secularism, a merely cultural achievement. It is the situation of maturity for men which God himself initiated when, in Jesus of Nazareth, he turned the world over to men as their responsibility by making men his sons and heirs.

People who find no meaning in faith outside I-thou relations with God and neighbor will not appreciate this view. But Cox has proposed that God has permitted a kind of neighbor-relation which does not automatically become an it-relation when it is no longer a thou-relation. There is still the you-relation, so familiar to the anonymous life of the city. God may even have allowed himself to be so situated in the scheme of things as to be satisfied to be addressed as "you." Van Buren's secular theology seeks an empirical foundation and expresses itself as a revision of the meanings in the traditional doctrinal outline. Van Buren was a close follower of Barth before his new affair with linguistic analysis, and the Barthian positivism has found a new form through him in the lingering positivism of linguistic philosophy. Cox, on the other hand, speaks for a group of theologians who find the quest for empirical validation something required not by modern secular man, but by the immature and religious, who still seek a sign. Secular meaning in Cox's view is found in the socio-political responsibilities which faith inspires and illuminates. In his way Cox may at last be introducing into theological understanding a non-analytical form of verification once sponsored by the American philosopher, Dewey. Truth is not something to be verified. Truth *is* in its verification. Theologically expressed, that could mean that "the love of God" is only true when a man is loving his neighbor.

4. Now one can see how in American theology God has been successively telescoped. His metaphysical independence as God has been telescoped into the historical reality of Jesus of Nazareth and from thence into the responsible relations of Jesus' followers to their society. What next step does that suggest? God could die out entirely. I would not want to claim that "the death of God theology" regards itself as the dialectical outcome of the views I have been reporting. But probably no current theological expression in America is more contrived to catch the secular ear than this one. "God is dead." Nietzsche's Zarathustra announced it. William Blake, Hegel, and Luther announced it before him. Today's world is just coming into that realization through the collapse of meaning in its God-words. William Hamilton and Thomas Altizer are the chief spokesmen for this view. They do not mean as many have, that theistic positions regarding God have died. Nor do they mean that God has been momentarily eclipsed. Nor do they mean that men have learned to remain silent about a God they no longer quite understand. They mean that God has actually allowed himself to die. Therefore, they are not atheists. They believe in a God who was. Nor are they deicides. They have not eradicated God through their rapier-like theological wit. God in his wisdom and love sought to redeem the world by letting it be without him. God's death is the objective reality at the base of our life today, which is the major barrier to our any longer speaking meaningfully about God. The form which the Christian confession must now take is to affirm the reality of God's

death. The holy history of the acts of God, when recapitulated by modern man, must now include the holy act of his death.

What the necrology of God precisely means in this view is necessarily vague. Possibly "death of God" states the case too strongly. Bonhoeffer's language about God "allowing himself to be edged out of the world" is probably more accurate, and sufficiently heady. These theologians do not seem to mean that God has really died, but that He is really absent. As Hamilton has said, "We are not talking about the absence of the experience of God, but about the experience of the absence of God." Therefore, God is not really present in the word of faith. He is dead for faith.

What is the theological structure of this view? Christology replaces theology and kenosis is redefined. God does not empty himself so as to become man. Rather, the man Jesus becomes the Christ by emptying himself and all the history which follows him of its godness. Christians who confess their faith in Christ at one and the same time confess the absence of God from history and the presence of man himself in his full humanity to the world in its complete worldliness. "My God, why hast thou forsaken me" is not a cry of dereliction but the essence of God's revelation in Jesus of Nazareth.

If I do not seem to have answered the question posed in my title, it is because I believe it is an answer which can only be judged by history, beginning with the reader himself. I have written the article, and have done it in the way I have, because I believe no theology can regard itself as mature which has not been openly engaged by these four positions.

20

MARTIN LUTHER KING

Black Prophet of the American Dream

Martin Luther King Jr. (1929–1968) was one of America's most controversial historic figures, both revered and reviled. At various times and by various admirers and detractors, he was described as saint, troublemaker, subversive, apostle of nonviolence, a great leader of the black community, and one of the century's most powerful preachers. No easy rubric emerges that would gain broad assent, but in my view he may be most accurately and enduringly regarded as a prophetic voice significantly addressing himself to America's destiny and the choice of values which will determine that destiny. Although he made no overt claim to theological acuity, such a claim has been entered on his behalf by intellectually distinguished contemporaries. In any event, King left a profound legacy of both thought and action. Behind the headlines of his brief, impactful life is to be found an amalgam of repetitious, even banal preachments and a serious, urgent revolutionary message and outlook that touches upon the major levels of human concern, from the Kierkegaardian self alone before God to vast ethnic, national, and transnational masses of people. Integral to this perspective is a deeply committed religious personalism related to King's program of social action. Historically, King's freedom movement, even though superseded by a more fragmented and partially more divisive one, set in motion a more honest and encompassing notion of America's democratic vistas—and brought to bear a decidedly Christian religious way of thought and action.

Martin Luther King was born in Atlanta, the son and grandson of black Baptist preachers who were also outstanding leaders of Atlanta's Negro middle and upper class.[1] He was educated at Morehouse College, Crozer Seminary, and Boston University, and the formative influences in his theological outlook were predominantly liberal. At Boston he studied with Brightman until the latter's death, and wrote his doctoral dissertation on Tillich and Wieman. The writings of Rauschenbusch and Niebuhr played a significant part in shaping his ideas, as did the more direct influence of such men as Benjamin E. Mays, George D. Kelsey, and L. Harold De Wolfe.

King was a pastor throughout his adult life. He was ordained at the age of eighteen and installed as assistant pastor of his father's Atlanta church. At 25, upon completion of his Ph. D. studies, he became minister of the Dexter Avenue Baptist Church in Montgomery, Alabama. Fifteen months later, in December 1955, he became the leader of a year-long boycott of that city's buses, a campaign of nonviolent, direct action against racial injustice. It established King's Southwide leadership of the nonviolent freedom revolution, which began on a wide scale in 1960 with the student sit-ins. The remaining years of King's life were devoted chiefly to that struggle. He will probably be best remembered for the dramatic campaign he led in Birmingham, Alabama, in 1963, and for the historic March on Washington which followed it, a march which brought some 250,000 people to the Lincoln Memorial to hear his stirring address, "I Have a Dream." That speech and his "Letter From Birmingham Jail," written the same year, are his best-known utterances. Several attempts on his life were made from 1956 onward. He was stabbed by an insane black woman in 1958, and on April 4, 1968, he was fatally shot by a white assassin.

Like their white Southern counterparts, the Negro Baptists have tended to depreciate serious theological studies until recently, and even at present neither has produced a major intellectual contributor to American Protestant thought. As

---

[1] See William Robert Miller, *Martin Luther King Jr.: His Life, Martyrdom and Meaning For the World* (New York: Weybright & Talley, 1968), and Coretta Scott King, *My Life With Martin Luther King Jr.* (New York: Holt, Rinehart & Winston, 1969).

early as the 1780s, such black Christians as Richard Allen and
Absalom Jones were preaching the gospel with eloquence, but
they were Northerners and Methodists. Articulate Negro religious intellectuals have appeared chiefly among men of Martin
Luther King's generation, and to a lesser extent among the
generation preceding his,—Kelsey, Mays, and Howard Thur-
man among the older men; Nathan Scott, Charles Long,
Gayraud Wilmore, Shelby Rooks, Eric Lincoln, Nathan Wright,
and a dozen others among the younger ones. To date, perhaps
Vincent Harding has shown the greatest promise of theological
originality. None of them, however, stands in the kind of
historic relationship to the black Baptist mainstream in which
King stood and in which he was not only rooted but remained
while reaching out to embrace the ecumenical movement.

King left no clearly definable body of theological writings as
such. He did not regard his role as that of a theologian except
in the sense that every thoughtful minister or layman is an
exponent and interpreter of some kind of theology. He was
primarily an activist, a pastor, a spiritual individual, rather
than a man engaged in the exploration of theological problems.
He was a personalist and an exponent of social Christianity,
largely in terms of influences already mentioned. To these
must be added the diffuse impact of Christian pacifism and
the perhaps larger and clearer impact of the leading ideas of
Mahatma Gandhi. The amalgam of all these strands is loose
and unsystematic, perhaps laden with inner contradictions,
but raw as it may appear it nevertheless comprises a legacy
significant enough to warrant serious study. King's style is
often an impediment, for it runs to the inflated and ornate
rhetoric of the Baptist preacher. Yet within the broad and
repetitious fabric of his writings and speeches and sermons
are imbedded the makings of a serious and distinctive theology embodying a synthesis of elements from personalism,
pacifism, Gandhism, and the inherited traditions of the Negro
Baptist church, bound together and transformed by pragmatic
experience both personal and social, and informed also by an
innate religious intuition, the sensibility of a man for whom
religious feeling was at least as real an experienced fact of

life as for Jonathan Edwards, Schleiermacher, or Bushnell. Herbert Richardson, in a preliminary article, goes so far as to call King America's great "unsung theologian."[2]

Subsequent scholarship may well establish an underground current, stemming from Edwards' ideas about conversion, emerging out of the black Baptist tradition in King's synthesis as the change of heart made possible through nonviolent moral and social action. Some of King's key concepts, such as the redemptiveness of suffering and the basic unity of mankind, are derived from Gandhi. But it is instructive to note the extent to which Gandhi's own thinking was steeped in a perfectionist, largely Tolstoyan Christianity. Gandhi's impact on King was pivotal, but as far as it had theological content or implications its force resulted in a crystallization of certain Christian motifs and secured their centrality in King's thought. There is not the slightest trace of syncretism, not a shred of Hindu cosmology in King's conception of human relationships or human destiny. Gandhi's nonviolence was a blend of Hindu and Christian concepts; King's was one that eliminated the Hindu elements and augmented the Christian ones with pragmatic secular correlates. To a considerable degree, King more closely resembles the 19th-century Universalist, Adin Ballou, whose Yankee concept of "moral resistance" found its way to Gandhi by way of Tolstoy.[3] King did not study Ballou, but he set aside the Gandhian-Tolstoyan elements and picked up what Gandhi had got from Ballou; insofar as he differs from Ballou it is in the direction of subsequent Protestant theology. However one chooses to state it, the result is an understanding of such non-violent moral resistance as part of a process of redemptive suffering structured according to the life and teachings of Jesus and verified in man's pragmatic experiences of repentance and forgiveness in interpersonal relations.

For King, the New Testament doctrine of reconciliation is

---

2 See Herbert Warren Richardson, "Martin Luther King—Unsung Theologian," *Commonweal*, May 3, 1968.
3 Tolstoy's *The Kingdom of God Is Within You* was the book from which Gandhi derived his idea of *satyagraha*. It contains a summary of Ballou's *Christian Non-Resistance*.

not confined to an expiatory event which took place when Jesus died on the cross. That sacrifice, rather, attests to the need and the possibility of reconciliation among men wherever they are estranged by sinful injustice. Like Rauschenbusch, King envisions salvation as having a decidedly social aspect, but he is more aware of its essentially interpersonal character —theologically as between the divine and human persons of God and Jesus, and existentially between persons involved in intergroup conflict. King is perhaps more aware than Rauschenbusch of the intermediate strata between the solitary individual and the total social structure; in particular he is more attuned to those involving direct confrontation between individuals and groups. For King, contends Richardson, the ultimate value in human life is not the exalted, holy love which the New Testament calls *agapē;* the ultimate human value is simple friendship, with all that this implies of personal respect and empathy. The *agapē* which produces self-sacrifice is not something compartmented and divorced from friendship but is rather its highest manifestation. The image of Jesus as friend, his divine sonship, and the traditional Baptist notion of the church as pre-eminently a fellowship community or gathering—these are integrally related parts of King's doctrine of man, and they all have direct application to the actual social problems which King sought to solve.

As a social visionary, King maintained a precarious balance between optimism and desperation, embracing both perfectionism and realism, and on different occasions he was capable of erring as much in the direction of restraint as of excess. The following address to the 1965 General Synod of the United Church of Christ was delivered a few weeks after the Selma-to-Montgomery march, which marked the height of his career and of the churches' involvement. Probably no statement of similar length, except his 1964 Nobel Prize Lecture, affords as good a general conspectus of his outlook and its inner structure. None so well expresses the theological or the churchly aspects of his concern, nor so forcefully summarizes and highlights the plight of the Negro and the challenge which the racial crisis poses for white American Christians.

MAN IN A REVOLUTIONARY WORLD*

America has brought the nation and the world to an awe inspiring threshold of the future. Through our scientific and technological genius we have built mighty bridges to span the seas and skyscraping buildings to kiss the skies. We have dwarfed distance and placed time in chains. We have carved highways through the stratosphere. Through the marvelous advances of medical science we have been able to cure many dread plagues and diseases, alleviate our pain, prolong our lives, and make for greater security and physical well-being. This is a dazzling picture of America's scientific progress.

But when we turn to the question of progress in the area of race relations, we face one of the most shameful chapters of the America scene. In spite of the jet-like pace of our scientific and technological developments, we still creep at horse and buggy speed in human relations. We must face the melancholy fact that one hundred and two years after the Emancipation Proclamation, the negro is still dominated politically, exploited economically, segregated and humiliated. Negroes, north and south, still live in segregation, housed in unendurable slums, eat in segregation, pray in segregation and die in segregation. How much of our national life can be summarized in that arresting phrase of Thoreau's: "Improved means to an unimproved end." Through our scientific genius, we have made of the world a neighborhood, but we have failed to employ our moral and spiritual genius to make of it a brotherhood. The problem of race and color prejudice remains America's chief moral dilemma.

This tragic dilemma presents the Church with a great challenge. In the final analysis the problem of race is not a political,

* An address, July 6, 1965, published as Appendix 14, *Minutes of the Fifth General Synod of the United Church of Christ,* 1965, pp. 236–244.
Reprinted by permission of Joan Daves. Copyright © 1965 by the Estate of Martin Luther King, Jr.

but a moral issue. As the chief moral guardian of the community the Church must work with passionate determination to solve this problem. The task of conquering segregation is an inescapable must confronting organized religion. It has always been the responsibility of the Church to broaden horizons, challenge the status-quo, and break the mores when necessary. In the words of the Old Testament, the Church is "Set over nations and over kingdoms, to root out and to pull down, to destroy and to overthrow, to build anew and to plant." We are called to be thermostats that transform and regulate the temperature of society, not thermometers that merely record or register the temperature of majority opinion.

Honesty impels us to admit that religious bodies in America have not always been faithful to their prophetic mission on the question of racial justice. In this area the Church has failed Christ miserably. In the midst of a nation rife with racial animosity, it too often has been content to mouth pious irrelevances and sanctimonious trivialities. Called to combat social evils, it has often remained silent behind the anesthetizing security of stained-glass windows. Called to lead men on the highway of brotherhood and to summon them to rise above the narrow confines of race and class, it has often been an active participant in shaping and crystallizing the patterns of the race-caste system. It has so often cast the mantle of its sancity over the system of segregation. In some communities of the South many Churches are the ready lackeys of state governments. In defiance of the supreme court's desegregation decisions, they allow their religious education buildings to be used for private segregated schools. Nothing so completely reveals the pathetic irrelevancy of the church, nothing so sharply illustrates the eclipse of its spiritual power as its failure to take a forthright stand on the question of racial justice. How often the Church has been an echo rather than a voice, a tail light behind the Supreme Court and other secular agencies, rather than a headlight guiding men progressively and decisively to higher levels of understanding.

If the Church does not participate actively in the struggle for economic and racial justice, it will forfeit the loyalty of millions and cause men everywhere to say that it has atro-

phied its will. In short, the Church must decide whether it
will assume the role of leadership or the role of pious irrelevancy. The Church must decide whether it will aggressively
lead men along the path of brotherhood or whether it will
remain more cautious than courageous, and more prone to
follow the expedient than the ethical way.

Of course, there are always those who will argue that the
Church should not get mixed up in such earthly, temporal
matters as social and economic improvement. There are still all
too many Churches following a theology which stresses the
total and hopeless depravity of all mundane existence and
which admonish men to seek salvation in escape from social
life and in preparation for an hereafter wherein all wrongs will
be automatically righted. But however sincere, this view of
religion is all too confined.

Certainly, otherworldly concerns have a deep and significant
place in all religions worthy of the name. Religion, at its best,
deals not only with the relations of man to his fellowmen but
with the relations of man to the universe and to ultimate
reality. But a religion true to its nature must also be concerned
about man's social conditions. Religion deals not only with
the hereafter but also with the here. *Here*—where the precious
lives of men are still sadly disfigured by poverty and hatred.
Here—where millions of God's children are being consigned to
degradation and injustice and where the habitation of men is
filled with agony and anguish. Any religion that professes to be
concerned about a future good "Over Yonder" and is not concerned about the present evils "Over Here" is a spiritually
moribund religion only waiting for the day to be buried. Such
a religion is the kind the Marxist likes to see—an opiate of the
people.

Now let us turn to some of the specific things that the
church and synagogue can do to face the challenges of this
day.

First, they must make it palpably clear that segregation is
morally wrong and sinful, and that it stands against all of the
noble precepts of our Judeo-Christian tradition. This includes
the legal segregation of the South as well as the *de facto*
segregation of the north. There are at least two reasons why

Christianity must affirm the immorality of segregation. The first has to do with the sacredness of human personality. Deeply rooted in our religious heritage is the conviction that every man is an heir to a legacy of dignity and worth. Our Judeo-Christian tradition refers to this inherent dignity of man in the biblical term the *image of God*. The innate worth referred to in the phrase the *image of God* is universally shared in equal portions by all men. There is no graded scale of essential worth; there is no divine right of one race which differs from the divine right of another. Every human being has etched in his personality the indelible stamp of the creator. Every man must be respected because God loves him. The worth of an individual does not lie in the measure of his intellect, his racial origin, or his social position. Human worth lies in relatedness to God. An individual has value because he has value to God. Whenever this is recognized, "Whiteness" and "Blackness" pass away as determinants in a relationship and "Son" and "Brother" are substituted.

Segregation stands diametrically opposed to the principle of the sacredness of human personality. It debases personality. Immanuel Kant said in one formulation of the categorical imperative that "All men must be treated as *ends* and never as mere *means*." The tragedy of segregation is that it treats men as means rather than ends, and thereby reduces them to things rather than persons. To use the words of the late Martin Buber, segregation substitutes an "I-It" relationship for the "I-Thou" relationship. The colloquialism of the southern landed gentry that referred to slaves and negro labor as "hands" betrays the "thing" quality assigned to Negroes under the system. Herein lies the root of paternalism that persists even today. The traditional southerner is fond of "His Negro" as he is of a pet or a finely tooled fire arm. "It" serves a purpose or gets a job done. The only concern is performance, not well being.

But man is not a thing. He must be dealt with, not as an "animated tool," but as a person sacred in himself. To do otherwise is to depersonalize the potential person and desecrate what he is. So long as the Negro or the member of any other oppressed group is treated as a means to an end; so long as he is seen as anything less than a person of sacred worth, the image of God is abused in him and consequently and proportionately lost by those who inflict the abuse.

A second reason why segregation is morally wrong is that it deprives man of that quality which makes him man, namely, freedom. The very character of the life of man demands freedom. In speaking of freedom at this point I am not referring to the freedom of a thing called the will. The very phrase, freedom of the will, abstracts freedom from the person to make it an object; and an object almost by definition is not free. But freedom cannot thus be abstracted from the person, who is always subject as well as object and who himself still does the abstracting. So I am speaking of the freedom of man, the whole man, and not the freedom of a function called the will.

Neither am I implying that there are no limits to freedom. Freedom always operates within the limits of an already determined structure. Thus the mathematician is free to draw a circle, but he is not free to make a circle square. A man is free to walk through an open door, but he is not free to walk through a brick wall. A man is free to go to Chicago or New York, but he is not free to go to both cities at one and the same time. Freedom is always within destiny. It is the chosen fulfillment of our destined nature. We are always both free and destined.

With these qualifications we return to the assertion that the essence of man is found in freedom. This is what Paul Tillich means when he affirms "Man is man because he is free" or what Tolstoy implies when he says, "I cannot conceive of a man not being free unless he is dead."

What is freedom? It is, first, the capacity to deliberate or weigh alternatives. "Shall I be a doctor or a lawyer?" "Shall I vote for this candidate or the other candidate?" "Shall I be a Democrat, Republican, or Socialist?" "Shall I be a Humanist or a Theist?" Moment by moment we go through life engaged in this strange conversation with ourselves. Second, freedom expresses itself in decision. The word decision, like the word incision involves the image of cutting. Incision means to cut in, decision means to cut off. When I make a decision I cut off alternatives and make a choice. The existentialists say we must choose, that we are choosing animals, and if we do not choose we sink into thinghood and the mass mind. A third expression of freedom is responsibility. This is the obligation of the person to respond if he is questioned about his decisions. No one else can respond for him. He alone must respond, for his acts are determined neither by something outside him nor by any part of him but by the centered totality of his doing.

From this analysis we can clearly see the blatant immorality of segregation. It is a selfishly contrived system which cuts off one's capacity to deliberate, decide and respond.

The absence of freedom is the imposition of restraint on my deliberations as to what I shall do, where I shall live, or the kind of task I shall pursue. I am robbed of the basic quality of man-ness. When I cannot choose what I shall do or where I shall live or how I shall survive, it means in fact that someone or some system has already made these *a priori* decisions for me, and I am reduced to an animal. The only resemblances I have to real life are the motor responses and functions that are akin to human-kind. I cannot adequately assume responsibility as a person, because I have been made the party to a decision in which I played no part in making.

Now to be sure, this may be hyperbole to a certain extent, but only to underscore what actually happens when a man is robbed of his freedom. The very nature of his life is altered and his being cannot make the full circle of personhood because that which is basic to the character of life itself has been diminished.

This is why segregation has wreaked havoc with the Negro. It is sometimes difficult to determine which are the deepest— the physical wounds or the psychological wounds. Only a negro can understand the social leprosy that segregation inflicts upon him. The suppressed fears and resentments and the expressed anxieties and sensitivities make each day of life a turmoil. Every confrontation with the restrictions is another emotional battle in a never ending war. He is shackled in his movements to tip-toe stance, never quite knowing what to expect next.

Is there any argument to support the withdrawing of life-quality from groups because of the color of their skin, or the texture of their hair or any external characteristic which has nothing to do at all with the life-quality? Certainly not on the grounds of morality, justice or religion. Nothing can be more diabolical than a deliberate attempt to destroy in any man his will to be a man and to withhold from him that something that constitutes his true essence.

The Churches have an opportunity and a duty to lift up their voices like a trumpet and declare unto the people the immorality of segregation. We must affirm that every human life is a reflex of divinity, and every act of injustice mars and defaces the image of God in Man. The undergirding philosophy of segregation is diametrically opposed to the undergirding philosophy of our Judeo-Christian heritage and all the dialectics of the logicians cannot make them lie down together.

Another thing that the Churches can do to make the ideal of brotherhood a reality is to get the ideational roots of racial prejudice. All race hate is based on fears, suspicions, and mis-understandings, usually groundless. The Church can do a great deal to direct the popular mind at this point. Through their channels of religious education, they can point out the irrationality of these beliefs. They can show that the idea of a superior or inferior race is a myth that has been completely refuted by anthropological evidence. They can show that negroes are not innately inferior in academic, health, and moral standards, and that they are not inherently criminal. The church can say to their worshippers that poverty and ignorance breed crime whatever the racial group may be, and that it is a tortuous logic to use the tragic results of segregation as an argument for its continuation.

A third effort that the Church can make in attempting to solve the race problem is to take the lead in social reform. It is not enough for religious institutions to be active in the realm of ideas; they must move out into the arena of life and do battle for their sanctities. First, the church must remove the yoke of segregation from its own body. Only by doing this can it be effective in its attack on outside evils. It is trite to say, but shamefully true, that in all too many instances the most segregated hour of America is eleven o'clock on Sunday morning, the same hour when many Christians are standing to sing, "In Christ there is no east or west;" and the most segregated school of the week is the Sunday school. How often the church has had a high blood pressure of creeds and an anemia of deeds!

There has been some progress. More and more churches are courageously making attacks on segregation, and actively integrating their congregations. But these stands must still be enlarged.

The Churches must become increasingly active in social action outside their doors. They must take an active stand against the injustices and indignities that the negro and other non-white minorities confront in housing, education, police protection, and in city and state courts. They must support strong civil rights legislation. They must exert their influence in the area of economic justice. Economic insecurity strangles the physical and cultural growth of its victims. Not only are millions deprived of formal education and proper health facilities, but our most fundamental social unit—The Family—is tortured, corrupted, and weakened by economic injustice. The church cannot look with indifference upon these glaring evils.

But those of us who have been on the oppressed end of the old order must be equally determined to go into the new age with love and understanding. To these we must add the dimension of forgiveness. We must realize that the forgiving act must always be initiated by the person who has been wronged, the victim of some great hurt, the recipient of some tortuous injustice, the absorber of some terrible act of oppression. The wrongdoer may request forgiveness. He may come to himself, and, like the prodigal son, move up some dusty road, his heart palpitating with the desire for forgiveness. But only the injured neighbor can really pour out the warm waters of forgiveness.

This is why it is my personal conviction that the most potent instrument the Negro community can use to gain total emancipation in America is that of non-violent resistance. The evidence of the last few years supports my faith that through the use of nonviolence, much can be done to raise the negro to challenge segregation and discrimination in whatever form they exist. Nonviolence in so many ways has given the negro a new sense of "somebodiness."

But not only has nonviolence given the negro a new image of himself; it has also thwarted the growth of bitterness. It has helped to diminish long repressed feelings of anger and frustration. In the course of respecting the discipline of the nonviolent way, the negro has learned that he must love the adversary who inflicts the system upon him. He learns in the midst of his determined effort to end segregation that a commitment to nonviolence demands respect for the personhood of his opponent.

Now the love referred to here is not something soft, and anemic. It is not emotional bosh. It is not spineless sentimentality which refuses to take courageous action against evil for fear someone might get hurt or be offended. Love is treating fellowmen as persons, understanding them with all their good and bad qualities, and treating them as potential saints. It is helping people with no thought of receiving anything in return. It is love facing evil with an infinite capacity to take it without flinching, to overcome the world by the Cross.

I believe that this is the type of love that must guide us through this rather turbulent period of transition. It will cause us to enter the new age which is emerging with a wholesome attitude. We will seek to rise from a position of disadvantage to one of advantage, thus subverting justice. We will not seek to substitute one tyranny for another. We will be imbued with the conviction that a philosophy of black supremacy is as injurious as a philosophy of white supremacy. God is not interested merely in the freedom of black men, and brown men, and yellow men; God is interested in the freedom of the whole human race.

I am happy to say that the nonviolent movement in America has come not from secular forces but from the heart of the Negro Church. This movement has done a great deal to revitalize the Negro Church and to give its message a relevant and authentic ring. The great principles of love and justice which stand at the center of the nonviolent movement are deeply rooted in our Judeo-Christian heritage.

A final challenge that faces the Churches is to lead men along the path of true integration until men and women are obedient to that which cannot be enforced by law.

Dr. Harry Emerson Fosdick has made an impressive distinction between enforceable and unenforceable obligations. The former are regulated by the codes of society and the vigorous implementation of Law-Enforcement agencies. Breaking these obligations, spelled out on thousands of pages in law books, has filled numerous prisons. But unenforceable obligations are beyond the reach of the laws of society. They concern inner attitudes, genuine person-to-person relations, and expressions of compassion which law books cannot regulate and jails cannot rectify. Such obligations are met by one's commitment to an inner law, written on the heart. Man-made laws assure justice. But a higher law provides love. No code of conduct ever compelled a father to love his children or a husband to show affection to his wife. The law court may force him to provide bread for the family, but it cannot make him provide the bread of love. A good father is obedient to the unenforceable.

In our nation today a mighty struggle is taking place. It is a struggle to conquer the reign of an evil monster called segregation and its inseparable twin called discrimination—a monster that has wandered through this land for hundreds of years, stripping millions of negro people of their sense of dignity and robbing them of their birthright of freedom.

Let us never succumb to the temptation of believing that legislation and judicial decrees play only minor roles in solving this problem. Morality cannot be legislated, but behavior can be regulated. Judicial decrees may not change the heart, but they can restrain the heartless. The law cannot make an employer love an employee, but it can prevent him from refusing to hire me because of the color of my skin. The habits, if not the hearts of people, have been and are being altered everyday by legislative acts, judicial decisions, and executive orders.

Let us not be misled by those who argue that segregation cannot be ended by the force of law.

But acknowledging this, we must admit that the ultimate solution to the race problem lies in the willingness of men to obey the unenforceable. Court orders and federal enforcement agencies are of inestimable value in achieving desegregation, but desegregation is only a partial, though necessary, step toward the final goal which we seek to realize, genuine intergroup and interpersonal living. Desegregation will break down the legal barriers and bring men together physically but something must touch the hearts and souls of men so that they will come together spiritually because it is natural and right. A vigorous enforcement of civil rights laws is gradually bringing an end to segregated public facilities which have been barriers to a truly desegregated society, but it cannot bring an end to fears, prejudice, pride, and irrationality, which are the barriers to a truly integrated society. These dark and demonic responses will be removed only as men are possessed by the invisible, inner law which etches on their hearts the conviction that all men are brothers and that love is mankind's most potent weapon for personal and social transformation. True integration will be achieved by men who are willingly obedient to unenforceable obligations.

Here, then, is the hard challenge and the sublime opportunity: To let God work in our hearts toward fashioning a truly great nation. If the Churches will free themselves from the shackles of a deadening status quo and, recovering their great historic mission, will speak and act fearlessly and insistently in terms of justice and peace, they will enkindle the imagination of mankind and fire the souls of men, imbuing them with a glowing and ardent love for truth and justice. They can transform dark yesterdays of hatred into bright tomorrows of love. Men everywhere and at all times will know that our Hebraic-Christian faith transformed the jangling discords of America into a beautiful symphony of brotherhood.

Any discussion of the role of the Church in race relations must ultimately emphasize the need for prophecy. May the problem of race in America soon make hearts burn so that prophets will rise up saying, "Thus saith the Lord," and cry out as Amos did, . . . "Let justice roll down like waters, and righteousness like an everflowing stream." The prophet must remind America of the urgency of now. The oft-repeated cliches, "The time is not ripe," "Negroes are not culturally ready," are a stench in the nostrils of God. The time is always right to do what is right. *Now* is the time to realize the American dream. *Now* is the time to transform the bleak and desolate midnight of man's inhumanity to man into a glowing daybreak of justice and freedom. *Now* is the time to open the doors of opportunity to all of God's children. *Now* is the time to change the pending national elegy into a creative psalm of brotherly love. St. Augustine's words speak to us as never before: "Those that sit at rest while others take pains, are tender turtles, and buy their quiet with disgrace."

Honesty impels me to admit that this type of forthright stand is always costly and never altogether comfortable. It may mean walking through the valley of the shadow of suffering, losing a job, or having a six-year old daughter ask, "Daddy, why do you have to go to jail so much?" But we are gravely mistaken if we think that religion protects us from the pain and agony of mortal existence. Life is not a Euphoria of unalloyed comfort and untroubled ease. Christianity has always insisted that the cross we bear precede the crown we wear. To be a Christian one must take up his cross, with all of its difficulties and agonizing and tension-packed content, and carry it until that very cross leaves it marks upon us and redeems us to that more excellent way which comes only through suffering. We as Christians and Jews face today that haunting statement of Whittaker Chambers: "At the heart of the crisis of our times lies the cold belief of millions, avowed and unavowed, that the death of religious faith is seen in nothing so much as in the fact that, in general, it has lost its power to move anyone to die for it." Every minister, priest and rabbi must continually submit himself to that test.

We must make a choice, will we continue to bless a status quo that needs to be blasted, and reassure a social order that needs to be reformed, or will we give ourselves unreservedly to God and His kingdom? Will we continue to march to the drum beat of conformity and respectability, or will we, listening to the beat of a more distant drum, move to its echoing sounds? Will we march only to the music of time, or will we, risking criticism and abuse, march only to the soul-saving music of eternity? More than ever before we are today challenged by the words of yesterday, "Be not conformed to this world: But be ye transformed by the renewing of your minds."

It is encouraging to be able to close an address to a national Church body on an optimistic note, for in the past year we *have* seen the Church of Jesus Christ rise up as never before and join the thunderous procession of committed souls in behalf of racial justice. One of the most inspirational moments of my life was the memorial service for the Reverend James Reeb when an Episcopal bishop, A Methodist bishop, A Greek Orthodox Archbishop, the president of the Unitarian-Universalist Association, a Roman Catholic monsignor, and two Baptist preachers conducted services in an A.M.E. church, with twenty to thirty top ranking officials of labor and civil rights organizations seated in the choir stand saying amen. I was sure that this alliance of conscience could only be a sign of the coming of the kingdom.

Selma climaxed a spirit within the white churches which had been growing since the early days of the movement and which had really begun to bear fruit following the Birmingham Movement. The summer in Mississippi and the hard work of the Churches had begun to show that the Church was really on the march in behalf of the "Least of these," God's black children.

But this must be considered only the point of climax for the awakening of the slumbering moral giant. The actual work to redeem the soul of America is still before us.

In spite of the progress which is being made in the field of race relations, there is still a mighty battle to be waged before "The sons of want can shout for joy." Joblessness will probably increase. Housing continues to grow more critical for the teeming hordes which continue to migrate into our cities in search for jobs and opportunity. Right now we are creating numerous problems for ourselves and our Nation by the failure to provide quality integrated education in our slums and ghettos.

Can the spirit of Selma continue to grow and spread to local congregations? Can the Church maintain the courage of its convictions amid the hard and bitter struggle ahead? It will take more than the spontaneity which has characterized past responses by the Church and the movement.

21

PAUL M. van BUREN

Christologist of Freedom

Paul Matthews van Buren (1924–   ), like many theologians of his generation, came to maturity during the ascendancy of neo-orthodoxy and then discovered challenging alternatives. Virtually cut off from American theological movements of the past and oriented toward the post-liberal European theologies of Brunner, Barth and Tillich, they found themselves thinking with a German accent and equipped with splendid instruments that somehow turned out not to be designed for life as these younger theologians found it. Van Buren's reaction against Barth is both typical and highly individual in its thrust toward a new Christian humanism.

Paul van Buren was born in Norfolk, Virginia, the son of a corporation executive. He was educated at public and private schools in Cincinnati and Glendale, Ohio, and at St. Paul's, a private Episcopal school in New Hampshire. His college years were spent in the U.S. Coast Guard, the U.S. Naval Air Service, and Harvard College, where he majored in political science and was graduated with honors in 1948. He received his B.D. from the Episcopal Theological School in Cambridge, Mass., in 1951, and was ordained a deacon and later a priest of the Protestant Episcopal Church. From 1951 to 1954 he studied under Karl Barth at Basel, immersing himself in the theology of Jean Calvin, which formed the subject of van

Buren's doctoral dissertation.[1] He still regards the latter as "one of the few things I have done which I think will stand up under fire"[2]—and indeed it is a solid piece of scholarship, a close internal critique of the heart of Calvin's theology, based on study of the original sources.

Like Reinhold Niebuhr's half a century earlier, van Buren's first and only parish ministry was in Detroit, where he served two years in the team ministry of a small church and one as curate of St. Paul's Cathedral, while also participating in the Detroit Industrial Mission. In 1957 he began his academic career as an assistant professor of theology at the Episcopal Seminary of the Southwest in Austin, Texas. There he first heard of analytic or linguistic philosophy and, in 1960 he began reading the works of Ludwig Wittgenstein and soon discovered "I wasn't playing Barth's game any more."[3] For van Buren the difference between Barth's and Wittgenstein's understanding of "the workings of our language" called in question the validity of the word "God" for our time. This issue is central to *The Secular Meaning of the Gospel* (1963), which attracted wide attention and led to his appointment to the faculty of Temple University in 1964.

Van Buren has retained his connection with the Detroit Industrial Mission through his position as a consultant. Hugh White, then the mission's director, first interested him in the writings of William James, in the summer of 1964; he had not read James before. The full impact of this influence has yet to be seen in van Buren's thought, but he found in James a kindred spirit, for quite before this time van Buren had arrived at a decidedly pragmatic conception of religion by an entirely different route. In his essay, "The Dissolution of the Absolute,"

---

[1] Published as *Christ in Our Place: The Substitutionary Character of Calvin's Doctrine of Reconciliation* (Edinburgh & London: Oliver & Boyd, 1957), with a brief introduction by Karl Barth.

[2] Quotations, unless otherwise attributed, are from a letter from van Buren to the editor, dated 17 August 1968.

[3] Language, according to Wittgenstein, has a variety of uses and a multiplicity of forms, each of which comprises what he calls a "language game." See Ludwig Wittgenstein, *Philosophical Investigations* (Oxford: Blackwell, 1958), pp. 31–33

which is reprinted here, it would be hard to determine whether his references to "pluralism" and "relativism" reflect Wittgenstein, James, or other sources.

Not only is van Buren's thought congruent with James's, but in broad outline it could well be viewed as an outgrowth of the Chicago school of Ames, Mathews, and Wieman—except that in fact these men did not influence him. For van Buren is as firmly opposed as any of the Chicagoans to a metaphysical or ontological interpretation of religion. Yet the conclusion to which his analysis of language points is a Christian humanism much like Ames's. The word "God," van Buren maintained, has no empirical referent; theological statements are noncognitive propositions which can be verified only in terms of the concrete behavior that corresponds to them. They are not statements about empirical reality but about intentions or attitudes expressing a viewpoint on life. Distinctive to van Buren is not only his linguistic method, however, for he presses the logic of his position farther than Ames. While Ames related his ultimate commitment to the historic church and retained a pluralistic concept of God as a center of value, van Buren proposed to dispense with the word "God" and to translate all statements about God into human terms. He does not start from scratch. He takes for his province not only the Christian gospel as found in the New Testament but as formulated in such documents as the Nicene Creed and the writings of Anselm and Calvin. Neither the church nor any specific secular society figures in van Buren's theology, which is in contrast to the Chicagoans. In this respect, one detects something of the existentialist element of Barth, or more properly of Kierkegaard. It might be said that, in *The Secular Meaning of the Gospel*, van Buren ends with a Christology from which "God" has been removed—an image of Jesus as a kind of transcendent human prototype, a man who uniquely typifies human freedom and who by "contagion" inspires this freedom in others. It is a freedom that surmounts religious rites and organizational structures, a freedom that overcomes the demands and the anxieties of the world. The resurrection takes on secular meaning in the freedom it conferred upon Jesus' followers, who became "men who were free to face even death without fear."[4]

Even more than Ames, van Buren regards the task of "theological exploration" as among "the humanities," and he presses farther (and in different terms) the notion of Christianity as an experiment. In his Fulbright lectures at Oxford in 1967–68, titled "The Logic of a Religion," van Buren sketched "a proposal for something which may be called a religion, but need not; which could be called a revision of or variation on Christianity, but surely won't be by the more orthodox. In any case, it is an attempt to develop . . . what seems to me to be worthwhile out of the Christian story, centering in what I call a moral ideal." In 1969–70, van Buren was revising these lectures with a view to their later publication. He is not a prolific writer; of his three books that have appeared in eleven years, the first was his Ph.D dissertation and the third, *Theological Explorations* (1968), amounts to his collected shorter writings *in toto*.

By citing parallels with earlier writers it is not intended to show that van Buren is derivative. His approach is highly original and distinctive in many ways, inside or outside the context of linguistic analysis. For just that reason it is all the more noteworthy that his explorations go in the same direction as the main body of American religious thought, with their accent on freedom, their focus on Jesus, their distaste for authoritarian absolutes. The essay that follows originally appeared as part of a symposium titled "The Secular Emphasis of Our Age—Its Values and Dangers." In an introductory statement, van Buren characterized his contribution as "one man's analysis of what has been and is going on in the society and culture in which I live, as it bears upon the religious enterprise as I am familiar with it." That society and culture to which he refers are not solely American but Western, and the implicit frame of reference is often European. Yet the viewpoint and the accent are American, and in no pejorative sense.

---

[4] van Buren, *The Secular Meaning of the Gospel* (New York: Macmillan, 1963), p. 128.

THE DISSOLUTION OF THE ABSOLUTE*

The world in which I live, and apparently not alone, is a world I should like to describe as following upon, or in the late stages of, a major socio-psychological shift in our culture, which I shall label "The Dissolution of the Absolute." It seems to have been the case, prior to this shift, that thoughtful men spoke not infrequently, and as though they had no thought of not being understood by their peers, of the Absolute, the Highest Good, or of Reality (with a capital R). This characteristic of language and thought has become increasingly difficult to maintain or recapture. The change has come about, so far as I can see, not as a result of a frontal assault on the idea of the Absolute, but by a process of dissolution or decay. The Absolute was not murdered, *Zarathustra* notwithstanding; it died of neglect.

The dissolution of the Absolute, the passing of a world view and a habit of thought, or its quiet displacement by another and different habit of thought, is a phenomenon that I have called a socio-psychological fact. With that label I wish to indicate how broad and basic a shift I have in mind, and how many ways there are of exploring and describing this change. One can, for example, ask about the causes and timing of the dissolution of that pattern of thought in which differing views about the Absolute were held to be of such importance that these differences could lead to heresy trials and burnings at the stake, not to speak of wars. I take this question about the causes and timing of the change to be a historical question which it is the proper business of the historian of Western culture to explore. Setting dates for this sort of cultural shift is a rather arbitrary business, but let me just suggest, as an illustration of the historical aspect of the problem, that if one were to write a history of Western Christianity, it might be more accurate to locate the fundamental turning point not in

* From *Religion in Life*, XXXIV, (Summer 1965), pp. 335–342.

the Reformation, as is often the case with Protestant histories of Christianity, but somewhere nearer the French Revolution. After all, Luther and Calvin stand in one world with Augustine and Aquinas, no matter how they may disagree about the details; whereas none of them fit easily, if at all, into the world of the Enlightenment. The gap between the Reformers and the Scholastics is small indeed compared with the gap between them all and such men as Rousseau, Voltaire, or Jefferson.

One can also ask about the extent of the dissolution, to what extent it is the case that people no longer seem to operate on the assumption of an absolute. This is a question which the sociologist might be in as good a position as any to explore. Or, if they were willing to study our society with the penetration shown in their study of some other societies, perhaps cultural anthropologists could help us to see the extent to which our values, attitudes, and patterns of thought betray a departure from those in which words such as "God," "providence," "destiny," and "absolute" seemed to function powerfully. The social sciences could help us see to what extent the Absolute has been dissolved out of our operative images of life and the world.

Or one can ask about the shape of this changed situation, how it looks when the dissolution has taken place. This can be opened up to some extent by the social sciences, but it can also be exposed by the works of writers, poets, and artists. The question of shape is in part an aesthetic question, and insofar as a quantifiable answer seems to fall short of satisfying our questions, the artists, writers, literary and art critics, and aestheticians can help us to see where we are today.

Further, there is a task of clarifying the dissolution and the logic of our new situation, which is, from one point of view, a philosophical question. Metaphysics I take to be not some sort of superscience which might provide us with new information about the universe or "Reality" of a rather esoteric or subtle kind. I know that there are theologians who speak as if ontology were some sort of penetration of the "structure of being," but I gather that few if any philosophers are impressed by this. A metaphysics or ontology, as I gather it would be taken by most philosophers today, consists rather of a proposal, one might say an invitation, to see what we already know in a particular way. Metaphysics does not give us something new to see (such as "being itself" or "the ground of being") in any other way than by giving us a new way to see what we have been looking at all along.

From this point of view, then, to speak of the dissolution of the Absolute is one way of indicating a shift which has occurred in our metaphysical assumptions. At this point, however, I find that philosophers seem to withdraw from what I take to be a serious and worthwhile enterprise: the attempt to formulate and clarify the logic of the commonsense metaphysics of our society. They say, quite correctly, that a major piece of this job is not their business: namely, the careful empirical study of what people in our society think and the way in which they think. That would properly be the business of the behavioral and social sciences to discover. Yet when it comes to the task of formulating and analyzing the workings of our commonsense attitudes, it would seem to me that the philosopher need not be so retiring. The disdainful remark that the common sense of today is only the poor leavings of the best thinking of yesterday and beneath the dignity of philosophical investigation, which I have heard from several philosophers, bothers me a bit. After all, the common sense of today is the pattern of thinking in which we do our major arguing and debating of the great issues of our society. I notice that philosophers appear just about as frequently as theologians among the lists of those thinkers called upon by government and industry to assist in dealing with the major issues of our time. Could it be that philosophers as well as theologians, admittedly for different reasons, have simply opted out of the society of common sense? If theologians are the more irrelevant to life today, it is because they have been even more disdainful of the realm of ordinary language and ordinary common sense. Be that as it may, I would still wish to urge that there is a philosophical task to be performed in our attempts to get clear about the commonsense understandings of our time, and if this task is not well done by competent philosophers, then it will be poorly and sloppily done by others.

The dissolution of the Absolute, then, is a broad cultural shift which may be investigated and documented from a number of angles. It is a change that has affected our thought and language in ways so fundamental that they are not always noticed. Few have taken as little account of this shift as have the theologically inclined, although it should be evident that religion and theology are as much or more touched by the dissolution of the Absolute as any area of human activity. One consequence of failing to see this change that has taken place has been a certain degree of linguistic and logical confusion, resulting from attempting to operate in a world without absolutes while using ideas and languages drawn from a world in which the idea of the Absolute had an important place. The confusion is not unlike that of the substitute player in a football game rushing onto the field firmly clutching a baseball bat.

A prime example of this sort of confusion may be seen in the use of the word "reality." Now on any showing, this is a tricky word, an odd sort of noun, like "sadness" or "beauty," which is derived from a reasonably clear usage in the adjectival form of the word. That is to say, we do not seem to have much difficulty when we use the word "real." There is little difficulty knowing what we mean when we say that a mirage, the appearance of water on the road ahead on a hot summer day, is not real. Or in doing an elementary experiment in refraction, we may see that a stick half immersed in water looks bent; but we know, or so we say without confusion, that the stick is really straight, in spite of appearances. In these cases the words "real" and "really" serve the purpose of touching base in or reminding us of a commonly agreed frame of reference. Empirically minded though we may be, we are also aware of the limitations of sense experience. Our senses are not infallible, we say. Things are not always what they seem; skim milk masquerades as cream. But we do have words such as "seem," "appear," and "masquerade," as we do have the working distinction between the uses of these words and the use of the word "real," because we do have that common network of ground rules to which we are to appeal with the word "real." If this, then, is how we use the word "real," what would be the meaning of "reality"? Well, in a great many cases "reality" is a word that refers to the whole of our understanding of how things are according to this same network of ground rules. So we might say that a man who is insane is a man who has "lost touch with reality." We mean that he no longer plays life's game according to the common rules. Or we say that a hypothesis seems "to conform to reality," by which we mean that it seems to fit fairly well into how we take things to be according to our commonly held understandings.

So far so good. That is, nothing is at all airtight about any of this, but we get along all right; we understand each other fairly well. Now along comes the knight of faith[1] and speaks of "reality breaking in upon us!" Or he speaks to us in the name of "absolute reality," or, even more confusing, his faith is placed in "an objective reality." And here I would suggest that language has gone on a wild binge, which I think we should properly call a lost weekend.

This knight of faith is presumably speaking English, and so we take him to be using words which we have learned how to use. Only see what he does with them. "Reality," which is ordinarily used to call our attention once more to our agreements about how things are, is used now to refer to what the knight of faith must surely want to say is radically the opposite of all of our ordinary understandings. Why not better say, "Unreality is breaking in upon us"?

I think we can say something about what has gone wrong here. There was a time when the Absolute, God, was taken to be the cause of a great deal of what we would today call quite real phenomena, from rain and hail to death and disease. God was part of what people took to be the network of forces and factors of everyday existence, as real and as objective as the

---

[1] "Knight of faith"—the allusion, facetious here, is from Kierkegaard. —ED.

thunderbolts he produced. But today we no longer have the same reference for the word "reality." The network of understandings to which the word points has undergone important changes. The word "reality" has taken on an empirical coloration which makes it now a bit confusing to speak of "reality breaking in upon us," unless we are referring to, for example, a sudden and unexpected visit from the police or a mother-in-law.

There is, however, another source of unclarity or confusion here, and that is the very fact of the dissolution of the Absolute itself. In the eleventh century the great theologian Anselm of Canterbury wrote a little essay containing an argument for the existence of God which continues to this day to occupy philosophers and theologians. I do not intend to explore Anselm's argument, but there is one contextual aspect of it which bears on our problem. Anselm was asking a certain question, the question about God, in such a way that he understood himself to be asking the one question which included and summed up every human question. And when he arrived at his answer, it was, as he conceived it, the discovery which was in some sense at once the answer to every human question. Indeed, I believe that this observation is true for all of the great traditional arguments for the existence of God. Those arguments were not trying to make a case for simply one entity, namely God, but for that which was the basis for and foundation of everything that is. Take away this frame of reference, this approach to these arguments, and they all become a bit silly.

Now the reason why most people today do regard these arguments as silly, the reason why we have difficulty accepting the answers or conclusions of these arguments, is because we simply do not know how to ask Anselm's question. We do not conceive it possible that there could be one answer which would entail and provide the answer to every question man can ask, in such diverse areas as, for example, politics, physics, mathematics, and aesthetics; so we are unable to ask after "God" in the way in which Anselm could. That being the case, we find it hard to accept his, or any of the arguments for the existence of God, as being persuasive. To speak of Absolute Reality is to speak in Anselm's world, not ours, both with respect to the word "Absolute" and to the word "Reality."

The change which I have called the dissolution of the Absolute has led to a pluralistic society and a pluralism of values and understandings. We are not in this world in one way; we live in our world in many ways, and it hardly seems to make sense to try to pull everything together under one heading. The sociologists call this differentiation, I believe, and another way of putting it would be to say that we have become relativists as well as pluralists. I am not saying, however, that we think everything is of the same or equal importance, or that we inhabit our various worlds or parts thereof in always the same and equal ways. Plurality does not entail equality of all the parts. It does mean, however, that life and the world are for us many different things, and that when we talk in a manner which convinces ourselves, we talk about "the whole" of life by talking in more detail or with more care about the various parts.

I touched on this in connection with Anselm's question and our inability to ask his question. The fact that Anselm and his world are part of our past may be taken as a clue to what I would call our monistic hangover, which, when it is particularly acute, makes our pluralist waking an agony. The monistic images of our past haunt us in the most unexpected and sometimes unwanted places. We may find, for example, when we try to think or speak of the universe, that we do not honestly want to spell "universe" with a capital "U." If we are asked about the extent of our small "u" universe, we may mention the rule of thumb which gives it a radius twice the range of the most powerful telescope, under the assumption that any presumed sources of light beyond that range are moving away from us at so nearly the speed of light that for all practical purposes (and isn't that a revealing phrase!) we can ignore them. And if we come closer to home, it is only out of habit that we speak of a "universe" at all. It really depends on how you approach it, we might say, for the "universe" of one discipline is but the background or a detail for another. All things considered, it appears to be more appropriate to speak of a polyverse.

But then that old monistic hangover begins to creep over us and tempts us to ask if there is not something fundamental to the human mind which leads us to keep on trying to pull things together, to see everything in some sort of interrelatedness, to devise laws and hypotheses in the hope of seeing how it all fits together into one whole. Perhaps at this point we need a bit of aspirin. Does the human mind actually do this, or is it more accurate to say that the human mind indeed tended to do this in the past out of which we have come? Perhaps we need to recall, for example, that historical study is one way of going at things, and it has developed and continues to develop its own methods. And physics is another way of going at things, with its own methods. And literary critics and biologists and painters also have their appropriate ways of exploring the world. Do we honestly think we shall come to understand any one of these ways, with its results, or indeed the whole of life, by somehow pulling them all together into one great system? What human knowledge was conceived of hierarchically—say on the model of a Gothic arch—it made sense to build comprehensive systems, and there could also be one queen of the sciences. But since the Gothic arch has been displaced by the marketplace as a model for human understanding, comprehensive systems have become strangely out of place, just as royalty finds itself out of a job in the context of the marketplace.

Pluralism means that we have granted that there are many ways of looking and seeing, many points of orientation, and that attempts to pull these all together into one grand scheme do not bring us closer to understanding how things are. The generalist has been displaced by the specialist in our society, in area after area of our common life. Insofar as this is true, insofar as this is how we think, we lose interest in Anselm's answer because we are not convinced he was asking the right question.

Relativism means that we appear to be coming more and more to a consensus that there is more than one way to look at any matter, and that what is said can be called true or false only in the terms provided by the particular point of reference. The student of art, for example, is encouraged to look at a given work of art in the light of the problems which the artist set for himself or were set for him by his situation. It is not a serious question for the student of art to ask what is the single greatest painting of all time.

Pluralism and relativism do not mean, however, that there are no distinctions to be made. One may have reasons for preferring one scale of values to another, one way of looking at a problem to another. But it is, I think we should agree, a mark of education and good sense to refrain from dogmatic statements which necessarily deny all merit to all other positions and points of view. One can hold serious commitments without universalizing them and without insisting that all who disagree are either knaves or fools. If relativism has an unpleasant sound, then let us call it tolerance. By whatever name, it is an important feature of the (secular) spirit of our age; and when we run into its denial, as in McCarthyism or Goldwaterism, most of us are at least uncomfortable. Somehow extremism has lost status, and if at moments it seems to make headway again, I think most of us regard this as a step backward, as a betrayal of what little progress civilization has made.

To ask theology and religion to accept the dissolution of the Absolute, to open their eyes to the world in which they live, is admittedly to ask much. It means that religion must not only become much more guarded in speaking of God (if not give this up altogether); it means also that more care be exercised in speaking of "unique revelation," "absolute commitment," and some single "ultimate concern." It is to ask of the life of faith that it be lived as a certain posture, involving commitments, but held in balance with many other commitments; a certain willingness to see things in a certain way without feeling obliged to say that this is the only way in which they can be seen. The question may fairly be asked whether theology and faith can survive this shift of focus; whether Christianity, for example, which has for so long proclaimed a monistic view of the universe, a single and unique point of reference as the only valid one, with a single and unique revelation of this truth, can learn to live in a world from which the Absolute has been dissolved. However one may choose to answer this in theory, we are in fact in the actual process of finding this out, for living when we do and as we are is not exactly a matter of choice. What are the values and dangers of this? Well, what are the values and dangers of being alive? They are the values and dangers of being who we are.

22

PETER L. BERGER

Sociologist

Peter L. Berger (1929–   ), like most American theologians of his generation, is more firmly rooted in European than in specifically American theological terrain. Unlike them, however, he was born in Europe and studied theology in America. Still more unlike them, he makes his intellectual home in the world of the social sciences and is fluent in the languages of Scheler, Durkheim, and Piaget.

Born in Vienna, Peter Berger came to the United States shortly after World War II and is now a citizen. He completed his baccalaureate studies at Wagner College in 1949, majoring in philosophy, and the following year he received his M.A. in sociology at the New School for Social Research. After graduate study in theology at Lutheran Theological Seminary in Philadelphia, 1950–51, he returned to the New School for a Ph.D. in sociology, conferred in 1954. He is now a professor in the Graduate Faculty at the New School and, since 1965, editor of *Social Research*.

Berger is the author of four books in the field of religion. He was director of research at the Evangelical Academy in Bad Boll, Germany, during the academic year 1955–56, and for five years prior to his New School professorship he was associate professor of social ethics at Hartford Seminary and director of its Institute of Church and Community. His first two books emerged from that setting in 1961—*The Noise of Solemn Assemblies*, a tough-minded sociological study of Protestant churches in America, and *The Precarious Vision*, a sociological examination of "social fictions and Christian faith", which comprises an astonishing range of scholarship—sociological, psychological, theological, philosophical, literary—and a distinctive viewpoint reflecting the existentialist tradition.[1] More recently, he has written *The Sacred Canopy* (1967) and *A Rumor of Angels* (1969), the former subtitled "elements of a sociological theory of religion" and the latter dealing with contemporary culture and the supernatural. He has edited or co-authored important books on the sociology of knowledge and of work, as well as *Marxism and Sociology* (1969), a collection of essays by East European social scientists. His basic volume, *Invitation to Sociology* (1963), presents what Berger calls a humanistic perspective on the subject, and it has been translated into several languages.

Berger is not the only present-day thinker who possesses credentials as both theologian and social scientist, but he is one of the few whose primary emphasis is in the latter field, and he is perhaps the only recognized theologian holding a sociological professorship at a completely secular institution. More to the point, from both disciplines he brings to bear on contemporary issues an informed and incisive analytical mind. If his theological frame of reference is predominantly European, so is that of the "secularizing" theologians under discussion in the following pages, which originated as the presidential address at the 1966 annual conference of the Society for the Scientific Study of Religion. It is not narrowly European, however; there are enough American accents in it to justify its inclusion in this volume if that were a decisive criterion. The subject of an American development of these theologies, if such is to occur, falls outside the scope of Berger's analysis, though it may be implicit in some of his remarks. Most of the issues discussed here are in fact trans-Atlantic—as seen not only by Berger but by Cox and Altizer. If in the future significant contributions to the discussion address themselves to American religious or socio-cultural factors, there is reason to expect that Berger will be among the most articulate

---

[1] Berger moves easily among such figures as Kierkegaard, Barth, Camus, Weil, Sartre, but he cannot be categorized simply as a Barthian, or follower of any single school of thought.

of the critics in both sectors. Whether this proves to be the case or not, what he has to say here already comprises a major contribution to the first phase of the debate.

A SOCIOLOGICAL VIEW OF THE SECULARIZATION OF THEOLOGY*

Considerable public attention in this country has recently been focused on a movement in Protestant theology variously described as "radical," "secular," or just plain "new." This attention has gone far beyond the confines of organized religion proper, even attracting comment from such venerable theological journals as *Time, Newsweek,* and *The New Yorker.* The newsworthiness of the movement has been enhanced by its connection with several other developments of wide public interest, such as the civil rights movement, in which there has also been a "radical" involvement by religious figures; the so-called "youth problem," which supposedly involves widespread disillusion with societal values, religious and other; and the long-lasting news field day provided by the Vatican Council. By now, such bywords of the "secular" theologians as "death of God" or "post-Christian era" have become standard topics of discussion at businessmen's Bible breakfasts and in book reviews in the provincial press. To the extent that public issues in our society are largely determined by the mass media, it is possible to say that the "new" theology has become a public issue.

The spectacle afforded by the movement is strange. Indeed, it has all the characteristics of a man-bites-dog story. The phrase "secular theology" itself strikes with intriguing dissonance, while phrases such as "atheist theology" or "religionless Christianity" seem to come from a script for the theater of the absurd. The strangeness of the spectacle does not dis-

* From *Journal for the Scientific Study of Religion,* XI, 1 (Spring 1967), pp. 3–16. This paper originated as the presidential address to the Society for the Scientific Study of Religion, 1966.

appear on closer scrutiny. Professional theologians declare that their discipline must begin with the presupposition that there is no God. Clergymen, even bishops, charged with the performance of public worship proclaim the senselessness of prayer. Salaried employees of religious organizations state that these organizations are destined to fade away—and the sooner, the better. To an outside observer, say a Muslim scholar of western religion, all this might well appear as a bizarre manifestation of intellectual derangement or institutional suicide. An observer familiar with the background of these ideas can, of course, show that they did not spring from nowhere, but this still does not explain why they have attained their peculiar virulence at this time, nor how they can be plausibly present themselves as the wave of the future. We may assume that any adequate explanation of the phenomenon will have to be multifaceted. However, a sociological view of the matter (more specifically, a view in terms of the sociology of knowledge) can add something to our understanding of what is happening. Before we attempt this, though, a closer look at the ideational content of the phenomenon will be necessary.

THE IDEATIONAL CONTENT

While the roots of these ideas are in earlier developments, particularly in post-World War II controversies within German Protestant theology, their explosion into public view may conveniently be placed in 1963, when John Robinson's *Honest to God* was first published in England. The book immediately produced a violent public controversy there, which was repeated in other countries as the book was translated. In this country, not surprisingly, the book rapidly achieved bestseller status, and the attention paid to this controversy by the mass media attained the crescendo appropriate to the style of our cultural life. Since then, a number of American figures have either associated themselves, or been associated by others, with Robinson's overall theological stance—notably William Hamilton, Paul van Buren, Gabriel Vahanian, Thomas Altizer, and, lately, Harvey Cox. Paul Tillich, apparently to his dismay, is widely regarded as a sort of elder statesman of the movement.

While the movement continues to be definitely Protestant, it
has found an echo both among *aggiornamento*-minded Catholics and among liberal Jews. It is safe to assume that the movement represents something much more significant than a curiosity of the Protestant imagination.

The various figures associated with the movement differ
considerably in their precise positions and in the level of theoretical sophistication. All the same, it is possible to identify a
central characteristic common to all of them—namely, a denial,
in various degrees and on different grounds, of the objective
validity of the supernatural affirmations of the Christian tradition. Put differently, the movement generally shows a shift
from a transcendental to an immanent perspective, and from
an objective to a subjective understanding of religion. Generally, traditional affirmations referring to other-worldly entities or events are "translated" to refer to concerns of this
world, and traditional affirmations about the nature of something "out there" (to use a phrase of Robinson's) are "translated" to become statements about the nature of man or his
temporal situation. For example, the resurrection is no longer
understood as a cosmic event, but as a symbol of human existential or psychological processes. For another example, Christian eschatology ceases to refer to the interventions of a
transcendent God, but becomes an ethical perspective on current political affairs.

It is important to understand that this general characteristic
of the "new" theology is anything but new. Rather, it stands
in a direct continuity with classical Protestant liberalism at
least as far back as Schleiermacher's "translation" of the
Lutheran *"Christus pro me"* into a concept of "religious experience." It is instructive in this connection to read Adolf
Harnack's great manifesto of Protestant liberalism, *Das Wesen
des Christentums,* first published in 1900, and imagine what
Time might say about it if it had just been written by a
"radical" seminary professor. The immediate European antecedents of the new theology are commonly given as Rudolph Bultmann and Dietrich Bonhoeffer. In the latter case,
it takes great selectivity to find legitimations for the current

positions in Bonhoeffer's writings (mostly, in the fragmentary and, by their very nature, ambiguous writings of the underground period, particularly the correspondence from prison). In the case of Bultmann, however, the connection with classical liberalism is not hard to see. The Anglo-American theologians cannot even claim newness with respect to the degree of their "radicalness." If Bultmann is not already radical enough, there are such figures of contemporary German-speaking theology as Friedrich Gogarten and Fritz Buri, not to mention once more, Tillich's daring "correlations" between the Christian tradition and modern secular thought. In addition to some of the conceptual tools, of which more in a moment, what is new here is, above all, the resonance of these ideas in a mass public. This fact by itself leads to the suspicion that there is a sociological dimension to the phenomenon.

In addition to the central characteristic indicated before, the secular theologians share a common presupposition, that the traditional religious affirmations are no longer tenable, either because they do not meet certain modern philosophical or scientific criteria of validity, or because they are contrary to an alleged modern world view that is somehow binding on everybody. In some cases it is not quite clear which of these two reasons (logically quite different) is the decisive one. Must the traditional affirmations be given up because we now know that they are false, or because we simply cannot put them over any more? Because of this confusion, the presupposition that the tradition is now untenable often hovers uneasily between questions of epistemology and of evangelistic tactics. Be this as it may, the conclusion typically comes out as a statement that "We cannot any longer . . . " maintain this or that element of the tradition, or cannot perhaps even maintain the tradition itself. This conclusion could, of course, result in the rejection of the theological enterprise as such or of the ecclesiastical institutions that embody the tradition—and we know that there are individuals who do just that.

The interesting thing about the secular theologians, however, is that they do *not* draw this conclusion. Not only do they continue to operate as theologians, but most of them do so within the context of traditional ecclesiastical institutions. That this creates a certain amount of practical strain is obvious and needs no elaboration here. The strain, however, is also theoretical. The problem of translation, consequently, is one of great urgency. In other words, if the situation is interpreted in such a way that "We cannot any longer," then a way must be found to deal with the tradition so that "We can again"—that is, can again exist as ecclesiastically involved theologians. It should be stressed as emphatically as possible that putting the problem in these terms *in no way* questions the sincerity of such an intellectual operation. On the contrary, the desire for sincerity is probably one of the strongest driving forces in this whole movement. The issue is not whether such an operation is sincere, but what theoretical procedures are required for it. In other words, given the problem of translation, where are the grammars?

Classical Protestant liberalism used various forms of philosophical rationalism or positivism to solve the same problem, as well as the newly refined tools of historical scholarship. To some extent, these methods are still used, both in the demolition and in the reconstruction phases of the translation enterprise. New conceptual tools have been added, derived from existentialism, psychoanalysis, sociology, and linguistic analysis (probably in declining order of importance). With the exception of the last, which understandably plays a greater part in the English branch of the movement and which in this country has been particularly employed by van Buren, these conceptual machineries permeate the entire ideational complex and often overlap in both of the above-mentioned phases.

It is important to see that these conceptual mechanisms have two applications. They may be used by some writers in the movement on a high level of theoretical sophistication, and yet have an ideological correlate on a lower level of popular consciousness. Take the application of existentialism to our problem, for example. Concepts derived from existential philosophy, particularly Heidegger's, are the standard operating procedures of Bultmann's particular translation exercise—to wit, his famous program of "demythologization." With system and consistency, the entire transcendental frame of reference of the Christian tradition is demolished, that is, consigned to the mythological world view that "we cannot any longer" maintain. (His one lapse in consistency, as was immediately pointed out by some of his critics, was the retention of an acting God.) The major items so treated are then translated into terms that makes sense within the frame of reference of an existentialist anthropology—a procedure, of course, of the most radical detranscendentalization and subjectivization imaginable. Thus transcendental ontology becomes immanent anthropology, and *Heilsgeschichte* becomes a kind of biography, the biography of the individual in terms of whose *Existenz* the reinterpreted tradition is still supposed to make sense. A similar procedure, employed with immense erudition and ingenuity, is at the center of Tillich's translation enterprise, and it is reiterated in one way or another (though rarely with the same intellectual force) by most of the figures in this movement. The sometimes awe-inspiring eggheadedness of the existentialist vocabulary must not be allowed to obscure the "pop" correlates of the movement. For example, existentialist *Angst* and alienation are not limited to seminary professors who have read Heidegger. To a remarkable degree, these experiences seem to be shared by suburban housewives. As a result, the translations undertaken by the seminary professors can be popularly applied by ministers with suburban housewives in their clientele. To use a Weberian term, there appears to be an "elective affinity" between certain ideas of Heidegger and the mentality of certain suburban housewives. The explanation of this, as we shall try to show presently, is to be sought *not* in a philosophical analysis of Heidegger, but in a sociology-of-knowledge perspective on the quasi-Heideggerian housewives.

Ideas derived from psychoanalysis (psychologism would probably be a better term) play a very prominent part in the translation procedures. The traditional religious affirmations are understood as symbols of (largely unconscious) psychological states and, as such, declared to have continuing positive significance. The optimistic twist to Freud's original understanding of religion that this entails is, in any case, consonant with (to pervert a phrase of Harry Stack Sullivan) the benevolent transformation that Freudianism underwent in America. Since psychoanalytically derived ideas are by now widely diffused in American society, almost instant relevance is guaranteed by an interpretation and, equally important, to an application of religion in these terms. At least part of the appeal of Tillich's theology may be explained by its ingenious combination of the conceptual mechanisms of existentialism and psychologism, both of them being ideational complexes that are, so to speak, "in the air" culturally. But, without in the least trying to denigrate Tillich's intellectual achievement in itself—for which one may have the highest respect, even if one totally disagrees with it—it should be emphasized that essentially similar procedures are employed on greatly inferior levels of sophistication. There, too, quasi-existentialist malaise is interpreted in psychologistic terms, psychotherapeutic measures are advocated to cope with the matter among people already predisposed to accept the diagnosis, and religion comes in as a "symbolization" in both the diagnostic and the therapeutic phases of the operation. There is, therefore, a very important link between Tillich and, say, Norman Vincent Peale—*not*, needless to say, in their statures as religious thinkers, but in the common relevance of their thinking in a psychologically inclined population. Louis Schneider and Sanford Dornbusch have given us an excellent analysis of this in their study of popular religious literature (*Popular Religion,* University of Chicago, 1958), and Samuel Klausner gives us a good picture of how the same relevance is being expressed in the programs of ecclesiastical institutions (*Psychiatry and Religion,* Free Press, 1964). Here, of course, the subjectivization of the traditional religious contents appears in pure form. Robinson's "Daddy on a cloud" has become a psychological datum, the "up there" is relocated "deep down within" human consciousness, and, in a truly impressive theoretical *salto mortale*, this very dissolution of theology into psychology is hailed as a vindication of religion.

Conceptual machinery derived from sociology can also be applied both diagnostically and therapeutically in the translation enterprise, and perhaps this is the point where I should acknowledge my own past share in both applications, with the added comment that these days I much prefer the diagnostic to the therapeutic role. Sociology can demonstrate easily enough that large segments of traditional religious lore have become irrelevant (that is, subjectively meaningless and/or practically inapplicable) to the man in the street. The conclusion may then be drawn that the remedy lies in reinterpreting the tradition so that it *will* be relevant (that is, subjectively meaningful and practically applicable). Cox's recommendation to the churches to "speak politically" is a good recent example of this—highly "relevant," of course, in a situation where churches and church people have been widely involved in the racial struggle, as well as, more recently, in the debate over American foreign policies. Here, particularly, the point should be stressed again that our analysis has *no bearing whatever* on the sincerity and intrinsic worth of these political activities. The point is, quite simply, that theology and ecclesiastical practice accommodate themselves to the reality presuppositions of the man in the street. The events and moral issues of Mississippi and Vietnam are real to the man in the street. The traditional religious affirmations about God, world, and man, very largely, are unreal. The sociologically derived programs for theology and church give cognitive as well as practical priority to the reality presuppositions of the man in the street over those of the religious tradition. Those with an inclination towards linguistic analysis as now fashionable in Anglo-American philosophy can perform essentially the same operation with different conceptual tools, for here too the reality of the man in the street is accorded a privileged cognitive status. There are some problems of application in both translation procedures, since, after all, there are significant variations within the species "man in the street." What is real and relevant to the young civil-rights worker is not necessarily so to the corporation executive. The general character of translation, therefore, will vary in accordance with the target audience addressed by the translators.

Whatever the particular conceptual machinery employed, the reinterpretation of the Christian tradition by the secular theologians entails an accommodation between the tradition and what is, correctly or not, taken to be modern consciousness. Nor is there any question as to where something must give way in this process, as between the two entities to be accommodated. Almost invariably, the tradition is made to conform to the cognitive and normative standard of the alleged modern consciousness. Our movement thus replicates to an amazing degree, in form if not in content, Feuerbach's famous program of reducing theology to anthropology.

THE INFRASTRUCTURE OF THE MOVEMENT

We have already indicated some of the practical consequences drawn from these theological developments. It would be very naive sociologically to think that there are not also practical, specifically social, roots for the theological developments. In other words, there is a sociologically graspable *Sitz im Leben,* a nontheoretical infrastructure, from which the theological ideas in question have sprung. Their self-avowed starting point is the disintegration of Christendom as a general and assumed universe of discourse in western culture. This disintegration, however, is itself an effect of broad historical forces that have created the modern world. Put differently, secularization in both society and consciousness is itself a phenomenon that must be explained. The usual explanations in terms of the growth of a rational and scientific world view (which is where Bultmann begins and where he is pretty generally followed by our secular theologians) are unsatisfactory for this reason, whatever their merits in particular cases. We strongly suspect that no explanation that remains only within the framework of the history of ideas is likely to serve as an adequate means to understand the phenomenon of secularization. The weakness of any such "idealistic" explanations is actually illustrated very well by the secular theologians as a case in point. Their general procedure is to relativize the religious tradition by means of certain modern ideas. It does not occur to them, on the whole, that these modern ideas, which serve as their criteria of validity or relevance, can themselves be relativized.

Let us grant Bultmann, for example, that people using electricity and radios generally find the miracles of the New Testament less than credible. Let us also leave aside here the question as to why, despite electricity and radios, these people still manage to find a place in their world view for luxuriant irrationalities of a nonreligious nature. Let us here even grant Bultmann (what should not be granted to him at all) that all these electricity- and radio-users share with him a scientific world view. But just this fact, if it were a fact, would cry out for explanation! And what equally cries out for explanation is the fact that Bultmann, and with him the entire movement, takes for granted the epistemological superiority of the electricity- and radio-users over the New Testament writers—to the point where the theoretical possibility that, after all, there may be a nonscientific reality that has been lost to modern man is not even considered. In other words, secularized consciousness is taken for granted, not just as an empirical datum, but as an unquestioned standard of cognitive validity. Otherwise, the possibility that there may be a cognitive need for modern consciousness to be *re*mythologized would at least make an appearance in the theological argument, if only for the purpose of rejecting it, not on tactical, but on epistemological grounds.

It is at this point that a sociology-of-knowledge perspective begins to be useful. The question as to who is ultimately right in his knowledge of the world—Bultmann, the electricity-using man in the street, or St. Paul—is, of course, bracketed in this perspective. What is asserted, though, is that all three exist and think in their own unquestioned worlds, that are themselves grounded in specific social infrastructures. Just as the religious tradition was grounded in such a specific infrastructure, *so also* are the ideas employed to relativize the tradition. The general blindness of the relativizing theologians to the relativity of their own debunking apparatus points directly to the need for analyzing the infrastructure of their own ideas.

Obviously, it is impossible here to discuss various possible explanations of the origins of secularization either in terms of the history of ideas or in socio-historical terms. We readily admit a certain partiality to the notion, frequently expressed by the theological figures that interest us here, that decisive impulses towards secularization may be found in Biblical religion itself. This notion, to our knowledge, was first elaborated systematically in Max Weber's understanding of the "disenchantment of the world," though, especially if one thinks in Weberian terms, it is well to keep in mind that this process was unintended and thus profoundly ironical. Nor is it our intent to quarrel with the various theories that explain the transformation of modern consciousness in terms of economic, technological, and social-structural terms. It is readily evident that so complex a phenomenon will have to be analyzed in multicausal terms, and it is evident, at least to me, that "ideal" and "material" factors will be found to interact dialectically in the historical chain of causes. However, there is one causal factor that is rarely emphasized in this connection and which we could consider to be decisive in the formation of an infrastructure capable of giving rise to modern secularized consciousness—namely, the pluralization of social worlds.

Christendom developed in a situation in which the great majority of people lived within the same overall social structure, as given in the feudal system, and the same overall world view, as maintained by the church as sole reality-defining institution. This is not to say that medieval society was monolithic or in a state of perfect equilibrium. There were strains within the social structure, as shown by the peasant uprisings, and there were challenges to the monopoly of the church, as expressed in the various heretical movements. All the same, Christendom provided both a social-structural and a cognitive unity that was lost, probably irretrievably, upon its dissolution at the beginning of the modern age. By the same token, the social world of Christendom was contained in a way that ours cannot possibly be. This, again, does not mean that there was no awareness of other worlds. There was always the world of Islam before the gates and the world of Judaism within the actual confines of the *res christiana.* These discrepant worlds, however, were only rarely capable of becoming threats to the unquestioned reality of the Christian world. The one was kept away at the point of the sword, the other carefully segregated, often enough also with the sword.

Our own situation, by contrast, is one in which discrepant worlds coexist within the same society, contemporaneously challenging each other's cognitive and normative claims. We cannot discuss here the various factors that have gone into this —the ideological schisms unleashed by the renaissance, reformation, and enlightenment; the opening up of strange lands (and ideas!) in the great voyages of discovery; the growth of highly differentiated and mobile social structures through urbanization and industrialization; the transformations of "knowledge" brought on by the invention of printing and, later, by mass literacy; the very recent impact of the mass media of communication; and so on. We can only stress the net result of this pluralization of worlds—that it has become very difficult to maintain, or, for that matter, to establish *de novo,* any monopoly in the definition of reality. Instead, our situation is characterized by a market of world views, simultaneously in competition with each other. In this situation, the maintenance of any certitudes that go much beyond the empirical necessities of the society and the individual to function is very difficult indeed. Inasmuch as religion essentially rests upon superempirical certitudes, the pluralistic situation is a secularizing one and, *ipso facto,* plunges religion into a crisis of credibility. The particular theological movement that interests us here must be understood, then, as emerging from a situation in which the traditional religious certitudes have become progressively less credible, not necessarily because modern man has some intrinsically superior access to the truth, but because he exists in a socio-cultural situation which itself undermines religious certitude.

We have so far avoided formulating our perspective in systematic sociology-of-knowledge terms, so as not to offend prematurely with the proverbial barbarity of the specialist's jargon. At this point, however, there must be at least some explication of the systematic features of the perspective. In this context, this must unavoidably be done in somewhat of an axiomatic manner. Let us first reformulate the above description of the background of our phenomenon in more systematic terms: The movement under consideration presupposes a *de-objectivation* of the traditional religious contents, which in turn presupposes a disintegration of the traditional *plausibility structure* of these contents. What does this mean?

DE-OBJECTIVATION

Human consciousness emerges out of practical activity. Its contents, pretheoretical as well as theoretical, remain related to this activity in diverse ways. This does not mean that theoretical consciousness, or "ideas," are to be understood as mere epiphenomena or as dependent variables determined in a one-sided causation by nontheoretical, non-"ideal" processes. Rather, theories and ideas continually interact with the human activity from which they spring. In other words, the relationship between consciousness and activity is a dialectical one—activity produces ideas, which in turn produce new forms of activity. The more or less permanent constellations of activity that we know as "societies" are, therefore, in an ongoing dialectical relationship with the "worlds" that form the cognitive and normative meaning coordinates of individual existence. Religious worlds, as much as any others, are thus produced by an infrastructure of social activity and, in turn, act back upon this infrastructure.

The socially produced world attains and retains the status of objective reality in the consciousness of its inhabitants in the course of common, continuing social activity. Conversely, the status of objective reality will be lost if the common social activity that served as its infrastructure disintegrates. It is very important to remember that these social processes of reality-confirmation and reality-disconfirmation apply to contents that, by whatever criteria of validity, the scientific observer regards as true, as well as to those he regards as false. Thus, the objective reality of astrological forces is confirmed by the same social processes that, in another society, confirm the objective reality of the scientific world view. The sociologist, of course, is not in a position of judge between the rival cognitive claims of astrology and modern science; he can only point out that each will be taken for granted in the specific situations where everyday social experience confirms it. Human theories and ideas, then, require specific infrastructures of confirmatory social interaction if they are to retain what William James aptly called their "accent of reality." If such infrastructures are strong and enduring, then the theoretical constructions grounded in them take on an objective reality close to that of natural phenomena—they are taken for granted with the same unquestioning certitude given to the "facts of life" encountered in the physical universe. Again, this holds for religious ideation as much as for any other. It is as "natural" to be Catholic in a Catholic milieu, as to be a Muslim in Arabia. What is more, we have good reason to doubt an individual's "Catholic consciousness" if he is transplanted to Arabia, and to doubt a Muslim's certitudes in the reverse case.

The social infrastructure of a particular ideational complex, along with various concomitant maintenance procedures, practical as well as theoretical, constitute its plausibility structure, that is, set the conditions within which the ideas in question have a chance of remaining plausible. Within the plausibility structure, the individual encounters others who confirm, by their attitudes and by their assumptions, that the particular ideational complex is to be taken for granted as reality. Among these others there may be authority figures, officially accredited reality-definers, who will from time to time engage in especially solemn confirmations, frequently by means of terrifying and awe-inspiring ceremonies. If the individual should, for one reason or another, develop doubts about the officially defined verities, the plausibility structure will usually provide various mechanisms of "mental hygiene" for the eradication of doubts. Put simply, the plausibility structure is to be understood as a collection of people, procedures, and mental processes geared to the task of keeping a specific definition of reality going. It does not require great sociological sophistication to see that such a social and social-psychological matrix is a condition *sine qua non* of all religious ideation. It is precisely for this reason that religion is a communal or collective enterprise. At the risk of offending theological sensitivities, we can state this fact quite simply by appropriating the sentence, *"Extra ecclesiam nulla salus,"* with the slight modification that *"salus"* in our context does not refer to a superempirical destiny of the individual, but to the plausibility of the religious contents represented by any particular *ecclesia* within this empirically available consciousness.

Strongly integrated plausibility structures will produce firm objectivations, and will be capable of supporting world views and ideas with a firm status of objective reality within the consciousness of their adherents. As soon as plausibility structures begin to disintegrate, this status of objective reality begins to totter. Uncertainty, doubts, questions, make their appearance. What was previously "known" becomes, at best, "believed." In a further step, it is an "opinion," or even a "feeling." In other words, the particular contents of consciousness that used to be taken for granted as "knowledge" are progressively de-objectivated. In the case of religious contents, the process can be readily understood by contrasting the state of, say, "living in a Christian world," with a desperate "leap of faith" into a Christian position, and, finally, with having some sort of a Christian label attached to one's "religious preference" or "religious interest." These last two phrases, which need no explanation in an American setting, express what has taken place in the de-objectivation of the religious tradition with admirable succinctness.

The excursion into general sociology-of-knowledge theory has, we hope, been useful. It should be clearer now in what way a sociology-of-knowledge perspective may be applied to the situation that interests us here. The recent history of western religion makes a great deal more sense in this perspective, into which it has been placed only rarely, if at all. To my knowledge, the closest to it may be found in the work of some contemporary German sociologists, notably Arnold

Gehlen, who coined the term, "subjectivization," for a broad range of modern cultural phenomena, and Helmut Schelsky, who applied Gehlen's notions to the sociology of religion. In any case, we would contend that our present religious situation can be understood much more readily if we apply to it the aforementioned concept of de-objectivation. The general background of the movement under consideration here is the reality-loss of the religious tradition in the consciousness of increasing numbers of people, something that is not to be ascribed to some mysterious intellectual fall from grace, but to specific and empirically available social developments. The secularization of consciousness and the pluralization of society must be understood together, as two facets of the same general and dialectical process. The important fact that this process has now burst beyond the confines of the western world and, as a result of modernization, has become a worldwide phenomenon, cannot be considered here, but should at least be kept in mind.

DEFENSE OR ACCOMMODATION?

The problem that poses itself as a result of the process of de-objectivation is simple—how to perpetuate an institution whose reality presuppositions are no longer socially taken for granted. The problem has an obvious practical side, which produces the headaches of all those responsible for the economic and general well-being of organized religion. There is an equally obvious theoretical problem of how to legitimize the continuing social existence of the institution and its tradition, in the absence of the massive reality-confirmation that previously sustained them. This, of course, is where the headaches of the theologians come in, or more accurately, of those theologians who continue to operate as legitimating functionaries of the institution. The manner in which our particular group of secular theologians has responded to the problem will be further clarified, we think, if we ask ourselves what options are possible in our situation in the first place.

There are two fundamental options, with variations within each—defense and accommodation. The institution may take on a defensive posture vis-à-vis the secularizing-pluralizing process, continue to affirm the old objectivities, and, as far as possible, go on with its own life and thought despite the regrettable developments on the "outside." Or the institution may accommodate itself to this "outside" in a variety of practical and theoretical compromises. Both options have been tried. Both entail considerable practical and theoretical difficulties.

The main practical difficulty of the defense posture is one of "social engineering." If one is to go on proclaiming the old objectivities in a social milieu that refuses to accept them, one must maintain or construct some sort of subsociety within which there can be a viable plausibility structure for the traditional affirmations. What is more, this subsociety must be carefully and continuously protected against the pluralistic turbulence outside its gates. Put a little rudely, one must maintain a ghetto. This is not very difficult in a modern society with mass literacy and mass communications, unless the subsociety can exercise totalitarian control over its territory and its population. The theoretical difficulties are directly related to this. One can repeat the old legitimations as if nothing had happened, in which case one risks, sooner or later, a complete collapse of plausibility. Or one may carry on a ceaseless theoretical warfare, a kind of permanent apologetic, in which case one risks, sooner or later, contamination by the very reality one is trying to keep out.

The extreme case of this choice is the closed world of certain sects, which exist as deviant reality-enclaves within the surrounding social world with which they maintain only the minimal relations required for economic and political survival. The old-line Amish settlements or the Hasidic communities in New York may serve as illustrations. Less extreme cases are, of course, more common. The most important example is the Catholic church, which until very recently has confronted the modern world almost everywhere in a posture of determined defensiveness and, as a result, has had to spend a good deal of its institutional energy on the maintenance of Catholic subsocieties. It is hardly fanciful to suggest that the social engineering difficulties just indicated account in large measure for the *aggiornamento* now in process, setting loose disintegrating forces that, we suspect, the official promoters of the *aggiornamento* will find hard to control.

Within Protestantism and Judaism, orthodoxy and neo-orthodoxy everywhere have had to go hand in hand with an energetic reconstruction of social milieus that could serve as plausibility structures for the reaffirmed objectivities of old. Thus, it is not so much a theological as a sociological imperative that led from the Barthian return to the tradition to the so-called "rediscovery of the church." To put it a little rudely again, one needs a pretty strong church as a social-psychological support if one is to believe what the Barthians want one to believe. We strongly suspect, incidentally, that the long dominance of neo-orthodoxy in European Protestantism had much to do with political situations on the "outside" that made subsocial self-enclosure morally appealing, and that the post-war decline in this domination is directly related to the loss of this essentially nonreligious appeal. In sum, orthodox or neo-orthodox positions in our situation inevitably tend towards sectarian social forms for their maintenance, which will be successful to the degree that people can be motivated to be sectarians—a stand that is contingent upon many, mostly nonreligious, factors quite beyond the control of ecclesiastical authorities.

The accommodation posture is obviously the more "modern" one. But it too has its great difficulties, which can be summed up in the simple question, "Just how far should one go?" Usually, the answer is first given in tactical terms, just as the entire accommodation process typically begins with an effort to solve the tactical problem—that is, the problem of getting one's message across to a recalcitrant clientele. One then goes as far as one has to for the pastoral or evangelistic purpose at hand. The difficulty with such a procedure is that there is a built-in "escalation" factor. The clientele is likely to become more, not less, recalcitrant in the secularizing-pluralizing situation, and one is consequently obligated to ever-deepening concessions to the reality presuppositions of the people one wants to keep or win. The difficulty attains a new dimension, however, as these presuppositions begin to infect the thinking of the tacticians themselves—again, an almost inevitable outcome under the circumstances. The question is then no longer, "Just how far should one go?" but, "How far must *I* go to continue believing myself?" When this point is reached, the floodgates are opened to a veritable onslaught of relativizing challenges to the tradition. In sum, the intrinsic problem of the accommodation option is that, once taken, it has the powerful tendency to escalate to the point where the plausibility of the tradition collapses, so to speak, from within.

The fierce opposition to concessions of even a minor sort among ultraorthodox elements in the religious institutions may thus be said to rest upon a rather sound sociological instinct, which is frequently absent in their more "open-minded" opponents. Therefore, quite apart from one's own intellectual and moral sympathies, one cannot deny a good measure of sociological sense to the authorities that squelched the modernist movement in the Catholic church a half century ago, or, for that matter, to the conservatives in the church today who fear that the *aggiornamento* will open up a Pandora's box of ecclesiastical and theological troubles. The history of a couple of centuries of Protestant accommodation can hardly be reassuring to them.

The Choice of the Secular Theologians

But it is high time that we return to our secular theologians. How is one to understand their place in the general situation that we have tried to describe? Historically, as already mentioned, the "new" movement stands in a continuity with classical Protestant liberalism. While its theological propositions are hardly more radical than at least some made long ago by the generations of Ritschl and Harnack, their overall posture seems more radical precisely because the disintegration of the plausibility structures has greatly accelerated since the period of the classical liberals. In any case, whatever one may think of the newness of the "new" theology, it stands at an extreme pole of the defense-accommodation continuum of theological postures—so extreme that it is very hard indeed to imagine any further steps in that direction short of the final self-liquidation of the ecclesiastical-theological enterprise as such.

Accommodation with the secular theologians has become total. The reality presuppositions of our age have become the only valid criteria for the handling of tradition. From the viewpoint of the conservative apologetician, the secular theologians have surrendered to the enemy. The more moderate liberal positions may be characterized as a bargaining procedure with secularized consciousness: "We'll give you the Virgin Birth, but we'll keep the Resurrection;" "You can have the Jesus of history, but we'll hold on to the Christ of the apostolic faith;" and so on. The secular theology disdains such negotiation. It surrenders all. Indeed, it goes farther in its abandonment of the tradition than most people who do not identify themselves with it. For example, the secular theologians show a greater willingness to abandon belief in a life after death than does the unchurched man in the street, who commonly retains some lingering hopes in this matter. And, at least in America, it seems that theologians today have a greater propensity to proclaim themselves as atheists than the average, theologically untrained skeptic. The whole thing reminds one strongly of the old story of the drunkard who carefully walked in the gutter so that he could not possibly fall into it. The transformation of transcendence into immanence, and the change from objectivity to subjectivity, is completed. The paradoxical result is that one can now feel safe from the secularizing and subjectivizing forces threatening the tradition. The worst, so to speak, has already happened—one has pre-empted it to oneself.

It is important, we think, to understand that this posture can be very liberating. Quite apart from the general rewards of feeling oneself to be "with it," there is the liberation of "going all the way," being done once and for all with the agonies of compromise. Indeed, this liberating quality, we suspect, is psychologically very much the same as that which comes from the opposite movement of the "leap of faith." All "radical" decisions have this much in common psychologically: to quote the punchline of a classic American joke, one is rid, once and for all, of "all those choices." In this case the choices include, at least, a good many theological ones. Every theologian must ask himself the question, vis-à-vis his tradition, "What do I believe?" And the answer, "Nothing!", can be as alleviating as the answer, "Everything!"

To think, however, that the fundamental problem of the *institution* can be solved in this manner is, obviously, mistaken. The practical and theoretical difficulties raised by secular theology for the churches are almost too apparent to elaborate. Practically, secular theology leads to programs of nonreligious activity that, by definition almost, are very hard to distinguish from similar programs launched under lay auspices. For example, it is not easy to retain any sort of marginal differentiation between psychotherapeutic or political-action programs sponsored by the churches or by purely secular organizations. The thought that one might just as well dispense with the "Christian" label is hardly avoidable sooner or later. There is thus a built-in self-defeating factor in all such programs of "secular Christianity." Very much the same problem arises on the level of theorizing. After all, a theoretical mind can usually stand only a certain amount of paradox. The particular paradox of engaging in the discipline of divinity while denying the divine is hardly likely to recommend itself to many people for very long.

CONCLUSIONS

Sociological prediction is dangerous business, as everyone knows who has tried it. We would not like to engage in it here. Yet some projections into the future are hard to avoid in an analysis such as this. If one projects a continuation of the movement under consideration here to the point where it becomes the dominant ideology within the Protestant community, one would also have to project that this community is on the brink of dissolution as an institution. This is not very likely, certainly not in America. There are powerful social functions carried on by the institutional complex of American Protestantism. Most of these, to be sure, are of an essentially nonreligious character, but there are strong reasons for maintaining at least a semblance of continuity with the traditional institutional legitimations. While in many ways American Protestantism is already secularized both in its social functionality and in its consciousness, there is no need to proclaim this from the rooftops as a theological verity. At the same time, the afore-mentioned difficulties for any sort of orthodoxy within our situation would certainly not lead one to expect a vigorous resurgence of antimodernism, unless, indeed, we are fated to undergo convulsions similar in intensity to those that brought the Barthian movement into a position of dominance in Europe in the 1930's. What is now happening in the Catholic com-munity seems to support this. If one is to make a prediction at all, then probably the safest would be that there will be no reversal in the secularization and de-objectivation processes, but that the extreme legitimations of these will be considerably blunted as they are diffused through the community and become respectable. The probable fate of the secular theology, once its appeal as the *dernier cri* in religion has passed, would then be its absorption into the legitimating apparatus of the institution (which, incidentally, is exactly what happened with classical liberalism). We strongly suspect that this process of neutralization is already taking place as these "challenging new insights" are integrated in various ecclesiastical programs. In this process, there is nothing to prevent the "death of God" from becoming but another program emphasis, which, if properly administered, need not result in undue disturbances in the ongoing life of the institution.

A few slightly less than scientific words in conclusion. The foregoing analysis has moved with some care within a sociolog-ical frame of reference. It goes without saying that this im-poses certain limits on one's view of these matters. The most important limit is that, of course, any question about the ultimate truth or error of the theological positions under consideration must be rigidly excluded from the analysis. When it comes to such questions of truth or error, the most that sociology can do is to make one aware of the socio-historical relativity of one's own cognitive presuppositions—an aware-ness that I, for one, would strongly recommend to the secular theologians. But I will take the liberty here of at least one little step beyond the proper limits of sociological inquiry.

If anyone should think that the previous analysis camouflages some strong position of certitude, I can only assure him that nothing could be farther from the truth. I cannot, I am afraid, lay claim to any certitudes, positive *or* negative, in the fundamental questions of religion. I can only claim a persistent and, at times at least, passionate concern for these questions. In speaking of de-objectivation and its consequences, therefore, I speak of something that involves myself. But perhaps it is precisely for this reason that I am somewhat less than amicably disposed towards those who claim to have reached the end of a road on which I still regard myself as traveling, regardless of whether they do so by proclaiming the "death of God" or His "undeniable" presence.

It seems to me that the essence of religion has been the confrontation with an *other,* believed to exist as a reality in the universe external to and vastly different from man—something that is indeed "out there," as Robinson puts it. The fundamental religious proposition, therefore, is that man is not alone in reality. Whether this is or is not part of the socially objectivated world view of a particular society is as irrelevant to its possible validity as, for instance, the absence from the world view of Zulu society of any notion of quantum theory is irrelevant to the validity of the quantum theory. The theological enterprise reduces itself to absurdity if it engages itself with the fundamental proposition of religion on any terms other than those of its validity. Is man alone in reality: Yes or no? If one is certain that the answer is "Yes," then, it seems to me, one could do better things with one's time than theology. In this respect one could learn from Marx. When he was certain that, with Feuerbach, the critique of religion was finished, he did not bother with it any more, but went on to concern himself with other things. But if one is *not* so certain that the religious proposition of an *other* confronting man in reality is only a gigantic illusion, then one can hardly dismiss the question about the validity of the proposition as irrelevant. In one way or another, inside or outside the traditional religious institutions, one will want to continue pursuing the question.

23

W. RICHARD COMSTOCK

Neo-Christian Philosopher

William Richard Comstock (1928–   ) is the founder of no new system, yet he has much to recommend him as a candidate for a major role in the radical transformation of Christian thought that began to take place toward the end of the 1960s. He speaks an idiom both American and international, with an accent at once distinctive and alert to past and future. His first book, an original interpretation of the Christian-Marxist encounter, was not completed until 1970.

Comstock was born in Bakersfield, California, the only son of Chauncey Mark Comstock and Antonina Vlasova. His paternal ancestry can be traced back to a Devonshire Puritan who settled at Providence, Rhode Island, in the 1660s and includes Kansas homesteaders who heeded the call of the West. His maternal grandfather, Aleksandr Popov, was another kind of pioneer, involved in Russia's great age of railroad building in the decades before the Revolution. One sees in Richard Comstock a certain bipolarity reflecting these origins—on the one hand, pragmatic, common-sensical, optimistic; on the other, a Dostoevskyan bent toward the mystical and ecstatic, a blend of visionary hope and brooding awareness of the world's suffering. He feels his intellectual task is not to flatten but to purify the religious sense—to refine and distill the raw brew with the instruments of common sense and logical scrutiny.

Educated at Berkeley High School and the University of California at Berkeley, Comstock received his religious training at First Presbyterian Church in that city, a Calvinist impetus that led him to Princeton Theological Seminary, where he took his B.D. in 1954. Ordained a minister of the

United Presbyterian Church, U.S.A., he served as an army chaplain for four years, mostly in West Germany, returning to Princeton for a Th.M. degree (1959) and moving on to Union Theological Seminary for his doctorate (1963) and a year as instructor. When the University of California formed a department of religious studies at its Santa Barbara campus, he joined its faculty and is now an associate professor.

Three thinkers have been decisive for Comstock's development—Paul Tillich, William James, and George Santayana. He was professionally associated with Tillich for a brief period before the latter's death, but his interest in Tillich's "grand view of religion as the element of depth in culture"[1] dates back to seminary days. From the matrix of Tillich's thought Comstock has moved toward the more empirical and scientific approach of James. He feels that the valid insights of idealism, phenomenology, and existentialism become distorted when detached from the physical, biological, and material order of existence; accordingly, Comstock aligns himself with James as philosophically a pragmatist and naturalist.

From Tillich's view of the religious symbol, Comstock has moved toward Santayana's more lucid appreciation of "the symbolic texture of all our knowledge claims, whether those of religion, common sense, art, or science. Santayana maintained an impressive balance between semiotic idolatry, which regards a particular system of symbols as an exact mirror of reality, and that agnosticism which holds that symbols are incapable of reflecting reality at all." In Santayana's view, as Comstock learned, language can illuminate reality without being exhaustive or infallible. In *Scepticism and Animal Faith*, particularly, the Harvard sage explores the relationship between man's critical faculties and his basic confidence in the cognitive powers of his body and mind. These themes were especially manifest to Comstock in his studies for his doctoral dissertation, which is a detailed study of Santayana as a religious thinker.

---

[1] Quotations, unless otherwise attributed, are from an autobiographical sketch drafted by Comstock at the request of the editor.

Comstock's first published work was a review of Teilhard de Chardin's *The Divine Milieu,* which appeared in the *Union Seminary Quarterly Review,* May 1962. Since then, a dozen articles have appeared—half of these since 1966. Notable among them is a superb assessment, "Theology After the Death of God" (*Cross Currents,* Summer 1966)[2], which provides a theological overview of the controversy that is more than a survey, contrasting "the holy secularism of Tillich and the radical secularism of Nietzsche"[3] and arraying in ordered perspective not only the viewpoints of van Buren, Altizer, Hamilton, Bonhoeffer, and Cox, but also those of Sartre, Camus, and Barth, with side glances at Tolstoy, Kafka, Buber, and Wittgenstein. Although Comstock's output has been small, it is marked by an originality that remains to be focused and defined but is at least partly the result of thorough scholarship which casts both wide and deep. Tillich, James, and Santayana are each in a sense eclectic, yet in each one finds "a specific worldview or visionary center that gave unity to his thought. Finally, each was concerned with the construction of a theology or philosophy of religion that was not a purely personal matter, but sought to express the visionary center implicit in our most contemporary and advanced culture." To such inclusiveness Comstock aspires, and it is this which energizes his scholarship and produces the cohesiveness in his interpretation of the death of God.

Again like Tillich, James, and Santayana, the emerging unity of Comstock's vision implies a comprehensive view of man, nature, and destiny—a synthesis correlating the insights of religion, art, and philosophy with "the most advanced scientific findings." What Aquinas did for the Middle Ages and their culture, what Tillich did for the Protestant Era, "must be redone for the cybernetic world into which we are now moving." The perennial questions of meaning, healing, God—

---

[2] This article, together with an illuminating postscript, appears in Bernard Murchland, ed., *The Meaning of the Death of God* (New York: Random House, 1967).
[3] *Ibid,* p. 235.

these will remain. In that sense, Comstock sees himself as traditional. But, he says, "the position will become revolutionary because one must willingly accept radical changes in form in order that the religious content may be properly conveyed in the new age of electronic media." Like others of his generation, Comstock is attuned to process—"the question is not 'what is man?' but 'what is man becoming?'" He regards the Teilhardian vision as an augury of theology's future, a future in which the theism of the West will enter into creative interplay with the "ecstatic languages of Brahman, Tao, Sunyatta," moving toward a truly "world" theology.

This synthesis, Comstock believes, will require more than logical and metaphysical analysis alone. "Feeling as well as thought must be considered. It is a matter of making whole again the divided sensibility of the modern mind. Somehow, religious aspiration and scientific rigor must be blended, yet in such a way that the autonomous integrity of each is maintained and not eroded." The task is not one for a single thinker but for a generation, some of whose representatives we have examined in previous chapters. It is too soon to predict Comstock's role or stature among this vanguard in years to come, but some substantial indication may be gleaned from his theological reflection on what might be termed the new symbolic language of electronic technology as seen in Marshall McLuhan. A great deal of superficial nonsense has been written about McLuhan by Christians who are eager to be considered up-to-date. Few have discerned, as Comstock does, the dimension of depth in McLuhan's frequently punny, cryptic, self-caricaturing literary analysis of postliterate culture. To use one of McLuhan's own terms, Comstock's essay may be regarded as a "probe" into what man's thought-forms are becoming. Even if this probe turned out altogether wrong, and I do not think it is, it would have lasting value as a new type of theological endeavor. If not outstanding as an achievement, it is at least important as a symptom and portent of tomorrow's theology—as much so as any of the efforts afoot in America on the threshold of the 1970s.

MARSHALL McLUHAN'S THEORY OF
SENSORY FORM: A THEOLOGICAL REFLECTION*

Marshall McLuhan characterizes his studies of the communications media as exploratory probes that are not to be accepted as a finished system but to be used as heuristic tools toward a more intimate awareness of the texture of our modern world.[1] In this paper I want to consider the implications of some of McLuhan's analyses for a more adequate understanding of the contemporary theological scene. McLuhan has admitted that his probes have such relevance, though he does not choose himself to point them out in any detail.[2] He does maintain that his studies can be of assistance to the bewildered modern who feels helpless and overwhelmed by the dramatic changes in human thought, style, and feeling that are now taking place. The sense of helplessness is caused by the manner in which these transformations of consciousness seem to occur relentlessly and yet without the conscious direction of those affected by them. McLuhan believes that his work can relieve this dilemma in two ways. At the very least, it can provide a greater awareness of the nature and focus of these events; thus: "It may be merely temperament in my own case, but I find some easing of the burden in just understanding and clarifying the

---

* From *Soundings,* A Journal of Interdisciplinary Studies, LI, 2 (Summer 1968), pp. 166–183.
[1] Interesting discussions of McLuhan are to be found in the following articles: Kenneth Burke, "Medium as 'Message,'" *Language as Symbolic Action* (Berkeley, 1966), pp. 410–418; John M. Culkin, "A Schoolman's Guide to Marshall McLuhan," *Saturday Review,* March 18, 1967, pp. 51–54, 70–72; Richard Kostelanetz, "Marshall McLuhan: Making the Unconscious Conscious," *Commonweal,* LXXXV (January 1967), 420–426; "Understanding McLuhan (In Part)," *The New York Times Magazine,* January 29, 1967, pp. 18, 37–50; *Newsweek,* March 6, 1967, pp. 53–57; Anthony Quintin, "Cut-Rate Salvation," *New York Review,* November 23, 1967, pp. 9ff.
[2] Gerald E. Stearn, "Conversations with McLuhan," *Encounter,* XXVIII (June 1967), 50.

issues."[3] Secondly, increased awareness of our present conflicts in consciousness "holds out the promise of reducing these conflicts by an increase of human autonomy."[4]

Such therapy, if available, will certainly be appreciated by the theologian and religionist who are witnessing dramatic shifts in attitude toward their traditional concerns that are frustrating for the reasons noted. Thus a radical secularism is experienced in which the traditional sense of the sacred seems to be almost entirely eroded. Or again, the "death of God" is announced, not because of some new empirical discovery or rational argument, but simply because the idea of God seems no longer relevant, important, meaningful. Both the felt presence of this God and the very notion of such a presence seem to have become inconceivable within the general framework of the world in which man is now living.

I propose to examine here some salient features of Mc Luhan's position that may possibly increase our understanding of this theological situation. I first want to examine McLuhan's notions of "sensory form," "ratio of the senses," and "hot" and "cold" media. If certain important clarifications of these crucial categories in McLuhan's thought are made, their implications for theology may be more easily perceived.

The Meaning of Sensory Form

The center of McLuhan's thought is concern with the question of the forms of human consciousness. In spite of significant differences, McLuhan is a continuator of the tradition of Hegel, Kant, and Cassirer, which has emphasized the integral connection between the content of consciousness and the symbolic form in which it is apprehended. Here is the basic meaning of McLuhan's famous aphorism that the "medium is the message."[5] Many critics who should know better have applied a

---

[3] Marshall McLuhan, *Understanding Media: The Extensions of Man* (New York, 1966), p. 59; hereinafter *UM*.
[4] Ibid., cf. Marshall McLuhan, *The Gutenberg Galaxy* (Toronto, 1962), p. 254, hereinafter *GG;* also see Marshall McLuhan and Quentin Fiore, *The Medium is the Massage* (New York, 1967), p. 150.
[5] *UM*, p. 23.

hyper-literal interpretation to this dictum and expressed dismay at its apparent denial of any relevance of content to consciousness at all. In spite of a few polemical passages in McLuhan's books which display obvious exaggeration for heuristic purposes, it is clear that such is not his intention.[6] Rather than being a denial of content, the dictum that the "medium is the message" is a brilliant example of the capacity of metaphoric compression to call attention to the integral relation between form and content, not the replacement of one by the other. Through this aphorism, McLuhan affirms that there is no neutral content unaffected by the medium that it only accidently inhabits, like a book in a box. To McLuhan, form and content are rather integral aspects of a single process, like the singing (the medium) of a song (the content).

However, in spite of his affinities with the idealistic tradition on this point, McLuhan's own contribution is an attempt to ground the medium of consciousness in the concrete texture of natural existence. McLuhan criticizes with telling effect idealists like Oswald Spengler, who are perceptive in their recognition of changes in human consciousness but naively view such changes as "the result of a special tremor" in "soul stuff" and thus miss the significant influence that material factors exert on them.[7]

McLuhan's basic approach is similar to Susanne Langer's, who accepts Ernst Cassirer's brilliant account of symbolic forms but seeks to provide for these forms a firmer natural and biological basis than her idealist teacher recognized. McLuhan's work can even be compared meaningfully to Karl Marx's project of turning Hegel right side up by showing that the forms of consciousness are determined by economic modes of production.[8] In McLuhan's case, it is, of course, technological media of communication which assume the determining role.

---

[6] *UM*, pp. 26–27; but cf. "Exaggeration, in the sense of hyperbole, is a major artistic device in all modes of art" (Stearn, "Conversations with McLuhan," p. 55).

[7] *UM*, p. 109.

[8] For some of McLuhan's opinions about Marx, see Stearn, "Conversations with McLuhan," pp. 55–56; *UM*, pp. 49–51.

McLuhan may be guilty of exaggerating the role of technical apparatus in the structuring of consciousness, though it is an exaggeration probably necessary to direct attention to a significant influence that might otherwise be completely ignored. Like other modern thinkers of many persuasions, McLuhan is describing a position that bypasses the sterile alternative of idealism or materialism. To him, consciousness is a real phenomenon, but in Aristotelian fashion we must consider it as a form only realized when organically incarnated in the system of bodily interactions between human self and natural world. Furthermore, this form is no immutable solidity, but a variable function of awareness occurring in the dynamic field of interaction between organism and environment, in which the bodily senses and their technological extensions are constitutive factors. Such an approach, when properly stated, does not commit its proponent to a mono-causal theory attributing the evolution of consciousness to one single factor, such as technological invention alone. Rather, we are presented here with a field theory of multi-dimensional functions in constant interaction.

McLuhan's main contribution to this transactional theory of consciousness is his description of the *form* of consciousness in terms of *sensory ratios*. This notion is very important and we must attempt to interpret it with care. First of all, the notion of a ratio refers to the interplay among the senses whereby, affecting and supporting one another, their combined deliveries provide multi-sensual awareness of a *common* world. On this point, McLuhan refers to the Aristotelian and Thomistic concept of a "common sense" that translates the "experience of one sense into all the senses" and presents the result continuously as a unified image to the mind.[9] McLuhan then plays on an etymological connection by linking this ratio of the senses to the basic idea of ratio-nality. Rational man is one who maintains adequate contact with his world through a properly functioning ratio of his senses.

This problem of contact is related to the important category of tactility. Three distinct though related meanings can be

---

[9] *UM,* p. 67.

recognized in McLuhan's argument. First, McLuhan often uses this term to refer to the basic sense of touch through skin and to the closely related sense of taste and smell.[10] Second, the meaning is then extended to refer to a "haptic" sense of organic touch through the integral reaction of the nervous system as a whole.[11] Finally, this meaning in turn is extended still further by McLuhan to refer to the basic "interplay between all the senses, that functional ratio whereby reality is truly 'felt' and 'grasped.' "[12] Thus:

> It begins to be evident that "touch" is not skin but the interplay of the senses, and "keeping in touch" or "getting in touch" is a matter of a fruitful meeting of the senses, of sight translated into sound and sound into movement, taste and smell.[13]

Another important aspect of McLuhan's account concerns the manner in which the emphasis or focus of attention placed on one particular sense can affect the ratio and interplay amongst all the senses. It is possible that an organism learns to depend mainly on eyes or ears to guide its more important behavioral transactions and thus develops a sensory ratio dominated by one or the other of these senses. However, it is important to distinguish this kind of dominance measured by amount of use from another kind of dominance created by the "heating" or "cooling" of a given sense.

Although McLuhan's definitions of "hot" and "cool" suffer from certain frustrating ambiguities, the basic idea is significant and worth attempting to clarify. We can apply these adjectives either to the senses directly or to technical media that are their extensions. "A hot medium is one that extends one single sense in 'high definition.' High definition is the state of being well filled with data."[14] Conversely, a cool medium provides low definition and a sparsity of data. For example, a photograph is "hot" as compared to a "cool" cartoon. This

---

10 *UM*, p. 116.
11 *UM*, p. 105.
12 *UM*, p. 67.
13 Ibid.
14 *UM*, p. 36.

distinction then leads McLuhan to observe, in his book *Under-standing Media,* that a cool medium requires more participation from the subject, who must fill in the low definition with his own interpretation, as when the few lines of a cartoon are taken to refer to a complex object or event.[15] However, the word "participation" is misleading, since in both hot and cool forms the subject is certainly involved, and there is the further complication that we also want to say that a cool medium may allow for more freedom and detachment from its structure, whereas the hot medium actually involves and ties down the observer to the high definition of its data. Thus, McLuhan has said: "This is cool, in that it is at once involvement and detachment."[16]

For these reasons, I think McLuhan has made his distinction with more clarity in *The Gutenberg Galaxy,* where he stresses the passive-active contrast more than the participational-non-participational one. McLuhan's point is that the cool medium requires more active interpretative energy on the part of the subject, whereas the hot medium forces him into a state of *passive* recognition and acceptance with a minimum of active response of his own. Thus: "The low definition imagery of the tactile mode compels the viewer into an *active* participant role."[17]

The Sensory Form of Visual Narcosis

In *The Gutenberg Galaxy,* McLuhan attempts to describe a particular ratio of the senses that has dominated the modern period of Western history from the fifteenth to the late nineteenth century. This epoch has been profoundly influenced by the development of Western science, the industrial revolution, and the astounding increase in technological invention. McLuhan calls it the Gutenberg Galaxy because he believes that one invention in particular—the printing press—has exerted a major influence on the sensory ratio characteristic of the period.

[15] *UM,* pp. 36–45.
[16] Stearn, "Conversations with McLuhan," p. 57.
[17] *GG,* p. 41 (italics mine).

McLuhan argues that in this period the visual sense assumed an unprecedented emphasis which was caused by the extreme "heating" to which it was subjected by the invention of movable type.[18] He points out that a technological medium that stimulates and "overheats" a given sense may have the effect of inducing a state of numbness or narcosis in the human participant. Just as Narcissus became entranced with his own reflection, so a human organism may be entranced into a state of numbed concentration through one sense that has been heated up to an unusually high degee and consequently allowed to dominate the consciousness.[19] McLuhan suggests that the biblical description of "idolatry" has affinities with this condition of hypnotic focus on a single set of highly defined, overwhelming data that has lost the capacity for dynamic interplay with the other senses.[20]

McLuhan points out that the hypnotic state or trance is a hallucinatory condition induced by the heating up of one sense (either sight or hearing) in a context in which the other senses are cooled down. Thus the hypnotic voice will dominate the consciousness in a darkened room. "The formula for hypnosis is one sense at a time."[21] The major thrust of McLuhan's argument is that man of the mechanical age has been dominated by a sensory ratio that can be characterized in terms of visual narcosis. One important feature of such a state is the loss of tactility, since, as we have already noted, tactility is the dynamic interplay of all the senses in contact with reality, whereas the extreme heating up of one sense necessarily diminishes or completely destroys such an interchange.

It is more important for our purposes to recognize the character of this sensory form than to follow McLuhan in his controversial theory about the technological determinants of its appearance. Nevertheless, the two are interconnected in his thought, so that the question of technological causes must be briefly noted. McLuhan argues that phonetic literacy gave

---

[18] *GG*, pp. 155–177; *UM*, pp. 84–90.
[19] *UM*, pp. 51ff.
[20] *UM*, p. 55.
[21] *GG*, p. 272.

man an eye for an ear.[22] In other words, writing served to increase the use of the eye in comparison with pre-literate societies, where the ear is much more important in orienting man to his physical environment and to the oral wisdom of his society.[23]

McLuhan's notion of sensory ratios provides a way of interpreting the character and evolution of human cultures that is sensitive to complexity and opposed to misleading simplifications. For example, although Greek and medieval societies developed writing skills, it would be a mistake to characterize them in a simplistic fashion as either "ear" or "eye" cultures exclusively. Rather we must see these civilizations as exhibiting, in the course of their long histories, fluctuating changes in sensory ratios. It is true that in comparison with a pre-literate society, certain aspects of Greek civilization develop more emphasis on the eye, as revealed in those judgments of Greek literature that rank sight as a sense superior to any of the others.[24] The crucial role of ideas as "forms of vision" (something to which we gain access through sight") in Plato's philosophy is a further case in point.[25] Aquinas continues this Greek tradition by echoing Aristotle in his observation that "among the senses themselves, sight has the most perfect knowledge, because it is the least material."[26]

Nevertheless, this evidence must be supplemented by the many examples of a continued openness to oral tradition, to the tactility that still pervades manuscripts and cursive writing, to such interesting data as the fact that medieval man was prone to accompany even his solitary reading with lip and vocal movements.[27] Thus McLuhan argues: "Throughout the centuries of manuscript culture it will appear that the visual

---

22 *UM*, p. 58.
23 *GG*, pp. 31–32, 45–47; *UM*, p. 144.
24 Rudolf Bultmann, *Gnosis*, trans. J. R. Coates (London, 1952), p. 3.
25 Paul Friedländer, *Plato: An Introduction*, trans. Hans Meyerhoff (New York, 1958), p. 16.
26 Thomas Aquinas, *Basic Writings of Saint Thomas Aquinas*, ed. Anton Pegis (New York, 1945), p. 797. See esp. Q. 84, Art. 2.
27 *GG*, pp. 92–93; cf. *GG*, pp. 82–111.

did not become quite dissociated from tactility, even though it diminished the auditory empire drastically."[28]

McLuhan then asserts that the "mass production of exactly uniform and repeatable type" generated a drastic "fission of the senses" in which "the visual dimension broke away from the other senses."[29] The basic features of the ensuing visual narcosis can be best described in short compass by considering its spatial aspects. According to McLuhan, the space in which objects appear to heated sight focusing upon data of precise definition is an affair of clearly visualizable dimensions extended along lines composed of repeatable, homogeneous points. Such a space presents its subject matter for scrutiny in patterns that are lineal, sequential, uniform. An eye trained by its attention to lines of uniform type now begins to organize all of its experience as punctiform repeatable units, each of which occupies a specific sequential place within the universal container of homogeneous space.[30] Time apprehension is also spatialized into a kind of linear sequence of homogeneous events taking place in infinite succession along a temporal line analogous to the visual spatial ones.[31]

McLuhan's point is misunderstood if it is interpreted as an attack on visual space as completely undesirable. Obviously the organization of experience in this form has been useful for many purposes. McLuhan's main purpose is to note that when this space is apprehended through a ratio that has been narcotized for the reasons already noted it assumes the form of an abstract illusion.

The main point to recognize is that since each of the senses conveys a spatial form of its own, there seems to be no necessity, other than the compulsion of a hypnotic tyranny, for assigning to visual space an ontological priority. For example, tactility as the sense of touch through skin reveals a space of relationship among kinetic pressures. Each center of energy

---

[28] *GG*, p. 81.
[29] *GG*, p. 54.
[30] *UM*, pp. 108–114, 117–119.
[31] *UM*, pp. 135–144.

generates its own tactile space rather than occupying a part of an abstract geometrical enclosure.[32] Or again, sound occurs in an acoustic space in which the aural data surround the hearer without occupying specific points on a visual line.[33]

Which of these spaces is the real space? The question is unnecessary when we accept the definition of tactility as referring to the dynamic interplay of all the senses. Then we experience the visual space of a "cool" eye in creative configuration with the spaces of the other senses that provides a complex engagement with a multi-spatial world which is probably the most adequate index of what is meant by the elusive term "reality." If McLuhan in places seems to have a negative attitude toward visual space, this is true only when it is separated from tactility and consequently functions as an illusion hypnotically claiming an exclusive reality it does not possess.

McLuhan finds his basic position expressed in an epigram by W. B. Yeats:

> Locke sank into a swoon
> The garden died.
> God took the spinning jenny
> Out of his side.

McLuhan's commentary reads:

> The Lockean swoon was the hypnotic trance induced by stepping up the visual component in experience until it filled the field of attention. . . . At such a moment "the garden" dies. That is, the garden indicates the interplay of all the senses in haptic harmony. With the instressed concern with one sense only, the mechanical principle of abstraction and repetition emerges into explicit form.[34]

THE THEOLOGICAL IMPLICATIONS

The implications of this narcosis for economics, political theory, philosophy are enormous. But our concern here is with its effect on religion and theology. Thus, it is intriguing to note

---

[32] *UM*, pp. 118–119.
[33] *GG*, pp. 41–43; McLuhan and Fiore, *Medium is the Massage*, p. 111; cf. Stearn, "Conversations with McLuhan," p. 52 and Don Ihde, "Some Auditory Phenomena," *Philosophy Today* (1966), pp. 227–235.
[34] *GG*, pp. 17–18.

how Mircea Eliade, without reference to McLuhan, has independently characterized profane space as

> homogeneous and neutral; no break qualitatively differentiates the various parts of its mass. Geometrical space can be cut and delimited in any direction; but no qualitative differentiation and, hence, no orientation are given by virtue of its inherent structure.[35]

Eliade has argued that religious man apprehends his world as a place capable of irruptions by sacred power that generates qualitative difference throughout the spatial contours of the cosmos. But if a narcotized visuality forces the profane form of homogeneous space to dominate the consciousness of modern Western man, it follows that the sense of the sacred will seem to erode, just as it has done in the last few centuries. McLuhan agrees with Eliade's description of the actual textures of "profane" and "sacred" spaces but regrets Eliade's failure to emphasize the technological forces involved in their differentiation.[36]

Again, according to the biblical tradition the living God was evidently first apprehended in forms of haptic immediacy and acoustic space lacking exact visual dimensions. The emphasis in the Bible on the word by which the world was created, the prophet addressed, and salvation preached to man is well known. It is true that visual imagery is also present; but most references to vision (though not all) are cool and lacking in precise definition. The divine "light" illuminates a spiritual path but does not focus the attention on precise detail. According to Hebrew tradition, to see God (with heated vision) is to die. To know God through all the senses in tactile interaction is to encounter the living God in concrete engagement.

It is no wonder, then, that biblical theology experiences a specially severe crisis when it enters the hypnotic world of visual space generated by a heated sense of light. On the pale abstract grid of homogeneous visual space, there seems no

---

[35] Mircea Eliade, *The Sacred and the Profane* (New York, 1957), p. 22.
[36] For McLuhan's views on Eliade, see *GG*, pp. 51–69; *UM*, p. 144.

point capable of "containing" the concrete tactile actuality of the living God. It is for this reason that Bishop Robinson was instinctively correct in pointing to the difficulty modern man has in believing in the God "out there." This phrase refers to the uniform lineal space where no homogeneous point has the requisite tactility to bear the concrete presence of the Divine. Hence, the philosopher complains that this God is meaningless, by which he means that he is inconceivable, i.e., cannot be seen as one of the "clear and distinct" ideas which, ever since Descartes have been so dear to visual man.[37]

To avoid misunderstanding it must again be stressed that the thesis presented here is not that an emphasis on visuality alone contributes to the erosion of the holy, as if hearing were somehow a more sacred sense than sight. The quality antithetical to sacred apprehension resides in the heating of vision and not in vision as such. An extreme concentration on sharp detail seems to induce a condition of passive disinterested scrutiny that destroys the haptic participation in which religious awareness is nurtured. For example, if one considers the attitudinal stance in a service of religious worship, it is clear that when sight, hearing, and the other senses are in tactile interaction, appropriate responses of adoration and commitment are possible. But if vision is heated up so that one "stares" fixedly at the participants of the service, the worship event is immediately secularized into a lineal sequence of meaningless actions.[38] Again, Sartre has given us his famous account of how we de-humanize each other through the intense "look" of stupefying scrutiny that destroys communal interactions.[39]

In this connection it is especially illuminating to examine the exact phrases in which the atheism of two important contemporary thinkers has been expressed. In one passage, Nietzsche announces the "death of God" through the words of the Ugliest Man who refuses to bear the objectifying "look"

---

37 McLuhan and Fiore, *The Medium is the Massage*, p. 146.
38 For McLuhan's views on worship, see *GG*, pp. 137–140.
39 Jean-Paul Sartre, *Being and Nothingness*, trans. Hazel Barnes (New York, 1956), pp. 252ff.

of the Eternal Observer. Similarly, Sartre expresses his youthful rebellion by demanding that God remove "his gaze."[40] Evidently the world of heated visuality is one in which man can only meet God by subjecting him to a de-sacralizing scrutiny and God can only meet man by fixing on him a de-humanizing stare.

EXORCISM OF VISUAL ENCHANTMENT

One of McLuhan's most important theses is that the rapid development of technical media utilizing electricity has profoundly affected our sensory ratios in the twentieth century. The fantastic speed of electricity ends sequence "by making things instant." We turn from a spatial form of sequential extension to one of "instant sensory awareness of the whole." Simultaneity replaces lineality.[41] In a paradoxical and unexpected manner, the radical use of electric media has contributed to the restructuring of our sensory ratios into spatial configurations more congenial to haptic and auditory forms.

> The tendency is to speak of electricity as painters speak of space, namely that it is a variable condition that involves special positions of two or more bodies. There is no longer any tendency to speak of electricity as "contained" in anything. Painters have long known that objects are not contained in space but that they generate their own spaces.[42]

So also electric media generate a "space" of simultaneous relations analogous to the non-lineal space of acoustic phenomena.

It is this transition that has made exorcism of the visual enchantment of the earlier mechanical age possible. McLuhan argues:

> The hybrid or the meeting of two media is a moment of truth and revelation from which new form is born. For the parallel between two media holds us on the frontiers between forms that snap us out of the Narcissus-narcosis. The moment of the meeting of

---

[40] Jean-Paul Sartre, *The Words,* trans. B. Frechtman (Greenwich, Conn. 1966), p. 64; Walter Kaufman, ed., *The Portable Nietzsche* (New York, 1954), p. 376.
[41] *UM,* pp. 27–28.
[42] *UM,* p. 301.

media is a moment of freedom and release from the ordinary trance and numbness imposed by them on our senses.[43]

This description of the present situation presents one curious difficulty for an observer of the theological scene. If the electric age is initiating a new sensory form more congenial to the structures of religious apprehension, why then do we find the cries about radical secularism and the "death of God" to be especially prominent at the very time when, if McLuhan is right, the situation generating these complaints has been transcended? To answer this question, another one of McLuhan's tentative suggestions is helpful.

McLuhan observes that the inauguration of a new medium always creates a lack of appreciation of its own implications, but at the same time heightens the awareness of the "content" of the preceding dominant form. Man had less aesthetic appreciation for nature while agrarian arts and crafts prevailed than when he entered the age of the machine; then "for the first time men began to regard nature as a source of aesthetic and spiritual values."[44] The same line of analysis could be applied to the present theological situation. If McLuhan is right, it might be that while the visual narcosis of the mechanical age lasted its full implications were not realized. Granted that during this period real religious distress was experienced in the tension between the desire for a concrete faith and the abstract visual form provided as its medium. But it is only because the theologian is now partially freed from this religiously numbing form that he sees so clearly that propensity of its spatial lines to strangle deity in its homogeneous net, and of its antiseptic dimensions to de-sacralize the concrete world.

Paradoxically, then, modern man announces the death of God at the very moment when the instruments of this death have been destroyed. With his consciousness still affected by the form he is now transcending, contemporary man announces the total erosion of the sacred at the very moment that new

---

[43] *UM*, p. 63.
[44] *UM*, p. ix.

sensory forms are enabling him to apprehend the sacred more concretely than ever before.

CONCLUSION

McLuhan's description of the characteristics of sensory ratio provides an important heuristic tool for the exploration of the pervasive forms of human apprehension. Some specialists will consider that he is guilty of imposing rigid and simple patterns on phenomena that are dynamic and complex. On the contrary, by showing us how ratios are in constant fluctuation and transition, McLuhan warns us against the application of inflexible descriptions to either individuals or societies. His generalities (such as the characterization of the mechanical age as dominated by a ratio of visual narcosis) must be considered as "ideal types" which are never completely embodied in any concrete person or society but which illuminate our understanding by distinguishing significant patterns and trends. The main emphasis of his thought is on the *variety* of ratios possible within a given culture and a given individual during the course of his development. McLuhan does not impose a single pattern on Greek, Hebrew, medieval, or modern cultures, but rather stresses the complex changes and permutations that can be observed in these phenomena.

The contemporary theologian sensitive to McLuhan's approach will be encouraged to direct his thought to the task of discovering the viable sensory form in which our contemporary theological experience may be structured and communicated. McLuhan provides fruitful suggestions rather than finished answers. One very helpful point is his refusal to argue for the superiority of either eye or ear media over the other.[45] This is not to deny that some fruitful comparisons between the two can be made, especially for the purpose of breaking the tyranny of an exclusive eye orientation that still has a lingering influence on our culture. Many persons, when first asked which sense is more important in orienting them toward their world, will answer sight, although further reflection will often cause

---

[45] *GG*, p. 68; cf. *GG*, p. 19.

this judgment to be changed. One psychologist has observed, however, that

> the importance of auditory experiences for the interpretation of reality is proven through observation of deaf children. . . . A world without sound is a dead world: when sound is eliminated from our experience, it becomes clear how inadequate and ambiguous is the visual experience if not accompanied by auditory interpretation. . . . Deaf persons are prone to paranoid interpretations of outside events.[46]

The importance of sound lies not only in its contribution to physical orientation but in the crucial role it plays in human contact through dialogue. Deafness isolates us from the human context of our being much more radically than does blindness.

Nevertheless, in our desire to free ourselves from visual narcosis we should not consider a counter-emphasis on the aural to be automatically salutary. In fact, McLuhan warns us that since sound assumes an all-inclusive spatial form, it can, when heated, assume an even more tyrannical function than vision. Thus the theologian and historian of religion should beware of idealizing a pre-literate situation in which communal dialogue and human participation in reality supposedly prevails. McLuhan suggests:

> Primitive man lived in a much more tyrannical cosmic machine than Western literate man has ever invented. The world of the ear is more embracing and inclusive than that of the eye can ever be. The ear is hypersensitive. The eye is cool and detached. The ear turns man over to universal panic while the eye, extended by literacy and mechanical time, leaves some gaps and some islands free from the unremitting acoustic pressure and reverberation.[47]

McLuhan's solution is to recommend neither a visual nor aural over-emphasis, but the development of a dynamic tactile interplay among all the senses. Thus he does not consider the accent on vision in the mechanic age to be itself undesirable;

---

[46] Clemens E. Benda, "Language, Consciousness and Problems of Existential Analysis (Daseinanalyse)," *American Journal of Psychotherapy* XIV (April 1960), p. 262; quoted in Amos Wilder, *The Language of the Gospel*, (New York, 1964), p. 19.

[47] *UM*, p. 44; cf. *UM*, p. 162.

he only regrets that the thinkers of the late Middle Ages did not succeed in creating a "new synthesis of written and oral education" that might have enabled man to assume a less hypnotic ratio of the senses during that period.[48]

It is in this light that the theologian should consider the religious implications of the new electric sensory form for religion. There is no doubt that McLuhan is fascinated by the congruence between electric configurations, Eastern wisdom, and the aesthetic theories of modern artists who have sought to reunite visual space with tactility.[49] Furthermore, if McLuhan is right an electronic sensory form has important congruities with religious vehicles of symbolic expression. Both are "inclusive and mythic in mode. The mythic mode of awareness substitutes the multi-faceted for point-of-view."[50] An electric emphasis on simultaneity even seems to approach the mystic consciousness in which all entities are immediately present.[51] No doubt there are certain religious perspectives from which the electric sensory ratio here described will seem extremely attractive. Yet McLuhan's warnings of the effects of visual narcosis are balanced by his judgment that "the principle of numbness comes into play with electric technology as with any other," though in this case it is not a single sense but the nervous system as a whole that may become numbed.[52] Consequently McLuhan also feels uneasy about the possibility of "naive immersion in the metaphysical organicism of our electronic milieu."[53] The electronic world could lead to "a phase of panic terrors, exactly befitting a small world of tribal drums, total interdependence, and super-imposed co-existence. . . . Terror is the normal state of any oral society, for in it everything affects everything all the time."[54]

---

[48] *UM*, p. 76.
[49] *UM*, p. 105, cf. *GG*, p. 82.
[50] *UM*, pp. 141–142.
[51] *UM*, pp. 84, 106.
[52] *UM*, pp. 53ff, 56.
[53] *GG*, p. 248.
[54] *GG*, p. 33.

Thus McLuhan encourages a positive appreciation of the way that the electric sensory form now supports a sense of organic participation and interaction that has transcended the extreme individualism of heated vision, where each man is a separate entity in a homogeneous mass. Yet he also encourages our reservations about the tendency of this participation to absorb all individuality in a single all-inclusive world cell that functions like "a single consciousness" completely controlling all its human parts through the manipulation of communication media.[55] Perhaps, then, the uneasiness we may now feel about an all-embracing electric world that is "static and iconic and inclusive" may point to a contemporary task of electric exorcism which we must perform.[56]

In one suggestive passage McLuhan observes that "had he encountered the electric age, Blake would not have met its challenge with a mere repetition of electric form."[57] Religious critics of contemporary secular culture would do well to take this suggestion to heart. The congruences between electric apprehension and mythic sensibility already noted should not cause the unwary thinker to embrace a new electric narcosis even while celebrating liberation from the older visual one. A vital relation between sensory forms that support simultaneity and those that focus on lineal sequence still needs to be worked out.

Since there is implicit in both Eastern and Western religious traditions a drive toward a unity that is total and inclusive, the sensory form of electric simultaneity does seem to have the affinities with myth and mysticism that McLuhan has noted. However, there is recognizable in the Judeo-Christian tradi-

---

[55] *UM*, p. 67, cf. *UM*, p. 41. McLuhan's attitude toward this all-encompassing organicism is ambivalent. If he hesitates before our "immersion" in this organicism, he also ruminates that "the Christian concept of the mystical body—all men as members of the body of Christ—this becomes technologically a fact under electronic conditions" (Stearn, "Conversations with McLuhan," p. 50).

[56] *UM*, p. 50.

[57] *UM*, p. 38.

tion, and in others as well, a counter-emphasis on time, creative becoming, and history that also must be taken into account and for which a heated electric medium focused on a static simultaneity seems an inadequate vehicle.

The example of Teilhard de Chardin is a case in point. McLuhan does a masterful job of showing how Teilhard's account of the human "noosphere" and its holistic interpretation of centers of separate consciousness is related to electric media rapidly bringing about the simultaneous participation of these separate centers in some kind of comprehensive consciousness of a simultaneous all.[58] McLuhan does justice admirably to this aspect of Teilhard's thought. But there is another side to Teilhard's vision, nurtured in biblical motifs, that focuses on the "future of man" which is not a part of a simultaneous present but a prospect ahead of the temporal flow of creative becoming. In this connection we must also consider R. Buckminster Fuller's reference to the "total interrelatedness and *nonsimultaneous* interaccommodation regularities of universal evolution."[59]

McLuhan would evidently not disagree with this accent on time and indeed has observed that "the moralist has instinctively translated my forward-looking discovery into backward-looking misanthropy."[60] What we have here is a question of emphasis, and the fact is that McLuhan has stressed the "brand-new world of allatonceness."[61] There is in all his work an interest in sensory and aesthetic "spaces" that far exceeds his perfunctory attention to time.[62] There is a consequent

---

[58] *GG*, p. 32. Cf. "Through the discovery yesterday of the railway, the motor car and the aeroplane, the physical influence of each man, formerly restricted to a few miles, now extends to hundreds of leagues or more. Better still: thanks to the prodigious biological event represented by the discovery of electro-magnetic waves, each individual finds himself henceforth (actively and passively) simultaneously present, over land and sea in every corner of the earth." (Teilhard de Chardin, *The Phenomenon of Man*, trans. Bernard Wall [New York, 1961], p. 240).

[59] R. Buckminster Fuller, *No More Secondhand God* (Carbondale, Ill., 1963), p. 33 (italics mine).

[60] Stearn, "Conversations with McLuhan," p. 56.

[61] McLuhan and Fiore, *Medium is the Massage,* p. 63.

[62] His main discussion of time is found in Chapter 15 of *UM*.

lack of attention to the time structures as distinct from the spatial ones of his sensory ratios.[63] Yet this emphasis can have a salutary influence on theology, which has recently been guilty of an exaggerated emphasis on time to the extent that it is sometimes suggested than only temporal categories (in contrast to rejected spatial ones) have theological relevance.[64] McLuhan can help us correct this over-emphasis of a valid insight. As we have seen, McLuhan's argument helps to show how some forms of "heated" space may be antithetic to theological apprehension, while other forms of aesthetic and haptic space are not. McLuhan has reminded us that it would be a mistake if attention to the importance of time for theological reflection obscured the importance and relevance of space as well.

Furthermore, McLuhan's works have suggested an avenue to future exploration which may consider the importance of a "hybrid" interplay among several sensory ratios. Thus the task before the contemporary philosopher of religion who is sensitive to the phenomena McLuhan has noted may be to show the dynamic relation between electric simultaneity *and* a continued openness to some temporal sequential growth. McLuhan, correctly understood, has announced not the dissolution of all lineal apprehension of reality but only its "cooling" and its reintegration into a tactile ratio of the senses. It may be that in the development of such a complex sensory ratio as this secular man will find the path to freedom from the narcosis of electric enchantment and the attainment of a consciousness fully awakened to the concreteness of the dynamic world.

---

[63] For an example of an analysis of sensory form that gives more attention to temporal factors see Ihde, "Some Auditory Phenomena," pp. 227–235.

[64] For example, Paul Tillich goes too far when he contrasts the biblical God of time with pagan gods of space (*Theology of Culture*, ed. by Robert Kimball [New York, 1959], pp. 38–39). A better balance is found in the discussion of the categories in *Systematic Theology*, Vol. I (Chicago, 1951), pp. 194–195.

THE AMERICAN HERITAGE SERIES

THE COLONIAL PERIOD

THE REVOLUTIONARY ERA TO 1789